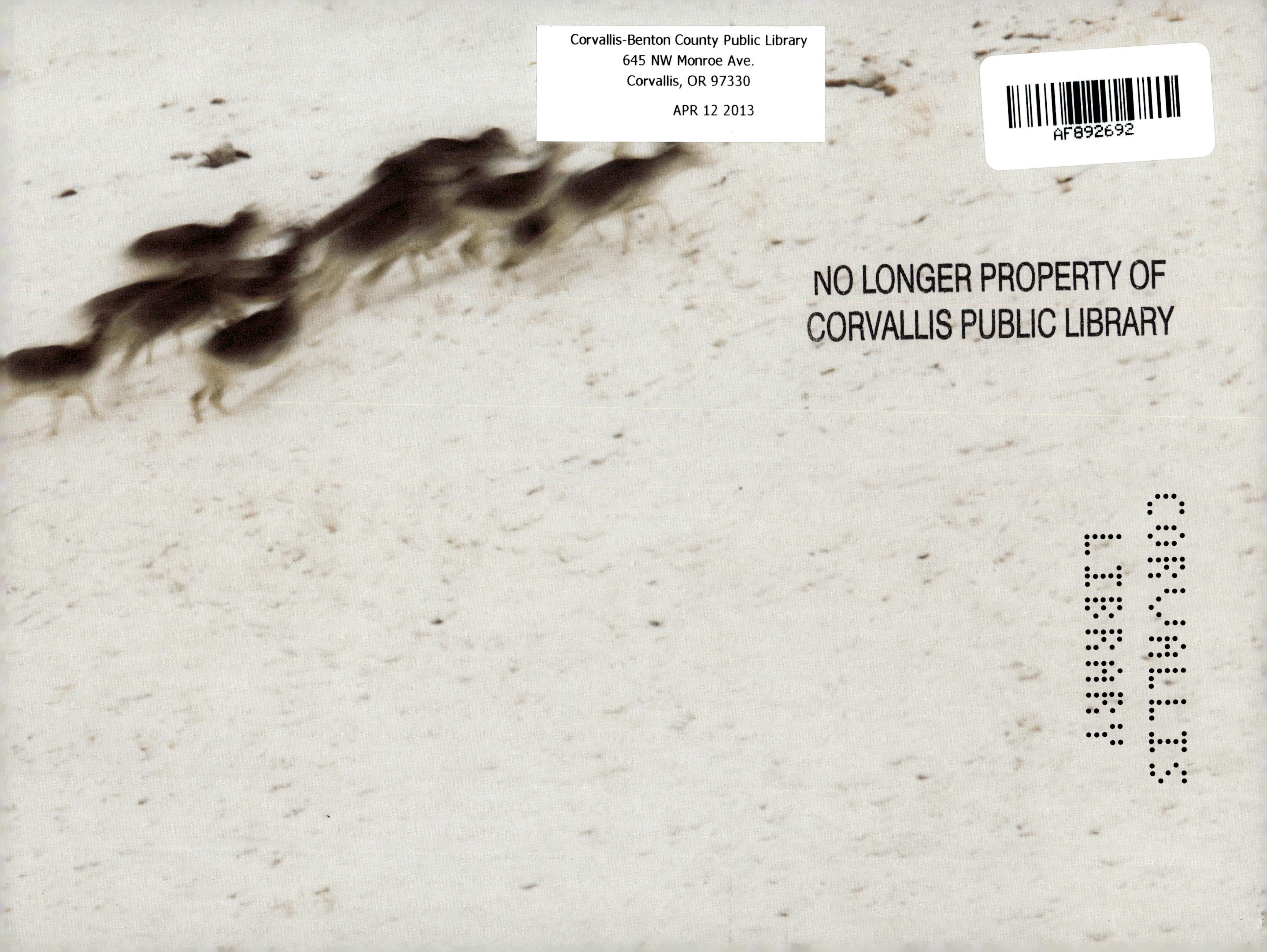

Corvallis-Benton County Public Library
645 NW Monroe Ave.
Corvallis, OR 97330
APR 12 2013

AF892692

NO LONGER PROPERTY OF
CORVALLIS PUBLIC LIBRARY

CORVALLIS
LIBRARY

LIBRARY
CORNELL

WILDLIFE WONDERS *of* CHINA

A Pictorial Journey through the Lens of Conservationist Xi Zhinong

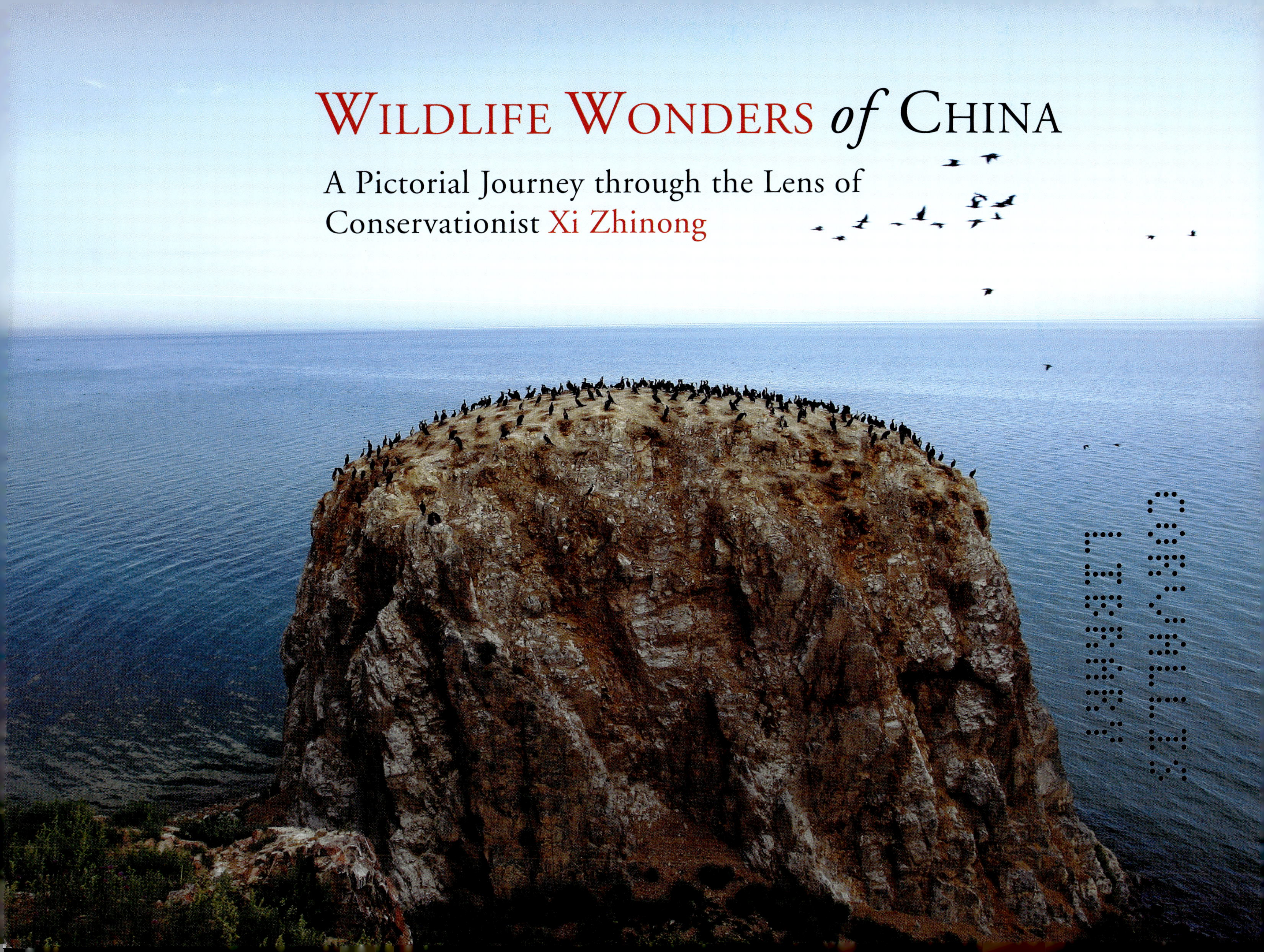

CORVALLIS LIBRARY

Copyright © 2013 Shanghai Press and Publishing Development Company

All rights reserved. Unauthorized reproduction, in any manner, is prohibited.

This book is edited and designed by the Editorial Committee of *Cultural China* series

Photographs: Xi Zhinong
Text: Xi Zhinong, Shen Cheng
Translator: Cao Jianxin
With Forewords by Rosamund Kidman Cox, Wang Song

Interior Designers: Yuan Yinchang, Li Jing (Yuan Yinchang Design Studio)
Cover Designer: Wang Wei

Copy Editor: Susan Luu Xiang
Assistant Editor: Wu Yuezhou
Editor: Yang Xiaohe
Editorial Director: Zhang Yicong

Senior Consultants: Sun Yong, Wu Ying, Yang Xinci
Managing Director and Publisher: Wang Youbu

ISBN: 978-1-60220-011-1

Address any comments about *Wildlife Wonders of China: A Pictorial Journey through the Lens of Conservationist Xi Zhinong* to:

Better Link Press
99 Park Ave
New York, NY 10016
USA

or

Shanghai Press and Publishing Development Company
F 7 Donghu Road, Shanghai, China (200031)
Email: comments_betterlinkpress@hotmail.com

Printed in China by Shenzhen Donnelley Printing Co., Ltd.

1 3 5 7 9 10 8 6 4 2

On endsheets
On the desolate Pamirs Plateau in the hinterland of Eurasia, a group of Marco Polo sheep is climbing the snow slope. They are named so in memory of Marco Polo and for the big beautiful horns in which he described them.

On page 1
Situated in the northeast of Qinghai province, Qinghai Lake is the biggest inland lake and the biggest saline lake in China. It is not only the birthplace of naked carps, but also the place for the propagation of numerous migrant birds.

This picture shows the Great Cormorant Islet close to the lakeside. On this small islet, there are hundreds of great cormorants building up their nests.

On pages 2 and 3
Yunnan snub-nosed monkeys are precious and rare species living on the steep snow mountains bordering on Yunnan province and Tibet in China. They live in alpine coniferous forests near the glacier snowline all year around.

Five kinds of snub-nosed monkeys, including golden snub-nosed monkeys, Guizhou snub-nosed monkeys, Yunnan snub-nosed monkeys, Tonkin snub-nosed monkeys (*Rhinopithecus avunculus*), and Myanmar snub-nosed monkeys (*Rhinopithecus strykeri*) recently discovered, have been put onto the IUCN Red List as endangered species. Among them, Yunnan snub-nosed monkeys, Guizhou snub-nosed monkeys, and Tonkin snub-nosed monkeys are one of 25 primates on the possible verge of extinction. Tonkin snub-nosed monkeys are only seen in the north of Vietnam, while Myanmar snub-nosed monkeys are found in the Gaoligong Mountains in Yunnan province in China. Golden snub-nosed monkeys, Guizhou snub-nosed monkeys, and Yunnan snub-nosed monkeys are unique to China and are deemed as "national treasures."

Thanks to proper protection, the number of Yunnan snub-nosed monkeys has been increasing yearly, amounting to over 2,500 in 2011. In the national nature reserve in the White Horse Snow Mountains in Yunnan province, a reserve with an area of more than 280,000 hectares, there are about 1,500 Yunnan snub-nosed monkeys in eight groups, an increase of about 300 compared to the number in 2004.

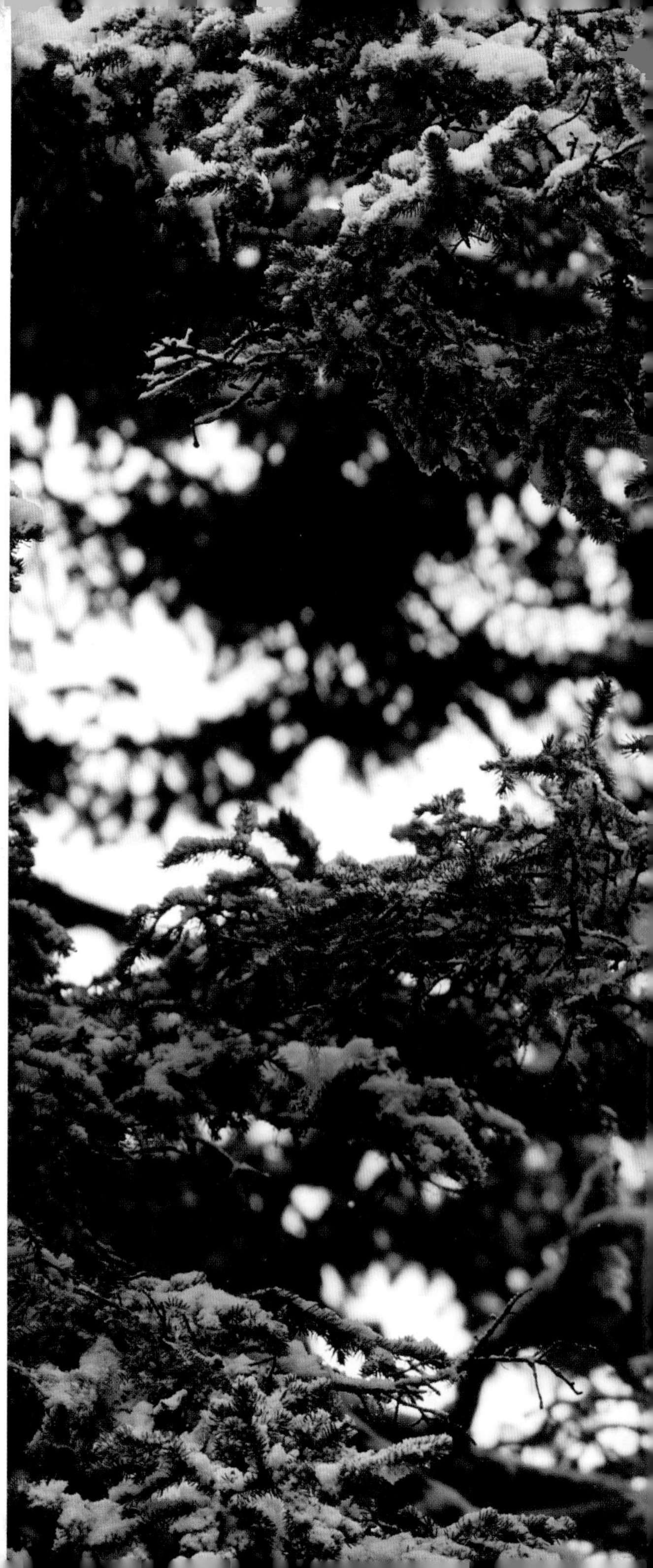

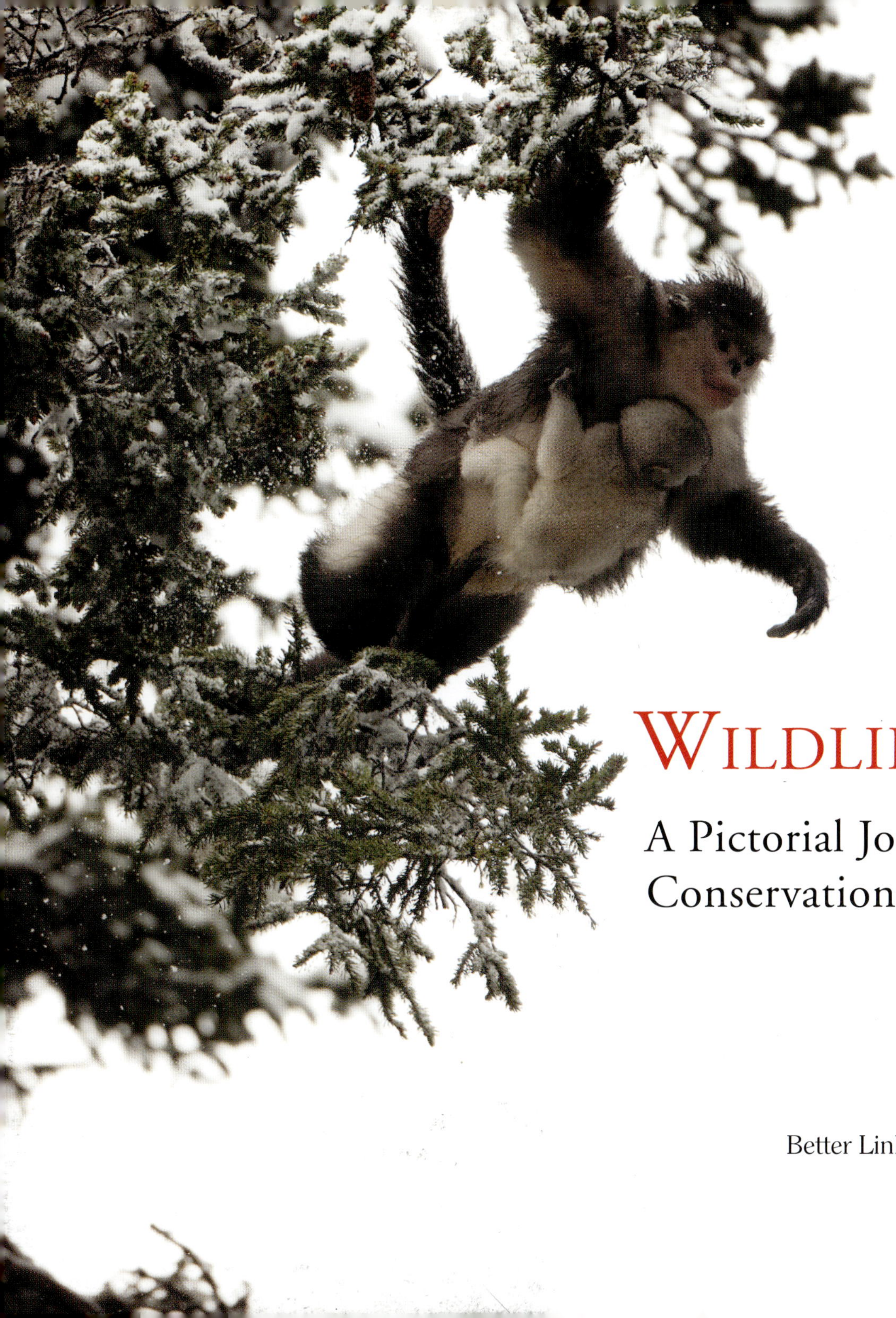

WILDLIFE WONDERS *of* CHINA

A Pictorial Journey through the Lens of Conservationist Xi Zhinong

Better Link Press

Contents

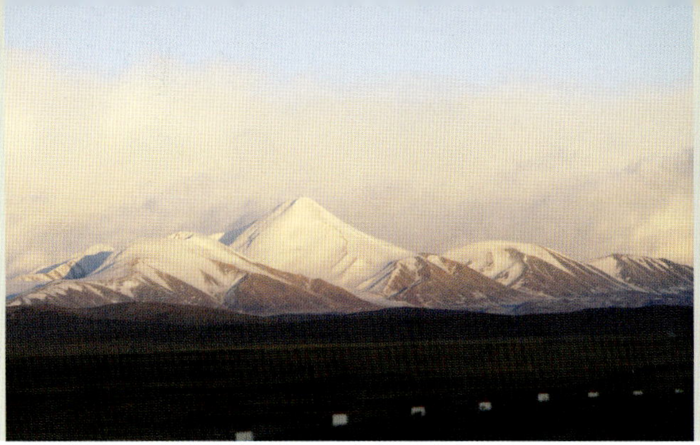

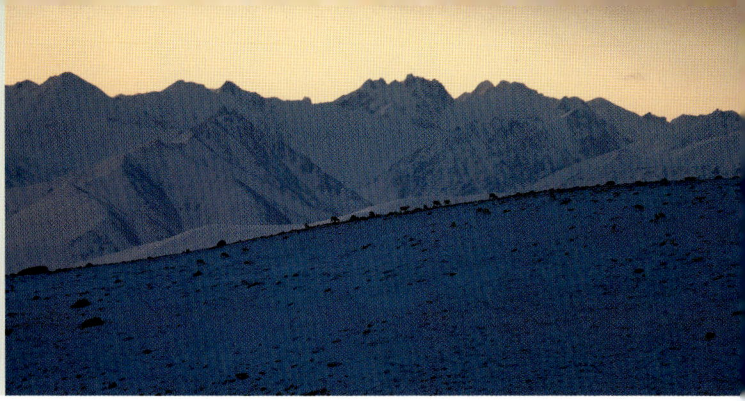

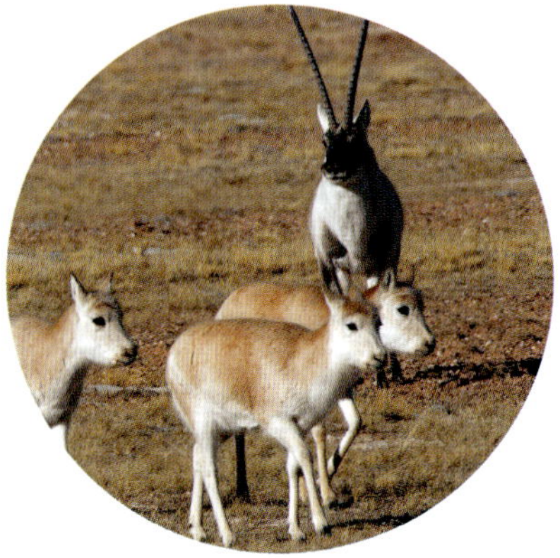

Tibetan antelope

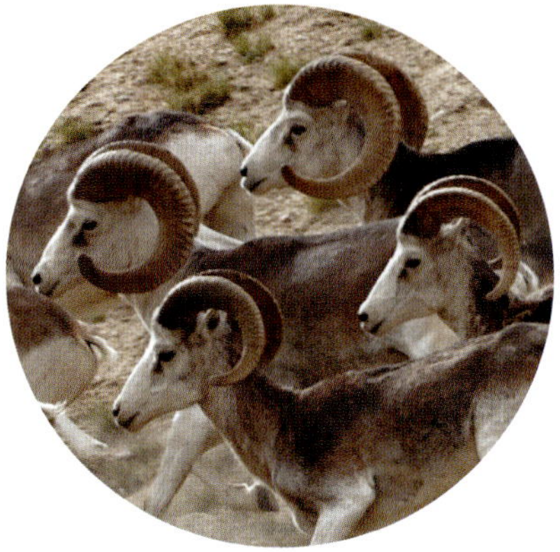

Marco Polo sheep

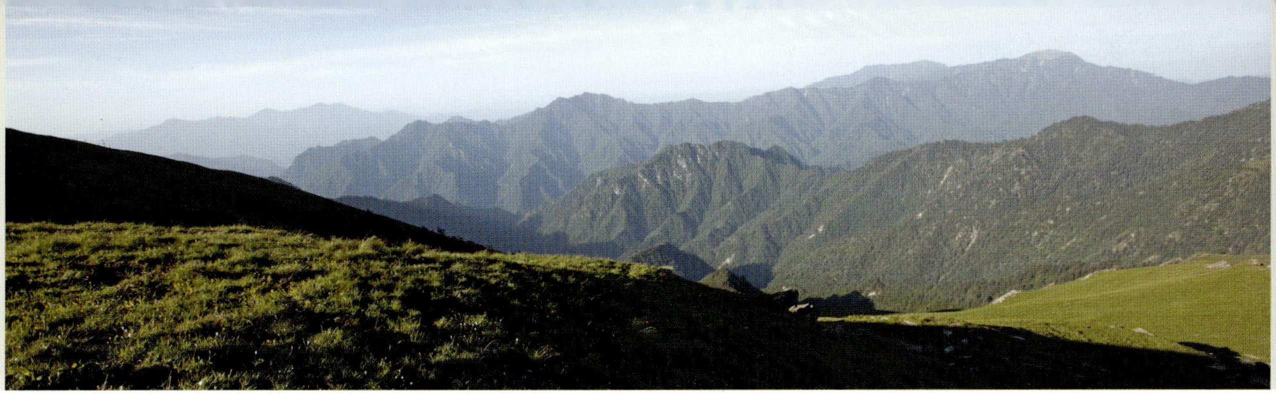

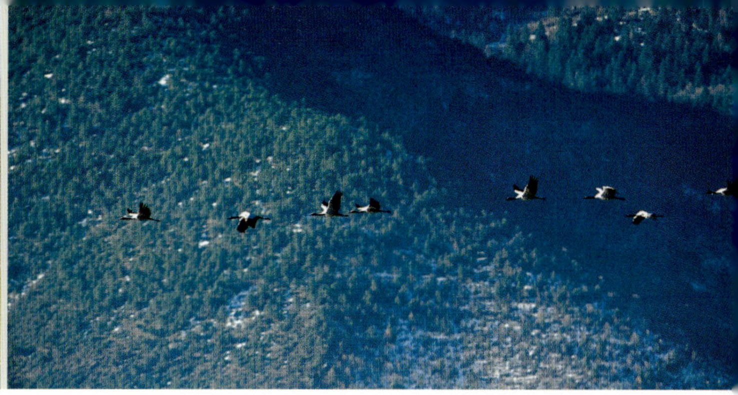

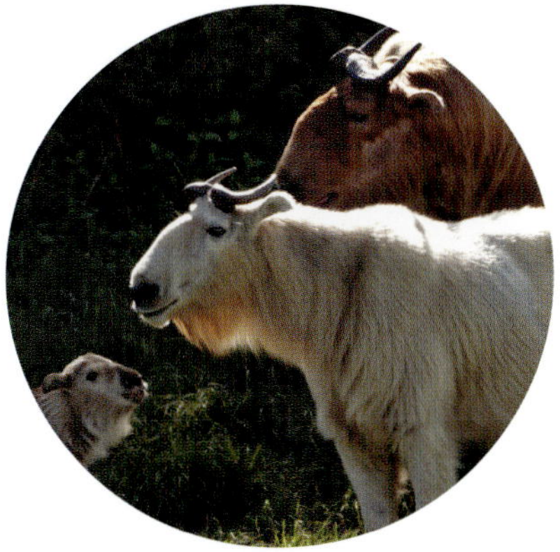

Takin

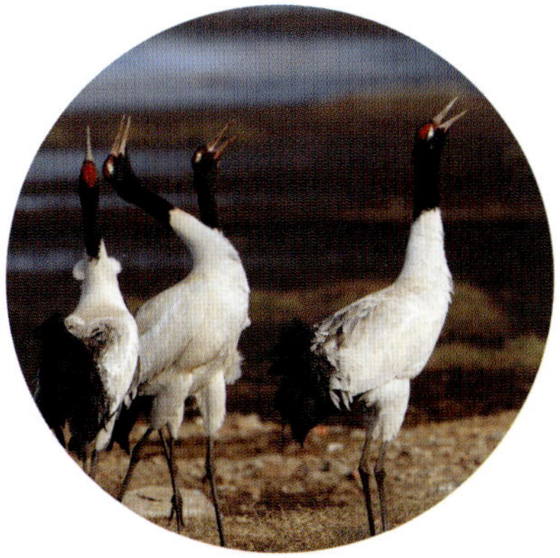

Black-necked crane

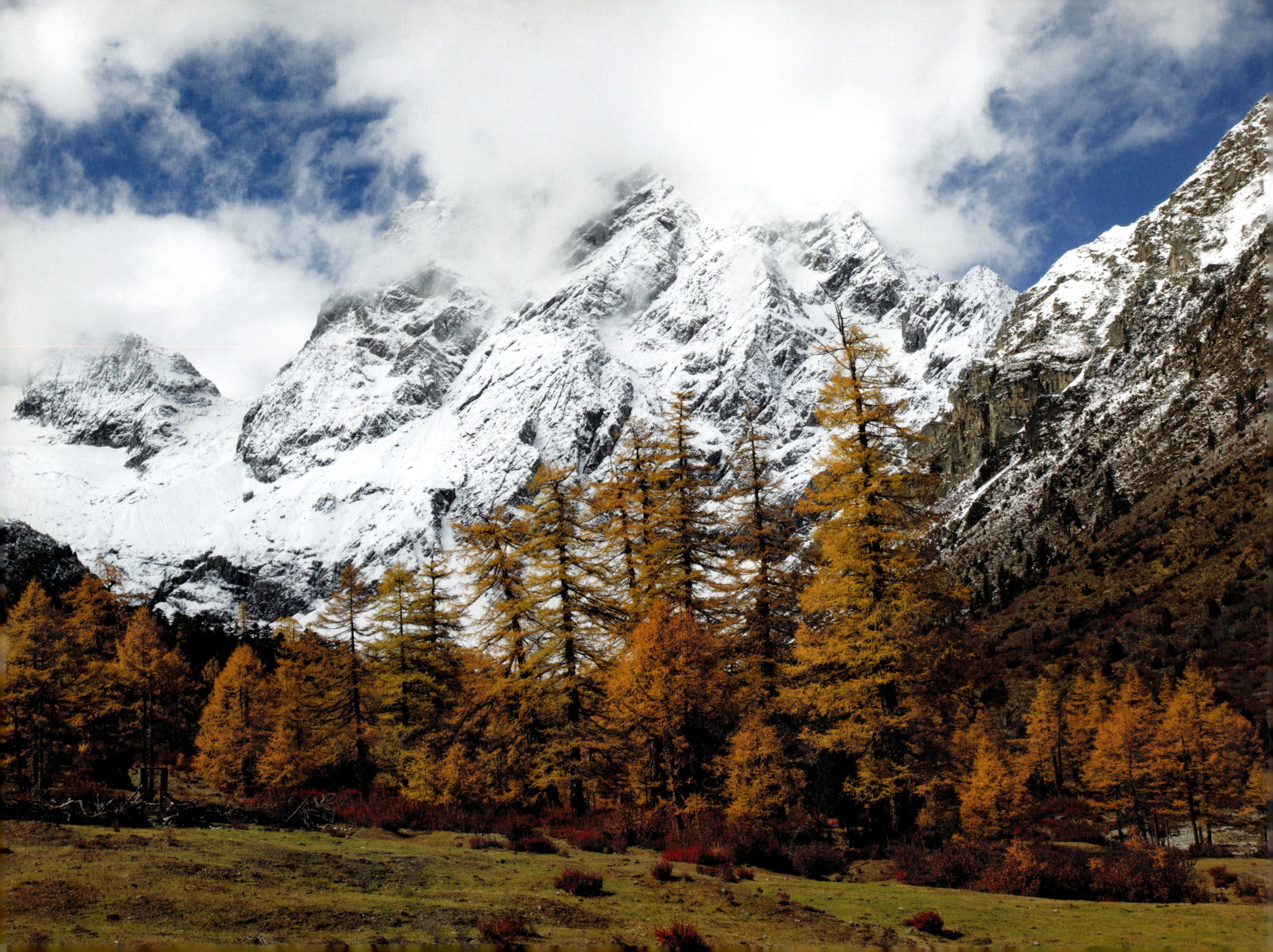

Photography Locations

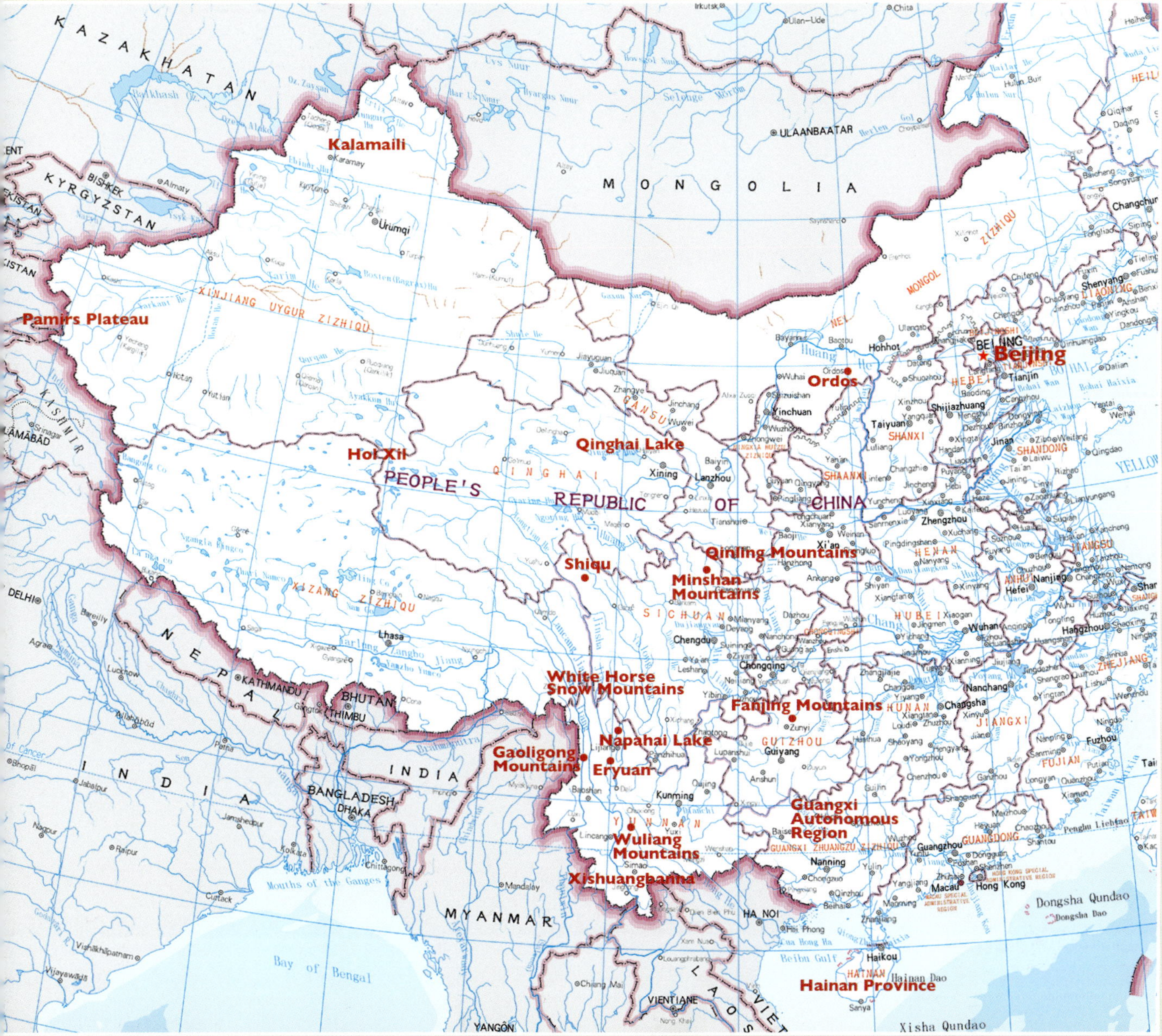

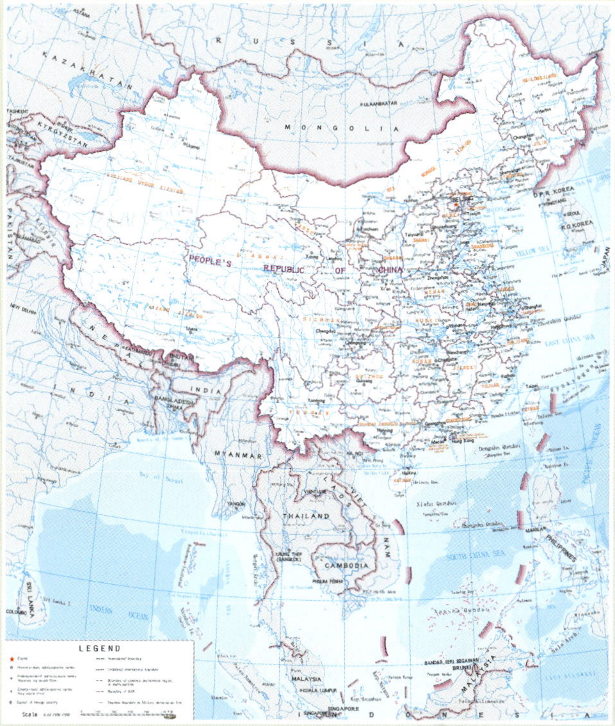

Map of China

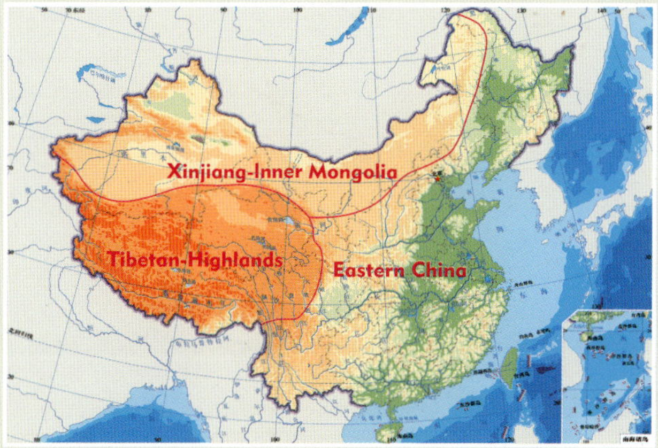

Three Wildlife Zones of China

On facing page
The White Horse Snow Mountains in Yunnan Province

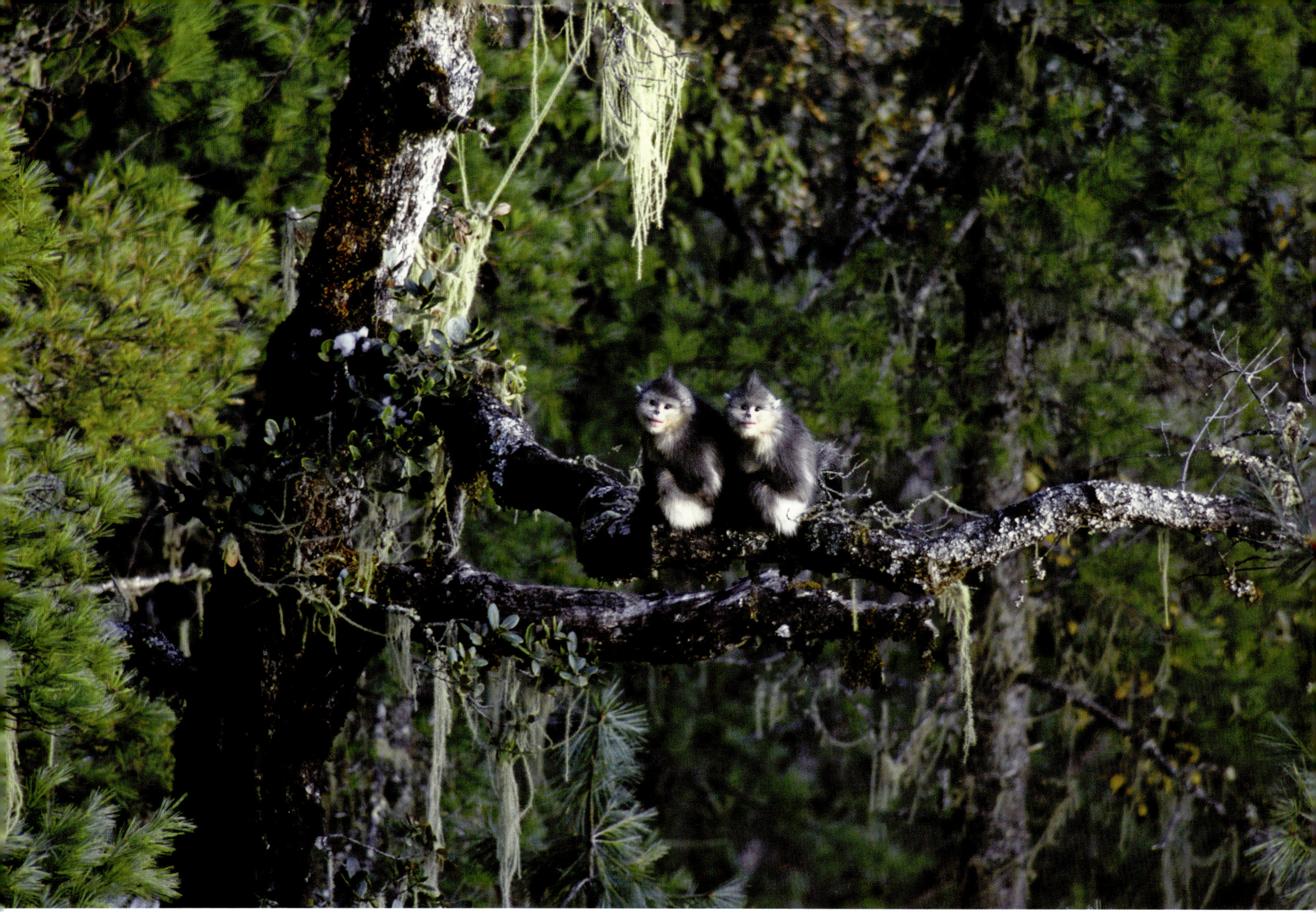

Foreword I The Power of Photography to Promote Conservation

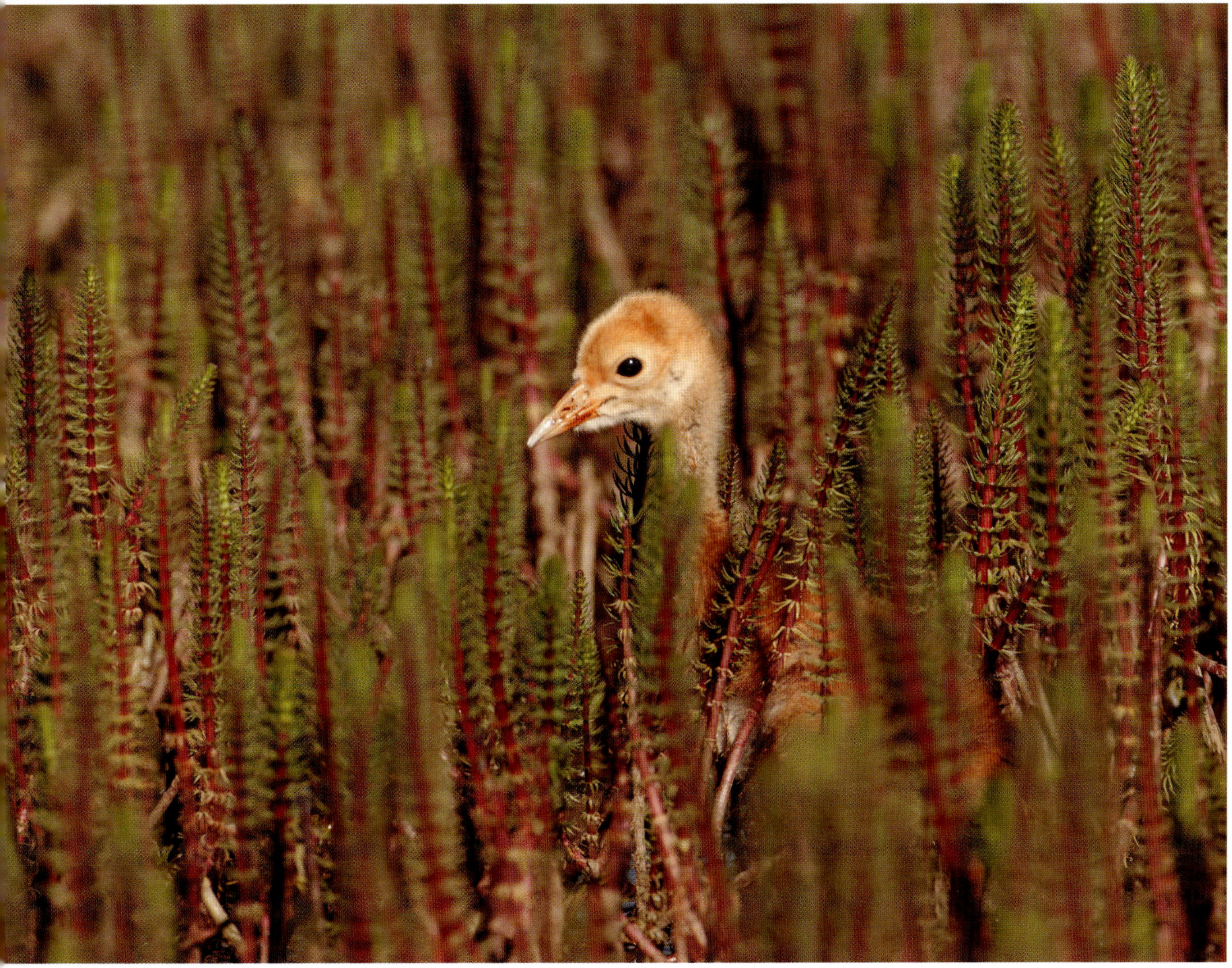

Some of the world's most extraordinary wildlife and wild places are to be found in China, and no photographer has done more than Xi Zhinong to reveal those wonders, both to his own countrymen but also to the Western world. This book is a collection of his truly memorable pictures.

Before Xi Zhinong's work began to get published, there were very few widely available pictures of Chinese wildlife, and certainly few taken in the wild. Most were portraits of captive animals, usually giant pandas and one or two bird species. Xi Zhinong's pictures of wild animals in extraordinary landscapes were therefore a revelation to most people who saw them. More than that, they have changed hearts and minds.

Xi Zhinong has used his photographs on behalf of his wild subjects and their environments, to highlight their plight and to campaign for their protection. That makes him a very special

Left
Black-necked cranes are the only kind of cranes living on the Tibetan Plateau. Each spring and summer, they fly in flocks to Qinghai Lake for propagation. Usually, a female black-necked crane produces one to two eggs, which are in turn taken care of by the female and the male. The cranes would break from the shell in a month or so. Because of bad climate, the survival rate of juvenile cranes is very low. Only 60% of them can survive after breaking from the shell in three days.

On facing page
This photo of Yunnan snub-nosed monkeys was taken in 2001 in which it won the Gerald Durrell Award for Endangered Species of Wildlife Photographer of the Year. This picture, which was not easy to come by, has saved Yunnan snub-nosed monkeys in the primitive forests in the White Horse Snow Mountains.

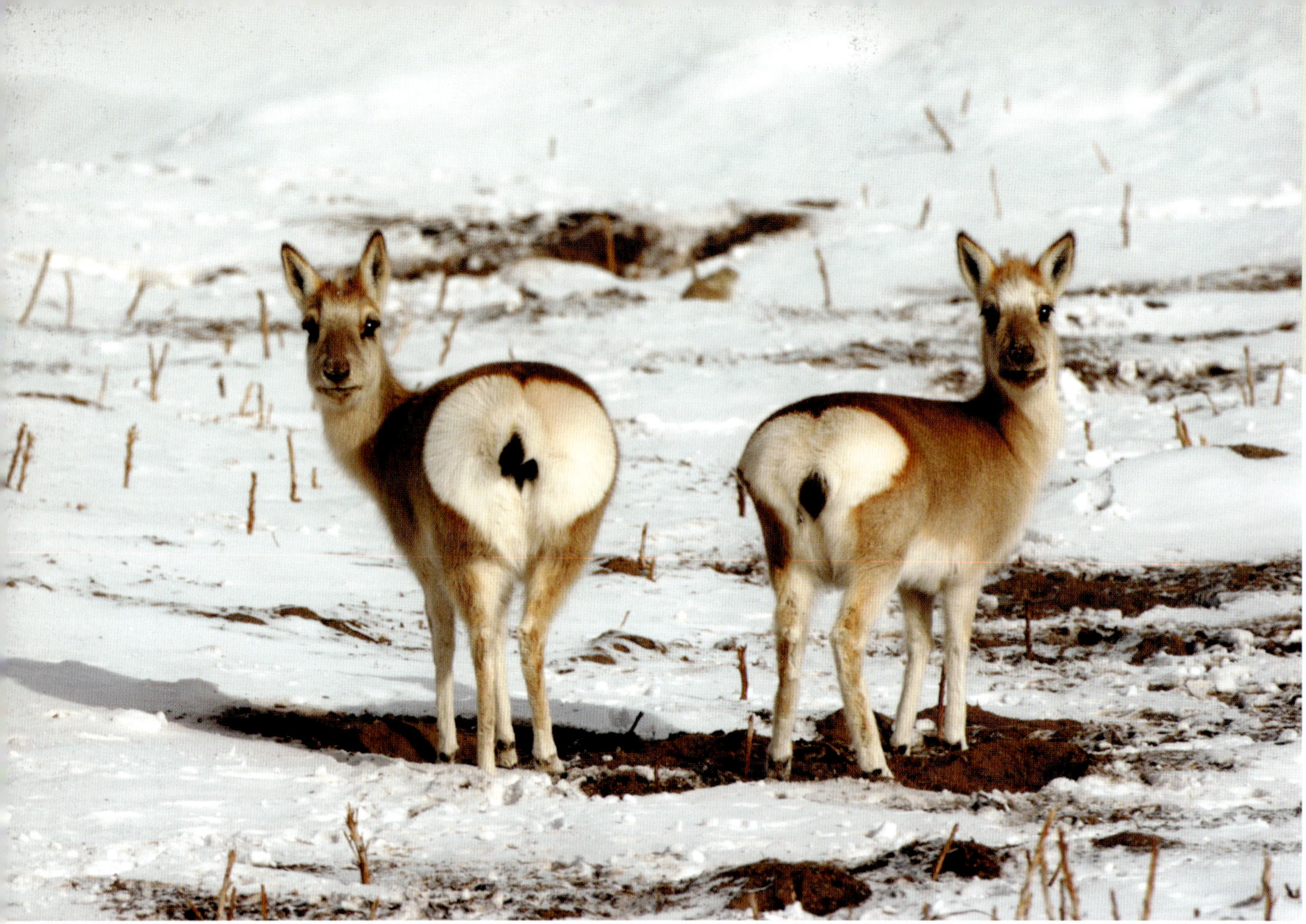

Hoh Xil is the biggest alpine area of the Tibetan Plateau. Human beings are unable to live here for a long time, but it is the paradise of wild animals. The purely white big buttock patches are the biggest feature of the Tibetan gazelles. They are commonly known as "white buttocks in the shape of loving hearts."

On facing page
As the moon slowly sinks into the horizon, the first ray of sunlight of the new day shines warmly over a small group of Tibetan antelopes.

wildlife photographer and a very deserving fellow of the International League of Conservation Photographers—still the only Chinese fellow to have been elected to the league.

I'll never forget the first picture by Xi Zhinong that I saw, back in 1999, when I was the editor of *BBC Wildlife* magazine. It showed two Asiatic-looking monkeys—monkeys that I'd never seen pictures of before—huddling together on the branch, not of a tropical rain forest tree, but of a huge lichen-covered conifer. It was both a mysterious and thought provoking picture, and I wanted to find out more about the species and the forest.

We published an article about them in the magazine, featuring not only Xi Zhinong's pictures—the first ones taken of Yunnan snub-nosed monkeys in the wild—but also the tale of their plight and the successful campaign by Xi Zhinong and his fellow Chinese conservationists, using photographs, film, and words, to stop the illegal logging of the monkeys' forest home.

In 2001, he went on to win a major award with a picture of the monkeys in the international Wildlife Photographer of the Year competition. As a result, the monkeys became known to literally millions of people worldwide. And in the following year, his film about the monkeys and their story won an award at the international Wildscreen Film Festival. Xi Zhinong's photographic campaign is now one of the most famous examples of the power of photography to promote conservation.

Photography really does have the power to change the way we think. A single image stays in the mind, and many of Xi Zhinong's pictures of endangered species are unforgettable—the intimate glimpse of takins touching noses (see page 106), the pair of symmetrical Tibetan gazelle (see page 10), and the Marco Polo sheep racing as if for their lives (see page 84 and 85), for example.

Xi Zhinong, with his Wild China Film team, has also been training others to take pictures of rare and wonderful creature so that the Chinese people can see what their national treasures are and want to conserve them. He has also championed wildlife photography in China, in the belief that more photographers will mean that more people value wildlife in the wild.

Xi Zhinong deserves the highest praise, and this book deserves the biggest audience possible.

Rosamund Kidman Cox
Former Editor-in-Chief of *BBC Wildlife* Magazine
Judge of the International Wildlife Photographer of the Year Competition

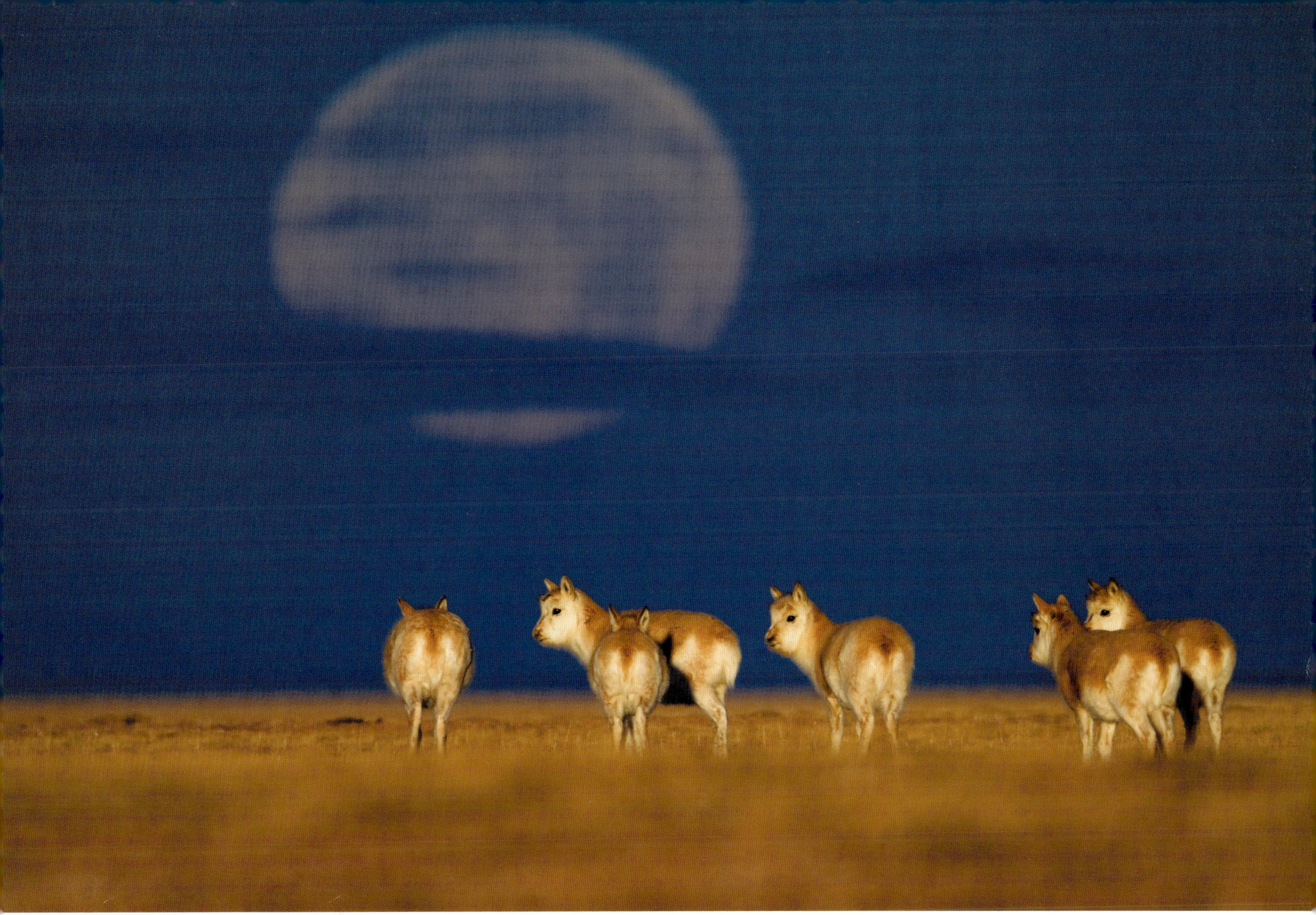

Foreword II
Wildlife Photography in China

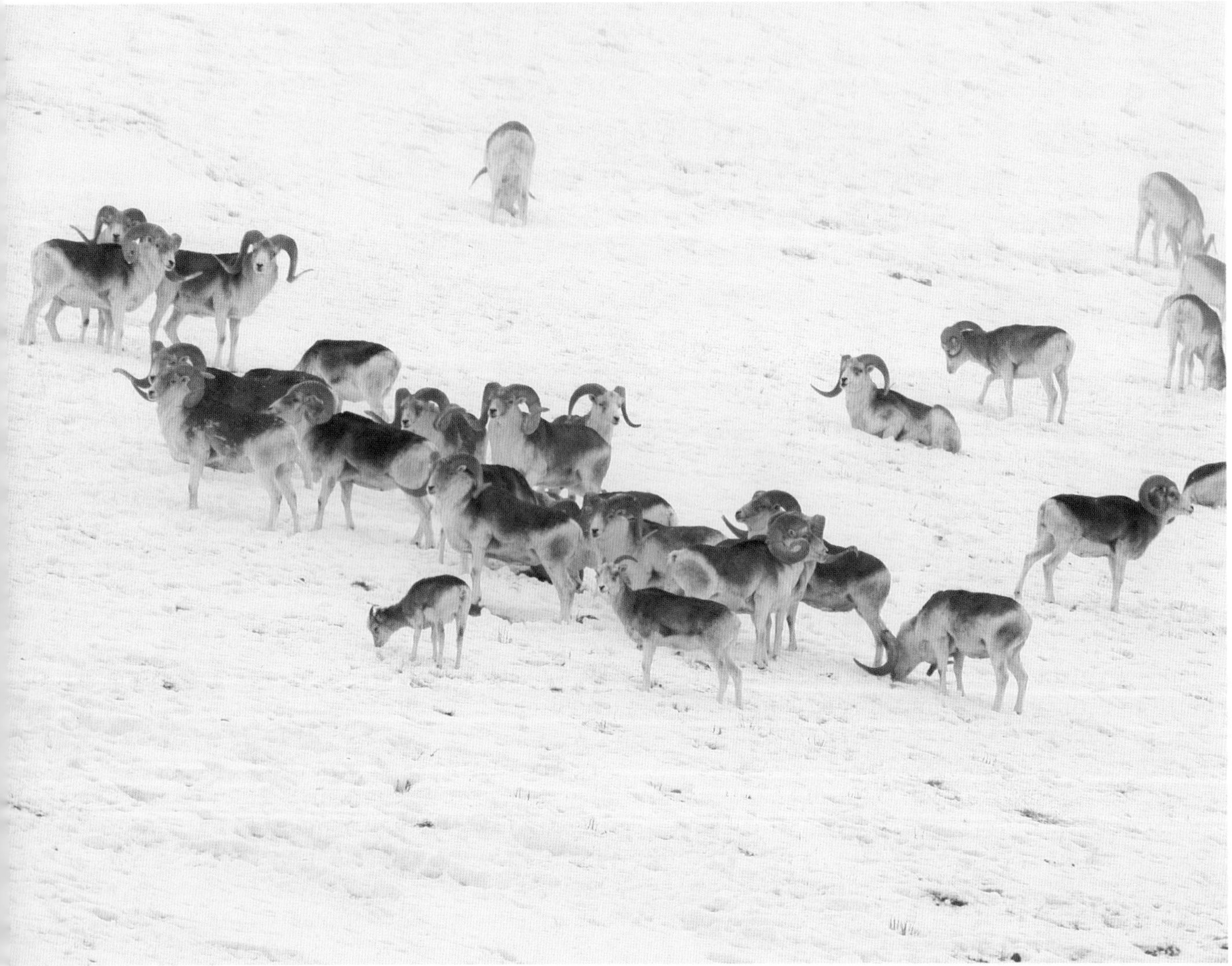

It is my great pleasure to see the publication of *Wildlife Wonders of China* by Xi Zhinong, a famous wildlife photographer. I have known Xi Zhinong for years and am very impressed with his enthusiasm and great experience in wildlife photography, as well as his efforts and contribution to wildlife conservation. For years, he has been promoting environmental conservation through the power of images. His work, *Wildlife Wonders of China* features a large number of breathtaking photos provide the readers and public with attractive features and information on China's wildlife.

China is recognized as a country with one of the richest biodiversity in the world. Its territory of 9.6 million square kilometers ranges from east to west almost across the whole of the Asian continent. From the desert to the taiga, from the temperate forests to the tropical forests, from the alpine mountains and the high plateaus to the flat expanse of the coastal alluvial plain—China is a vast country rich in fauna and flora. For example, there are over 500 and 1,300 species of mammals and birds respectively; boasting a greater diversity of species compared to that of Europe or North America as a whole.

As the biggest sub-species of argalis, Marco Polo sheep have a pair of huge curved horns which are said to be 1.8 meters long. They move around on gentle slopes of undulating high mountains 3,000 meters above sea level and in expansive gullies, serene places with abundant grass. They live on Pamirs Plateau bordering China, Pakistan, Afghanistan, and Tajikistan. Now, there are only about 6,000 left behind as they are on the verge of extinction. Cooperation among a number of countries concerned is required for protecting this species.

In China, there are four sub-species of takins. Among them, *B.t.bedfordi* in the Qinling Mountains that run across central China from the east to the west is the biggest. *B.t.bedfordi* is grey-white all over and interspersed with golden color, giving it a majestic appearance. There are less than 5,000 *B.t.bedfordi*, which have become an advantageous species in this area thanks to the establishment of the Qinling Mountains nature reserve and ecological corridor, as well as increasing awareness of protection among people.

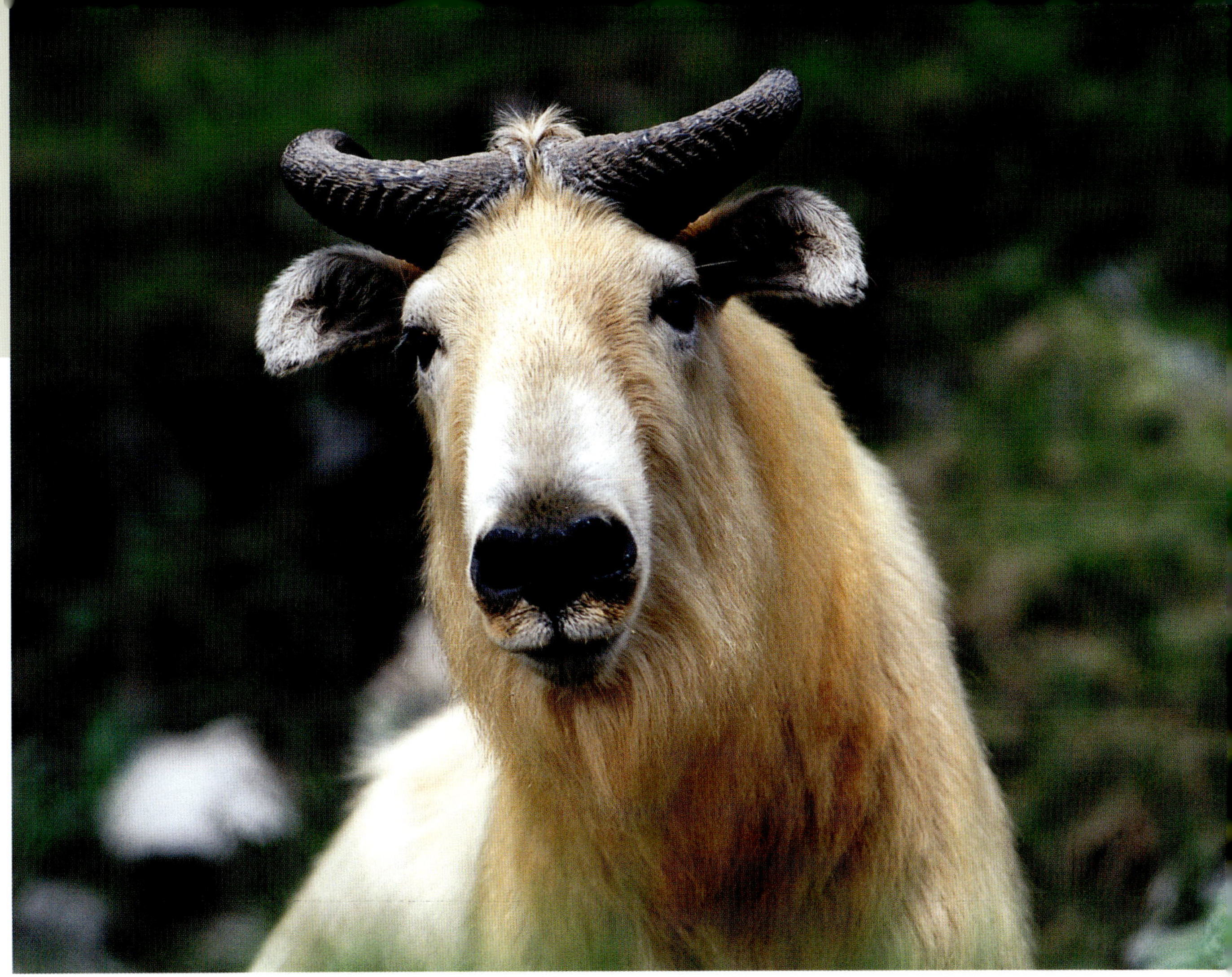

However, there was less emphasis on the field study of wildlife in China in the past decades; not many academic monographs, and certainly not an abundance of more attention drawing works such as colored field guides, illustrated books, or wildlife photographic collections. Large-scale field study only enjoyed a brief period of attention in the 1950s – 1960s, and since then was replaced mainly by molecular biology in the labs. Comprehensive knowledge about Chinese wildlife is still lacking, and wildlife photography even less developed. The first series of black-and-white photos of the giant panda in its natural habitat was taken at the Wanglang Panda Reserve, Sichuan, in 1968. At present, (excluding individual species such as the giant panda, the snub-nosed monkey, the takin, and the cranes) the majority of wildlife species in China remain in anonymity, with no existing documentaries or pictures dedicated to them. For instance, there are not many photos or films of wild cats (such as the snow leopard, the leopard, clouded leopard, lynx, desert cat, golden cat, etc.) or deer (such as white-lipped deer, sika deer, moose, sambar, etc., or bovines). Even though the public can appreciate the wildlife in zoos, they would be hard-pressed to imagine where and how the creatures live.

Nowadays, wildlife conservation in China is a great challenge brought about by a long history of unsustainable use and logging. Over the years, many species have been over hunted for their fur, skeletons, meat, glands, and other derivatives for fashion or cuisine. The Saiga antelope has been hunted to extinction in China for its skin, meat, and parts used in Traditional Chinese Medicine, especially its horns. Meanwhile, the previously abundant musk deer and pangolins of China are now greatly endangered due to over harvesting and over consumption for their musk and scales respectively. Unfortunately, such endangered species are not given the limelight, as more iconic species such as the giant panda receive greater popularity and conservatory awareness. This is a pity, as the awareness of, and familiarity with wildlife is one of the keys to encouraging changes in the otherwise entrenched, negative behavior in China.

The recent development of photographic technology leads to higher quality still-photos and films of wild animals that are an important resource for establishing research on a particular wild animal. A more intuitive understanding of the wild animal may be gained through those images

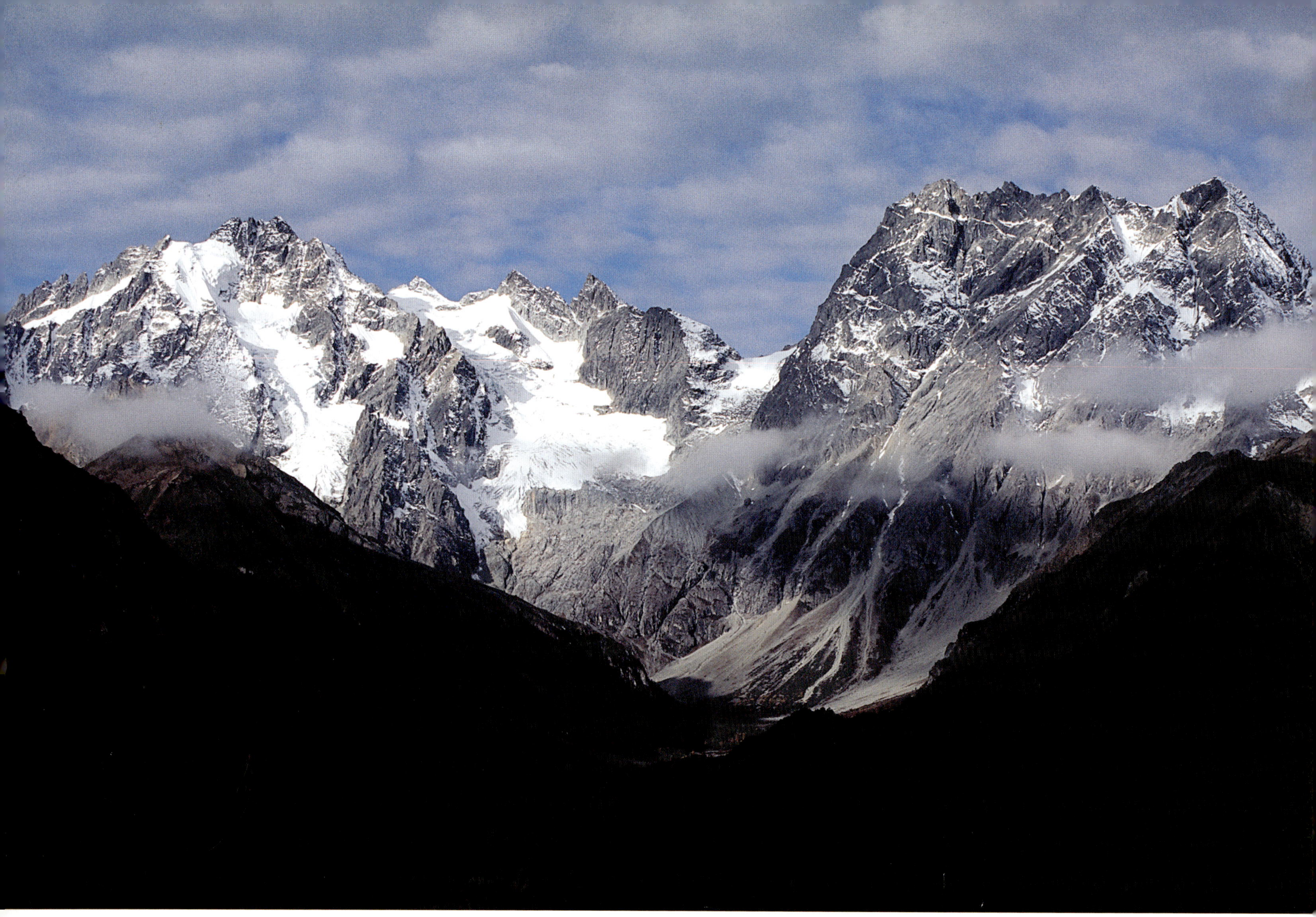

On facing page
The White Horse Snow Mountains, with the ridge that looks like a galloping horse, is situated in Yunnan province in southwestern China. It has rich vegetation, thus enjoying its reputation as the "kingdom of alpine animals and plants in the cold temperate zone."

Pictures taken of Yunnan snub-nosed monkeys have prevented an expanse of primitive forests in the White Horse Snow Mountains from being cut down. Meanwhile, the process of protecting Yunnan snub-nosed monkeys has become the symbol of the rising awareness of environmental protection among people in China.

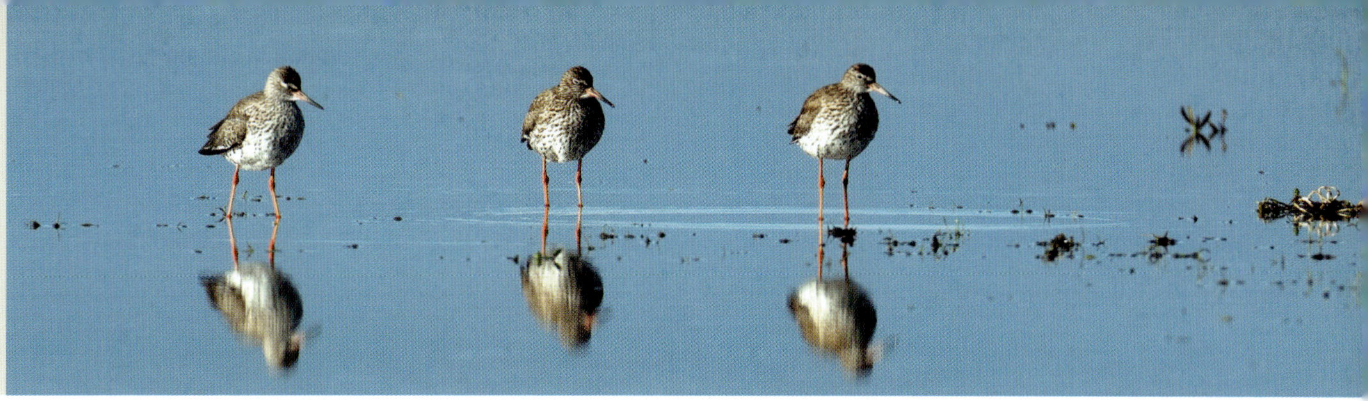
Three common redshanks stand quietly in the water, with their figures reflected on the calm surface. As an extensively distributed bird, common redshanks go through the period of propagation on the Tibetan Plateau through eastern China, flying to the Yangtze River Valley and southern China to spend the winter.

just as observing the animals in their natural habitat can. In this regard, the publication of various media concerning wildlife for the public, especially for children, should be encouraged. Such publications should also inform the public of the current status of, as well as the urgency for an increase in wildlife and biodiversity conservation by linking the threats that all the species and ecosystems are facing.

In his new publication *Wildlife Wonders of China*, the author exhibits a total of fifty-nine species of wildlife, with images taken during the past three decades. It gives the readers visuals as well as information on those endemic and endangered wildlife; providing further understanding on where and how those creatures live, and what we can do to save them.

Since the United Nations Conference on Environment and Development (UNCED) in Rio in 1992, there has been a greater emphasis on sustainable development both domestically and internationally. More attention should be paid to wildlife and biodiversity conservation in the future in order to prevent extinction, as well as further emphasis on sustainable development.

In the beginning of the 1990s, when Xi Zhinong was working for the TV program titled *Animal World,* he started to commit himself to work in wildlife photography and wildlife conservation. His work has always impressed me. The first shot of the endemic and critically endangered species of primates in northwest Yunnan, the Yunnan snub-nosed monkey, eventually saved its natural habitat and forest from logging. His field survey also disclosed the crime of the smuggling of the Tibetan antelope in western Qinghai, which had also resulted in large-scaled public awareness of the conservation actions for the unique plateau creature. In 2008, Xi Zhinong published his first volume of *Wild China.* It included many of his wildlife photos, taken mainly in southwest and northwest regions, including the snub-nosed monkey, the takin, the argali, and the Tibetan antelope in their natural habitats.

Based on these conservation and naturalist activities, he founded his NGO—Wild China Film—a small but active organization working in wildlife conservation. A number of conservation public awareness activities were sponsored and carried out by his organization, including lectures, workshops, and wildlife photography training courses. In 2010, Xi was involved in the launch of the China Endangered Species Image Plan, aimed at encouraging more photographers to record wildlife facing the crisis of extinction.

During the past decade, he has won a number of awards domestically and internationally, such as: the Conserving the Mother River Award (2001); the Gerald Durrell Award for Endangered Species (*Yunnan Snub-Nosed Monkey*, 2001); the Wildscreen Festival TVE Award (*Searching for the Yunnan Snub-Nosed Monkey*, 2001); the Malay Bear Award of Singapore Asian Wild Animal and Environmental Film Festival (2007), etc.

As mentioned above, Xi Zhinong is an aspiring conservationist and a leading wildlife photographer. However, he also leads a refreshing lifestyle. When we were working together, I found him enjoying simple meals instead of the stereotypical banquets of a "celebrity." He prefers to be out in the fresh air, and further displayed his love for the environment even in everyday life by asking the driver to shut down the air conditioning when we were travelling together on a bus.

Photographers could play an important role in education by means of producing the visuals to show the values, ecological functions, and threats facing biodiversity. For all these reasons, the publishing of Xi's fully illustrated book of wildlife is timely in further promoting field surveys and the increased publication of similar materials for the purpose of conservation, eco-tourism, public education, and awareness.

I am quite sure that, following this publication, more and more colorful guide books and pictorial monographs will appear.

Wang Song
Researcher of Institute of Zoology, Chinese Academy of Sciences
Secretary General of China National Committee for International Union of Biological Sciences

Preface

Along with five thousand years of long history, the far eastern land of China possesses a vibrant wildlife and natural sceneries little known to the public. I felt very lucky to have gone deep into places almost without human activities to visit those rare species on the verge of extinction, including Tibetan antelopes, wild yaks in Hoh Xil, Yunnan snub-nosed monkeys in White Horse Snow Mountains, and giant pandas in the depths of the Qinling Mountains. They gave me opportunities to record their beauty, curiosity, tranquility, and serenity. The expressions in their eyes have touched and inspired those who have a chance to see these pictures.

My childhood was spent playing in the field, enjoying the beauty of Mother Nature in my hometown. It has been so natural for me to grow from a bird-raiser boy to a young man who held a camera and became a wildlife photographer.

In 1983, I worked as an assistant photographer for a science educational film called "The Paradise of Birds." We went to Napahai Lake, Zhongdian prefecture in Yunnan province to photograph black-necked cranes. At that time in China, with a limited amount of equipment, close-up shots were not available. Therefore, someone borrowed a specimen of a black-necked crane and placed it in the grass to help to complete a close-up shot. A staff from the zoo was invited to assist us by catching the birds and binding them with strings. However, after having done this, no one could remember to set these poor little birds free. On the next day these young birds that were about to leave the nest all died, leaving me heartbroken. Since then, I was determined to learn photography, taking photos of those free flying birds in the wild, and this started my career of wildlife photographer.

In 1990, joining a three-month wildlife field survey mission with Kunming Institute of Zoology of Chinese Academy of Sciences (CAS), I visited Dulong River, which was closed to external world without road access. According to the ecological location, there should be many endemic species living in Dulong River region, yet unfortunately squirrel was the only and the "biggest" live animal we could meet during the mission period. Moreover, it was skulls of takins, fur of red gorals, and steel wire traps that were ubiquitous in the area instead. This mission experience appalled me to focus my lens more on general environmental issues rather than birds only.

Nearly 30 years of my work in the wilderness represents also a period of rapid economic growth in China, symbolized by unprecedented pressures and threats facing the ecological environment and wild animals. In 1992, when I went to White Horse Snow Mountains region to photograph the Yunnan snub-

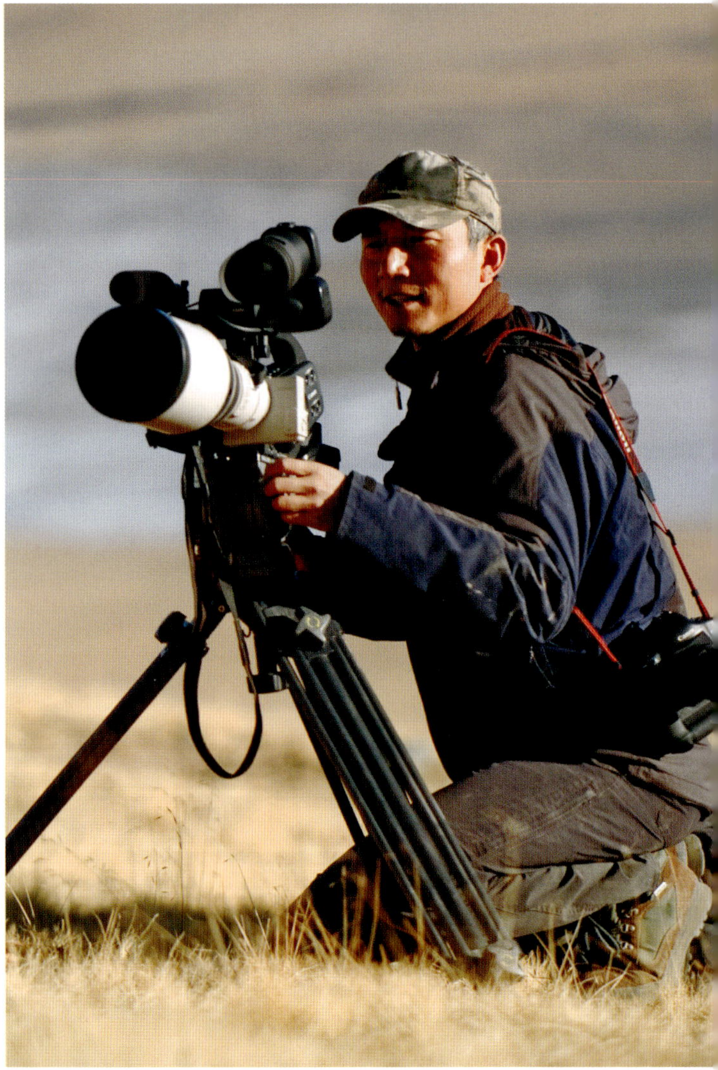

Picture taking in wilderness often lasts for several months. Staying at a place for several days in a row is nothing strange in order to "wait for" the main subject.

nosed monkey, I started to look at wildlife poaching issues. During the winter of 1997, together with the anti-poaching patrolling team, I went to Hoh Xil. My works of the dead Tibetan antelopes from that trip astonished the general public. From the eyes of the dead antelopes, we see selfishness and greed of human beings, at the same time pureness and innocence.

When I am photographing Mother Nature, I always carry a sense of responsibility, a devout heart behind the photos are much more important than the image itself. Only with passion and love for Mother Nature can photo itself be compelling. These years, attributed to all great efforts from normal individuals, government, and mass media wildlife conservation is gradually making progresses despite considerable hurdles met consistently.

In China, it is quite difficult to photograph wild animals. On the one hand, wild animals are very much afraid of human beings, making it extremely

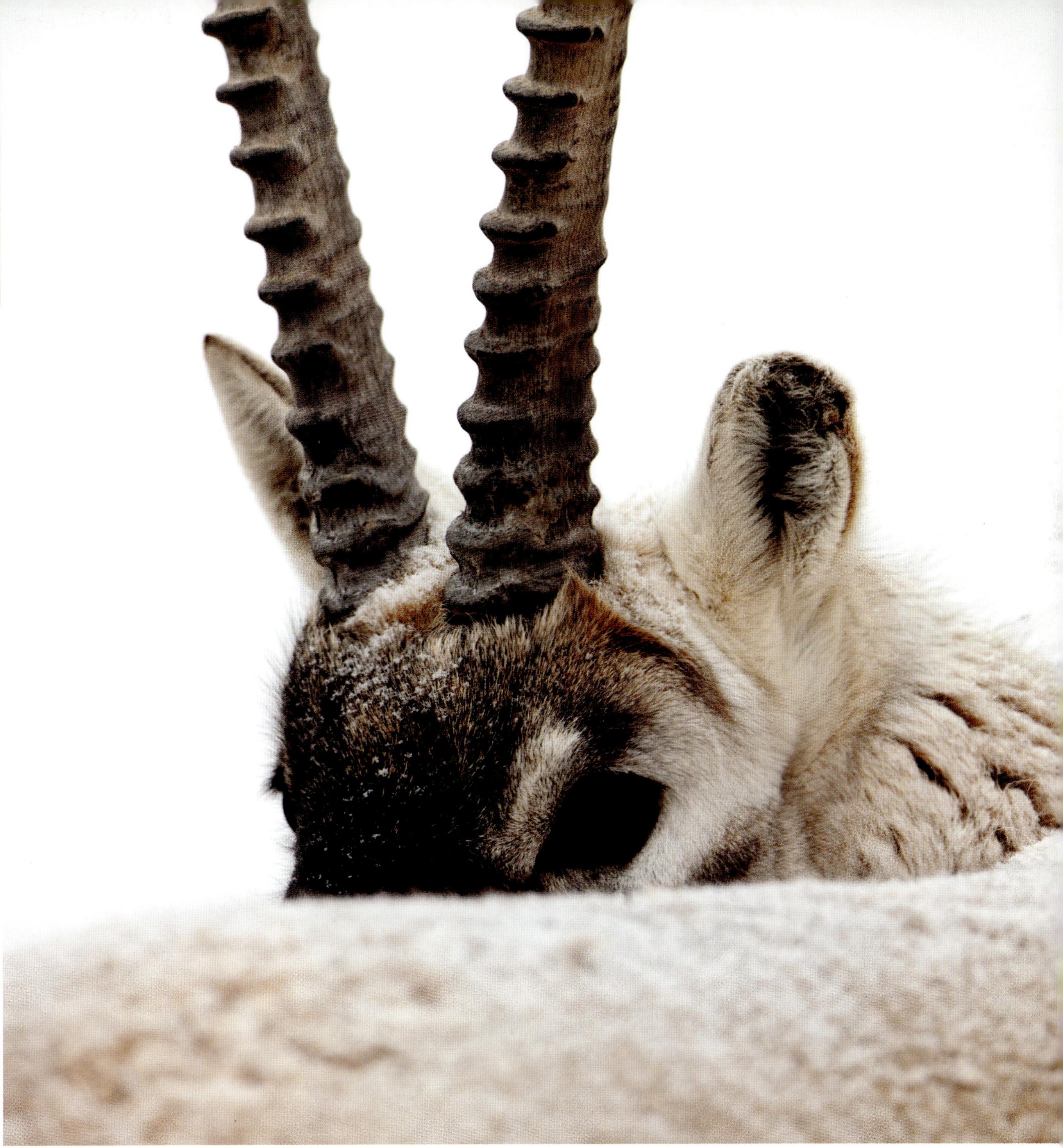

Hoh Xil, where Tibetan antelopes live, is marked by thin air, very dry and cold weather. The annual mean temperature is always below zero. The Tibetan antelope in the photo is covered with thin snow and the male one from behind has perhaps seen the enemy, hence the expression of vigilance.

The photographer once went deep into Hoh Xil without human beings to expose the mad behaviors of illegal hunters, to let people know the truth of shahtoosh shawl and to draw extensive attention to Tibetan antelopes.

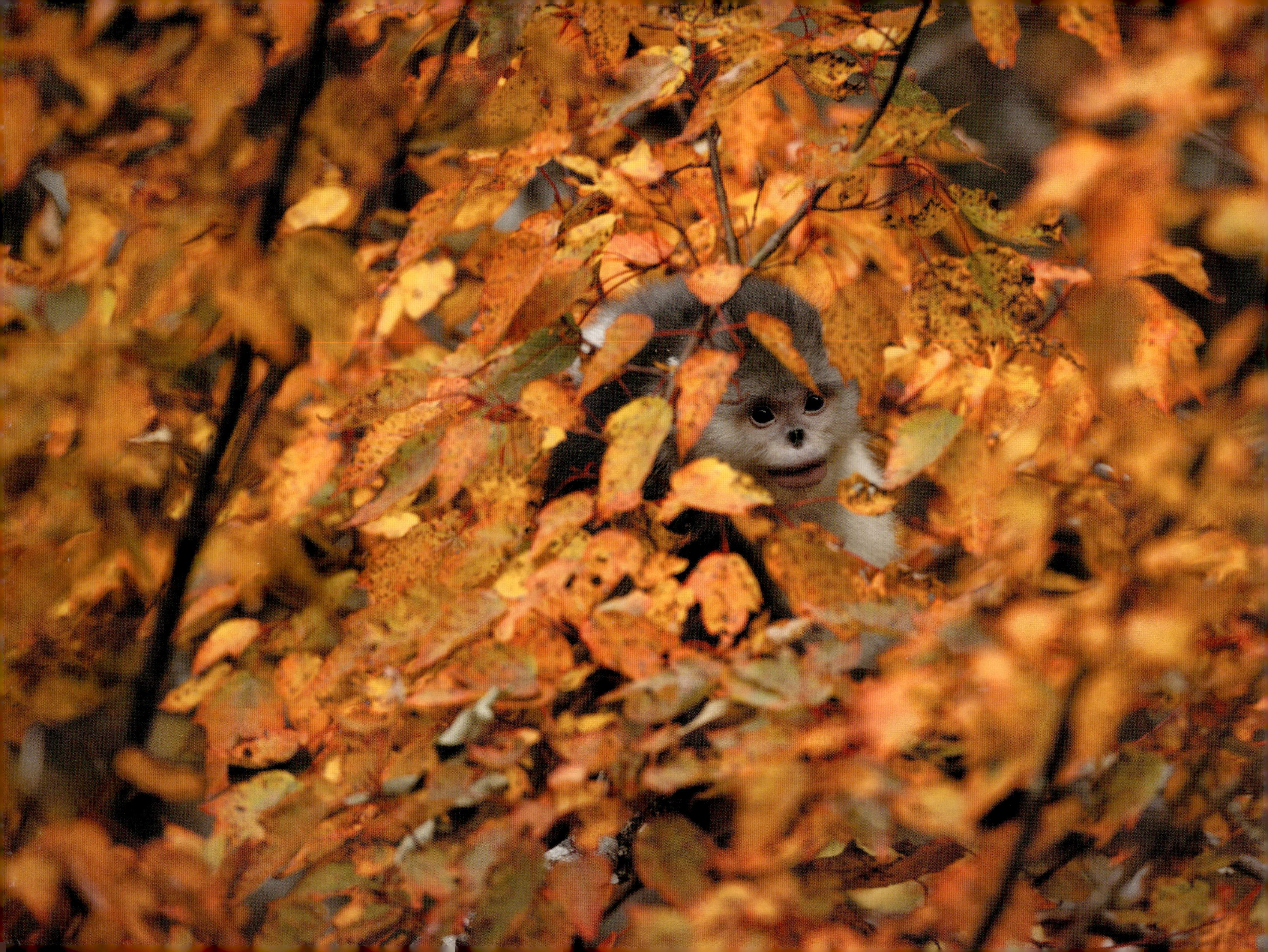

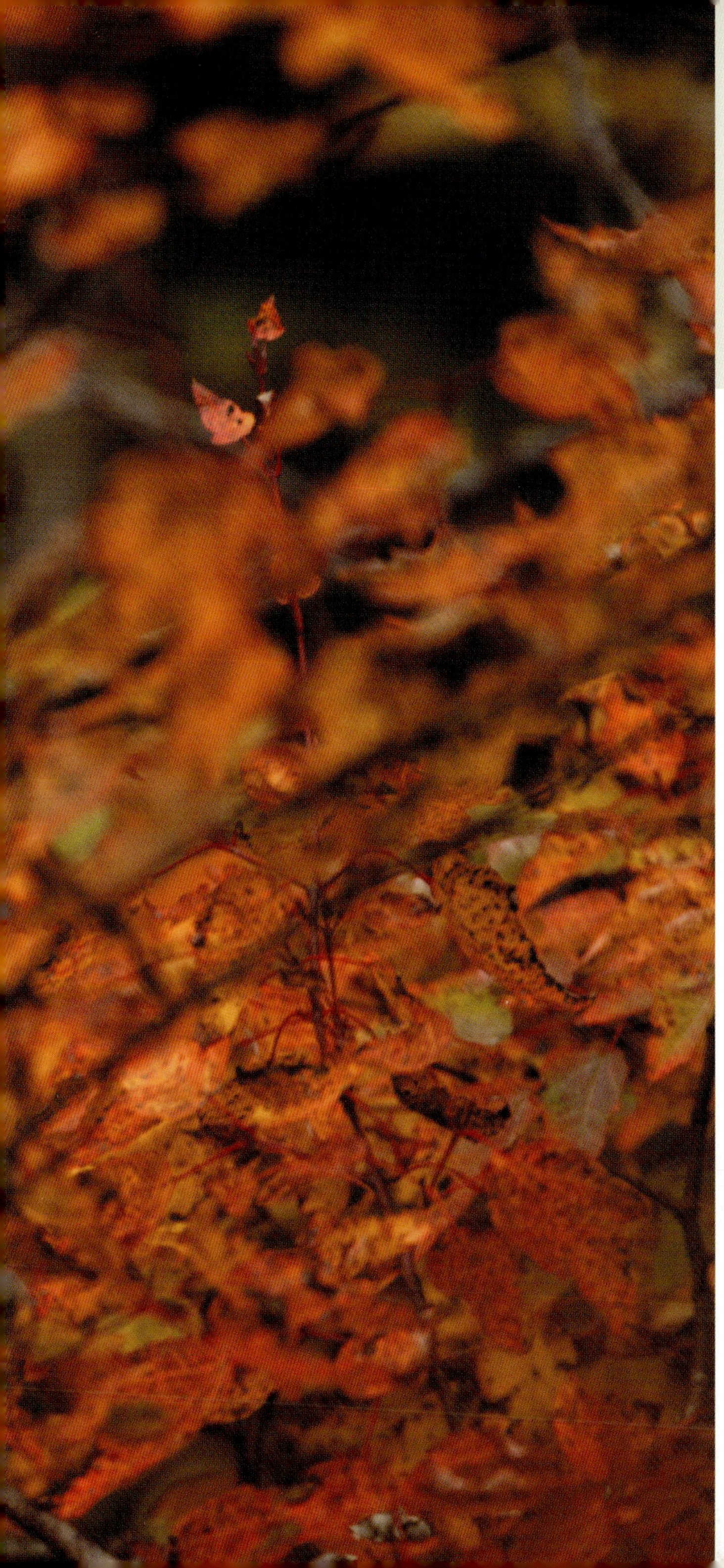

hard to see them in the wilderness. Moreover, data and information on wildlife is quite limited due to inadequate field research of wildlife. Hence, often times, photos taken by wildlife photographers are able to provide evidence and data for science research. Lots of my works were the first science evidence for those species to be seen alive in field: Yunnan snub-nosed monkeys crossing flowstone shoals and the snow mountain-pass, or the first photo in over a hundred years capturing Przevalski's parrotbills (see page 133).

Luckily enough, I could have chance to reach and be close to the spectacular and wonderful Mother Nature, I made close contact with various wildlife and played hide-and-seek with them. I witnessed spruce Yunnan snub-nosed monkey mother leaping across the forest with their children (see page 63), I captured the grand scene of hundreds of Tibetan antelopes migrating in the chilly wind and snow, and unexpectedly I met with takins over the ridge of the Qinling Mountains (see page 13).

Mother Nature can't speak like human, nor can wildlife. I expect my photos and works could speak for them. From the first day I picked up the camera, I took it as a tool. It is the photographer's responsibility to capture the touching message from the Mother Nature then passing it to a broader audience. I hope those images would compel and motivate for conservation efforts. I believe the power of image, I also believe this power will be able to inspire for actions contributing to conservation. Of course, one person is far from enough to achieve this goal, we should also take advantage of websites, various publications, photo exhibitions, and public campaigns, to share the astonishing beauty and pristine image of nature and wildlife with the public.

This book is a record of my wilderness adventures in the last two decades, covering over half of the nation. This includes three wildlife zones: Tibetan-Highlands alpine region, Xinjiang-Inner Mongolia dry-land, and monsoon region of Eastern China. You will find particular vegetation types and species in those three zones.

The chapters of this book try to follow the rationale of the abovementioned three zones, yet there might be some overlaps in term of species as same species can be found in more than one region. I also try to introduce some species following the photographing location. Considering bird is the major migrating species in my book, and there is a huge spatial and latitudinal difference between their breeding and winter resting sites, a separate chapter is devoted especially to focus on migrate birds.

A Yunnan snub-nosed monkey occasionally shows its face amidst the broad-leaved forests at low sea level. The photographer hopes to reveal the beauty and sorrow of Mother Nature through pictures, so as to let more people know, pay attention to, and participate in the protection of wild animals.

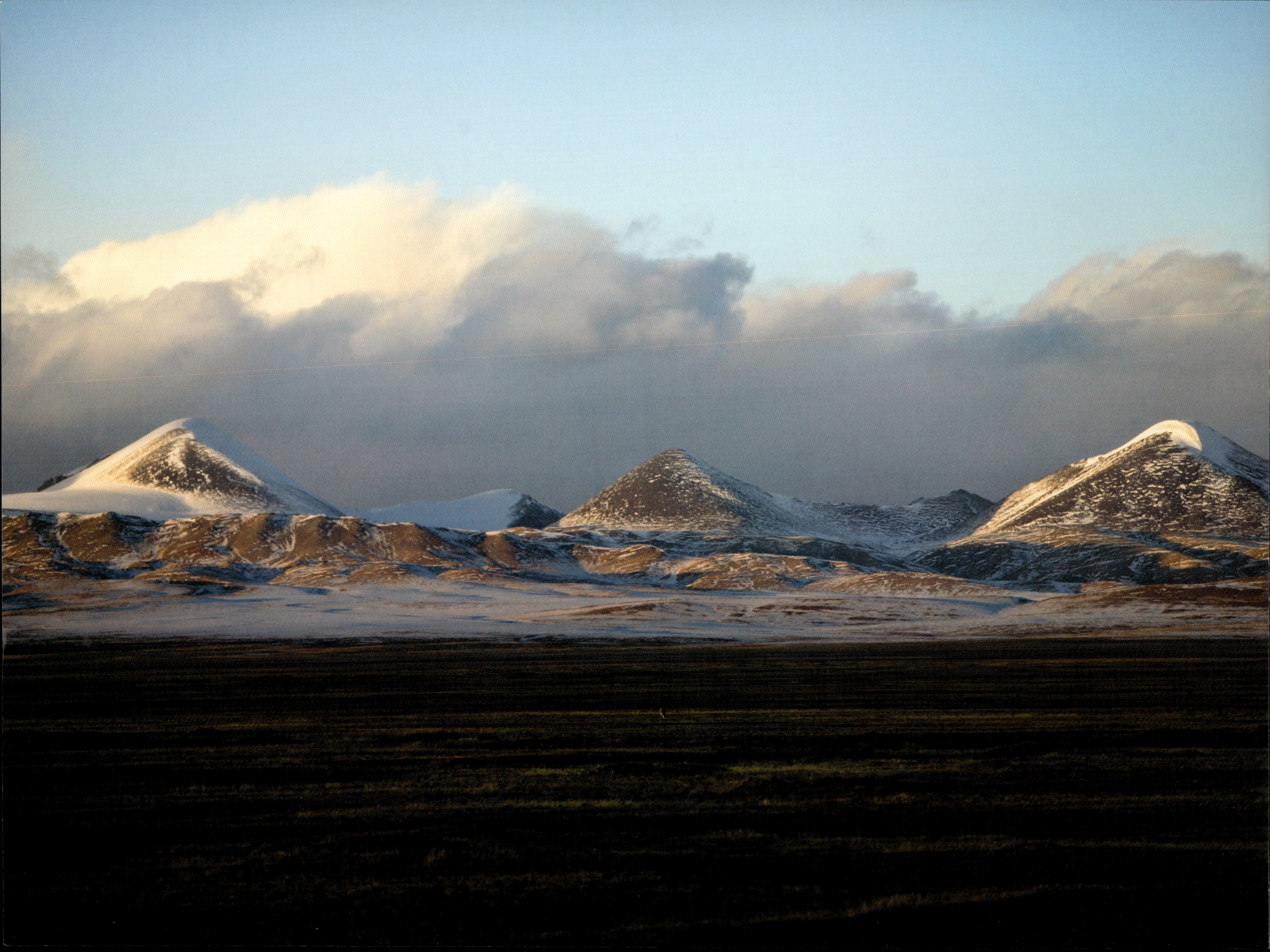

Part One
Tibetan-Highlands

As the biggest plateau in China and the one with the highest sea level in the world, the Tibetan Plateau (Qinghai-Tibetan Plateau) covers an area of 2.4 million square kilometers. It is reputed as "the roof of the world" and "the third pole." In the long process of geological growth and natural evolution, the plateau has formed a system of natural ecology marked by various types.

The Tibetan Plateau is a very unique and natural geographic area both in China and in the world. Covering 25% of the total area of China, it extends from the Kunlun Mountains, Altun Mountains, and Qilian Mountains in the north to the Himalayan Mountains in the south. This plateau averages over 4,500 meters above sea level, including mountains exceeding the snow line 6,000 to as high as 8,000 meters above sea level. In terms of topography, it also includes the outlying Pamirs Plateau and Hindu Kush Mountains as well as high mountains in the western cross-fault mountains

This area is featured by thin air, low temperature, and strong wind. With an annual mean temperature of below 0℃, it does not have a real summer. Its highland vegetation is marked by dwarf and sparse plants. Most parts of it fall into inland valleys with lots of lakes and the water is salty due to drought.

Five rivers in the world originated from the Tibetan Plateau. To its south, there is Yarlung Tsangpo River as the upper stream of Brahmaputra River, in addition to Nujiang River (i.e. Salween River), and Lancang River (i.e. the upper reach of Mekong River), as well as the famous Yangtze River and Yellow River.

Qinghai Lake, 3,200 meters above sea level in the northeast of the plateau, is the biggest lake in China with a water area of 4,400 square kilometers. However, like other lakes in this region, Qinghai Lake is witnessing a constant drop of water level.

A harsh environment characterizes the Tibetan Plateau, and the Himalayan Mountains have become the biggest partition in regards to the distribution of animals between Europe and Asia. However, Qaidam Basin, formed by the abrupt fall of the northern verge of the plateau, connects this natural area with the arid area of northwestern China, hence bringing some animals living under the highland climate to the Tibetan Plateau, such as goitered gazelles, horned larks, and Pallas's sandgrouses. Although there are not many kinds of animals on the Tibetan Plateau, some special animal species used to living under highland climates are seen here, such as Tibetan antelopes, wild yaks, several kinds of pikas, black-necked cranes, Tibetan rosefinchs, and Tibetan buntings. Despite their small number, local residents seldom do harm to them due to the passive nature of their religions. As a result, this region became the "paradise" of wild animals. Because of their special value, Tibetan antelopes were once hunted on a large scale, leading to a sharp drop in numbers. Now, they have become the most important animals under protection. Some other kinds of large animals have also been brought under protection in this region, such as Tibetan gazelles, wild yaks, argalis, blue sheep, kiangs, and snow leopards.

The Tibetan Plateau, also known as the "roof of the world."

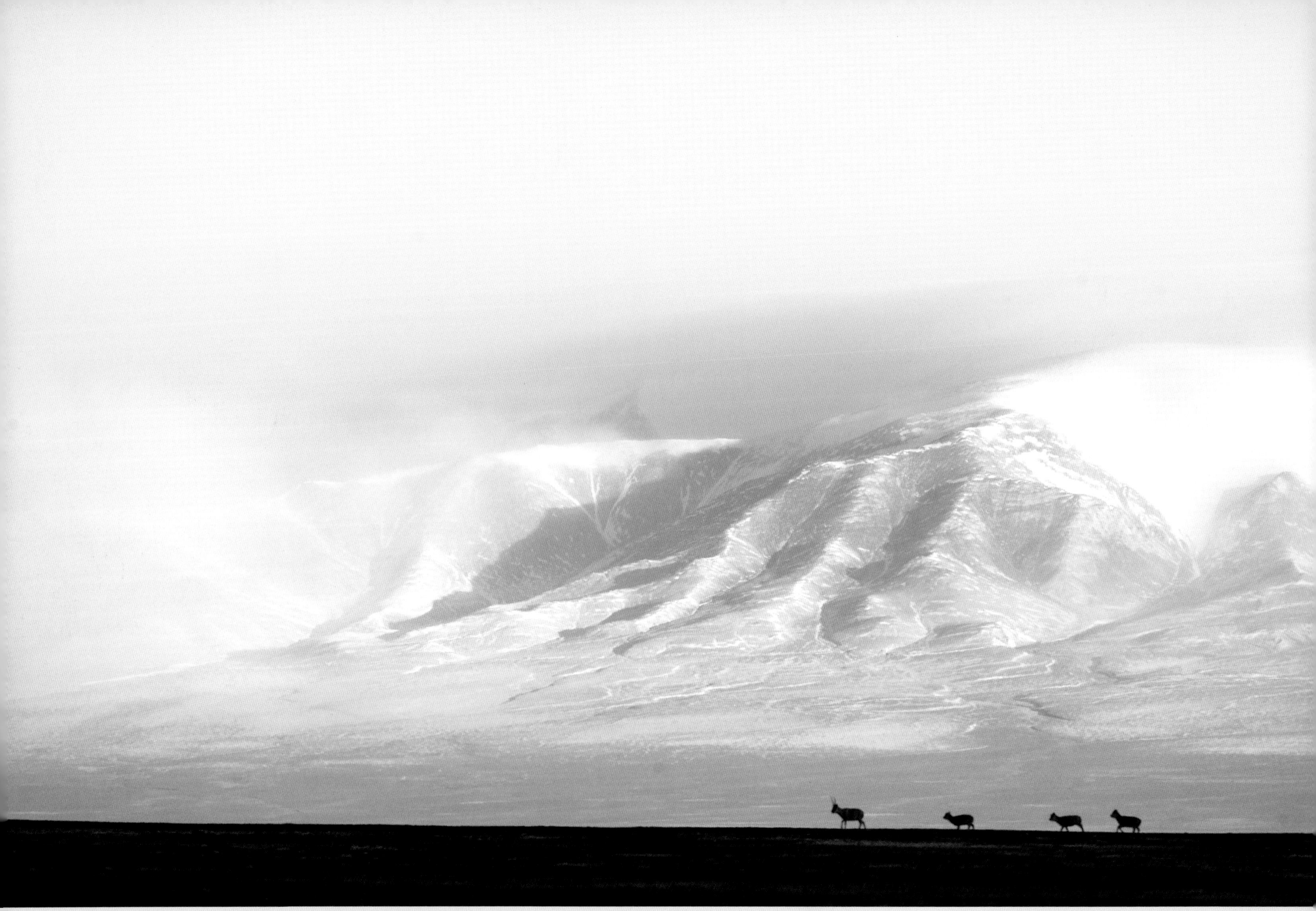

Chapter One
Hoh Xil—The Home of the Tibetan Antelopes

As one of the regions that best preserves the primitive eco-environment in the world, Hoh Xil is also one of the nature reserves of the largest area, the highest sea level, and the richest resource of wild animals and plants in China. It includes the Changtang Steppe in the northern Tibet Autonomous Region, the area to the south of the Kunlun Mountains in Qinghai province, and areas bordering the Xinjiang Autonomous Region with Tibet and Qinghai province. Without geographic screens, Hoh Xil is marked by high and steep terrains, has an average sea level of over 5,000 meters, severe cold climate, little rainfall, and lots of wind. It is known as "a forbidden area for human life" because of its big regional difference and harsh natural conditions, which make it impossible for human beings to live here for a long time. But because of this, Hoh Xil has created unique conditions for the survival of wild animals on the plateau, having become "a paradise for wild animals." There are wild yaks, Tibetan antelopes, kiangs, white-lipped deer, and brown bears as wild animals run rampant in the Tibetan Plateau. As shown by data, Hoh Xil is one of the regions with fairly rich animal resources in China, with over 230 kinds of wild animals.

Since the mid-1980s, along with a large influx of gold rushers and illegal hunters, wild animals in Hoh Xil have been hunted unscrupulously, leading to sharp drops in a number of species. In the past, Hoh Xil had criss-crossed car-ruts and abandoned gasoline tanks as well as dead bodies and skulls of those wild animals.

It is a long and arduous job to protect Hoh Xil and restore it to its primitive ecology. Gratifyingly, activities of various volunteers are unfolding in Hoh Xil, aiming to make it a tranquil home for wild animals without killings and destruction through the efforts and participation of the whole society.

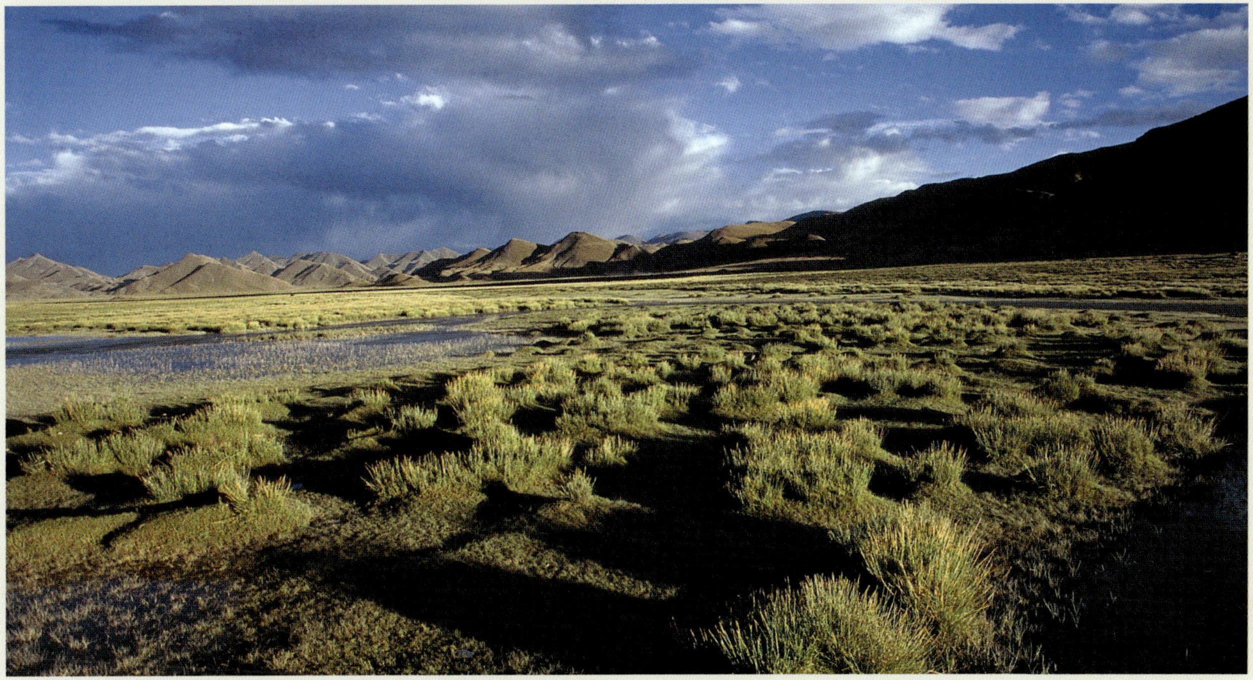

On facing page
The snowy mountains of Hoh Xil stretch continuously amidst the clouds and mists as Tibetan antelopes walk across the horizon.

Changtang Steppe represents the highland grassland of the Tibetan Plateau, which is marked by extremely fragile vegetation. Once damaged, it cannot be restored or it will take a very long time to restore. Ungulates live under unique conditions of climate and survival in this area.

Tibetan Antelope

Pantholops hodgsonii

IUCN Red List: Endangered

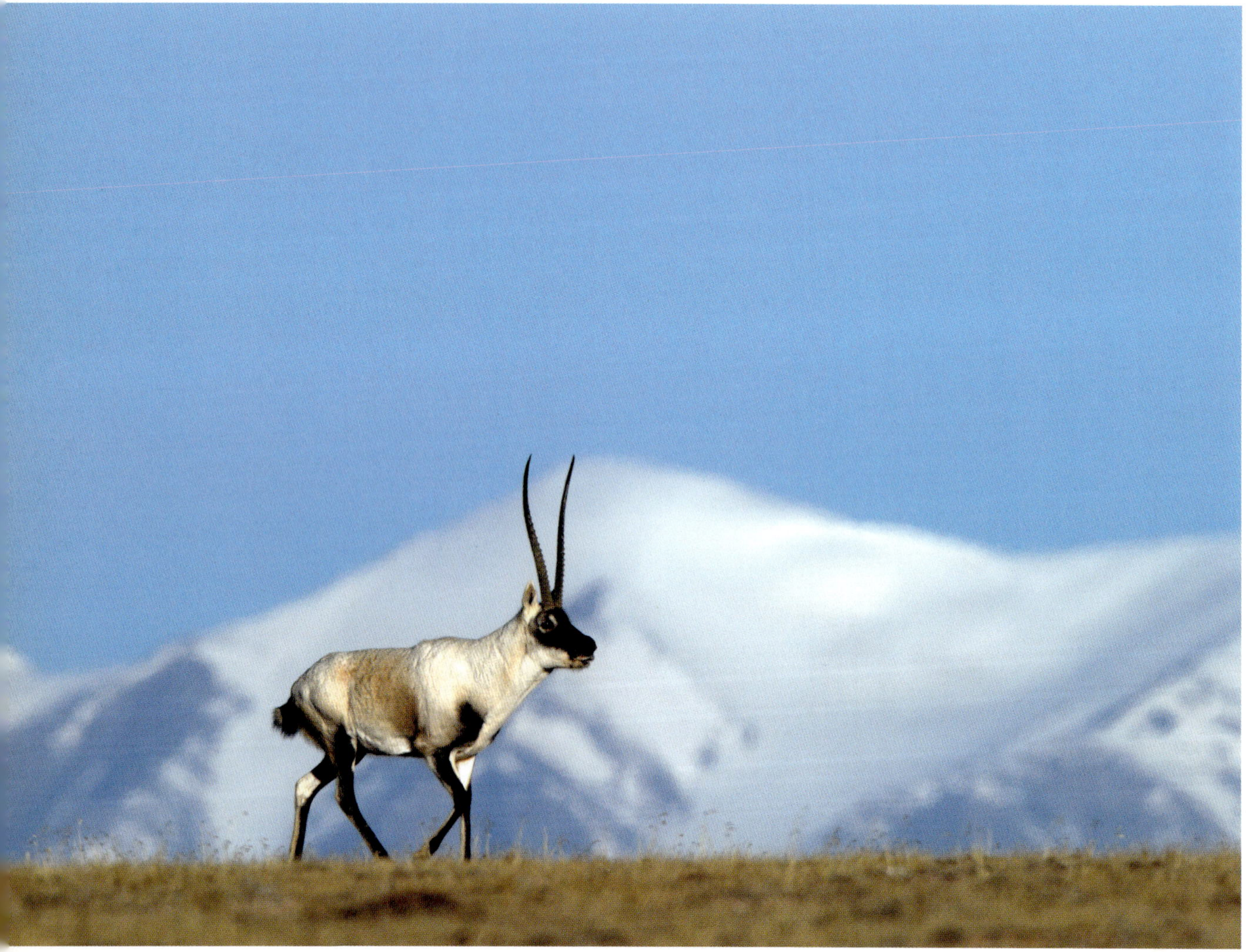

Deserts on the Tibetan Plateau are marked by thin air, very dry and cold climate, and a mean temperature below zero annually, hence keeping people away. Despite its status as "a forbidden area for human life," it is the home for Tibetan antelopes to propagate and live.

For hundreds of years, the bodies of Tibetan antelopes have been evolving to adapt themselves to such a harsh environment. Even in an environment of thin air, they can also continuously run for over ten kilometers at a speed of 80 to 100 kilometers per hour. Ordinary carnivores can by no means catch up with them.

In the period between each May and June, female Tibetan antelopes move to the place that they have been going to for generations for propagation. Their female babies also follow them to become familiar with the route. One month before propagation, pregnant antelopes get together and move along the set route from Sanjiangyuan Area (literally Three Rivers Source Area, here the three rivers are the Yangtze River, the Yellow River and the Lancang River) to such

The snout of the Tibetan antelope is convex and round while the nostrils are flanked by a walnut-shaped thing, like two air-clips, which serves to expand the volume of the nasal capacity for breathing in more oxygen.

On facing page
The adult female is taking her children back to their habitat.

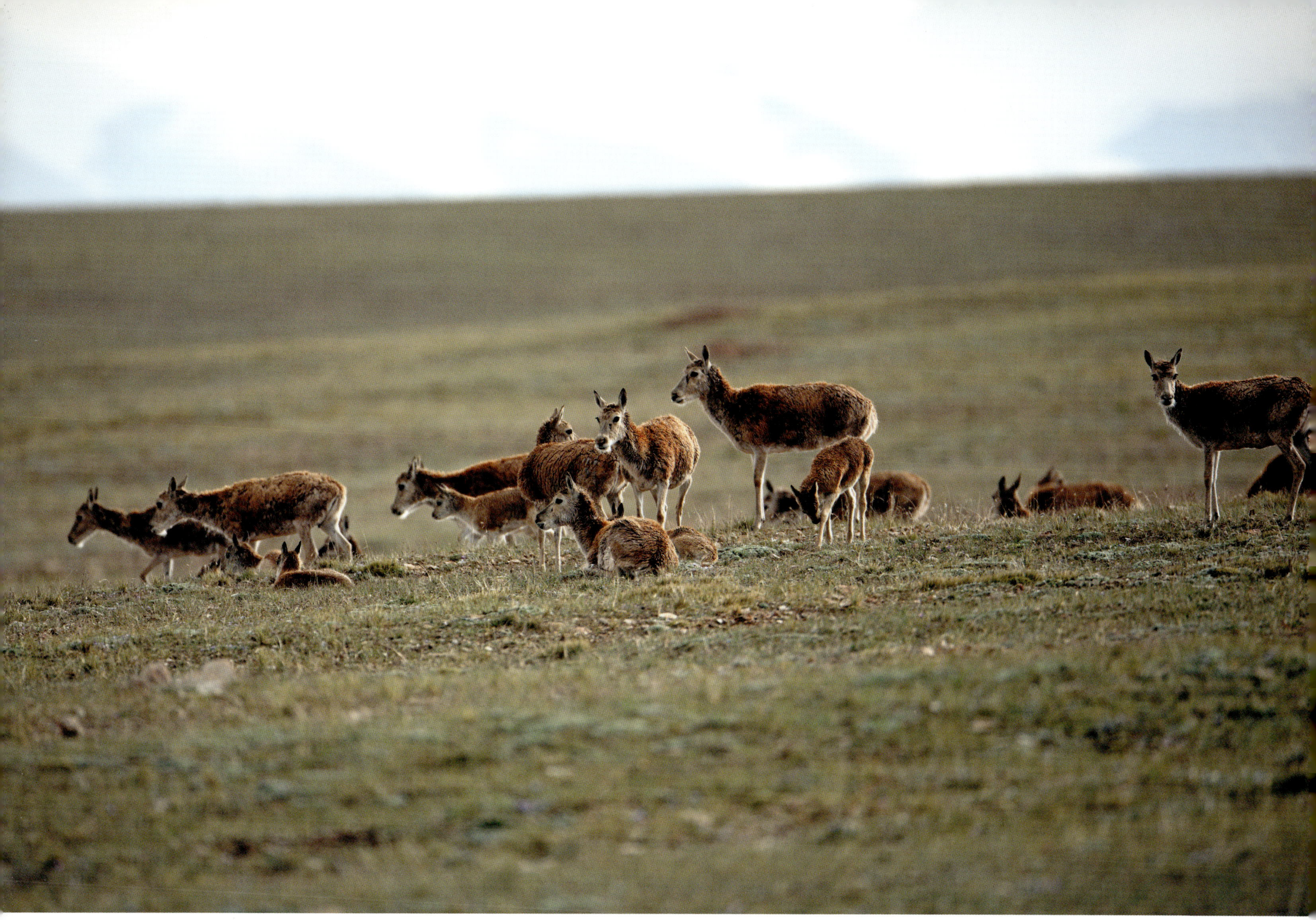

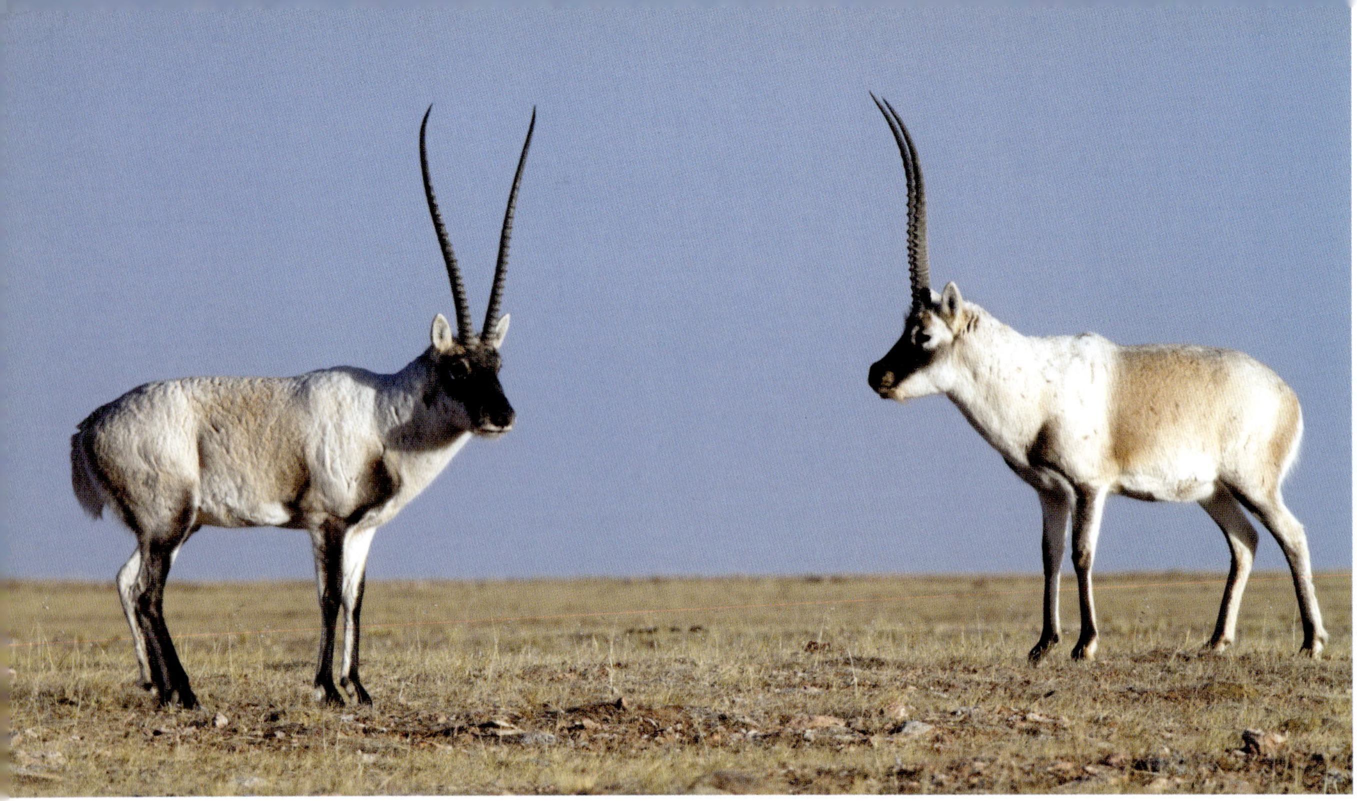

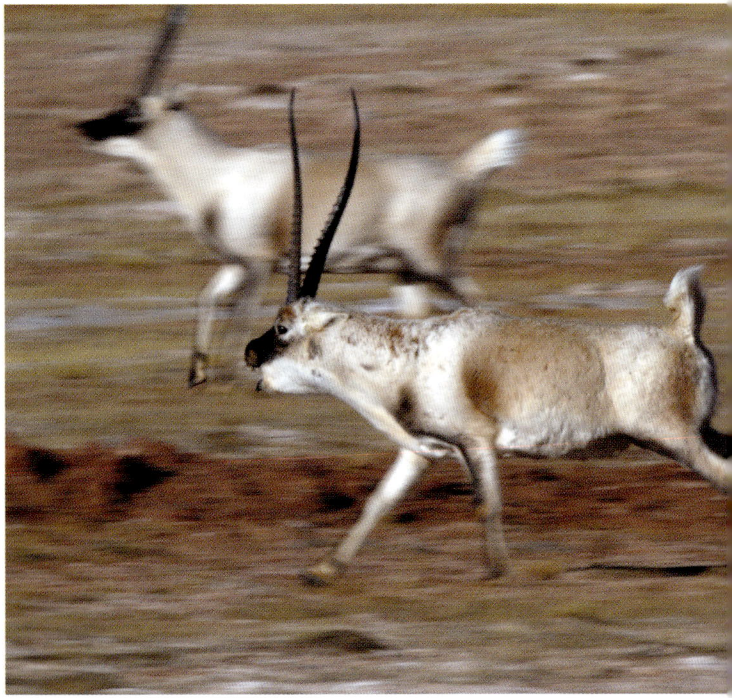

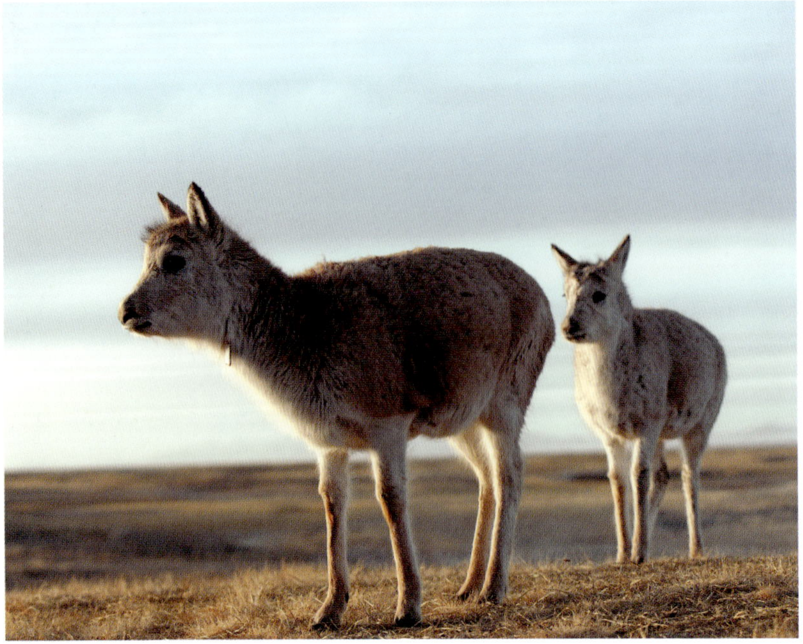

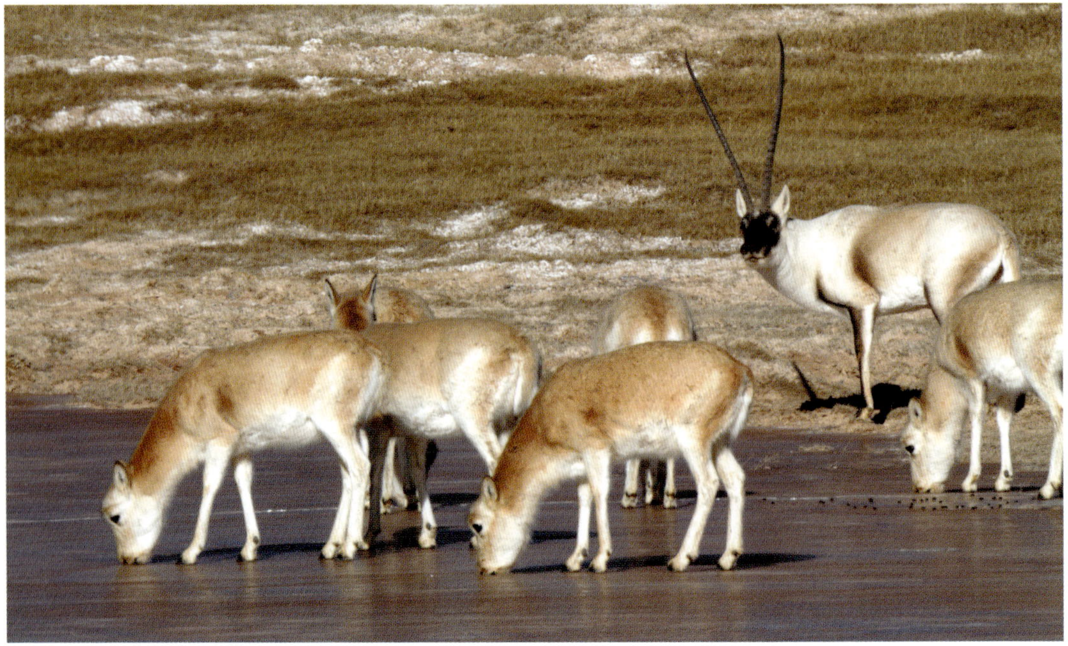

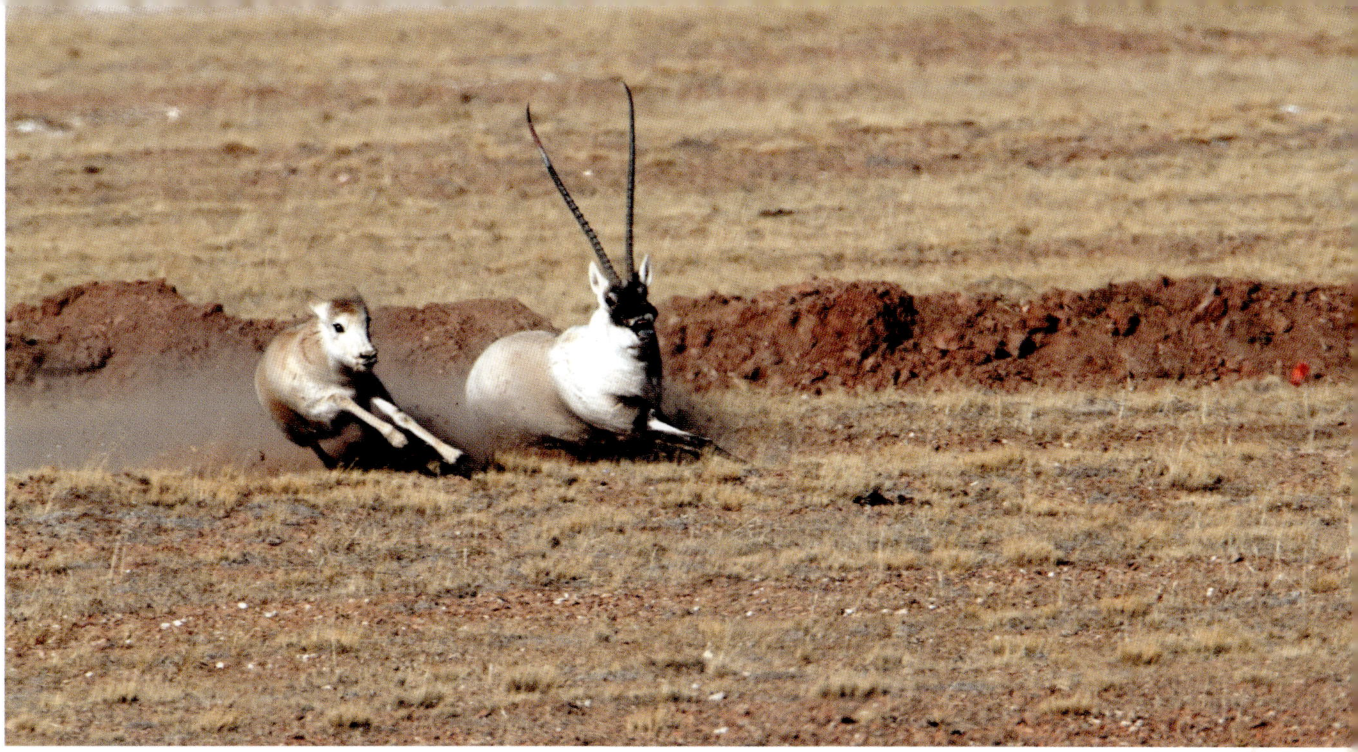

On facing page, above left
In the rutting season, the male Tibetan antelope wears a "wedding coat" of black and white with a pair of long horns pointing directly at the sky. In order to win over more females, male Tibetan antelopes must fight with one another. Two male Tibetan antelopes are confronting each other, ready to fight at any moment.

On facing page, above right
Two male Tibetan antelopes begin to run and chase after each other, making it almost impossible to take a picture of them.

On facing page, below left
Female antelopes quietly watch as two male antelopes fight fiercely with each other.

On facing page, below right
The male Tibetan antelope, as the final winner, proudly takes his "concubines" to the domicile. The "concubines" leisurely licks from the frozen icy river while the male Tibetan antelope is on the alert for other male Tibetan antelopes or a potential attack from wolves.

Right
Male Tibetan antelopes work very hard during the mating season. They have to guard their female partners against other male Tibetan antelopes. A female Tibetan antelope runs away and to bring his "sweetheart" back, the male Tibetan antelope takes a very spruce and swift turn to close the space between them.

Below
The mating is finally taking place.

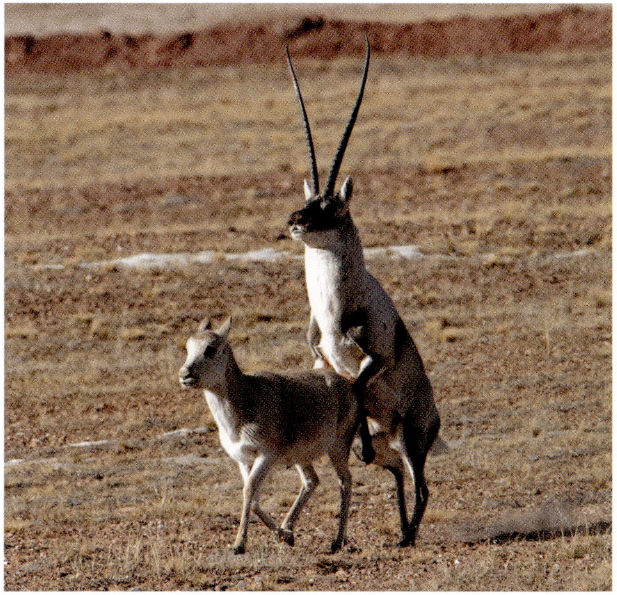

places as Ulan Ul Lake, Zonag Lake, Hoh Xil Lake, and Sun Lake. Female antelopes would travel together when meeting with each other on the way because they have to overcome various kinds of hardships and dangers. However, the mode of migration by Tibetan antelopes in Changtang of Tibet and in Altun Mountains of Xinjiang is quite different. They would divide themselves into groups of different sizes with each group having its own place for spending winter and propagation, rather than getting together at a unified place for propagation. After giving birth to calves, female Tibetan antelopes stay at the place of birth for about one month and then take their calves that are already able to run to embark on the long journey to return to their respective habitats.

Male Tibetan antelopes do not take part in the migration, since they need to reserve their energy for another "battlefield." The end of each autumn and the beginning of each winter is the rutting season. Just like hearing a soundless order, Tibetan antelopes in this period would automatically gather on the expansive meadow. "Polygamy" is practiced among Tibetan antelopes. Generally speaking, a male antelope have several and even dozens of female ones. There would be fierce fight among male antelopes, competing for female antelopes. Inexperienced and weak male antelopes would be injured and even stabbed to death. While chasing at a high speed after female ones, male antelopes would be injured because of their long and sharp horns.

Because of their life in a highland climate, Tibetan antelopes develop a very warm under wool that is used for producing the shawl known as shahtoosh shawl, a traditional garment among the people of Asia. Each summer, Tibetan antelopes undergo a change of fur that is abandoned to the wind. Slaughter is the only way to get the fur before it is shed. However, only 100 grams of fur is

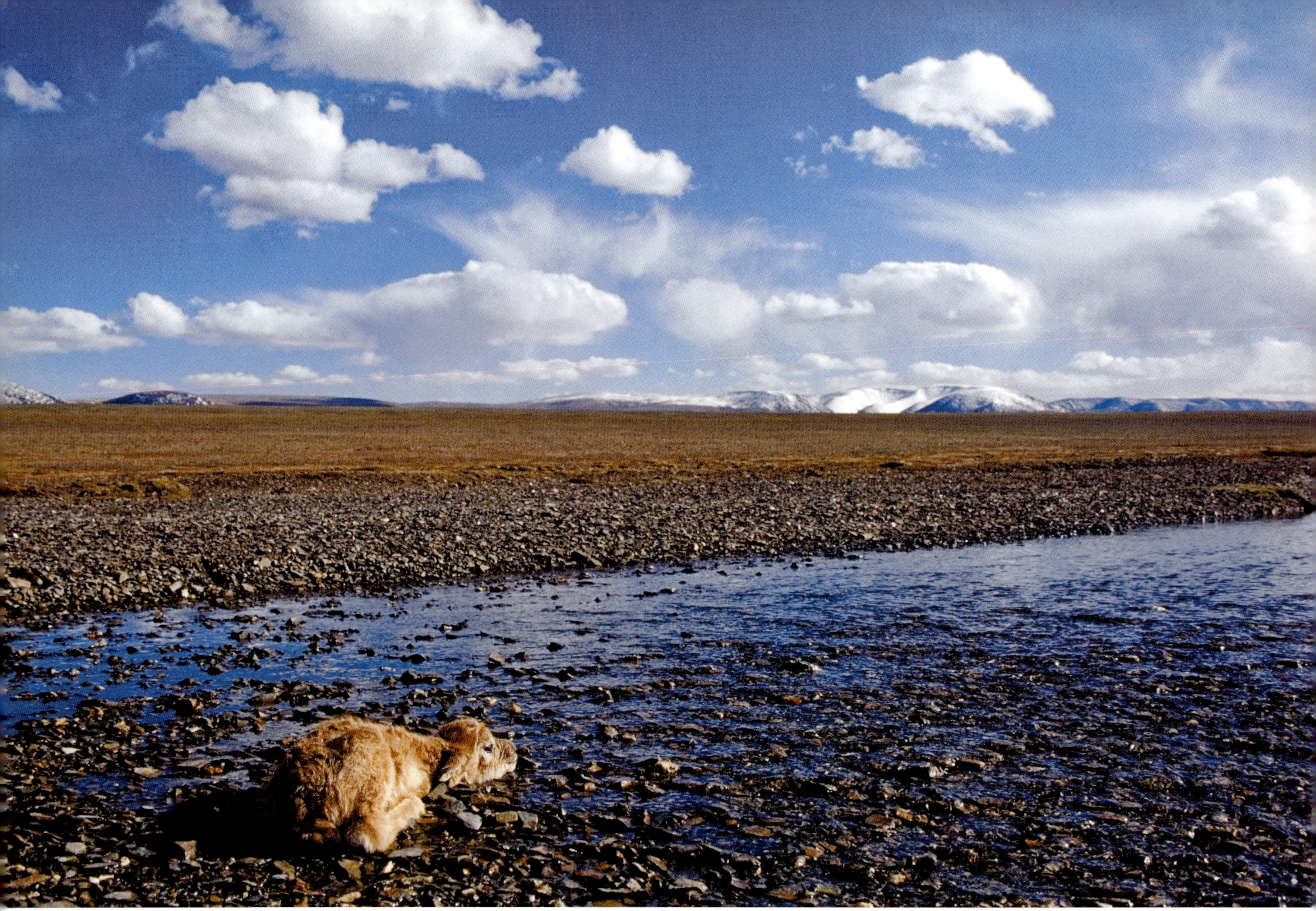

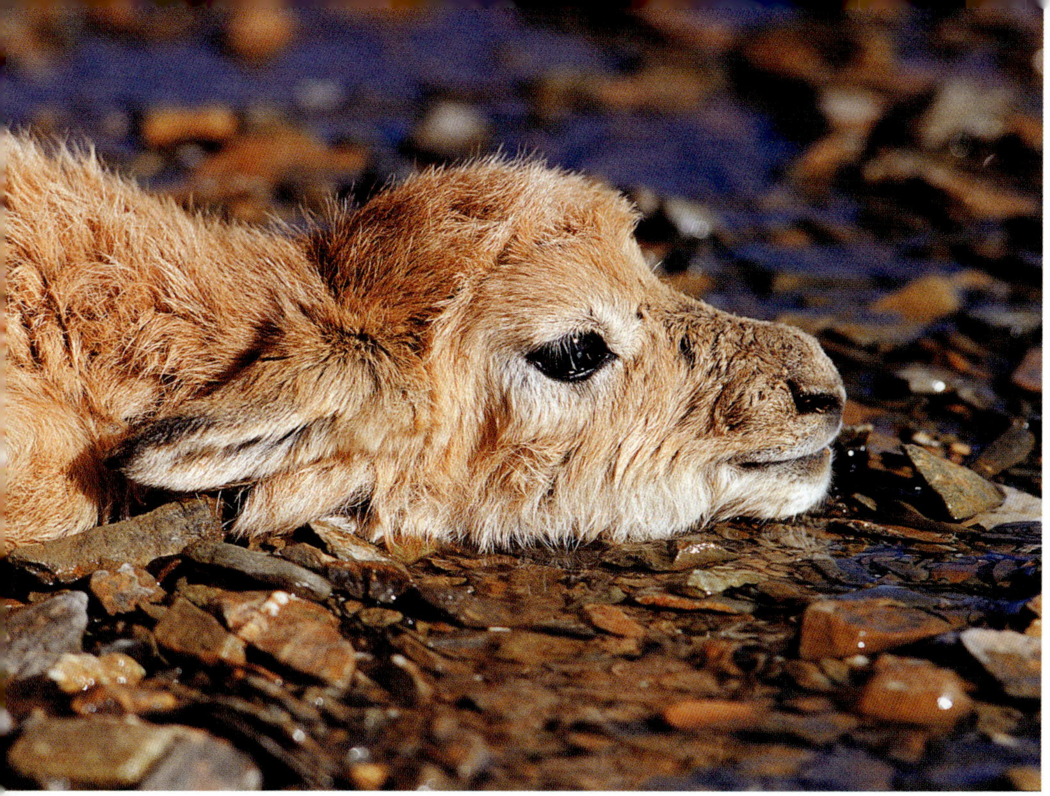

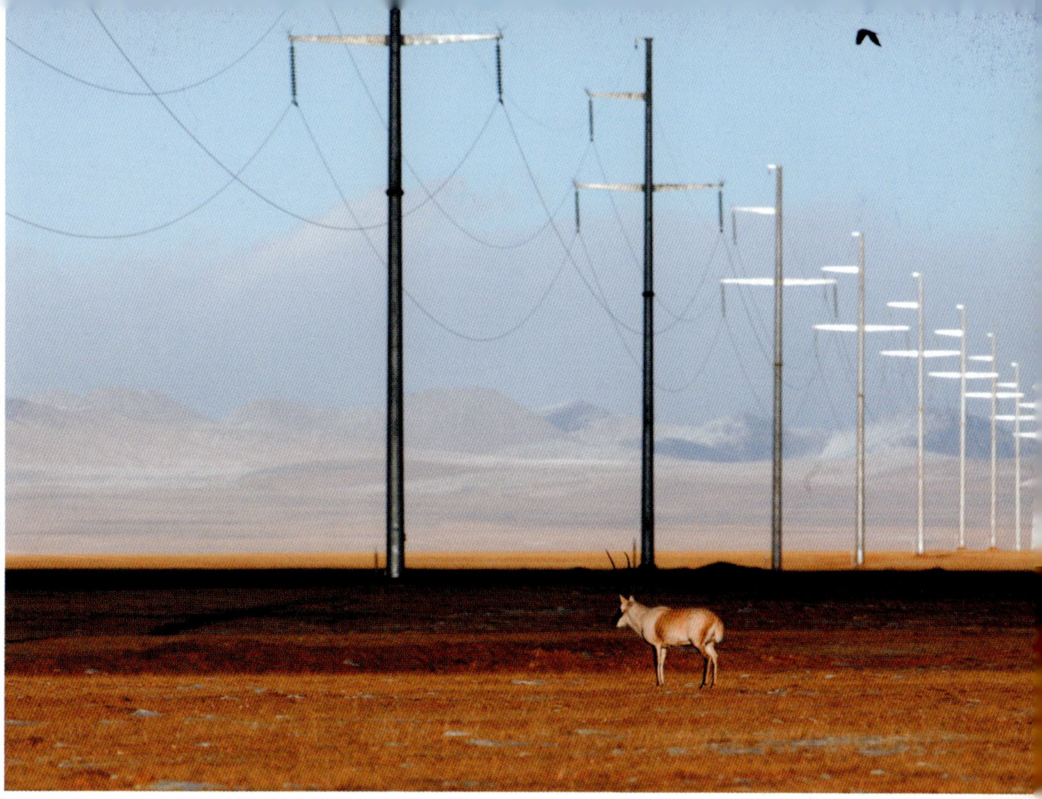

On facing page and the above left
This is a Tibetan antelope calf only a few days old, crouching motionlessly on the flooded land. It knows by instinct to stay motionless until its mother comes back.

Above right
Tibetan antelopes are trying to adapt and co-exist with human beings.

available on an antelope. A shahtoosh shawl of two meters long and one meter wide probably requires 300 to 400 grams of pure fur, equivalent to the life of three Tibetan antelopes. As the shahtoosh shawl has been brought to Europe and Northern America, it has become the fashion enthusiastically favored by the rich, thus fating Tibetan antelopes to the bottomless abyss. Great profit in the international market has directly led to massive slaughter of Tibetan antelopes and poachers even kill pregnant antelopes at the place of their propagation.

In the early 20th century, there were at least over one million Tibetan antelopes. However, in a short period of one century, the number of Tibetan antelopes has dropped dramatically from over one million to less than 100,000. In 1995, there were only an estimated 75,000.

With the efforts and appeal of Chinese and international organizations of protection, in 1997, Tibetan antelopes were listed into species of Appendix I of *Washington Convention*, i.e. *Convention on International Trade in Endangered Species of Wild Fauna and Flora* (species of Appendix I refer to those that are threatened with extinction and are/or may be affected by trade). Measures for protecting Tibetan antelopes in the chains of production and trade of shahtoosh shawl have gone into action and international cooperation has dealt effective blow at illegal hunting and smuggling. In 2008, Tibetan antelopes became the mascot of the Olympic Games in Beijing, having further enhanced international perception of Tibetan antelopes.

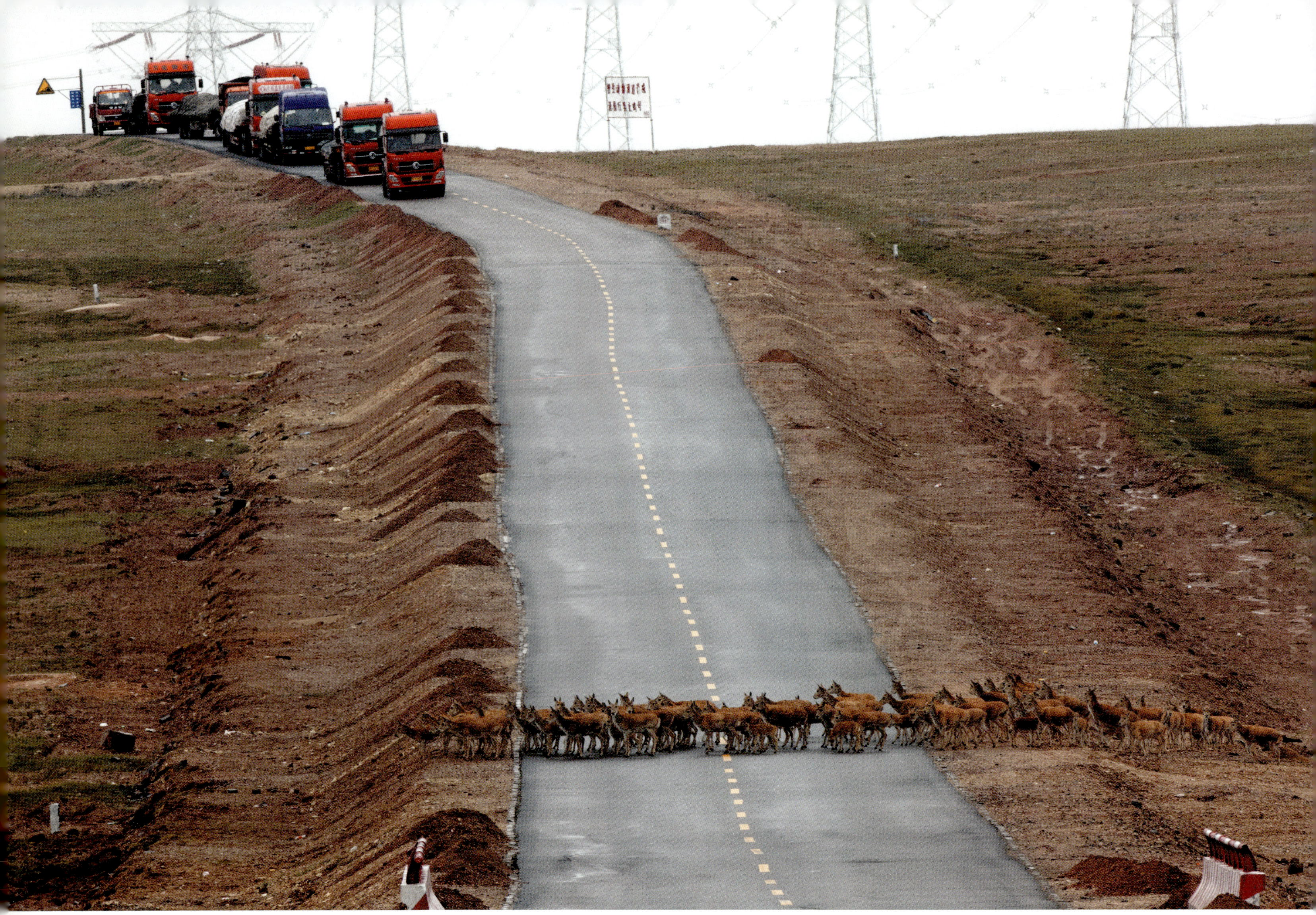

Protecting Tibetan Antelopes

In the summer of 1998, as a photographer, I took part in an investigation of the propagation place of Tibetan antelopes in the Altun Mountains Nature Reserve. This was the first time that human beings entered the propagation place of Tibetan antelopes.

Our destination was a breeding ground at the foot of Ulugh Muztagh peak. Upon entering this area, we found new and dense car ruts that must have been left behind by poachers. Immediately after that, we saw vultures hovering in the sky. Following the car ruts and heading to the place where the vultures landed, we quickly discovered the first pile of dead Tibetan antelopes, with their blood still fresh and eyes pecked to a mess by vultures. The blood of a female antelope remained uncondensed with her children lying next to her. As revealed by their size and hair-color, they were born only in one or two days ago, not yet ready to open their eyes to see this world as they died of hunger. Some were drawn out by vultures from the womb of their mothers even before they were born!

The Altun Mountain Nature Reserve work staff travelling with us was also shocked, as they originally believed that poachers would kill Tibetan antelopes when their wool is the thickest in winter. They did not expect the poachers to sneak into the propagation place of Tibetan antelopes that was unknown to the outside world! After leaving the first pile of dead Tibetan antelopes, in a walking distance of less than 200 meters, we found the second pile of dead Tibetan antelopes. Before reaching our camp for the night, we had discovered three piles of this kind. As shown by statistics after the investigation, we found eleven piles with 84 dead Tibetan antelopes which was the number of female antelopes, excluding the number of calves. The biggest pile included 24 female antelopes and 15 calves, which died right after they were born.

In the winter of 1998, the investigation team again looked into the mating of Tibetan antelopes. At the camp, team members could hear bumping resulting from fierce fight among male Tibetan antelopes every evening. In this investigation of over 20 days, we saw less than 200 Tibetan antelopes at an important place of their mating.

In the summer of 1999, when the team went there again, it was found that the number of Tibetan antelopes killed was ten times as much as that in 1998! As many as over 1,000 dead female Tibetan antelopes were seen on the ancient land of their propagation, in addition to over 1,000 calves which were just born! These weak lives need protection of our full efforts.

In December of 1997, I went with an anti-poaching patrolling team to an area without human beings the first time, an area covering several thousand square kilometers in Hoh Xil, Qinghai province. This was a 14-day patrol in winter. In this period, we took pictures of blood-shedding Tibetan antelope fur in piles in Golmud. After returning to Beijing, we presented a video of the illegal hunting of Tibetan antelopes and an anti-poaching campaign for TV, revealing for the first time the situation concerning the existence of Tibetan antelopes in China, and informing related units and environmental protection organizations of the tragic sight of slaughtered Tibetan antelopes. Within a short period of time, Tibetan antelopes became a hot topic in the public, prompting related governmental departments to begin to protect Tibetan antelopes and strike at poachers.

On facing page
After giving birth to calves in Hoh Xil, the female Tibetan antelopes take their newborn calves to cross the Qinghai-Tibet Highway.

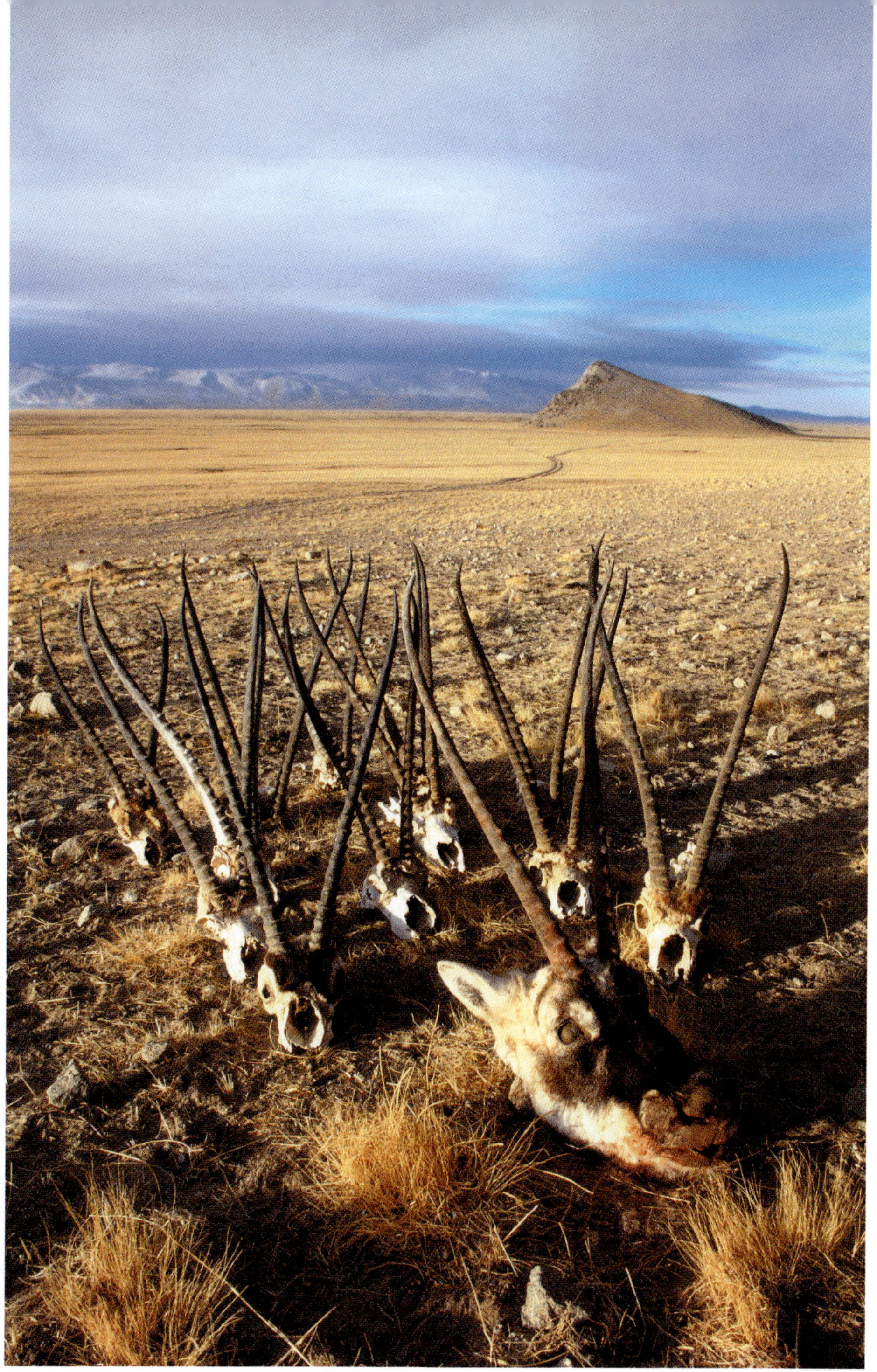

Right
While taking pictures in the Altun Mountains, the photographer placed the skulls of male Tibetan antelopes as evidence of crimes committed by illegal hunters.

Wild Yak

Bos mutus

IUCN Red List: Vulnerable

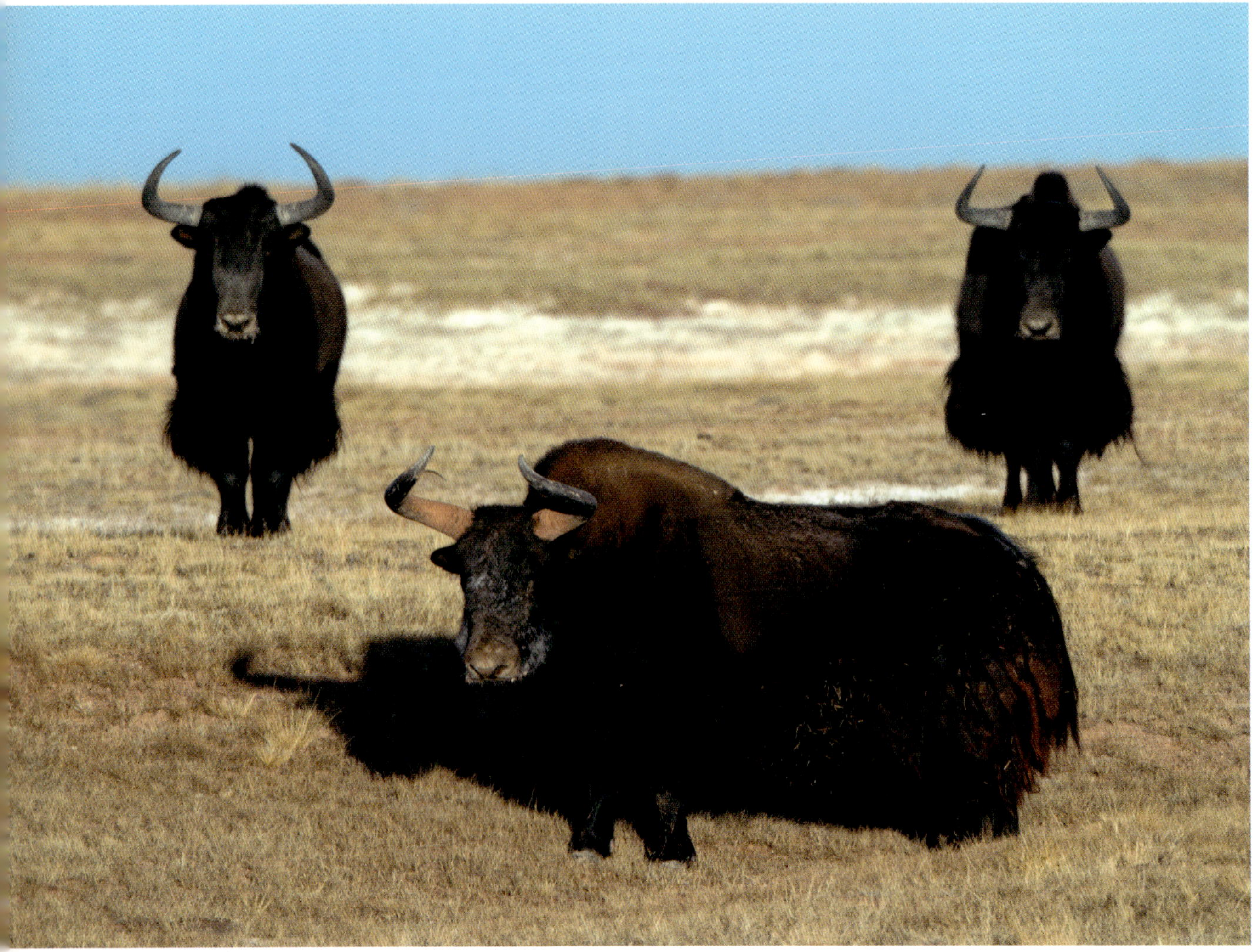

As animals unique to the Tibet Plateau, wild yaks are the ancestors of the domestic yaks. They are typical highland animals with lungs and hearts that are bigger than those animals living in areas of low sea level and have an extraordinary ability to supply oxygen to the blood, hence being able to live in various environments such as an alpine meadow 3,000 to 6,000 meters above sea level, high mountains and peaks almost without human beings, mountain basins, highland grassland, and highland desert steppes. In the summer, they can even reach places of 5,000 to 6,000 meters above sea level, moving around in the lower part of the snow line.

With hard teeth and a strong ability to collect food, wild yaks are characterized by digestive organs larger than an ox's. They look for food chiefly at night and in the early morning, and their food mainly includes such highland desert plants as sedges and sagebrushes. Their special tongue structure enables them to eat cushion plants. In the daytime, they stand on the steep cliffs of desolate mountains, ruminating or lying down for rest and sleep.

They have an acute sense of smell. In case of danger, male ones would surely bear the brunt to protect the group. When their enemy is approaching, wild yaks would look down with their tails turning up and then start to run wildly around, disappearing all of a sudden. They enjoy living in groups. Except for a few males that tend to move

On facing page
One wild yak seems to be waiting for an opportune moment to make a move as two others stand quietly in the back.

Above right
Wild yaks looking for food in the Wild-Yak Gully in Qinghai province.

Below right
Wild yaks are the biggest wild animals on the Tibetan Plateau. An adult male can weigh as much as a ton. In the winter, there is little rainfall on the Tibetan Plateau. Wild yaks lick snow to quench their thirst while eating grass.

around individually, wild yaks, male and female, old and young, would be together, as few as several and as many as hundreds and even thousands in number. Old male ones are introverted, often living away from groups in the summer with three to four of them staying together.

Wolves in groups are their major natural predators. They often surround old, young, and weak yaks, forcing the latter onto the ice and prey on them when they slip down. Although excessive hunting of wild yaks has been brought under control, domesticated animals still graze on the living space of wild yaks.

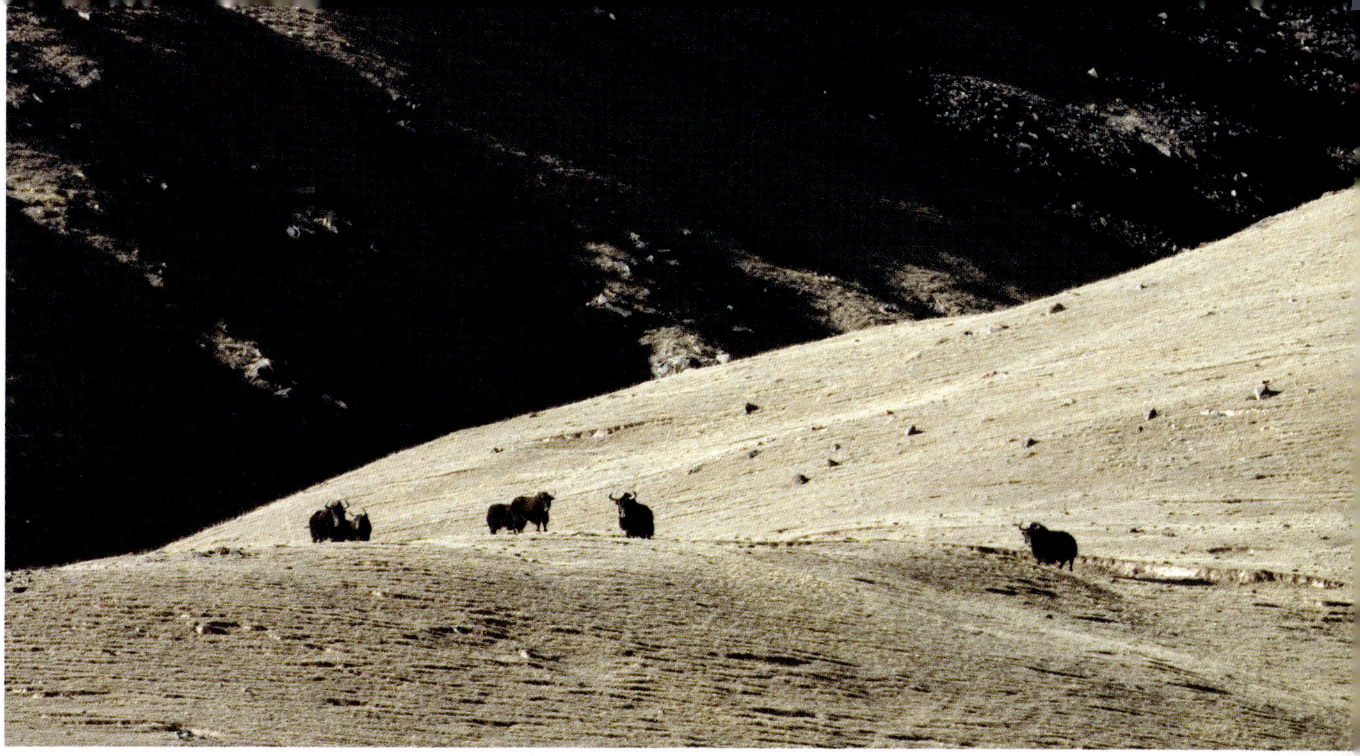

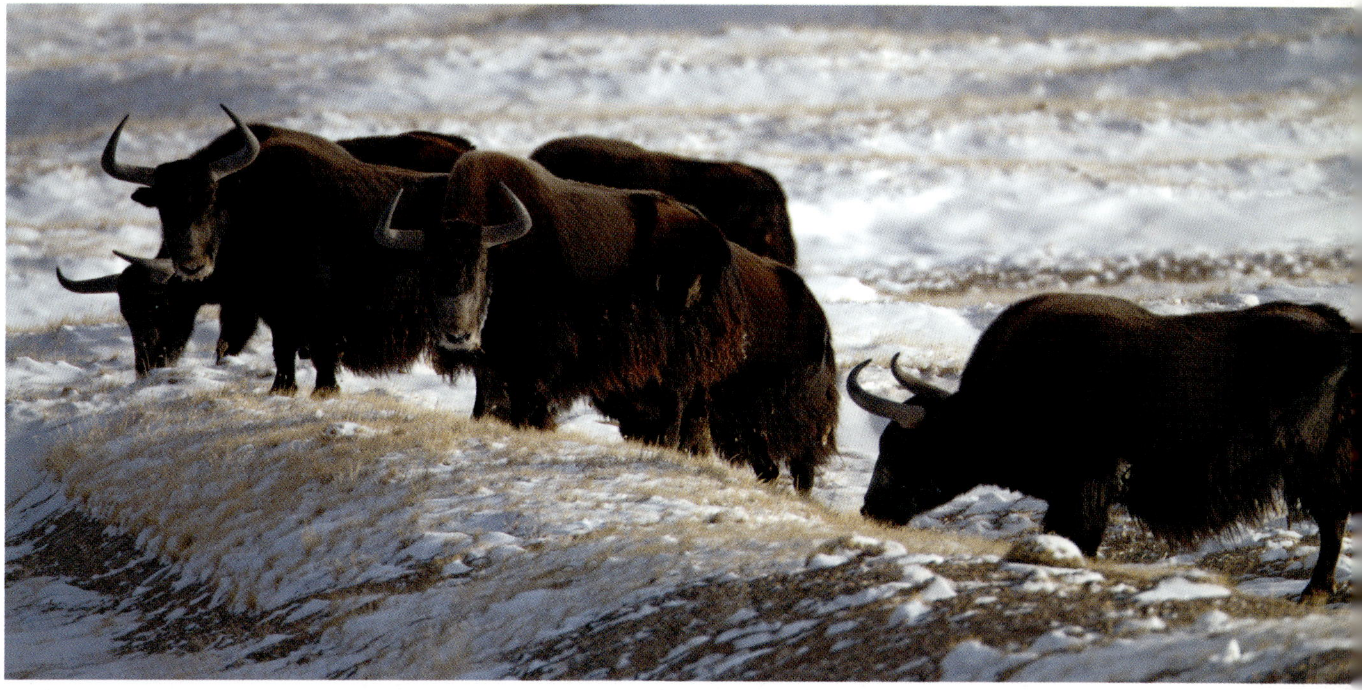

My Unexpected Encounter with Wild Yaks

In one winter, for picture taking, I went to a plateau of about 4,300 meters above sea level in Aksai of Gansu province. This was a desolate piece of land. After searching for several days, I finally found a group of wild yaks eating grass on a slope about one kilometer away. Covered by the terrain, my companions and I walked quietly toward them along an icy river. When we climbed onto a slope, wild yaks suddenly appeared at a place only 100 meters away from us. It was an unexpected encounter between human beings and wild animals. Over 50 robust wild yaks instantly got ready for a fight. Horns of all male yaks were unanimously directed at us. I thought it was a golden opportunity for me and I kept taking pictures of them. Luckily, for reasons unknown to us, wildly running yaks abruptly took a turn at a place 30 to 40 meters away from me, rushing thunderously toward the other side of the icy river.

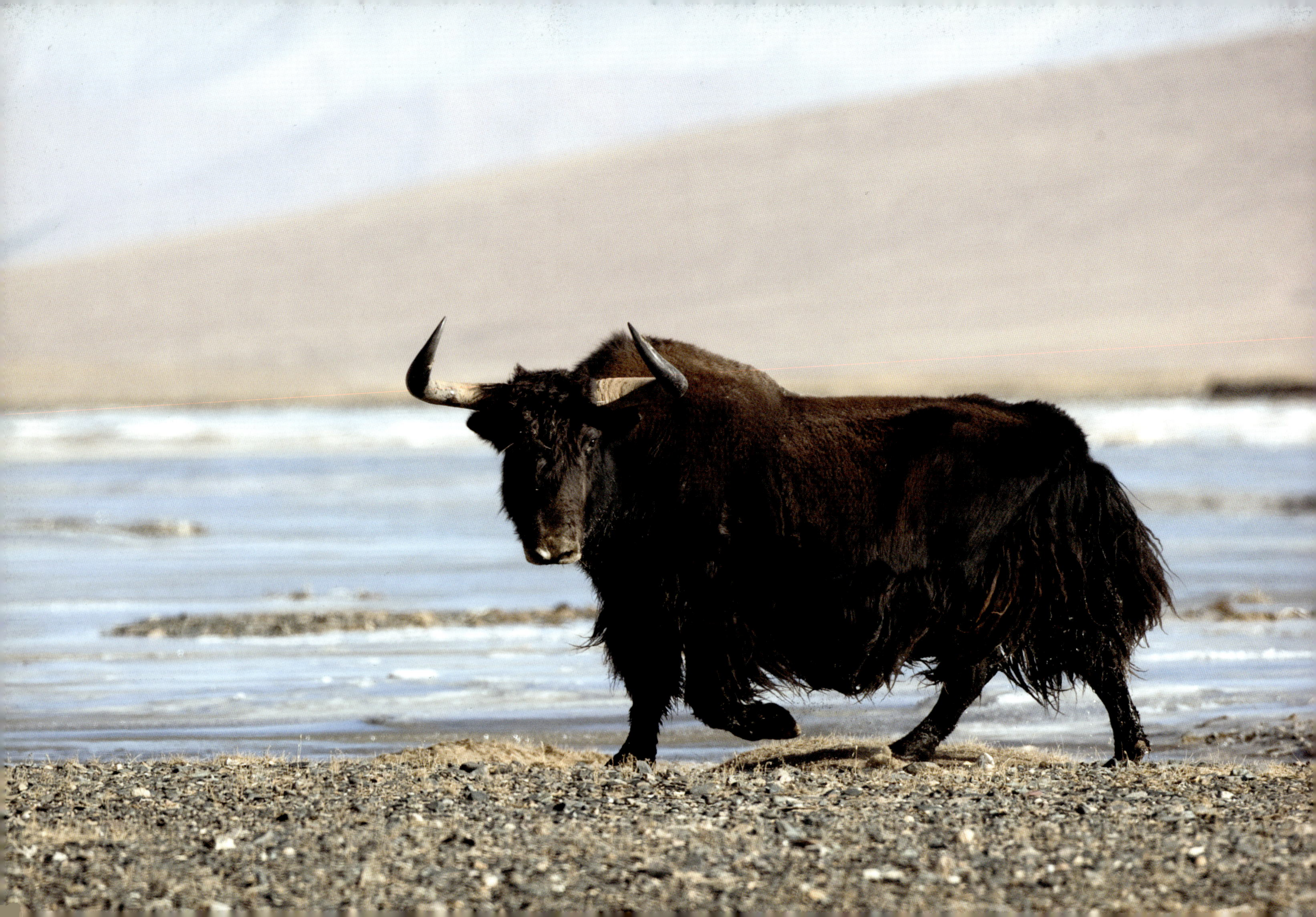

On facing page
A wild yak performs an elegant waltz while running.

Below
This huge wild yak is like a lonely hero quietly strolling in the vast, expansive wilderness.

Far below
Wild yaks are seen along the Qinghai-Tibet Railway.

Right
A hot-tempered wild yak is running towards the photographer. Its big fan-like tail is standing up, its nostrils are puffing, its limbs are kicking up dust, and its horns seem to be ready to attack the "intruder" at any time. Its convex back adds to its fierceness.

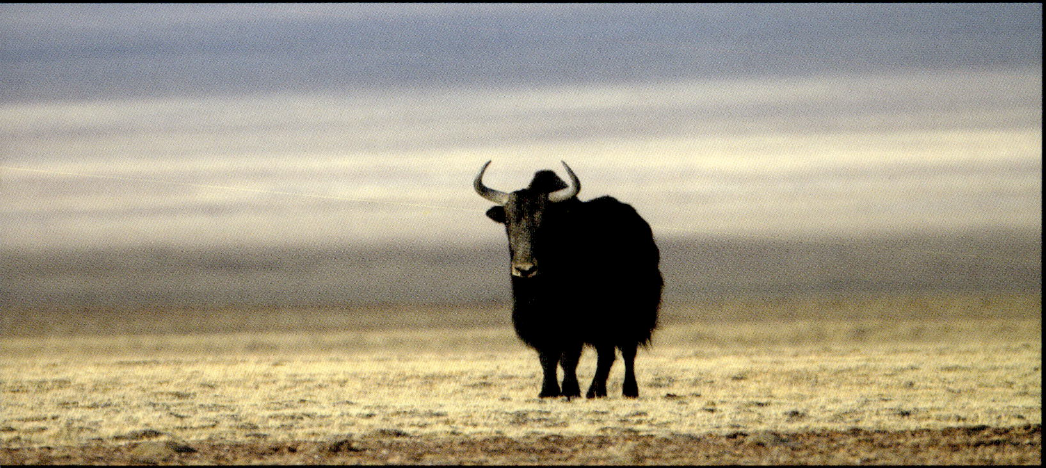

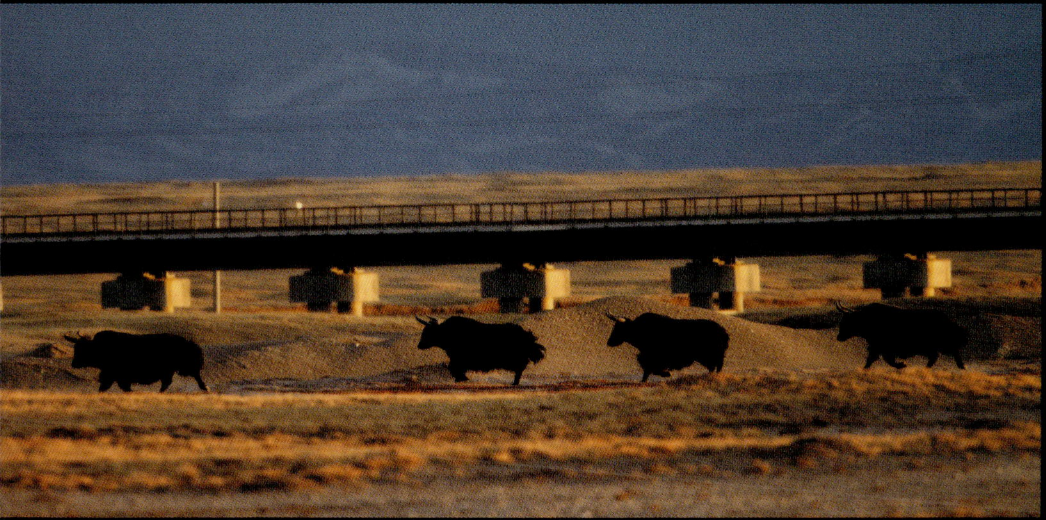

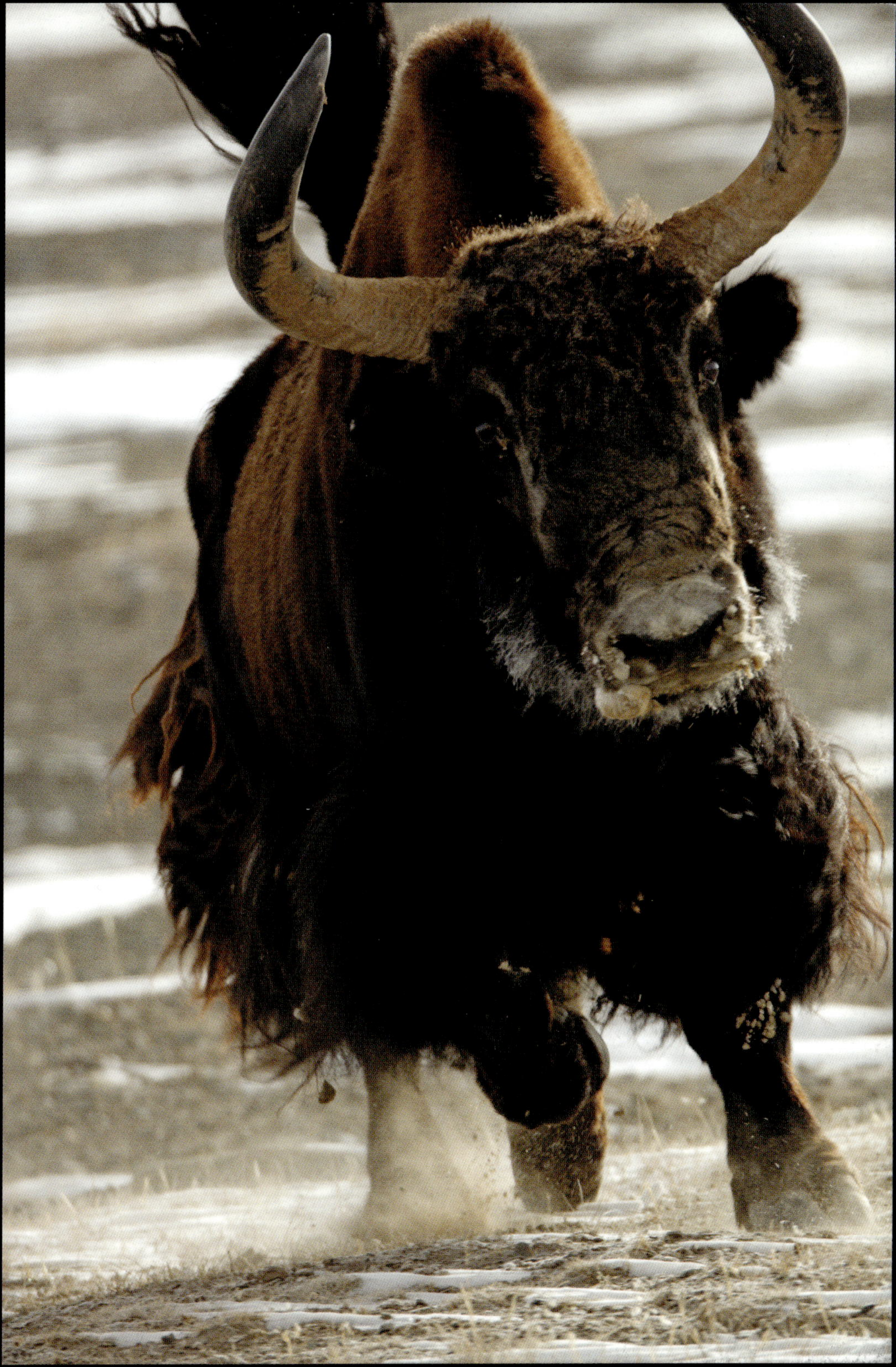

Tibetan Gazelle

Procapra picticaudata
IUCN Red List: Near Threatened

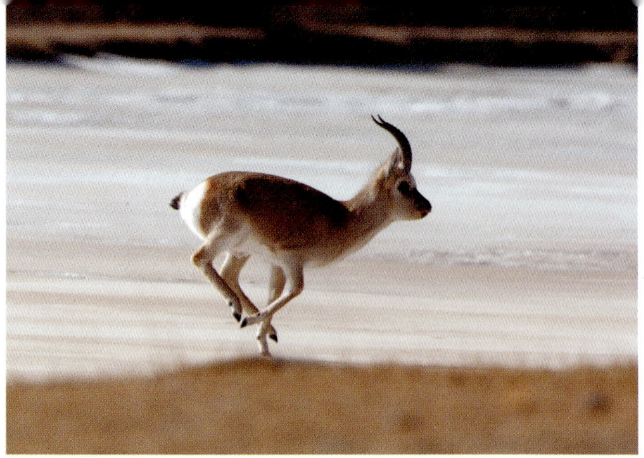

Tibetan gazelles run with their limbs above the ground, displaying a beautiful posture.

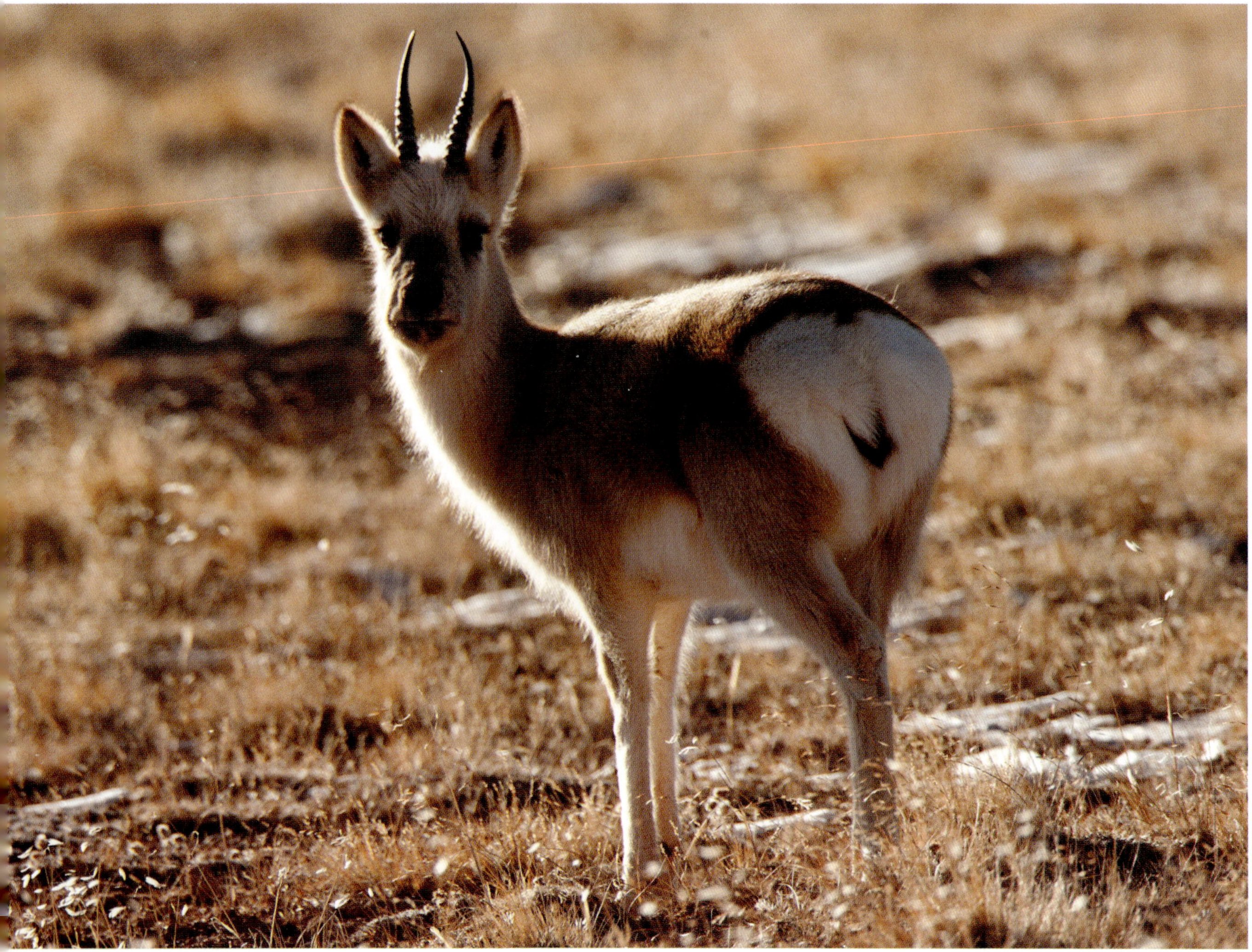

In Hoh Xil, apart from Tibeten antelopes, there is another kind of commonly seen "antelope" named Tibetan gazelle, also known as goa. It is quite small and the male one has slender and fairly long sickle-shaped horns, rising almost parallel from the forehead and then bending slightly backward. They are mostly characterized by purely white and large buttock patches with a short tail almost concealed within the hair. Their snow-white buttocks shine under sunlight while running, just like a mirror hung on the body. Therefore, they are also called "Mirror Sheep."

Tibetan gazelles are typical plateau-based animals, with their habitats of 3,000 to 5,100 meters above sea level. Although they can live almost in all kinds of grassland environments, they are mostly

Left
A Tibetan gazelle is looking back on the grass.

On facing page
Tibetan gazelles, often mistaken for Tibetan antelopes, can be easily seen on the Tibetan Plateau. Their eye-catching heart-shaped white buttocks mark the difference between them and the antelopes.

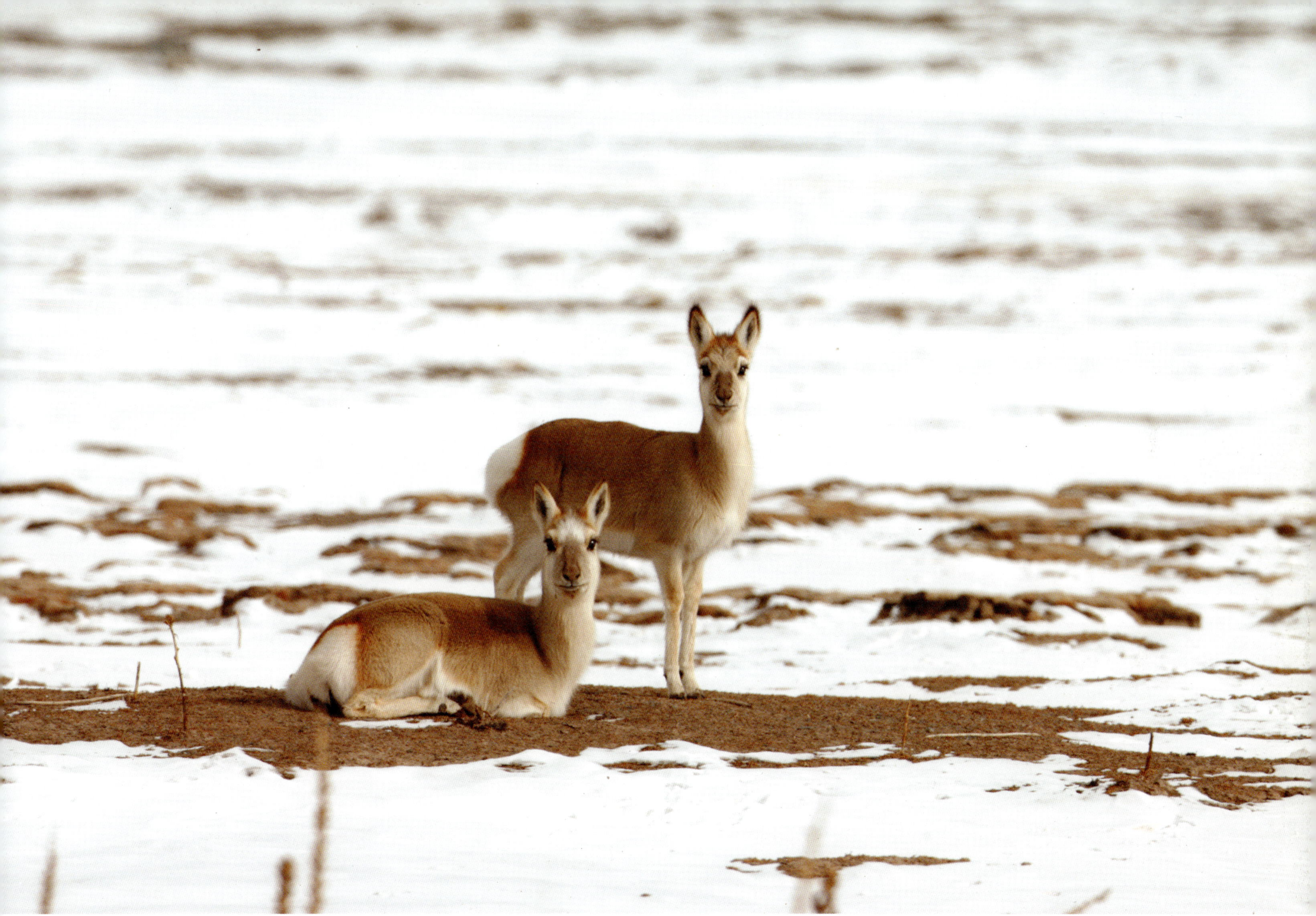

Above right
Tibetan gazelles are innately vigilant and agile, and they generally move in groups. Scenes such as this of them occur frequently. They become jumping small white spots that gradually disappear into the distance until they cannot be seen in the depth of desert.

Below right
A group of Tibetan gazelles and domestic yaks are quietly and harmoniously looking for food on the same grassland.

seen on highland meadows and arid steppes, with a few of them on the plateau desert and semi-desert.

They are especially fond of places with lush herbs and abundant water source. Without a fixed range of activities, they often roam around in groups ranging in different sizes in different seasons. The groups are bigger usually in winter and spring, often amounting to dozens in a group and sometimes a big group of over a hundred gazelles. In summer and autumn, they are in a small group of several to over ten gazelles, while some roam by themselves. Instead of having an acute sense of smell, they have very good hearing and vision. Thanks to their quick wit and vigilance, they escape rapidly while encountering the enemy, stop at a distance, look back, and then run continuously, or they rest and eat at the original place. They chiefly eat plants of the sedge family and grass family. Tibetan gazelles move around agilely and run rapidly on the plateau. Wolves and lynxes are their major natural predators.

In the past, there were hoof-oriented animals which could be seen almost everywhere on the Tibetan Plateau. However, their number has dropped sharply nowadays and their range is shrinking quickly. In the long run, they are very likely to be extinct.

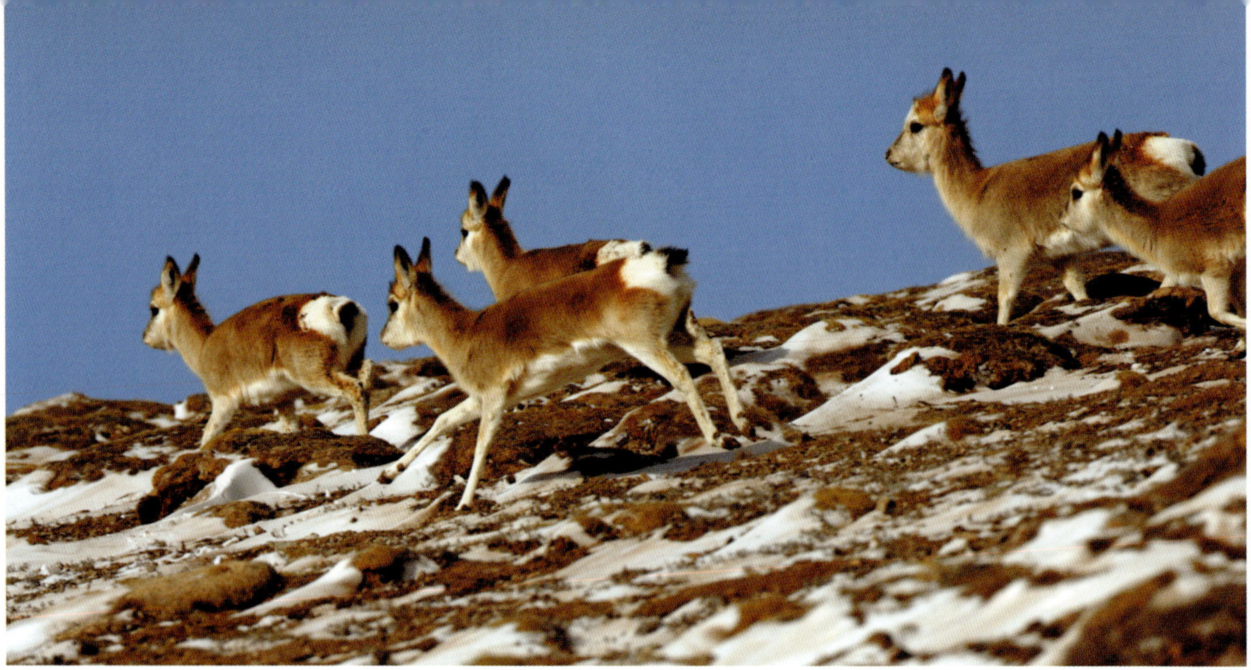

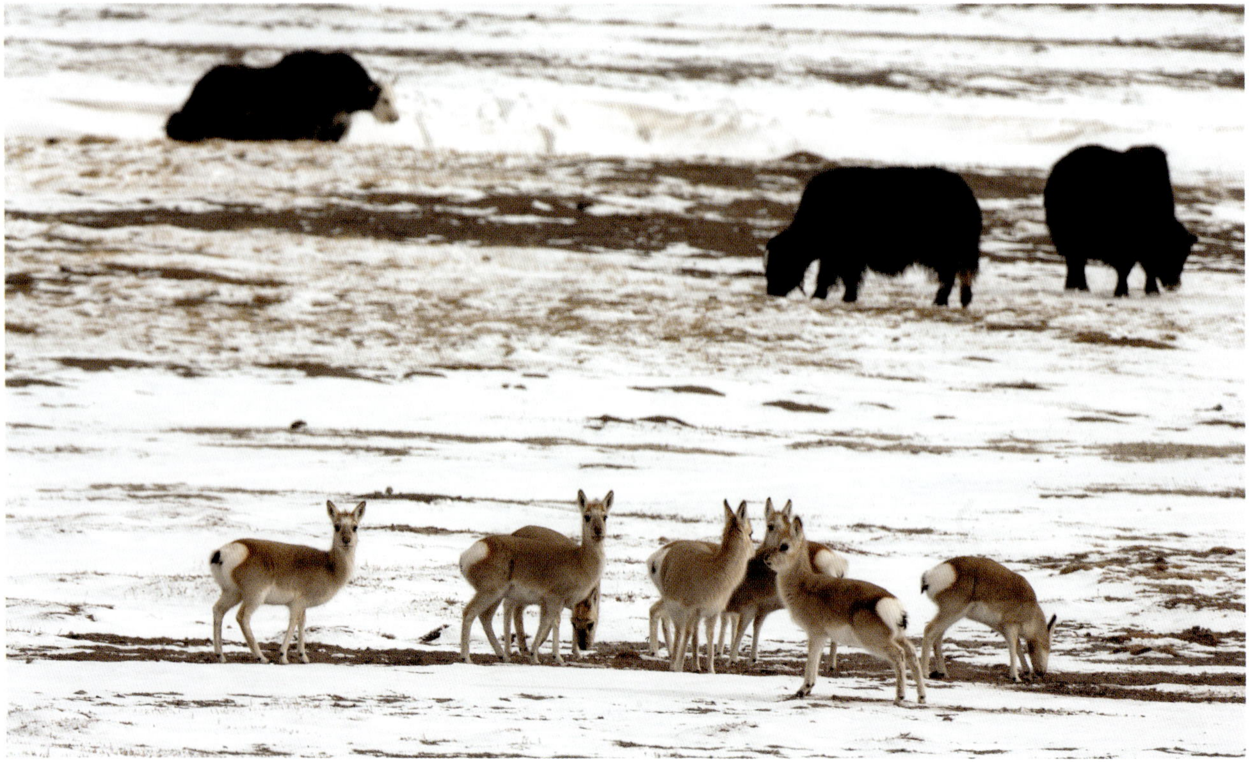

Kiang

Equus kiang

IUCN Red List: Least Concern

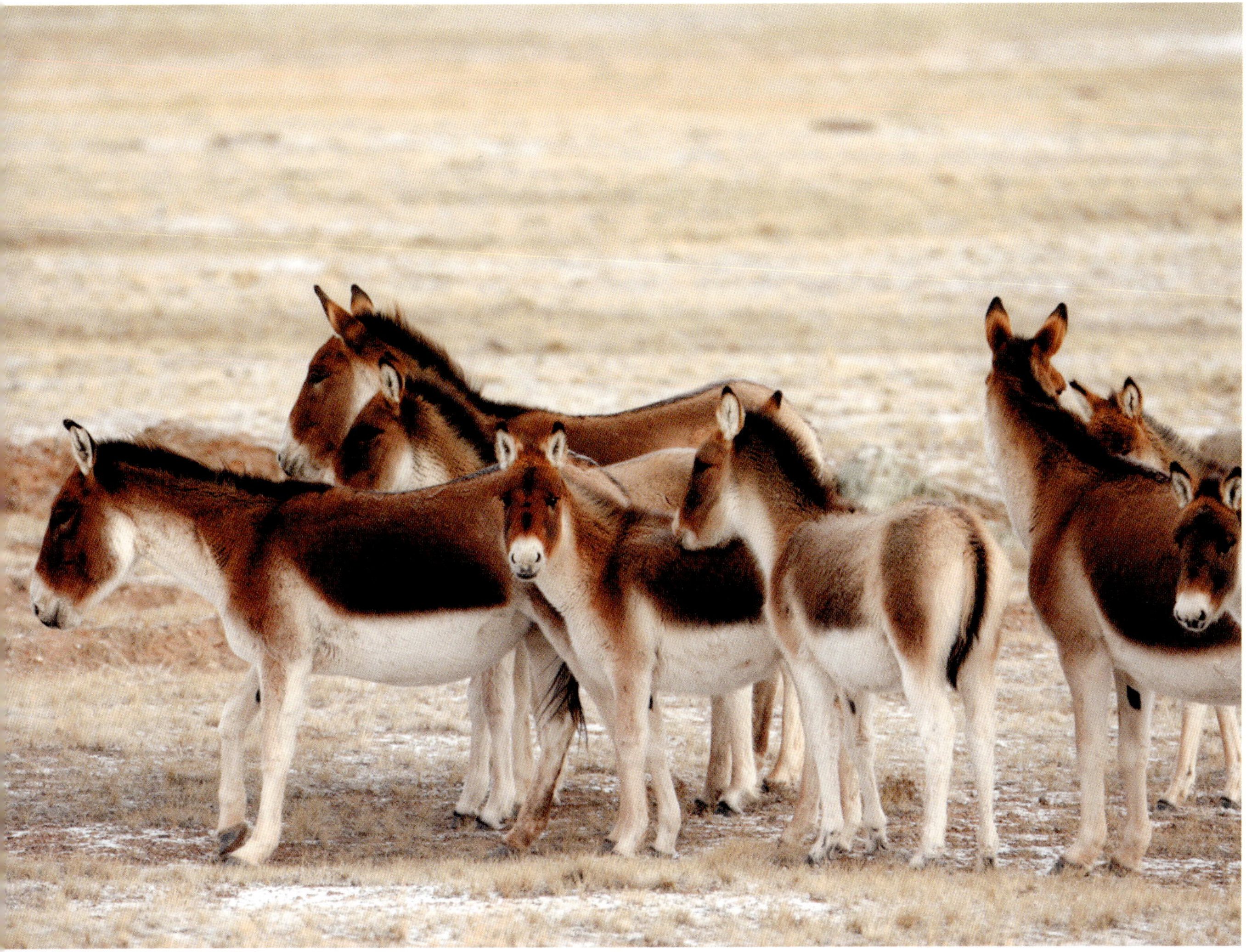

Living in an area of 3,600 to 5,400 meters above sea level, kiangs are marked by an acute sense of vision, hearing, and smell. With a strong running ability, they can go as fast as 45 kilometers per hour. All this can help them find and avoid wolves. In addition, they have a very strong ability to deal with the elements.

Kiangs move around in groups. Usually, a group consists of a robust male kiang and over ten female ones. They gather in large herds and move around. From the early morning, they set off from deserts or hills to drink water at the source. For most of the day, they gather on the grassland near the water source to look for food and to rest. At dusk, they return to the depth of the desert. From their habitat to the place of the water source and grassland, they run for over 20 kilometers everyday, with an obvious feature of migration. Sometimes, they stay with such even-toed ungulate as Tibetan antelopes, feeding on high-mountain plants, and can go several days without water.

In mid-May, they undergo a change of fur. In the mating season from July to August, kiang groups moving around form themselves into a

This could be a big family of kiangs, with adults at the front, followed closely by two foals.

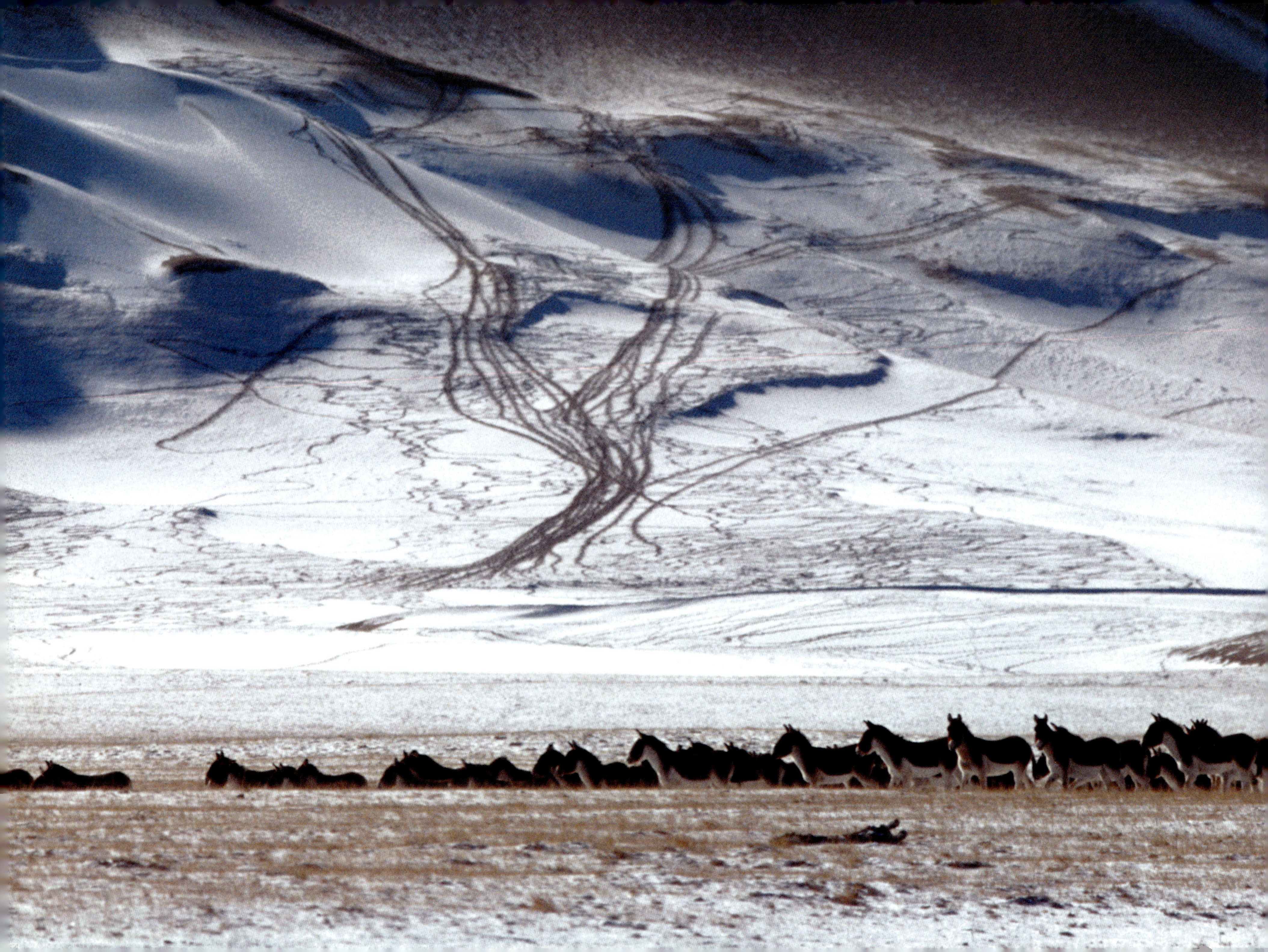

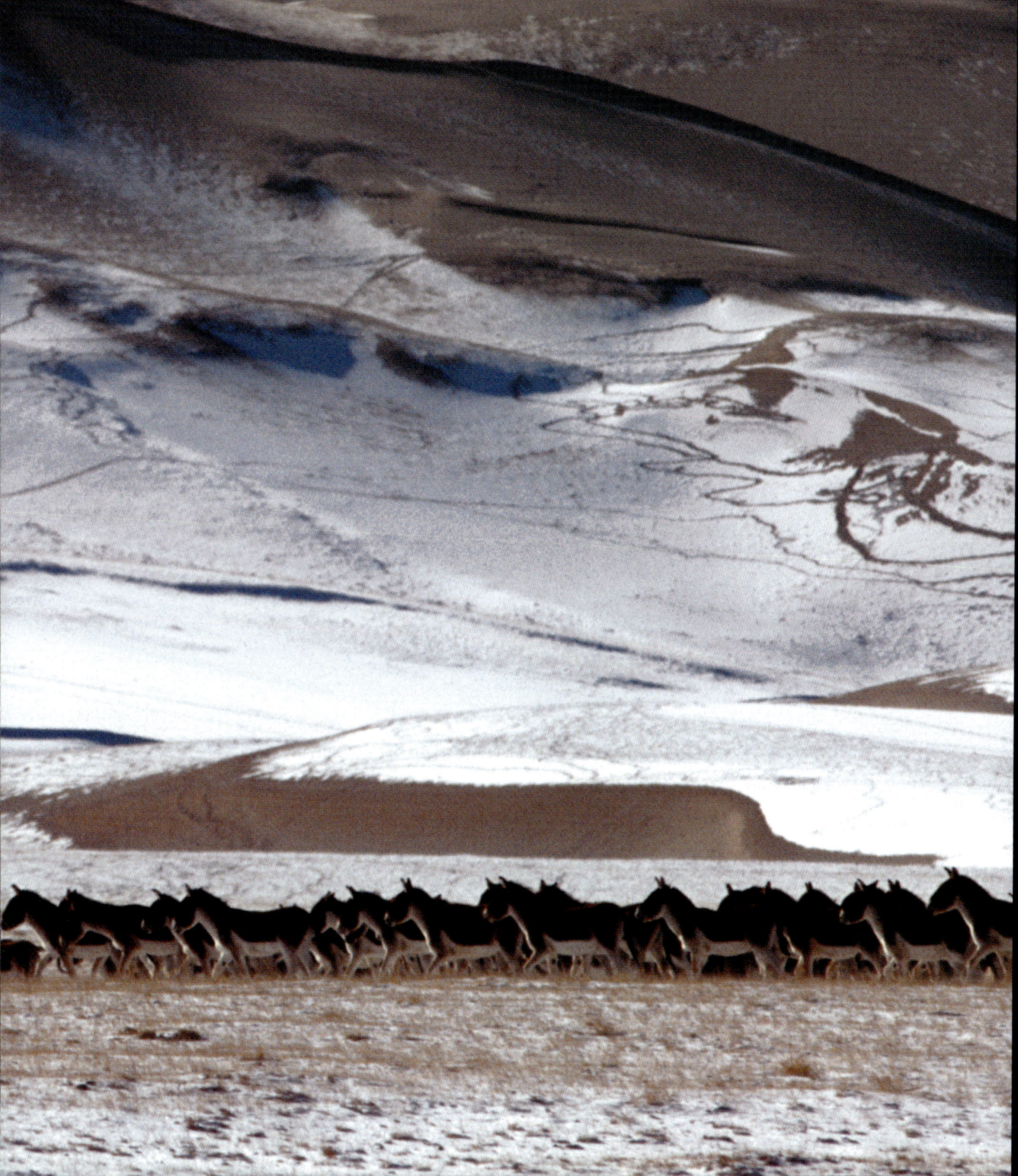

A large group of kiangs are seen on the expansive flood land in front of snowy sandy mounds. It is a spectacular scene that can be compared with that of the Serengeti National Park in Africa. The kiangs walk in a single file, with the males in front, the foals in the middle, and the females in the rear, and always in that order. There will be an obvious "kiang track" through which they trample.

On page 42
At noon, a terrible wind is blowing hard on the snowy plateau. The mountain top in the distance is covered with snow and mist. Under dazzling sunlight, a lonely kiang runs in the desolate wilderness.

big group of a spectacular scene. There would be fighting among male kiangs that bite each other or kick with their rear hoofs, trying to drive their opponents out of the group. They undergo the change of fur in mid-August and become fat and strong, with the scope of their migration being gradually extended. In the period from June to July the following year, female kiangs give birth to foal.

The life of kiangs is also encroached on and interfered with by excessive human grazing, gold rush, and poaching, leading to a sharp drop in their number. Besides, due to constant expansion of pastureland into areas without human beings, such wild animals as kiangs have become animals not welcomed by human beings because they "snatch" the herbage of domestic animals. The spectacular scene of hundreds of kiangs eating and resting together has not been seen for many years.

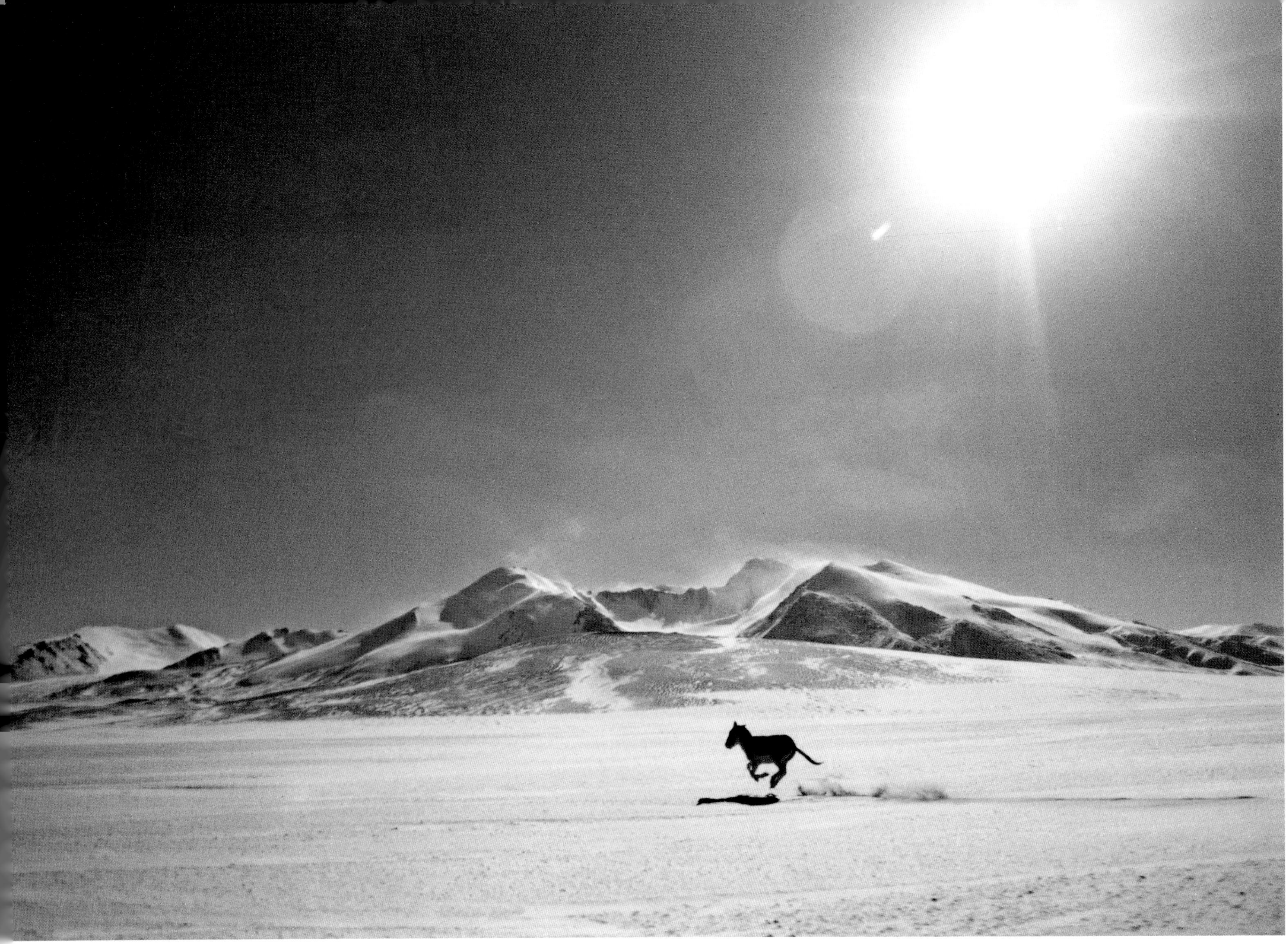

Red Fox

Vulpes vulpes
IUCN Red List: Least Concern

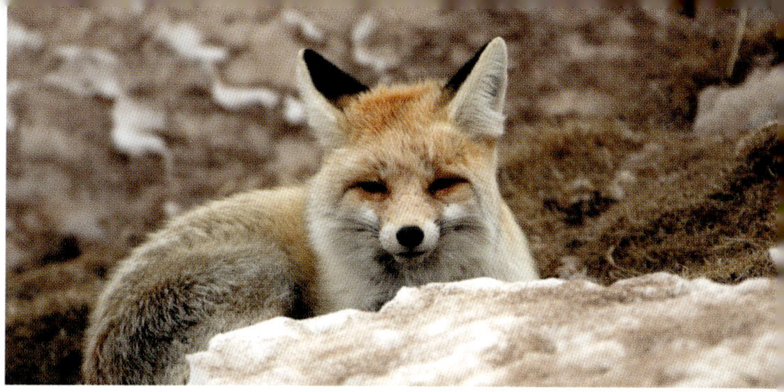

Maybe just having been fed to the fullest, this red fox is squinting at the lens while crouching behind a pile of snow.

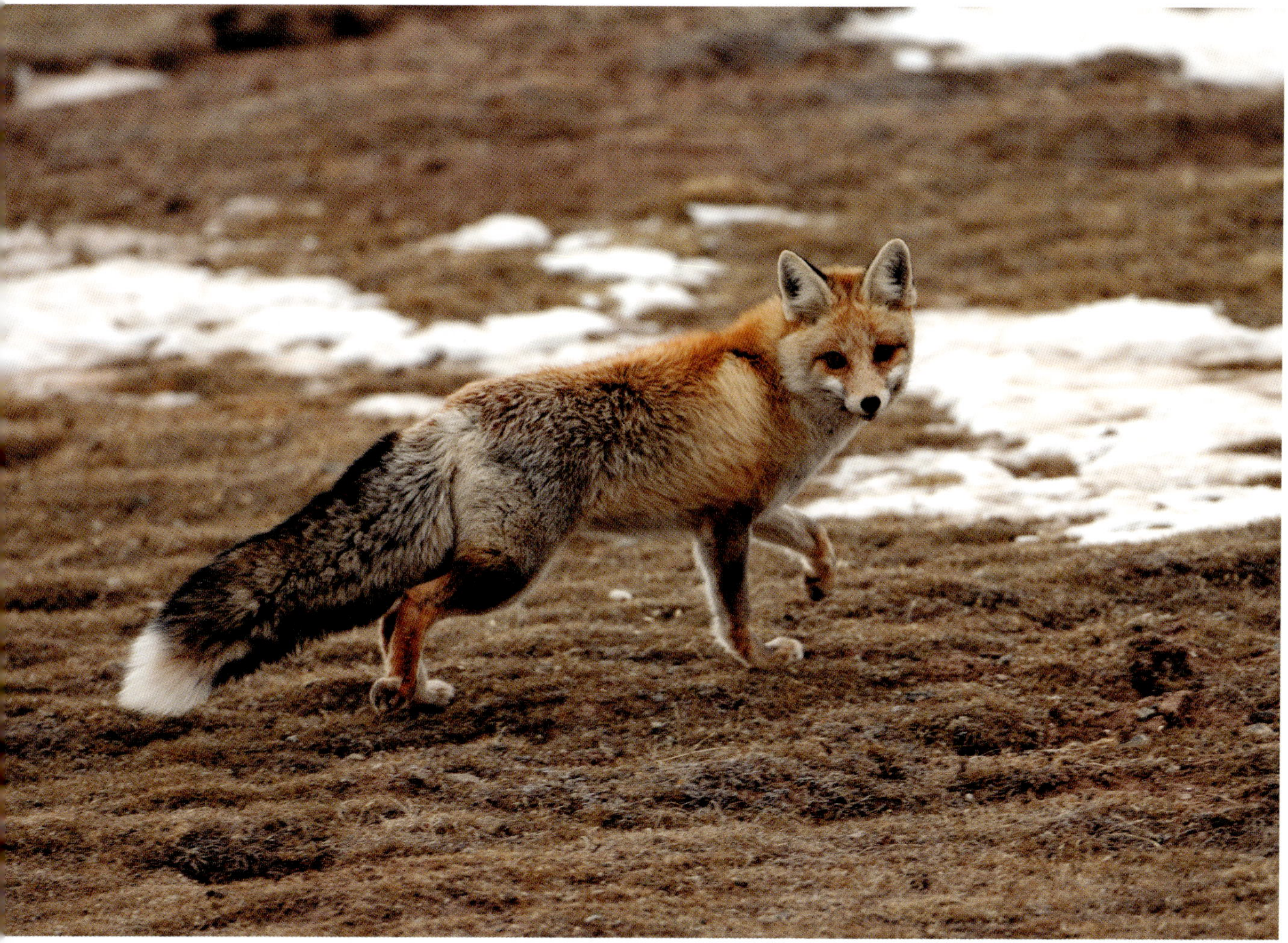

Red foxes are not often seen in China, though they are the most extensively distributed with the greatest adaptability.

In the Vuples genus, red foxes are the biggest, the most commonly seen, and the most famous kind. A red fox is 50 to 90 centimeters long and usually weighs 5 to 10 kilograms. With strong adaptability, red foxes are fond of spacious areas and bushes criss-crossed by vegetation.

Red foxes are marked by very good memory, a well-developed sense of hearing and smell, as well as agile and durable movement. In addition to hunting for preys like other kinds of canine animals, they often lay ambushes. Apart from the period of propagation and breeding kits, they generally live independently. They usually set out at night and sleep in the cave in the daytime. Their long tail serves to prevent moisture and keep them warm. However, in desolate places, sometimes they also set out to look for food in the daytime. Despite their short legs and feet, they have very sharp claws. Running very fast, they can go as quickly as over 50 kilometers per hour chasing after prey. They are good at swimming and climbing trees. They are opportunists—their food ranges from small rodents, rabbits, various pheasants, birds, frogs, snakes, insects, and even some berries and plants. They eat rotten food occasionally.

On the Tibetan Plateau, like Tibetan foxes, red foxes also play an important role of keeping the rat population under control. Therefore, poisoning rats and pika exerts a great impact on them. Excessive hunting of red foxes for their fur poses even a bigger threat to them.

Tibetan Fox

Vulpes ferrilata

IUCN Red List: Least Concern

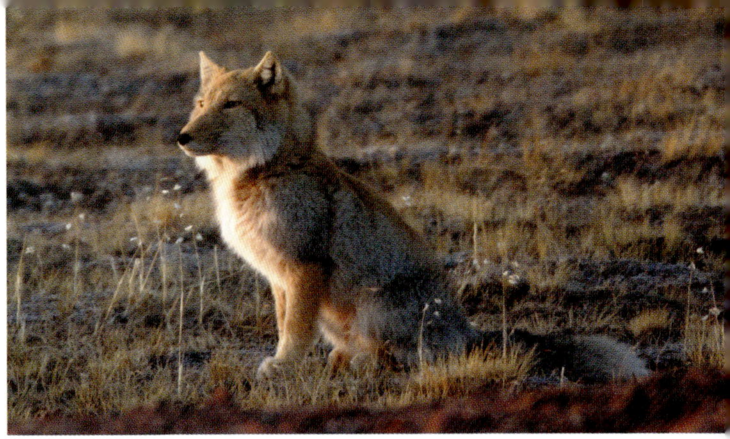

This Tibetan fox is crouching on the grass and looking around, ready to jump into action as soon as something unusual happens.

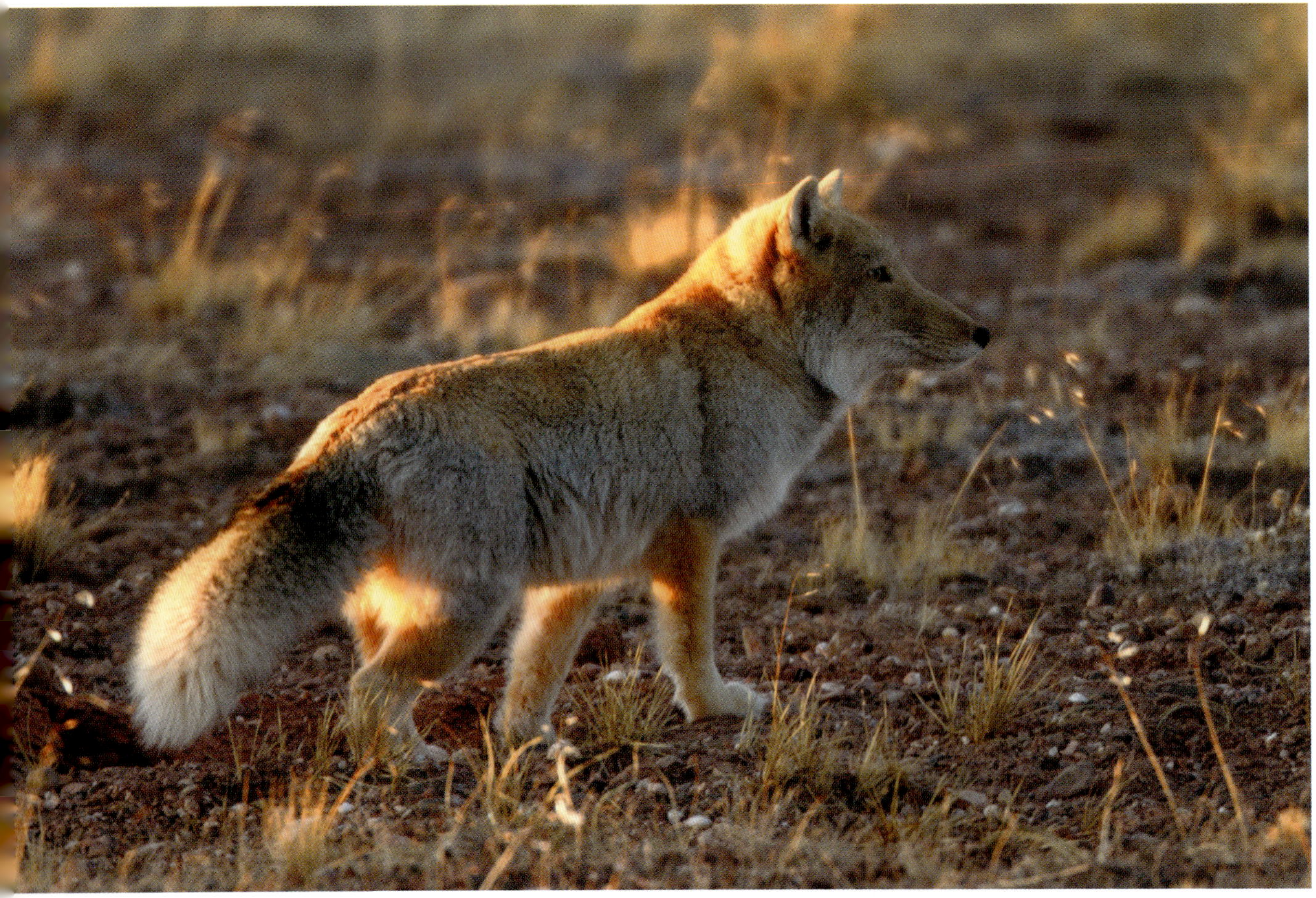

Quite short and round, a Tibetan fox is similar to a red fox in size. Its tail is obviously short and its fluffy and short tail-hair is a far cry from that of a red fox. Its ears are shorter than those of a red fox. An adult Tibetan fox has a big funny face and its fur is slightly inferior. It has a white abdomen, light-grey body sides, and light brown-red back. Though it is not eye-catching, its appearance conforms to the surrounding environment, with a very good ability to camouflage itself.

Tibetan foxes are typical plateau animals. In terms of the range, they live in the smallest area as compared with two other kinds of foxes, i.e. red foxes and corsac foxes in China. They are only seen on the Tibetan Plateau, including most or some areas of Tibet, Qinghai and Sichuan provinces.

Tibetan foxes are fond of moving around and looking for food at dawn or dusk in a spacious environment, in addition to often roaming around in the daytime. On the Tibetan Plateau, red foxes are often seen looking for food or resting along the roads and easy slopes in the mountain. Upon hearing sounds, they escape quickly, or run while looking back. They can dig for caves for themselves and sometimes use caves of marmots as their own habitat. The red fox's cave generally has two openings piled around with lots of mud and pebbles dug out from the depth of the cave. They chiefly eat various pika, woolly hares, in addition to some birds like snowfinches and horn larks sometimes.

The number of red foxes has dropped sharply due to excessive hunting for their fur. Poisoned pikas also pose a danger to them as they can also be affected by the poison.

Grey Wolf

Canis lupus

IUCN Red List: Least Concern

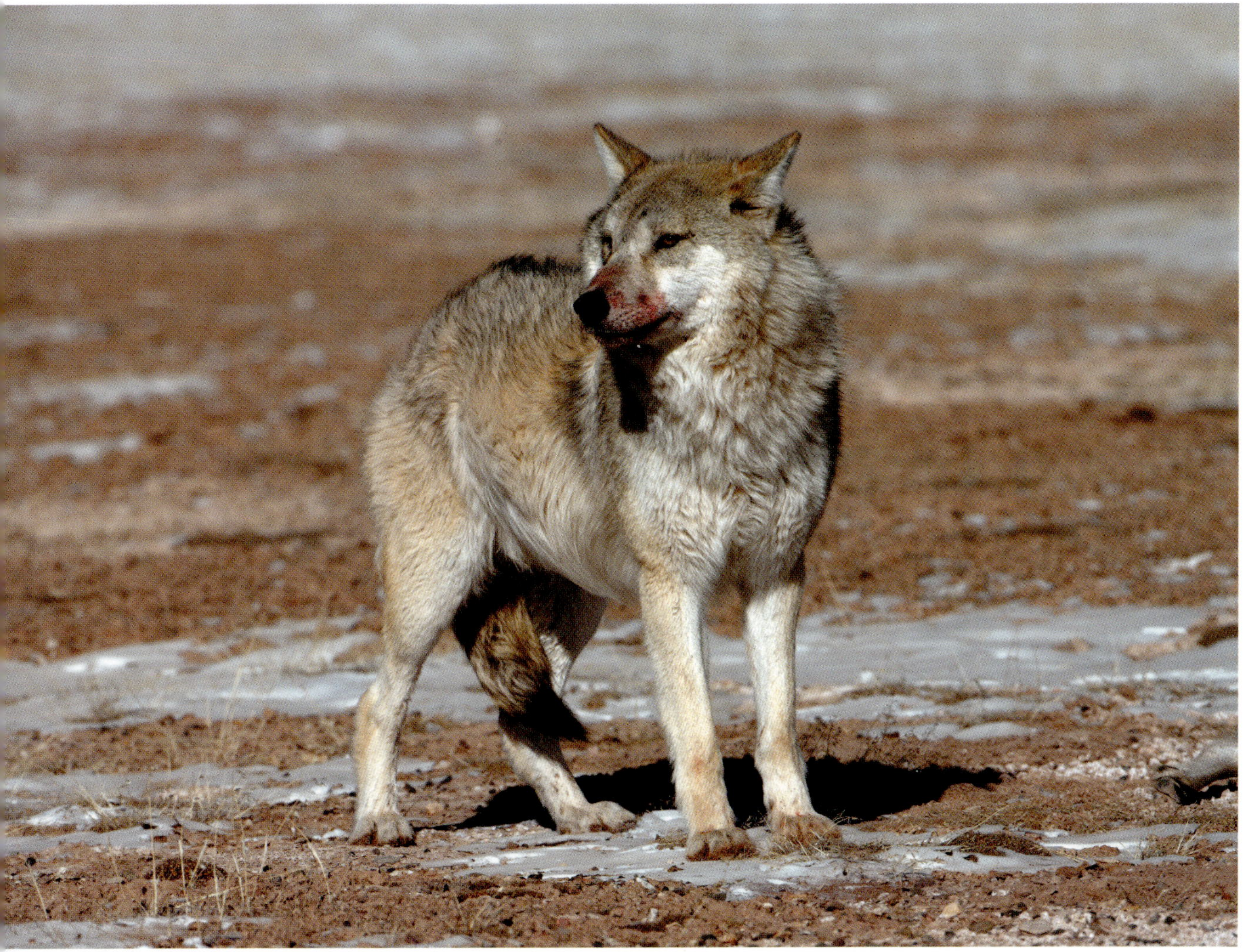

Wolves are mammals that were extensively distributed around the world, including Eurasia and North America. Nowadays, however, wolves are hardly seen in most of their former habitats. In China, there are four sub-species of wolves, which were extensively distributed in the ecosystem ranging from the Tibetan Plateau, Sanjiangyuan wetland, Tianshan Mountains, and the great plains of the Yangtze River. Despite their great adaptability, which enables them to survive under very harsh environment, they are rarely seen on the plain of Northern China, the vast areas along the middle and lower reaches of the Yangtze River, due to dense human population and huge environmental pressure there. Due to the relatively sparse human population on the vast pastureland in northern China and northwestern China, there is still a large space for them. On the other hand, these areas have many wild ungulates, ox, and sheep as their prey.

Their soles can easily adapt themselves to cold areas. Little webs between their toes enable them to be more agile on the snowy ground. As digitigrades, wolves can have their weight well distributed on the accumulated snow. Their front paws are slightly bigger than their back paws. The front paws have

Grey wolves, always detested and hunted by people, have become rare animals in China. Nowadays, they can only be seen in far away Hoh Xil.

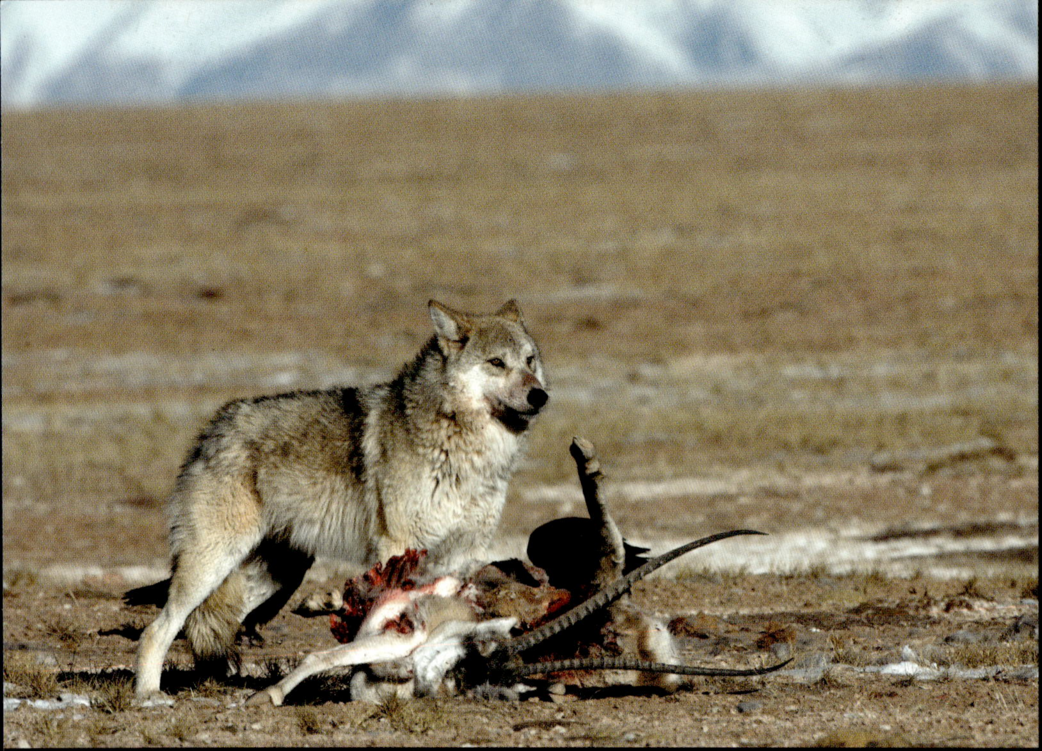

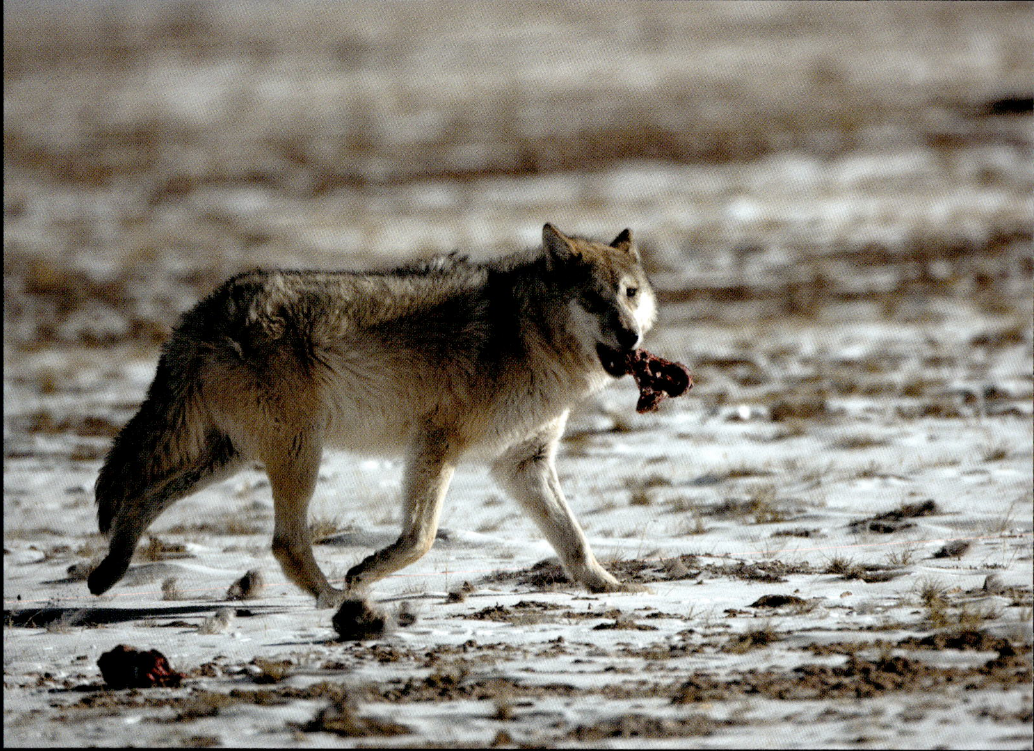

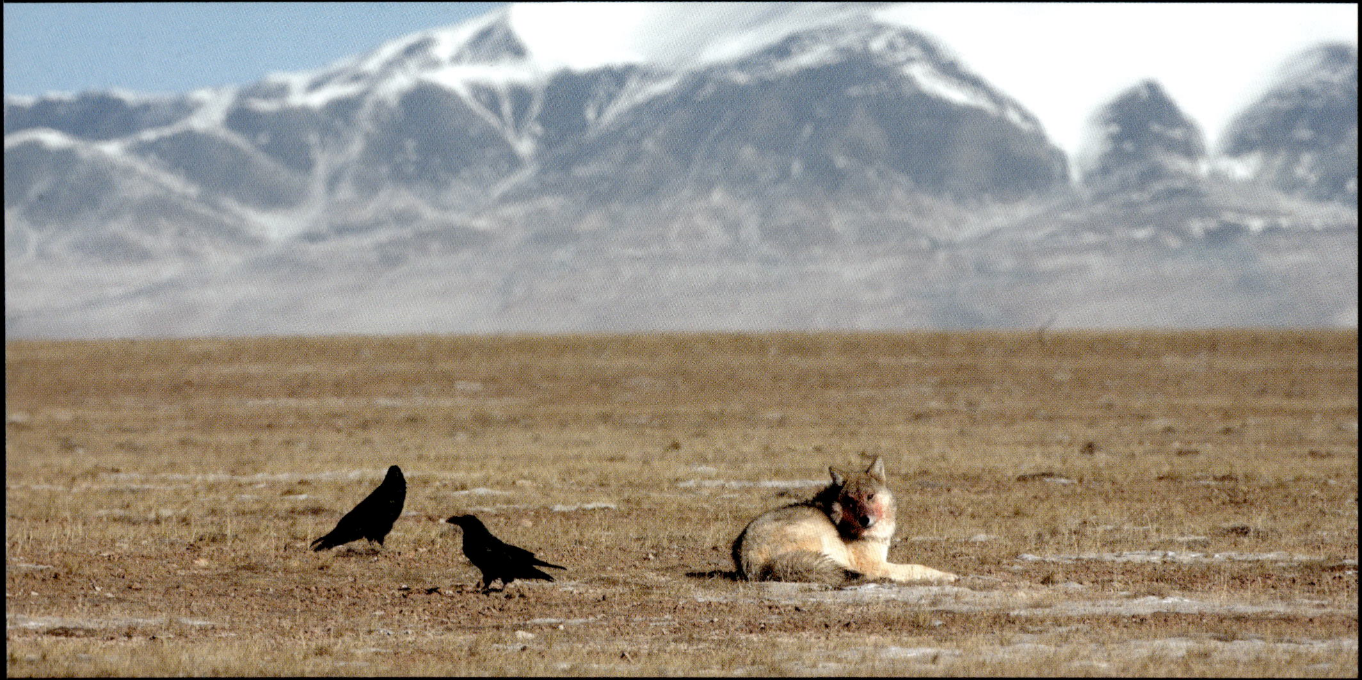

Above left
Winter is the season that wolves on the Tibetan Plateau anticipate most since they can very easily get hold of Tibetan antelopes injured in the course of chasing each other or dead antelopes.

Above right
Such a scene can sometimes be seen on the Tibetan Plateau: wolves wander around Tibetan antelopes that do not care at all while eating grass at their leisure. This is because both of them know their own strength. A wolf can only get a hold on a Tibetan antelope only when the latter accidentally stumbles during a fierce chase.

Left
A wolf that has just feasted crouches on the ground, with the fresh blood of a Tibetan antelope still seen on its face.

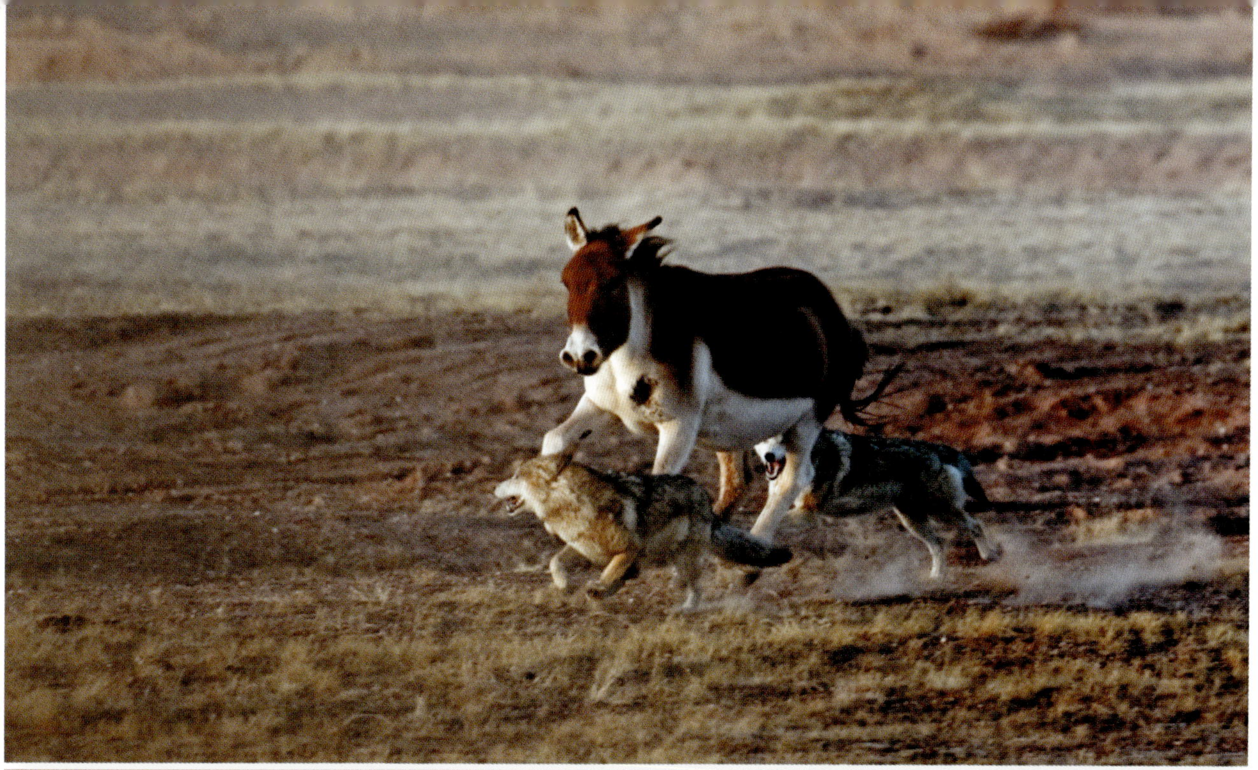

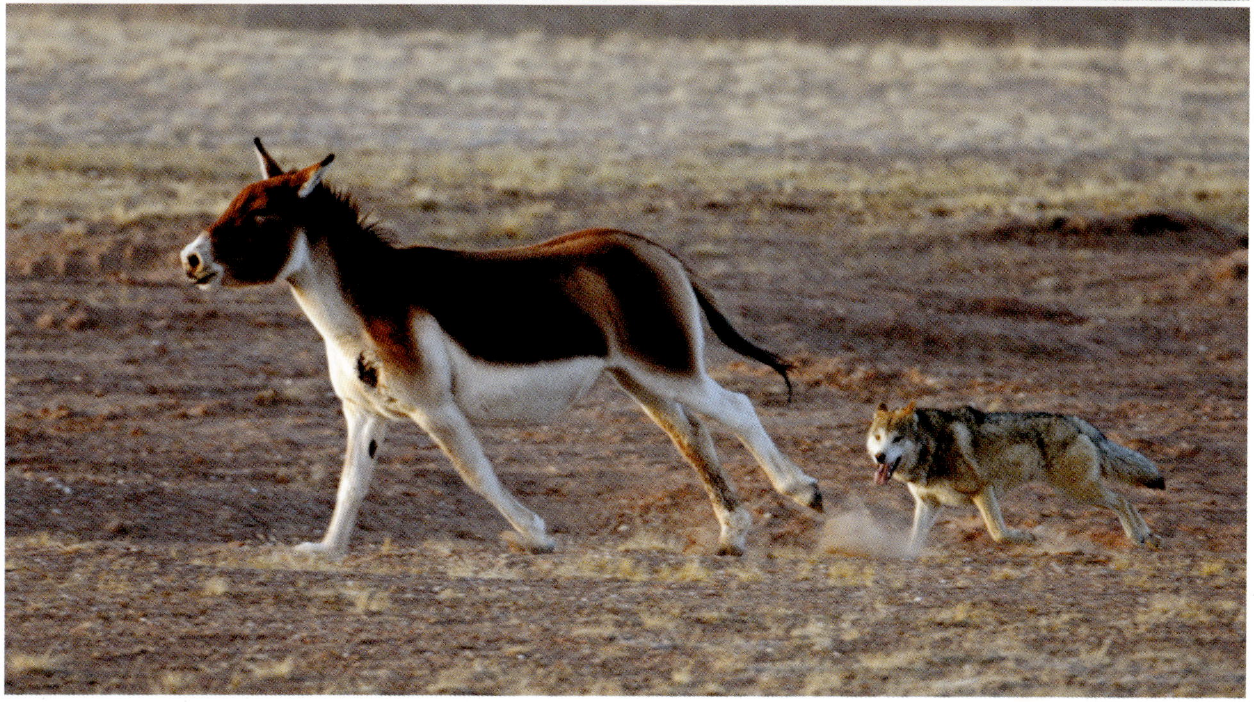

1
2

A group of kiangs ran wildly across. With the dust gone, one kiang is left behind and is attacked by two grey wolves, one in the front and one in the rear. The kiang has to run with all its might to break through.

five toes each, but their back paws do not have an upper toe. Hair on their paws and the slightly blunt claws help them to get hold of the wet and slippery ground. Their special blood vessels prevent their paws from being frozen on the snowy ground. The gland between their toes emits odor left from their footprints, helping them to record their own track while providing clues to other wolves about their location. In cold weather, wolves can regulate their body temperature since their blood flow can be kept considerably away from their skin. The adjustment by way of keeping themselves warm via their paws is independent of other parts of their body. Wolves can have a temperature slightly higher than that which is vulnerable to tissue frostbite when their paws touch ice and snow. All these can help them live in such highland areas as Hoh Xil.

Although wolves are not fastidious about prey, they chiefly eat medium and large ungulates. In Hoh Xil, Tibetan antelopes, Tibetan gazelles, kiangs, and even wild yaks can become their prey. Wolves would stay in groups to get prey and run continuously for 20 minutes at a speed of 56 to 64 kilometers per hour. In areas concentrated with herds of cattle and sheep, wild ungulates cannot compete with domestic animals. Many wolves are forced to catch these cattle and sheep raised by people. Therefore, wolves are regarded as harmful animals and hunted on a large scale by people for a long time.

Plateau Pika

Ochotona curzoniae

IUCN Red List: Least Concern

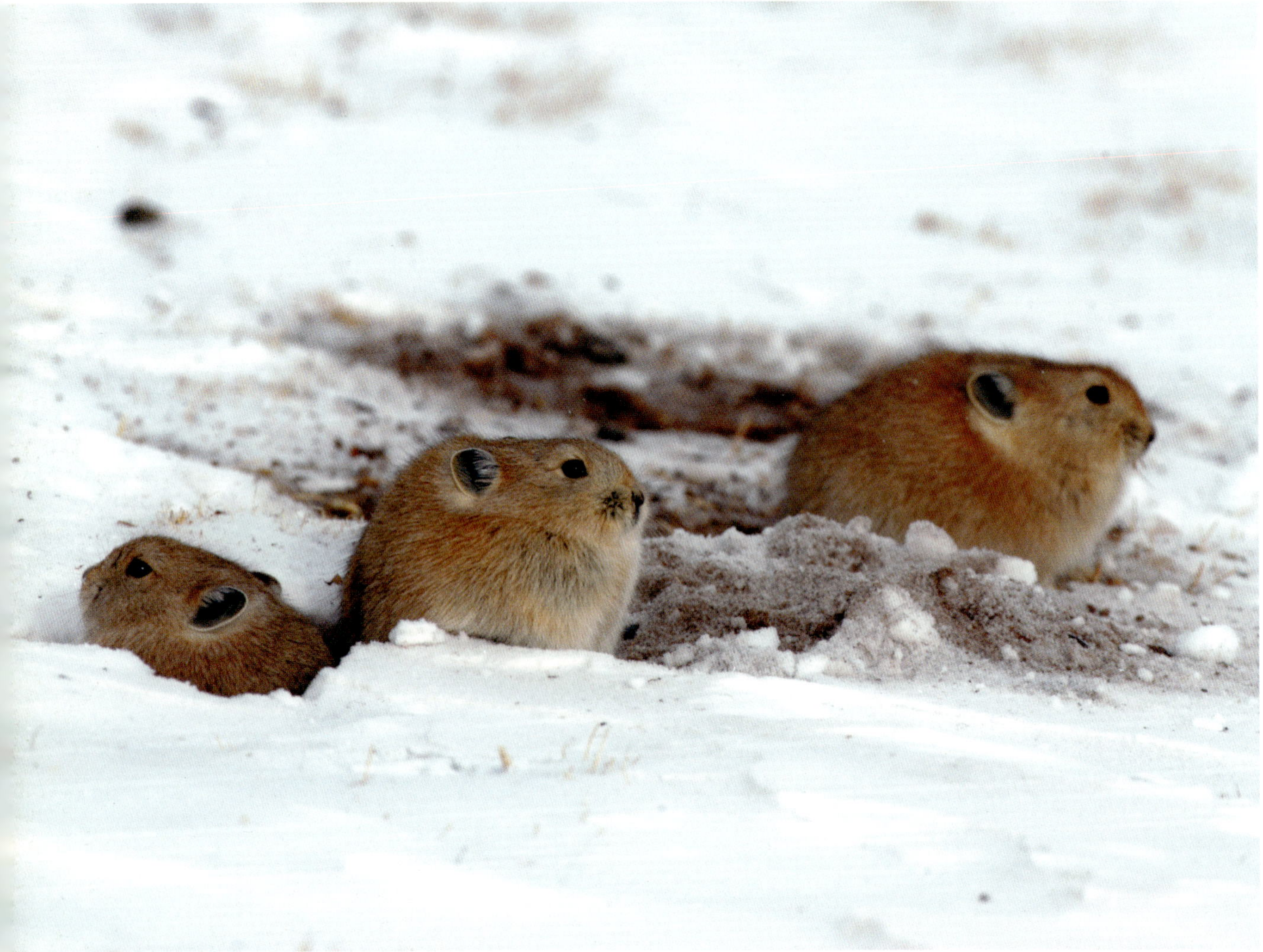

Looking like rats, plateau pikas do not have long ears but they are close relatives of rabbits. They live on alpine meadows, steppe, or deserts. They are graminivore, strictly speaking.

They live in a family unit, with the range of activities spanning no more than 25 meters. Because of the harsh living environment on the Tibetan Plateau in winter, many pikas die of the freezing cold and a few survive until the following year. Adult pikas that have survived winter give birth to three nests of litters in summer and they all live together. Most small mammals move around at night, but plateau pikas are active in the daytime. They can be seen screaming, jumping, and running. They are very unique, since some of them practice monogamy, some follow polygamy and a few practice a system of more husbands and more wives, with three phenomena in co-existence. This cannot be found in other kinds of animals. Usually, pikas of different families attack each other. We saw two running pikas on the Tibetan Plateau, possibly the mutual chase of male pikas between two families. Plateau pikas can utter six different kinds of sounds. Adult pikas utter long and hurried "Yi—" when seeking for a mate. Juvenile pikas utter relatively low and tender sounds. Along with

As an inseparable link in the ecosystem on the Tibetan Plateau, they can take minerals and microelements needed by other kinds of animals out of the earth's surface. They themselves are also preys of small and medium carnivores.

Right
Plateau pikas live in a family unit. A young pika and its mother are protruding their heads out for a look.

Below
1 2 3
A plateau pika crouches leisurely on the grass. Suddenly, it looks up, probably having heard whistles of a bird of prey in the sky or found an enemy ahead. The vigilant pika immediately begins to run for its life on its four small short legs.

the increase of the number of family members since younger pikas are weaned from breasts, the number of pikas increases by a big margin in summer, with each hectare having over 300.

Plateau pikas make themselves key species on the Tibetan Plateau due to the high density of their cave system. Almost all predators would take them as prey and their caves are occupied by many kinds of birds and lizards as habitats. Digging for caves also enables soil to absorb more water before monsoon season comes around, to reduce soil erosion, and increase the rate of nutrition circulation of the meadow. However, they are poisoned to death in large numbers since herdsmen believe that they are animals harmful to pastureland.

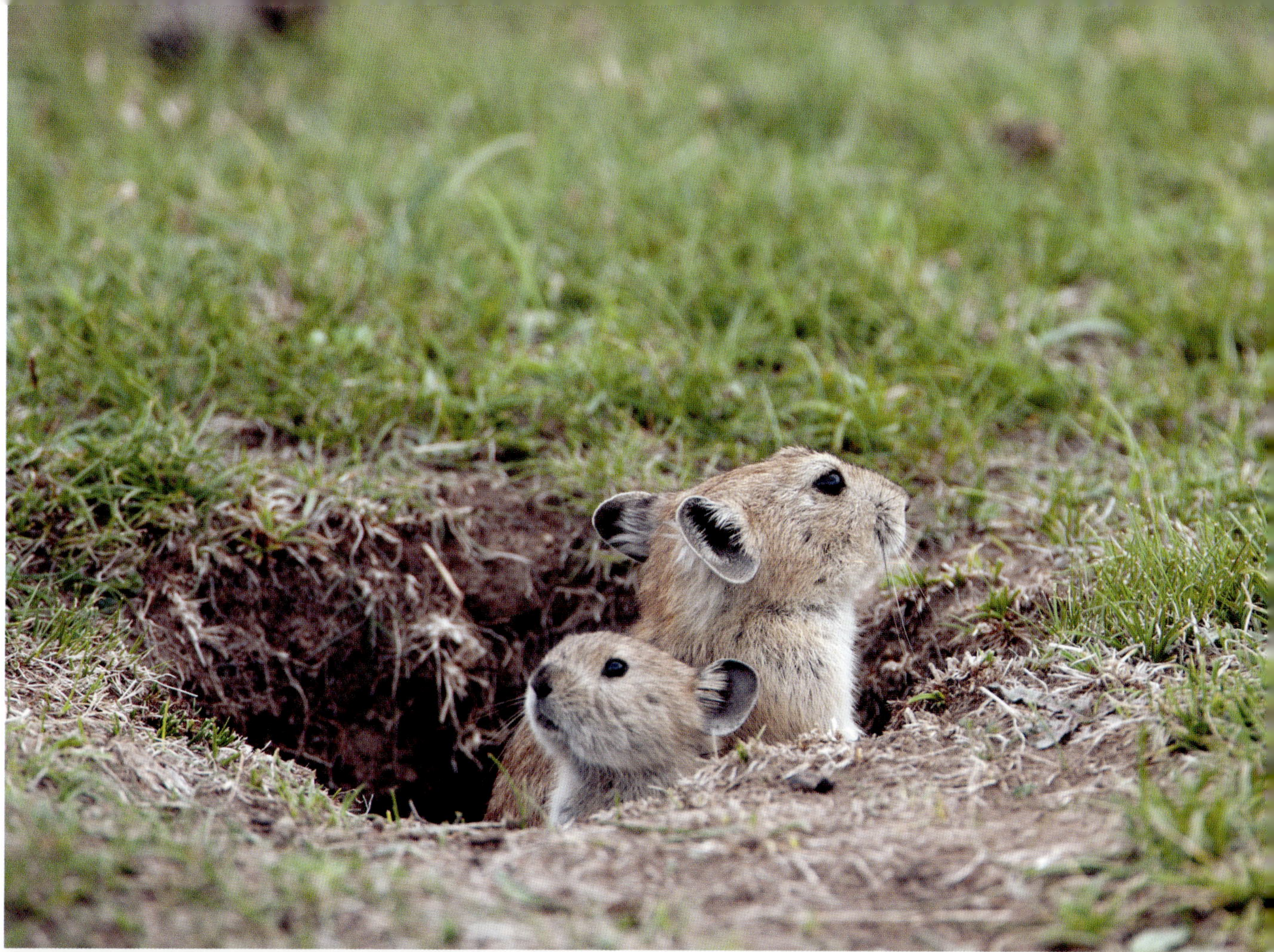

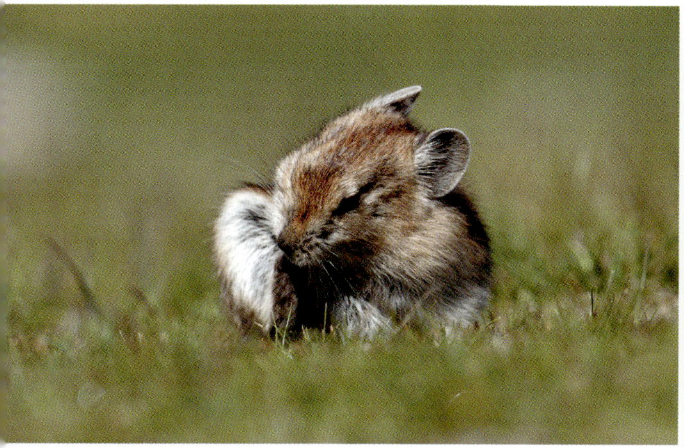

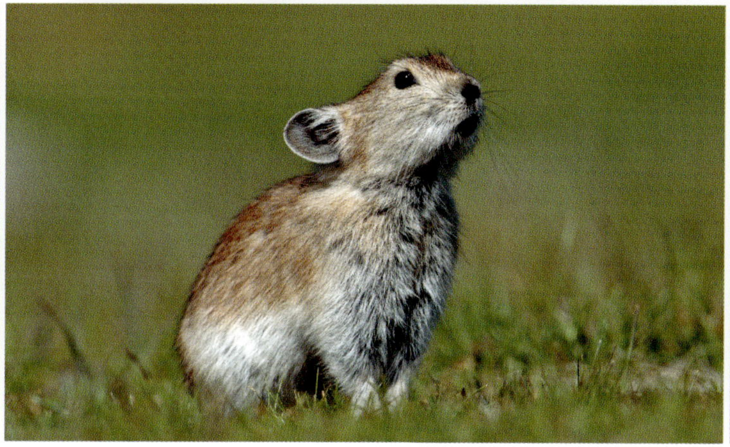

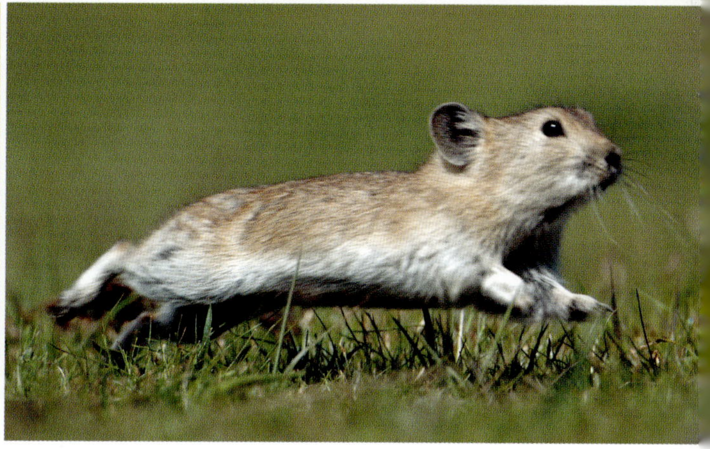

Saker Falcon

Falco cherrug

IUCN Red List: Endangered

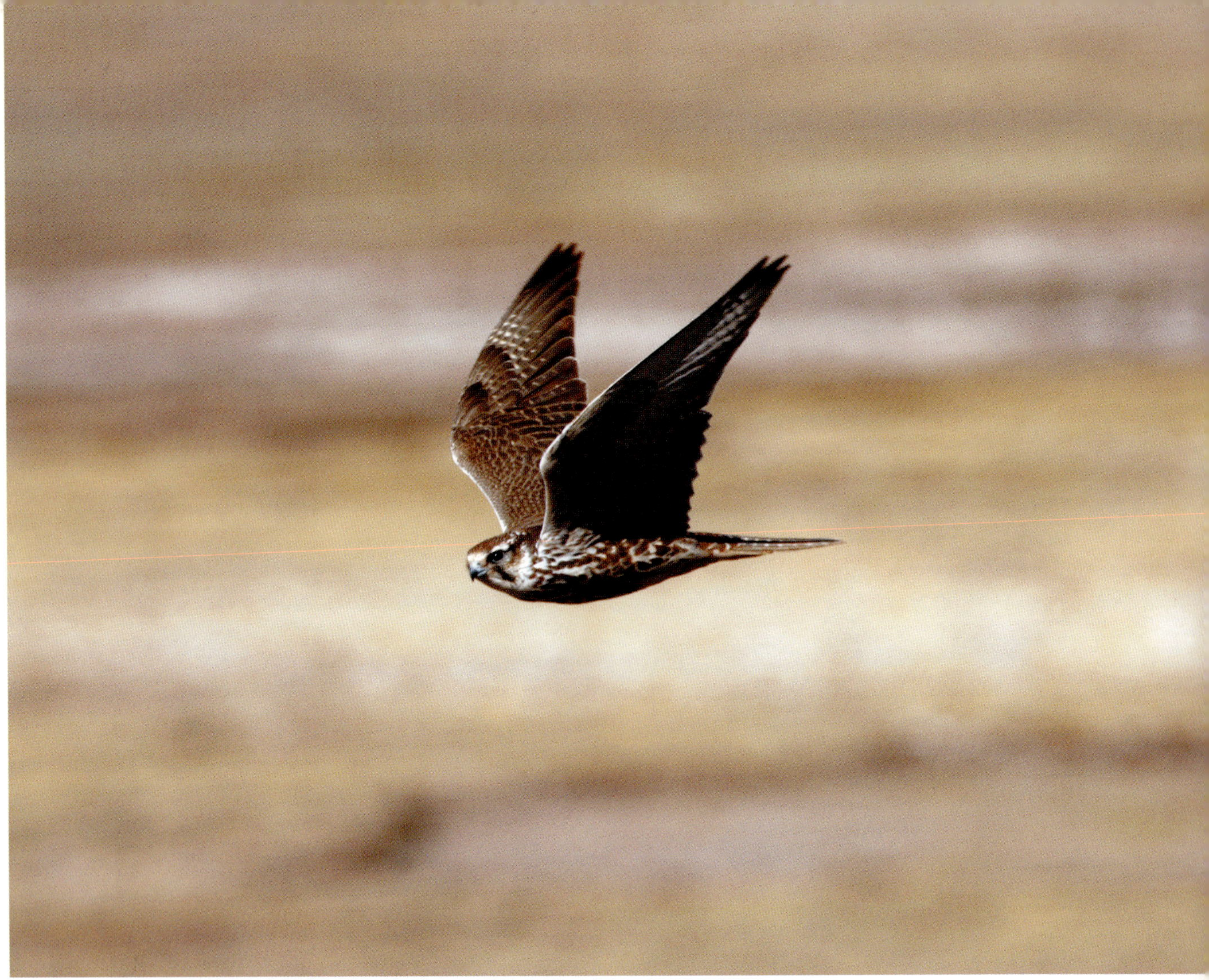

Next to gyrfalcons, saker falcons are the second-most widely distributed falcon. They are seen all over the forest steppes in Eurasia, ranging from Hungary, Mongolia, and central China. Although a few of them can be seen in many places in China, they are chiefly distributed in northern China and central China, such as Xinjiang, Tibet, and the Inner Mongolia autonomous regions.

They have strong adaptability to the environment, particularly in desert and arid zones. Their spruce figures flying across the sky are often seen over such expansive areas as mountains, valleys, grassland, wilderness with sparse trees, and rocky hills. Saker falcons are characteristic of high-mountain and plateau large falcons.

Saker falcons chiefly eat small and medium birds, rabbits, and rodents. Like fighters in the air, they attack such flying small birds as tits and larks. After catching up with their prey, they would hit hard at them with their wings until the latter lose their flying ability and fall down. Then, they would dive to catch them. On the Tibetan Plateau, saker falcons are one important in controlling the population of pikas.

At present, there are only 35,000 to 40,000 saker falcons in the world. China is one of the countries with a significant population of saker falcons. Huge demands for them due to traditional falcon-hunting in China and Middle East countries, illegal hunting, and smuggling in large numbers have led to sharp reductions of the number of saker falcons in northwestern China, directly threatening the survival of this species. The propagation density in Xinjiang, the major area for the propagation of saker falcons in China, is less than one pair/per 1,000 square kilometers. In addition to the threat of poisoning, the long-term killing of rats and pikas has also resulted in the lack of food for saker falcons and other birds of prey.

When spotting their prey on the ground, the saker falcon would fly like a high-speed plane to the space above the prey with its narrow wings, which can reduce resistance to occupy the commanding point. Then, it would withdraw its wings so the feathers can be on a vertical par with its body while the head retreats into the shoulders. At a speed of 75 – 100 meters per second in a 25-degree angle, it dashes at the prey. At the instant moment of approaching the prey, it would spread its wings slightly, hit or catch the prey with its rear toes of its claws.

On facing page

Because of the photographer's sudden arrival, a saker falcon has spread its wings to fly from the ground.

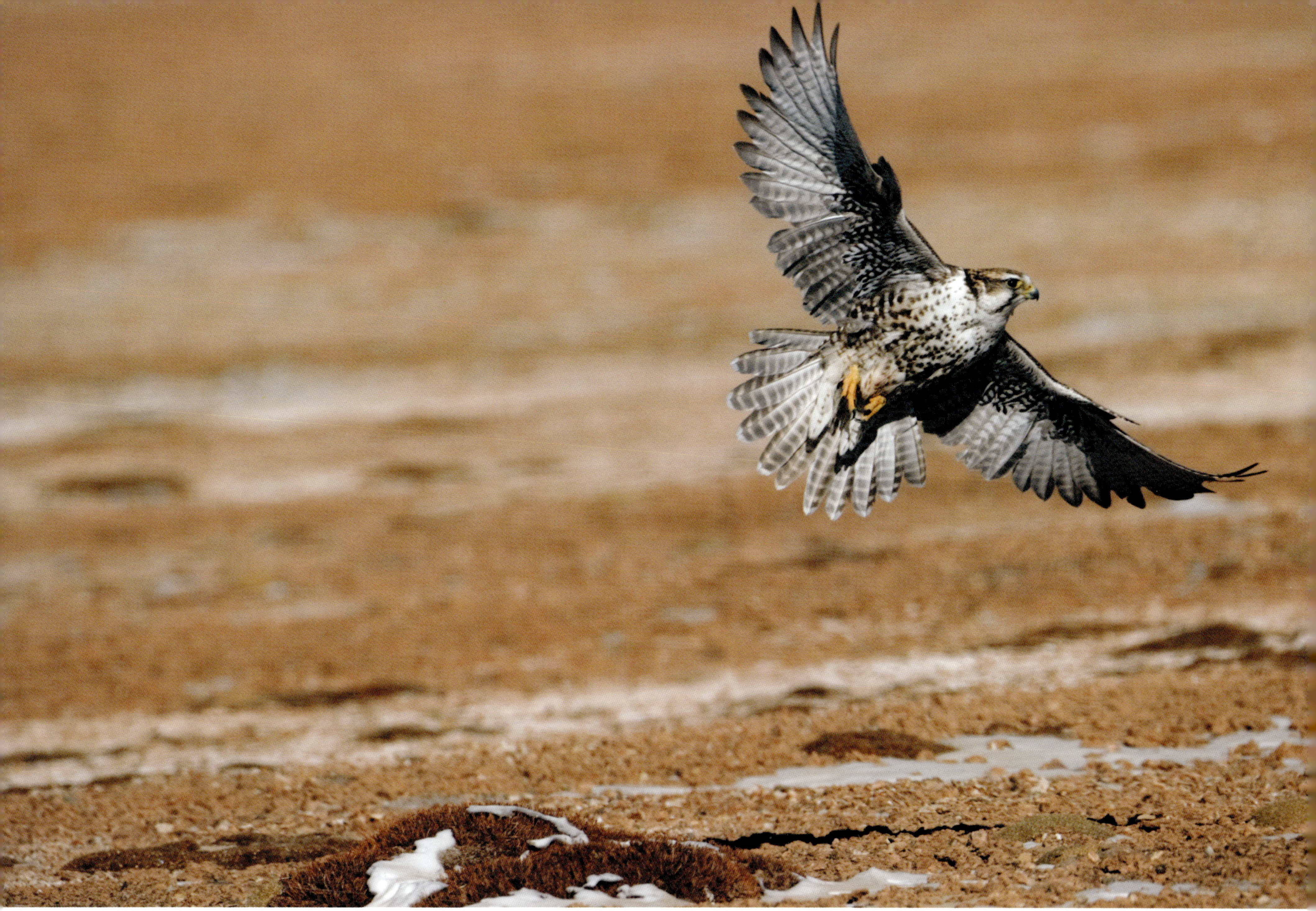

Himalayan Griffon

Gyps himalayensis
IUCN Red List: Least Concern

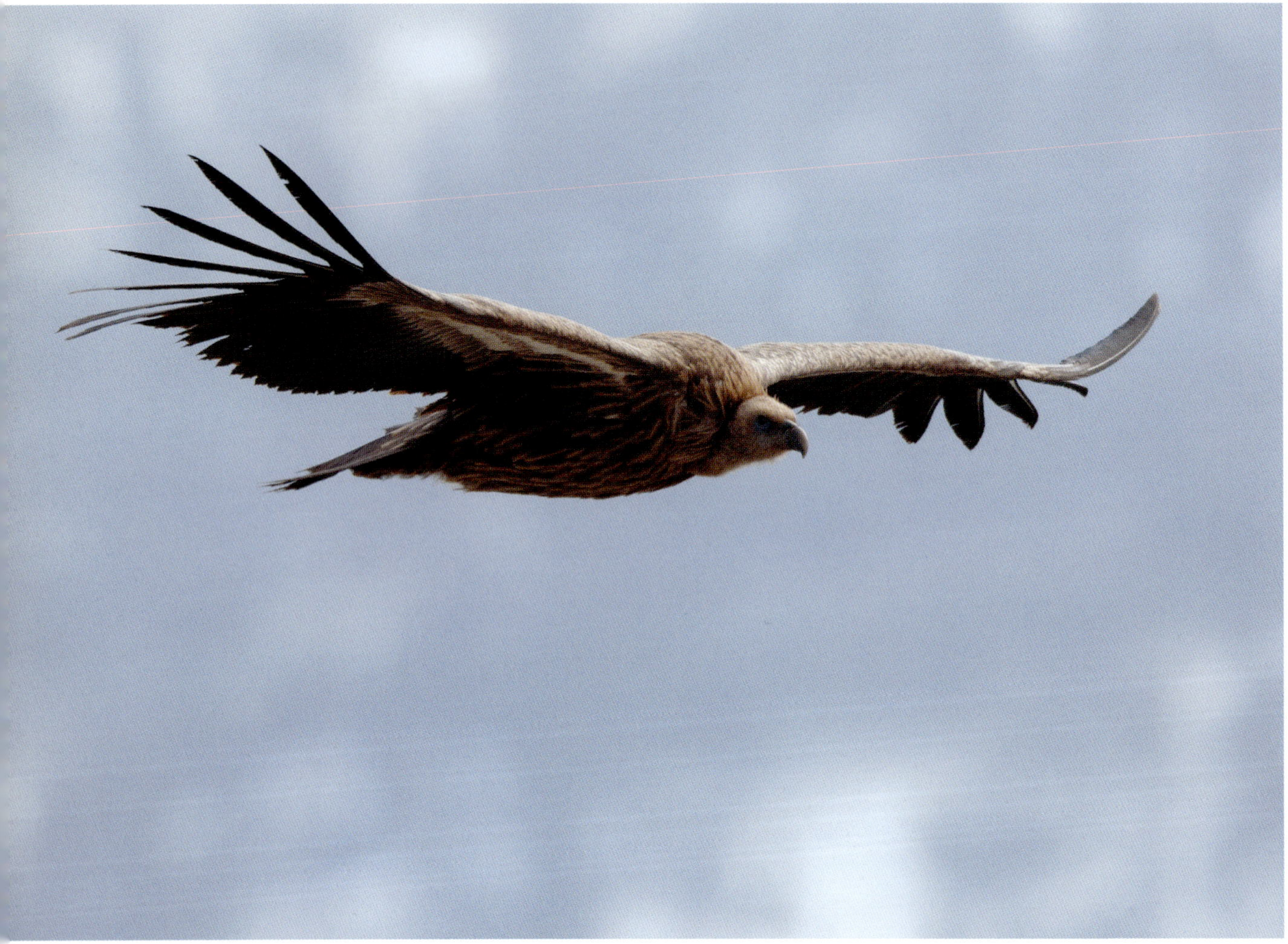

A Himalayan griffon hovers in the sky with its huge wings. Its excellent eyesight helps it to identify prey in the far distance.

Probably the biggest and heaviest birds in the Himalayas, Himalayan griffons are about 90 to 120 centimeters long and weigh 8 to 12 kilograms.

Living in high mountains and plateaus, they are often seen in tundra forests in upper alpine forests, plateau steppes, deserts, and rocky areas. Sometimes, they appear in the sky above the snow line. The propagation mostly takes place in the mountain of 2,000 to 6,000 meters above sea level. Sometimes in the winter, they are also seen at the foot of mountains.

Himalayan griffons generally do not attack other animals. The function of their claws has degenerated to the extent of not being suitable for hunting. With a very acute sense of vision and smell, they often hover in the sky to look for dead bodies on the ground. They also flock to dead bodies when smelling rotten meat and sometimes attack each other while snatching the food.

So far, they are the only birds that are closely connected with the traditions of an ancient nationality. Since Buddhism was brought into Tibet, Himalayan griffons have been in close connection with the unique life concept of Tibetans. In Tibet, people carry the human corpse to their venue, cutting it into pieces to feed them. It is an auspicious sign to have the corpse eaten completely by Himalayan griffons, as Tibetans believe that Himalayan griffons can take the soul of the deceased to paradise. Himalayan griffons, regarded as "immortal birds of Tibet," are held in high esteem by Tibetans.

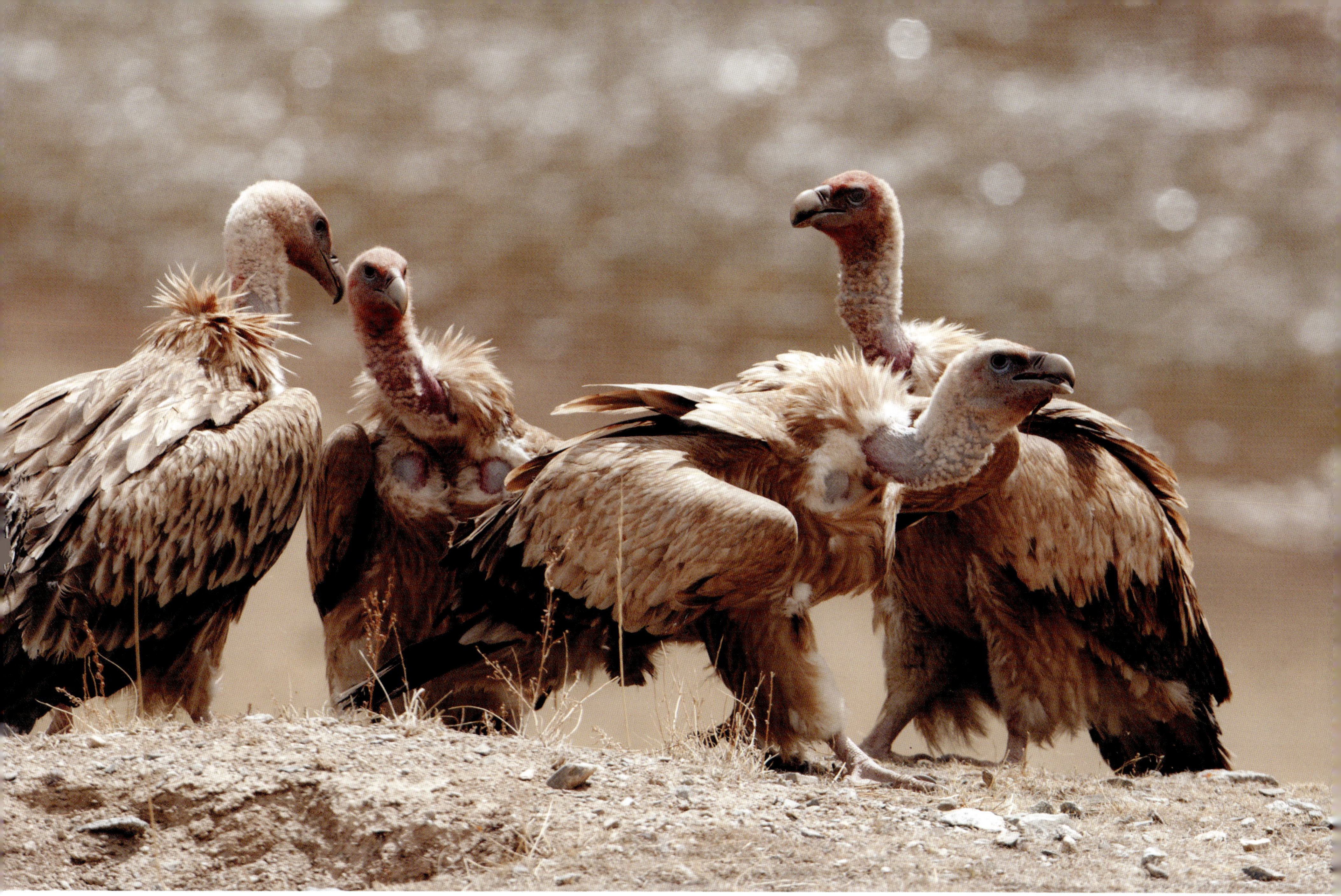

As a big bird of prey that can easily be seen on the Tibetan Plateau, they eat the corpse of various animals, resulting in the name "cleaners on the plateau." They either fly in the sky or stay in a group on the ground or on rocks to rest.

Lammergeier

Gypaetus barbatus
IUCN Red List: Least Concern

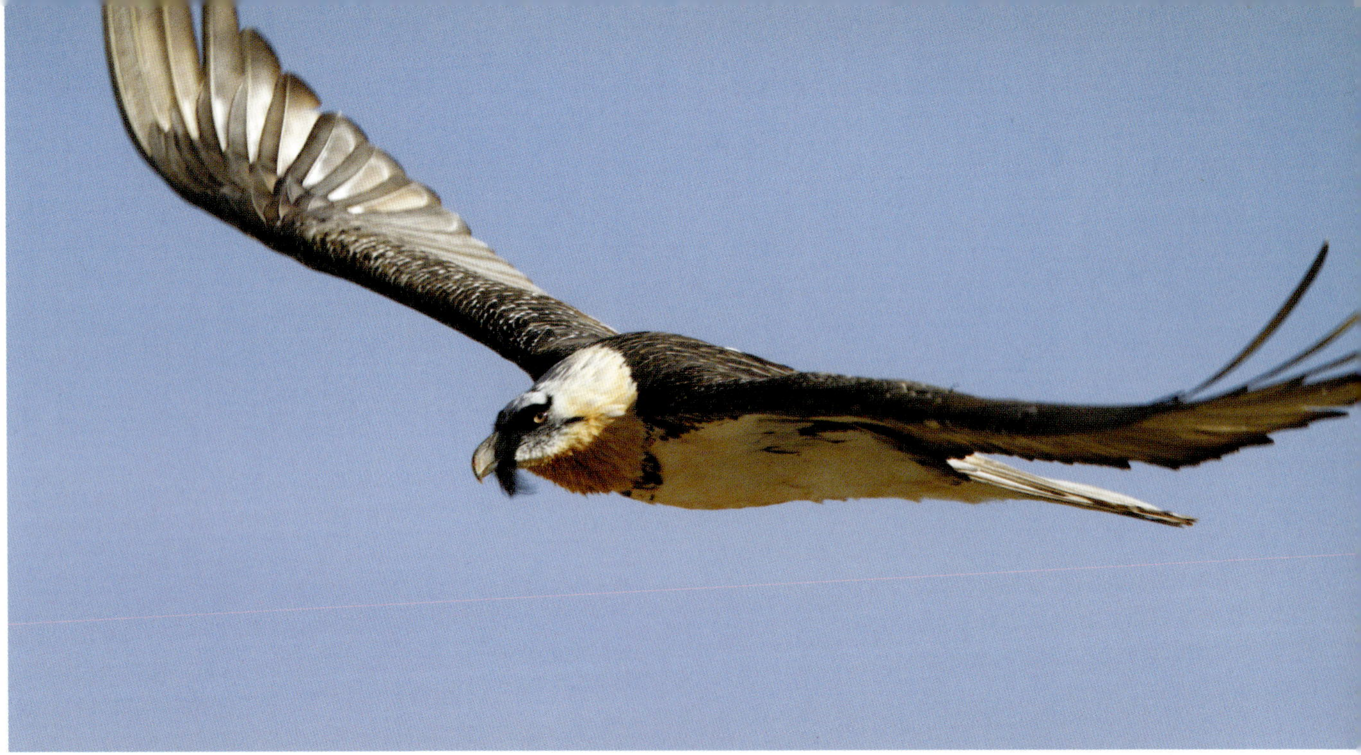

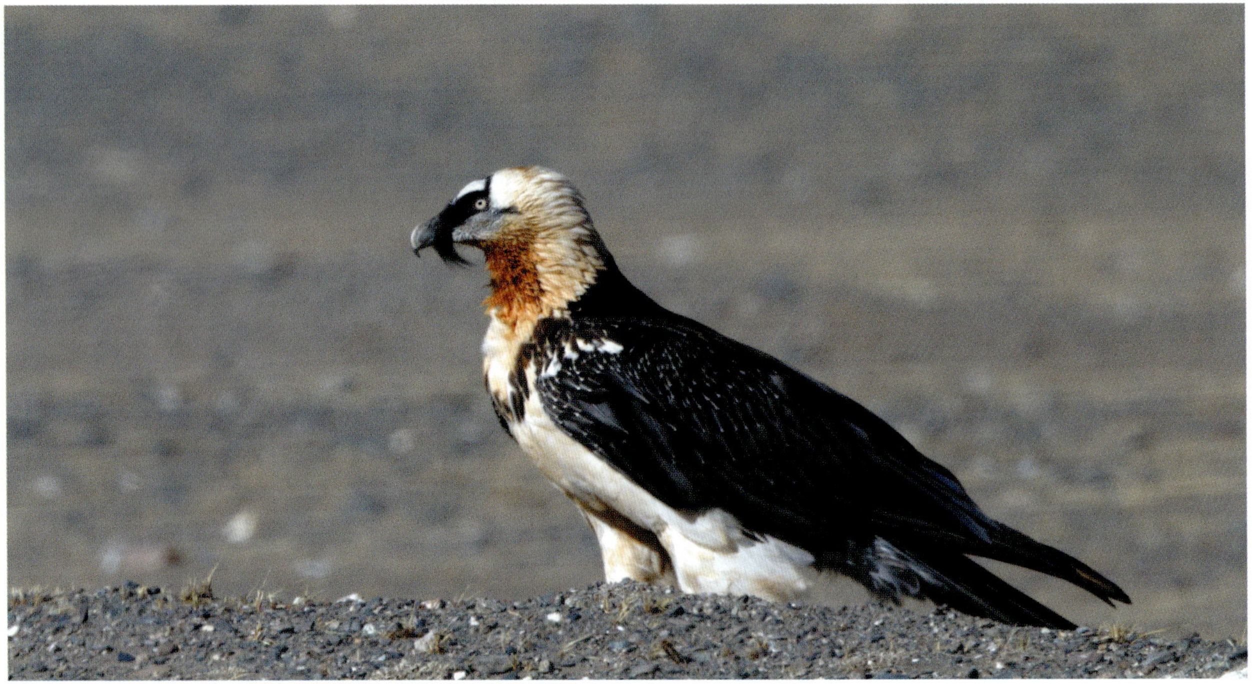

Also named bearded vultures, lammergeiers mainly live in areas of naked rocks of 500 to 4,000 meters above sea level. Such large fierce birds of prey eating rotten food are often seen in mountains interspersed with gulleys, plateau, and grassland. They can fly over the highest peak of over 8,000 meters above sea level in the Himalayan Mountains. In seasons of non-propagation, they mostly stay with Himalayan griffons in groups. Having found a dead body, they would first hover for observation and then land at a place 50 meters away from the spot. After making sure that there is no danger, they would flock to the dead body. Lammergeiers chiefly eat bones, making their diet quite unique.

Another feature of lammergeiers is their hatching relationship. They not only live in pairs, but also in trios (two males and one female). During the hatching period, two or three lammergeiers live together and jointly take care of their nest. They often fight among themselves for the best place for building the nest.

Though they are in danger in Europe, the number of lammergeiers is quite stable on the Tibetan Plateau. Like vultures and Himalayan griffons, they play an important role in the funeral traditions of Tibetans.

Above right
A lammergeier spreads its wings in flight. Huge in size, the wings of lammergeiers can be as wide as three meters.

Below right
Lammergeiers are marked by a black beard.

Little Owl

Athene noctua
IUCN Red List: Least Concern

Little owls are the most extensively distributed and the most commonly seen small owls in the Palearctic Realm (Palearctic Realm is an animal-oriented geographic sub-region chiefly based on Eurasia, covering Europe, Africa, and Arabia to the north of the Tropic of Cancer, Himalayan Mountains and Asia to the north of Qinling Mountains). They can be seen in the entire northern China. Though most owls are birds of prey at night, in order to avoid competition with other large owls at night, little owls mostly choose to be out at dawn or dust during the winter.

Prior to propagation, little owls usually move around on their own. They sleep in the daytime and set out at night. From the end of February to April, they have been more active in the daytime with more frequent chirps. The female little owl and the male little owl fly in pairs, chasing after each other. We can see them sing nicely in an antiphonal style. Some of the feathers on the abdomen of the female little owl begins to fall off, forming naked "hatching spots." From late April to mid-May, the female little owl would lay 5 to 7 white and nearly round eggs, and immediately start to hatch them. During this time, the male little owl has to look for food almost day and night and protect the female while she is hatching eggs. In the end, juveniles would leave for a place 50 to 200 kilometers away from their parents to settle down.

In China, owls are regarded as inauspicious birds and the chirps of little owls at night are even more unwelcomed. In northwestern China, the poisoning of rats is the major threat that leads to the little owls inadvertently being poisoned.

Right
A little owl is standing at the commanding point, flying back and forth to catch its prey at any moment.

Below
Under a warm sunshine at dusk, a little owl is crouching on the enclosure, waiting quietly for the appearance of a prey.

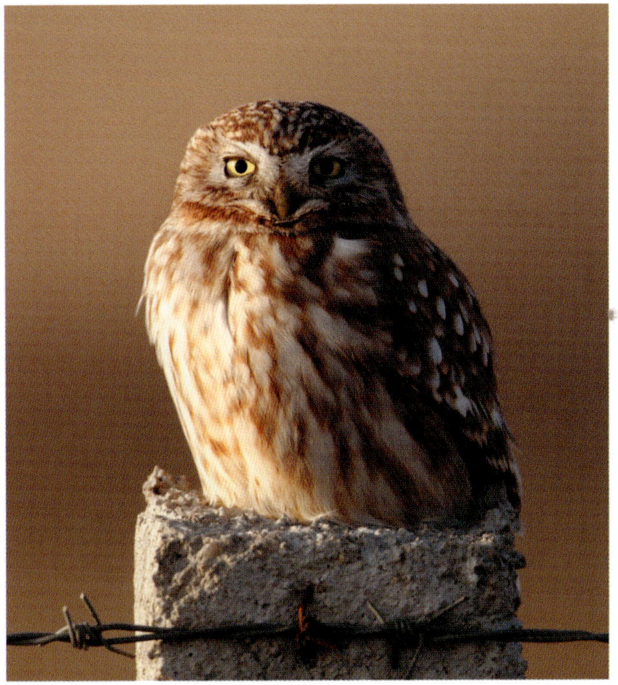

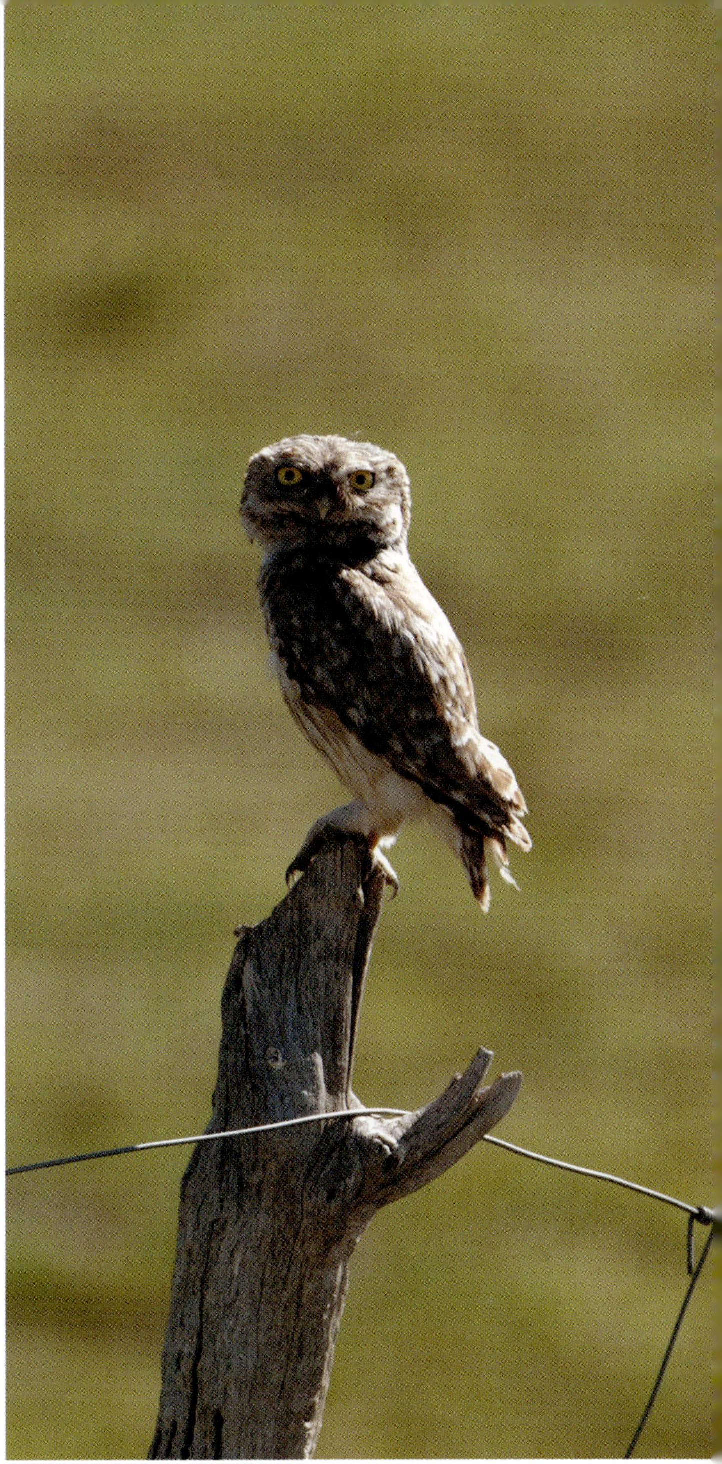

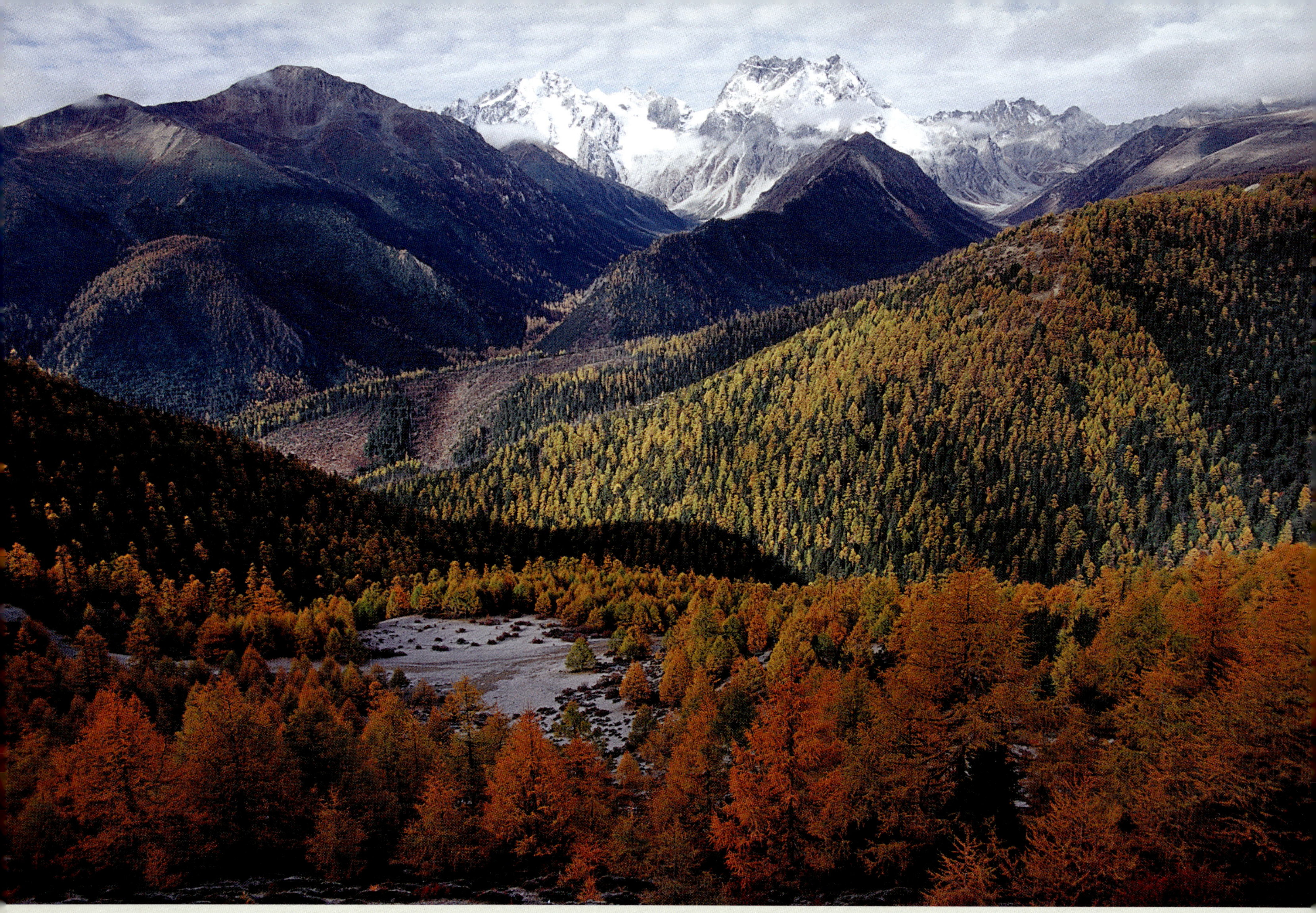

Chapter Two

White Horse Snow Mountains—The Yunnan Snub-Nosed Monkeys' Abode

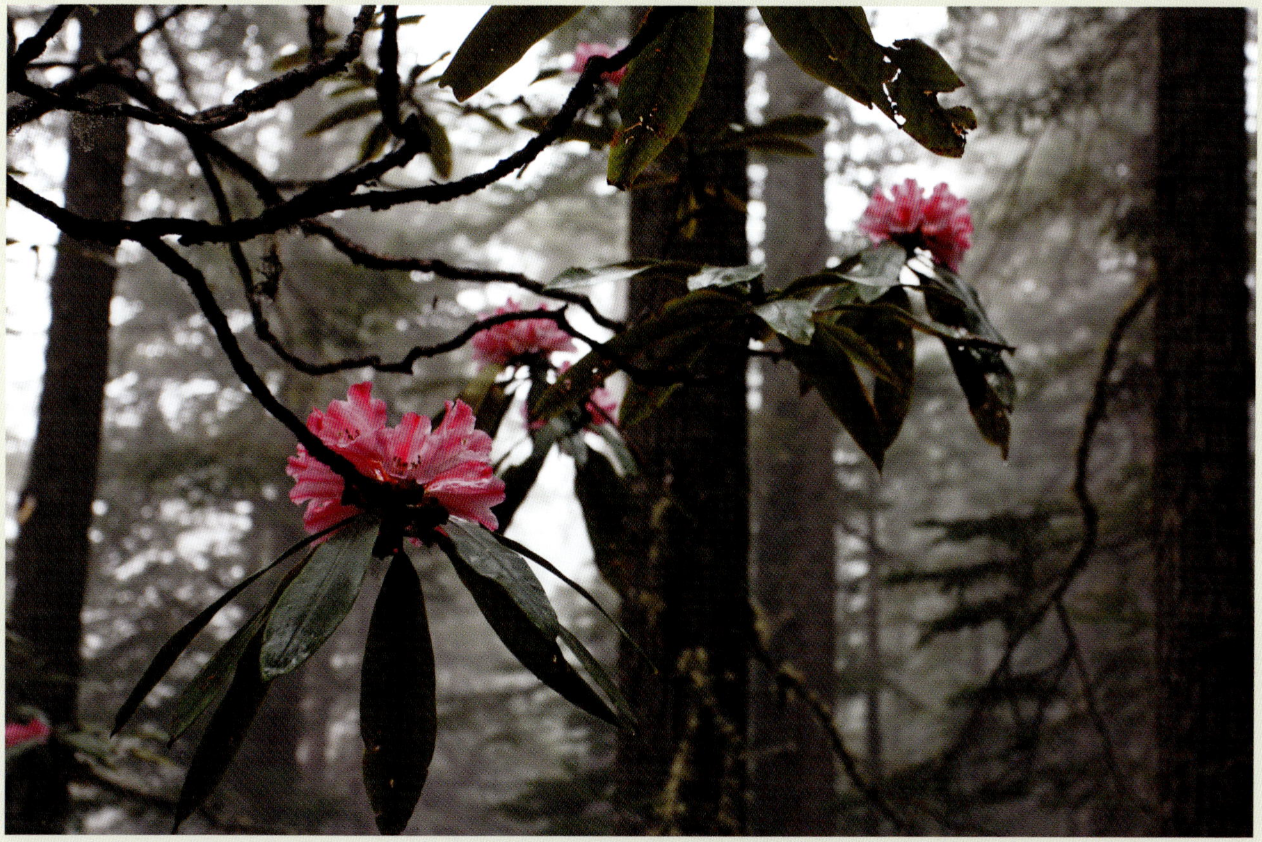

This is the typical habitat of the Yunnan snub-nosed monkeys, with gorgeous rhododendrons in blossom amidst firs.

The mountain's name came from its ridge, which looks like a galloping white horse. Covering a total area of about 190,144 hectares, it is at the highest sea level and the biggest natural and primitive forest reserve in Yunnan province. The towering Yunling Mountains in the reserve extends from the north to the south. There are 20 peaks of 5,000 meters above sea level. Zhalaqueni Peak is as high as 5,640 meters above sea level and its height changes according to the elevation of the sea level. The climate is marked by dry-heat in the valley and severe cold in the mountain. Vegetation is featured by obvious vertical distribution. Within an area of less than 40 square kilometers, there are 7 – 16 kinds of plants equivalent to the plant distribution belt extending several thousand kilometers from the south to the north across China.

It is reputed as "the kingdom of animals and plants in alpine areas," providing the best habitat for wild animals. Wild mammals in the protected area include large Indian civets, small Indian civets, clouded leopards, and Tibetan eared pheasants. Yunnan snub-nosed monkeys, which were never seen despite their reputation, live in White Horse Snow Mountains all year round, as it is the center of the forest resources in this region.

On facing page
Zhalaqueni Peak, the main peak of the White Horse Snow Mountains.

Yunnan Snub-Nosed Monkey

Rhinopithecus bieti
IUCN Red List: Endangered

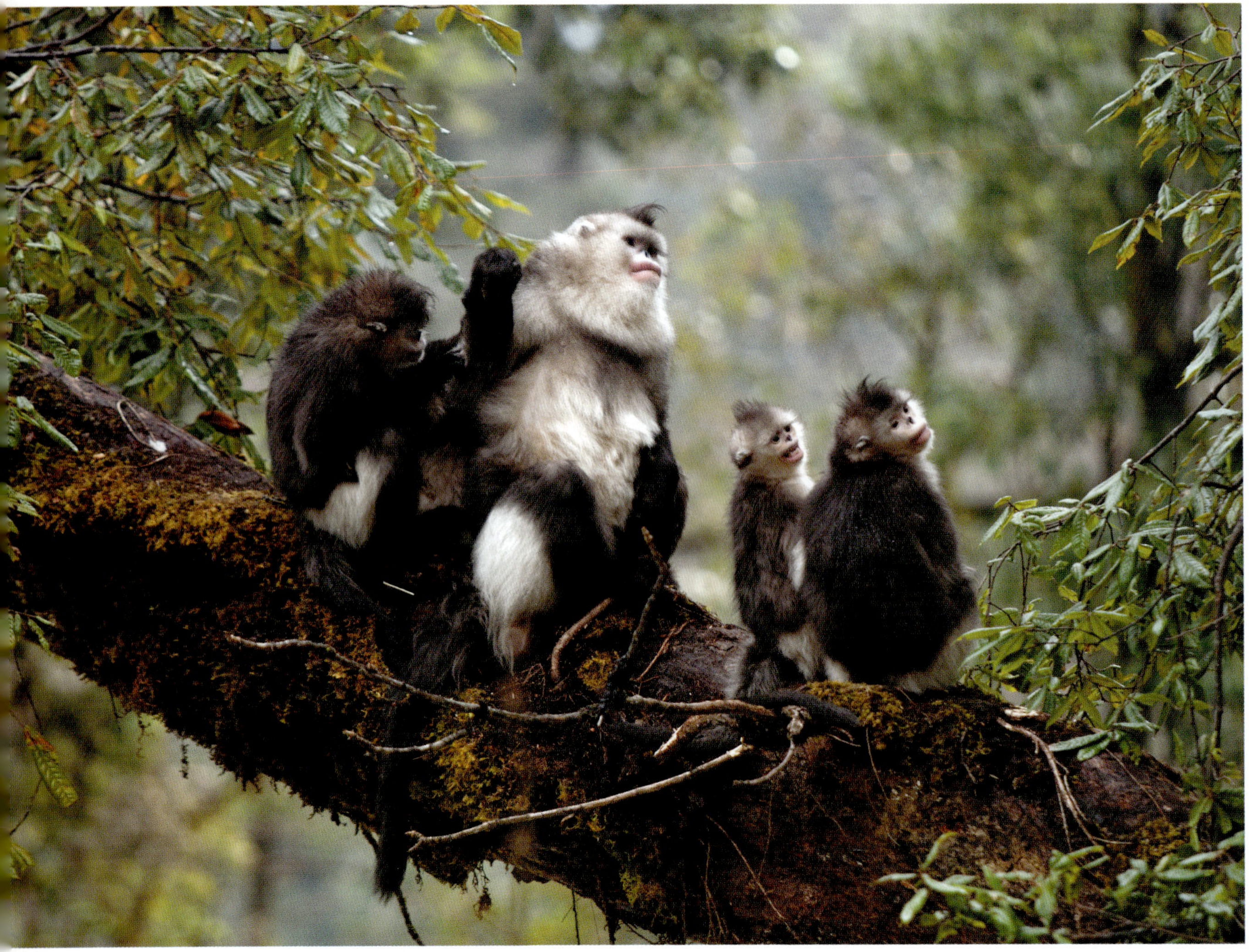

Also named black-white snub-nosed monkeys, Yunnan snub-nosed monkeys are rare and famous animals on the verge of extinction in the world. They are very special in the family of snub-nosed monkeys. Despite their name as "snub-nosed monkeys," they actually do not have golden hair and they are slightly bigger than golden snub-nosed monkeys. The discovery of Yunnan snub-nosed monkeys can be traced back to the sample collected by museologists in 1871 in Deqin county, Yunnan province. In 1890, French missionary Monseigneur Biet and his partners acquired more samples in their research into this kind of black-white monkeys. These samples were all transported to National Museum of Natural History (Paris, France). With these samples, French zoologist Milne Edwards named this species and gave scientific description respectively in 1897 and 1898. In 1904, British museologists also got a fur sample of a Yunnan snub-nosed monkey in the Samage area of White Horse Snow Mountains. In over fifty years, there had been little knowledge of this species and some people even believed that they had disappeared from the earth.

It was not until 1962 that scientists at Kunming Institute of Zoology of the Chinese Academy of Sciences got eight incomplete pieces of grey-black monkey fur in Deqin county, once again

Combing each other's hair is a behavior among primates for showing affection.

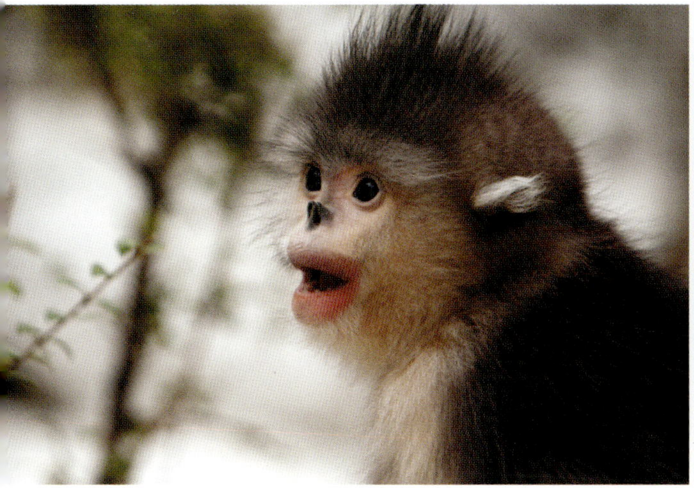

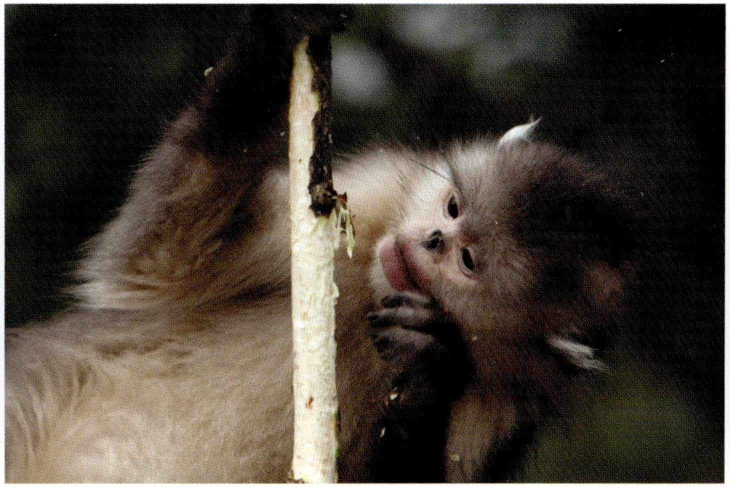

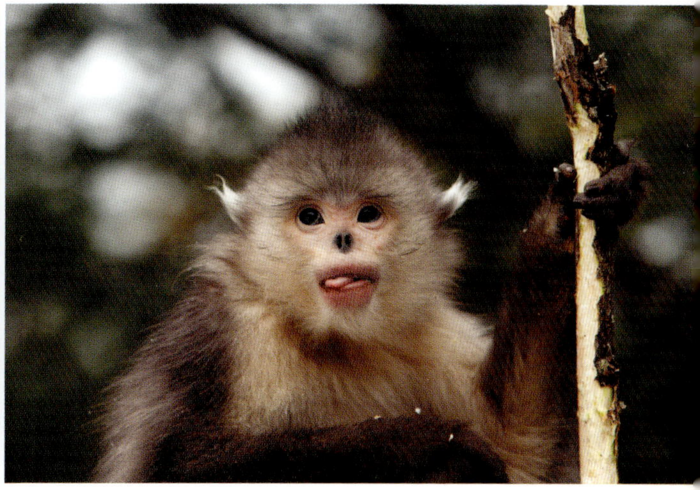

rediscovering the Yunnan snub-nosed monkeys and gradually uncovering their mysterious veil. Yunnan snub-nosed monkeys are only seen in southwest China, or rather, in northwest Yunnan province and in a narrow area of southeast Tibet, extending from Yunlong county in the extreme south of Yunnan province to Mangkang county in the extreme north of Tibet. They live in alpine coniferous forests of 3,000 – 4,700 meters above sea level. As the most indomitable primates living on high mountains where there are almost no human activities all year round, they are primates living in places at the highest sea level in the world, in addition to human beings. Even in winter with ice and snow all over, they will not move to places at low sea level.

Yunnan snub-nosed monkeys form family units consisting of 20 to 300 in number. Each family includes a male and 2 to 3 females as well as their children, practicing "polygamy." Family members take care of one another and live together on high firs, jumping from one fir to another. They eat tender buds and *Bryoria nepalensis*, a kind of lichen attached to the fir. In summer, local people can also see them eat newly protruded bamboo shoots and tender bamboo leaves. From the early morning till the dusk, people would see them collect food and find lots of fir branch-tips left behind by them. Since *Bryoria nepalensis* can only provide low energy and Yunnan snub-nosed monkeys live at such cold places at high sea level, they need to spend more time than other kinds of primates do in collecting food and rely on special micro-organism in their stomach to help their digestion, so as to acquire enough energy. There are some changes of plant varieties for their food collection due to different seasons. However, they never eat the crops of local villagers. That's why they can live in harmony with people for a long time and are regarded as "super-spirits" by local people of minority nationalities.

One of the major reasons for the rapid reduction of the number of Yunnan snub-nosed monkeys was that they were hunted in large numbers for their fur. In the 1970s, the number of Yunnan snub-nosed monkeys in Deqin county was less than 1,000. In ten years from 1971 to 1981, the number of Yunnan snub-nosed monkeys hunted in this region amounted to over 430. At present, this species is still threatened by traps set for catching musk deer. The loss of their habitat is another severe threat against them. In the period

1 2 3

Due to the lack of food in the winter, barks have become the staple for this sub-adult female Yunnan snub-nosed monkey.

The Campaign for Protecting Yunnan Snub-Nosed Monkeys

In 1995, due to financial difficulties, the government of Deqin county of Yunnan province planned to cut down an expanse of forests in the south of the White Horse Snow Mountains, which would directly threaten the survival of a group of Yunnan snub-nosed monkeys. At once, I appealed to the public for help. My letter for help and the pictures of Yunnan snub-nosed monkeys taken drew attention from many scholars and media in Beijing, hence starting "the campaign for protecting Yunnan snub-nosed monkeys" organized by university students, media, and a new force of environmental protection in China. In the end, Deqin county stopped the cutting down of this expanse of forests, protecting the Yunnan snub-nosed monkeys that lived there. With "China's Green Revolution" as the topic, the American magazine *Newsweek* reported this campaign of protecting Yunnan snub-nosed monkeys, stating: "this will be the watershed of awareness of environmental protection from Chinese people."

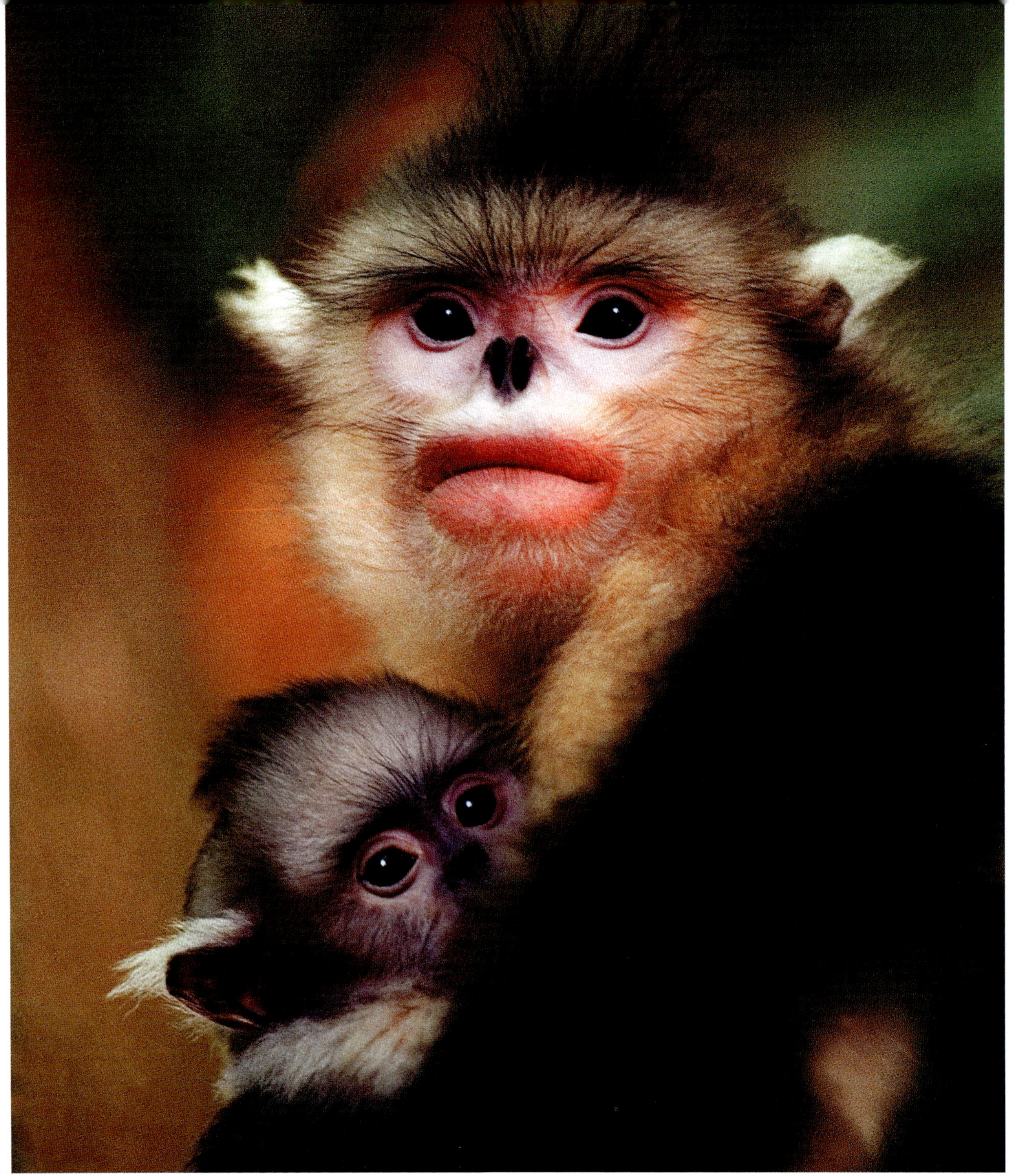

The expression in the eyes of this pair of Yunnan snub-nosed monkeys (mother and baby) has touched so many people, becoming the symbol of the rise of the environmental protection movement in China.

The Journey of Looking for Yunnan Snub-Nosed Monkeys

My relationship with Yunnan snub-nosed monkeys can be traced back to the beginning of the 1990s. In order to take pictures of the real state of such unknown species unique to China in the wilderness, I started my journey of looking for Yunnan snub-nosed monkeys in 1992. At that time, the investigation team set out for forest-based land in Amugulu. Once there, we found monkey droppings of about one week old and mountain ash leaves collected by them. New hope seemed to appear once again, but it was almost dark so we had to sleep on it. However, maybe our hope was too much, because we found nothing the following day.

On the third day, we had to return to our camp. On the way, none of us said anything. At four o'clock in the afternoon, we reached the forest nearest to our camp. As exhausted members of the team were climbing slowly, one shouted, "Monkey droppings!" On a fallen tree, we saw a small pile of shining monkey droppings right in front of us. We could tell that this pile of droppings were left behind one hour ago at most, judging from the color and luster as well as the extent of separation. We were all sure that they must be ahead! Our days of searching were fruitful. Looking around, we found monkey droppings on the ground, stones, and azalea branches, and some seemed to steam. Obviously, a group of them was just passing by. The discovery of monkey droppings was like an injection of cardiac stimulant into every one of us. It only took us 20 minutes to climb up to the mountain pass despite a vertical height of nearly 400 meters. At the pass, shouts of young monkeys were heard on the opposite side. A family of Yunnan snub-nosed monkeys was seen on a protruding fir through larch branches. Like spirits of a snow mountain, Yunnan snub-nosed monkeys appeared before our lens at last. We finally saw them through a long trudge on mountains paths at night and watched in ice cold cowsheds!

Two Yunnan snub-nosed monkeys on a tree.

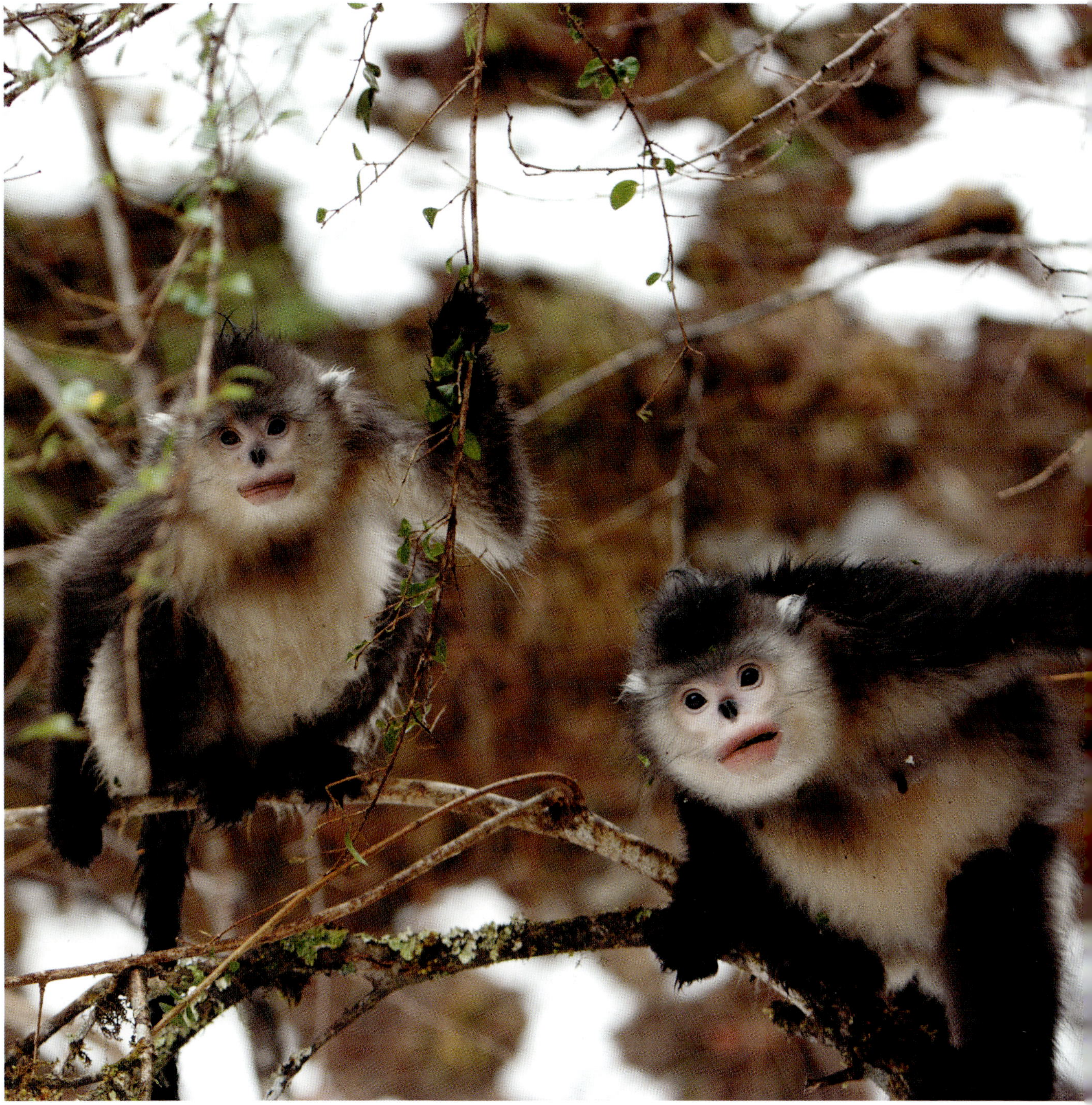

from 1958 to 1997, commercialized lumbering due to the needs of timbers and reclamation of forest-based land for grazing domestic animals had reduced the area of their habitat by 31%. So far, there are only 15 groups of them totaling over 2,000, thus making them very precious. Severe environmental breakdown caused by human activities has made these 15 groups almost separate from one another. It is not possible for monkeys in these groups to accomplish the exchange of genes.

Research into Yunnan snub-nosed monkeys in 1978 came to the attention of the Chinese government. The year 1983 witnessed the establishment of the first national nature reserve aimed at protecting Yunnan snub-nosed monkeys—White Horse Snow Mountains Nature Reserve of Yunnan province. *Laws for protecting Wild animals in China* promulgated in 1989 took Yunnan snub-nosed monkeys as grade-one key animals under national protection. The movement for protecting Yunnan snub-nosed monkeys initiated in 1996 brought this mysterious species to public attention. In 1999, Yunnan snub-nosed monkeys became the mascot of Kunming International Horticultural Exposition, quickly enhancing their reputation. Since then, Yunnan snub-nosed monkeys have become one of the wild animals receiving the greatest attention in China.

It is indeed a difficult question to answer in terms of the state of Yunnan snub-nosed monkeys, since we do not understand them very much.

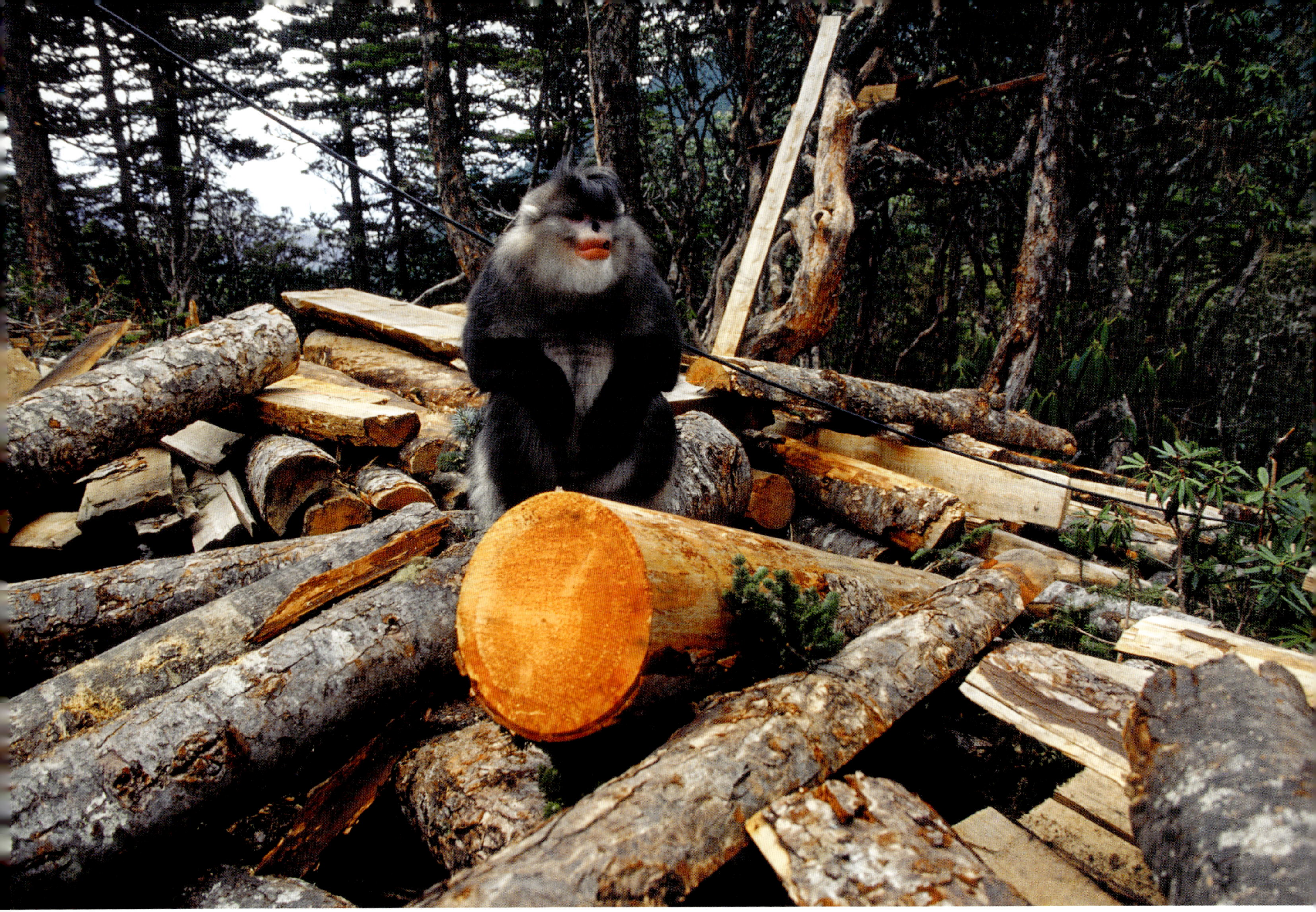

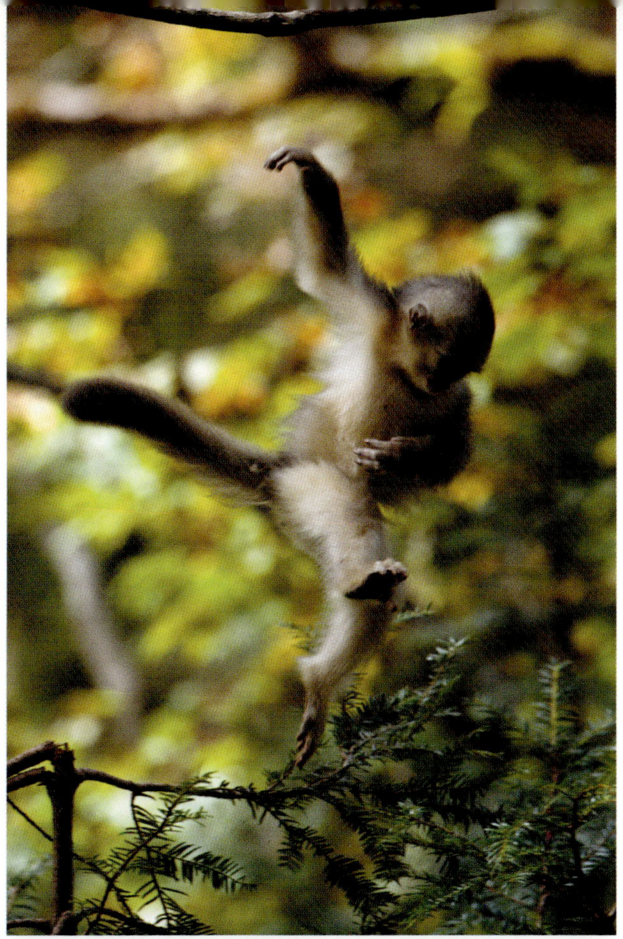

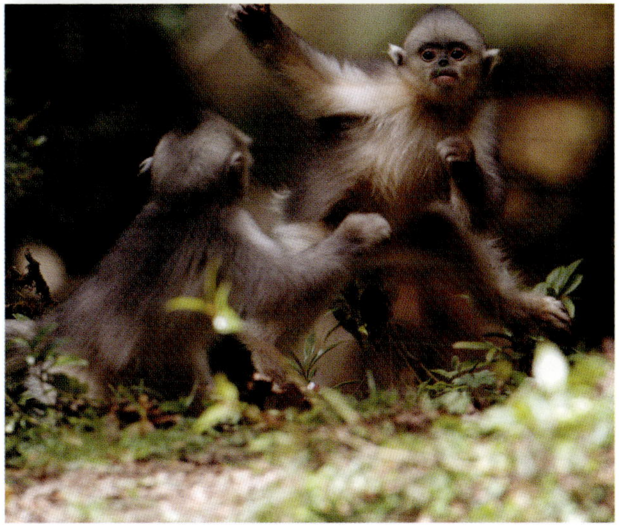

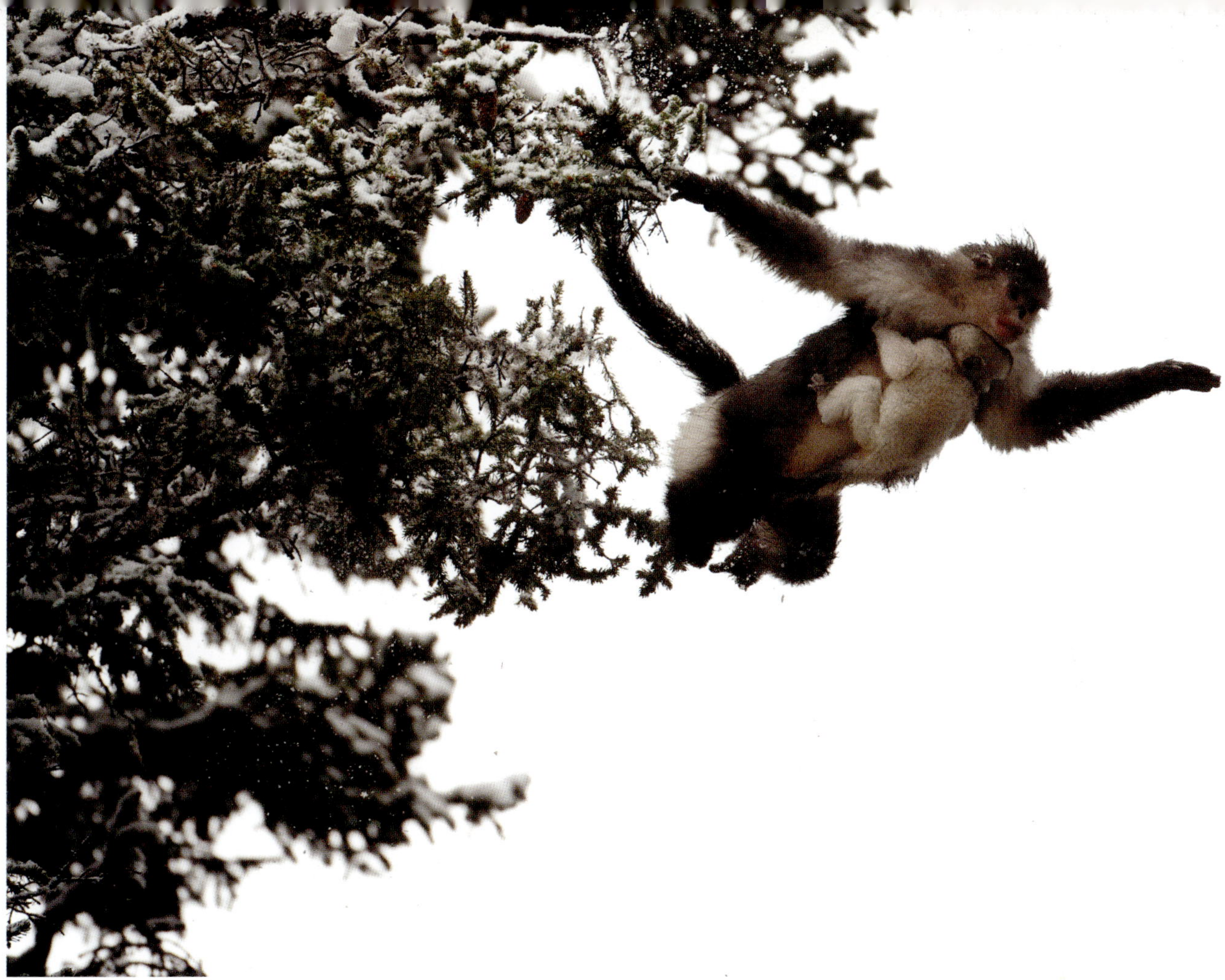

On facing page
A male Yunnan snub-nosed monkey sits alone after its failure in competition. Fragmented forests due to human activities are the major threat to the survival of the Yunnan snub-nosed monkeys.

Above left and below left
When not eating and sleeping, juvenile Yunnan snub-nosed monkeys play to their hearts' content. These two little monkeys chase after each other, jumping and leaping across trees with agile movements. Here, their postures seem to resemble those of kung fu masters.

Above
When a group of monkeys move away, almost all the family members would jump from the same position. This mother, holding her baby closely in her arms, leaps easily towards an opposite tree.

With the cease of commercialized lumbering of trees, massive destruction of their habitat and the threat of the disappearance of large areas have been eliminated, theoretically speaking. However, low-quality and low-efficiency consumption and utilization of forest resources due to the traditional ways of production and the lifestyle of the local people are still nibbling at precious primitive forests in the northwest of Yunnan province. The shrinking habitat of Yunnan snub-nosed monkeys is still going on.

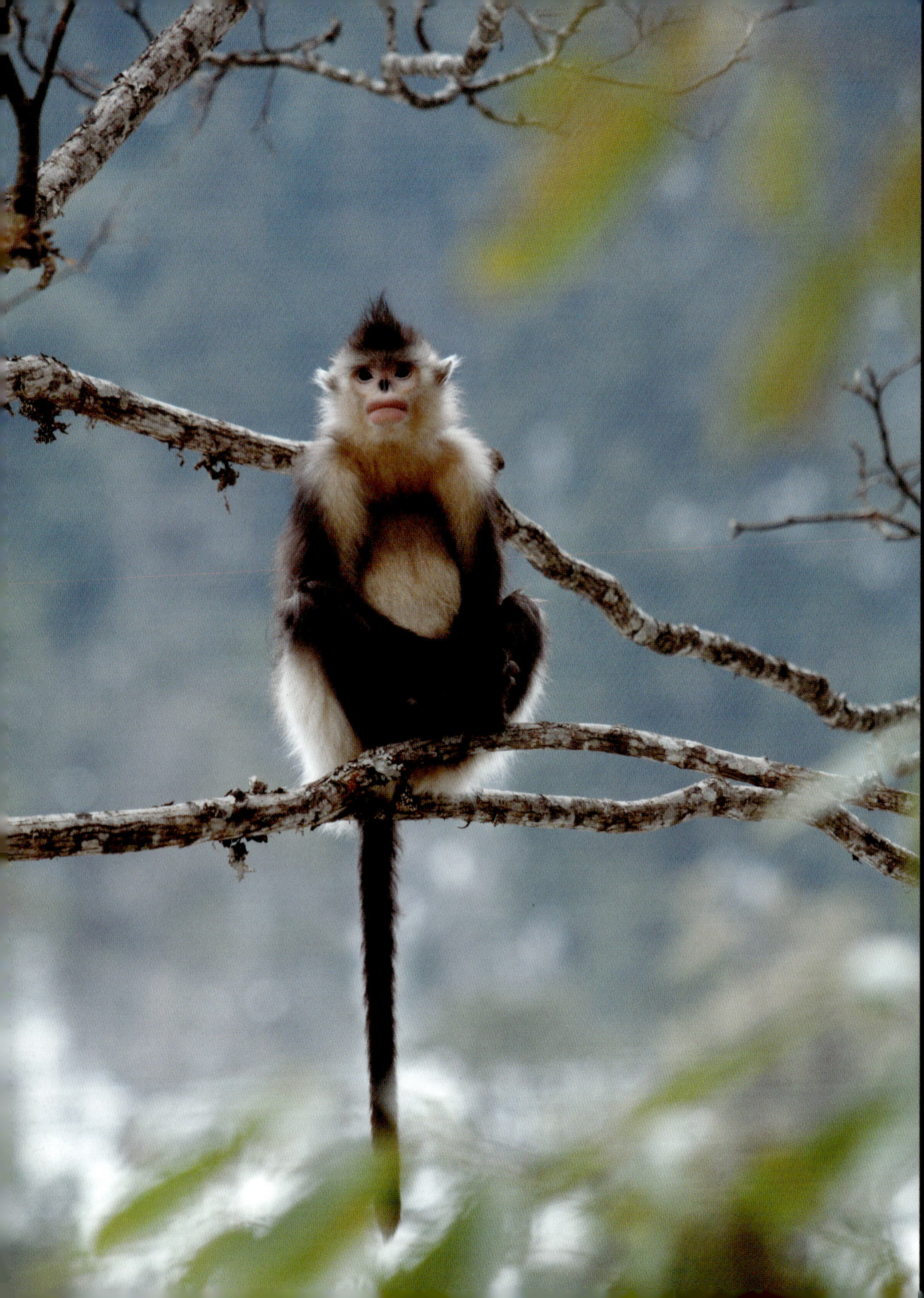

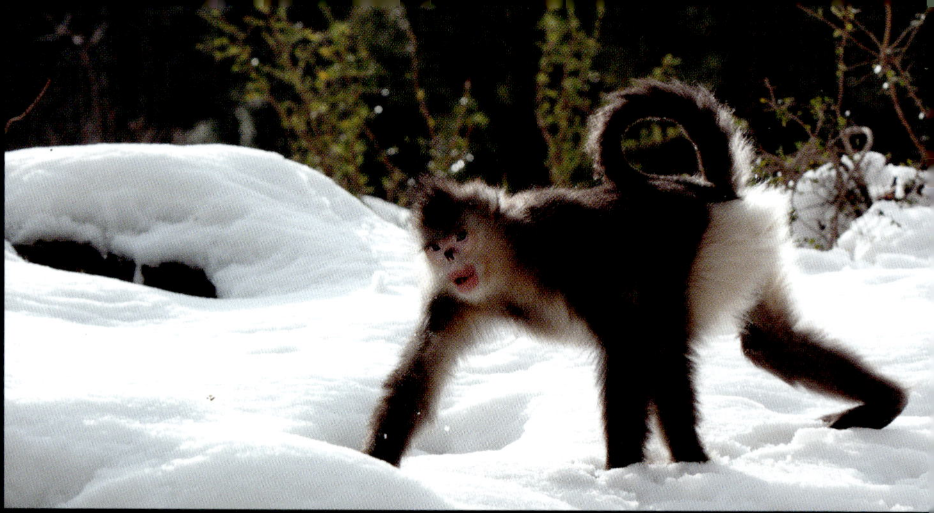

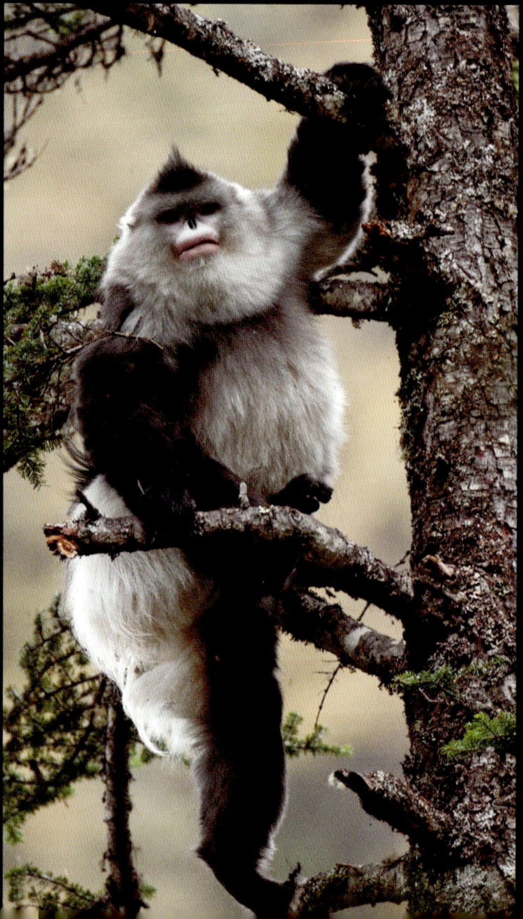

Far left
A male Yunnan snub-nosed monkey is sitting on fine tree branches with its legs crossed, appearing serene and peaceful. From a distance, it looks like a Taoist priest deep in the mountain and forest with profound Taoist cultivation.

Above
The amount of time that the Yunnan snub nosed monkeys spend on the ground is almost the same as that spent on trees.

Left
A big male Yunnan snub-nosed monkey can weigh as much as 40 kilograms. The alpine coniferous forest composed of high firs and spruces is the habitats of the Yunnan anub-nosed monkeys.

On facing page
Yunnan snub-nosed monkeys have pink faces, bright red lips, and a "punk" hair style very similar to those of human beings.

On page 66
It often snows in areas inhabited by the Yunnan snub-nosed monkeys, which is why they also have another name—snow monkeys.

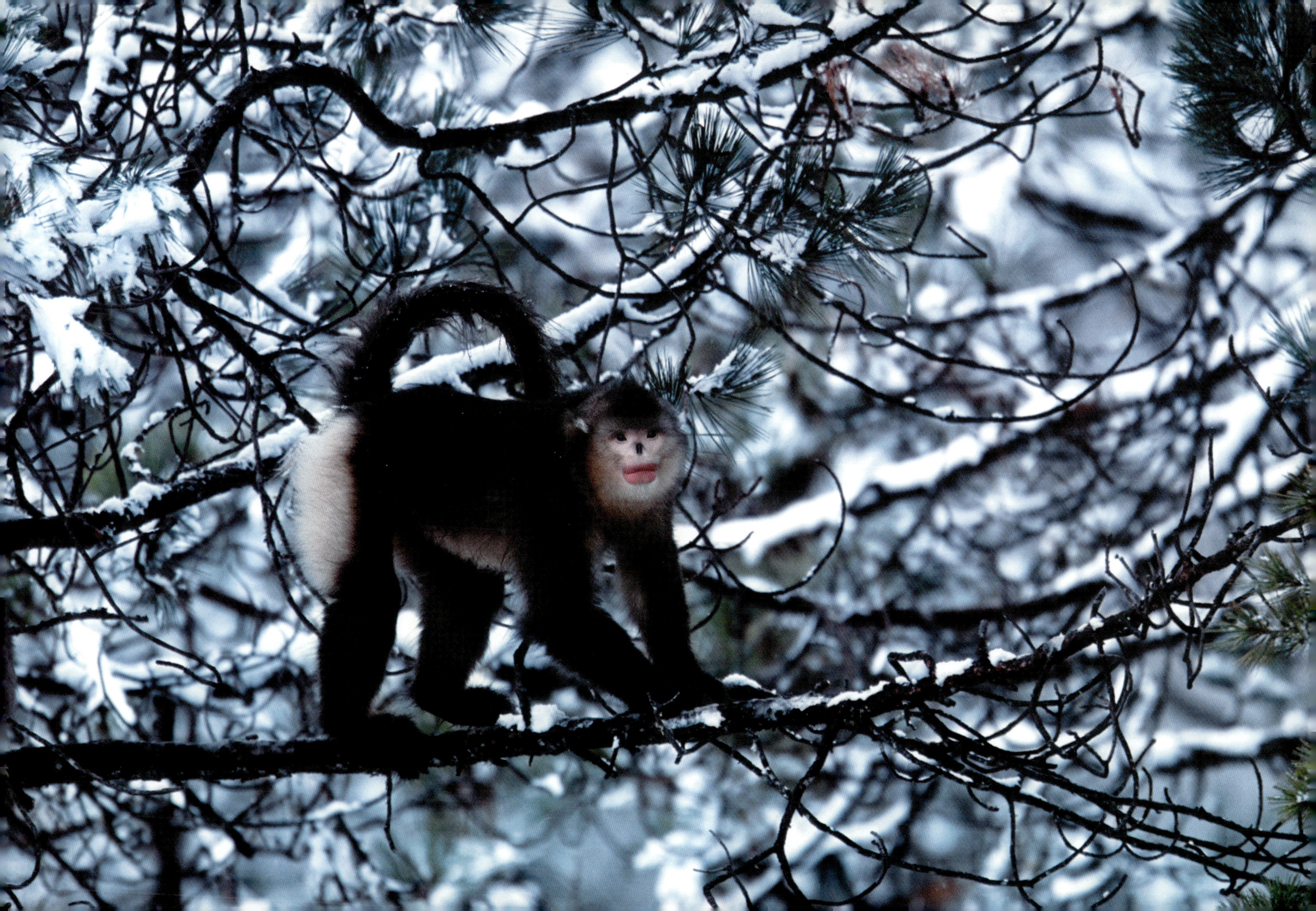

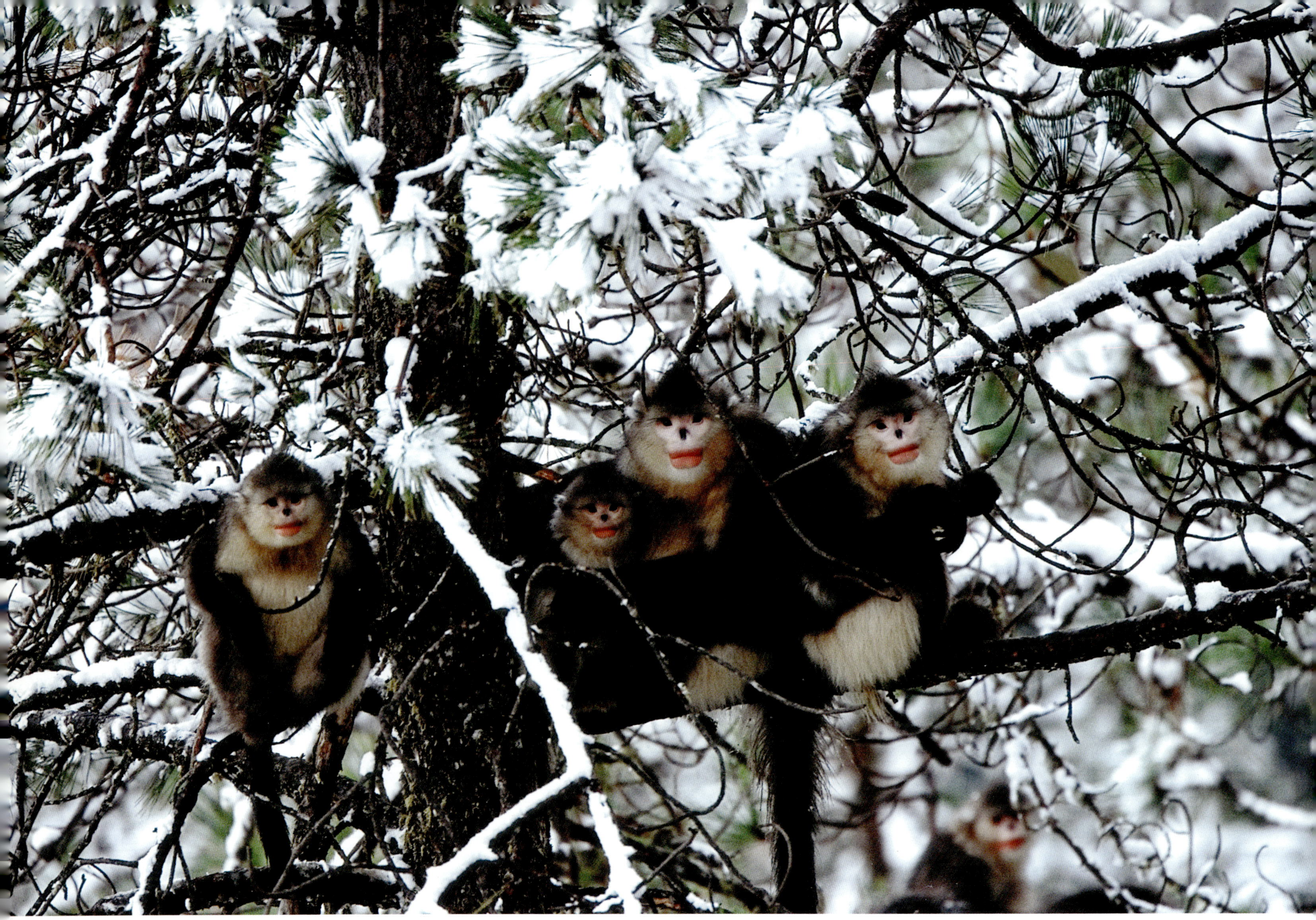

White Eared Pheasant

Crossoptilon crossoptilon

IUCN Red List: Near Threatened

Living in western China, they are chiefly distributed in eastern Tibet, southern Gansu and Qinghai provinces, Yunnan province, and western Sichuan province. As long as one meter, they are the biggest of the four species of eared pheasants.

In winter, they stay in a small group of 10 to 60. In the daytime, they eat ferns, moss and lichens in alpine coniferous forests, mixed forests, bushes, and steppes. They also eat some insects as animal protein. Sometimes, they would also get together to look for highland barley seeds in areas inhabited by Tibetans and near temples. In the vicinity of some temples, local lamas offer food and protection for them.

At night, white eared pheasants choose to stay on tall and lush alpine oaks, where they cannot be easily found by birds of prey.

Starting from each May, white eared pheasants in groups would begin to disperse. The adult female and adult male would propagate while some adults still live in groups. Those in the period of propagation build up nests with spruce branches, lichens, withered grass and feathers in bushes, under fallen trees, and even in caves in the forests. Twenty-five days of laying eggs, they would hatch out 5 to 7 babies.

Since the forests inhabited by white eared pheasants are the major timber resources for local people, the forest lumbering is constantly reducing the area in which the beautiful pheasants live. Excessive hunting for their eggs and tail-feather has also aggravated the extent of extinction on the part of this species.

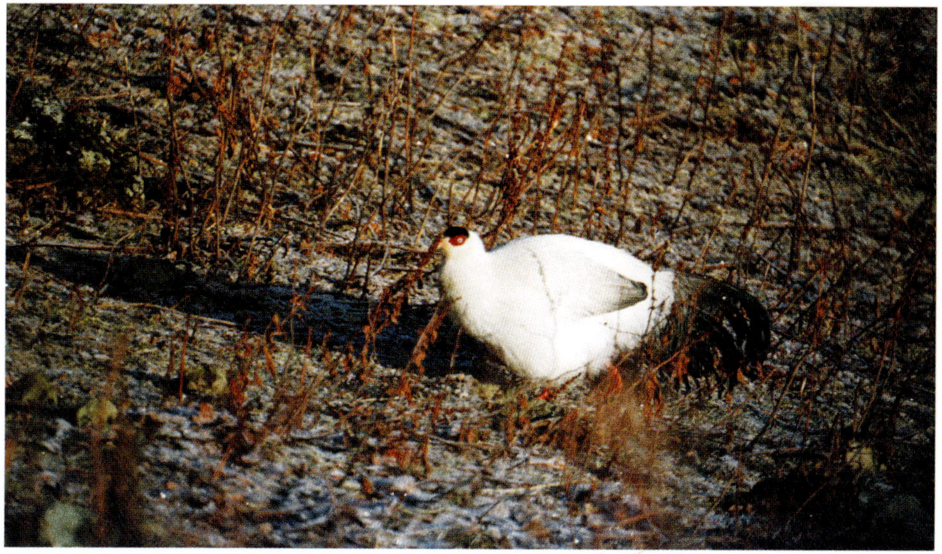

Under the early winter morning sunshine, a white eared pheasant from the forest is looking for food in an open space of pastureland.

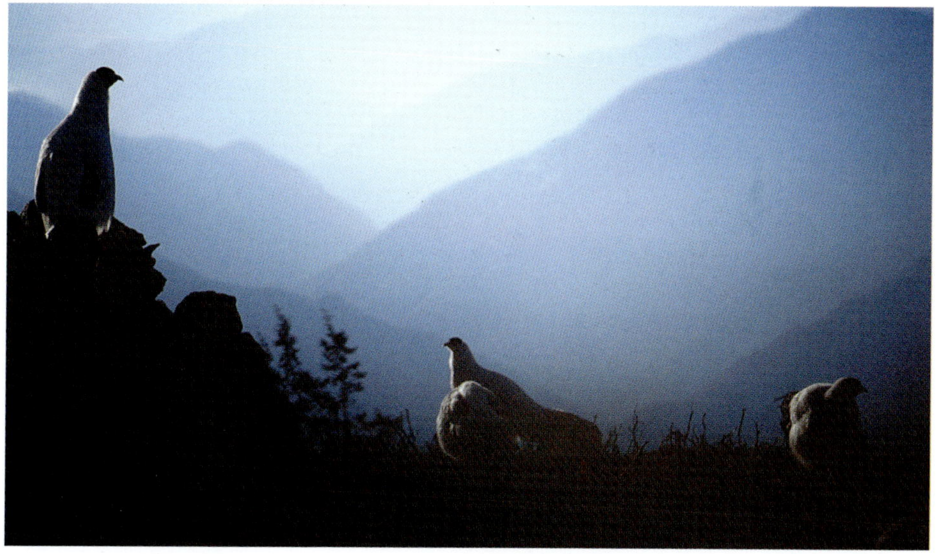

A good opportunity finally presents itself after three nights of waiting in a cold grazing shed. A white eared pheasant is looking for food and jumps onto a rock on the left. The photographer was lucky enough to have captured this nice scene.

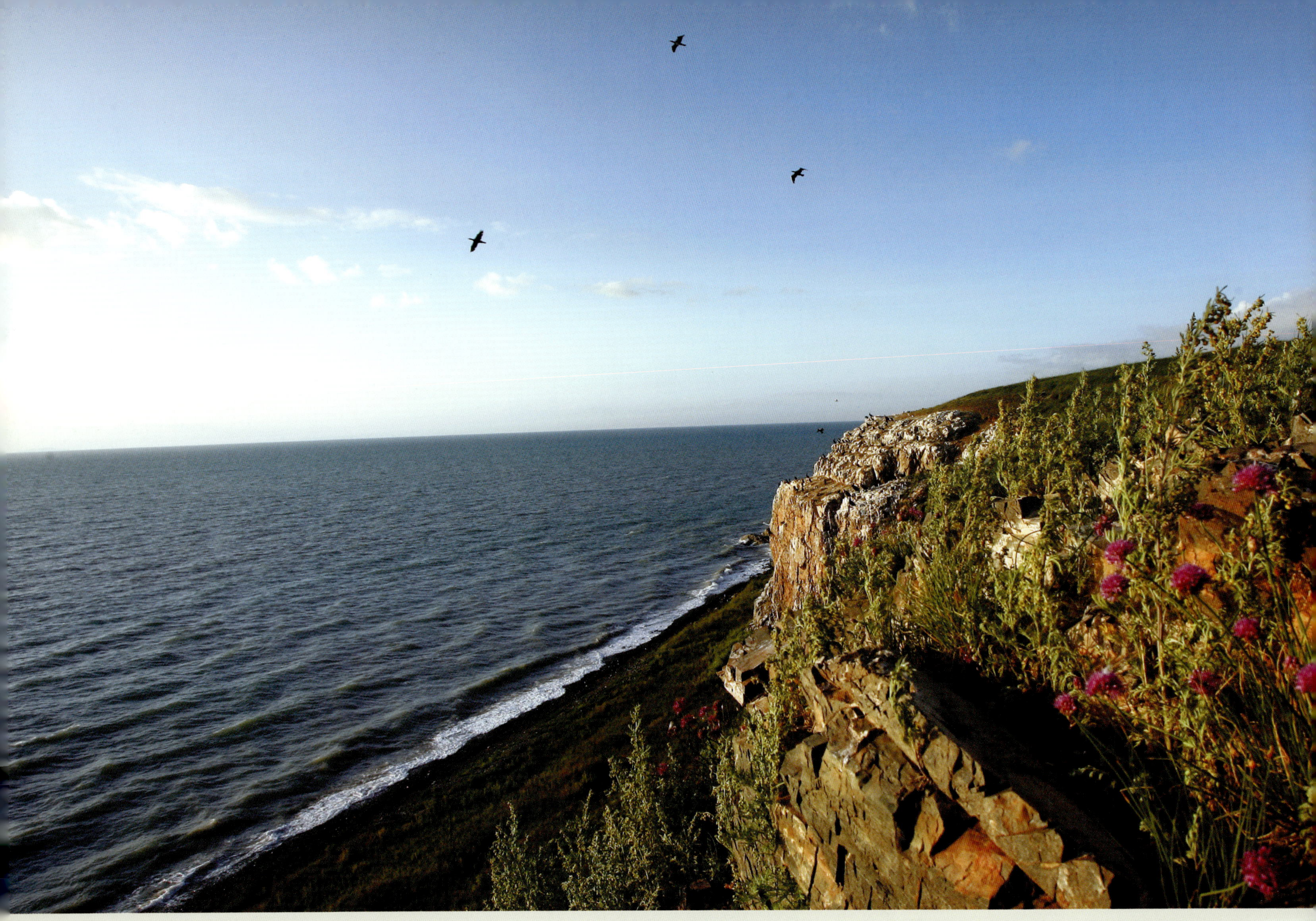

Chapter Three

Qinghai Lake—The Sanctuary for the Survival of the Przewalski's Gazelles

Situated in Qinghai Lake Basin in the northeast of Qinghai province, Qinghai Lake is the biggest inland lake and the biggest saline lake in China. Located in the northeast of the Tibetan Plateau, it is marked by expansive areas, vast grassland, numerous rivers, lots of grass, and a serene environment. Influenced by the plateau continental climate, it enjoys ample sunshine, with a cold winter and a cool summer and little rainfall. Towering mountains surround the lake 3,600 to 5,000 meters above sea level. Between the foot of the mountains and the lakeside, there is vast and flat plain, and the lake is just like a huge jadeite plate inlaid into it, hence constituting a spectacular scene set off by mountains, the lake, and grassland.

Located in the west of Qinghai Lake, though the Bird Island only covers an area of 0.11 square kilometers, it has over 100,000 migratory birds in spring and summer, including cormorants, bar-headed geese, Pallas's gulls, ruddy shelducks, and brown-headed gulls. In each May and June, the bird island is bustling with lots of juvenile birds whose chirps can be heard over one kilometer away. In July and August, birds either fly through the clear sky with a pleasant breeze, or swim on the lake. The lakeside is the home of another spirit, the Przewalski's gazelles. In recent years, due to comprehensive influence of the changes in the natural environment and human activities, the water level of Qinghai Lake has dropped down, in addition to the aggravation marked by more deserts along the lakeside and the reduction of vegetation. In spite of all these, Qinghai Lake has become the shelter for Przewalski's gazelles. Now, Przewalski's gazelles are one of the ungulates on the verge of extinction in the world. Protection of Qinghai Lake is the only hope of keeping Przewalski's gazelles from extinction.

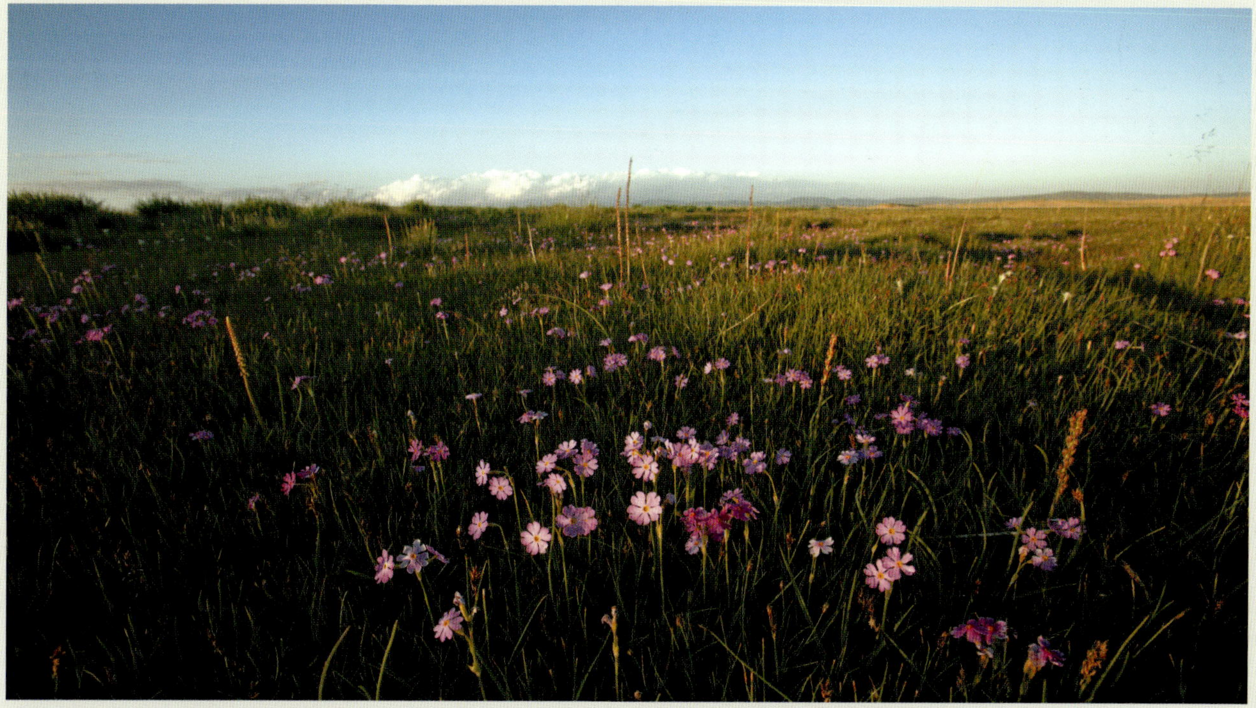

On facing page
In the early sunshine, a group of great cormorants return from looking for food.

The flowers blossoming around Qinghai Lake.

Przewalski's Gazelle

Procapra przewalskii
IUCN Red List: Endangered

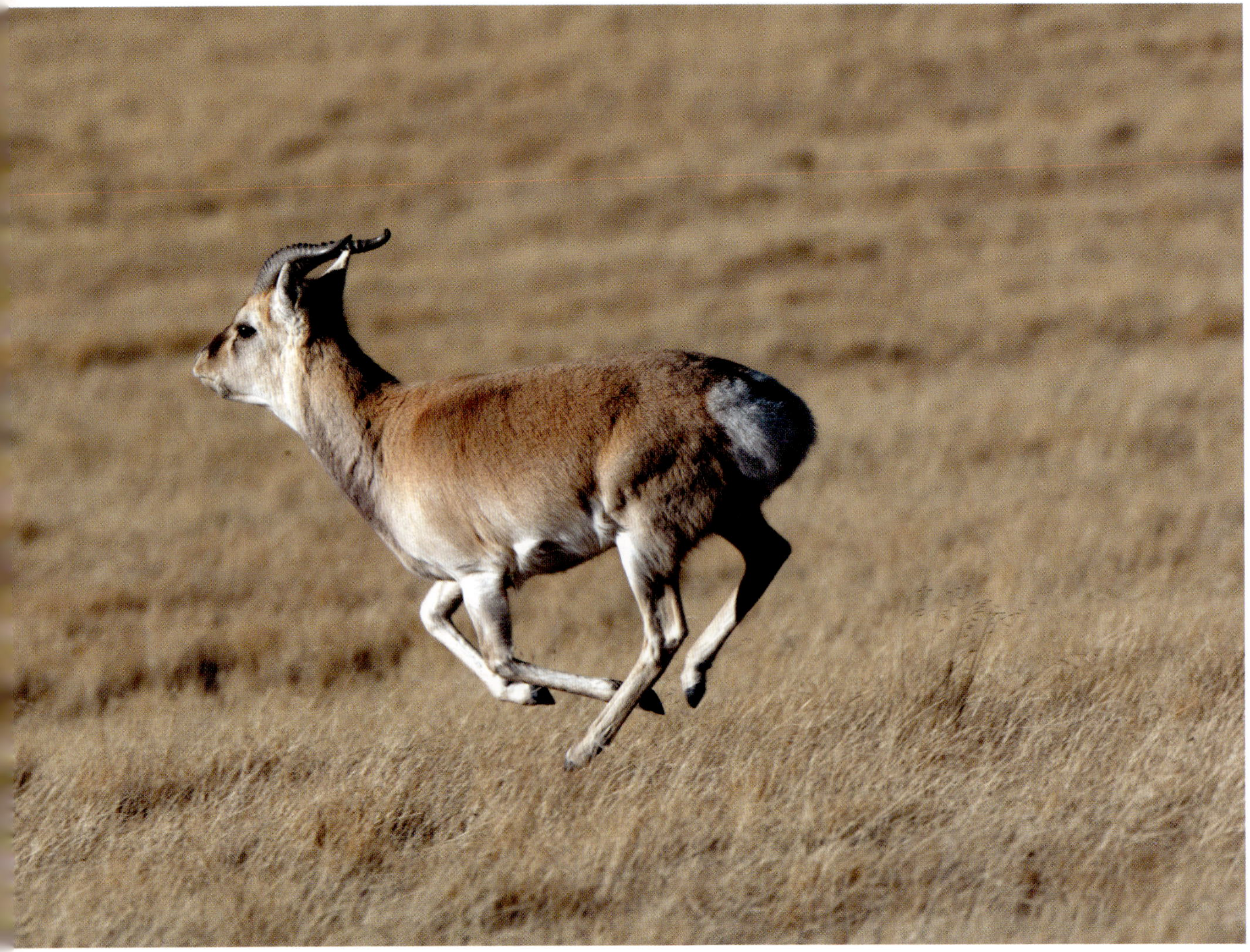

In the period between 1872 and 1873, Przewalski, a Russian museologist, took an investigative team and reached the Tibetan Plateau via the Inner Mongolia Plateau and the Alxa Plateau. This investigation team collected 130 pieces of animal fur and skulls of over 40 kinds of mammals. Among them, some small antelopes, the *Gazella cuvieri,* were later regarded as a sub-species of Tibetan gazelles. In 1949, Russian zoologist Stroganov confirmed it as an independent species after having studied samples collected by the Animal Research Institute of the Academy of Sciences of the former Soviet Union.

As animals unique to China, Przewalski's gazelles are seen in Qinghai province, the west of Inner Mongolia, the north of Gansu province, and Ningxia Autonomous Region in China. They live in quite flat semi-desert steppe of less than 3,400 meters above sea level. They never go to higher mountains, nor do they go to pure gobi desert. Sometimes, they migrate in groups according to different seasons. In winter, they migrate in groups to the south where there is rich vegetation, thinner accumulated snow, and abundant water source, and then come back in summer. They chiefly look for

When running, a Przewalski's gazelle looks like a shooting arrow, with its front and rear limbs close to each other, the rear limbs kicking forcefully backward, the body jumping up high, and propping up forcefully while falling down. Such leapfrog running gives its body an undulating and exceptionally beautiful curve above the ground.

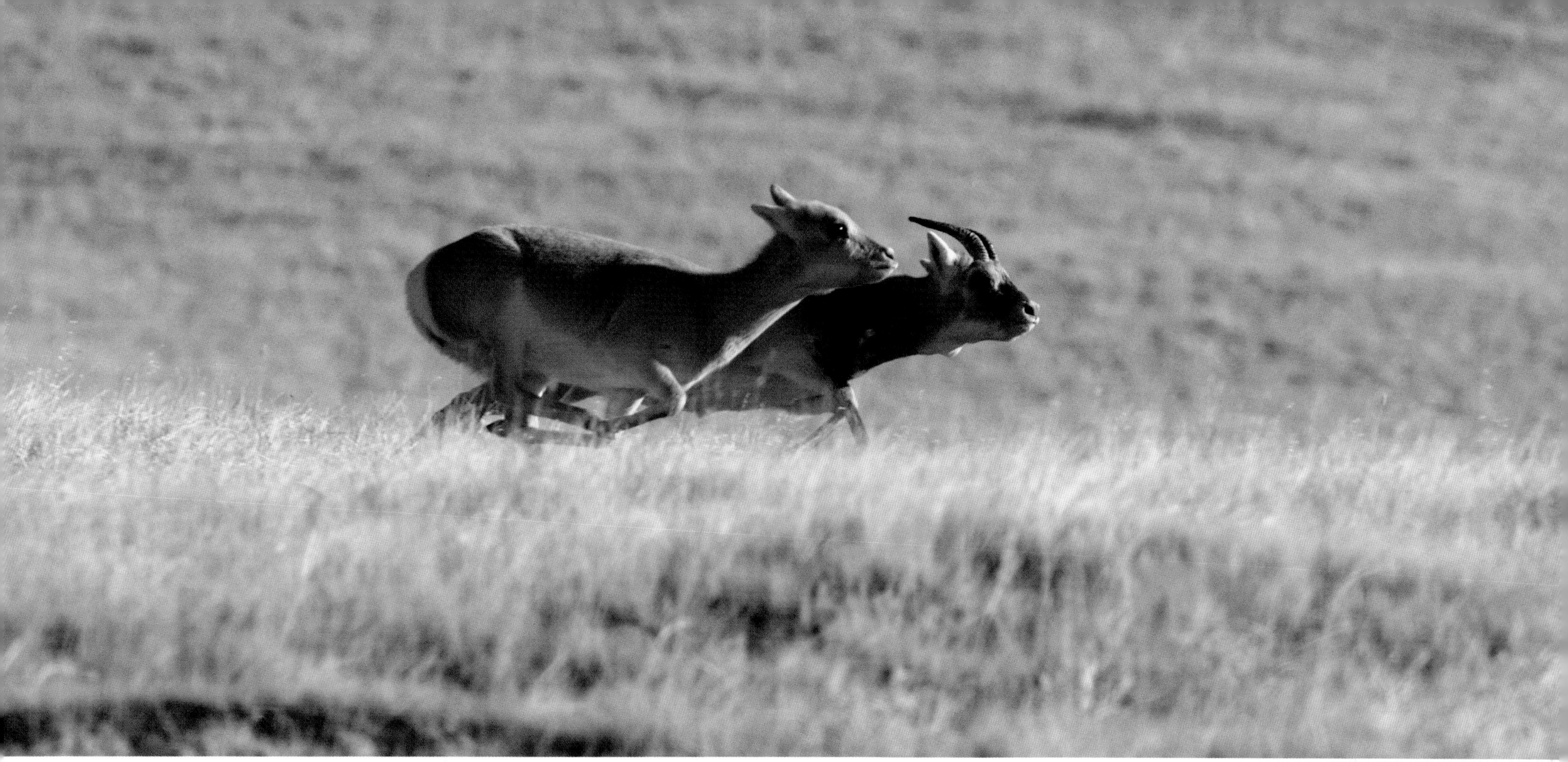

The chase for love is a competition of physical strength.

food on grassland, eating tender branches, stems, and leaves of the grass family, the sedge family, and other psammophyte vegetation. In winter, they eat dried grass and withered leaves, ruminate, and rest on sandy mounds.

Przewalski's gazelles are fond of living in groups and the number of each group ranges from 50 to 60. They are marked by rapid and agile movement. Despite their poor sense of smell, they have a well-developed sense of vision and hearing, as well as vigilance, enabling them to escape from the enemy. Also, they have a strong ability to endure thirst.

At the end of each November when there is northern wind blowing hard from the grassland and Qinghai Lake is frozen, Przewalski's gazelles enter the winter rut in which there are fairly big groups of propagation formed by female Przewalski's gazelles and male ones. Uttering loud screams, male Przewalski's gazelles occupy one mating spot after another on the grassland and move around them. Standing in the center of the mating spot, they frequently call female partners, but refuse to let other male ones get in. In this period, still just like other seasons, female Przewalski's gazelles move out of the sandy places to look for food on grassland. The mating spots of male Przewalski's gazelles are set up along the way where the females must traverse everyday. When female Przewalski's gazelles pass by the mating spots, male Przewalski's gazelles would take this opportunity to copulate with them. Female Przewalski's gazelles give birth to the offspring in July, usually a single one each time. Within a few minutes after its birth, it is able to stand up. After concealing itself for a few days in the grass, it is able to run together with its mother.

Along with frequent human activities, pastureland for Przewalski's gazelles is seriously degenerating and the area of desertification is gradually expanding. For years, the living space for them has been getting smaller and smaller along with the breakdown of their habitats, due to constant building of houses around Qinghai Lake and the expansion of cultivated land. At present, around Qinghai Lake, there are only 3 to 4 groups of Przewalski's gazelles, with a total number of less than 200 to 350. The small groups and separation between them have led to inbreeding and the reduction in the number of groups. Enclosures on the pastureland have further obstructed the activities of the remaining Przewalski's gazelles.

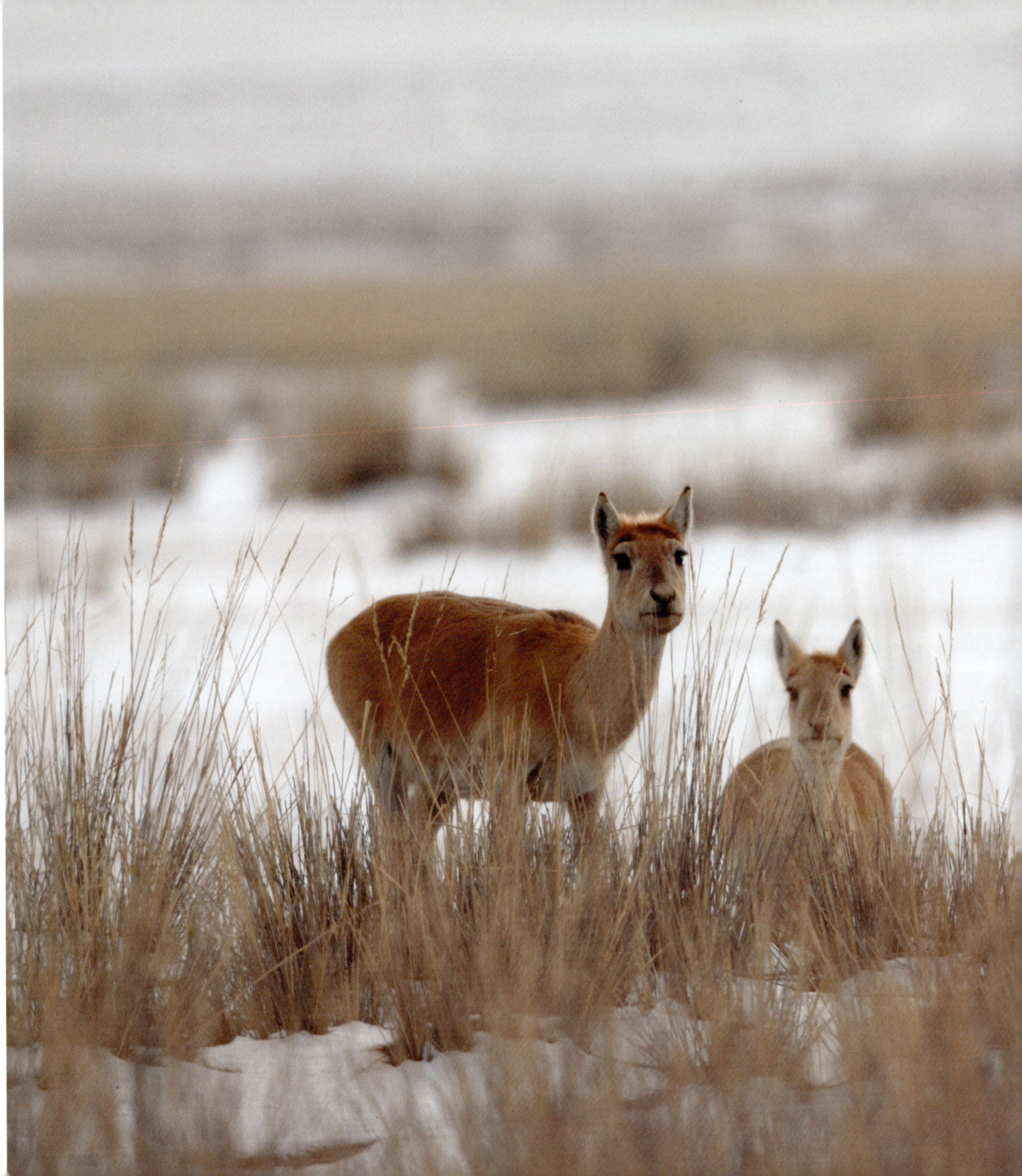

Przewalski's gazelles live in flat mountain basins and semi-deserts beside Qinghai Lake. Several Przewalski's gazelles or dozens of them form a group. They tend to form a bigger group in the winter.

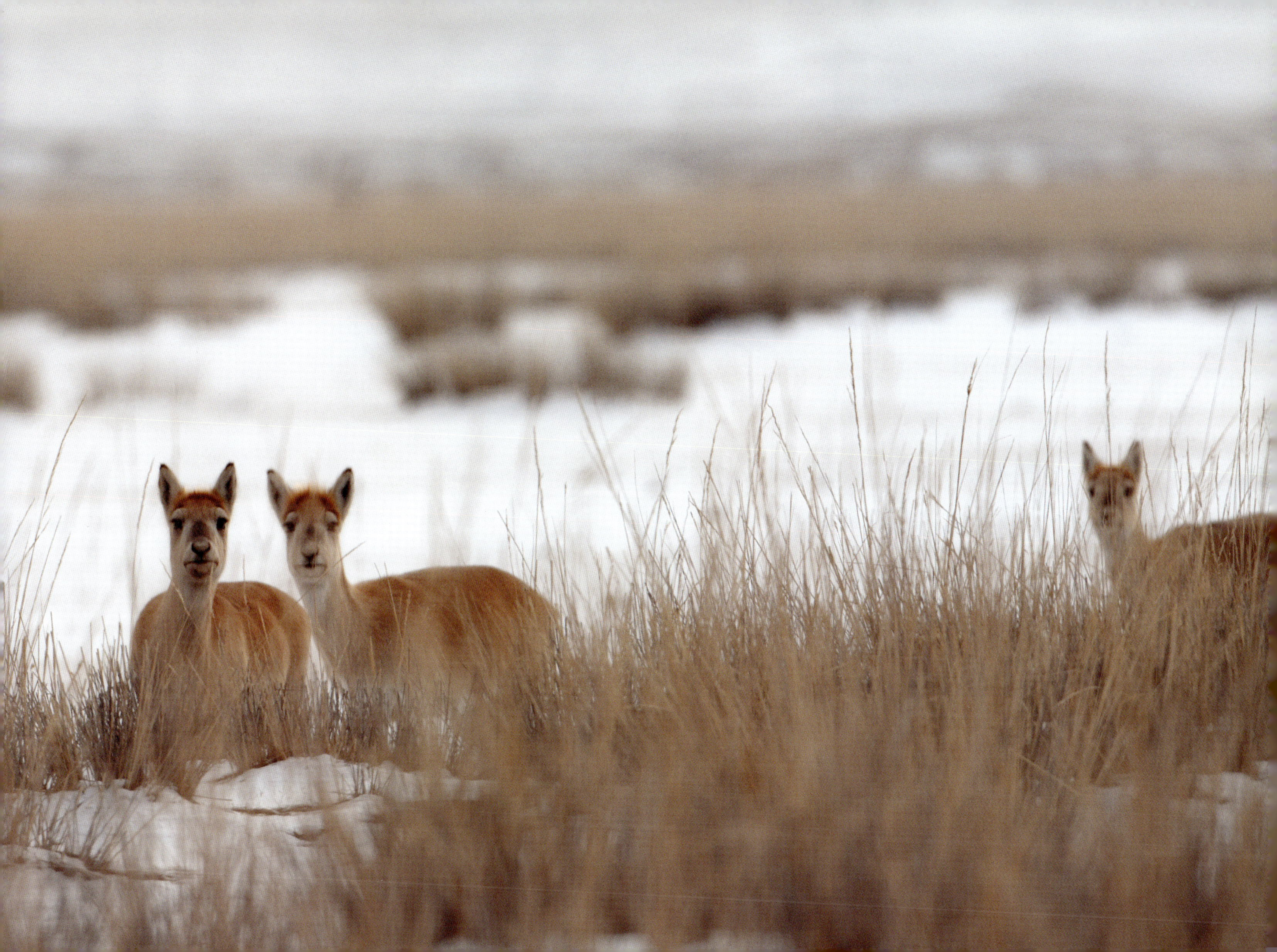

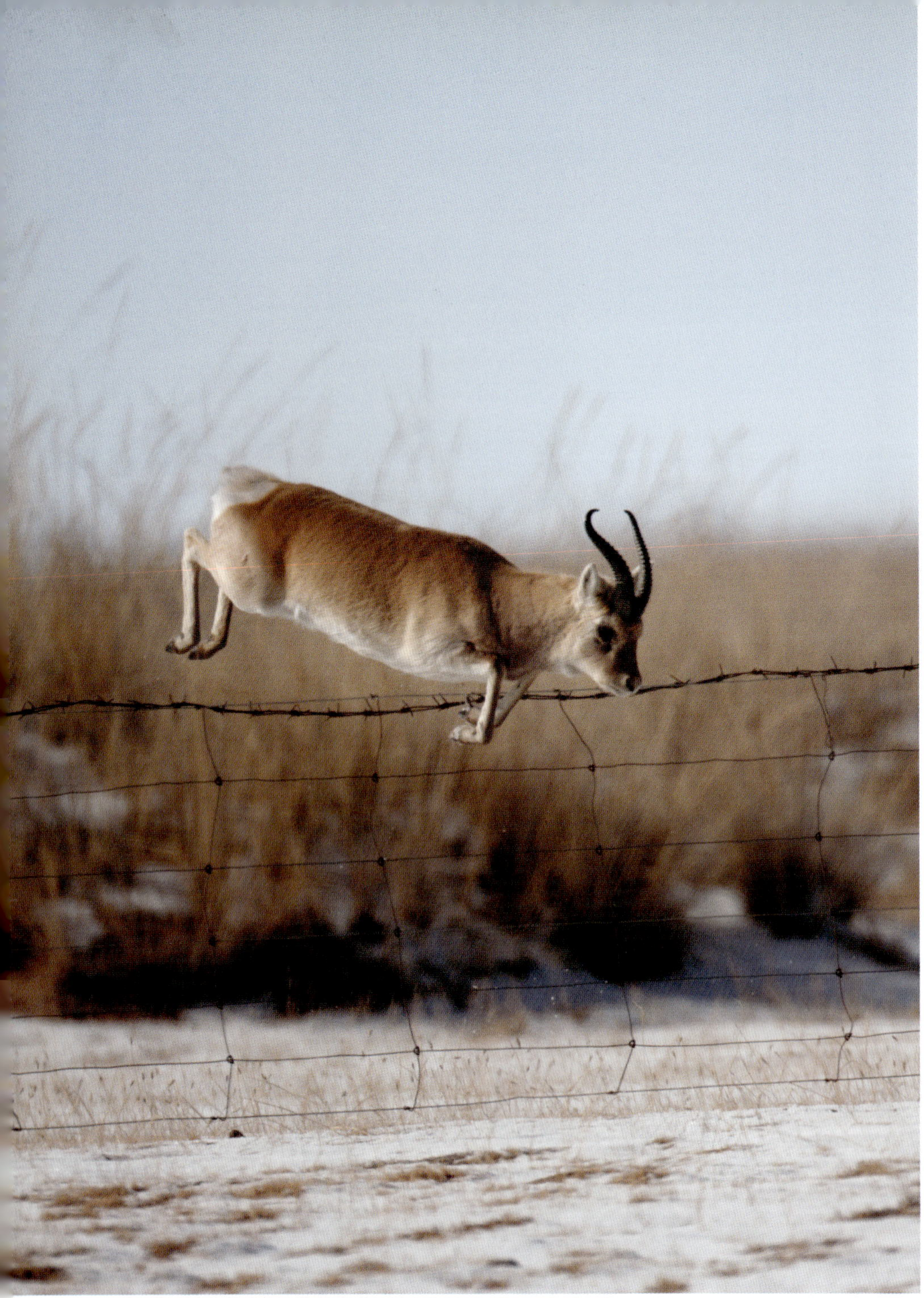

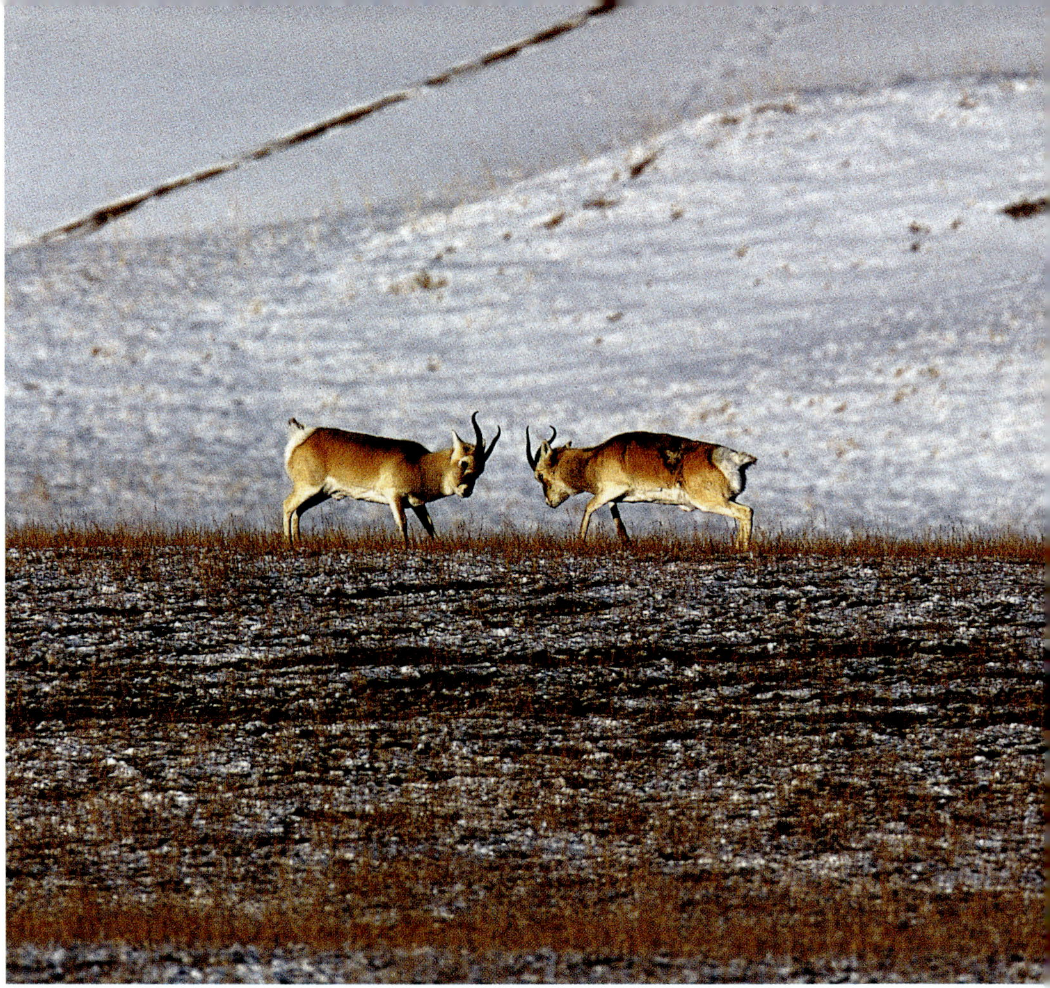

The foot of a sandy mound with the first snow is the "fight ground" for Przewalski's gazelles.

The habitat of Przewalski's gazelles has been carved up into pieces by the enclosures of herdsmen. In order to survive, this heartbreaking scene of a Przewalski's gazelle breaking through an enclosure is a daily occurrence.

Great Cormorant

Phalacrocorax carbo

IUCN Red List: Least Concern

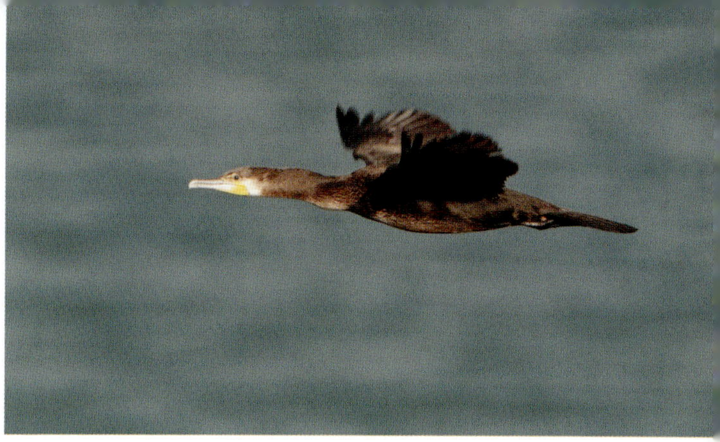

A great cormorant flying over Qinghai Lake.

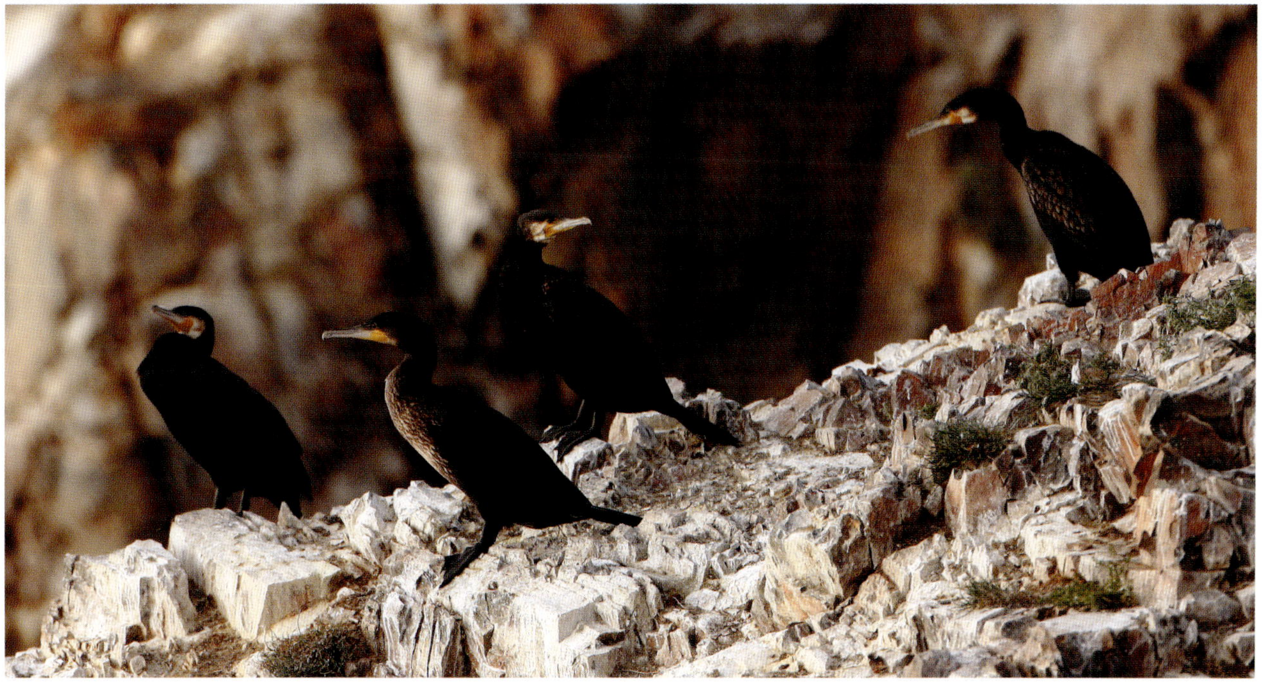

Bald stone-cliffs by Qinghai Lake are places where great cormorants like to build up their nests.

Qinghai Lake is frozen each December, with the freezing period lasting for six months. In the west of the lake, there is a 0.11-square-kilometer Bird Island on which there are over ten kinds of migratory birds, including bar-head geese, Pallas's gulls, and cormorants numbering as many as 100,000. Propagation of these birds relies heavily on naked carps, a fish unique to Qinghai Lake.

Cormorants are a kind of waterfowl that is divided into five species in China. Among them, great cormorants are the most commonly seen. They are distributed in numerous lakes and on marshland across China with fish as their food, since they are first-rate divers and extraordinary fishers. Usually, they live by the water, keeping a close eye on the fish under the water. Once finding prey, they would dash to the water surface with 100% success. They would dive 1 to 3 meters under the water to chase after fish groups in 30 to 45 seconds. Because of low visibility, they spot fish with their developed under water hearing.

The propagation period of great cormorants takes place between April and June. Usually, they are in pairs while building up the nest. The pair would be basically formed when they reach the place of propagation. In groups, their nests are built by the lakeside, riverside, or on trees of marshland. Sometimes, there are ten nests on a tree. Some of them also build up nests on rocky places by the lakeside or riverside, or on the islets in the center of the lake. Nests are built with withered tree-branches or water-weeds. They enjoy making use of old nests. Usually, they would repair old nests and build up new ones not long after they reach the place for propagation. They lay 3 to 5 eggs in each nest, with the female and the male hatching them in turn. The hatching period is about 28 to 30 days. Nestling great cormorants are naked without any feather when they are born. About two weeks after they are born, there will be feathers all over their bodies. They are able to fly and leave the nest after the feeding of 60 days or so.

Naked Carp

Gymnocypris przewalskii
IUCN Red List: Not Evaluated

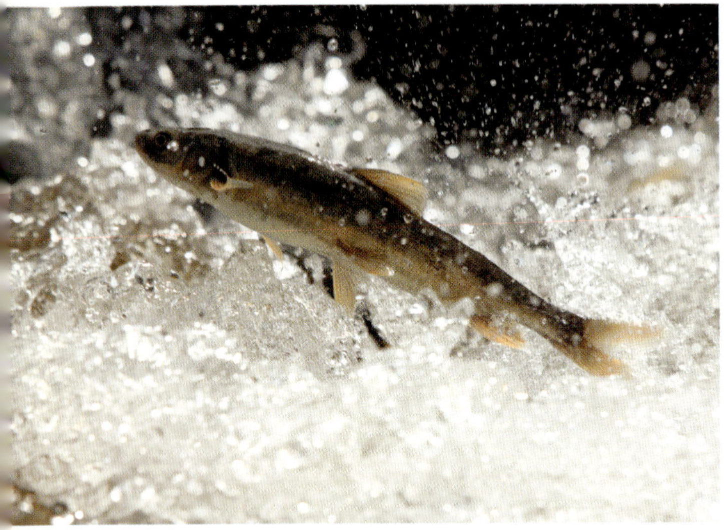

Despite a swift current, naked carps shouldering the mission of propagation leap forward one after another to head to the traditional place for laying their eggs.

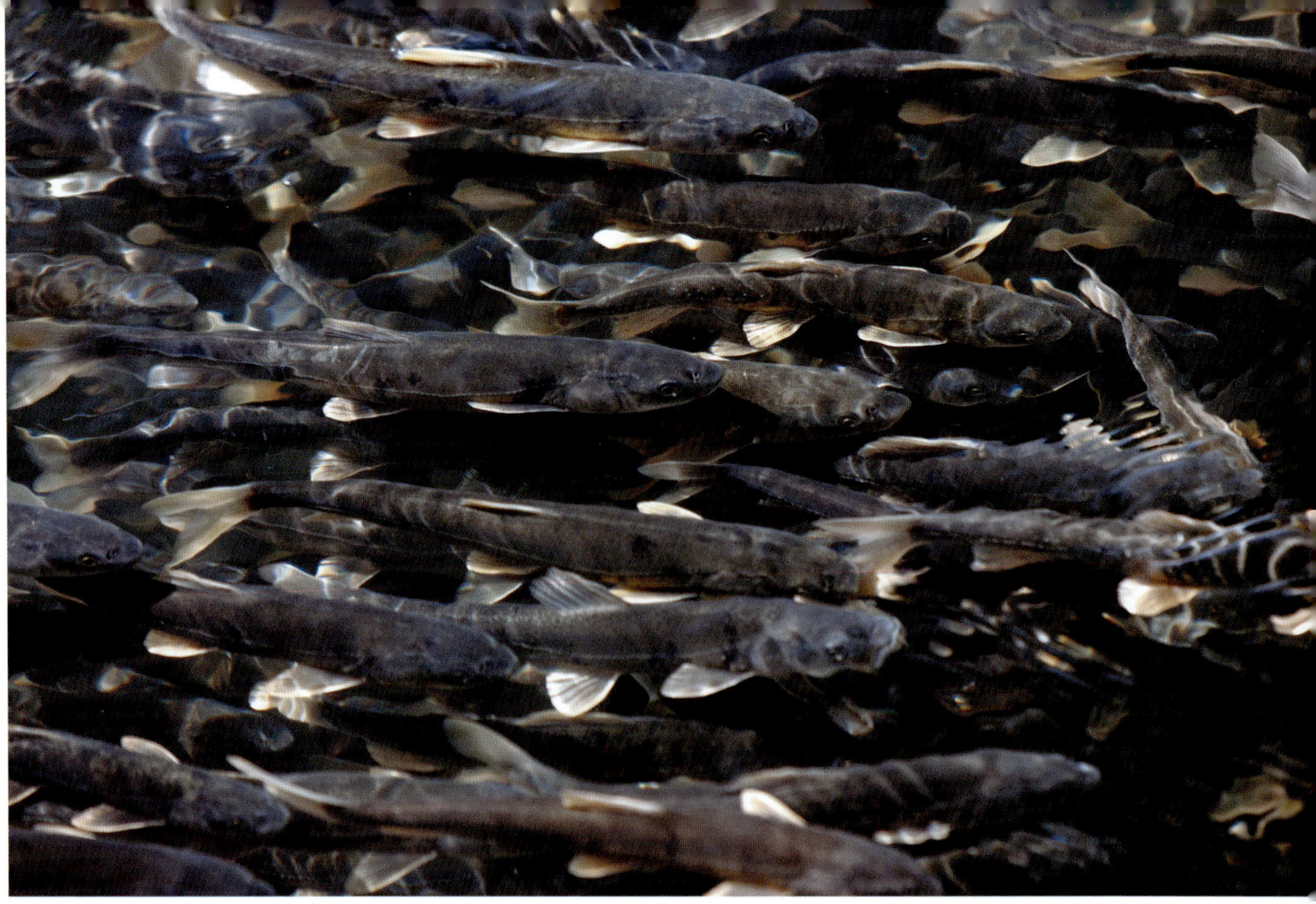

In late June, along with the rising temperature, accumulated snow on the mountains around Qinghai Lake begins to thaw, increasing water flow into the lake. Sexually mature naked carps aged 3 to 4 in Qinghai Lake also start their migration. Lots of naked carps get together, swimming upstream to look for a suitable place to complete their eternal mission—propagation.

Naked carps are special fish in cold saline fresh water that evolved due to the long-term geographic separation of Qinghai Lake. Distributed in Qinghai Lake and rivers around the lake, they appear long and slightly flat, with a cone-shaped head, a round and blunt kiss, as well as fine and narrow upper and lower lips. They grow quite slowly due to a special environment of their existence. It takes each naked carp 7 to 8 years to weigh 0.25 kg, and 11 to 12 years to weigh 0.5 kg.

As the major fish in Qinghai Lake and rivers attached, naked carps account for over 95% of all kinds of fish in the lake. Lots of birds seeking for habitats and propagation in Qinghai Lake take naked carps as their main food. Therefore, naked carps occupy a core position in the entire ecosystem of Qinghai Lake.

Since the 1960s, hundreds and thousands of *mu* (15 *mu* is equal to 1 hectare) of land around Qinghai Lake has been reclaimed into farmland. People have built dams on 108 rivers flowing into Qinghai Lake. Many rivers have dried up, leading to the obstruction of passages for propagation. Consequently, naked carps cannot lay eggs in the fresh water, resulting in the death of lots of naked carps at the river-mouth. Meanwhile, owing to excessive fishing and the killing of eggs in groups, the number of naked carps in Qinghai Lake has dropped sharply by over 80%, making it very difficult to restore the normal situation. In 1982, the local government started to seal off the lake and ban fishing, artificial propagation, and release of fish-fry, as well as build up fish passages across dams. As a result, the number of naked carps in Qinghai Lake has been increasing gradually in recent years.

Chapter Four
Other Areas

Mountain Weasel

(Shiqu, Sichuan Province)

Mustela altaica

IUCN Red List: Near Threatened

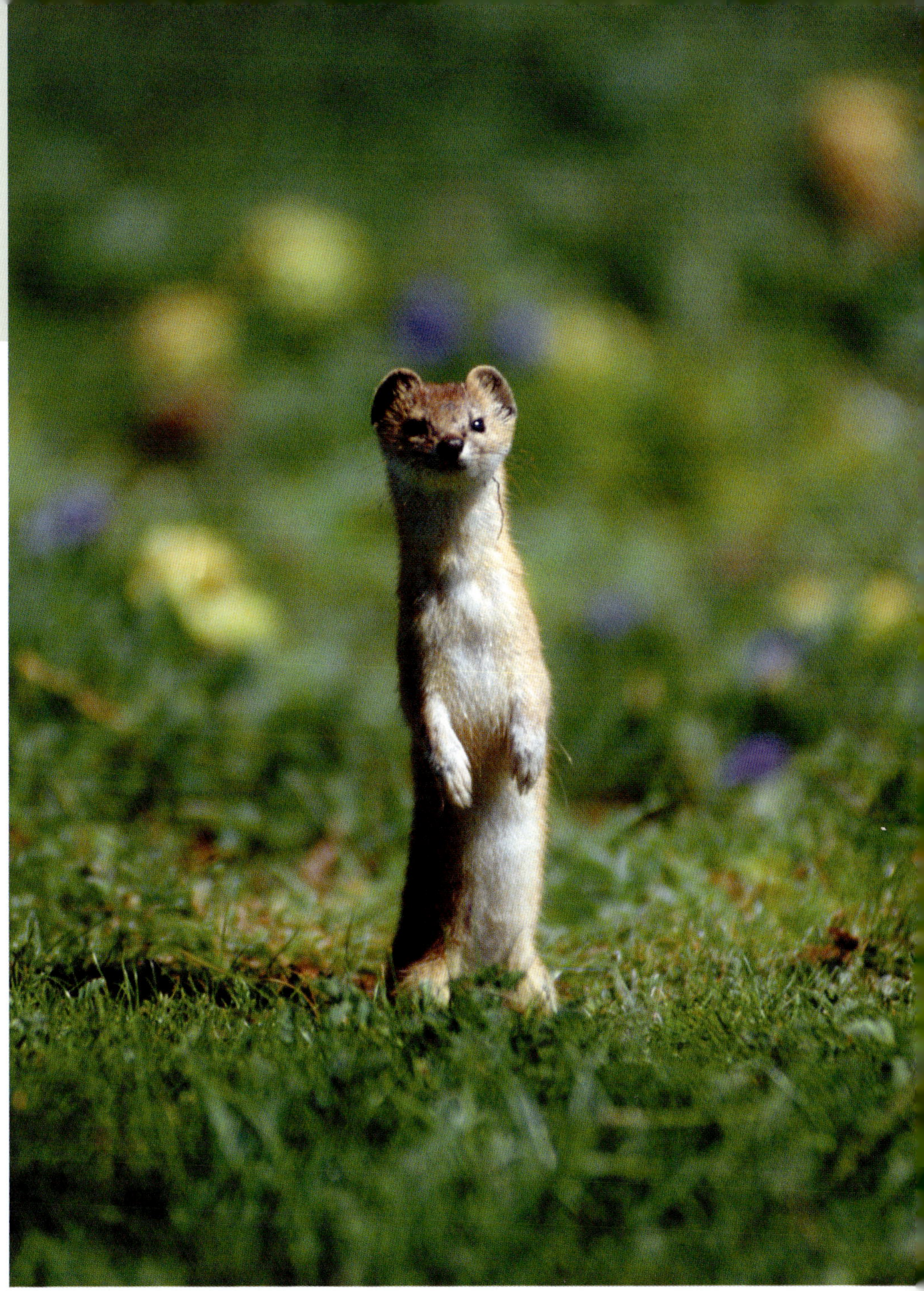

Among weasels distributed in China, mountain weasels are one of the two smallest kinds. As carnivores in a strict sense, they usually hunt at night. Plateau pikas and some small rodents are among their major food.

They are not afraid of human beings who approach them for observation within a distance of two meters. However, due to such human activities on the alpine meadow from excessive grazing, they find it more and more difficult to find food and shelter. Some herdsmen would poison pikas as "harmful animals," which also poisons the mountain weasels. Also, more and more highways and vehicles on the plateau also pose a threat to them.

Usually living on alpine meadows and rocky slopes at over 3,500 meters above sea level, they are often seen shuttling across scattered stones, cracks in ridges between fields, and various holes to chase after pikas. This mountain weasel stands up as if posing for the photographer.

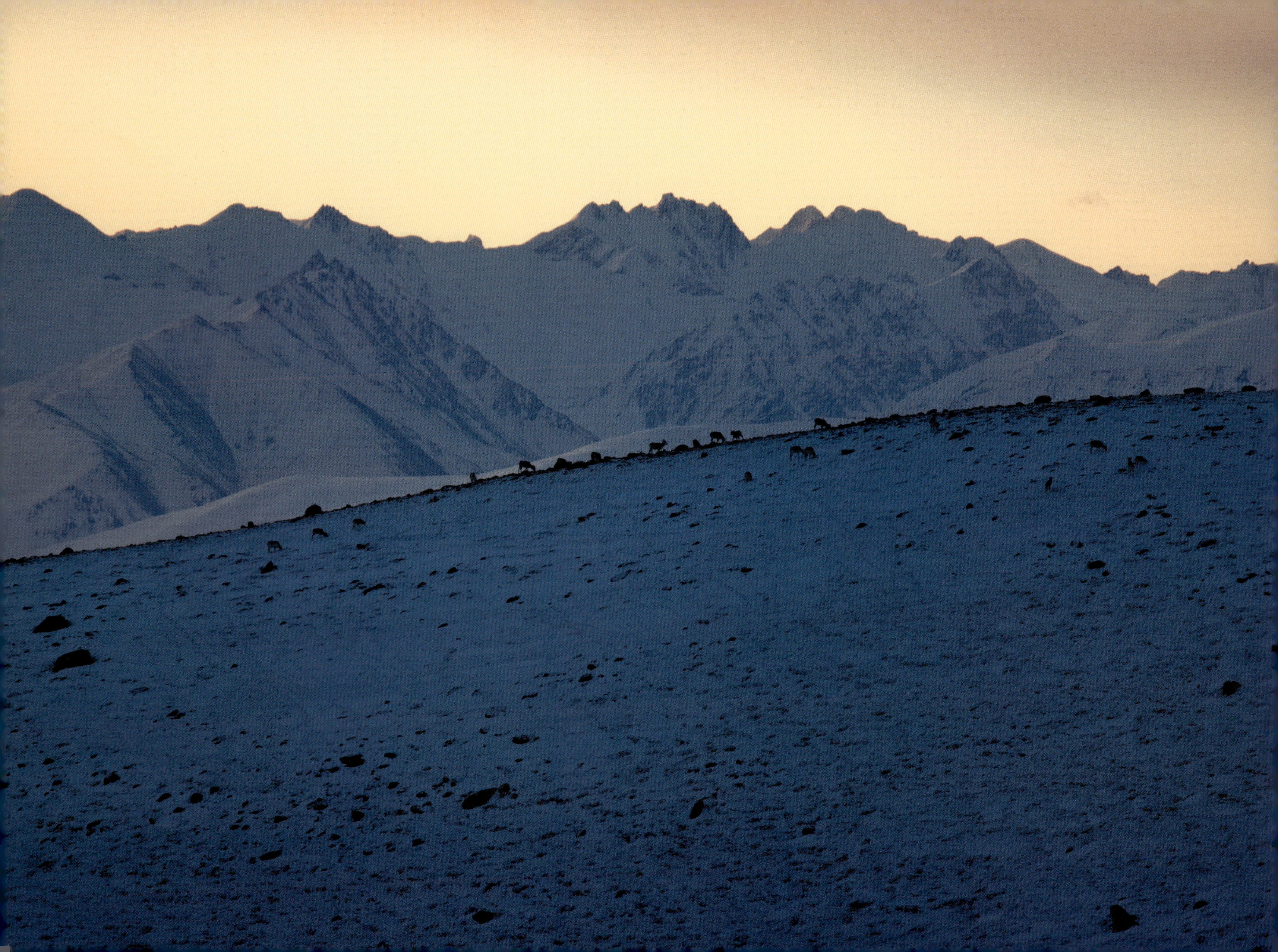

Part Two
Xinjiang-Inner Mongolia

The arid area in northwestern China is also called the plateau area of Xinjiang-Inner Mongolia. As part of a vast steppe as well a desert area of Eurasia, it accounts for 30% of the total territory of China, including Inner Mongolia, Xinjiang, Ningxia, the northwest of Gansu province, and the north of Shanxi and Shaanxi provinces. This area consists of a series of low-lying basins mostly of 500 to 1,000 meters above sea level. It is arid in its west and semi-arid in its east since the region is encircled by mountains far away from the sea, with little influence of tropical monsoon in the summer.

The deserts of China are located in this area. Covering an area of 327,000 square kilometers, Taklamakan Desert (i.e. a place of absolute death), the biggest and the harshest desert in China, lies in the bottom of Tarim Basin in the vicinity of the northern part of the Tibetan Plateau. Tianshan Mountains and Altai Mountains are two mountain ranges in the Xinjiang-Inner Mongolia region, with their peak ridges completely covered by glaciers. These two mountains have separated boundless deserts and stream water from mountains moistens narrow and very important fertile areas along the marginal places.

This area is divided into two parts, i.e. steppe and desert. The steppe zone only covers 1/4 of the total arid Xinjiang-Inner Mongolia area. With expansive and flat terrain, most of the steppe is 1,000 to 1,500 meters above sea level. Due to the increasing distance from the sea and gradual reduction of annual rainfall, natural vegetation has changed from desert to desert steppes. Owing to the influence of monsoon, the annual rainfall also changes greatly, resulting in imbalanced annual yield of grass and obviously affecting the stability of food for animals. Desert zone covers 3/4 of the total arid Xinjiang-Inner Mongolia area. Situated in the center of Eurasia, very far away from the sea and encircled by a series of high mountains and plateaus, this zone is marked by severe drought, vast deserts, and gobi desert full of pebbles with a most spectacular scene. Desert vegetation of this zone is chiefly composed of small shrub and sub-shrubs.

As compared with Eastern China, animal groups in Xinjiang-Inner Mongolia are featured by simple structure since almost all of them are species adaptable to drought. Large and medium ungulates enjoy an extensive range of activities, with a small number in the unit area and a fairly big corresponding area of protection. The forest-based environment, oasis, and wetland are attractive to some migratory birds from non-arid areas. Relatively speaking, there is a rich variety of animal species. In the past, commonly seen species include kulan, Mongolian gazelle, argali, goitered gazelle, chukar, and sandgrouse.

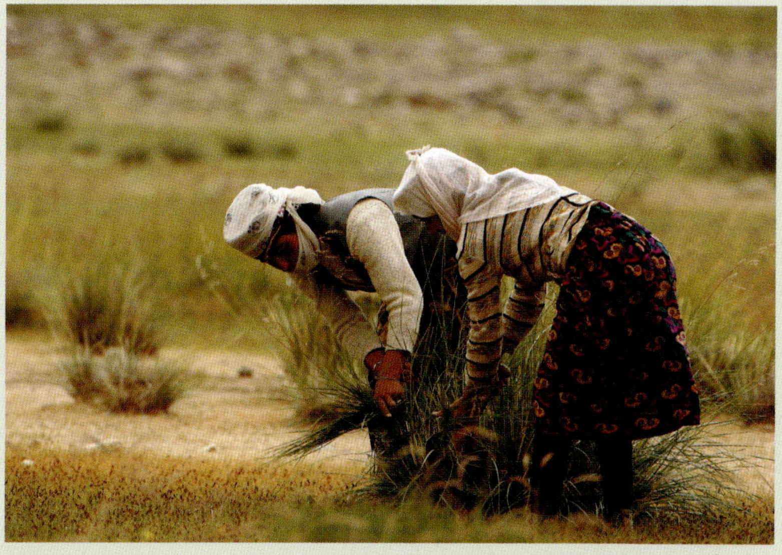

On facing page
When it is noon in Beijing, the Pamirs Plateau in the extreme west is just ushering in the dawn.

Tajik people on Pamirs Plateau are mainly engaged in husbandry in addition to farming, leading a semi-settled and semi-nomadic life.

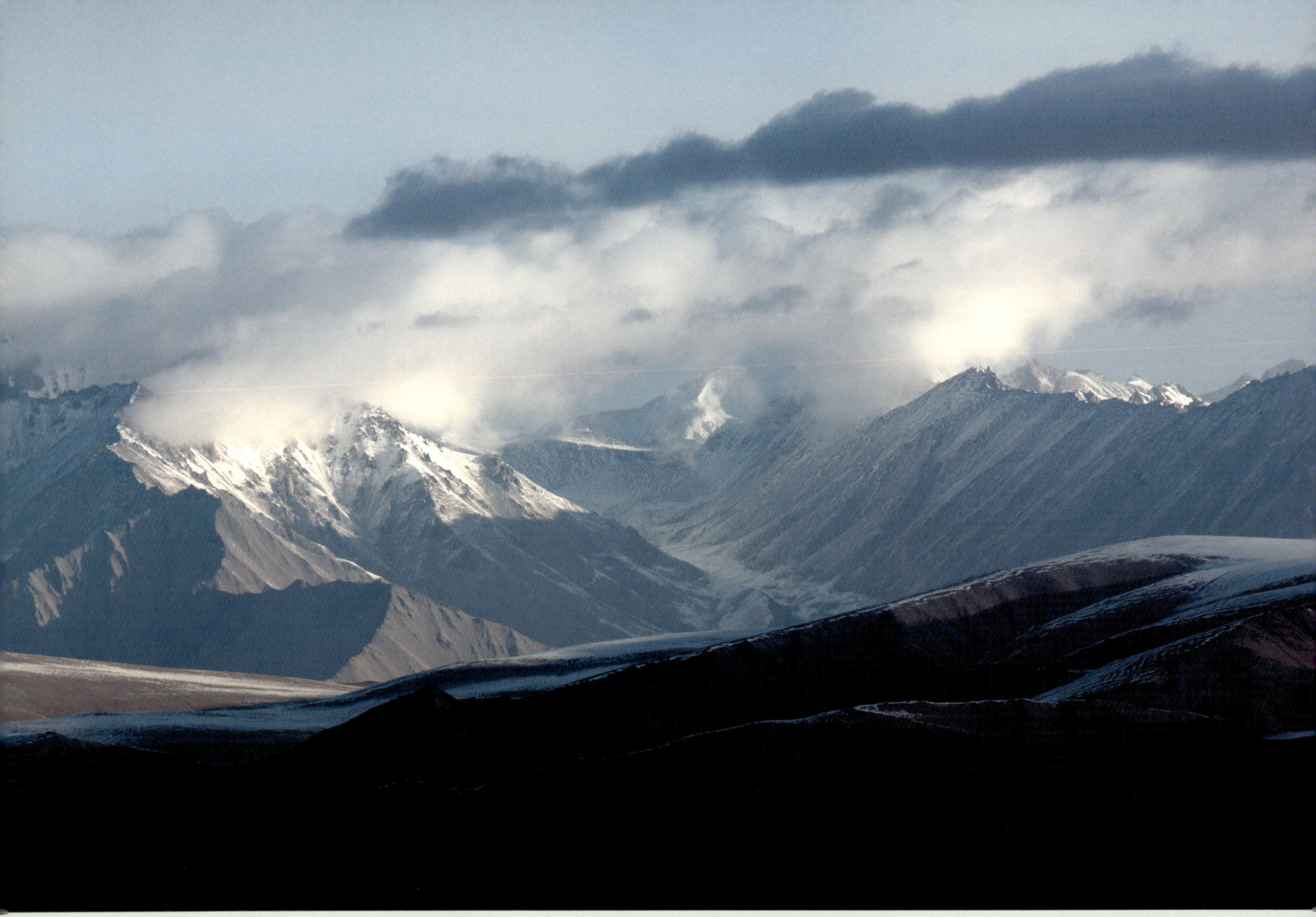

Chapter Five
Pamirs Plateau—The Marco Polo Sheep's Paradise

Asia is marked by a high terrain in the middle and low-lying areas around. In the center, there is a huge mountain-confluence convergence of several huge mountain ranges, i.e. the Himalayan Mountains, Karakoram Mountains, Kunlun Mountains, Tianshan Mountains, and Hindu Kush Mountains. There is a plateau with towering snow peaks, i.e. Pamirs, which is called "the roof of the world" together with the Tibetan Plateau.

Pamirs had been the crucial gateway on the Silk Road, first opened by the Emperor Wu of the Han Dynasty. Within the boundary of China, Kongur Tagh, 7,719 meters above sea level, is the highest peak of Pamirs. The Pamirs Plateau is marked by highland climate. As a forceful center regarding the function of modern glaciers, the Pamirs Plateau has over 1,000 glaciers, with obvious vertical changes of natural sceneries and various ecological environments. Therefore, the Pamirs Plateau is also called the source of all mountains and the home inhabited by numerous animals. Among all kinds of animals, huge horns of Marco Polo sheep and their fierce fight are also the most vivid impression left by the Pamirs Plateau on me. Marco Polo sheep are the biggest subspecies of argali. Over 700 years ago, according to a legend, Marco Polo recorded them in the Pamirs Plateau during his visit to the Orient. Apart from Marco Polo sheep, there are also many kinds of birds, such as horned larks, snowfinches, ground jay, sandgrouses, and snowcocks. However, some rare bird species are on the verge of extinction.

In recent years, as people have started to emphatically improve the eco-environment, the environment of the Pamirs Plateau and areas nearby is improving gradually. Public awareness and protection of birds is on the rise. The number of migratory birds in the winter and the number of non-migratory birds in Xinjiang are increasing. The presence of these beautiful spirits has brought vitality to the expansive plateau and vast deserts.

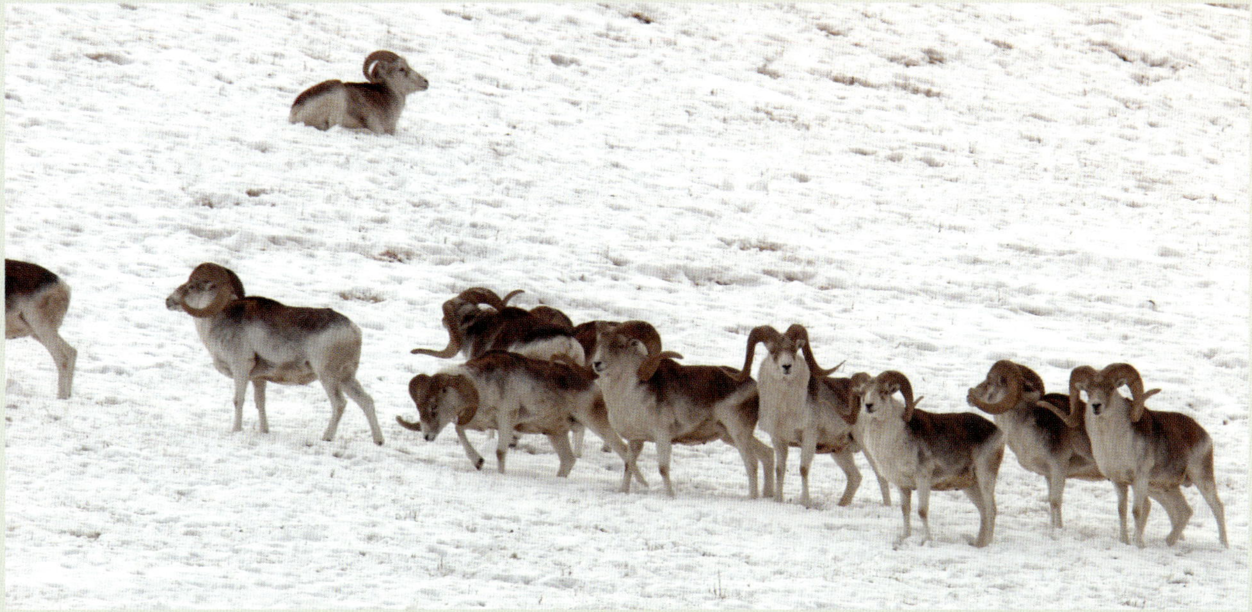

On facing page
The spectacular peaks of the Pamirs Plateau present themselves indistinctively amidst clouds and mist.

A group of male Marco Polo sheep gather on the snow ground, ready for a fight at any moment.

Marco Polo Sheep

Ovis ammon polii

IUCN Red List: Near Threatened

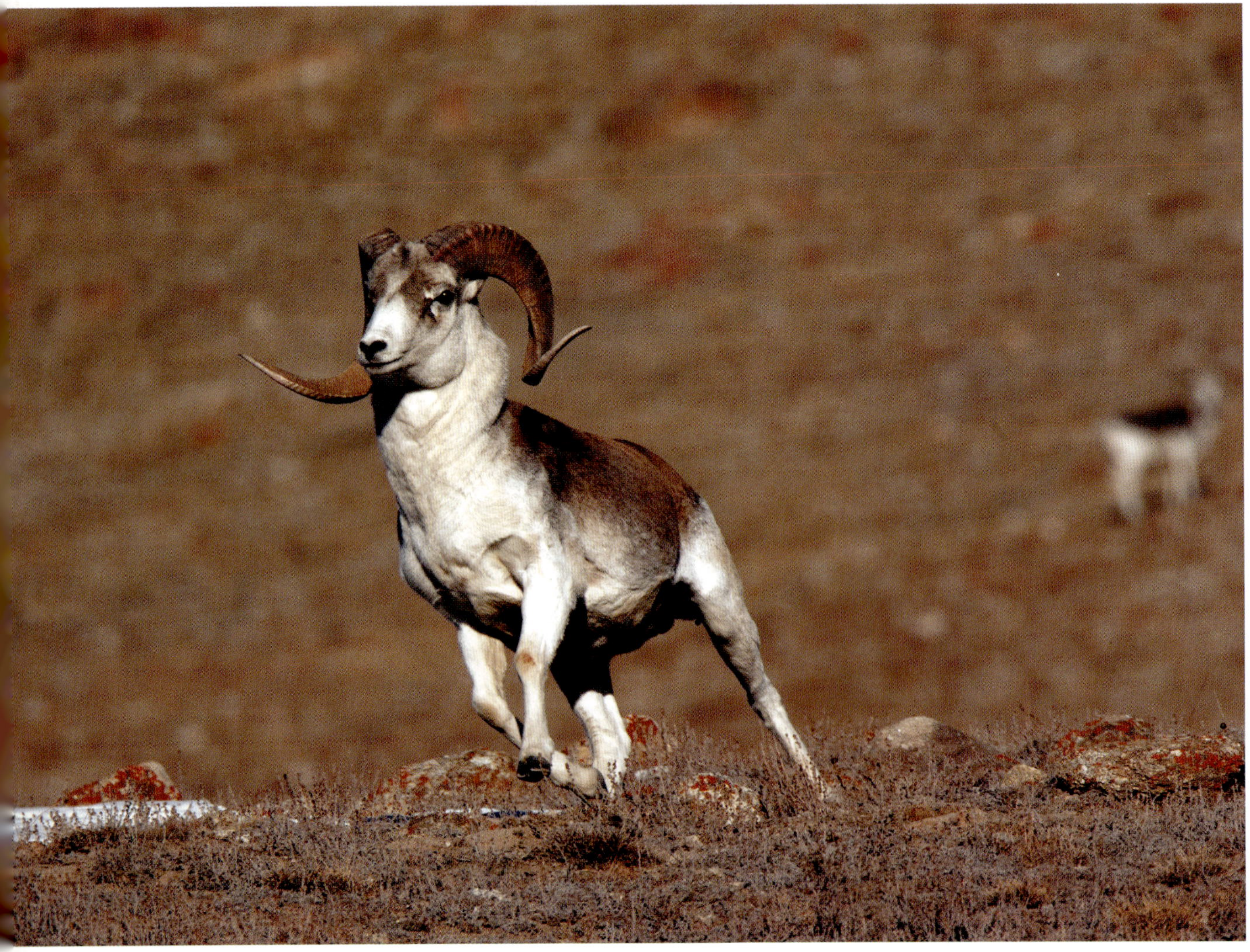

Tashkurgan Nature Reserve of the Pamirs Plateau is typically featured by plateau desert and its west is covered with glaciers of over 5,000 meters above sea level. Typical arid steppe vegetation is seen in the area of 3,700 to 4,700 meters above sea level. There are mainly short bushes and needlegrass of the grass family, except for a few moist places grown with sedges and plants of other grass families in the form of meadow. This is roughly the environment for the existence of Marco Polo sheep.

The legend about these beautiful animals can be traced back to the late 13th century. At that time, Italian traveler Marco Polo, on his way to China via the expansive central Asian grassland, recorded many novel things. While passing the Pamirs Plateau, he saw a kind of huge goat with a pair of big and robust horns.

In 1838, a British museologist got a pair of argali horns in an area bordering China and Afghanistan. Later the sample was sent to the British Museum and it is still there. In 1840, British museologists finally took that sample for a type of species and named it *Ovis ammon*. In memory of Marco Polo and the beautiful big-horn goats described by

As the most beautiful of all the argalis, the Marco Polo sheep gets its name from the Italian traveler.

On facing page, pages 84 – 85
On the slope with sparse vegetation on the Pamirs Plateau in the summer, a large group of male Marco Polo sheep runs up, with the elders bearing the brunt and the younger ones bringing up the rear.

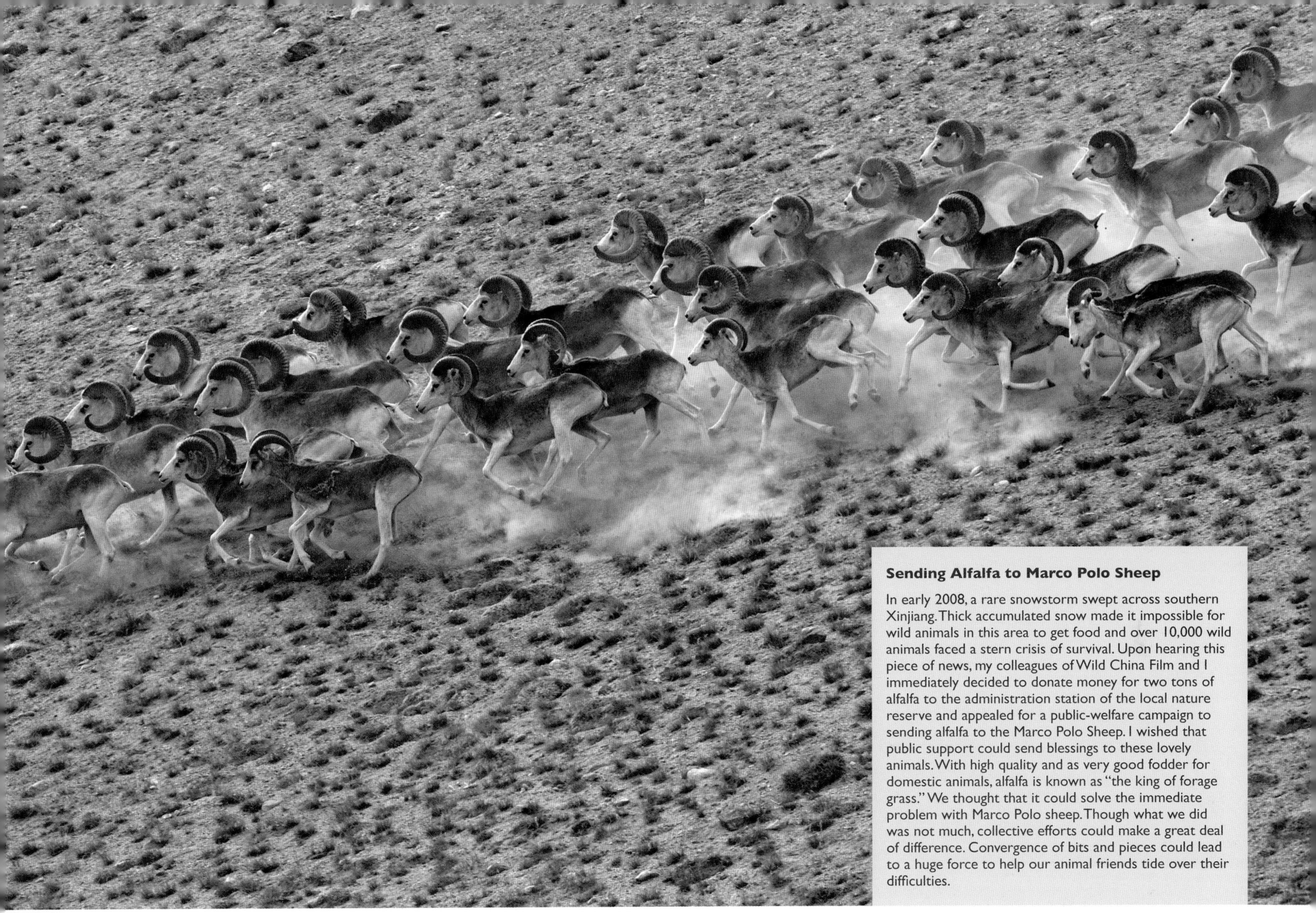

Sending Alfalfa to Marco Polo Sheep

In early 2008, a rare snowstorm swept across southern Xinjiang. Thick accumulated snow made it impossible for wild animals in this area to get food and over 10,000 wild animals faced a stern crisis of survival. Upon hearing this piece of news, my colleagues of Wild China Film and I immediately decided to donate money for two tons of alfalfa to the administration station of the local nature reserve and appealed for a public-welfare campaign to sending alfalfa to the Marco Polo Sheep. I wished that public support could send blessings to these lovely animals. With high quality and as very good fodder for domestic animals, alfalfa is known as "the king of forage grass." We thought that it could solve the immediate problem with Marco Polo sheep. Though what we did was not much, collective efforts could make a great deal of difference. Convergence of bits and pieces could lead to a huge force to help our animal friends tide over their difficulties.

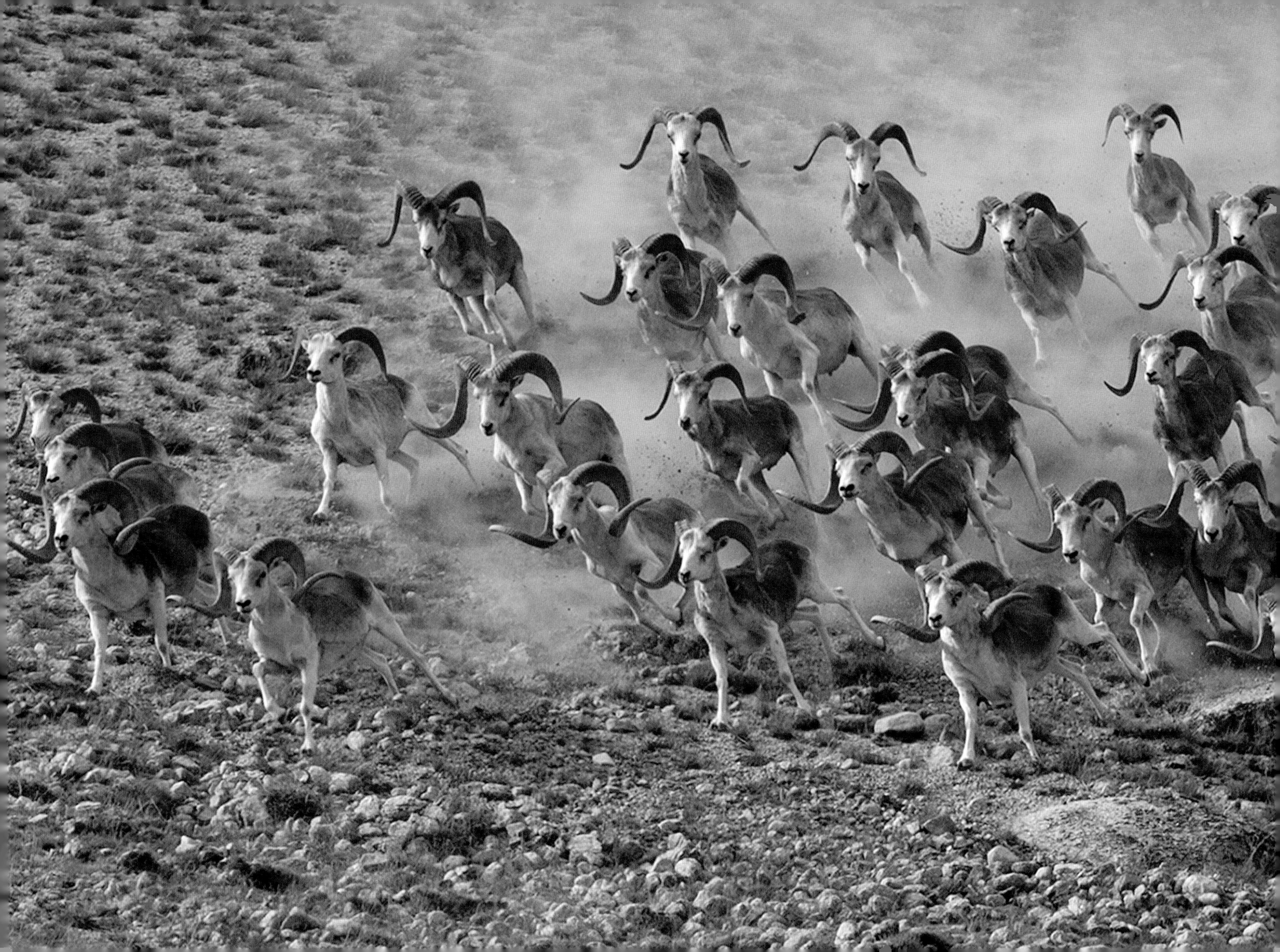

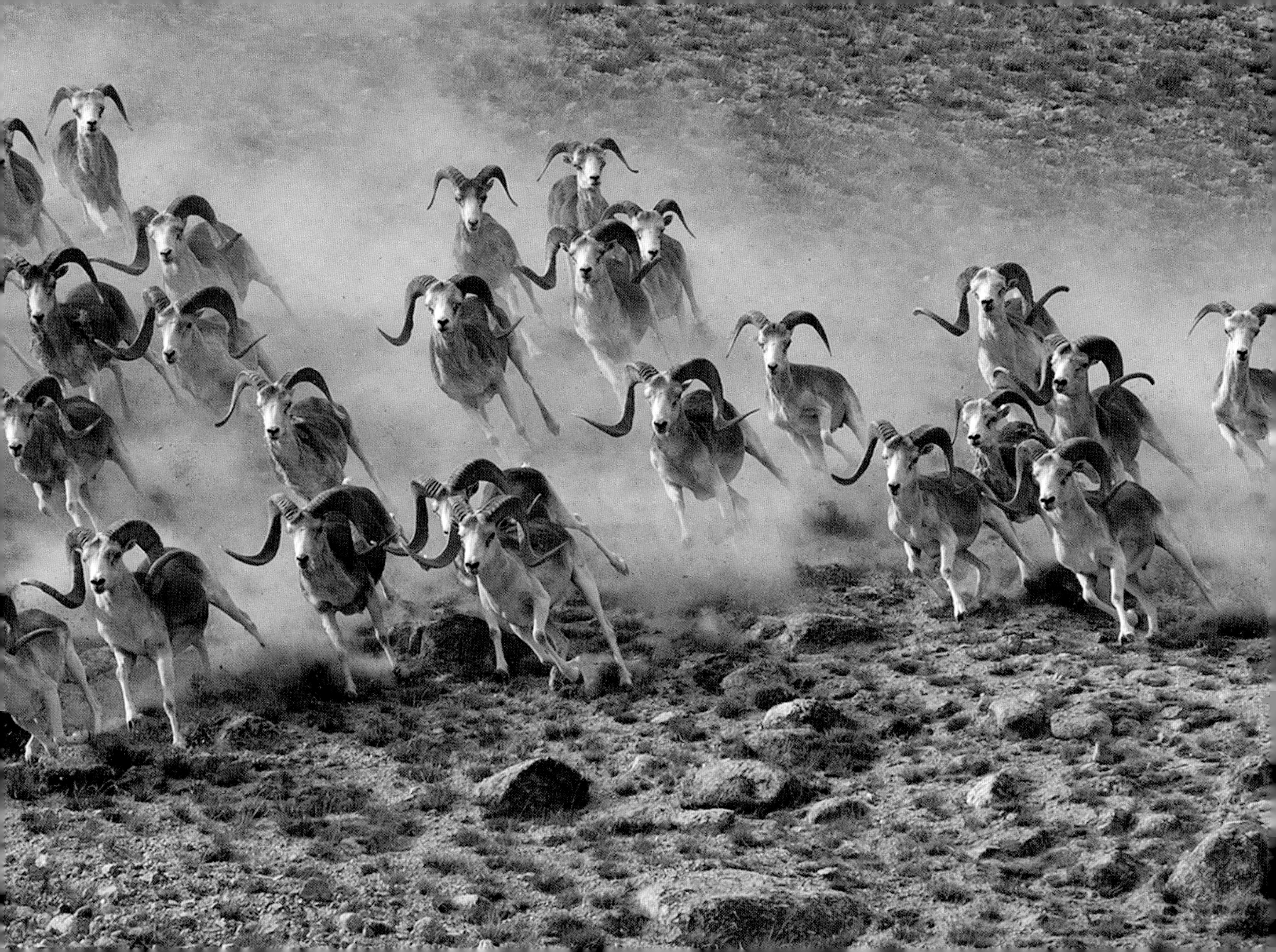

Beautiful Big Horns of Marco Polo Sheep

In October 2005, an investigation into Marco Polo sheep was jointly launched by Xinjiang Wildlife Conservation Association and Wildlife Conservation Society (WCS), in order to get to know the status quo of the existence of Marco Polo sheep in the Pamirs Plateau, Xinjiang. I was lucky to be the photographer for this investigation team. The Pamirs Plateau is very different from the plateau I was familiar with in the past, i.e. snow-peaks extend to the high sky; the sun is still there at eight p.m.; gifts given by elegant and warm-hearted Tajiks to us upon our first meeting; the lake-blue eyes of Tajik young girls. All these made me feel the splendid spectacle of our motherland amidst the atmosphere of surreal novelty.

On November 12, I rushed to the camp of 4,300 meters above sea level to wait for the fight among Marco Polo sheep. The further I walked toward Dabudaer, the more the mist was over the mountains alongside. The snowfall stopped, the mist dispersed gradually, and the sunshine presented itself. Looking out into the distance, I found the gulley at which the camp was located was still mist-shrouded. When we approached the gulley-mouth after a two-hour trudge, a group of female Marco Polo sheep with lambs was in the way. As we slowly got closer to them, they began to band together, moving toward the slope. It was not until we walked on a par with them that they started to run up to the slope and then stopped at a short distance from us. Some began to eat grass and some gazed at us vigilantly. Looking up with binoculars, we saw that on the slope at the back of our camp, there was a group of ewes standing up there, putting on a show of force while looking at us. On the snow-slope opposite to a house, seven to eight rams were crouching there for a rest.

After a few minutes, a patch of mist was floating over the valley, blocking our sight from the snow slope and sheep opposite to us. With the mist dispersed, we discovered a flock of rams squeezing together and the horns of some of them were rubbing with one another gently. With careful counting several times, we found that there were as many as over 140!

All of a sudden, this flock of rams began to be agitated. A young one, with its fore-leg raised, ran almost in a vertical posture against another one. We saw two big and zigzag horns bump against each other, with the sound of the bump heard only afterwards. Soon, another young ram ran out, suddenly and quickly chased after the one beside him. The one being chased, instead of showing any weakness, also began to run wildly on the snow-ground. This was an exciting scene! After chasing for two rounds, the one at the upper side suddenly turned its head, galloping and then bumping downward heavily. I kept taking pictures of this wonderful sight until these two opponents finally disappeared from my sight.

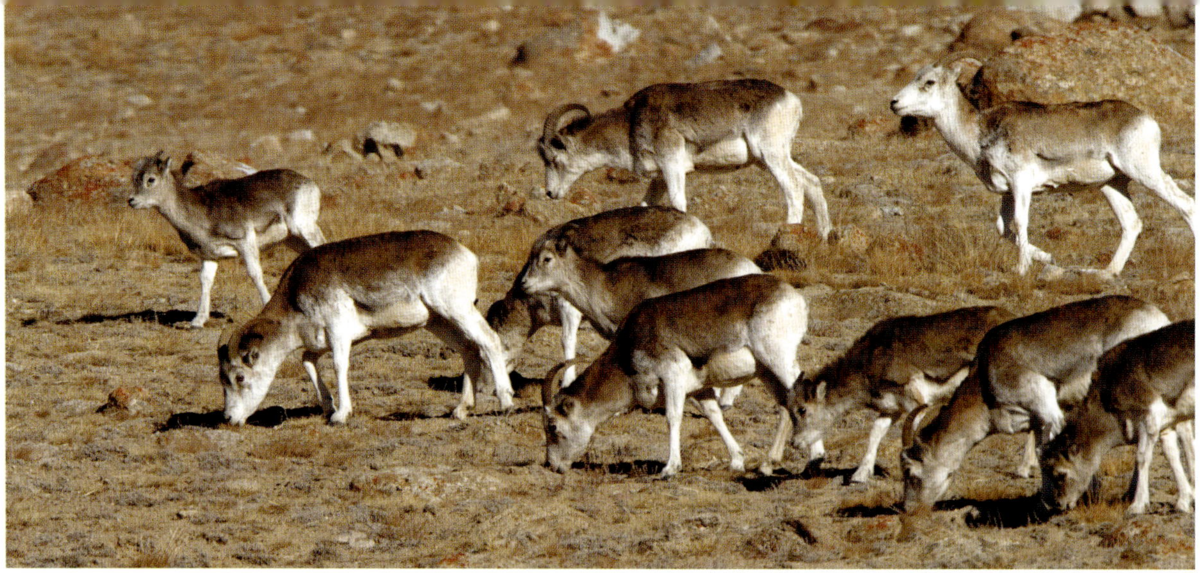

A group of Marco Polo sheep consisting of females and lambs are oblivious to having their pictures taken by photographers.

On facing page
A group of Marco Polo sheep have left behind a zigzag route on the thick accumulated snow of the Pamirs Plateau.

him, zoologists termed a sub-species of *Ovis ammon* as "Marco Polo sheep" (*O. a. polii*).

Marco Polo sheep, as the biggest sub-species of argali, are regarded as the biggest wild sheep in the world. Its size can be compared to a donkey since its shoulder height is 1.2 meters and its weight is 250 kilograms. The big and zigzag horns of the ram can be as long as 1.9 meters. They do not have a particular area for activities. Instead, they shuttle across different valleys, looking for tranquil places with ample grass. For most of the time during the year, rams and ewes are in a state of separation and they respectively form flocks of different sizes and move around in different areas. This is a typical behavioral mode of sex separation. It is not until the mating season in winter that rams would gather around ewes, attempting to set up spouse groups of their own and gain mating rights. Local people jokingly call this period of time a season of marriage among sheep.

Rams need to fight for their position to enable them to have spouses. The horns are their major weapons, plus their thick and robust necks and forceful running. All rams look for their own opportunities. They demonstrate their force before their opponents or start provocation with such actions as chasing, head raising, and side pushing. The fiercest fight would be violent bumps with their horns. Each bump would shock the valley. From November to December, the valley is full of bustling Male Marco Polo sheep.

Marco Polo sheep are world-famous thanks to their robust bodies as well as huge and beautiful horns. In the period from the mid-19th century to the first half of the 20th century, Marco Polo sheep were one of the most wanted collections of animal samples, sharply reducing the number of them.

As estimated, there are about 1,000 Marco Polo sheep in China. With regard to the sub-species of argali, the number of Marco Polo sheep is slightly more than *Ovis ammon jubata* and *Ovis ammon ammon*. However, illegal hunting and the spread of diseases are reducing the number of Marco Polo sheep.

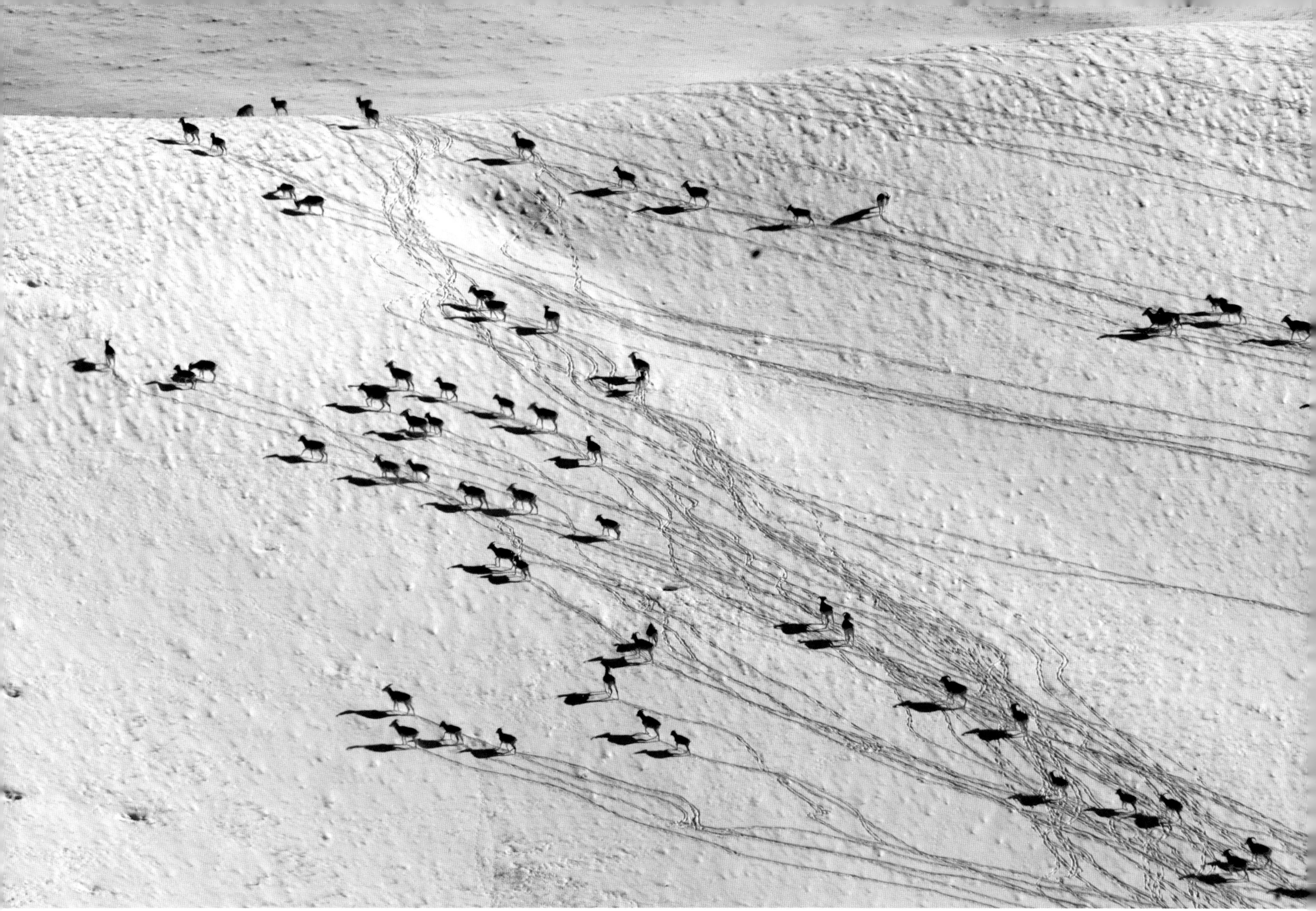

Blue Sheep

Pseudois nayaur

IUCN Red List: Least Concern

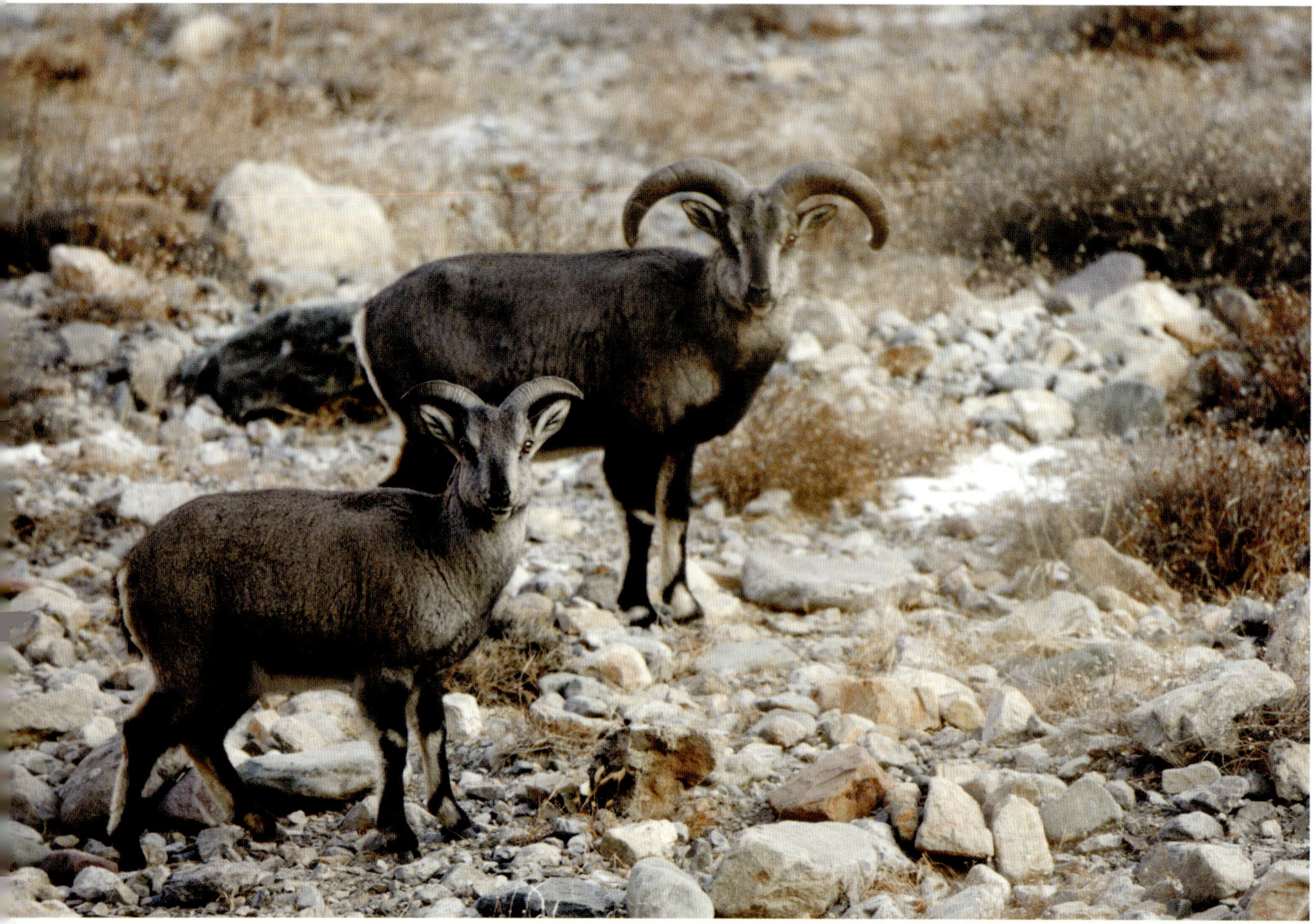

Horns of the blue sheep extend upward first, spread on either side, and then bend backward slightly half way. The surface on the horns is quite smooth with sharp ends, the base of the horns has some coarse and unclear horizontal edges, and the transaction is either round or triangle.

As a species endemic to the Tibetan Plateau, blue sheep are of a medium size. A male weighs 50 to 70 kg. It has a narrow and long head, short and small ears. The body is marked by greenish grey while its mouth and face are mixed with grayish white and black. The male horn is about 60 centimeters long and the longest is 84.4 centimeters. Though not as unique as the horns of the argali and Siberian ibex, their horns look great due to their especially robust shape. Blue sheep are distributed in Tibet, Xinjiang, Qinghai and Gansu provinces, and western Sichuan province, as well as Loess Plateau in the northeast. Generally, they live on the plateau meadow and alpine naked rocks of valleys. They do not go to forests, but mainly look for food on slopes. As ruminant herbivores, they chiefly eat club moss and lichens as well as bush branches and leaves.

Generally, they move around in groups. In areas of steep terrains with scattered food, they usually form into a small group of less than ten. On expansive meadow, they form into a big group of over 100 at most. They move around in the morning and afternoon, and crouch on the ground to rest or stand near rocks.

Though hunting has always been a threat to them, their biggest danger comes from competition with domestic animals grazed by human beings. They are apt to fall ill because they are not able to resist the diseases carried by these animals.

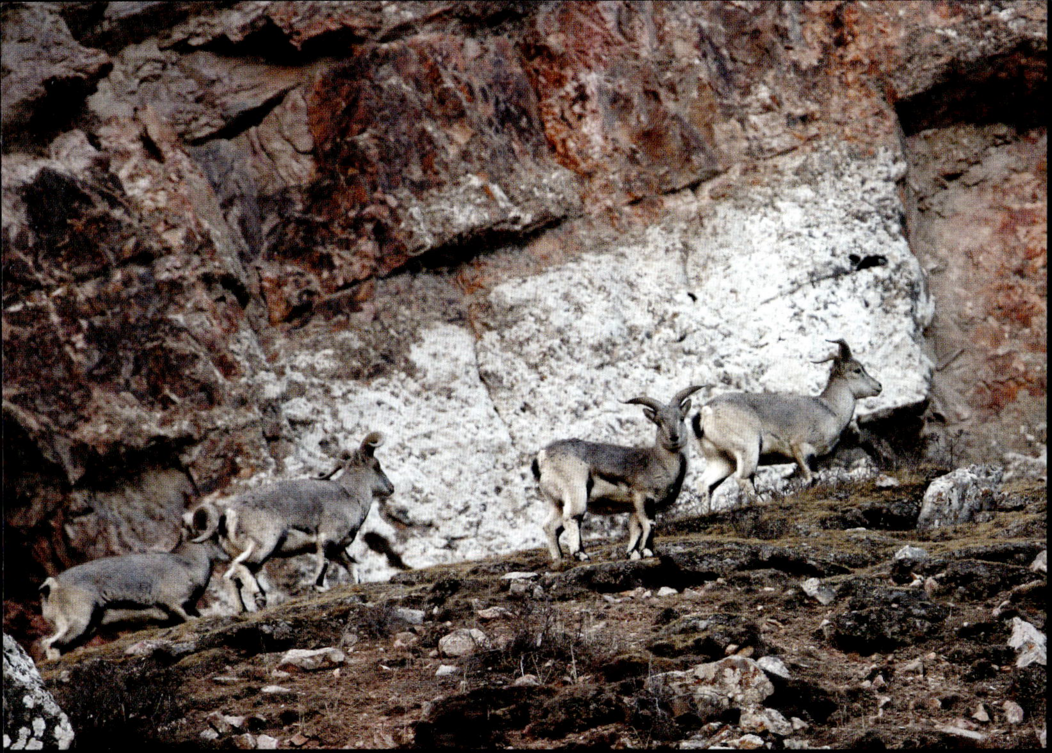

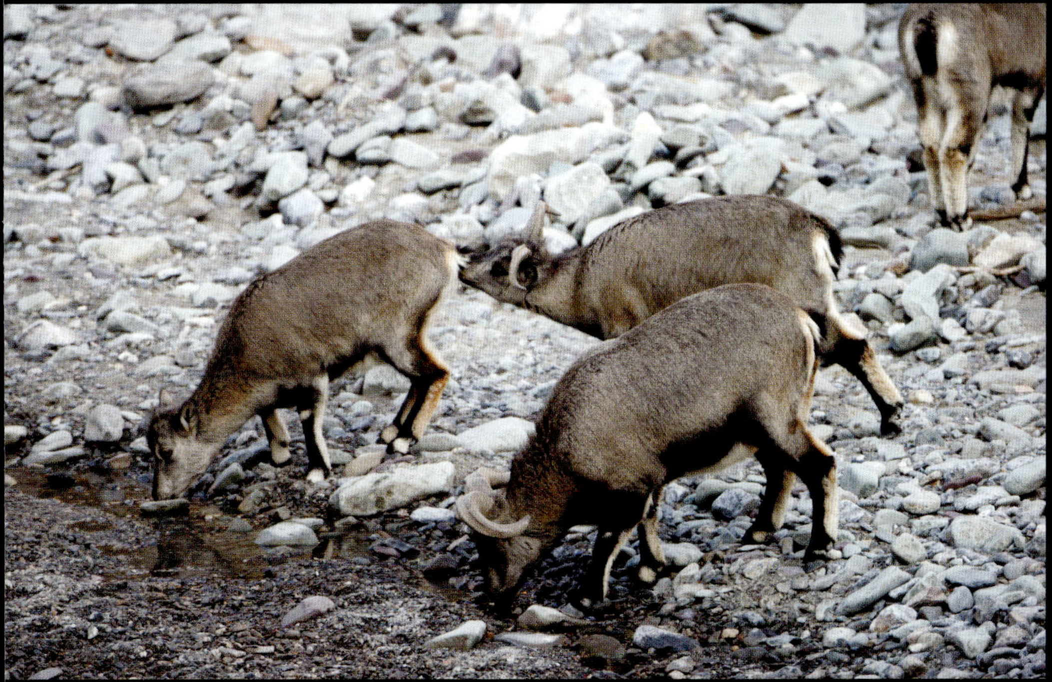

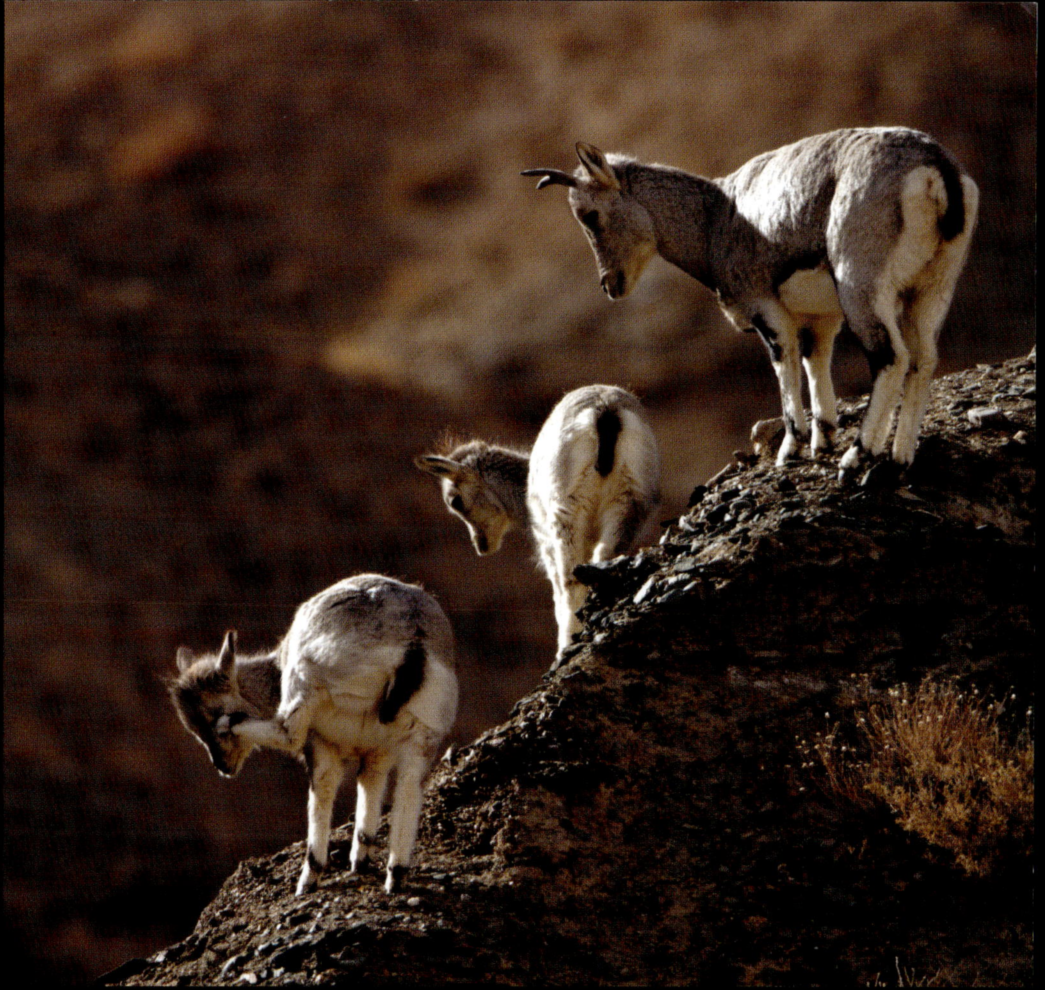

Above left
The blue sheep are very good at moving around on steep cliffs where they can climb as long as there is a ledge wide enough for them to stand on.

Below left
The blue sheep often drink water at fixed places and they have to lick ice and snow in the winter.

Above
As it is difficult to get food on the plateau in the winter, the female is taking the lambs to look for food at higher places.

Siberian Ibex

Capra Sibirica

IUCN Red List: Least Concern

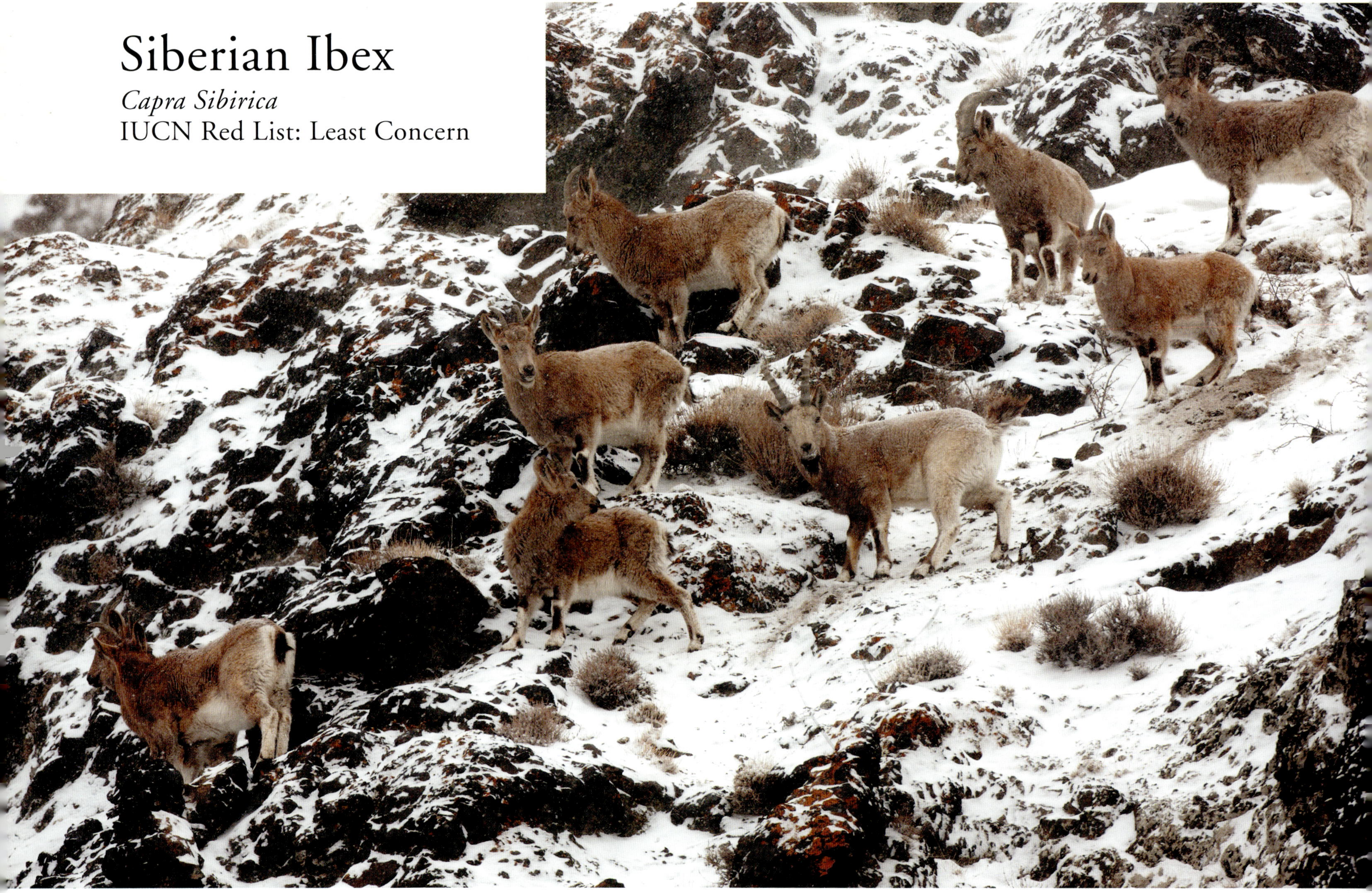

On facing page
Amidst wind and snow, a small group of Siberian ibexes are seen on the half slope. Very good at climbing and jumping, they have very strong hoofs, elastic heel joints, toes as firm as pliers, and legs with robust muscles, enabling them to climb steep and slippery slopes that are almost vertical.

Because of their great vigilance, the photographer only has a little time to take pictures of them. They flee upon hearing the slightest of sound. As a result, the photographer only took a picture of its black short tail and a pair of long horns. Both male and female Siberian ibexes have horns, but male ones have especially long horns, as long as over 140 cm, bending backward in an arc shape. Though not in a rotating way, the bending angle of their horns can be half or 2/3 of a circle, just like two bent knives inserted upside down into the head.

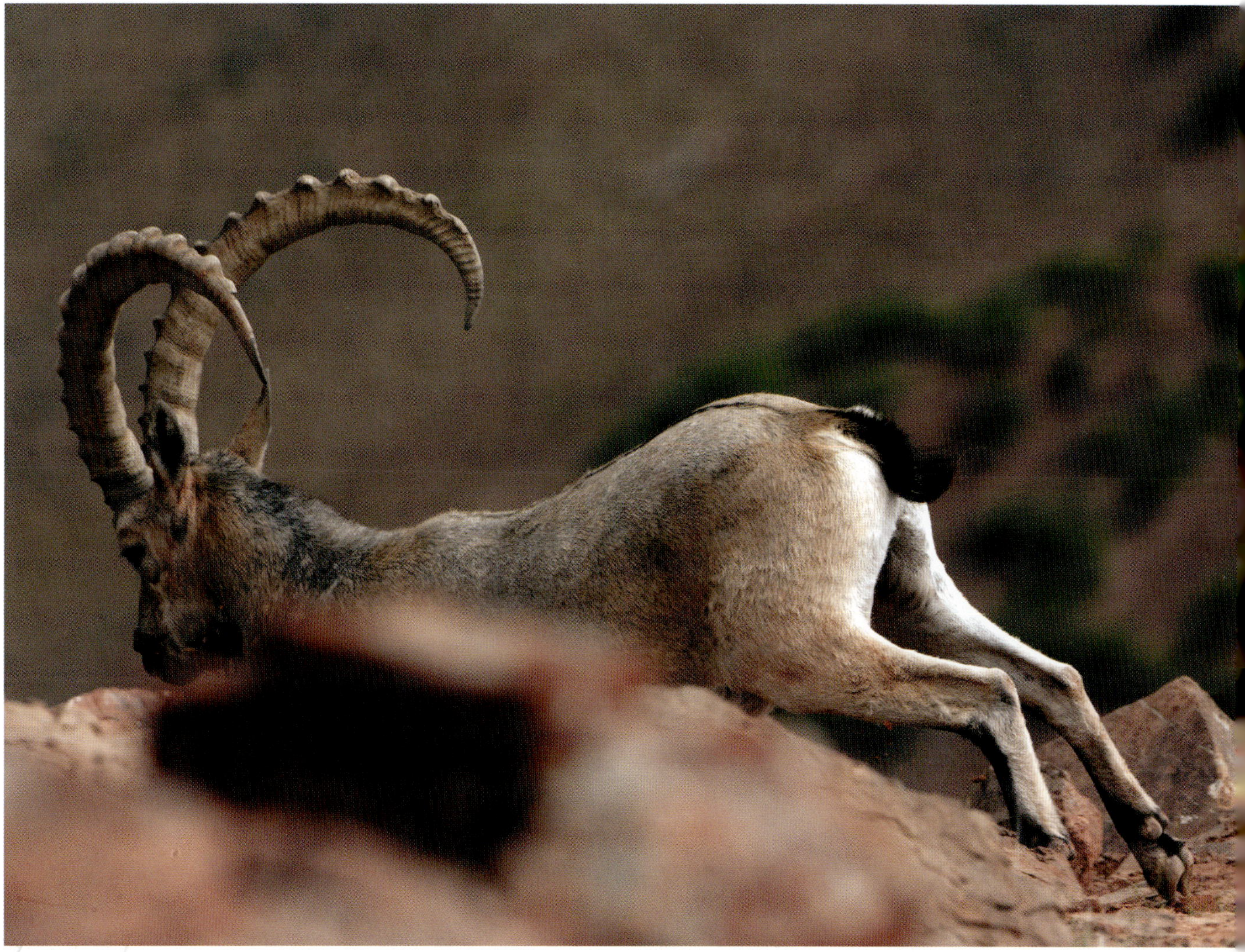

As a kind of typical wild goats, Siberian ibexes look like domestic goats but much bigger. A Siberian ibex is 115 to 170 centimeters long with a shoulder height of 100 centimeters or so and weighs about 50 kilograms.

Such a large ungulate is spread out in western Inner Mongolia, northwest of Gansu province and Xinjiang. As one of the mammals living at the highest sea level, they can be found on naked rocks of the plateau and amidst jagged broken stones of 3,500 to 6,000 meters above sea level.

With various kinds of grass as their food, they mostly crouch on naked rocks to rest, and look for food and water on alpine meadows at lower altitude only in the morning or at dusk. They are fond of group activities. Generally, a group is composed of four to ten. A bigger group consists of dozens and even over a hundred. A robust, vigilant male leads the group. In the course of looking for food, two to three females set aside to be on sentry. They stand on huge rocks not far away from the group, looking around. In case of danger found, the whole group would quickly climb up to steep cliffs to escape from snow leopards and lynxes, their natural predators.

In the period from the 1960s to the early 1980s, due to indiscriminate and excessive hunting, the number of Siberian ibexes had dropped, particularly in places populated by people. Siberian ibexes are gone in Qilian Mountains of Qinghai province and eastern Kunlun Mountains. In 1989, they were designated as the first-grade animals under national protection, leading to considerable reinforcement of protecting them and giving publicity to the protection, hence considerable withdrawal of large-scale hunting, rapid propagation, and considerable rise in their number. In some areas of Tianshan Mountains, Siberian ibexes have become the dominant species.

Golden Eagle

Aquila chrysaetos

IUCN Red List: Least Concern

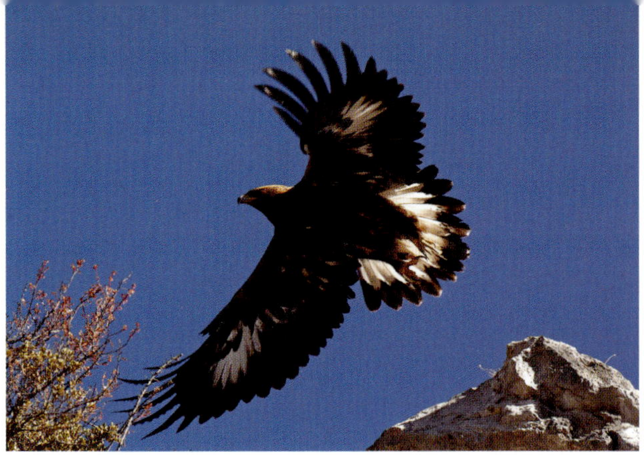

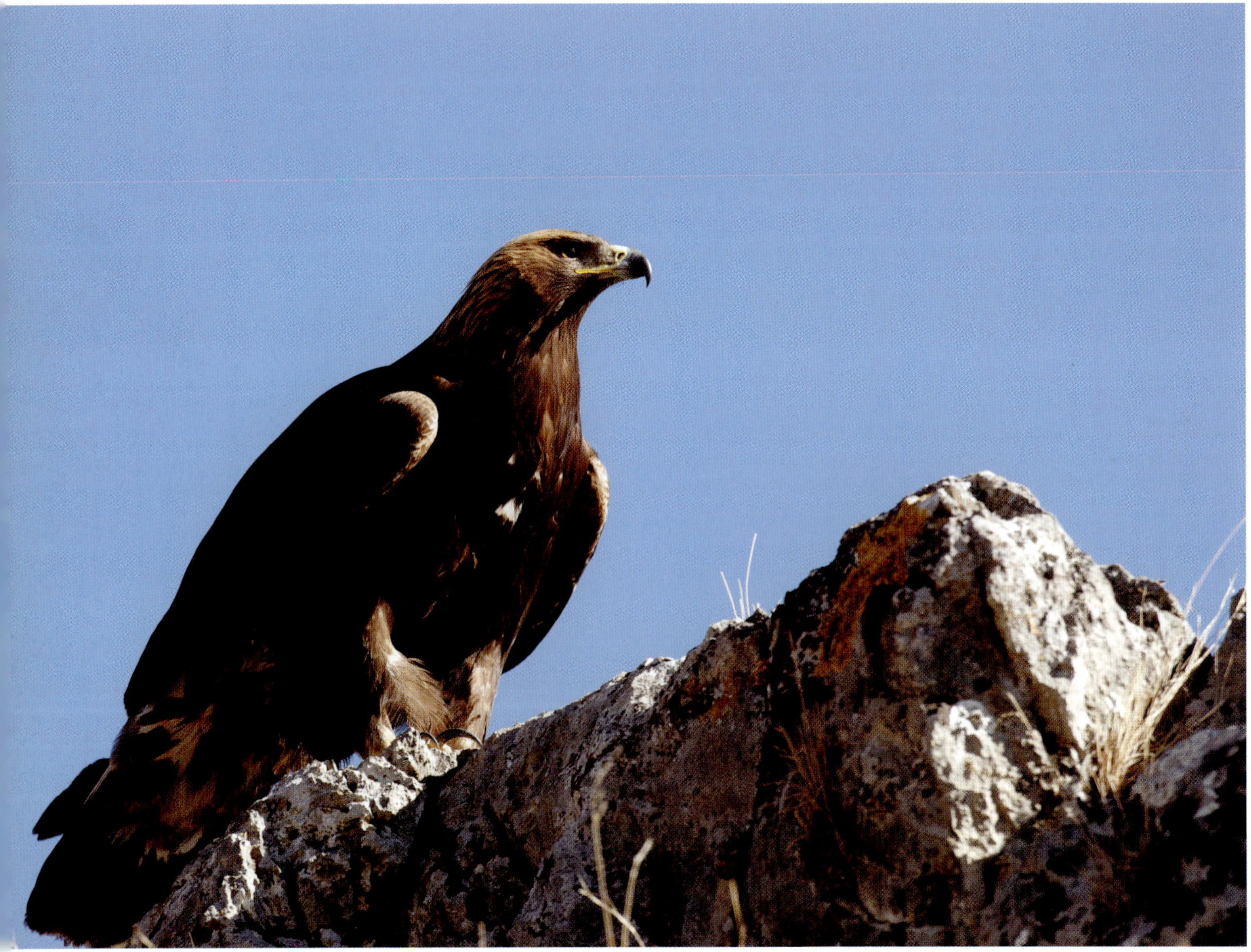

Golden eagles are the most well-known eagles in the world. The term "golden" is derived from the golden feathers extending from the back of their head to their nape. Most parts of their body are covered with brown feathers. There are white feathers on the tail and under the wings of the juveniles and sub-adult golden eagles.

Distributed extensively, they are seen all over Eurasia, Japan, North America, and northern Africa. In China, they are spread out in northeast China, north China, northwest China, southwest China, and some areas in southeast China. They are fond of looking for and hunting preys in expansive or semi-expansive areas. They can also be found in areas at low sea level, though they mostly live in mountains. In the season of migration, they often hunt on wetland converged by waders and shorebirds. Instead of being fastidious about their choice of preys, they attack birds and animals of medium size and above, even big goats. Usually, they would get hold of the head of their prey with

Left
The body of the golden eagle is perfectly structured for hunting. They are one of the fiercest birds of prey thanks to their acute vision, robust wings, and feathers conforming to aerodynamics as well as a sharp beak and claws.

Above
A golden eagle can be as long as one meter and its wings, when spread, can be as wide as 2.5 meters. Their wings are long and forceful.

one claw, and with the other claw break into their prey's lungs to speed up its death.

Usually, monogamy is practiced for many years between the male and the female. In the season of propagation, they would build up nests on tall arbors in coniferous forests and coniferous and broad-leaved mixed forests and woodlands, about 10 to 20 meters above the ground. In areas without many trees, they also build up nests on steep cliffs, concave stone-ledges, eroded cracks and shallow caves. Above the nest, there is mostly a protruding rock as a shelter against rain. Most of the nests face the sun under the lee at steep places inaccessible to climbers. The nest is shaped like a plate of accumulated withered tree-branches. With a very big structure, it is nearly two meters in outer diameter and 1.5 meters high. Inside, the nest is laid with fine tree-branches, pine needles, grass-stems, and fur.

Tajik people in the Pamirs Plateau are accustomed to taming golden eagles. Consequently, illegal hunting resulting from it has become one of the major threats to the local golden eagles.

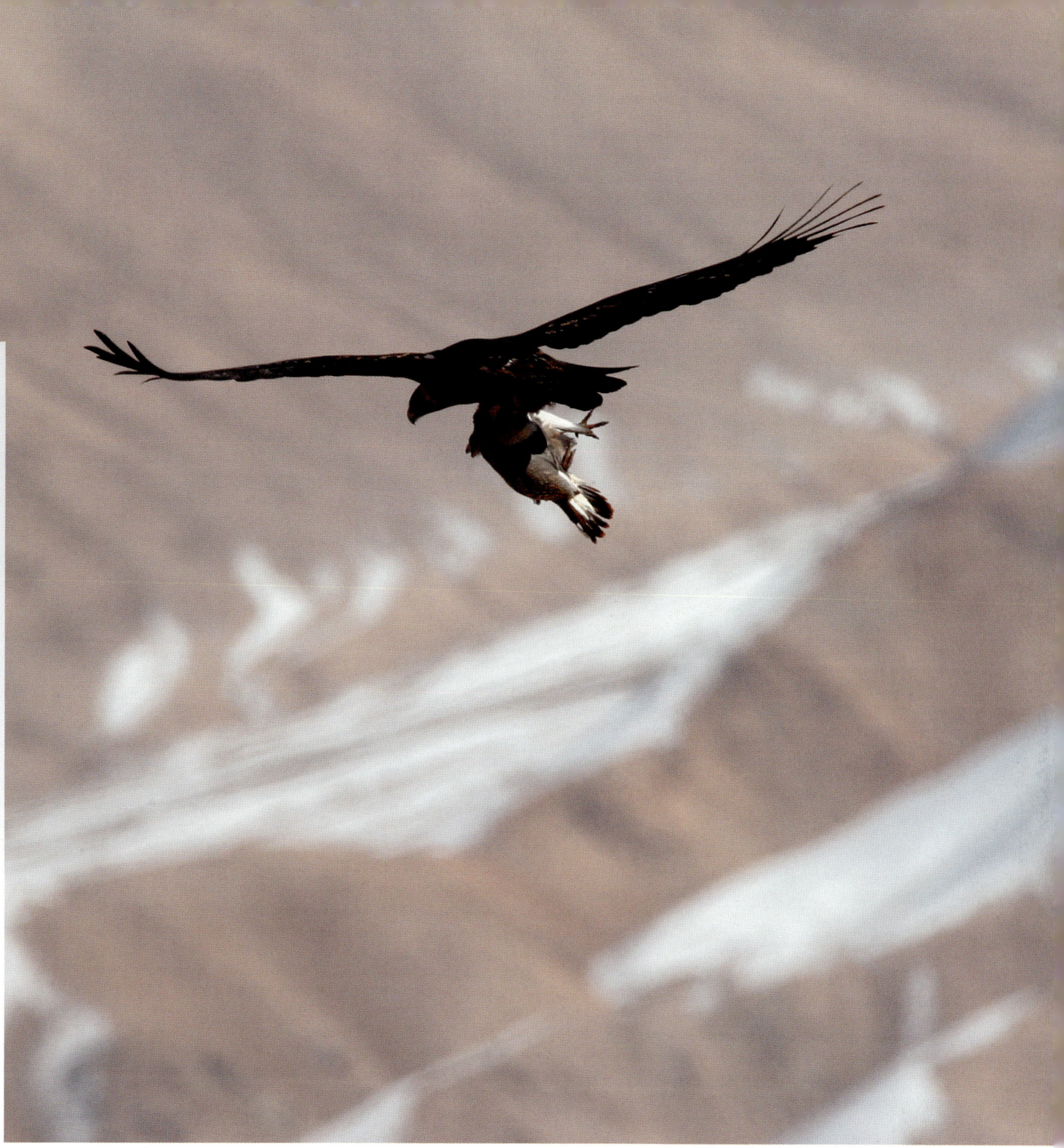

In the sky above the valley, a golden eagle is flying across like a glider. In an instant, it catches a Himalayan snowcock.

Himalayan Snowcock

Tetraogallus himalayensis

IUCN Red List: Least Concern

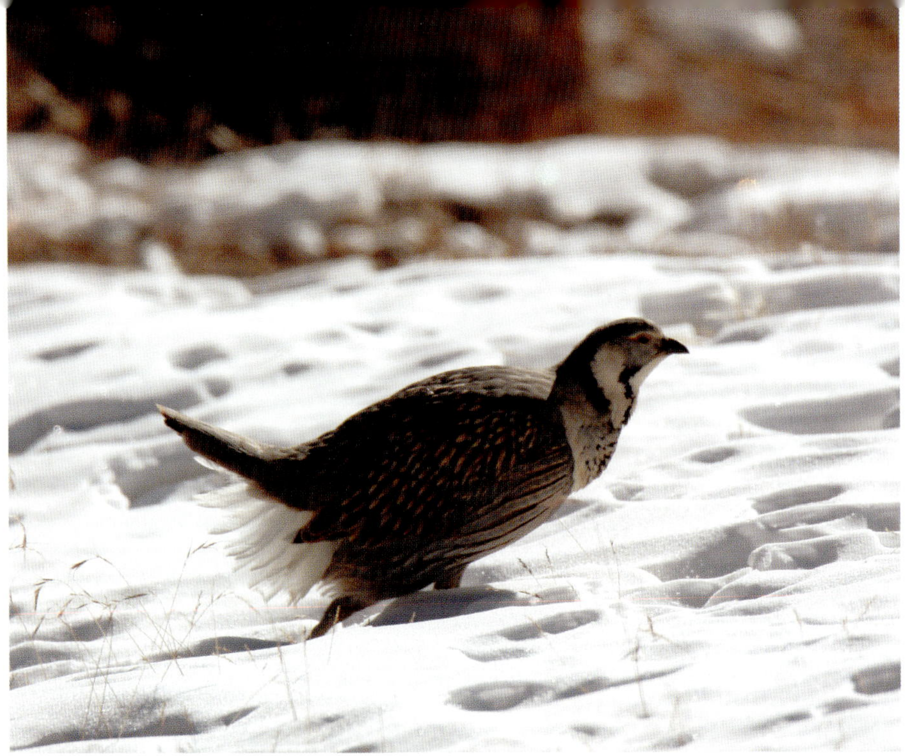

Right

Even at 40 degrees Celsius below zero, they can still live leisurely.

Below

Several Himalayan snowcocks are flying at a low level. The tail feathers of them are like small fans.

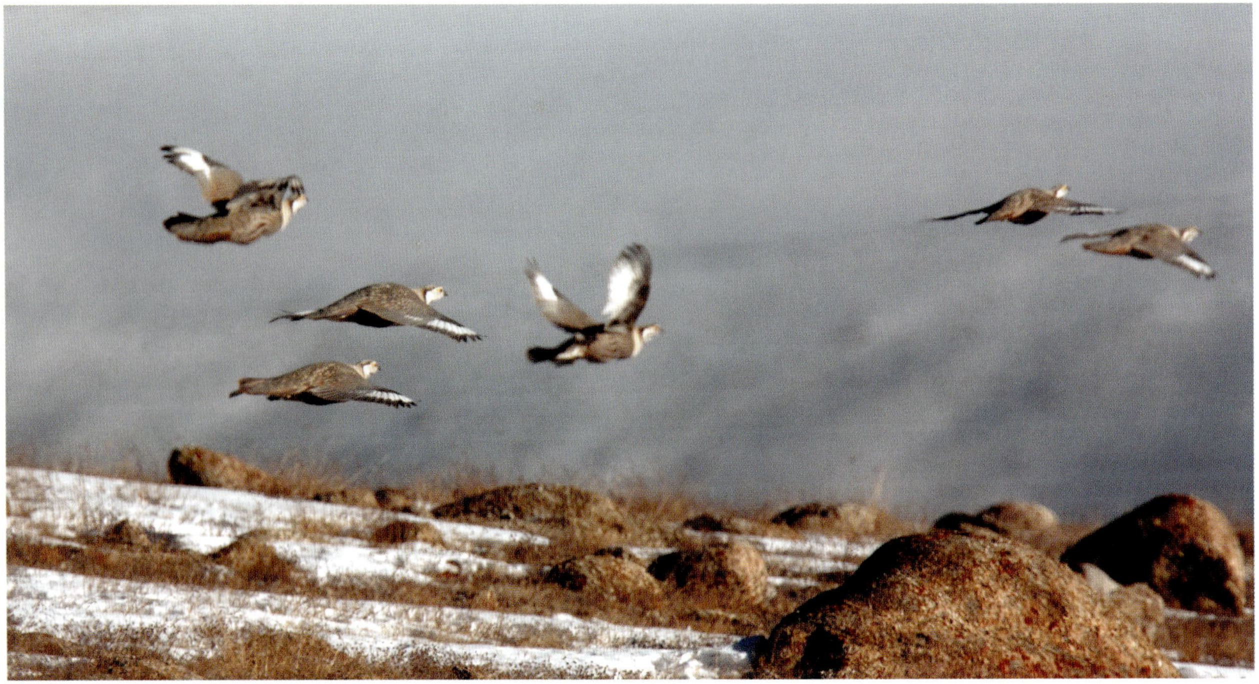

Snowcocks are pheasants located in places at the highest sea level in the world. Generally, they are seen at the place of 3,000 to 6,000 meters above sea level, above the snow line. Himalayan snowcocks are often found in high mountains in western China.

With a big body, a Himalayan snowcock is about 52 to 60 centimeters long and weighs about 2 to 2.5 kilograms. They are marked by vertical migration. In summer, they usually move around amidst bushes of alpine naked rocks, shrubs, and meadows near the snow line of high mountains with perpetual accumulated snow, or grasslands of mountain forests. In winter, they migrate to shrubs or grassy slopes of alpine steppes 2,400 to 3,200 meters above sea level.

Himalayan snowcocks mainly eat plants. In spring, they chiefly eat fescue, cinquefolia, and wild chive. In summer and autumn, they chiefly eat crazyweed and fescue. In winter, they mainly eat fescue, as well as some insects, such as grasshoppers and beetles. Very often, they look for food at the places trampled upon by ungulates or in their droppings.

Each April, they begin to fall into groups and look for spouses. Propagation is over at the end of July, lasting for over 100 days. Unlike many kinds of pheasants, Himalayan snowcocks practice monogamy in the period of propagation. Though the male does not repel the second female to enter its area, its spouse does and she unrelentingly drives the intruder out of their area.

Horned Lark

Eremophila alpestris

IUCN Red List: Least Concern

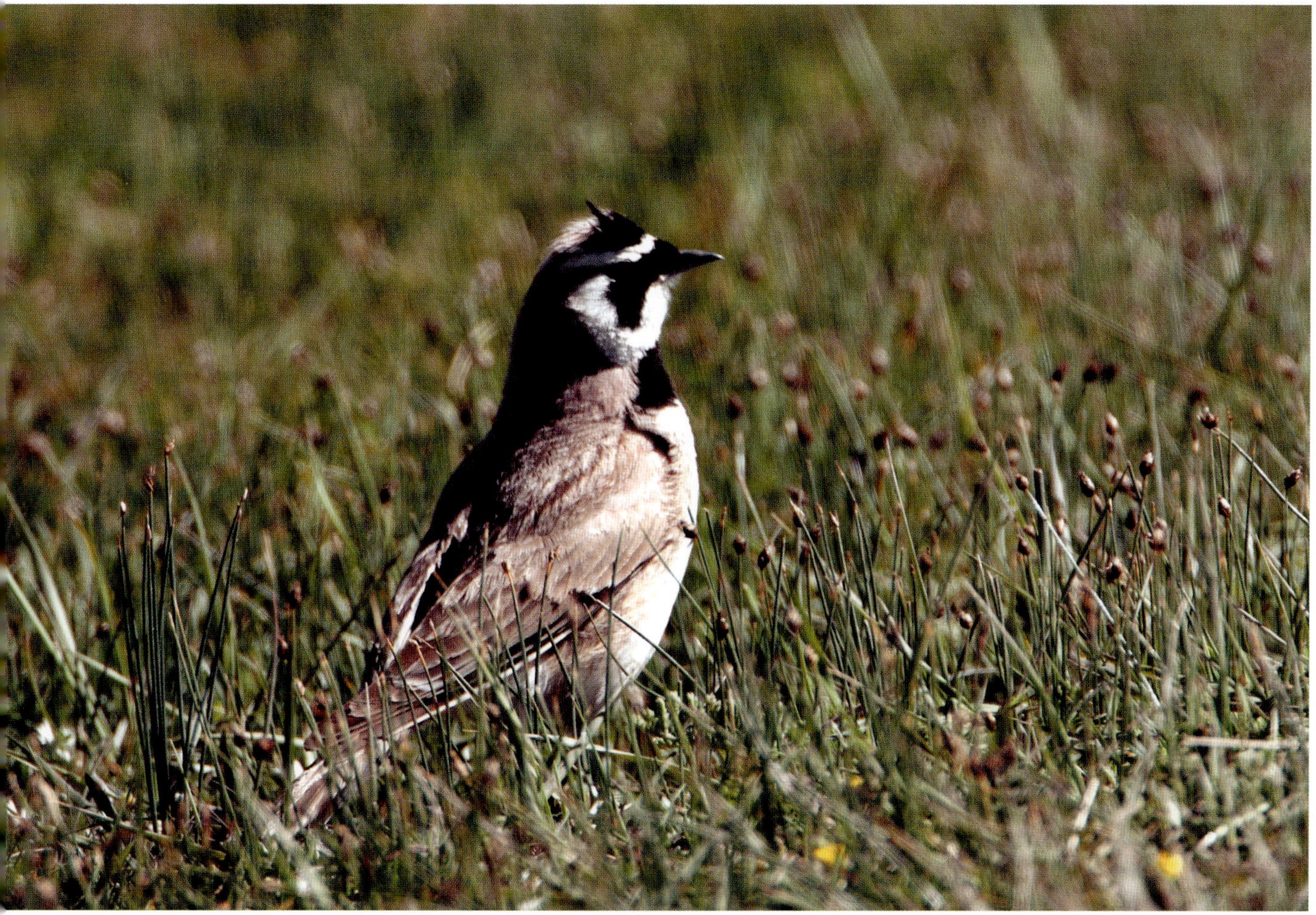

The upper part of the horned larks appears brown and grey-brown and there are wide black stripes between their lore and crown. On both rear sides of the stripes are black feathers perched behind the head like horns. Females are similar to males, but they do not have horn-like feathers on the sides of their heads.

With a body length of about 17 cm, the horned lark is a small songbird extensively distributed in the Americas, Indian Subcontinent, and southwestern China. Living on arid mountains, grasslands, rocks, and in deserts, they mostly move around in groups during the period of non-propagation. Very often, they fly just above the ground in a short distance or run, and eat insects and grass seeds.

Their propagation takes place on desolate arid plains and in cold deserts at high sea level. In winter, they go to short-grass land and lakeside. Their nests are built near the grass roots or in bushes. In the shape of shallow cups, their nests are made up of assorted grass, hair, bird-feathers, and fibrous roots. The nests are covered by drooping grass against the harm of wind and strong sunshine. In the period between May and July, 2 to 5 eggs are laid in each nest. The eggs appear light brown or nearly white, with dense brown fine spots. In turn, the male and the female take care of the hatching which lasts for 12 to 13 days. Juveniles which were just born have fine feathers only on some parts of their body. They grow very quickly, staying in the nest for only 11 days. In this period, they are fed by parents chiefly with larva. The higher the sea level, the less the number of eggs in each nest and the bigger the egg-size. With the strategy of big eggs in a small nest, horned larks deal with harsh natural environment at places of high sea level. However, due to dual pressure of low temperature and the lack of oxygen at places of high sea level, the growth rate of juveniles has dropped.

Chapter Six
Other Areas

Goitered Gazelle
(Kalamaili, Xinjiang Autonomous Region)

Gazella subgutturosa
IUCN Red List: Vulnerable

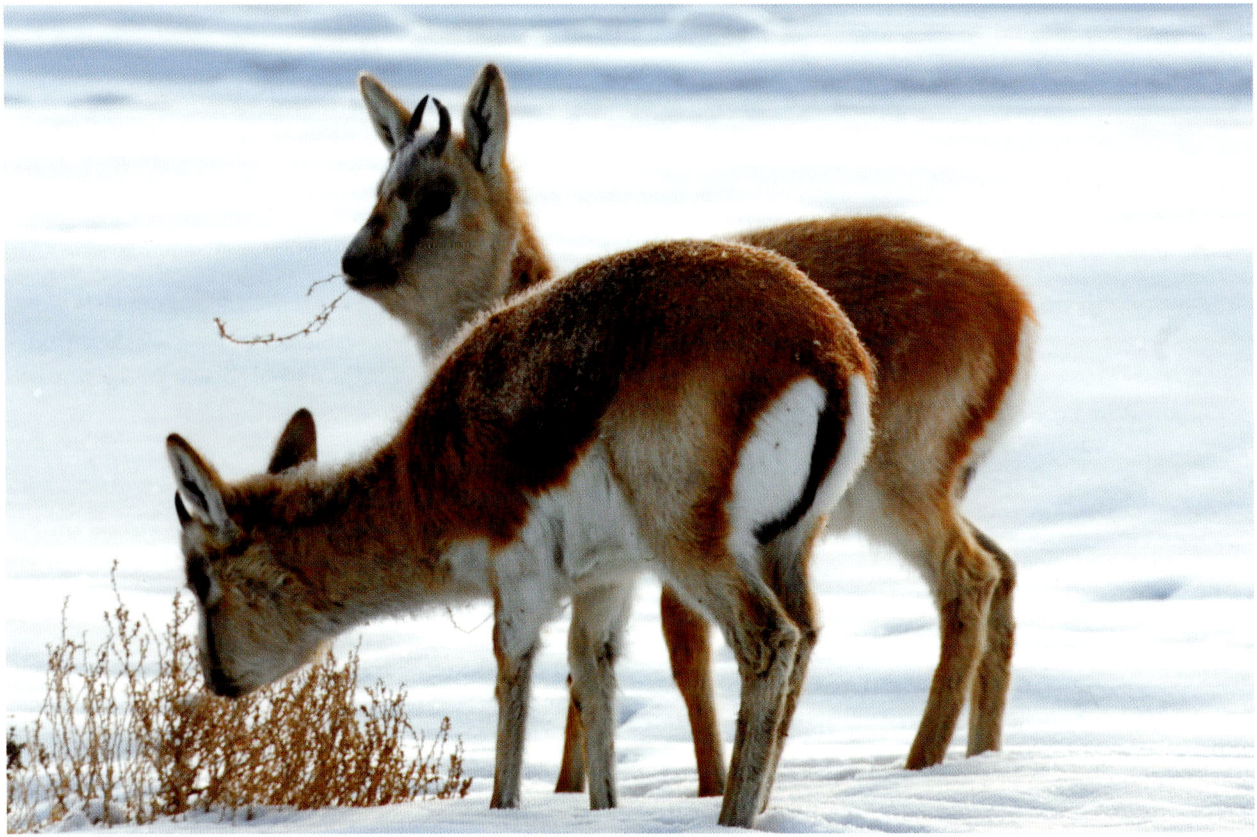

Also called black-tailed gazelles, goitered gazelles are important ungulates living in the deserts and semi-deserts in Eurasia. They mate in the period from December to January. In this period, the male's throat becomes inflated like the head of a gander, hence the name goitered gazelle. The word "goitered" refers to the expansion of the thyroid. In fact, it is the expansion of its throat cartilage, rather than thyroid. In summer and autumn, they mostly fall into a small group of 4 to 6 or move around individually. In the period from October to November in early winter, they fall into a big group and then into smaller groups.

Usually, they look for food in the morning and at dusk, with sagebrush and plants in the grass

In the winter, withered grass seen amidst the snow is the precious food for the goitered gazelles.

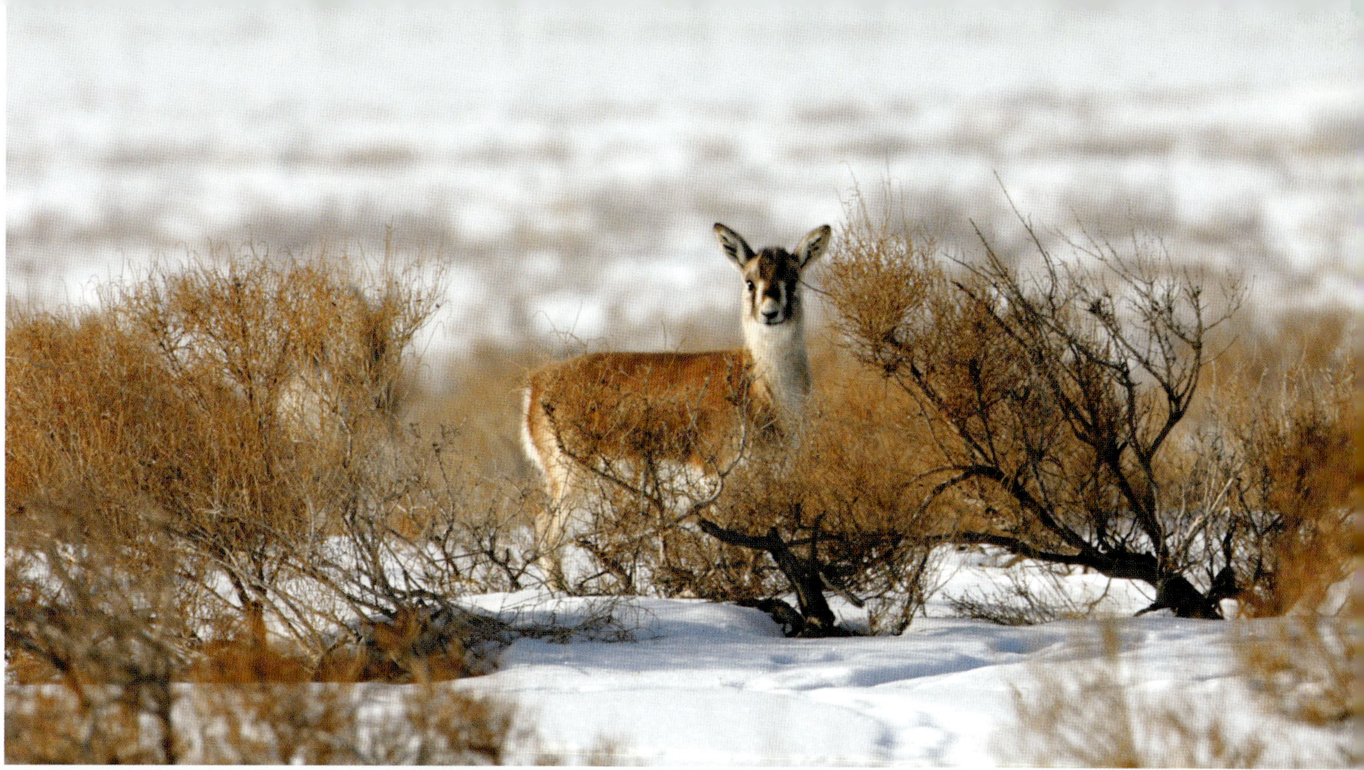

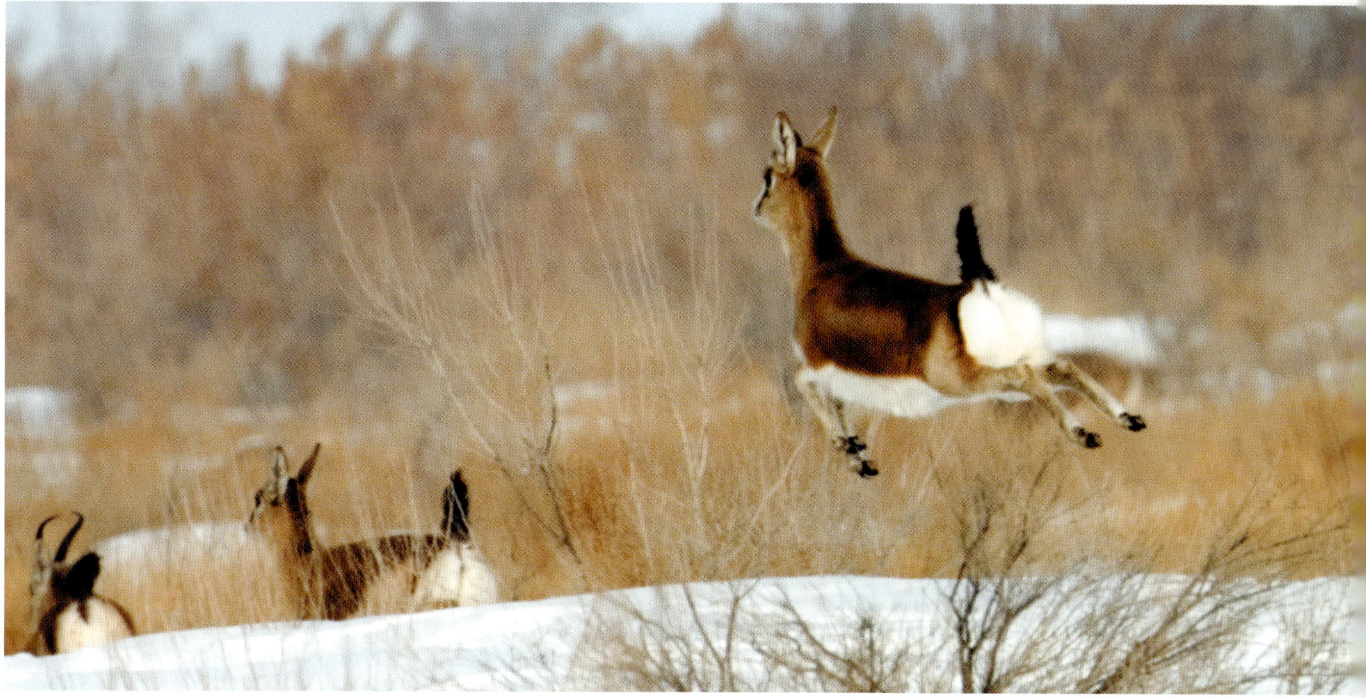

With a very strong running ability, it is good at running on the gobi desert or strolling across willows. Marked by agility and timidity, it flees instantly upon hearing any slight sound.

family as their main food. However, they seldom drink water as they are very capable of enduring thirst. Male ones are fond of fighting with horns, or stand vertically like human beings with their rear legs as support, looking around for observation.

Generally, they become sexually mature at the age of one. A few female ones begin the rut when they are five months old, but most of them are able to propagate at the age of 18 months. Each year, the period from November to January is the major season of their mating. In this period, males occupy places near the route along which female move around. In the early period of propagation, male goitered gazelles stay at their own places in the daytime and depart to look for food in the evening. With the passage of 5 to 6 months, females all give birth in May. Usually, a female gives birth to 1 or 2 offspring. Fifteen minutes after they are born, infants would be able to stand up to suck milk. In the first two months, each time after breastfeeding, the mother would hide her infants. After two months, the infants are able to move around with other adults. After five months, they will be weaned from the breast.

In the early 20th century, farmland and mining development, as well as excessive grazing of domestic animals, led to the loss and degeneration of the habitats of goitered gazelles and the shrinking

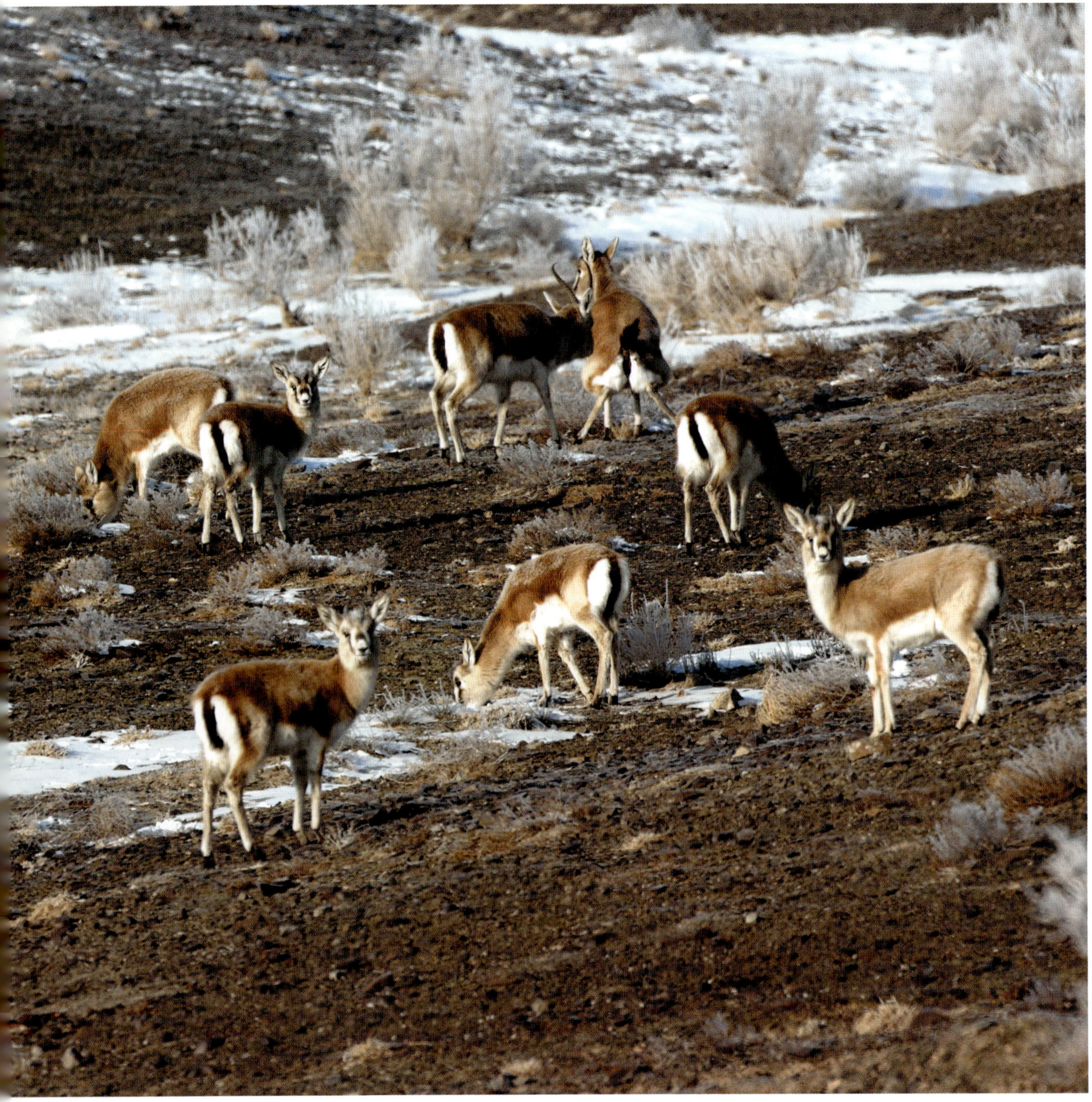

Left
Generally, goitered gazelles choose to live on plains, the quiet gentle hills, as well as in valleys and on plateaus, trying to keep away from the steep mountains, gullies, and areas with human presence.

Below
A goitered gazelle is hurrying across the road with its small upright black tail as its most eye-catching feature.

of the range for their activities. Though they are still often seen in some areas in northwestern China, the species quantity has dropped. Moreover, they are actually spread out in remote and out-of-the-way places or nature reserves, becoming separated populations.

With the establishment of Kalamaili Nature Reserve, illegal hunting in the locality took a turn for the better, in addition to the influence of climate change. As a result, the number of goitered gazelles has increased to over 20,000.

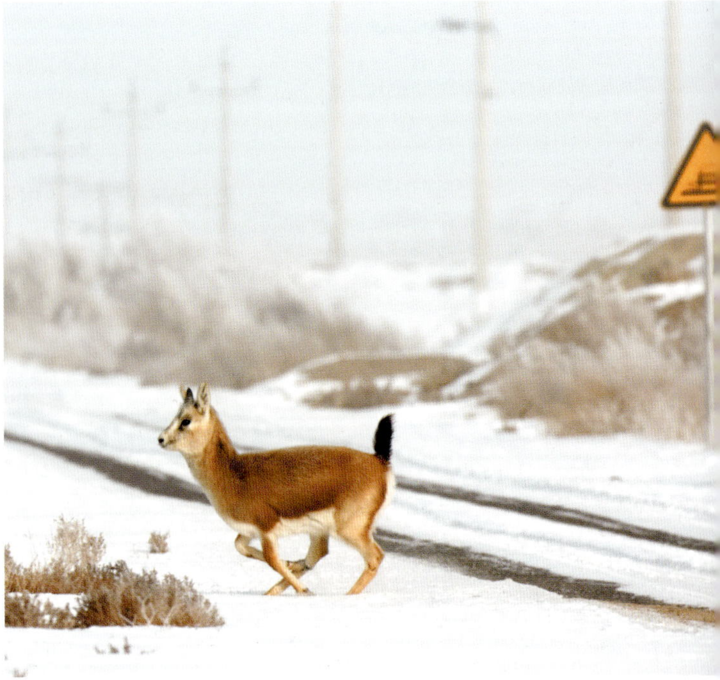

Relict Gull (Ordos, Inner Mongolia Autonomous Region)

Larus relictus

IUCN Red List: Vulnerable

In 1931, Ejnar Lönnberg, a Swedish museologist, wrote for the first time about the relict gull sample discovered in Ejin Banner, Inner Mongolia, China. However, he believed that it was the mutation of the brown-headed gull in the Orient. It was not until 1971 that a small independent genetic stock was found in Alakol Lake, Kazakhstan. As a result, the reproductive isolation between relict gulls and brown-headed gulls was recorded, making sure that the former is an independent species. Therefore, relict gulls became one of the birds recognized the latest by people.

The Hongjiannao Lake bordering Ordos of Inner Mongolia and Yulin of Shaanxi province is the biggest desert freshwater lake in China, as well as the biggest place for the propagation and inhabitation of relict gulls. Relict gulls are fond of living in saline or freshwater lake on the expansive plain, in deserts and semi-deserts.

Each March, relict gulls migrate northward successively. At this time, they wear brand new and gorgeous feathers, getting ready for a long flight to the nest area and attract partners of the opposite sex to become spouses. Some of them get acquainted during migration, becoming spouses. Most of them become spouses after reaching the place of propagation.

In recent years, coal mining near Hongjiannao Lake has stepped up its pace, leading to the change of subsurface flow, the formation of new subsurface streams, the influx of Hongjiannao water into goaves of coal mines, and the large reduction of water areas. So far, due to the absence of water supply, the water area of Hongjiannao Lake has been reduced from 105,000 *mu* (7,000 hectares) in 1996 to 60,000 *mu* (4,000 hectares). The water level drops at a rate of 60 centimeters each year and water quality is deteriorating continuously, having greatly affected the propagation of relict gulls and the success rate of their propagation.

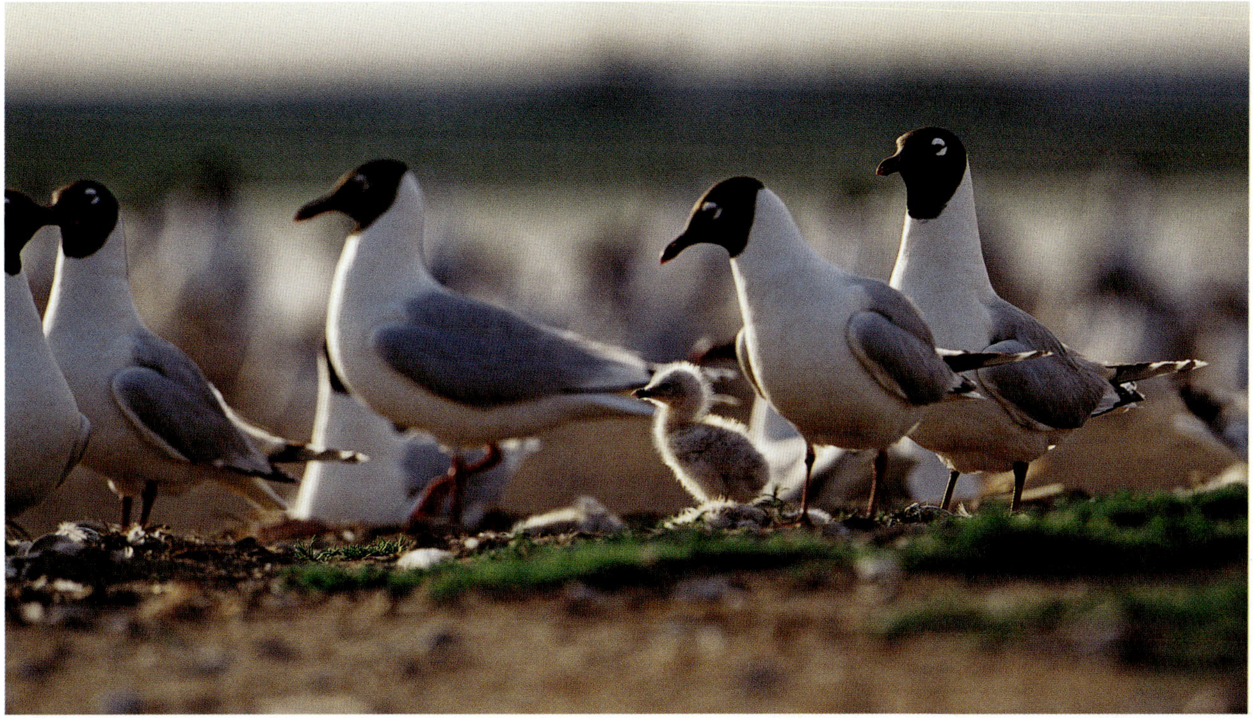

A saline lake surrounded by the desert in the Ordos of Inner Mongolia Autonomous Region was once the biggest place of propagation for relict gulls. Under the setting sun, the photographer has taken a picture of mother relict gulls with a newborn juvenile.

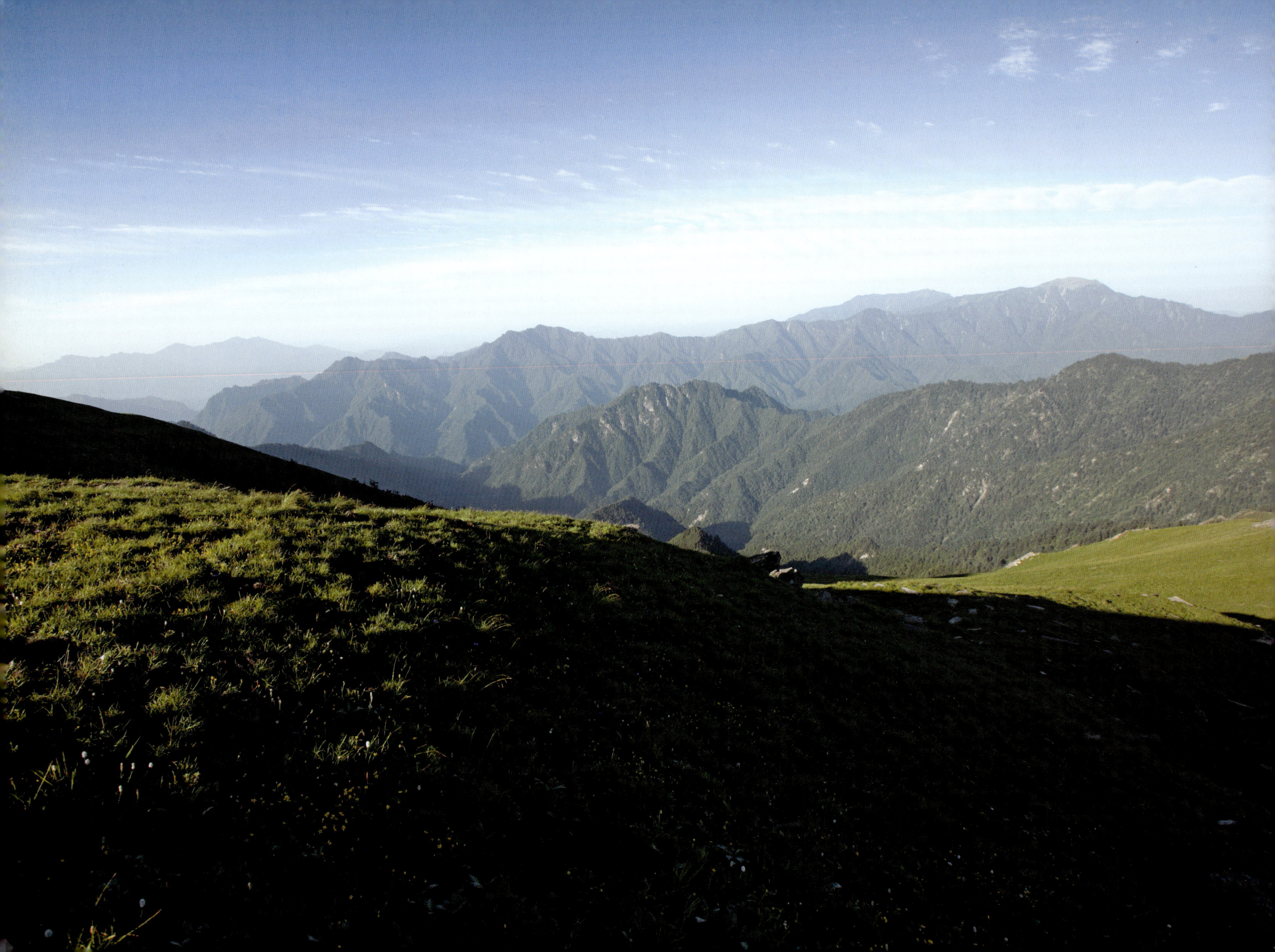

Part Three
Eastern China

Eastern China faces the sea, with inland plateaus at its back, including the Loess Plateau, Sichuan Basin, Yunnan-Guizhou Plateau, and Hengduan Mountains on the second geographical flight of stairs, as well as coastal plains and hilly areas on the third geographical flight of stairs, covering about 45% of the total land area of China. The warm and moist natural environment accommodates about 95% of the Chinese population.

As part of the monsoon area of eastern Asia and southern Asia, eastern China is obviously influenced by summer monsoon, resulting in quite high degrees of humidity in different parts, with forests as the major vegetation across the entire area. All these are undoubtedly favorable conditions to animals adaptable to living in forests.

Except for the Hengduan Mountains, eastern China is marked by low terrains and most parts are less than 1,000 meters above sea level, particularly in the east. Several important rivers originated from the Tibetan Plateau flow into the sea via this area, with the Yangtze River and the Yellow River being the most famous. In the eastern part, there are expansive alluvial river-valleys and coastal plains. Plains in the south are dotted with eye-catching limestone.

As an area of nature characterized by the richest bio-diversity in China, eastern China with various natural environments has also provided habitats for a diversity of living creatures. Various kinds of forests have provided desirable homes for a number of Cervidae family animals as food for many kinds of medium and large carnivores, tigers in particular. Almost all non-human primates live in eastern China. Tropical seasonal rain forests in the southwest and southeast are habitats with the richest bio-diversity where there are animals of typical tropical features. Mammals include elephants and a variety of gibbons while birds include hornbills, parrots, and sunbirds. Various kinds of waterfowls are seen in numerous lakes, marshes, and river-mouth deltas in the Yangtze River valley and Yellow River valley, including mandarin ducks, many kinds of shorebirds and cranes, which are provided with places for propagation and wintering. In the mountainous forests of Sichuan province and Qinling Mountains, there are a variety of the most eye-catching precious animals such as giant pandas and golden snub-nosed monkeys.

This is also an area that people exert the most extensive and profound influence on Mother Nature. Most parts that can be reclaimed have been opened as farmland, or secondary forests and bushes. Most of the natural forests are gone, with some of them preserved in areas under protection or in a few remote and out-of-the-way mountainous areas.

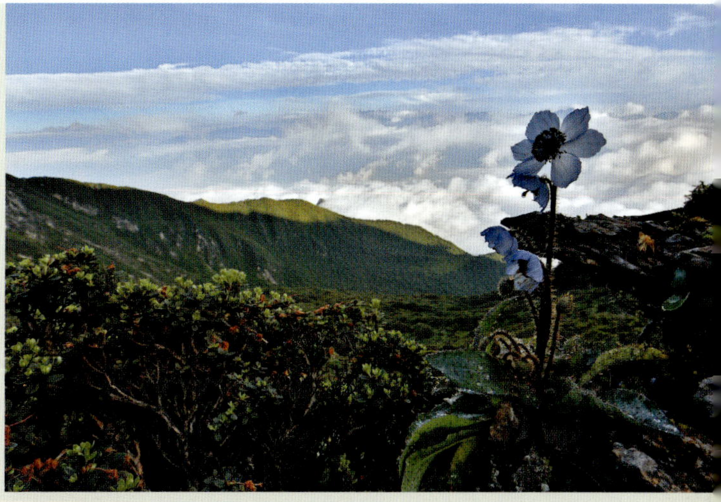

The humid climate of the Eastern China region has given birth to diversified vegetations. This picture shows a blue poppy (*Meconopsis spp.*) in full bloom on the Minshan Mountains, which generally grows on the flowstone beaches of high mountains and the front edges of glaciers over 3,000 to 4,000 meters above sea level. They are famous for their big flowers, gorgeous color, and graceful shape, and are one of the most eye-catching flowers among alpine plants.

On facing page
Compared to the Xinjiang-Inner Mongolia region and the Tibetan-Highlands, Eastern China is marked by warmth, humidity, and lush vegetation.

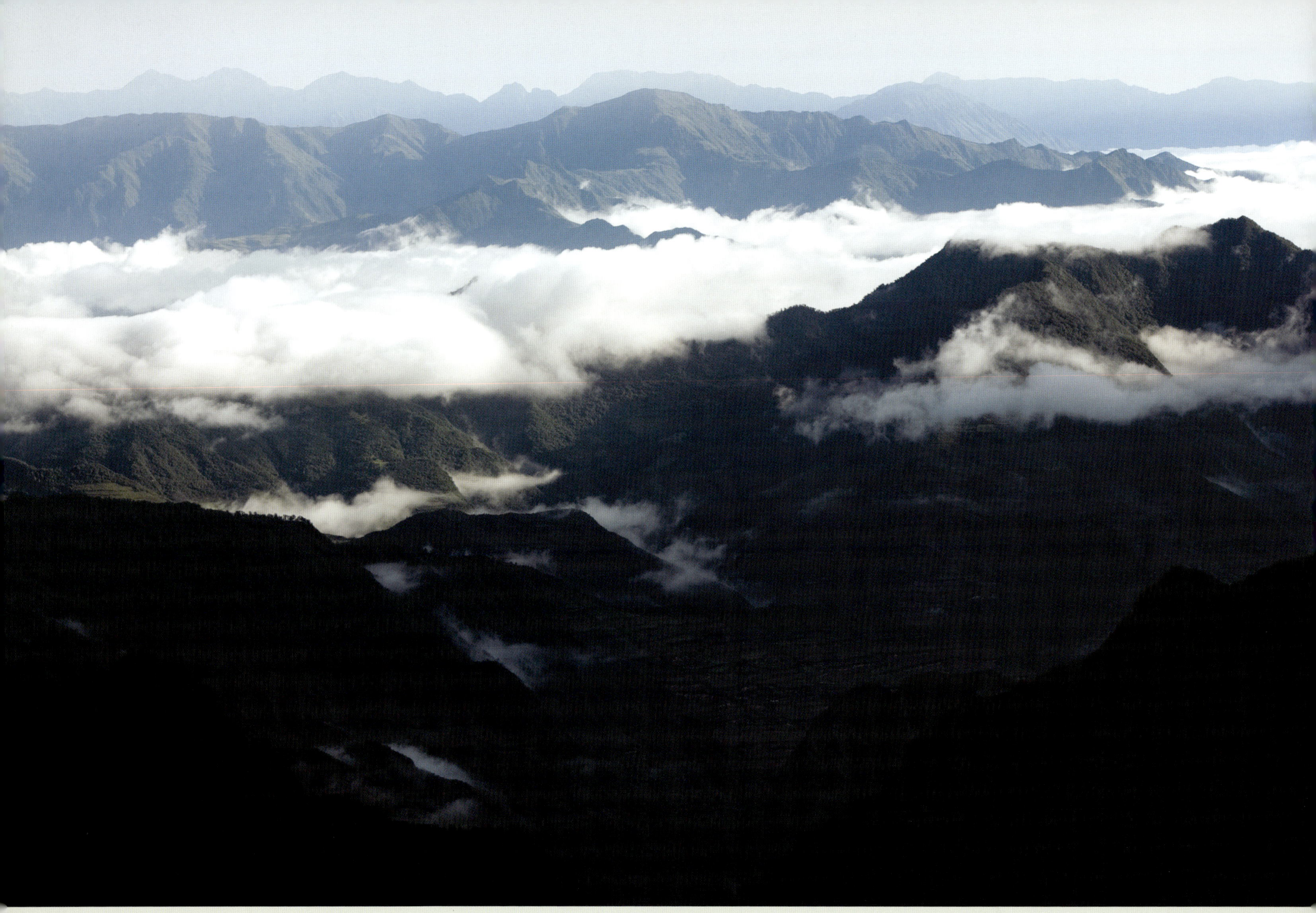

Chapter Seven

Qinling Mountains and Minshan Mountains—The Habitats of the Takins

Starting from the south of Gansu province via the south of Shaanxi province and the west of Henan province, Qinling Mountains traverse central China from the east to west, extending about 1,500 kilometers. The Huaihe River of Qinling Mountains known as the life line of the Chinese civilization, is the most important dividing line between southern China and northern China. With expansive areas, Qinling Mountains provide precious habitats for ancient life on earth. Some people speak highly of Qinling Mountains as the Central Park of China. Nourished by climate screens and water source, these mountains, having given birth to civilization, have formed very unique natural sceneries. The most important is that there are many kinds of precious and rare animals. Among them, giant pandas, golden snub-nosed monkeys, takin, and crested ibises are renowned as the Four treasures of Qinling Mountains.

Extending over 700 kilometers from the south to north, the Minshan Mountains are situated between Sichuan province and Gansu province. As the most important screens of eco-safety in western China, Minshan Mountains are the water divide between the Minjiang River, Fujiang River, and Baishui River (literally White Water River) of the Yangtze River drainage system and Heishui River (literally Black Water River) of the Yellow River drainage system. They are designated by the World Wild Fund for Nature (WWF) as one of the 25 areas under first-priority protection in the world. Xuebaoding Mountain (literally Snowy Treasure Peak), the main peak of Minshan Mountains, is 5,588 meters above sea level, with overlapping peaks and deep valleys around. At places of over 5,000 meters above sea level, there are modern glaciers and many remains of ancient glaciers. The Minshan Mountains are composed of sandstones, slates, limestone, and granites of jagged terrains. There are such trees as spruces in western Sichuan province, firs of the Minjiang River, and Chinese red pines and oaks. At places of over 3,800 meters above sea level, there are alpine bushes and meadows. The Minshan Mountains are also marked by numerous alpine lakes mostly concentrated in Jiuzhaigou Valley of Nanping county in Sichuan province. In forests, there are many kinds of precious and rare animals under protection. Jiuzhaigou Valley is also the place with giant pandas of the greatest density and the biggest number in China.

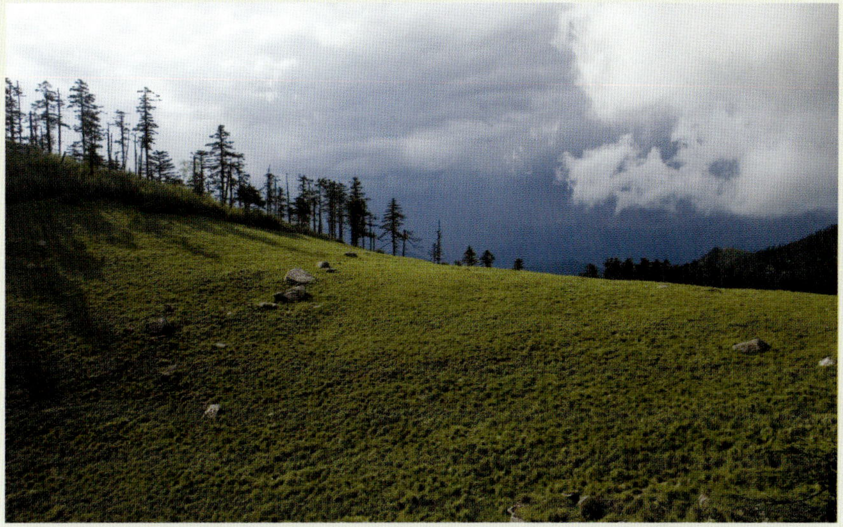

The Qinling Mountains, as it traverses central China, is also known as the "central mountain" of China. It is the dividing line of the climate between southern China and northern China, the water divide of water systems between southern China and northern China, and the converging hub of species between southern China and northern China.

On facing page
The Minshan Mountains, always known as "Minshan Mountains extending five-hundred kilometers" is just like a dragon zigzaging across thick white clouds.

Takin

Budorcas taxicolor
IUCN Red List: Vulnerable

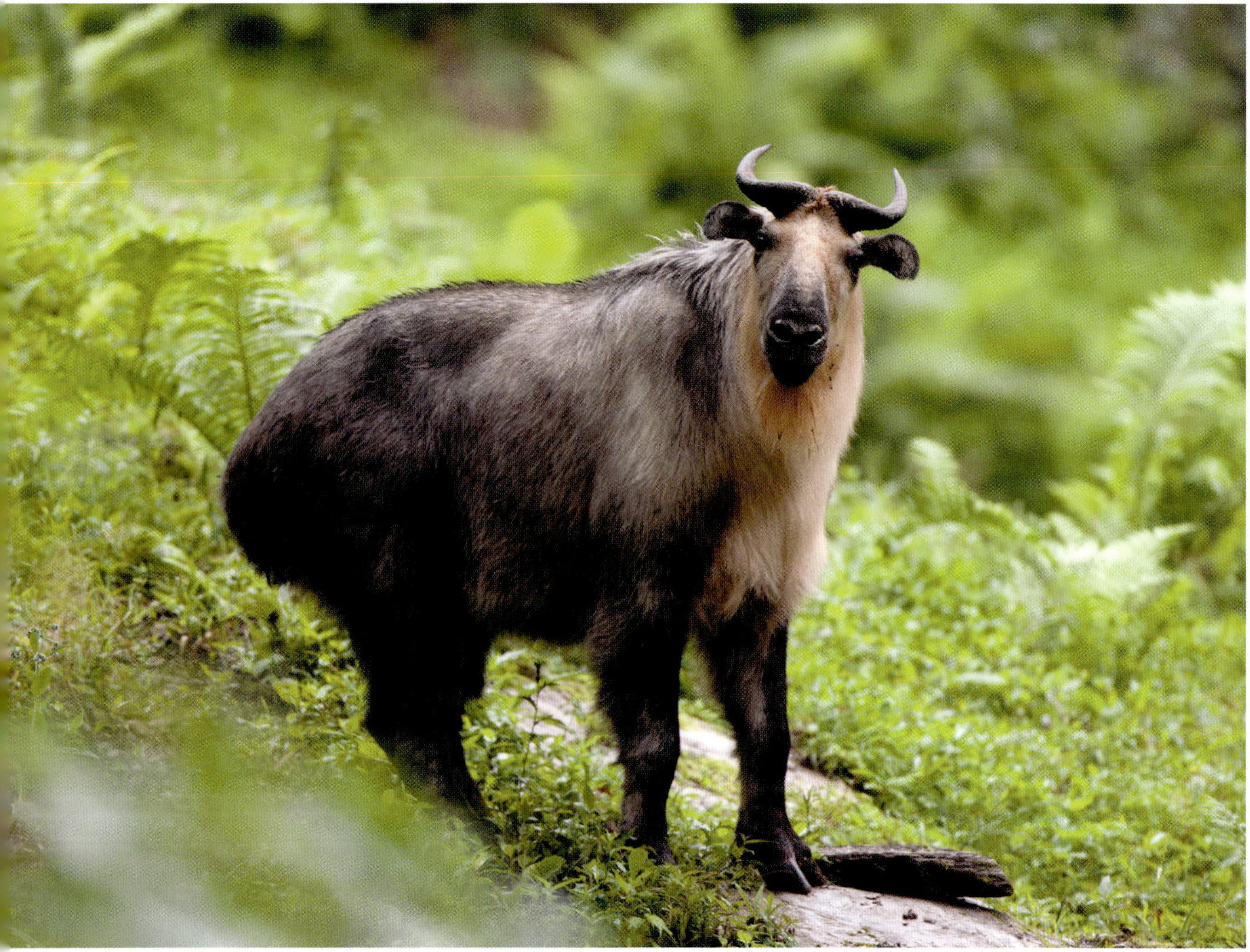

Commonly called the white sheep, the takin is a species unique to Asia. Closer to antelopes in terms of classification, they are chiefly distributed in the mountainous forests in Shaanxi, Sichuan and Yunnan provinces, and Tibet. Among them, *B.t.tibetana* and *B.t.bedfordi* are two sub-species unique to China. As one of the internationally acknowledged precious and rare animals, takins are very rare in the world. The number of *B.t.bedfordi* is very small, amounting to about 5,000 at present.

In the form of 3 to 5 families, takins move around and rest together, but each family is relatively concentrated. From June to July, the period of their propagation, several groups of them would converge on a slope. Adult male and female takins during this period of reproduction can freely choose partners.

As alpine animals, *B.t. bedfordi* would move to places at different sea levels in different seasons, i.e. "vertical migration." In the spring, accumulated snow over low mountains would thaw first, along with the budding of green grass. Takins would gather in a big group of as many as 100, going to river-valleys of low mountains of less than 1,600 meters above sea level. At this time, pregnant female takins over nine months would give birth to calves under the warm sunshine.

Takins are large forest mammals quite representative in China. They have robust limbs and wide hoofs, as well as dense and fluffy hair. The *B.t.tibetana* is featured by a deeper color that is close to black.

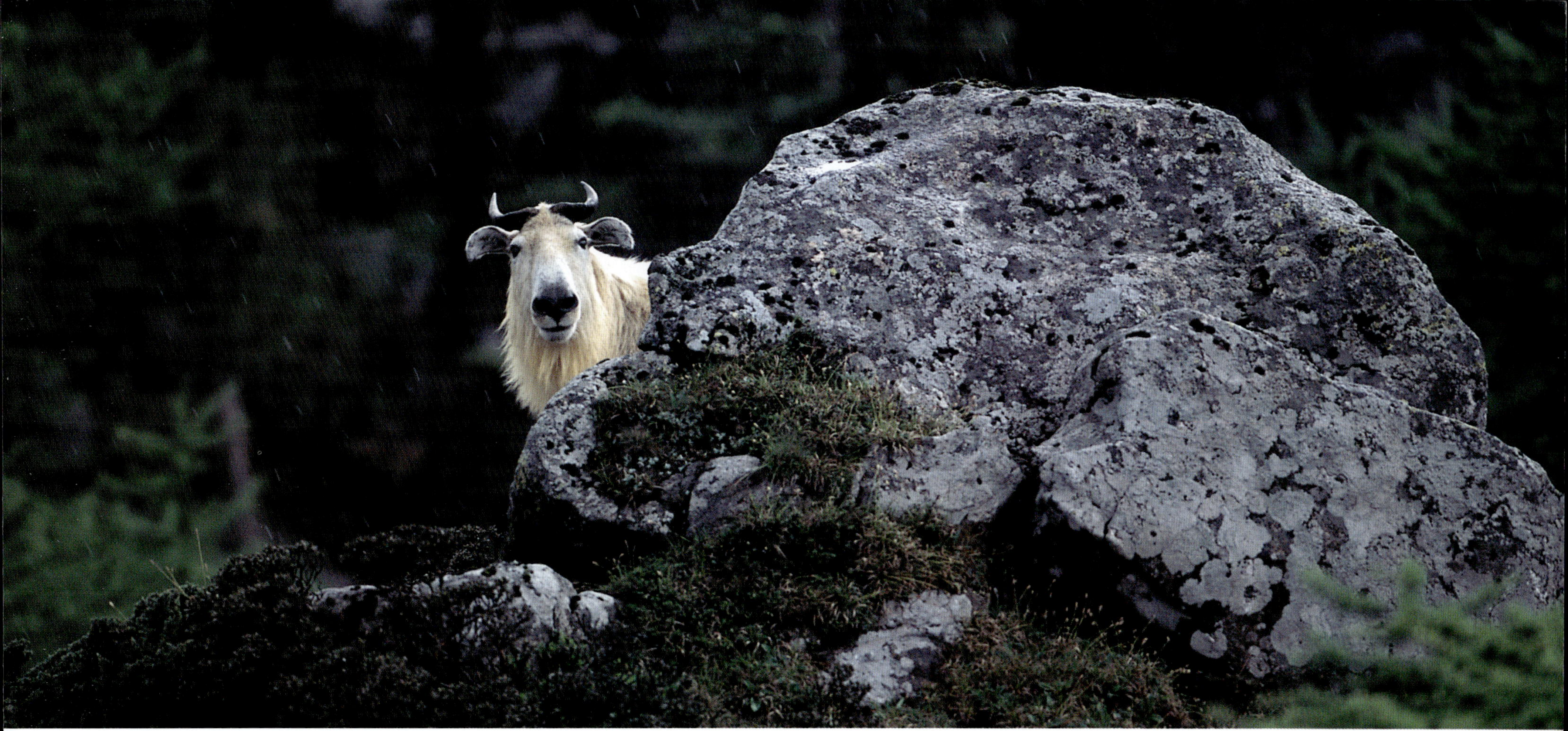

After a sudden hailstorm, a curious takin stretches its head out from behind a jagged rock.

In the summer, along with the rise of temperature, plants on low mountains begin to ate in addition to the increase of mosquitoes and flies. Takins would move from low mountains to alpine meadows of 2,200 to 4,000 meters to look for food in order to shake off the disturbance from these pests. They also make use of this period to absorb more nutrition and reinforce their physique to prepare for the time of mating. In the autumn, along with the sharp drop of temperature in high mountains, grass and trees begin to wither. With their respective family unit, they once again move to places at low sea level to look for fresh plants.

Winter is the harshest for takins, since they are susceptible to the cold, hunger, and diseases. Therefore, they move from places at low sea level to the forests of 1,800 to 2,000 meters above sea level, feeding on barks and lichens. Some old and weak takins would be hunted by their natural predators due to their slow movement, or eliminated due to their weak physique in severe cold weather. When spring comes around, those that have survived the winter are winners adaptable to Mother Nature.

In the habitats of takins, roads and railways built have broken their homes into pieces. Takins, who usually could stay together, have been confined to one isolated place after another. The increased population of human beings has aggravated the consumption of forest resources. A large expanse of forests has been cut down and transformed into farmland. Except for a few nature reserves at present, primitive natural forests are gone. Illegal hunting of takins still takes place due to the demands for their meat. Nowadays, almost all sub-species of takins are on the verge of extinction.

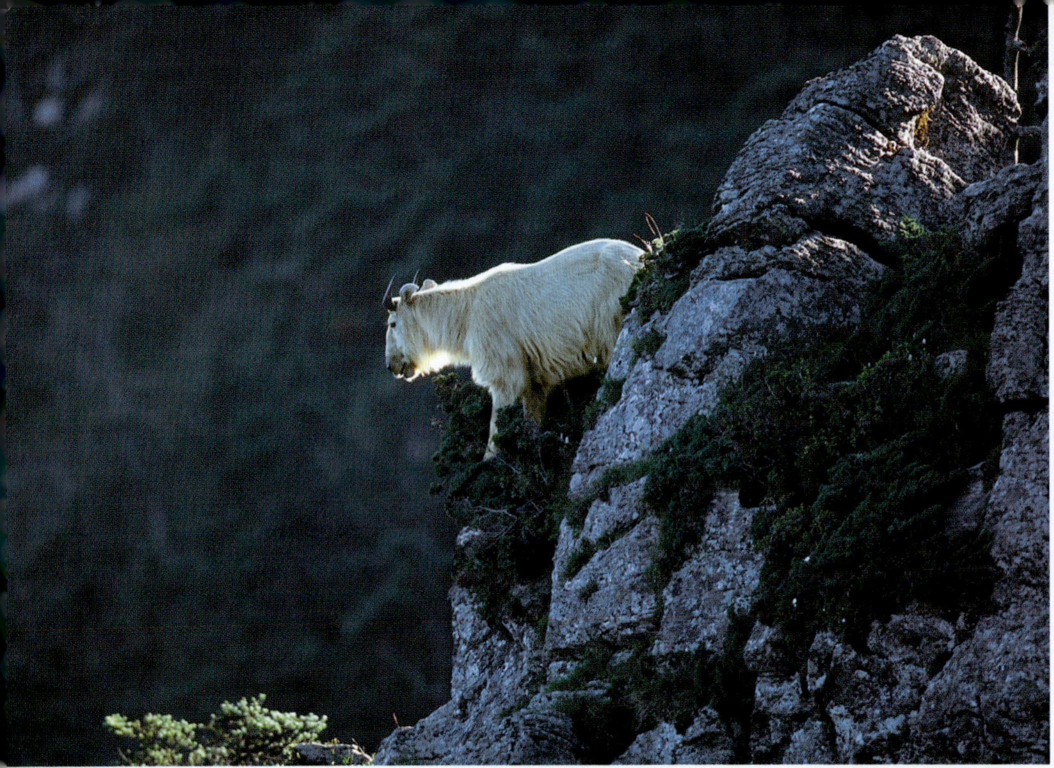

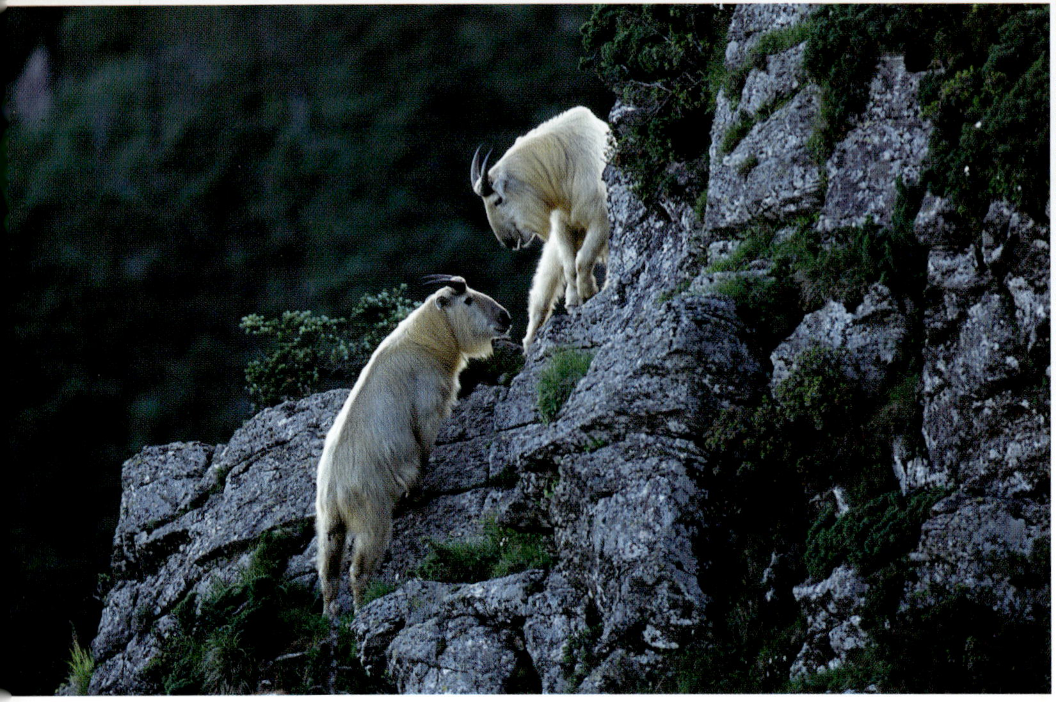

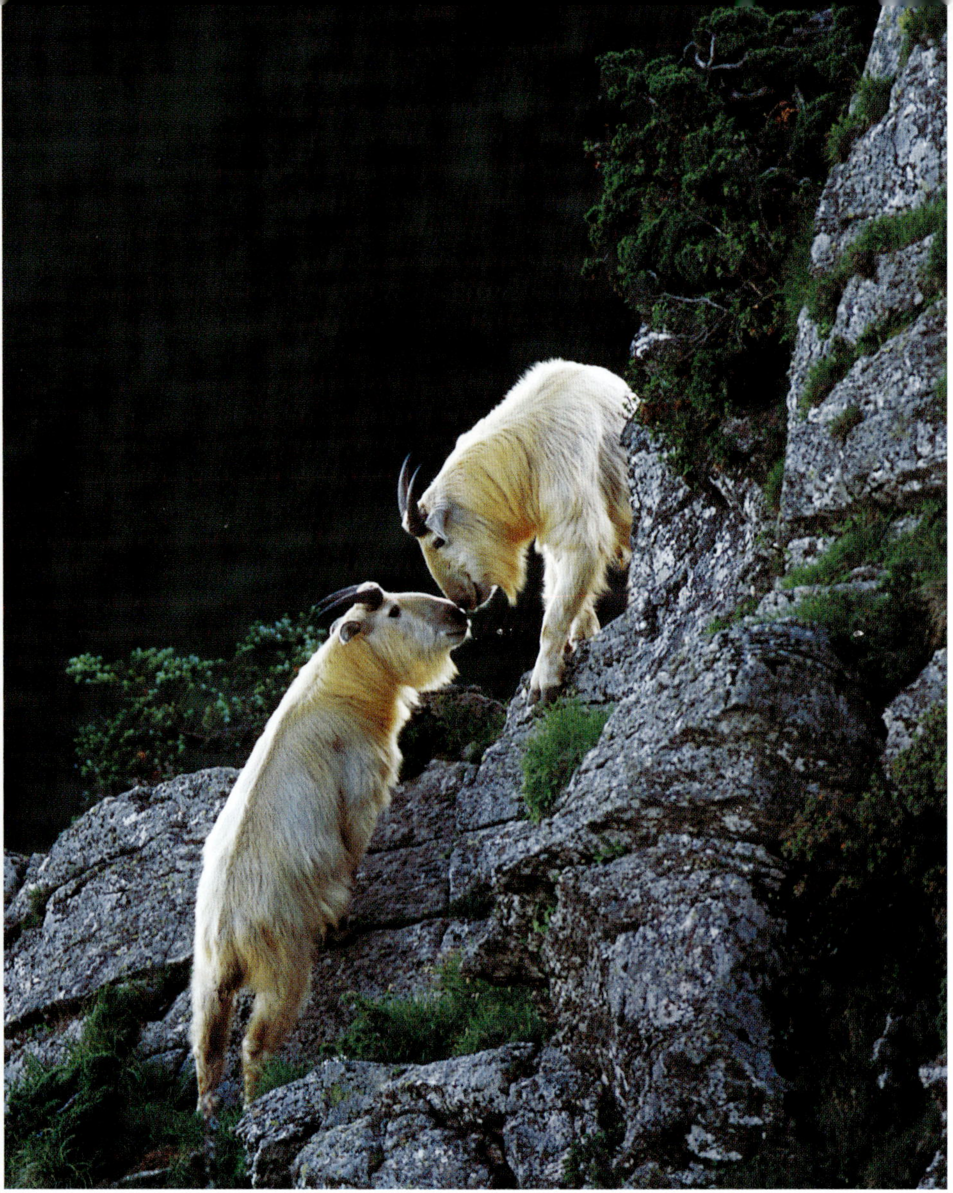

1 2 3

At dusk, a takin has climbed onto the cliff, with the light of the setting sun on its body. It meets another takin unexpectedly. When approaching, they greet each other by gently touching their noses, as if saying, "How are you today?"

On facing page
A calf takin seems to have heard the call of its mother. It even strolls toward the place where the photographer is hiding himself, so close that the photographer cannot focus his lens.

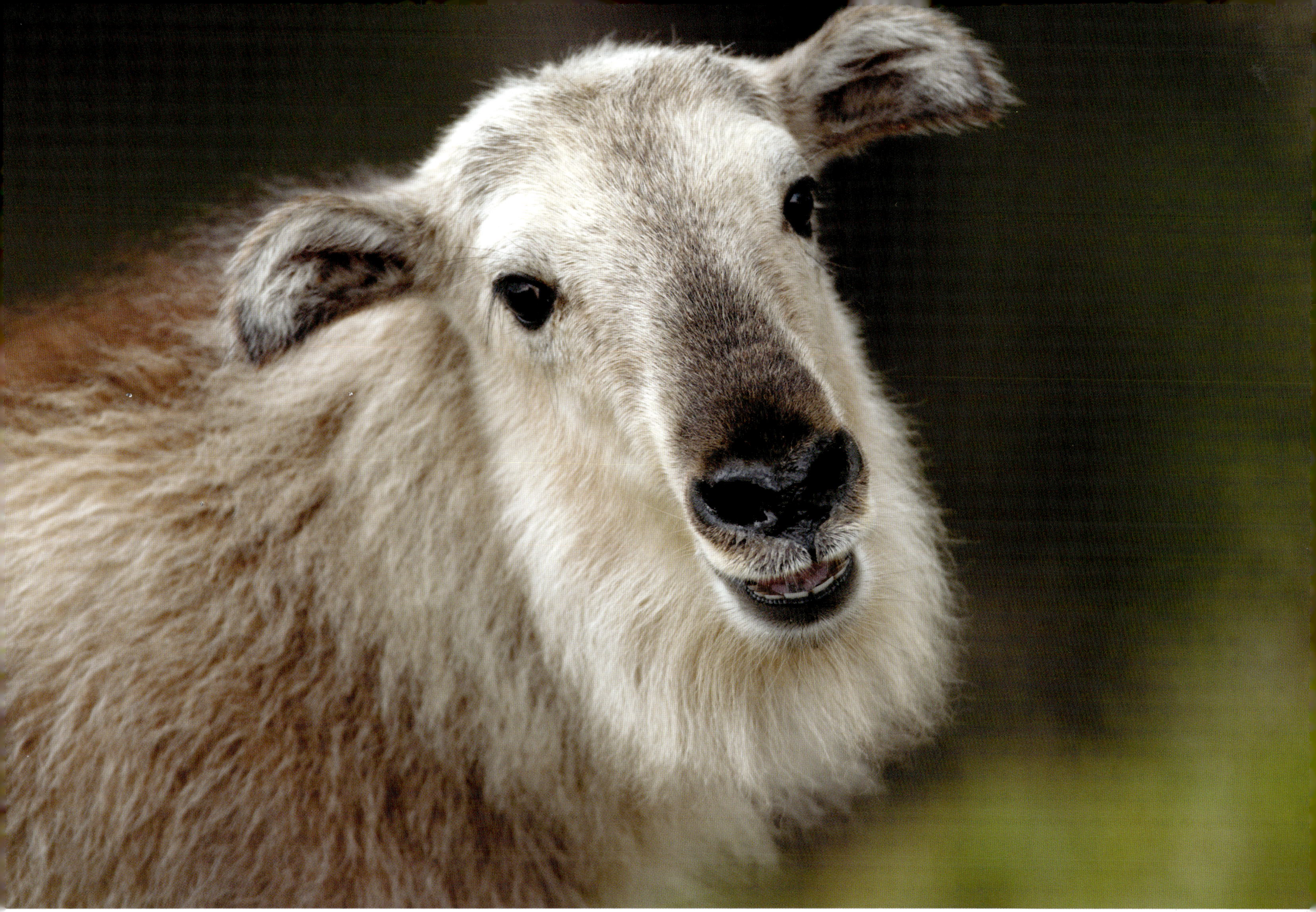

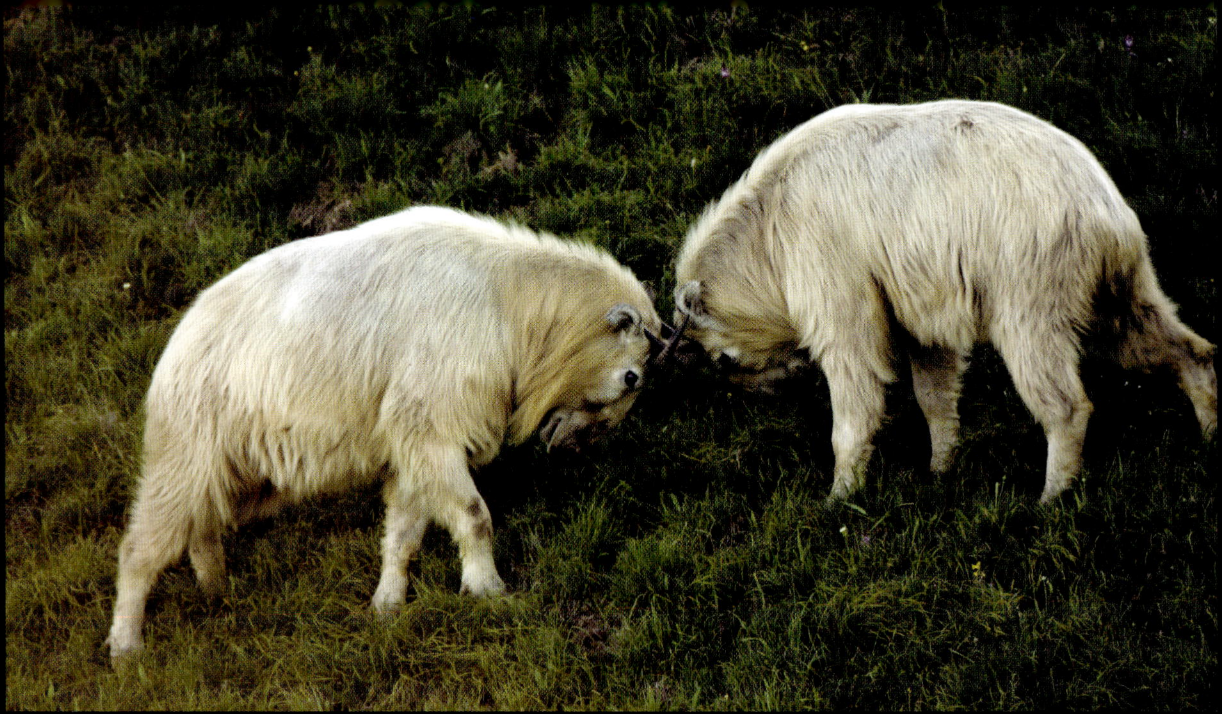

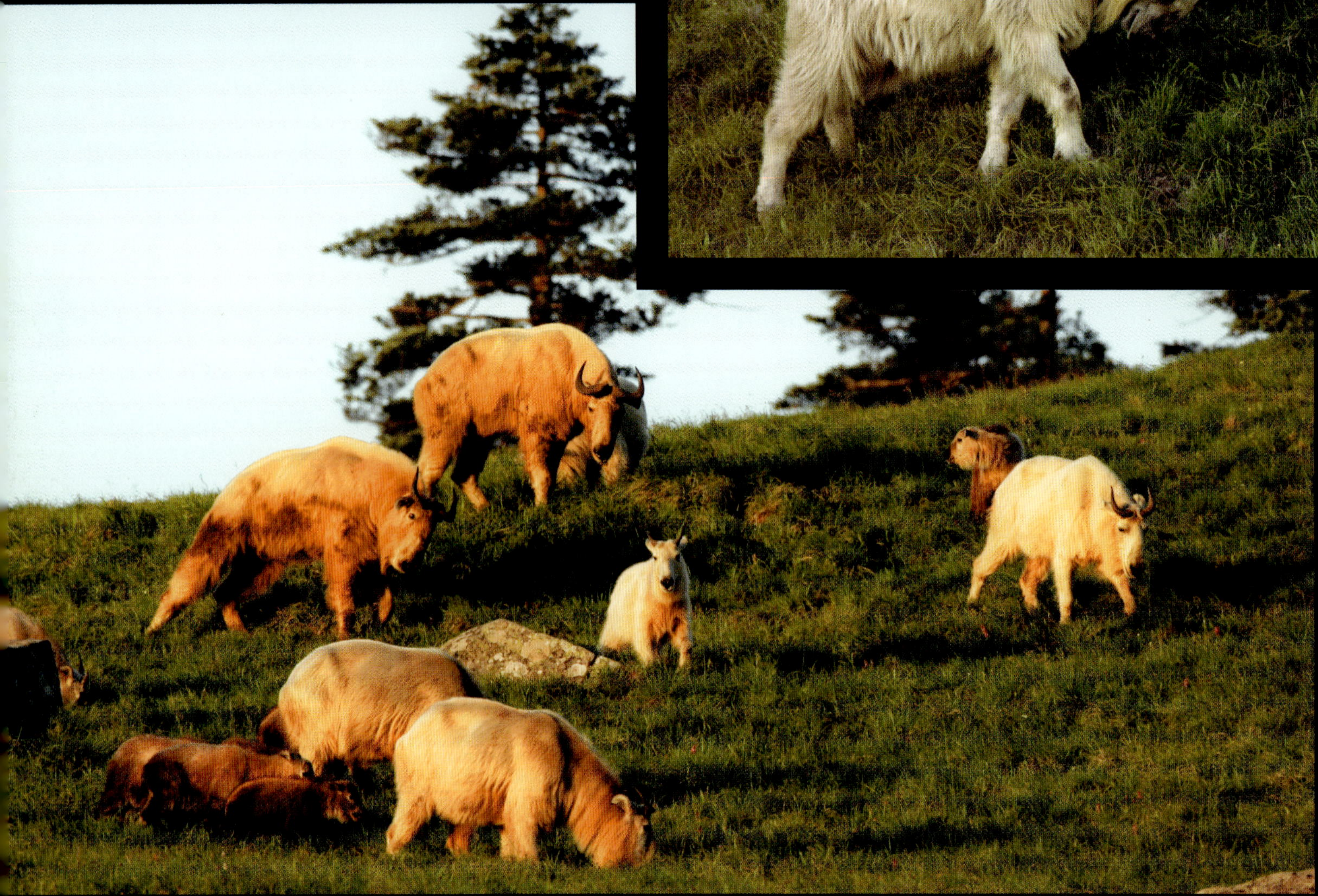

Above
On the alpine meadows in the summer, thanks to an agreeable climate and plenty of food, it is the season for takins to mate.

Left
Facing the rising sun, these takins are already looking for food on the alpine meadows of the Qinling Mountains.

On facing page
On the mountain ridge of the Tangjiahe Nature Reserve, a group of takins run towards the morning sun. Like most herbivores, takins are fond of living in groups. The number of a group ranges from ten to over a hundred. There are usually three forms, i.e. family group, community group, and gathering group. The family group, as the basic unit of the takins, is often composed of ten or so, with adult females, young males, and calves as members. Adult females assume the post as "heads" of the family group and always advance ahead of the group during migration. When looking for food as a group, they always stand guard on a high place.

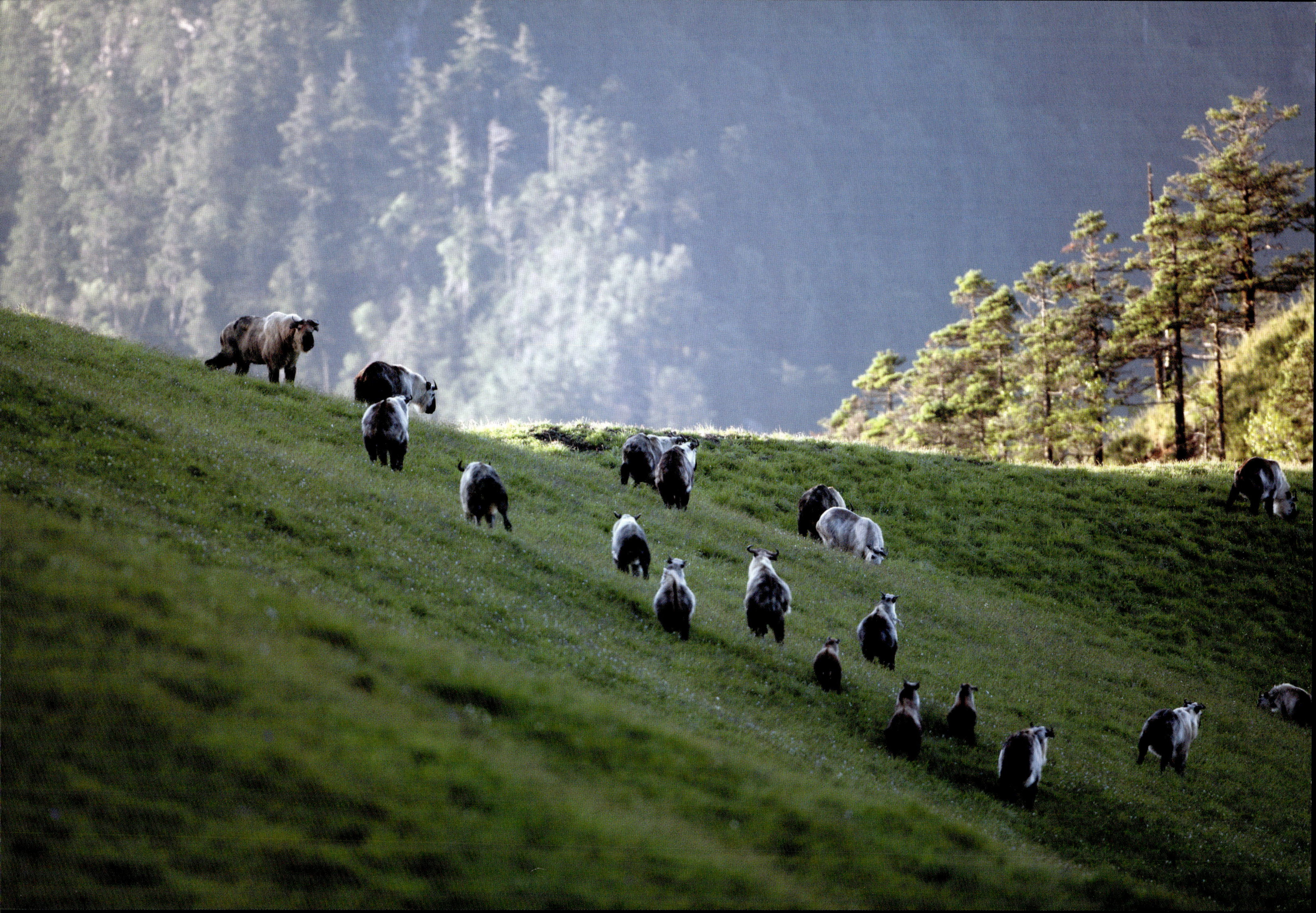

Giant Panda

Ailuropoda melanoleuca
IUCN Red List: Endangered

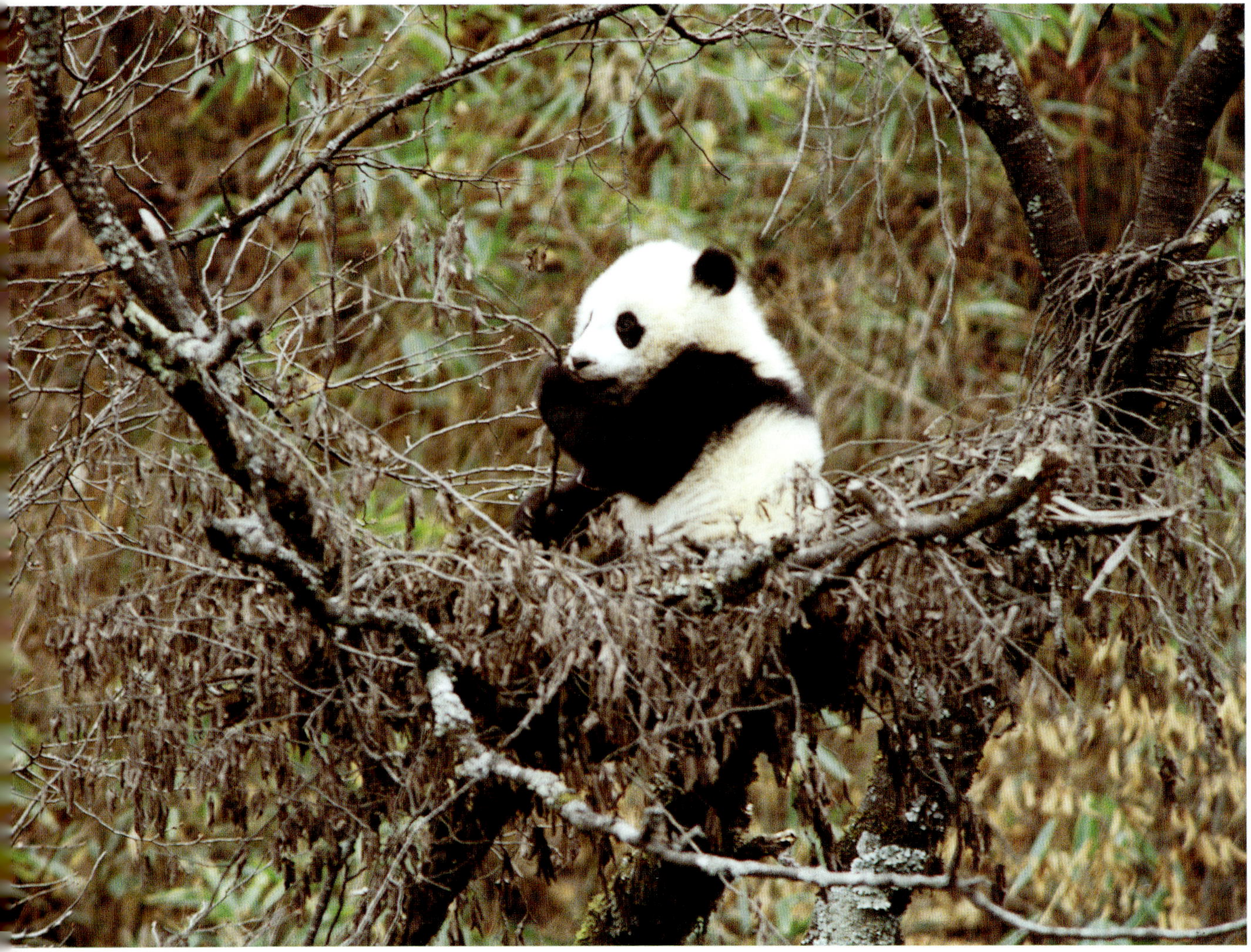

Giant pandas are one of the animals most well known to people. They are very much favored thanks to their black and white fur-color. In 1961, they were marked by the WWF right after its establishment, hence making them the most important symbol of species conservation.

They mainly live in areas with deciduous broad-leaved forests, coniferous and broad-leaved mixed forests, sub-alpine coniferous forests, and subtropical mountain bamboo forests. With great agility in the wilderness, they are good at climbing trees and run very fast when encountering danger. Like their bear relatives, adult pandas almost have no natural predators.

At present, there are two sub-species of giant pandas, i.e. *A.m. melanoleuca* and *A. m. qinlingensis,* which are respectively seen in Minshan Mountains of Sichuan province and the southern areas of Qinling Mountains in Shaanxi province. *A.m. melanoleuca* are very similar to bears, since they are marked by a big and long head and small teeth. *A. m. qinlingensis* are very similar to cats rather than bears, since they have a

At six-month-old, the giant panda is already agile and particularly good at climbing trees. Gaint pandas enjoy living alone. Each gaint panada has its own area for activities. Except for the rutting period, it usually lives by itself and moves around at night and in the daytime.

On facing page
Deep in the Qinling Mountains in March, this six-month-old panda is waiting on a tree for the return of its mother. It makes a wry expression at the camera and naughtily stretches out its small tongue.

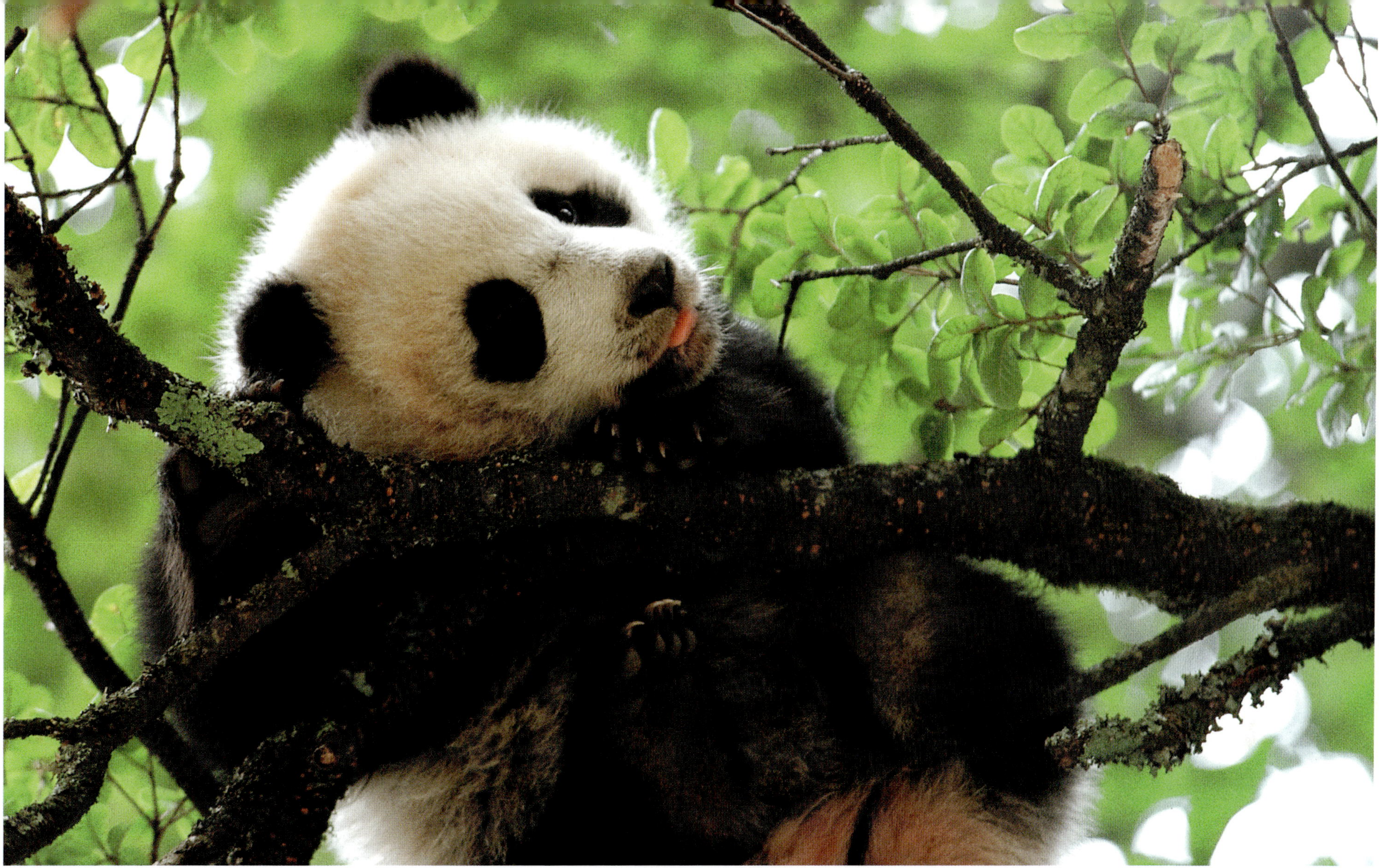

round head, a small skull, and big teeth, making them all the more lovelier. Therefore, *A. m. qinlingensis* are reputed as beauties among national treasures.

As carnivores, pandas sometimes prey on some small animals like bears do. A few of them eat meat occasionally, but they mainly eat bamboo. A panda eats bamboo of 10 to 20 kilograms per day and gains enough nutrition only after chewing for thousands of times. In recent years, the number of pandas has been declining since they are very fastidious about food and they cannot get enough bamboo due to the enormous development of bamboo groves.

Historically, pandas were quite extensively distributed in China. However, propagation of pandas in the wilderness is facing crisis due to destruction of their habitats, environmental pollution, and species separation. Thanks to the work of protection for many years, the number of wild giant pandas in some areas is beginning to rise. The panda became the mascot of 2008 Olympic Games in Beijing.

Golden Snub-Nosed Monkey

Rhinopithecus roxellana
IUCN Red List: Endangered

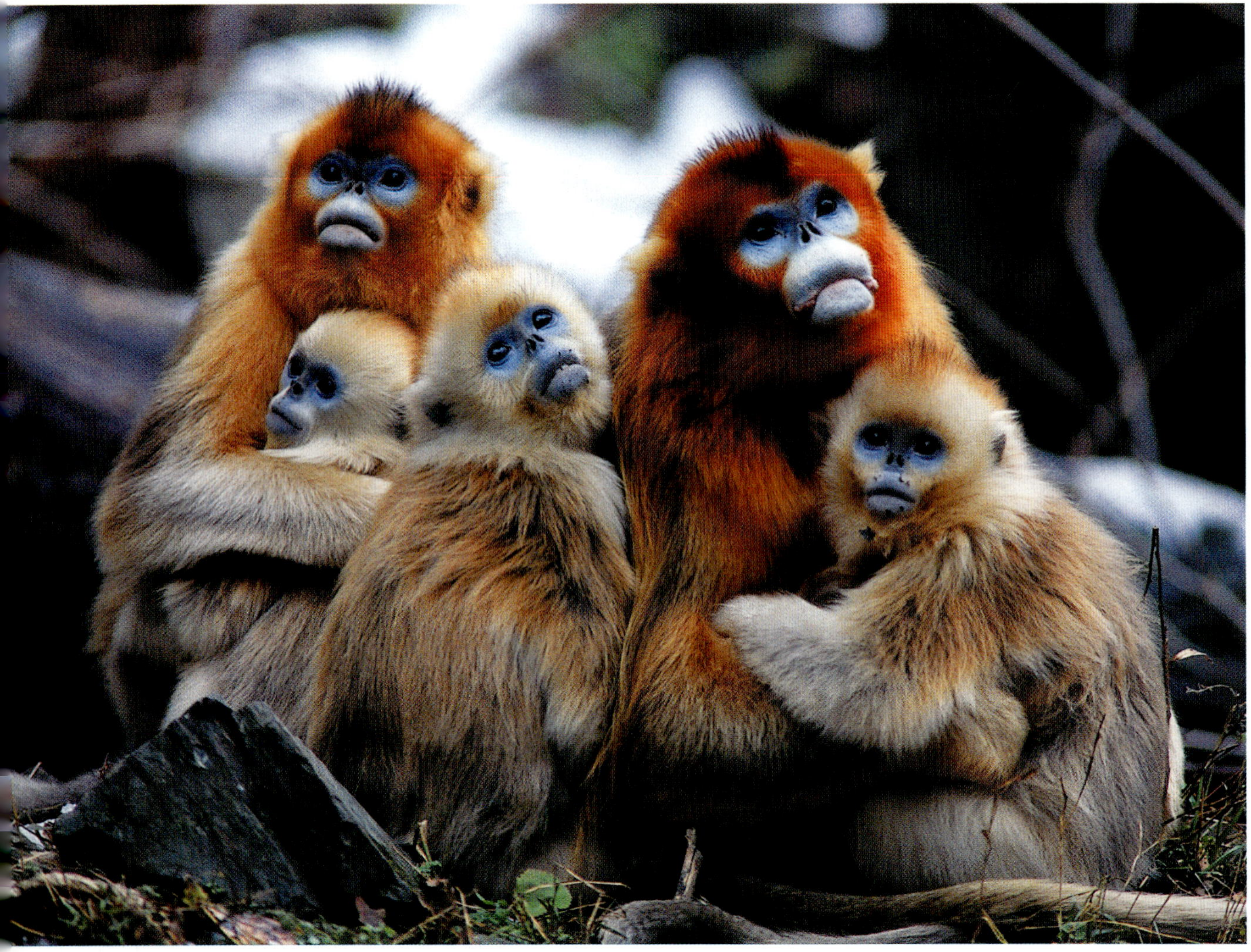

Golden snub-nosed monkeys are distributed in Minshan Mountains and Qionglai Mountains in Sichuan province, Qinling Mountains in southern Shaanxi province, Motianling Mountains in southern Gansu province, and Shennongjia Mountains in Hubei province. They live in coniferous and broad-leaved mixed forests of 2,000 to 3,000 meters above sea level. With the feature of vertical migration, they move around in mountain forests at high sea level in the summer and go to areas at low sea level in the winter. They have their own range of activities and relatively fixed routes. Golden snub-nosed monkeys are a sub-species seen in the extreme north among all those sub-species of Colobinae. Moving around in the daytime, they eat different kinds of food, e.g. tree-leaves, tender tree-buds, flowers, bamboo shoots, fruits, barks, insects, and bird's eggs.

They tend to live in a group of ten to over a hundred. The biggest group in Qinling Mountains has over 600. Each group has a few males and more females. Very often, as the leader, a big male takes

Three adolescent monkeys throw themselves closely into the arms of their parents. Part of a polygamous family, there is one or two more mothers and adolescents that have not come to participate in this photograph. Golden snub-nosed monkeys have a unique appearance; their face is blue with an upward turned nose and a big protruding mouth. An adult male has a dark-red "tumor-like" lump on either side of its mouth. Covered with golden hair, it has a brown-red face and neck-sides. The hair over the shoulder on the back of a male can be over 50 cm long, resembling a golden mantle. They deserve their name since they truly have golden hair among all the snub-nosed monkeys.

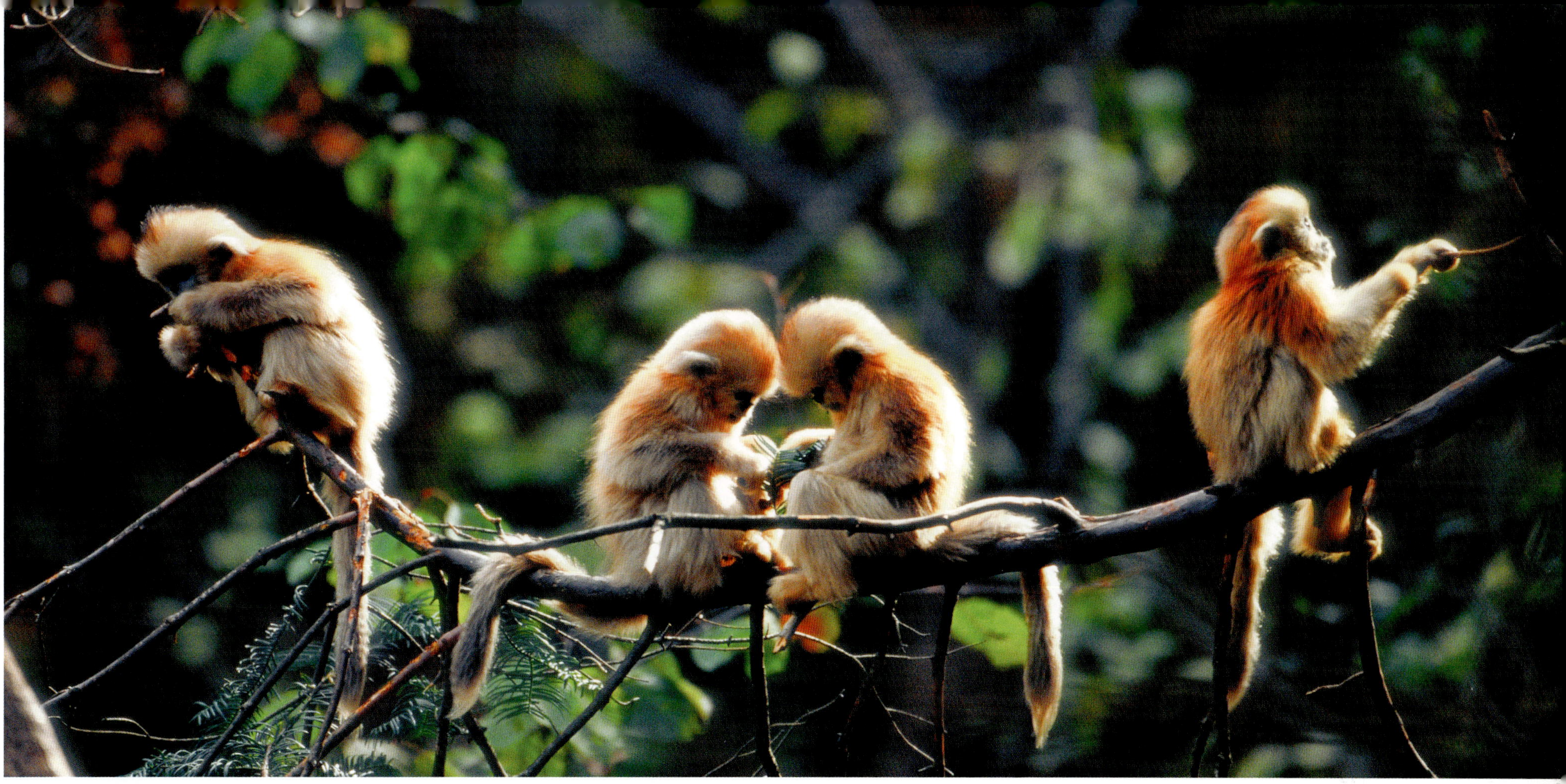

Playing is the most important link in the growth process of small monkeys. They learn to survive and grow up during the course of play.

many monkeys, male and female, old and young, to move around in the mountain forests. There is a sense of hierarchy that is not very strict and the ratio between the males and the females is 1:2 or 1:3. Along with the change of seasons, they often move up and down on mountains. They look for food at places at higher sea level in the summer and at lower sea level in the winter. Their natural predators include leopards, wolves, and hawk eagles. When finding enemies each time, they would call out an alarm and flee with the old and the young. Except for the occasional fight between two males, they are intimate and kind to each other, often combing hair and hugging among themselves, as well as holding each other during sleep. They would quickly hug each other or hum a little after slight frictions. Female monkeys have strong maternal instinct. All female monkeys love and take good care of infants and that they would vie with each other to hug newborn babies in their group. The period of their pregnancy lasts for seven months or so. Female monkeys become pregnant in the summer or autumn. They give birth in the spring or early summer, with one baby at a time. Newborn babies appear iron-grey in color, with red hands and red lips, a considerable color-contrast to adult monkeys. The breast-feeding period lasts for at least one year.

Golden snub-nosed monkeys have very beautiful golden fur that was regarded as a rare treasure as early as in ancient times. It is said that their fur provides very good warmth and effectively gets rid of moisture. It is also regarded by people of minority nationalities as an object of warding off evils. Also, their bones, meat, and inner organs can be used as medicine. All this make them prey to hunting by people. The most serious destruction took place in the period between

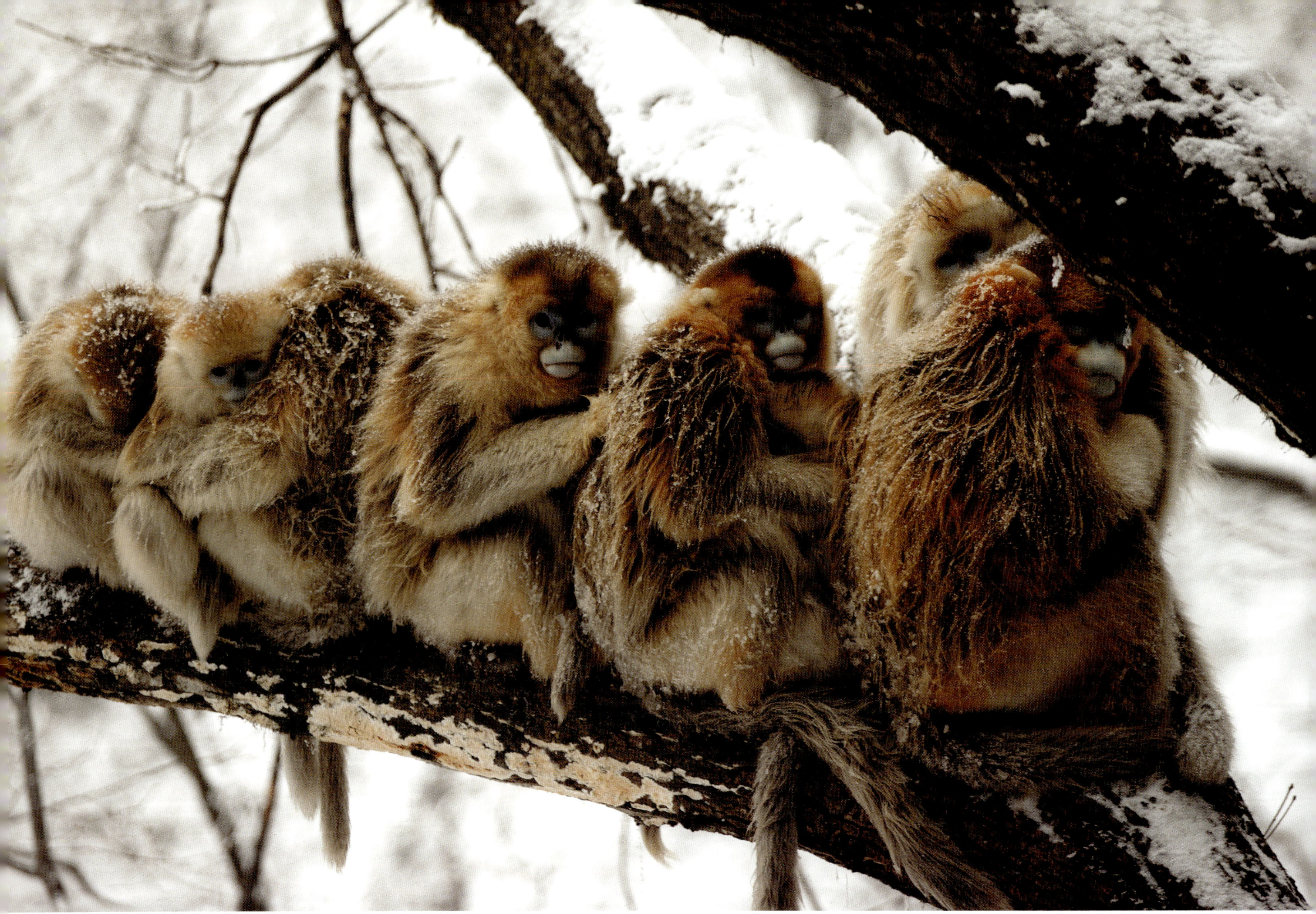

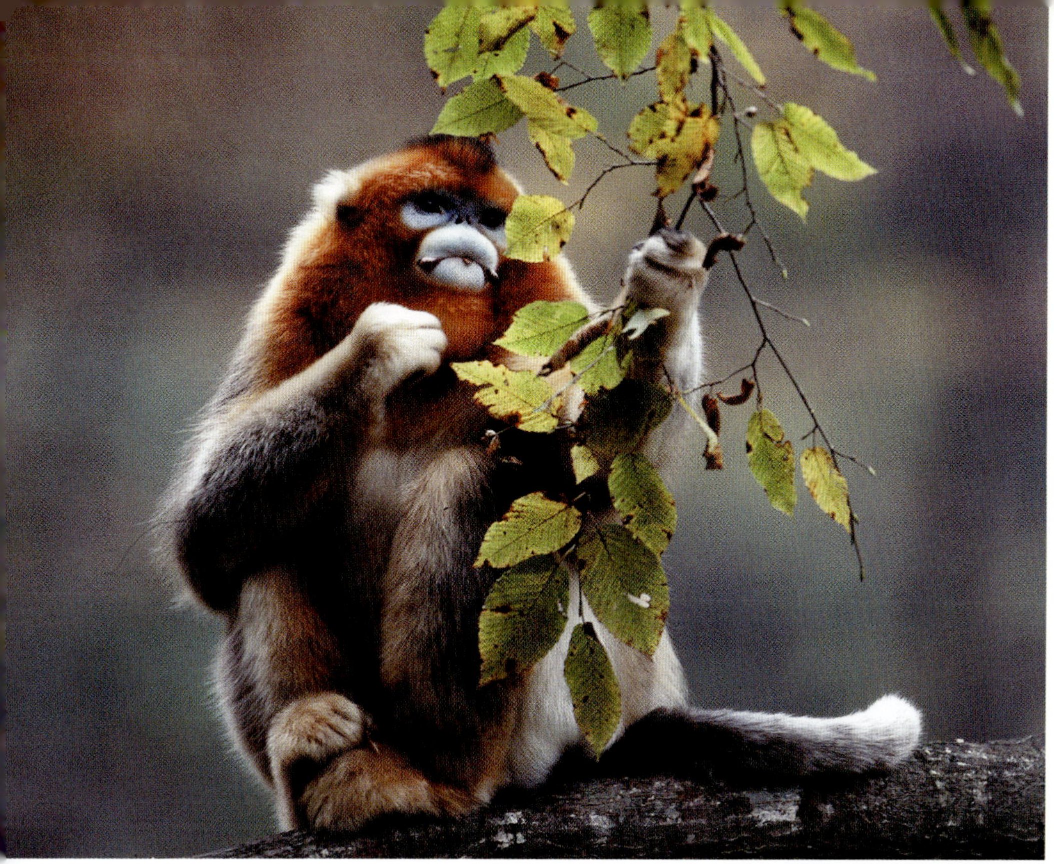

1963 and 1974. In Sichuan province only, 300 were killed according to incomplete statistics.

The habitats of golden snub-nosed monkeys are overlapped with those of giant pandas. Since the protection of giant pandas through the establishment of nature reserves started earlier, golden snub-nosed monkeys have appeared in many places. Compared with Guizhou snub-nosed monkeys and Yunnan snub-nosed monkeys, the number of golden snub-nosed monkeys is the greatest. Along with the implementation of policies by the Chinese government in fully banning the cut down of natural forests, habitats of golden snub-nosed monkeys have been brought under protection. Thanks to the pressure from the public as well as laws and decrees, illegal hunting has disappeared.

On facing page
In the cold winter, with their golden hair frozen with ice and frost, they nestle up against one another to keep themselves warm.

Above
Leaves begin to turn yellow in the Qinling Mountains in the autumn. A big male adult monkey is sitting on the trunk and holding a bunch of drooping leaves, perhaps thinking, "Oh my leaves, can't you be greener and more tender?"

Right
The mother is looking at the camera while holding her baby in her arms. The baby is looking timidly around.

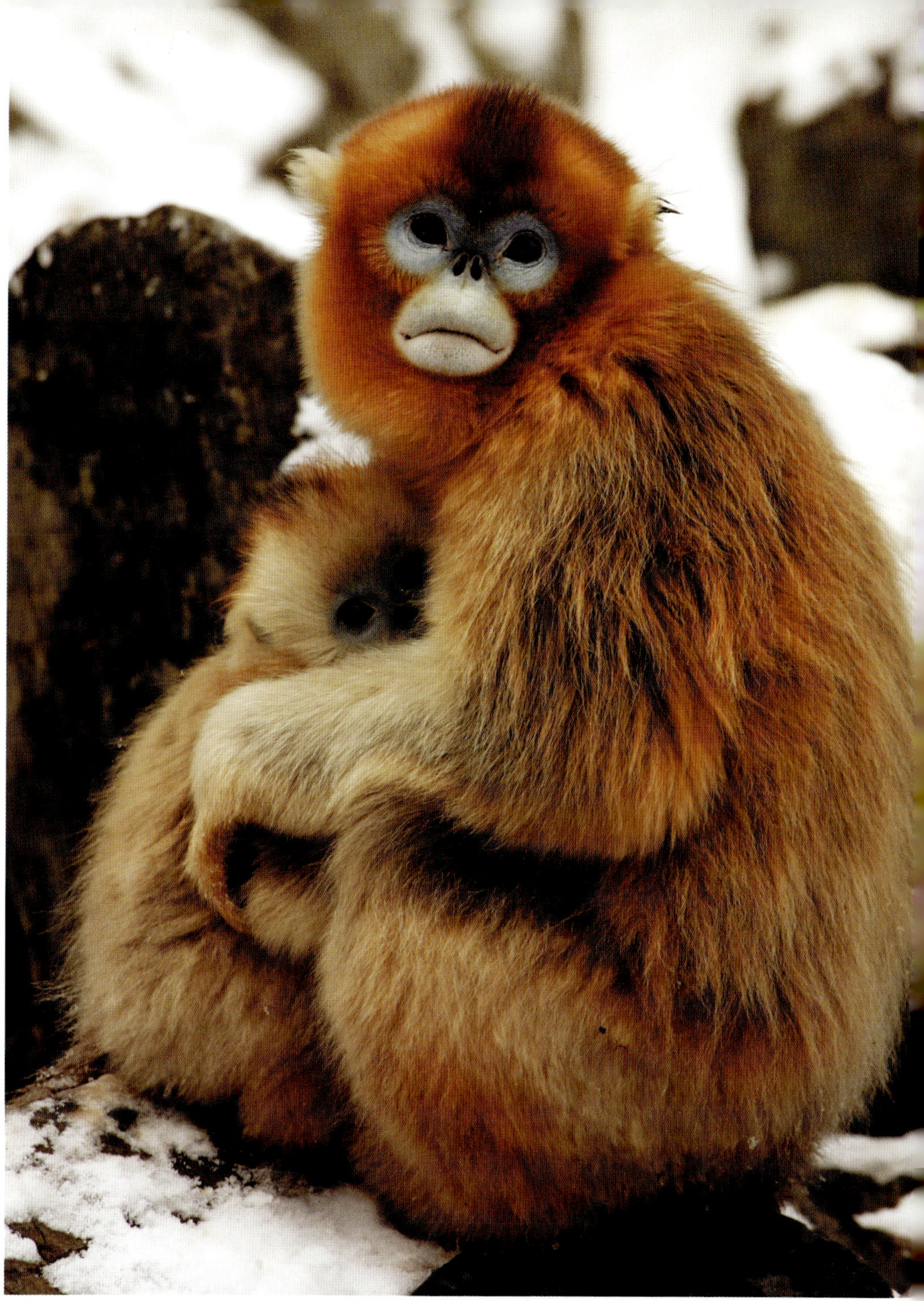

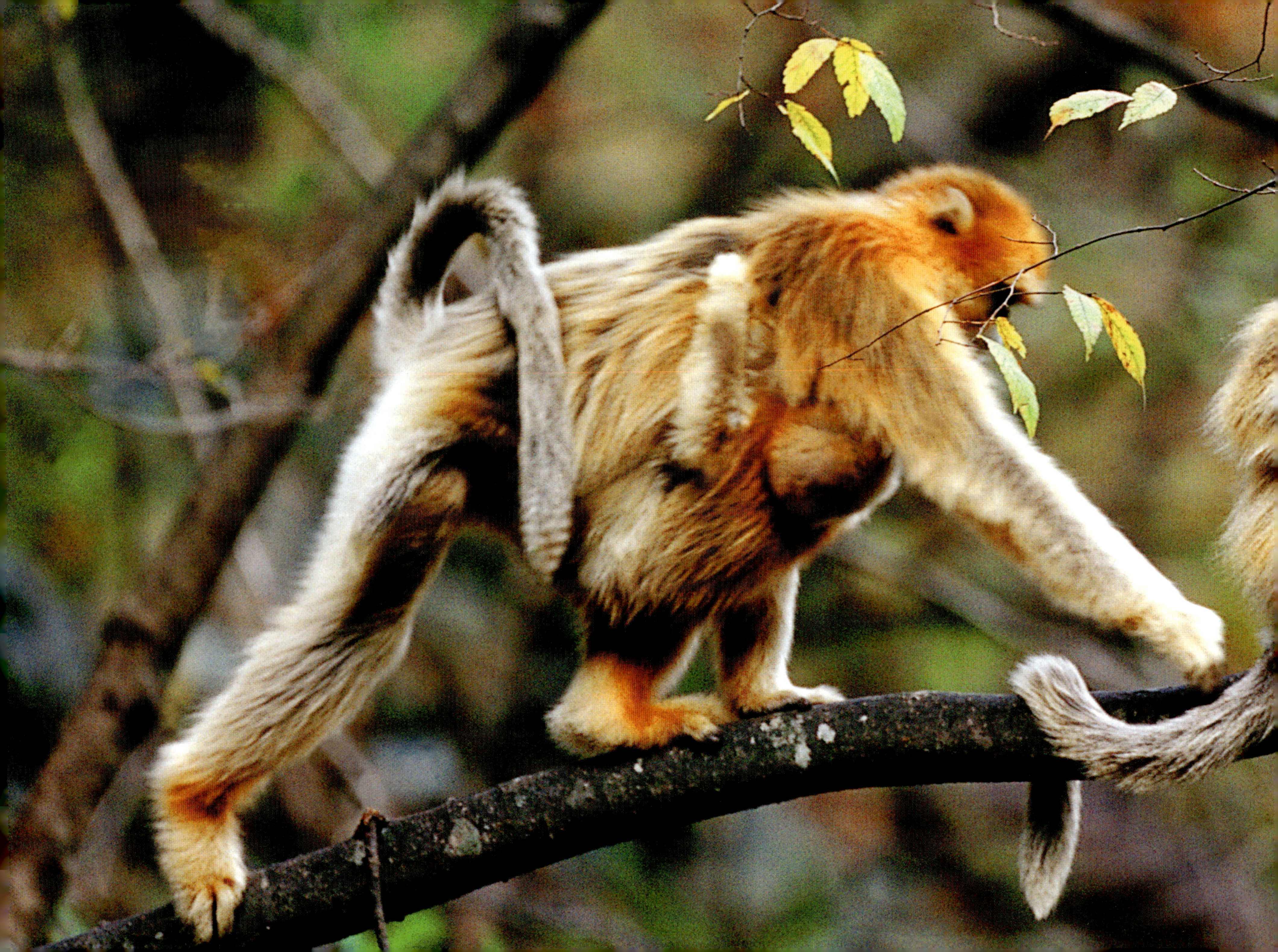

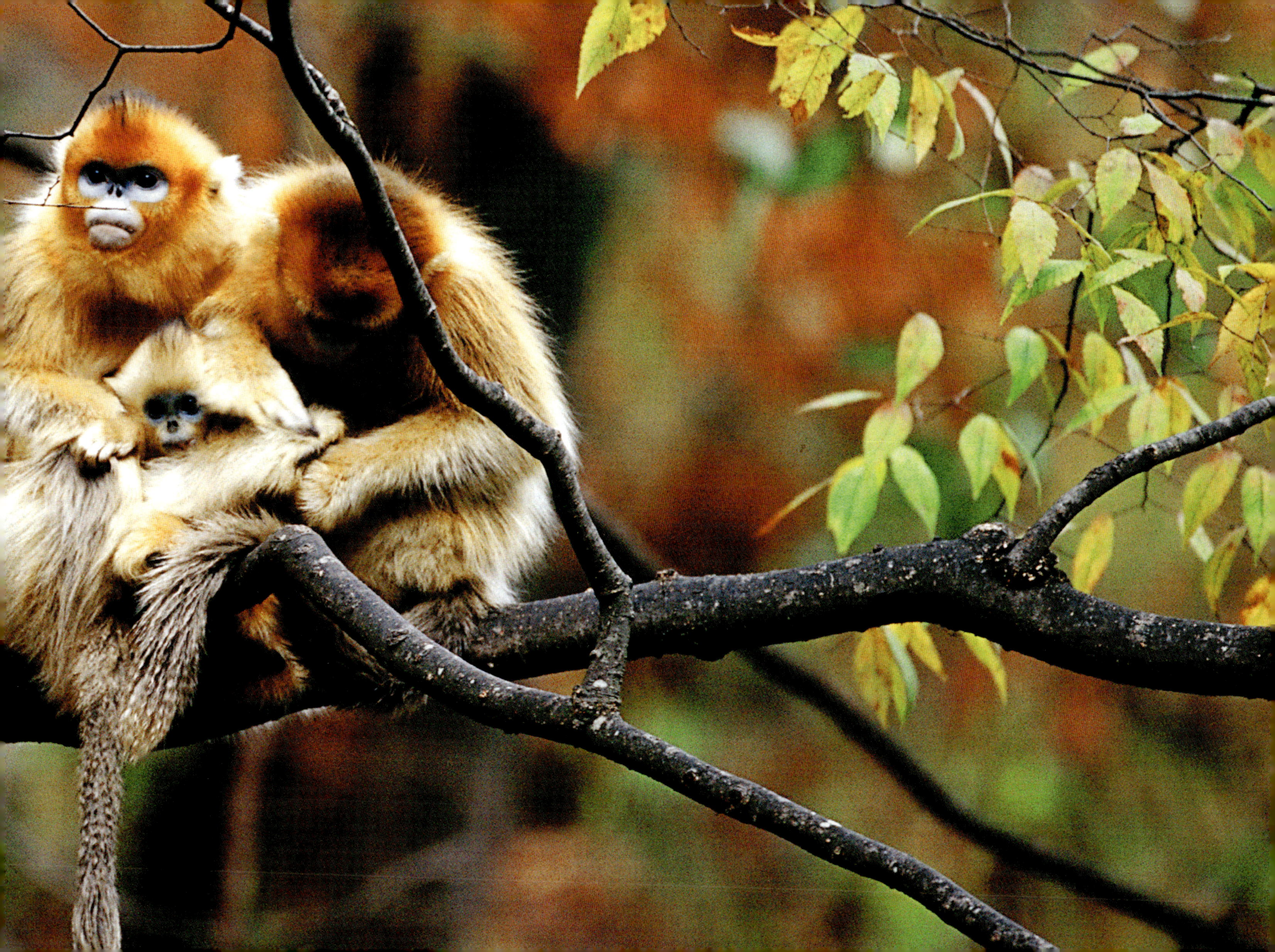

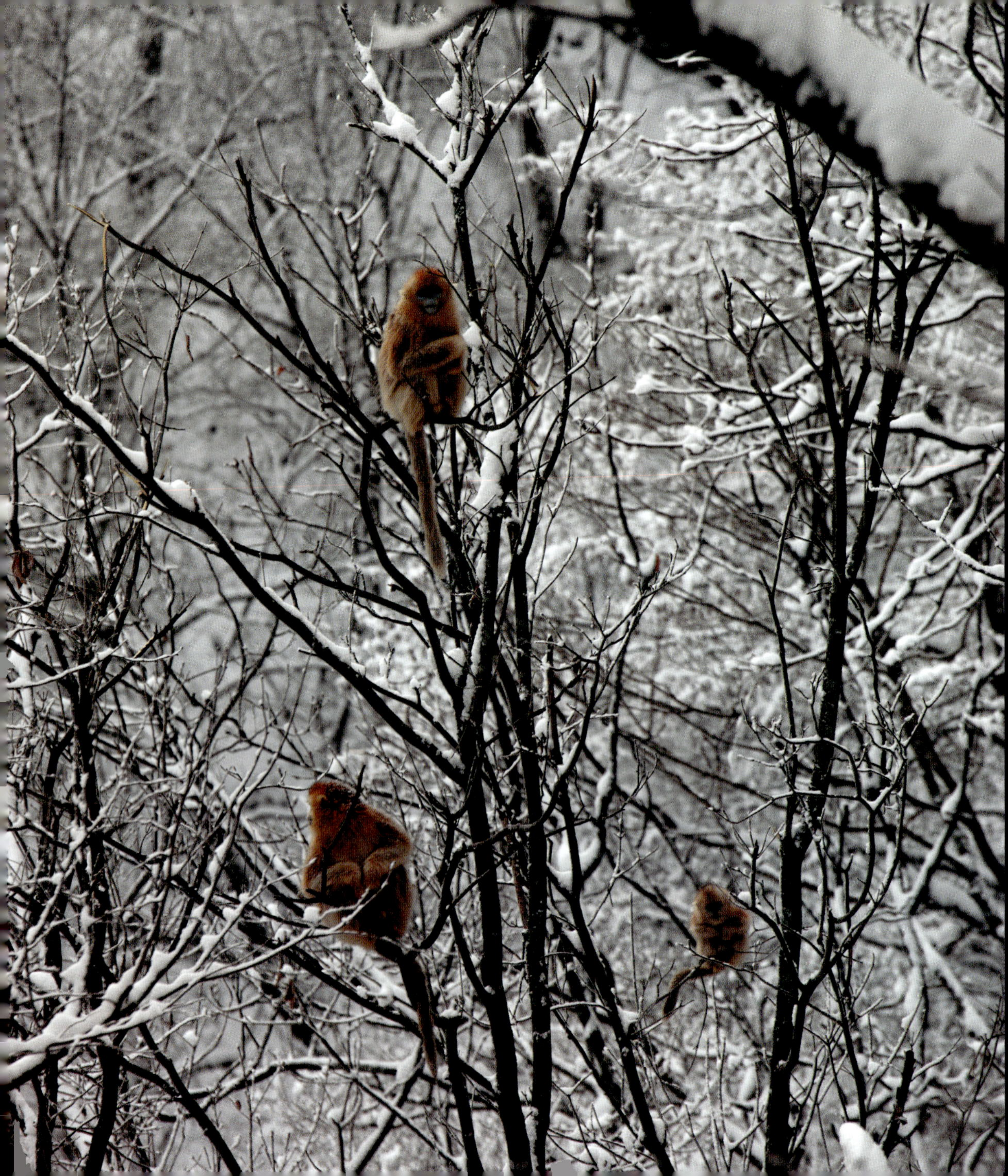

On previous spread
On an autumn afternoon, three mothers are sharing their experiences about child rearing.

Left
When the Qinling Mountains is covered with heavy snow, they have to feed on barks.

Below
As recorded by a high-speed shutter, a rapidly running small monkey is like a ballet dancer on the snowy ground.

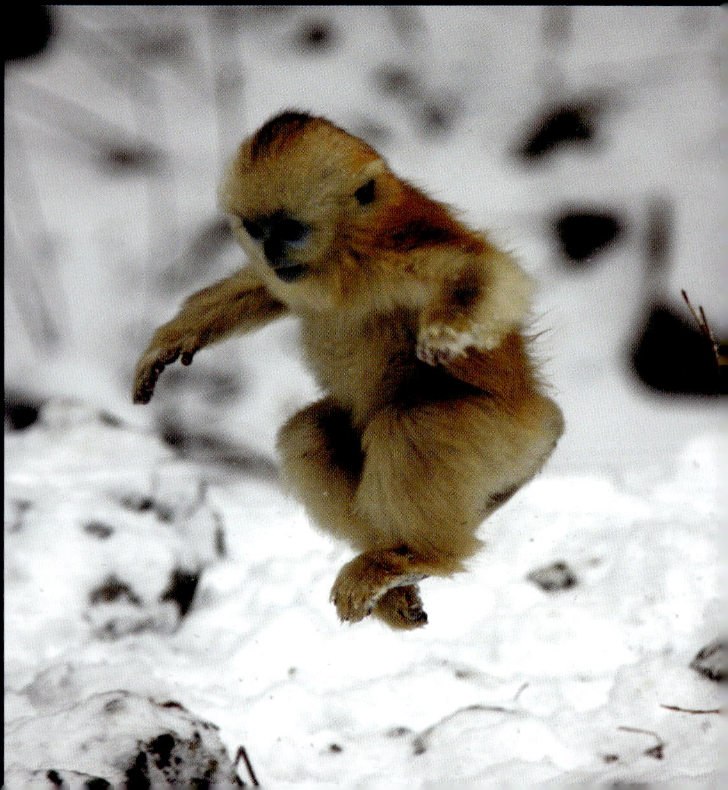

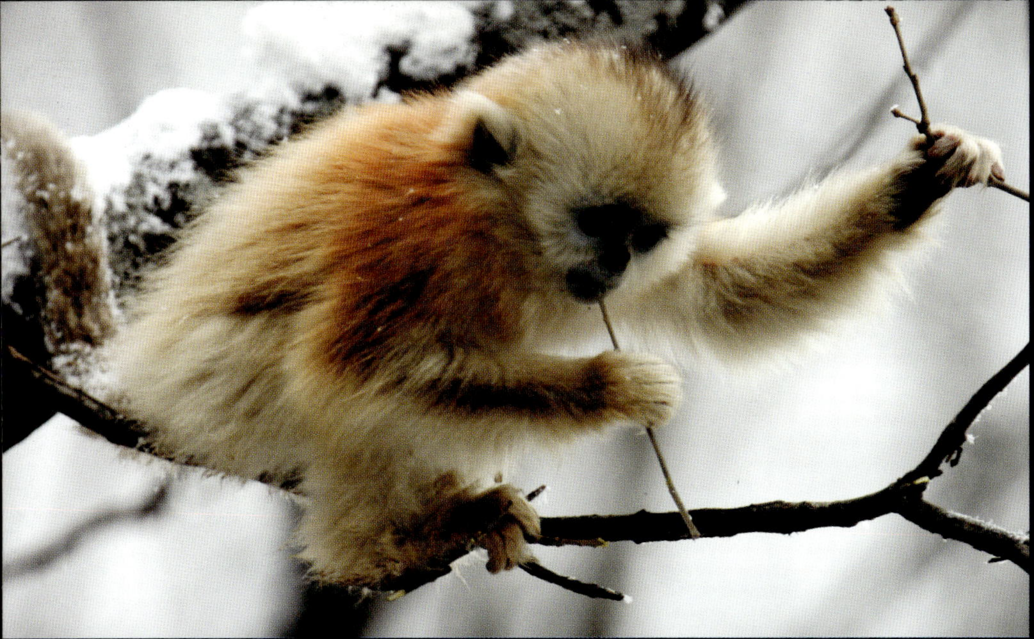

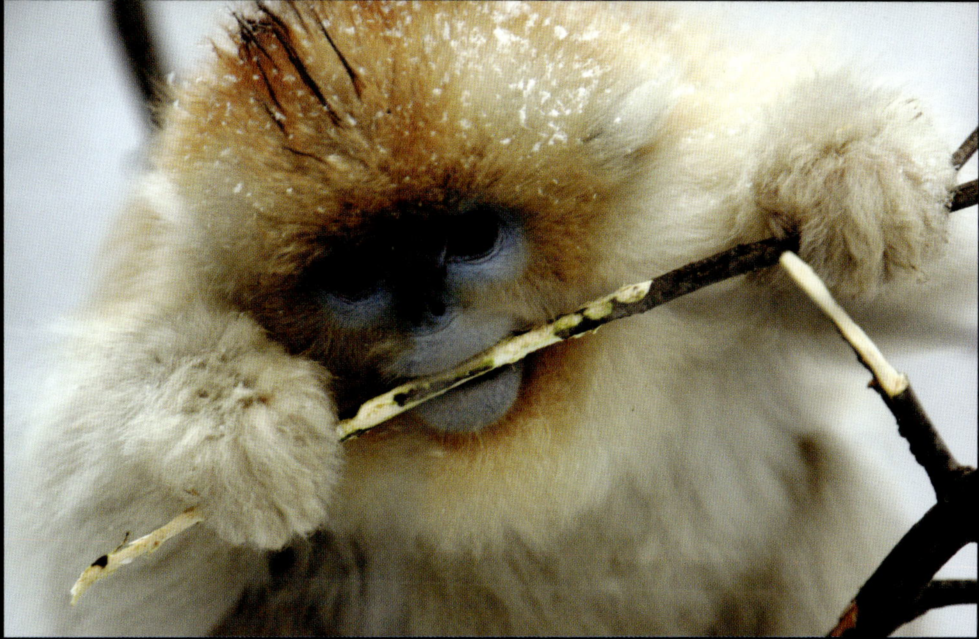

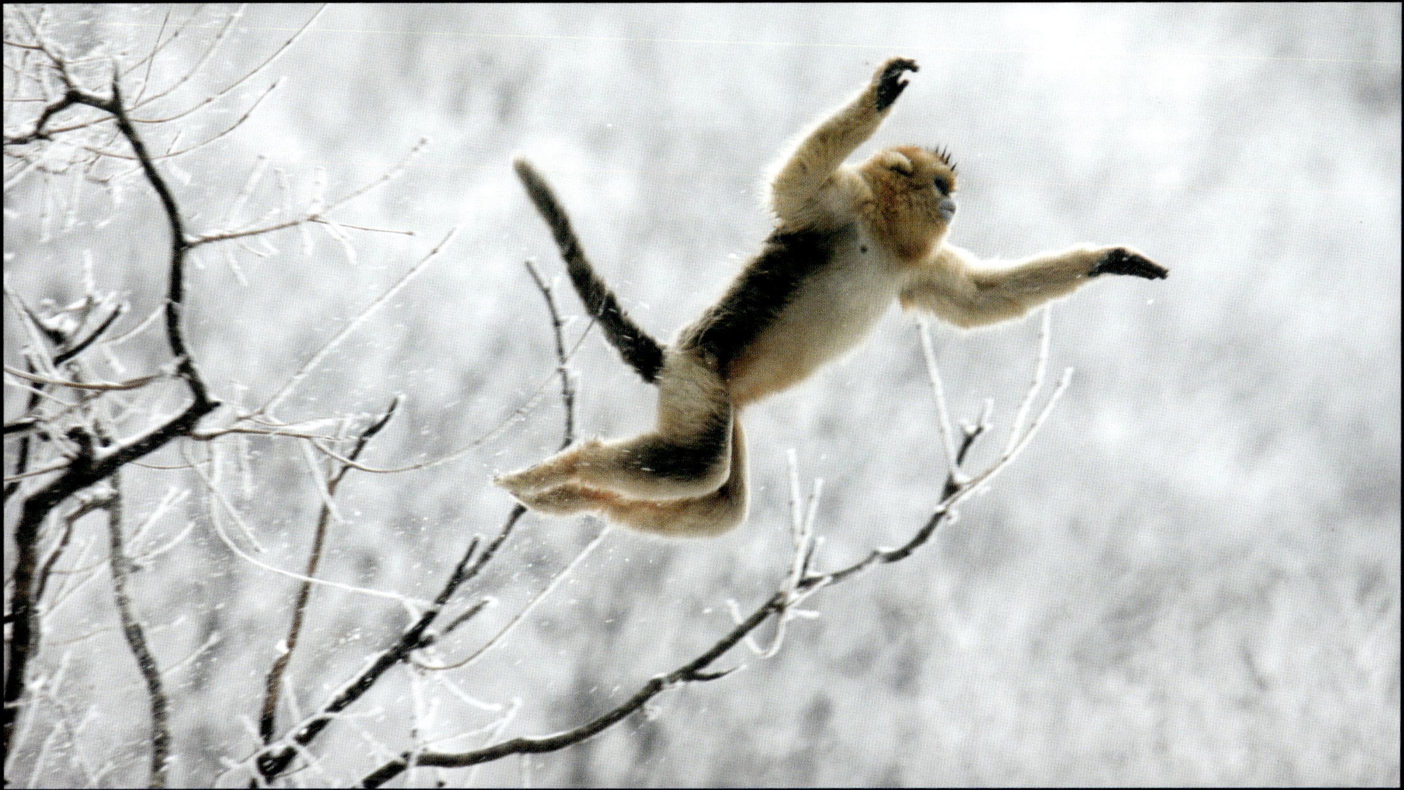

1 2

As the whole valley is covered with heavy snow, small monkeys are gnawing on barks.

Left

High-speed continuous shooting has caught the instant moment when a big male monkey is leaping freely way.

Chinese Goral

Naemorhedus griseus
IUCN Red List: Vulnerable

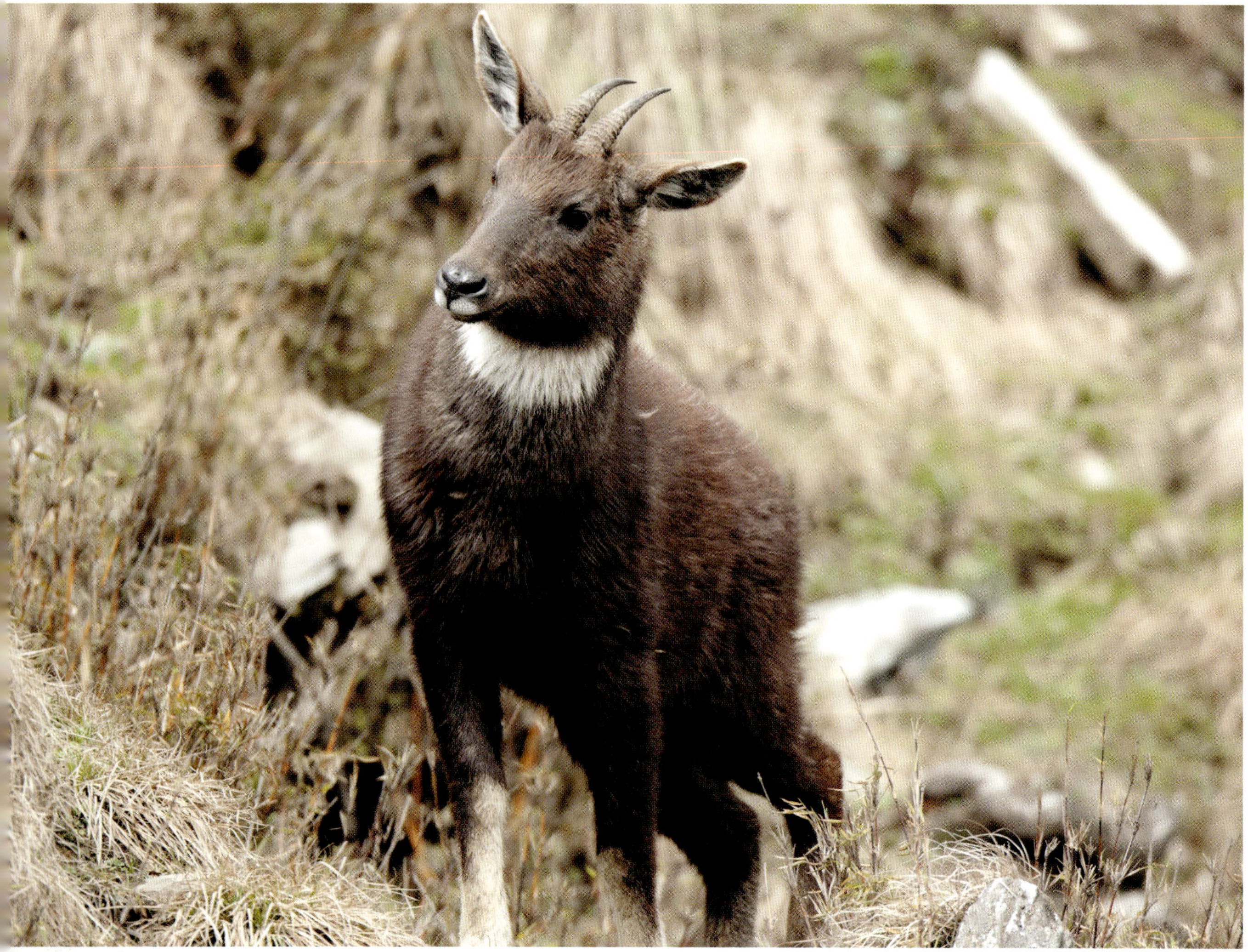

Gorals are a kind of small goat-antelope. Under their coarse and fluffy hair, there is fine hair like sheep wool. They can be found in areas across the Himalayas, Siberia, northern India, Indo-China Peninsula, northeast China, and the Korean Peninsula in the east. So far, all four kinds of gorals known in the world are seen in the rugged mountains of China.

Chinese gorals are the most extensively distributed and the most commonly seen among the four kinds, i.e. they are found in northern China, eastern China, southern China, and southwestern China. Though they are as big as goats, they do not have a beard. A Chinese goral is 110 to 130 centimeters long and weighs 40 to 50 kilograms. Both the male and the female have black short and straight horns.

Living in mountain forests of over 4,000 meters above sea level, they move around either individually or in small groups, eating various green grass, tender branches, and the leaves of bushes and fruit. Mostly coming out in the morning and at dusk, they are very good at leaping and climbing on steep cliffs. Generally, they dig into the earth to rest at places with a shelter along rocks. Sometimes,

They are quite extensively seen in China. Their hair changes according to the different areas. Generally, they are grey-brown with brown patterns on the back and a white stripe on the throat. Their limbs are short and evenly distributed and their hoofs are narrow and robust. They have black, short, and straight horns of 15 to 20 cm long, bending slightly inward with sharp ends.

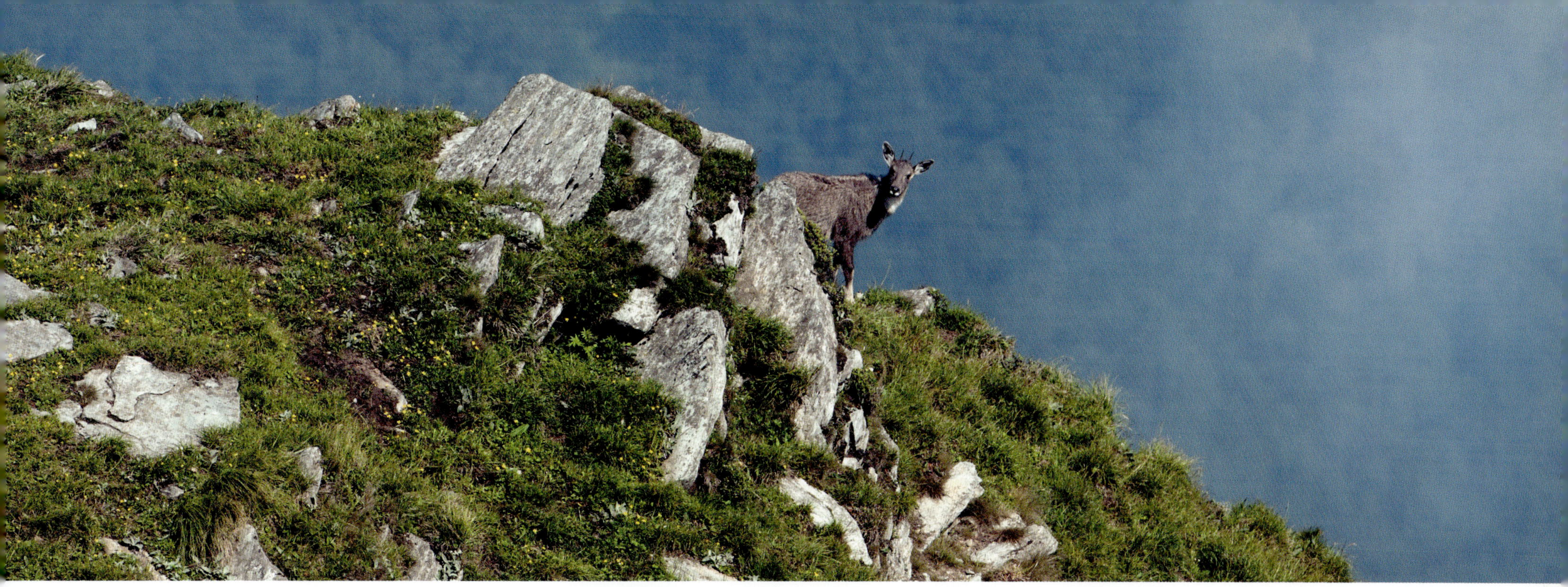

Above
Chinese gorals are very good at jumping and climbing on cliffs. Places under rocks are ideal for them to rest. This goral has protruded its head from its small den, wondering who has disturbed its sleep.

Right
In the summer, meadows on high mountains are fully covered with flowers. A Chinese goral is roaming amidst the flowers.

they rest on protruding rocks. They have a very acute sense of vision and hearing which help them escape from their natural predators in time.

Male Chinese gorals usually live on their own, but sometimes fall into a pair or a small group. They begin to rut in late autumn and early winter. The pregnancy period of female Chinese gorals lasts six months or so, with a single offspring or two each time.

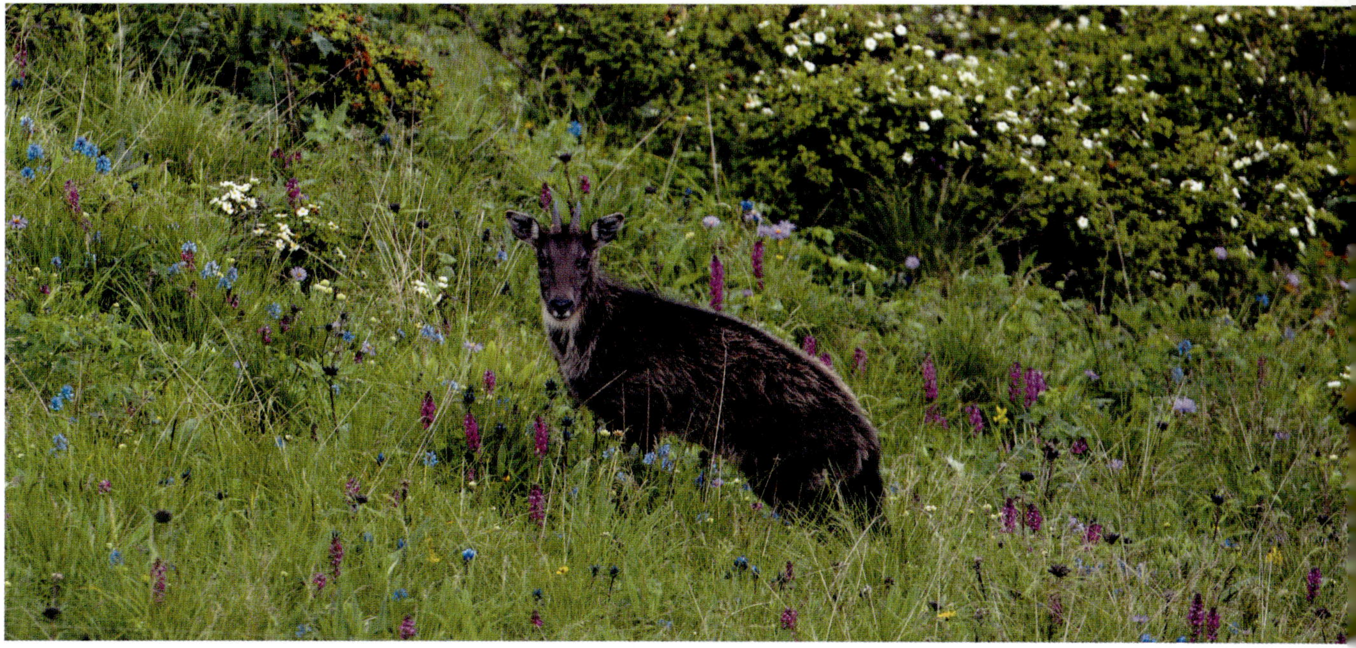

Sambar

Rusa unicolor

IUCN Red List: Vulnerable

As the biggest deer in the tropical and subtropical areas, a sambar is 140 to 260 centimeters long with a tail of 20 to 30 centimeters long. It weighs 100 to 200 kilograms and the biggest can weigh over 300 kilograms. The male sambar has a pair of large and rugged antlers. They have only three tines. The longest antlers can be up to 100 cm. They are found all over in the tropical and subtropical areas in southern and southwest China, including Hainan province and Taiwan. They live in forests, bushes, hills, and secondary marshes. Without fixed dens, they are marked by vertical migration along slopes, extending to places of 3,700 meters above sea level. With a large range of activities, they seldom go to places far away from water, but they would sometimes risk going to farmlands. They eat grass, leaves of small trees, ferns, and fruit.

Sambars are very adaptable to rugged mountains, since their hard hoofs enable them to move around in mountain forests full of rocks and pebbles. Their four limbs are long and forceful, making it easy for them to stroll back and forth across steep ravines.

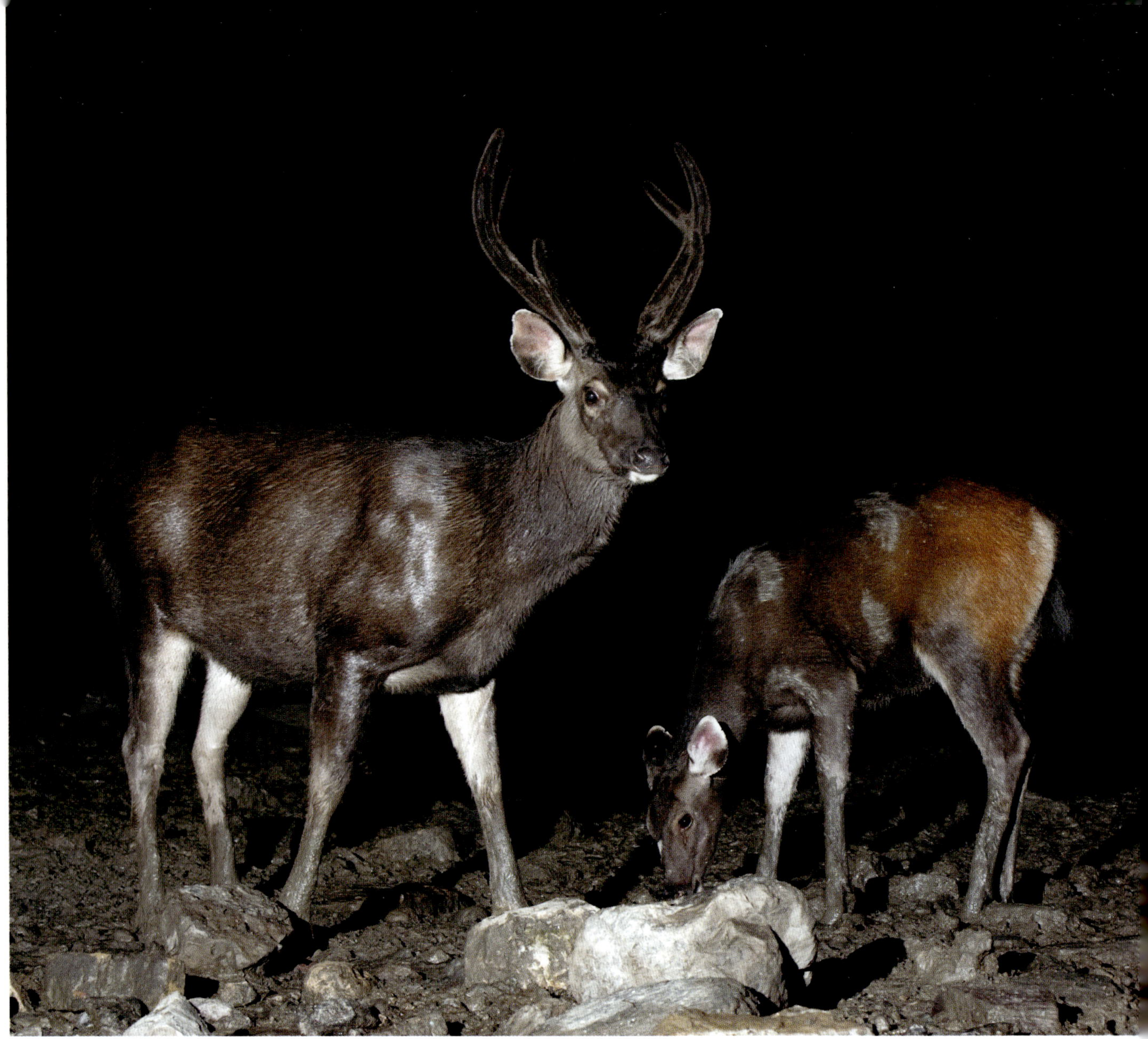

When night falls, a group of sambars lick salt at a deserted work shed. In the daytime, they hide themselves in the dense woods.

They often move around in a small group of less than five. In the period of propagation, a male and a female can be seen roaming together. But male sambars often move around alone during non-propagation time. They mostly start activities in the early morning and at night. In the daytime, they hide themselves amidst dense vegetation and look for food in more expansive places in the evening. They can often be found at places where they can lick salty soil, with which they can have minerals, particularly when males are in the period of growing new horns.

Chestnut-Throated Partridge

Tetraophasis obscurus
IUCN Red List: Least Concern

As birds unique to China, chestnut-throated partridges are found chiefly in rocky areas with pines, firs, coniferous, and coniferous and broad-leaved mixed forests, as well as azalea bushes. They generally move around in small groups.

Chestnut-throated partridges are marked by a strong adaptability to the natural conditions of high mountains. They are fond of drinking water by small streams and chiefly feed on plants. Their food changes according to different seasons. In the period from April to May, they mainly eat plant roots. In the period from August to September, they eat lots of fritillaries. After September, they eat berries, nuts, and seeds.

Their propagation takes place in the period from May to June, in which they mostly move around in pairs and sometimes in small groups composed of sub-adults. They build up two kinds of nests. In addition to building up nests in holes under steep cliffs and rocks, bushes, and weeds on the ground, they also build up nests on trees, which is unique in the family of pheasants.

Not long after they were born, the juveniles would be able to leave the nest to look for food together with their parents. When encountering danger, the mother would scream while running away, and then all the juveniles would flee in different directions at once, quickly sneaking into grass or rock-cracks. They will not come out until their mother screams a call for their return after the danger is over.

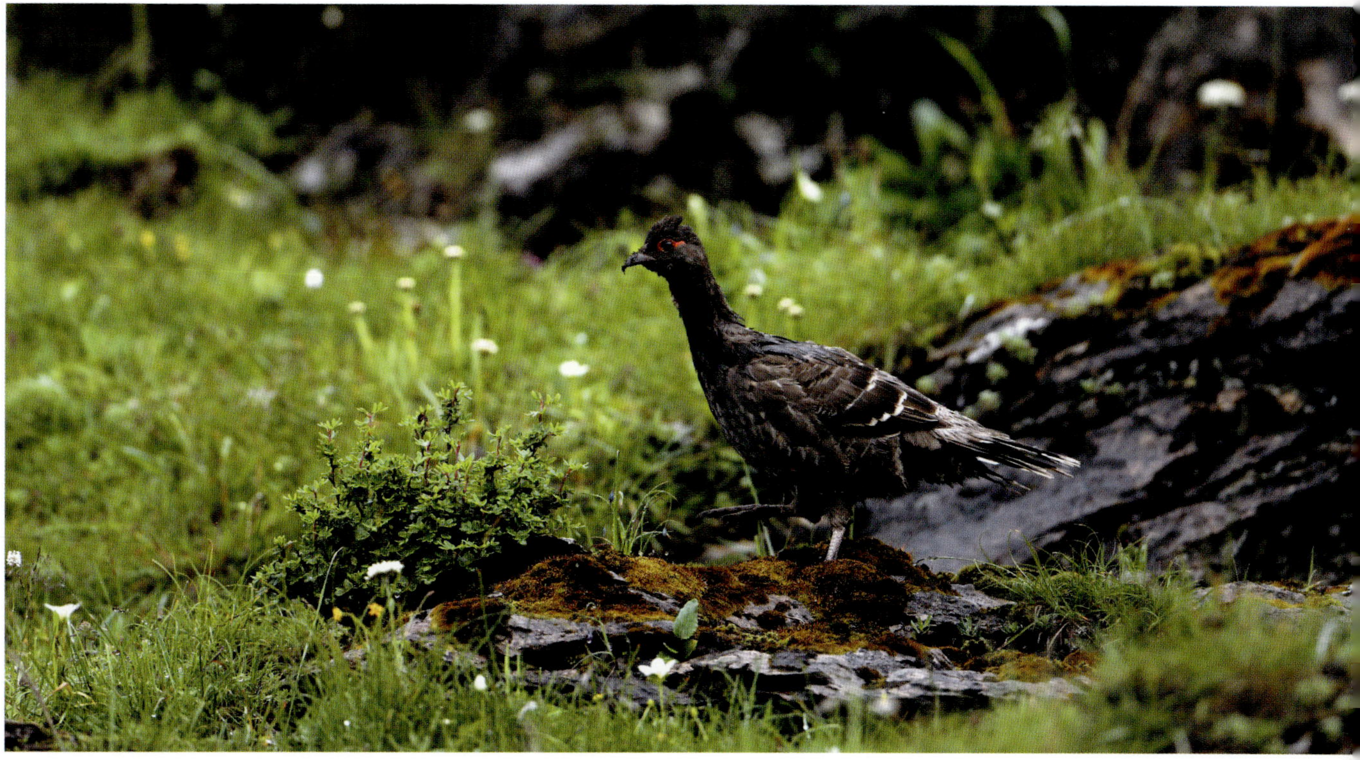

In the early morning, after a day of pouring rain, a chestnut-throated partridge steps out of the bush.

Due to the high sea level at places of their inhabitation, as well as restriction of terrains and topography, no continuous distribution among the groups can be formed. Moreover, economic activities of human beings in sub-alpine mountains have been increasingly frequent in recent years, resulting in more and more threats and damage to the environment of their existence. Being that illegal hunting and picking of bird's eggs take place from time to time, it affects the normal propagation of chestnut-throated partridges.

Crested Ibis

Nipponia nippon

IUCN Red List: Endangered

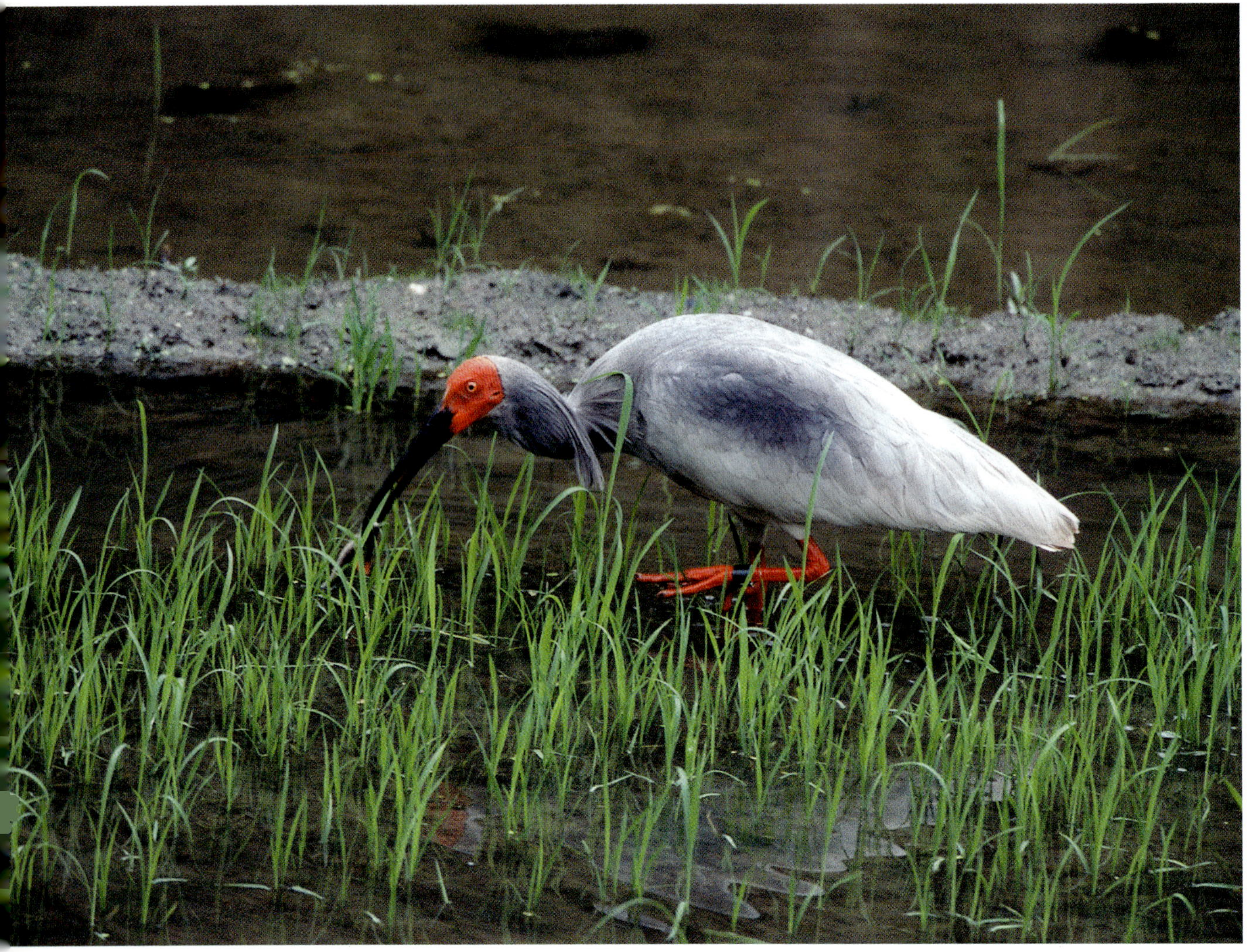

As a kind of medium-size water bird, common folks regard crested ibises as a lucky omen, leading to the name "auspicious birds." They live in temperate mountain forests and hills that are mostly in the vicinity of paddy fields, river beach, pools, streams, and marshes. Introverted, calm, and timid, they tend to fall into pairs or small groups. With higher demands for the habitats, they only like tall trees for resting and building nests and paddy fields and marshes with food available, as well as a tranquil environment without natural predators.

Spring is the season for their propagation. Adult males and females become spouses, which then leave the group that was formed during the winter. They are scattered on tall arbor trees, such as cork oaks to build nests and lay eggs.

Two to four eggs are laid in each nest. Eggs appear blue-grey or light green with black brown spots. The male and the female hatch eggs in turn, and the hatching period lasts for about 28 days. The upper part of the juveniles has light grey fine feathers and its lower part has white fine feathers. Their feet are orange red. In turn, parents spit out semi-digested food to feed them and eager

During the season of propagation, their napes emit a kind of lead-grey substance, which they try to smear all over their body to make themselves dark in order to reduce the chances of being discovered by their predators.

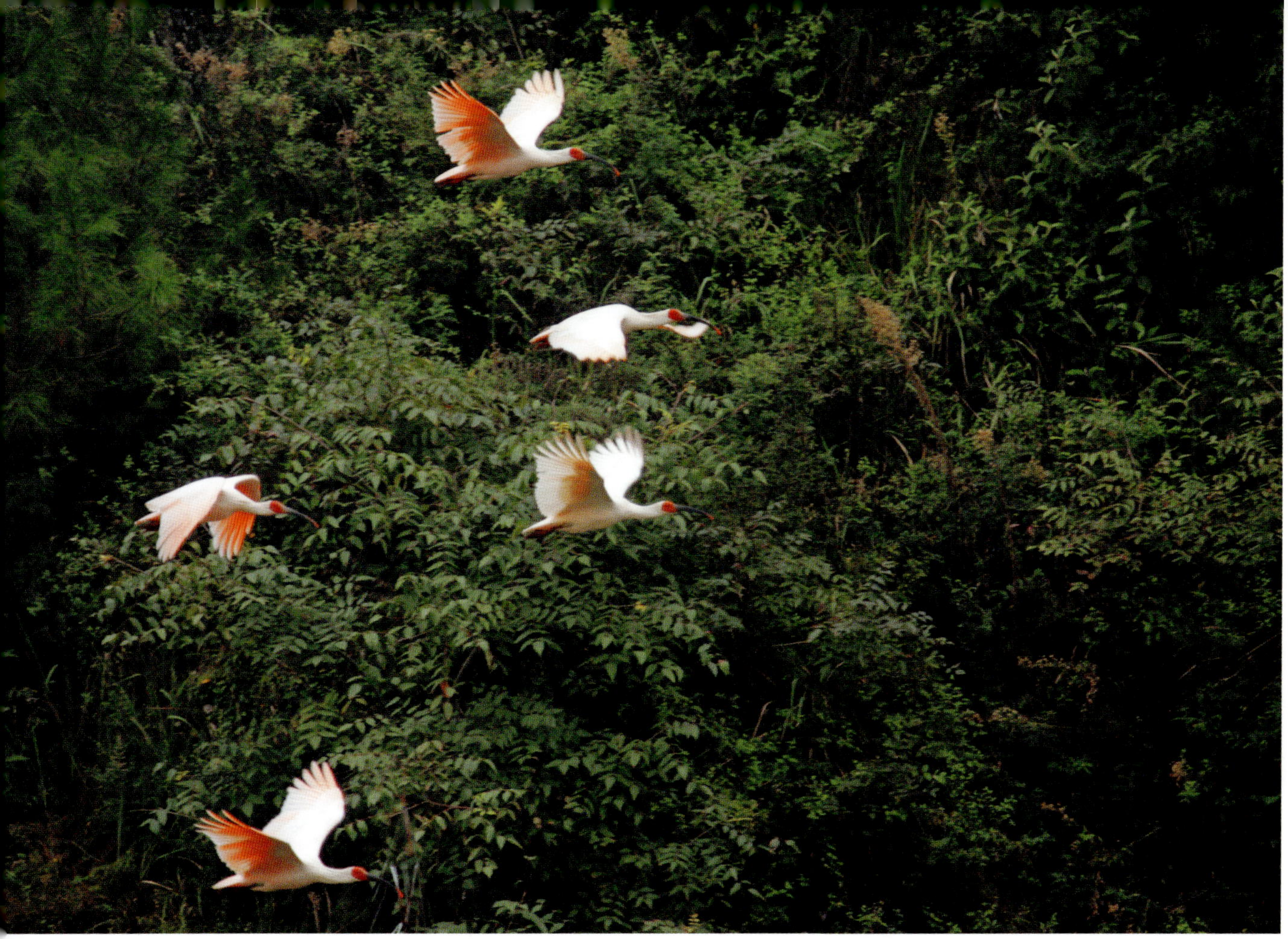

Left
With propagation over, their gorgeous feathers reappear and look like rubies under the sunshine.

Below
On a pine tree on the southern slope of the Qinling Mountains, a mother crested ibis is feeding her babies. The face of an adult crested ibis is vermeil, while the face of an infant crested ibis is orange-yellow. Their beak is fine, long, and curves downward. Their napes are covered with a willow-leaf-shaped crest composed of dozens of long thick feathers.

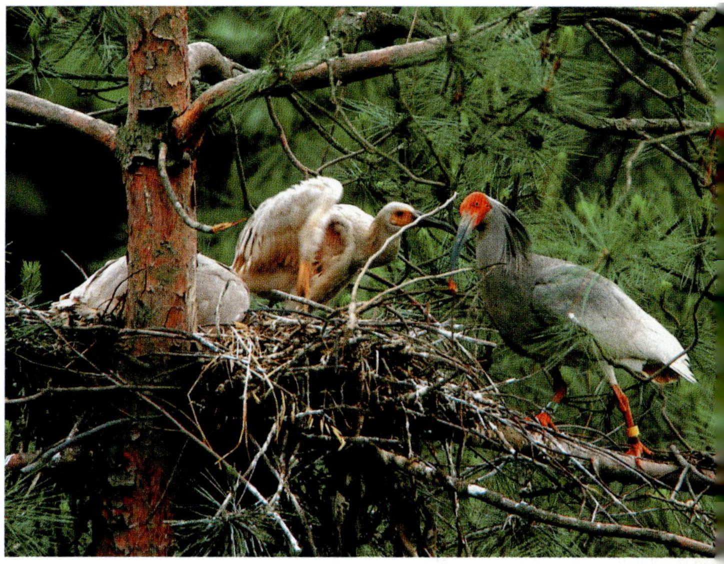

juveniles vie with each other to extend their long bills into the mouth of their parents, who forcefully shake their necks to spit out the food as quickly as possible. With this done, parents would help the juveniles clean the droppings in the nest by picking away tree-branches at the bottom of the nest so that the droppings can leak through, or they would pick away pieced cushions stained with droppings and then bring new nest materials and cushions as supplements. Immature crested ibises grow very quickly under the meticulous care of their parents. In sixty days, they would be able to fly freely with their parents. They would become sexually mature at the age of three or so and have been known to live as long as 37 years.

There are many reasons for them to be on the verge of extinction. Among them, environmental pollution is the major one. The change of farmland cultivation has reduced the area of paddy fields, the main habitat for them. What is worse, they have no place to build their nests since tall trees around their habitats have been cut down.

After the first crested ibis sample was acquired in 1964 in China, there had been no report on them in the period from 1964 to 1981 for nearly 20 years. In May 1981, seven crested ibises were discovered in Yangxian county, Shaanxi province. In order to salvage these seven crested ibises, the government promulgated a series of policies of protection and set up a nature reserve. In 1986, a center for breeding and propagating crested ibises was established in the Beijing Zoo. In 1989, artificial propagation of crested ibises was a success. By 2007, three groups of artificially bred crested ibises had been brought into the wilderness, amounting to 1,000 crested ibises.

Golden Pheasant

Chrysolophus pictus

IUCN Red List: Least Concern

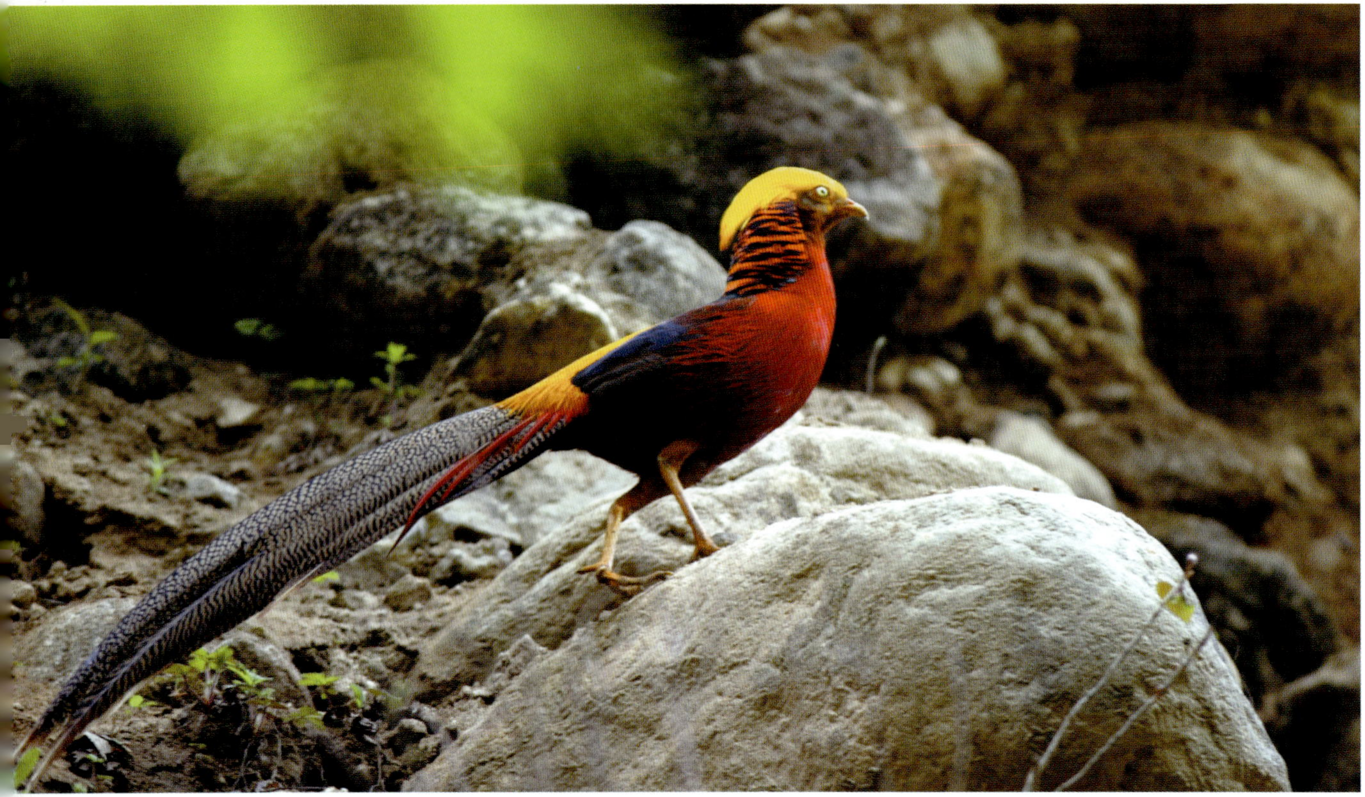

The golden crest of a male golden pheasant emits tender, soft, and silky luster. Though quite long, the crest smoothly covers the back of the neck instead of forming a phoenix-head structure. Its neck-side and the back of the neck are covered with fan-like golden feathers. The neck is densely covered with blue-black feather fringes, forming a "shawl" with black patterns on a red base. Its face, throat, chest, and abdomen are all covered with bright red feathers and long tail-feathers, making it fully magnificent.

Golden pheasants are unique to China, and the Qinling Mountains is one of the core areas for their distribution.

They live in broad-leaved forests, coniferous and broad-leaved mixed forests, woodland and shrubs at forest edges, in addition to the areas amidst short trees and bamboo groves on rocks and steep slopes. In winter, they often move around and look for food on grassy slopes on the forest edge and farmland. They stay in groups. Particularly in the autumn and winter, the number of a group can be as many as over 30. In the spring and summer, they are also seen moving around individually or in pairs.

They are good at running. They would spread their wings to slide when encountering low rocks or a small patch of open space. They fly quickly, agilely, and freely across the forest. They move around mostly on the ground in the daytime, particularly in the morning and afternoon. At noon, they would hide themselves in a place to rest. In the evening, they would perch on arbor trees such as pines and oaks near gulleys and steep rocks. While getting onto trees, they would leap from lower branches level by level in a spiral manner, or jump from small trees nearby. When night falls, their wing flaps can often be heard while they fly onto trees. Very often, they perch on side-branches of crown trees four meters above the ground. Usually, they do not perch on trees in a group, but on a number of nearby trees separately.

For a long time, male golden pheasants have been targets of illegal hunters due to their gorgeous feathers, the decorative value of their fur for export, and live exhibition. Even in today's nature reserve, there is still illegal hunting of such pheasants.

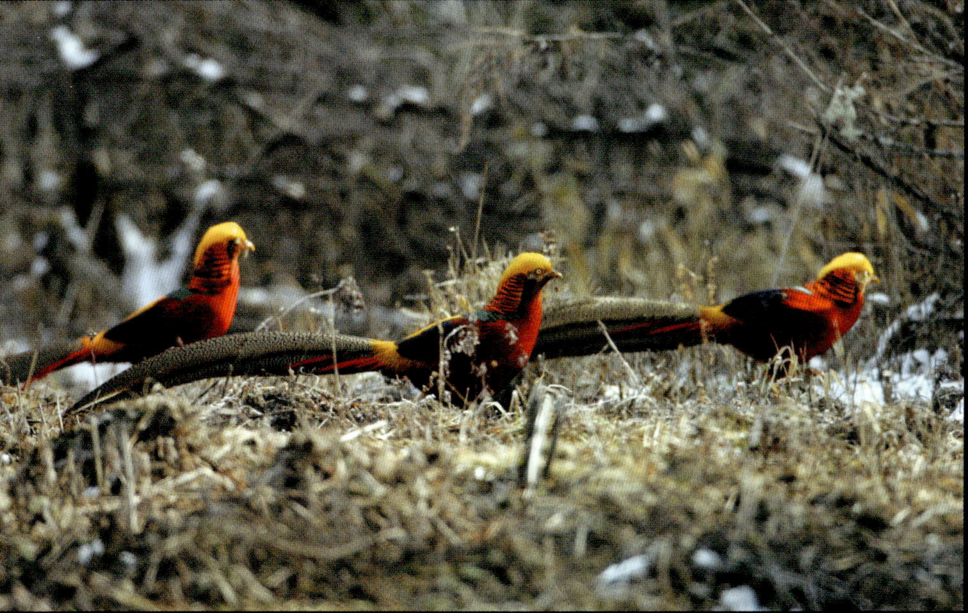

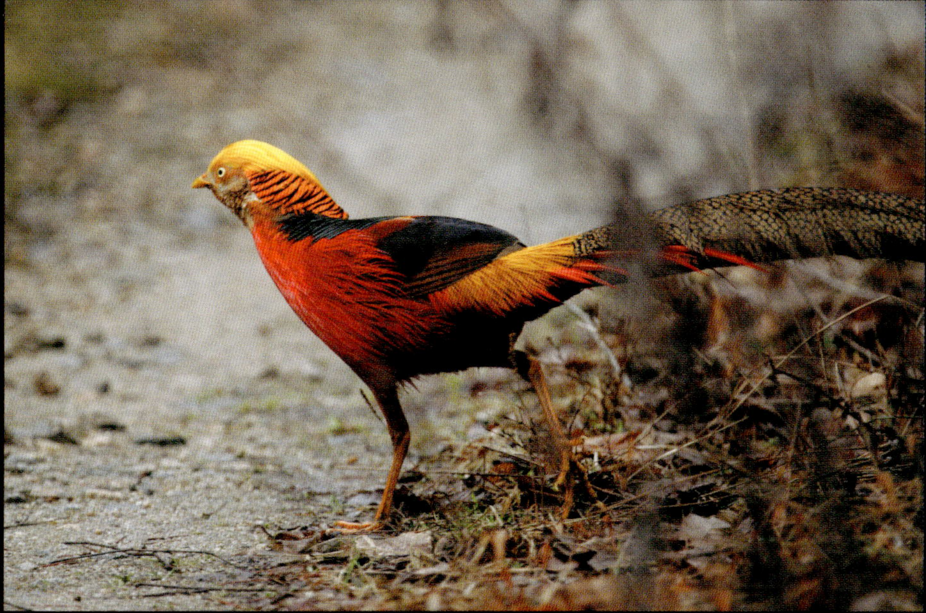

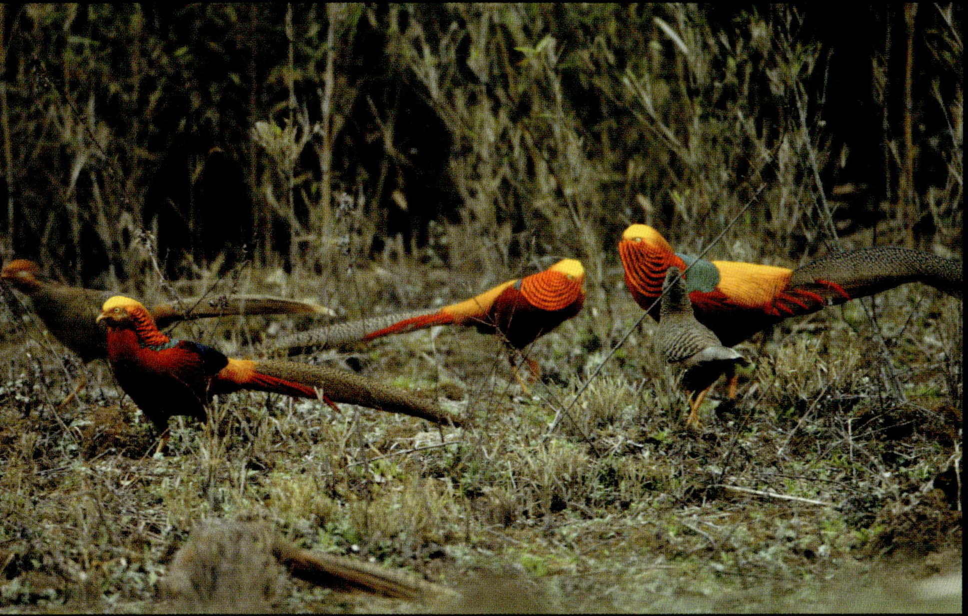

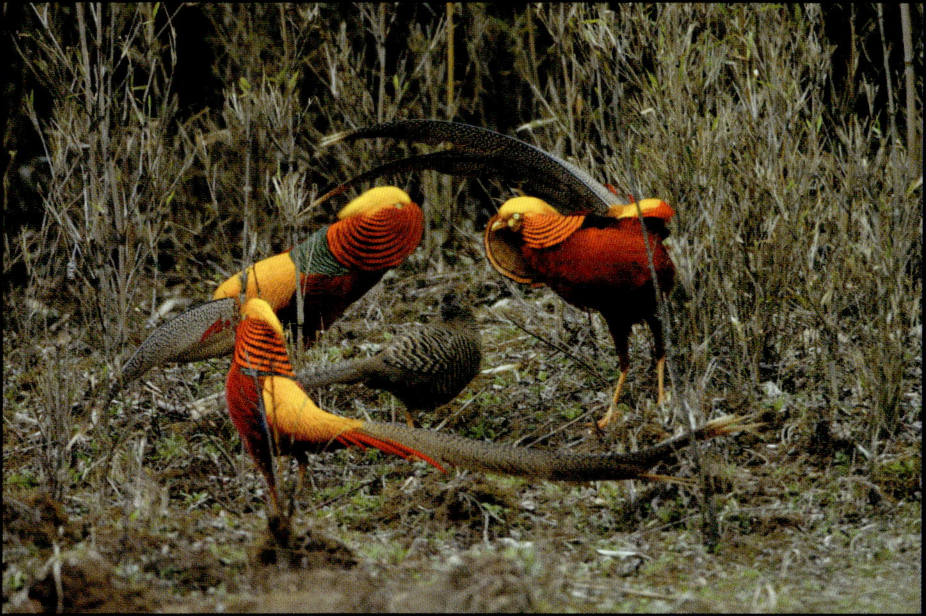

1 2
3 4

Early spring happens to be the time for golden pheasants to mate. Three males take a fancy to a female without prior arrangement. One of them has decided to take action first, and the other two lose no time chasing after the female when they sense the urgency. Three males circle the female, trying to spread all their colorful feathers. They unfold and extend their "tiger-skin shawl," which they usually put behind their head, to cover their head just like flowery fans, dance along with rhythmic pace around the female with their tail feathers trembling up and down. Looking exceptionally majestic, they silently watch the female for her reaction.

Chinese Monal

Lophophorus lhuysii
IUCN Red List: Vulnerable

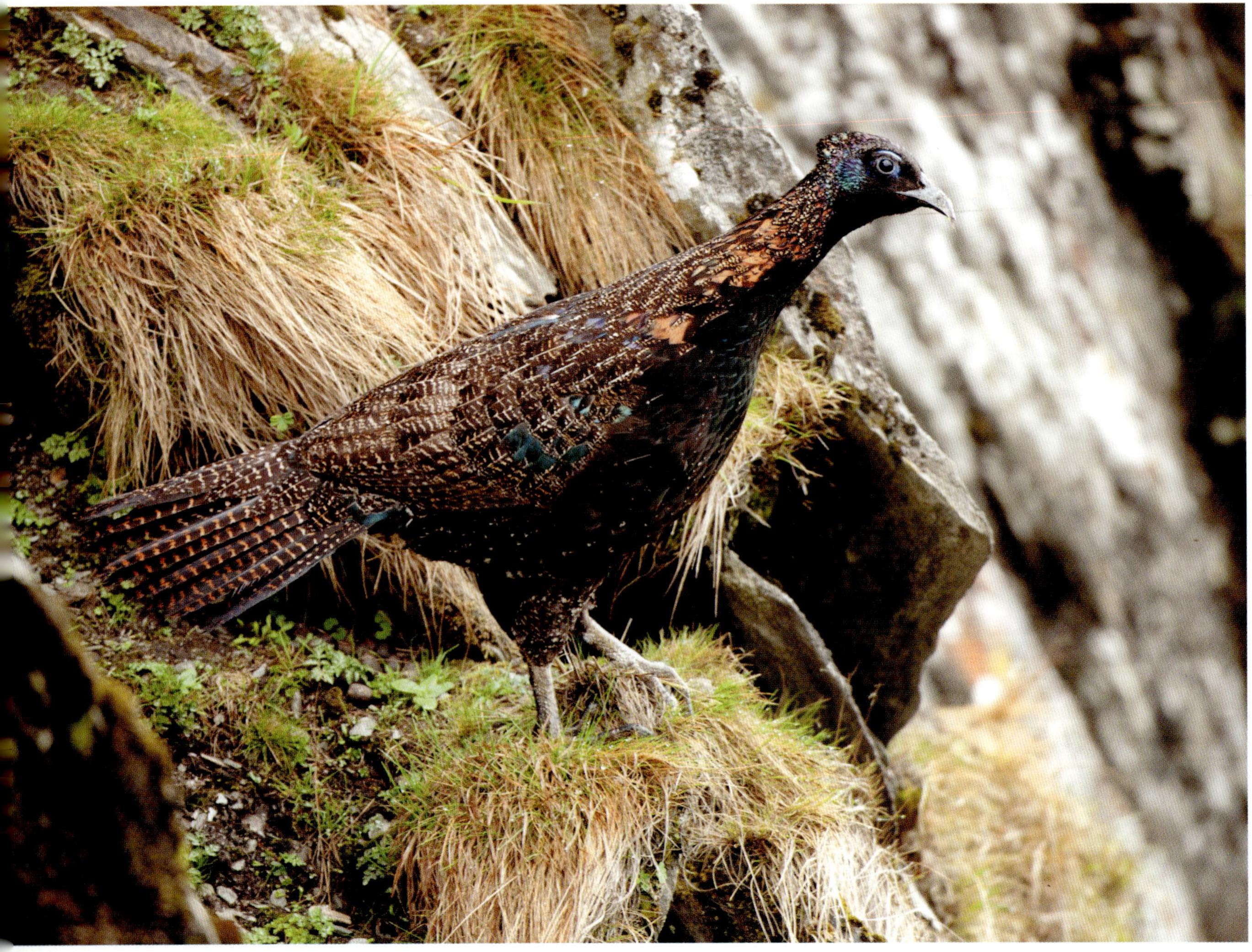

Chinese monals are seen in southeastern Qinghai province and southern Gansu province, as well as Baoxing, Kangding, and Pingwu in Sichuan province, China. They are called by local people as "fritillary chicken" because they enjoy eating fritillary bulbs. They are also termed as "eagle chicken" since they have very hard hook-shaped beaks that very much resemble eagle beaks.

Chinese monals are often seen in pairs or small groups. In the winter, they also sometimes form a bigger group of 8 to 9 and even over 10. They move around in the daytime, often on mountain ridges. At night, they perch amidst dense bushes or on low tree branches. Sharp witted and vigilant, they would stretch their necks to look around. Upon finding danger, they would sneak into bushes or flee at once.

Their habitats are meadow and bushes at high sea level whose ecological capacity is undesirable. Grazing and medicinal herb collection by local people has caused considerable damage to their habitats. Also, because of their fairly big size, they are hunted by local people as a food source.

This is an immature male Chinese monal already having metal-like shining feathers. After becoming an adult, it will have brilliant rainbows feathers.

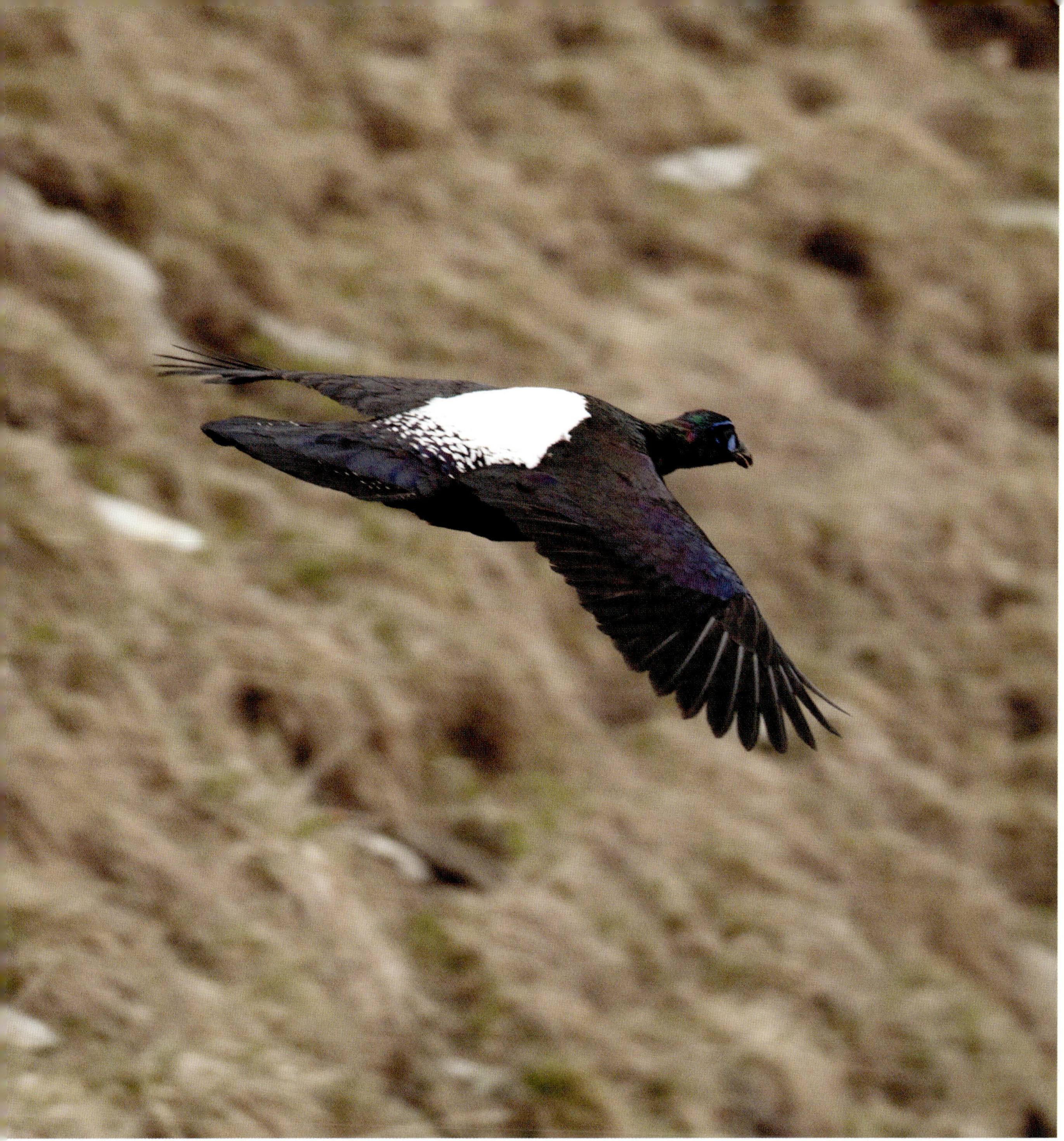

Chinese monals have robust legs and are good at running. Though not good at flying, in case of an emergency, they can glide from a higher place to a low place by taking advantage of the air flow. Chinese monals live on meadows on high mountains, in bushes, and areas with naked rocks at about 3,000 to 5,000 meters above sea level. They are particularly fond of living in bushes on high mountains and on meadows coupled by bushes with many cliffs and rocks.

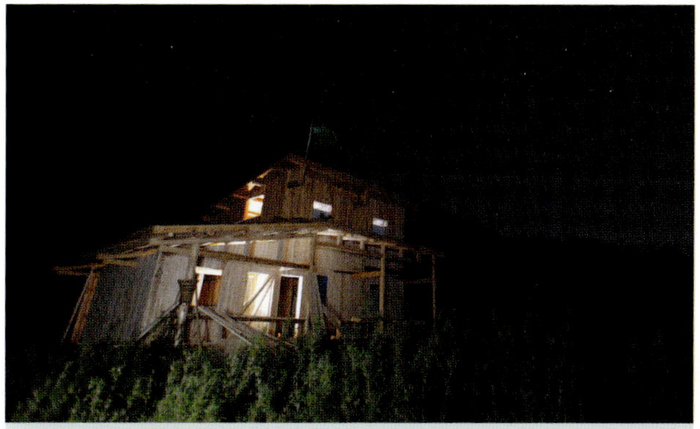

The Building of Small House for Chinese Monals

A severe earthquake hit Sichuan province on May 12, 2008, inflicting serious loss on the Tangjiahe Nature Reserve 140 kilometers away from the epicenter in Wenchuan. Over 1,000 animal samples in the museum, including giant pandas, snub-nosed monkeys, and takins, were all destroyed. Therefore, workers of science investigation and protectors of wild animals and plants were badly in need of a station for their work. In 2009, I took the lead in inviting Xie Yingjun, an architect in Taiwan, to design it for us. It was then named "Big-Thatched-Hall Station for Science Investigation of Wild China" and its other name was "Small House for Chinese Monals." Without a single steel bar in the entire structure, the roof was planted with grass and the wall was built with mud. Interior facilities were made of recycled environmentally friendly materials as much as possible. Then, 12 representative volunteers went to Tangjiahe, taking part in the construction in the hopes that this small house could provide better conditions for taking pictures of more Chinese monals and other kinds of animals.

Blood Pheasant

Ithaginis cruentus

IUCN Red List: Least Concern

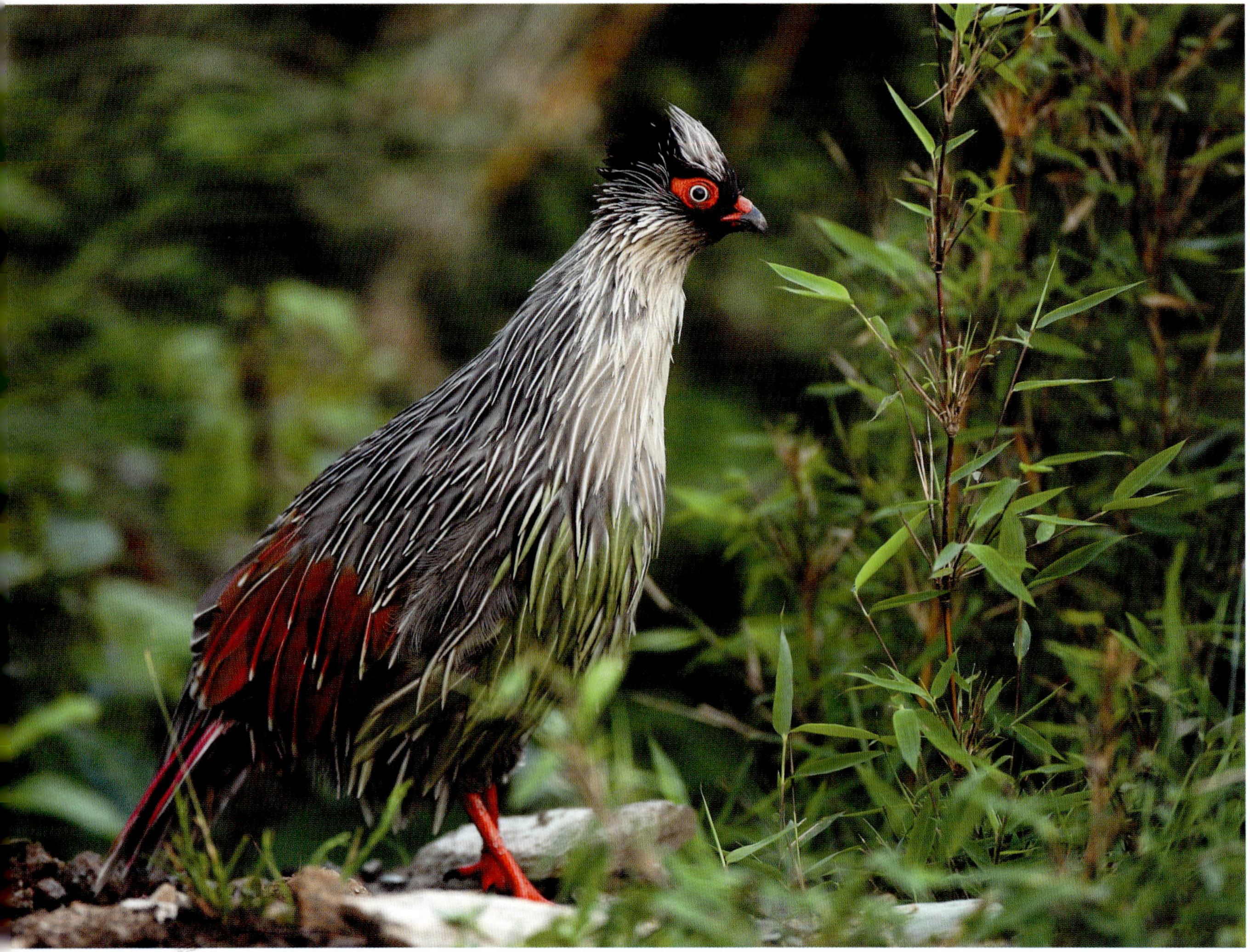

As pheasants in highland mountain forests and bushes, blood pheasants mainly live in coniferous and broad-leaved mixed forests of 2,000 and 4,500 meters above sea level. Marked by vertical migration according to different seasons, they often move around in groups. They chiefly eat plant seeds as well as insects.

Their propagation takes place in the period between April and July, with slight differences depending on the different areas and sea levels. Sometimes, a few male ones with bright-colored feathers can be seen fighting fiercely until a valiant one wins. The winner would walk proudly toward the female, who will appear very tender and docile. Then they would become a couple, living and moving around together all the time and starting a family life. Those male blood pheasants without spouses would roam around in a small group of 3 to 5.

Female blood pheasants begin to lay eggs in early May in bushes, under rocks or beside big fallen logs in the forest. They would find a concave place for their secret shelters, pick up some fallen leaves, lichens, pine needles, sagebrushes, and fine

The name is derived from the blood-red feathers of the male pheasants. Blood pheasants usually begin to move around at dawn. They keep on looking for food until dusk and rest on pines and firs with low tree branches. At noon, they take a short break under rocks or tree shades.

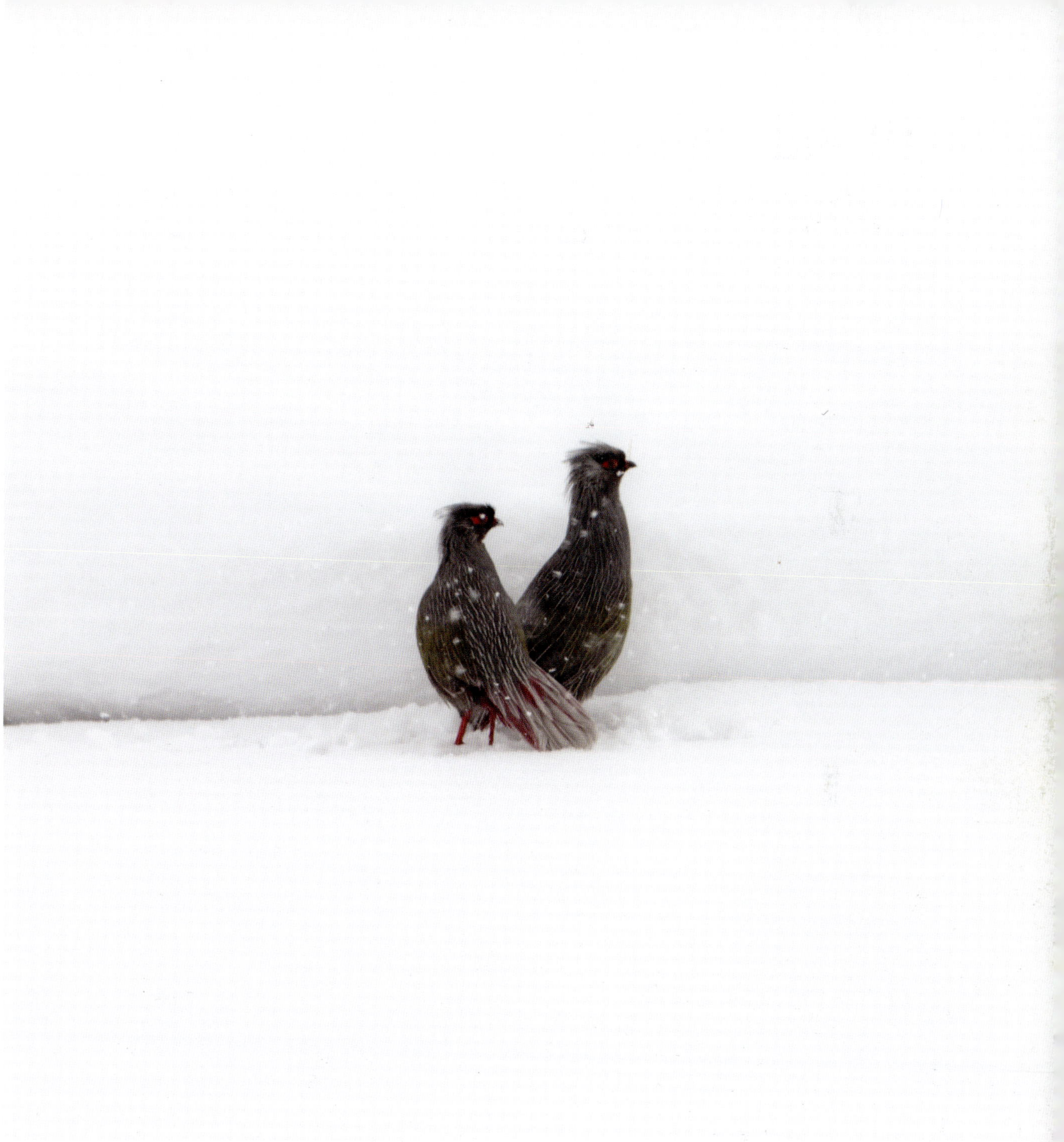

Two blood pheasants nestle up against each other amidst the falling snow.

roots, pressing them down with their bodies to form a loosely structured nest. Some female blood pheasants would build up the nest in the tree hole at the tree root, laying their own feathers under tree leaves on withered tree branches. The nest is in the shape of a shallow plate. A female blood pheasant would lay 3 to 9 eggs. It is a hard job to hatch eggs since the female blood pheasant has to spend one to two hours to look for food, and the rest of the time is spent hatching eggs attentively. In a rainy day, the female blood pheasant has to stay in the nest all the time to spread her wings for shelter against the rain, in order to maintain the temperature for hatching. Before going out to look for food, the female blood pheasant would always put some withered grass blades or feathers on the eggs, and they only go no farther than 100 meters from the nest to look for food.

When the female is hatching eggs, the male would patrol around the nest for fear that other pheasants would approach the nest. The hatching of 28 to 29 days would bring infants out. With their fine feathers becoming dry, they would leave the nest and roam around with their parents. If encountering danger, they would quickly sneak into earthen holes and grass until the danger is over. They would not appear until they hear the call of their parents. Such marvelous instinct enables them to escape from the harm for their predators.

Blue Eared Pheasant

Crossoptilon auritum

IUCN Red List: Least Concern

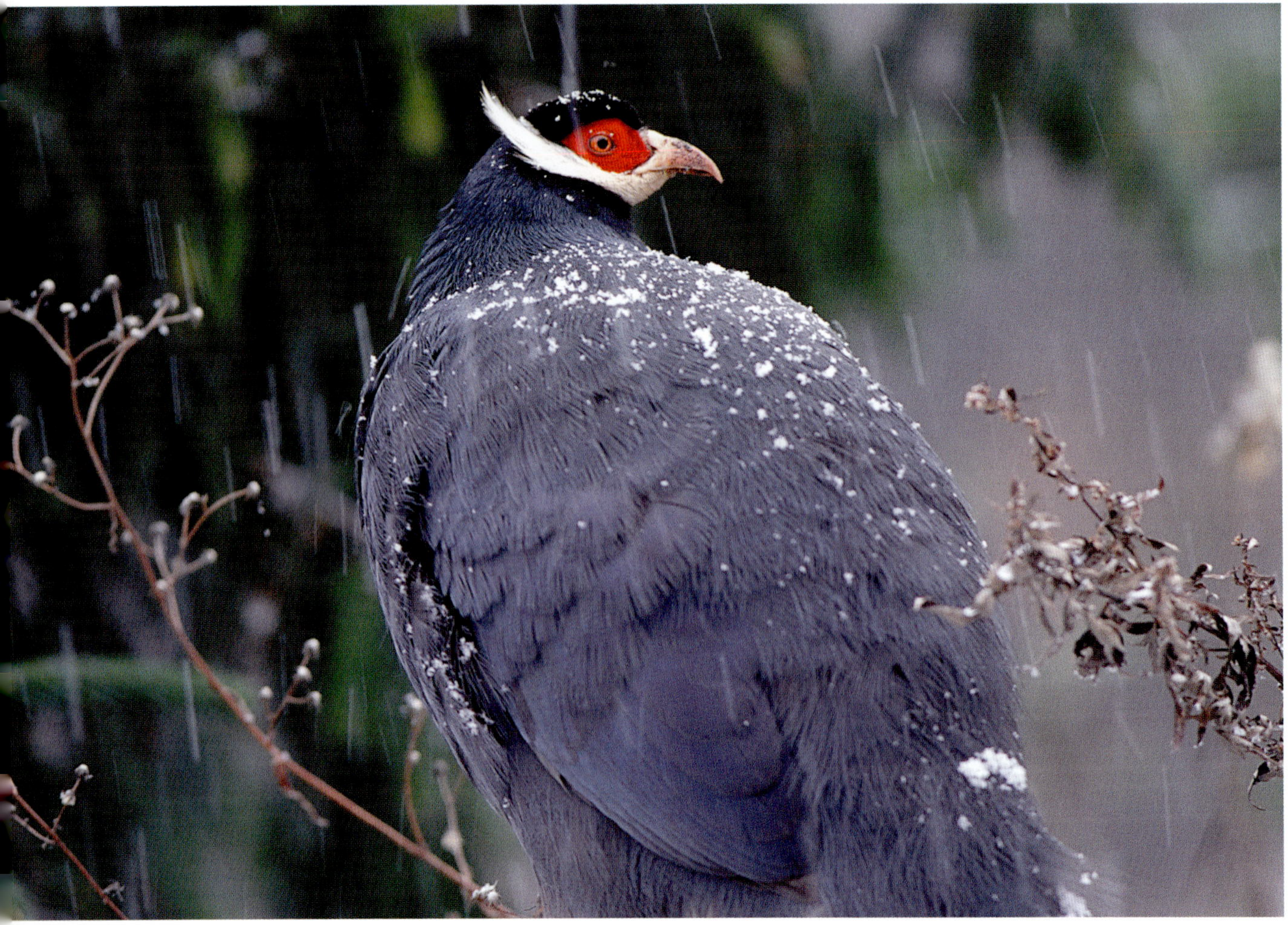

Like their closest relatives the white eared pheasants, blue eared pheasants have big fluffy tail feathers. But they are larger, with their bodies extending 96 cm. Their feathers are blue-grey and their white coverts are longer.

As a kind of pheasant unique to China, they are distributed in eastern and northeastern Qinghai province, southern Gansu province, Ningxia and northeastern Tibet (Tanggula Mountains), and northern Sichuan province. Blue eared pheasants live amidst spruces and oaks, or bushes like willows and bush cinquefoil of 2,500 to 3,400 meters above sea level. They form a group of 10 to 30 and begin to move around at dawn, looking for food in the forests. They mainly eat plants, chirping from time to time while eating. At noon, they would hide themselves in bushes and would not be active until dusk. They spend their nights in groups on trees with lush branches and leaves. Instead of flying, they jump from lower branches to higher ones, until reaching the branches near the top.

In the period from March to June for propagation, blue eared pheasants often hide themselves amidst tree branches or grass, making it difficult for them to be discovered. During this time, they would propagate in pairs and there are often fights among the males. After successful mating, the female lays their eggs in the nest built on a slightly concave place shaded by trees, with 6 to 12 eggs in each nest. Their nest looks like a plate with very simple materials, i.e. tree leaves, tree branches, grass, and lichens together with feathers, making it warm and comfortable. After autumn, they would move in groups down to gullies or expansive bush oriented grassland with water.

Przevalski's Parrotbill

Paradoxornis przewalskii
IUCN Red List: Vulnerable

As small birds unique to China, they are only distributed in alpine coniferous forests, bamboo, and bushes in river-valleys of 2,440 to 3,050 meters above sea level, in Minshan Mountains between Zhuoni county in southern Gansu province, and the Songpan area in northwest Sichuan province. They are typical species distributed in narrow areas. So far, there are only four areas of distribution, i.e. Minxian county, Zhuoni county, and Zhouqu county in Gansu province and Jiuzhaigou Valley in Sichuan province. Discovery in Gansu province is based on the record in 1886 and no other discovery has ever been made over the past 100 years since. In the period from March to May from 1986 to 1988, foreign bird observers consecutively reported the discovery of Przevalski's parrotbills in small groups in arrow bamboo shrubs near Jiuzhaigou Valley Nature Reserve, but without video records. Therefore, Przevalski's parrotbills have always been the rarest passerine birds in China, with their samples kept in Russia.

Since the 1950s, large scale commercialized cut down of forests and land reclamation have greatly reduced and broken the area of natural forests that are typical habitats of Przevalski's parrotbills, which may be the biggest reason leading to their dwindling number. For instance, it has been found that through investigation in Minxian county, the place where a type specimen of Przevalski's parrotbills were discovered, coniferous forests suitable for the existence of Przevalski's parrotbills are gone. The small number of Przevalski's parrotbills may also be attributed to their habits of relying too much on bamboo groves. Nowadays, since typical habitats of Przevalski's parrotbills have been overlapped with those of giant pandas, the former have been brought under quite effective protection.

Full Records of Przevalski's Parrotbills

In July 2007, Dong Lei, another bird-photographer, and I took the first picture of Przevalski's parrotbills in Tangjiahe Nature Reserve, Sichuan province. On that day, we were returning to Big-Thatched-Hall Station as mentioned above from the top of a mountain at 3,200 meters above sea level in Tangjiahe. When reaching a place at 2,600 meters above sea level, we found spectacled parrotbills in large groups mixed with streak-throated fulvettas on protruding bushes amidst bamboo groves. I took a lot of pictures quickly. In between, I took a picture of a parrotbill that was different from the spectacled parrotbills, a parrotbill that stood on the bush for two seconds. We doubted that it might be the Przevalski's parrotbill from legend. Rushing back to the camp, I compared it to the Przevalski's parrotbill sample in the book, confirming that the bird I took a picture of was none other than a Przevalski's parrotbill. My unexpected encounter with a Przevalski's parrotbill left behind the first video record of such rare birds discovered more than 100 years ago.

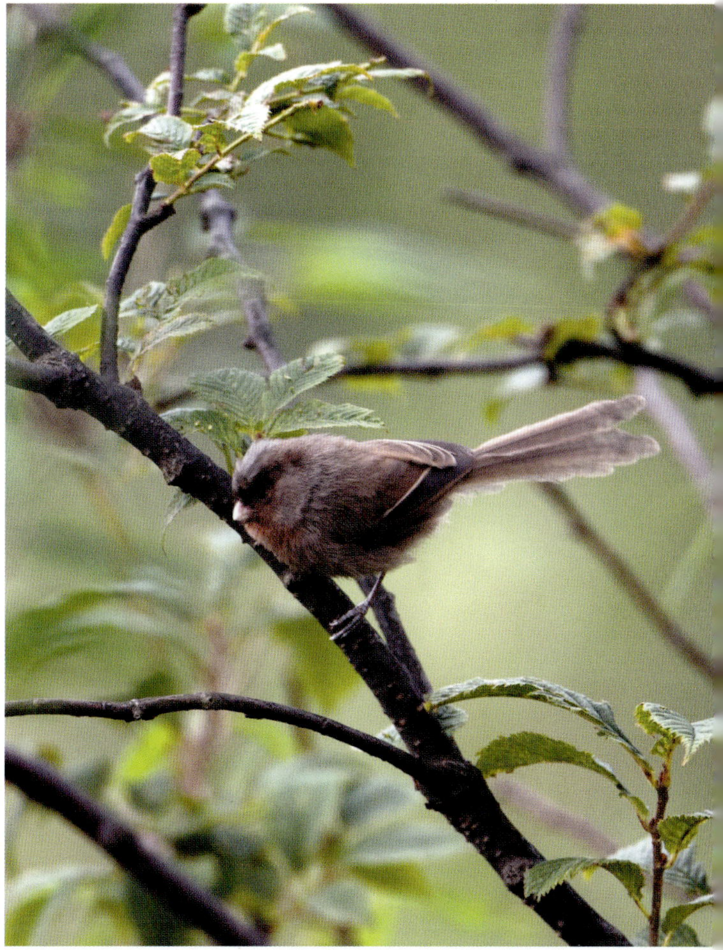

They were considered extinct for a time. However, their delicate figures on tree branches being photographed once again prove that true images can offer forceful evidence for scientific research.

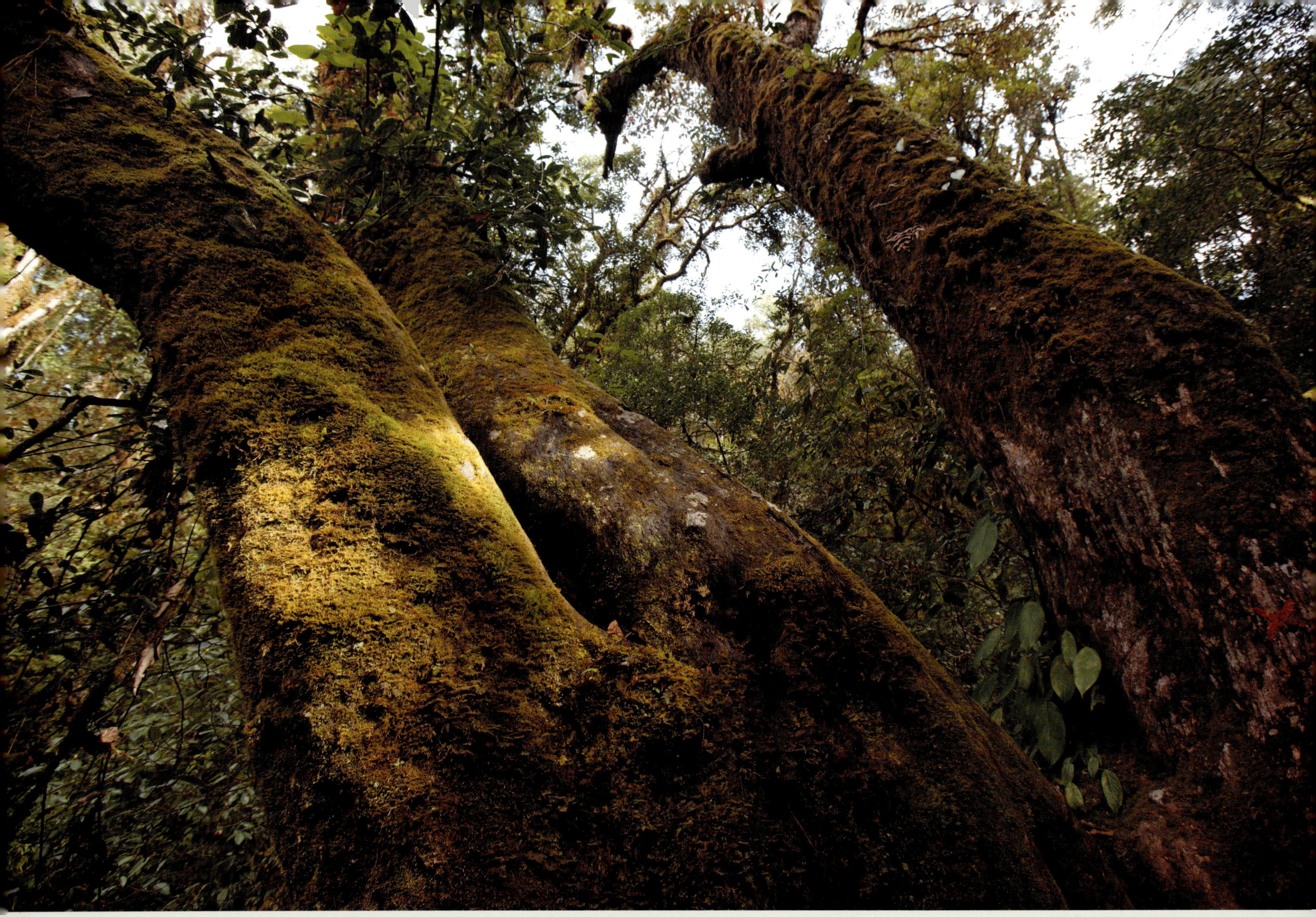

Chapter Eight
Gaoligong Mountains—The Dwelling of the White-Browed Gibbons

Situated in the western longitudinal valley in the west of Yunnan province, the Gaoligong Mountains are marked by high terrains in the north and low terrains in the south, linking with the Tibetan Plateau in the north and the Indo-China Peninsula in the south. Its special terrains, topography, and climate transform it into a corridor for the transit of wild animals and plants, and a shelter for wild animals and plants of the glacial period of the Tertiary and the Quaternary, and forming a framework of "complex species of animals and plants, with new and old ones, the transit between the south and the north as well as the confluence between the east and the west."

There are extremely rich forest resources along with precious and rare animals and plants everywhere. There is big tree rhododendron (*Rhododendron protistum* var. *giganteum*), the biggest rhododendron in the world. As a primitive and ancient plant, it was first discovered in 1919 in the primitive forests on the Gaoligong Mountains at 2,100 to 2,400 meters above sea level. In China, big tree rhododendron is only distributed in the Gaoligong Mountains. Between 20 to 30 meters high, its biggest base diameter can be 330 centimeters. At present, the actual number of its distribution is not clear. According to the existing data and identifications of type specimen, there are only several or over ten of them. The biggest rhododendron in the Gaoligong Mountains, known as "the king of the big tree rhododendron" is 30 meters high with a base diameter of 307 centimeters. As the biggest single rhododendron, it is estimated to be over 400 years old.

In 1992, the Gaoligong Mountains National Nature Reserve was designated by the WWF as a Grade-A Nature Reserve (the most important in the world). In 2003, UNESCO formally approved the Gaoligong Mountains National Nature Reserve as a member of the World Network of Biosphere Reserves. Various ecosystems of forests of the Gaoligong Mountains have given birth to a wide variety of precious and rare animals, such as the white-browed gibbon, black musk deer, Phayre's langurs, Sclater's monals, and green peafowls. Among them, the most eye catching is the white-browed gibbon, a kind of large primate, reputed to be "the dancing spirit of the Gaoligong Mountains."

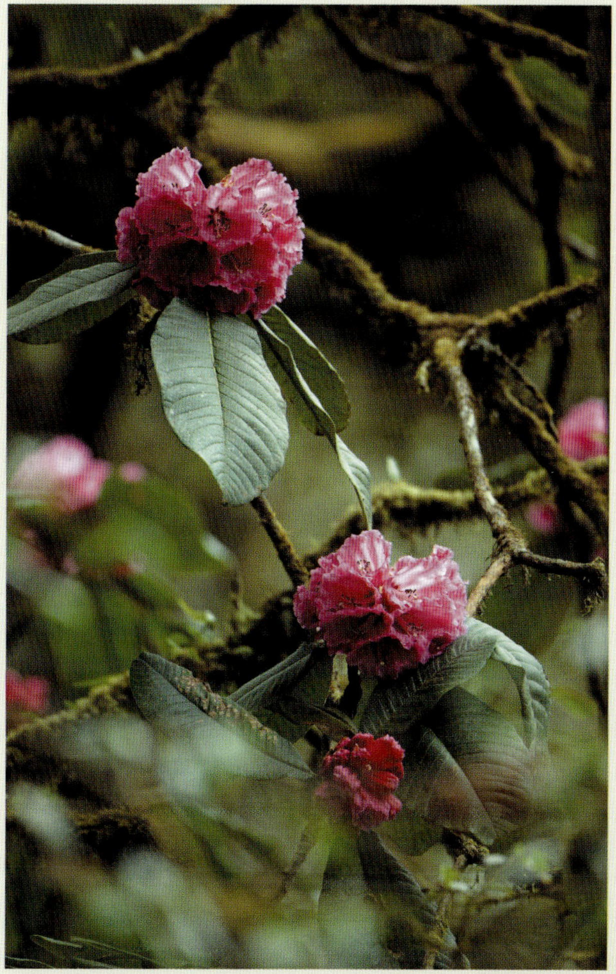

On facing page and right
Deep in the primitive forests of the Gaoligong Mountains, blossoming big tree rhododendrons look like rubies towering into the sky.

White-Browed Gibbon

Hoolock leuconedys

IUCN Red List: Near Threatened

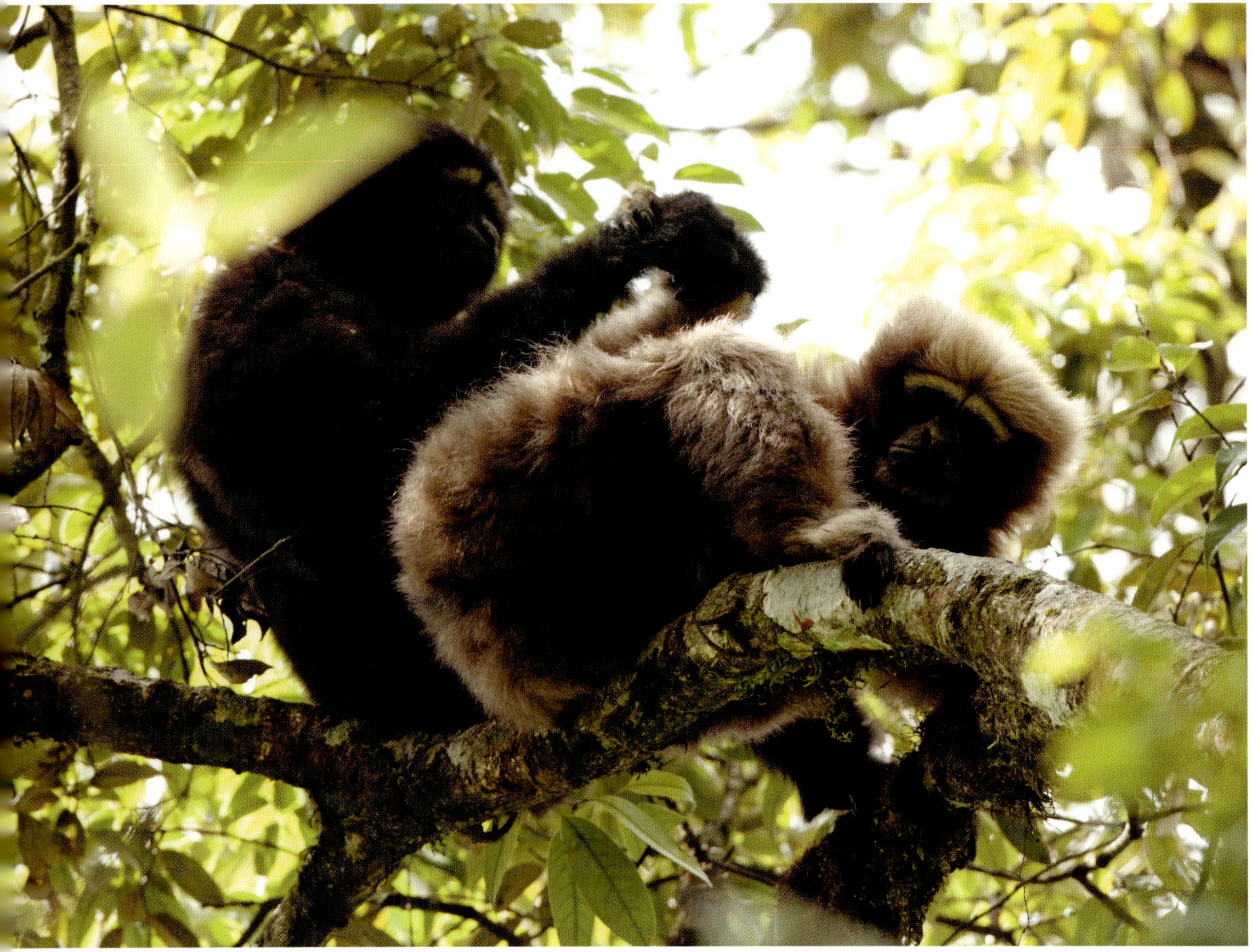

Gibbons are not monkeys, but apes. In addition to orangutans, chimpanzees, and gorillas, gibbons are the closest relatives to human beings. They all live in forests with tall trees in the tropical and subtropical areas in southern Asia. They are "acrobats in the high sky" among all the animals. Despite their small size—a gibbon is less than one meter high when standing up—its forelimbs are especially long and its arms can be as long as 1.5 meters when they are stretched out. Their hands can almost touch the ground when they stand up. Two agile long arms and hook-shaped long hands enable them to jump across trees just like on the ground. They look for food, play, rest, seek for spouses, give birth to, and nurture their young all on trees.

Gibbons have enlarged throat sacs, which inflate when they scream, making the scream extremely loud. Known as "singers" among the mammals, gibbons are particularly fond of calling, in the form of a "solo" for male gibbons, a "duet" between male and female gibbons, and a "chorus" for male gibbons and their family members. It is especially the case with a spectacular "chorus." Generally, adult male gibbons would sing first, followed by the quivering echo of the female

The males' bodies are brown-black while the females' look light brown. Their crest is quite long and hangs down to the back of the head, hence resulting in a flat vertex. The thick and dense brow is the most eye-catching feature of the white browed gibbons.

gibbons as well as the monotonous response from the sub-adults in the group. The tune gradually rises, clear and loud, shocking the valley. This habit of theirs is either the signal of interaction and expression of sentiments within the group, or the means to show their presence against invasion.

White-browed gibbons live in mesic evergreen broad-leaved forests and deciduous broad-leaved forests in the Gaoligong Mountains at 2,000 to 2,500 meters above sea level. Generally, they mostly eat many kinds of fruit, fresh tree branches, tender leaves, and flower buds, as well as insects, small birds, and bird eggs.

Unlike the Yunnan snub-nosed monkeys, they practice monogamy and form a small group of 3 to 5 together with their babies, occupying an area of about 30 to 40 hectares. Early every morning, white-browed gibbons would scream loudly and such "singing" can be heard several kilometers away. The other name of "hoolock" comes from their scream. White-browed gibbons declare the ownership of their family area through "singing" and the "chorus" of female white-browed gibbons is also an important way of consolidating family relationship.

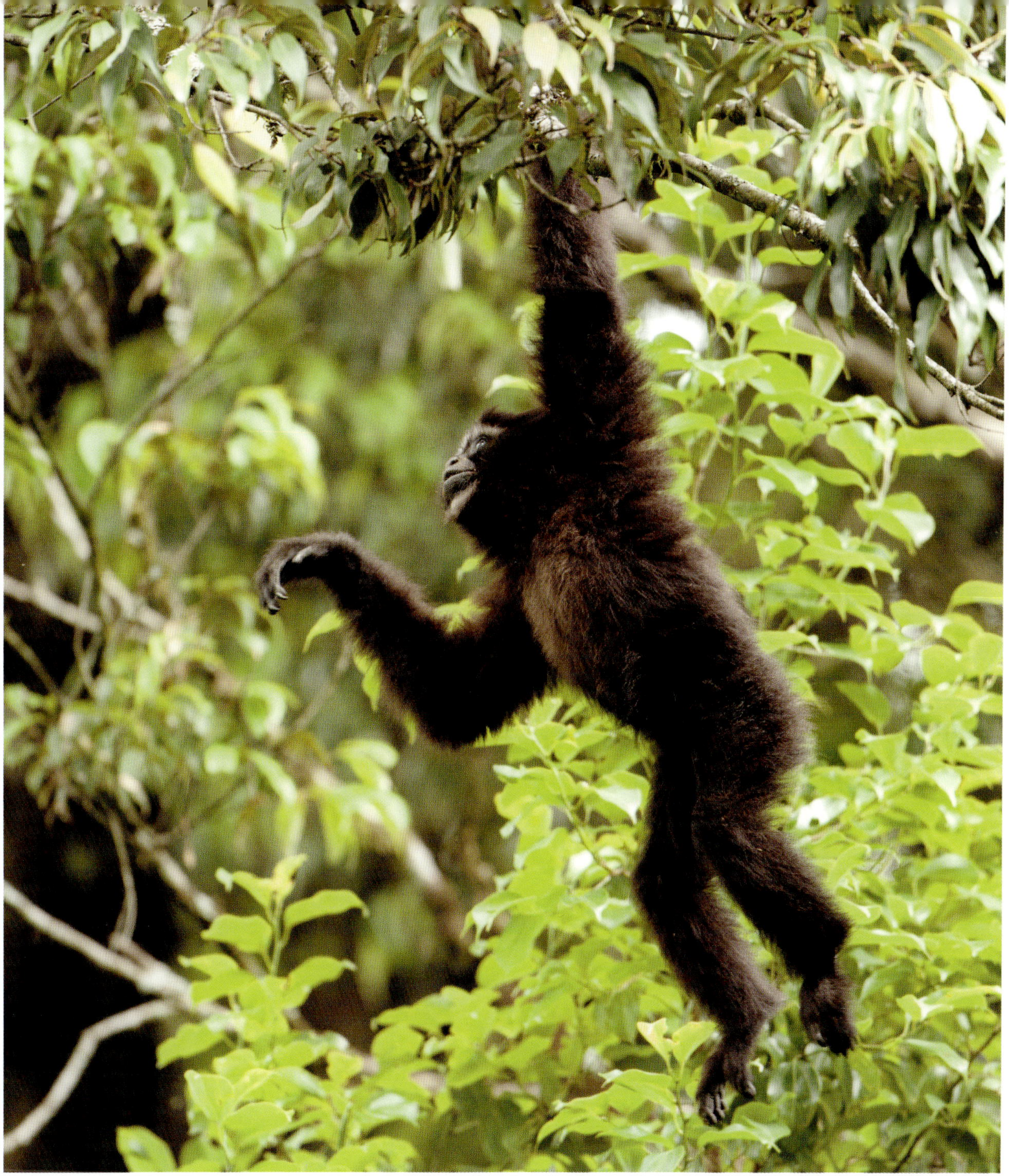

They can hang on the tree branch with a single arm and curved legs. They sway back and forth and advance like a swing. The distance of one move in the air can be three meters. It can swing 8 to 9 meters continuously, like flying across trees.

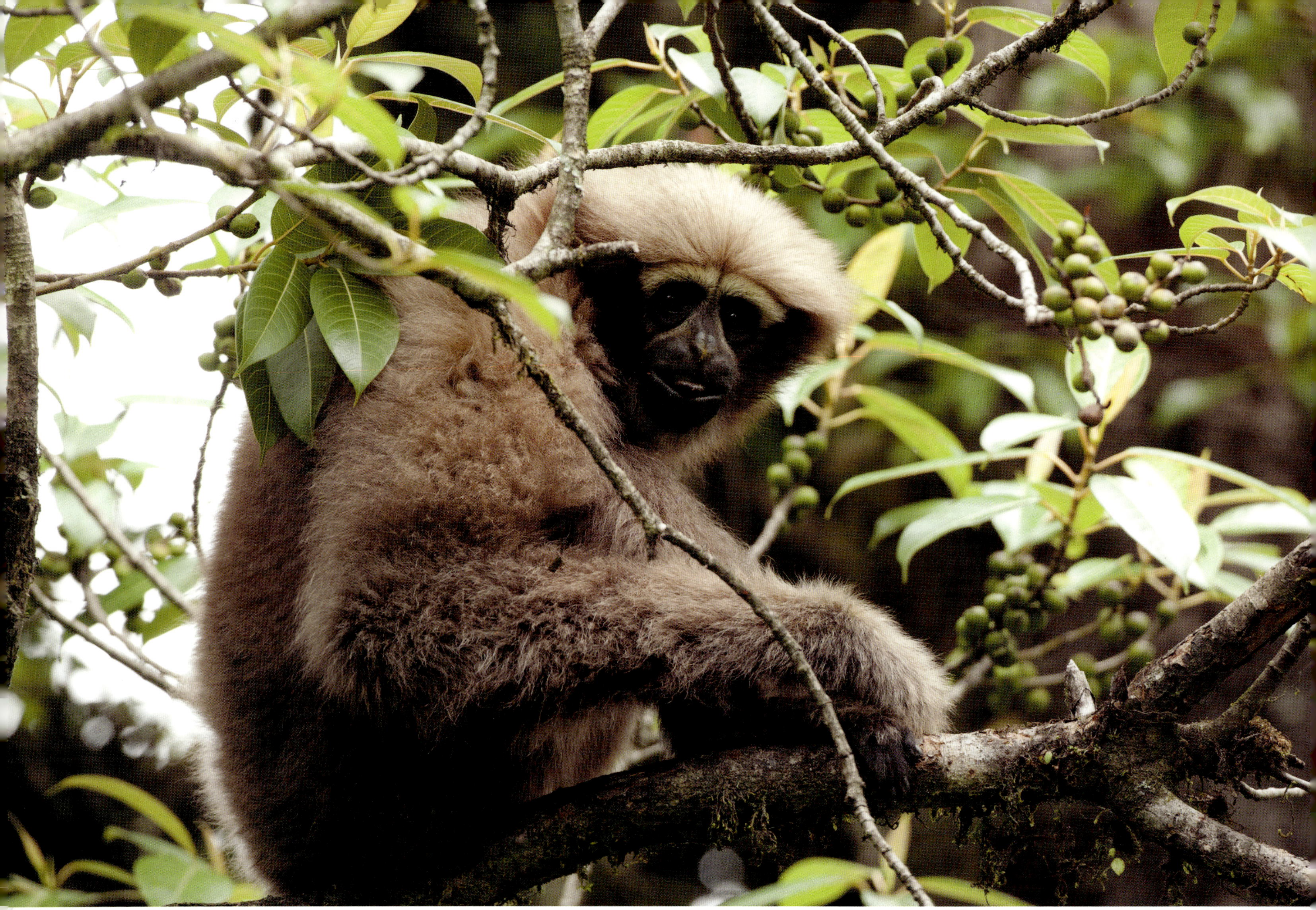

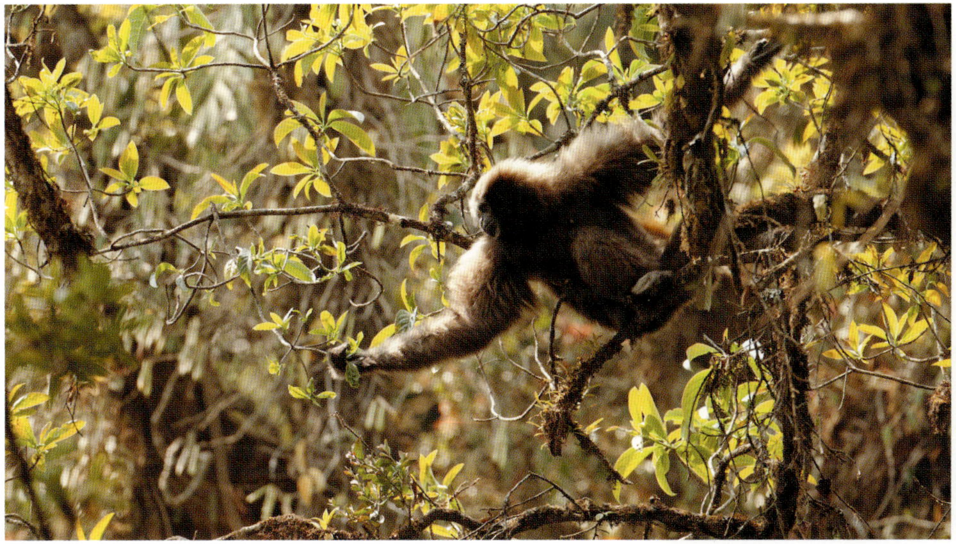

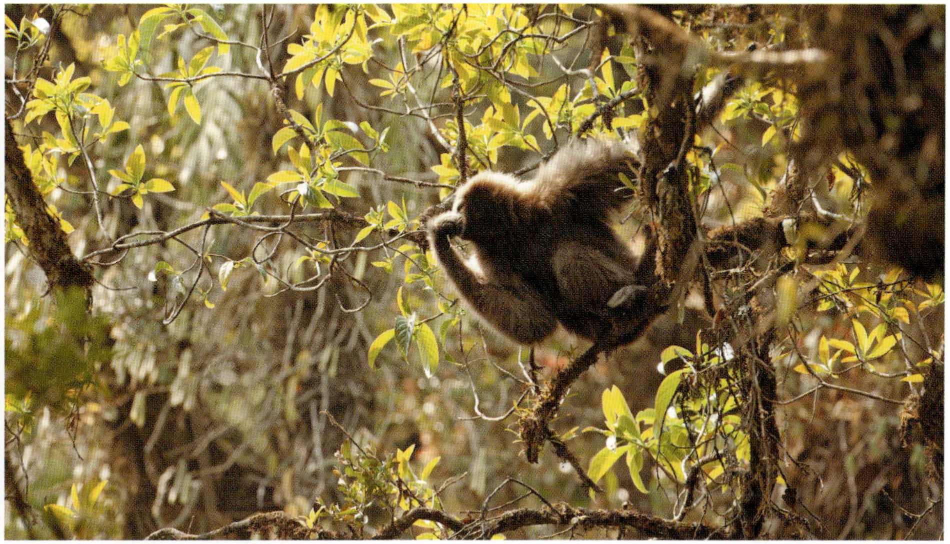

Above lefe and right
This white-browed gibbon is hanging on a tree, effortlessly eating food.

On facing page
A white-browed gibbon is sitting at ease on a tree, enjoying a nice meal of a small wild fruit.

Right
The baby swings closely in the arms of its mother across the trees.

At present, there are only less than 100 white-browed gibbons in China. Damage to their habitats is the major threat to their survival. Hunting for their meat and traditional medicinal ingredients from their bodies is the second reason for their endangerment. Meanwhile, their younger generation suffers from a weakened ability to survive, the decline of propagation because of the sparse distribution of existing white-browed gibbons, long distance separation between groups, and the serious phenomena of inbreeding. Sexually mature young gibbons depart from groups and lose the opportunity of propagation due to failure to find mates. These elements have brought white-browed gibbons to the verge of extinction, which requires salvation with no time to spare from people.

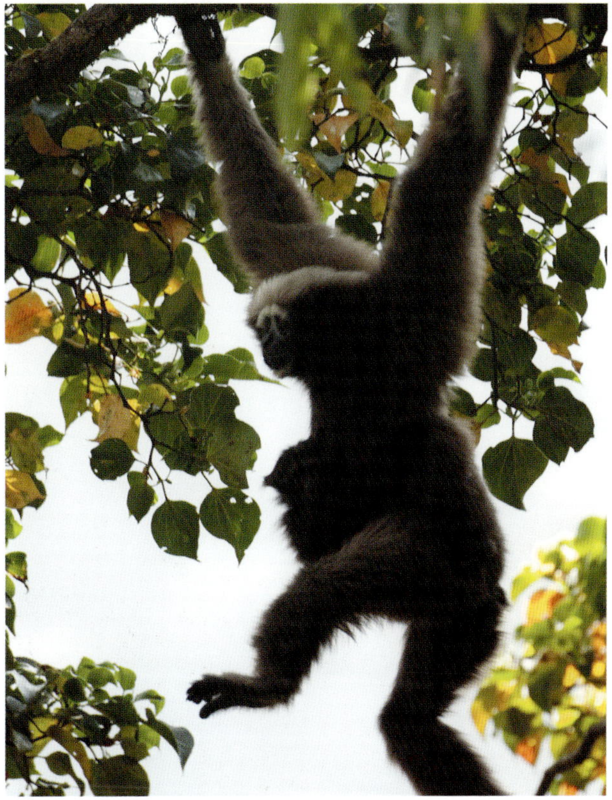

Listening to Gibbons Calling

On March 28, 2007, for the first time in the Gaoligong Mountains National Nature Reserve in Yunnan province, I succeeded in taking pictures of the white-browed gibbons, which I had failed several times in my previous attempts. This was indeed a very exciting day for me. At the end of March, while walking on the flower petal covered ground in the Gaoligong Moutnains, my partners and I came to an open space in the woods, with warm sunshine filtering through the tree tips, plating my lens with a layer of nice color. Loud chirps from woodpeckers could be heard in the far distance, with leaf warblers, rufous-vented yuhina, and chestnut-tailed minla joining the early morning chorus.

At 8: 41 a.m., the first gibbon calling was heard. Though not loud enough, it brought hope to the ancient Gaoligong Mountains. At 9: 16 a.m., there was another loud gibbon calling, immediately followed by nice ones of different lengths and frequencies, with the real climax taking place! Amidst the center of the chorus, the gibbons calling out one after another shocked my tympanic membrane and soul. This was not a chorus that I heard for the first time over ten years ago in the urban zoo, the chorus of man-bred black crested gibbons, white-cheeked gibbons, and white-browed gibbons, but the declaration of the re-vitality of Gaoligong Mountains!

Phayre's Langur

Trachypithecus phayrei

IUCN Red List: Endangered

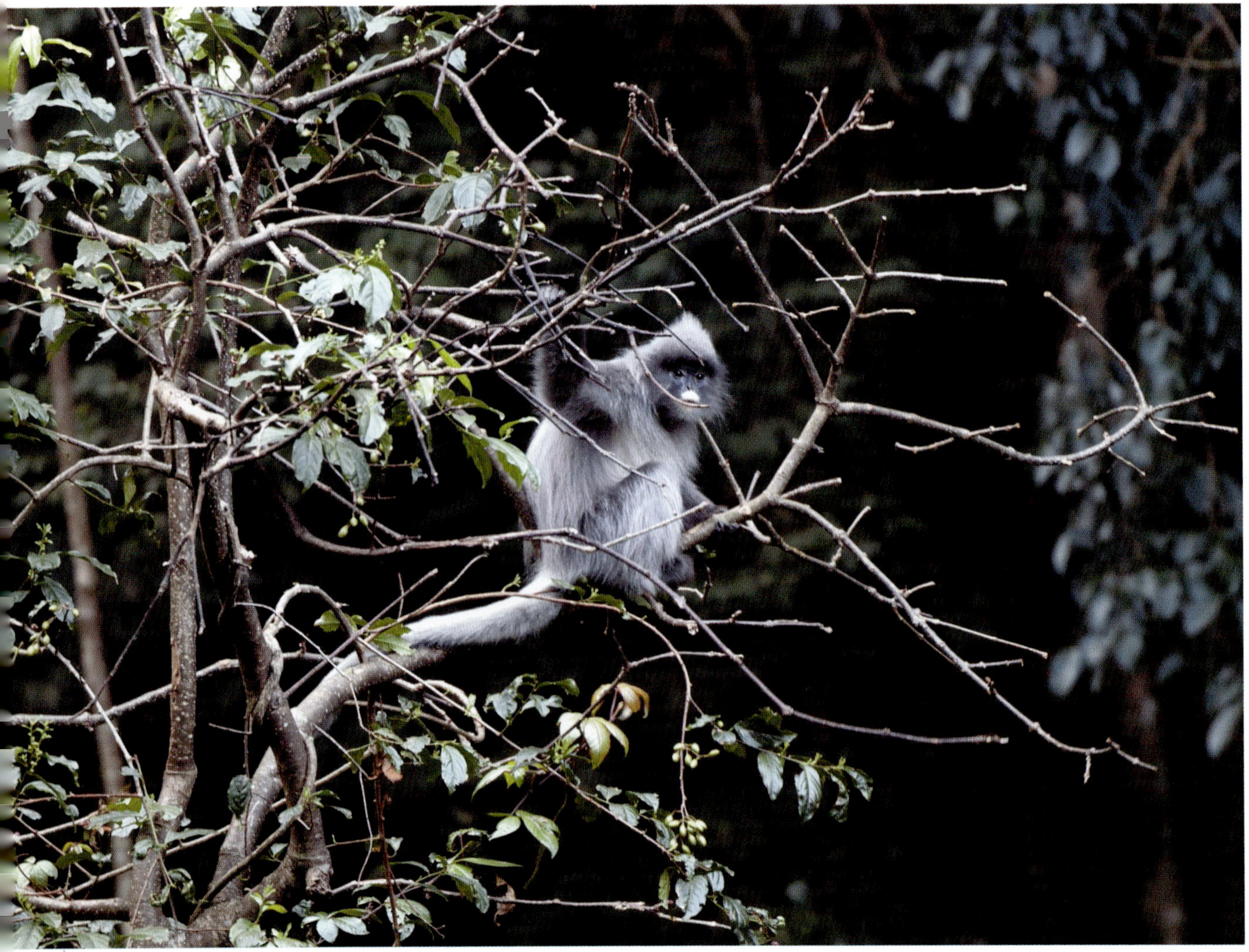

Phayre's langurs (Murphy's leaf monkeys) are only distributed in southern Yunnan province, China.

In China, there are two sub-species of Phayre's langurs, i.e. *T. phayrei shanicus*, which is distributed in Dehong prefecture in western Yunnan province, and *T. phayrei crepusculus*, which is distributed in southwestern, southern, and central Yunnan province. As typical arboreal leaf monkeys from tropical zones in Southeast Asia and southern Asia, Phayre's langurs mainly live in tropical rain forests and seasonal rain forests along the river and low-lying valleys, as well as tropical monsoon evergreen broad-leaved forests in southern Asia. The sea level of their habitats is less than 1,200 meters.

Phayre's langurs mostly move around, look for food, play on trees, and often come down to drink water in ponds with nitrate. Each group consists of about 50 to 60. They start to move around mostly before and after dawn. The period from 9:00 to 12:00 a.m. is the peak time for their frequent activities. They would rest at noon and often play or sit quietly in trees. The period from 4:00 to 7:00 p.m. is another peak time for their activities. When it gets dark, they would sleep

A Phayre's langur weighs 5 to 10 kilograms with an average length of 500 mm. It is covered with silver-grey hairs and its face has obvious light blue-white eye-sockets. Its long tail helps it to keep balance while moving around on a tree. Therefore, its tail exceeds its body and can be as long as 800 mm.

on nearby tall trees with dense and lush branches and leaves. They chiefly eat nuts, seeds, tender buds, and petioles, as well as fresh branches, tender leaves, flower buds, bamboo shoots, small birds, and insects, amounting to over 80 kinds.

For Phayre's langurs, the period of their mating and propagation take place between August and November. They give birth to infants in the period between February and April the following year. Pregnancy lasts for six to seven months and the period of breast-feeding lasts for about four months. Infants appear golden all over three to four months after they are born. Five months later, they will have light and grey hair and will be sexually mature at the age of three or four.

A number of a specific group of Phayre's langurs have disappeared due to the disappearance of their habitats caused by the cut-down of forests and excessive hunting for acquiring Chinese medicinal ingredients from their bodies. China has set up over ten nature reserves in areas distributed with Phayre's langurs, having brought their habitats under protection.

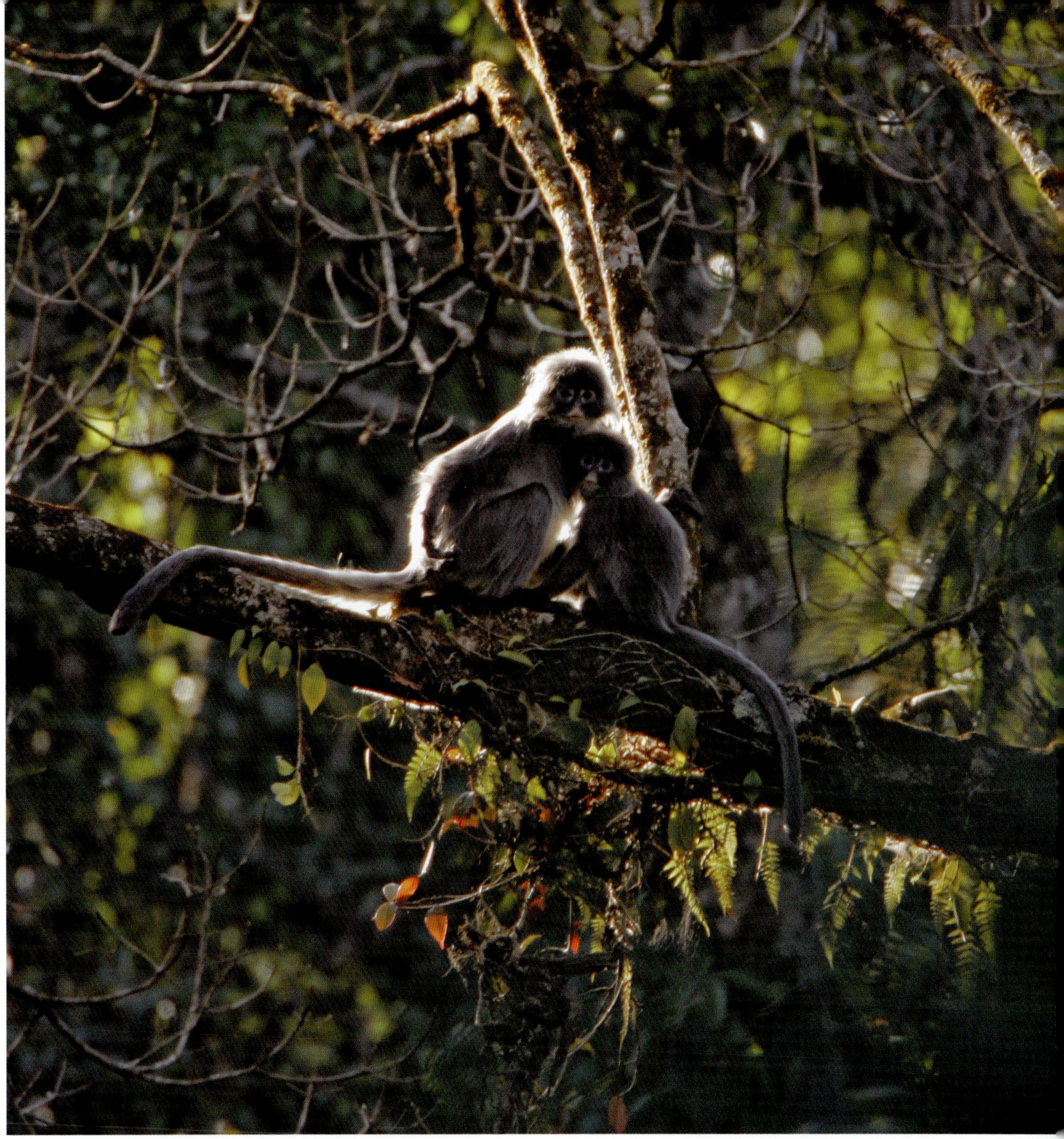

This pair of mother and baby Phayre's langurs is enjoying the warm afternoon sunshine in the dense forest.

Golden-Throated Barbet

Megalaima franklinii

IUCN Red List: Least Concern

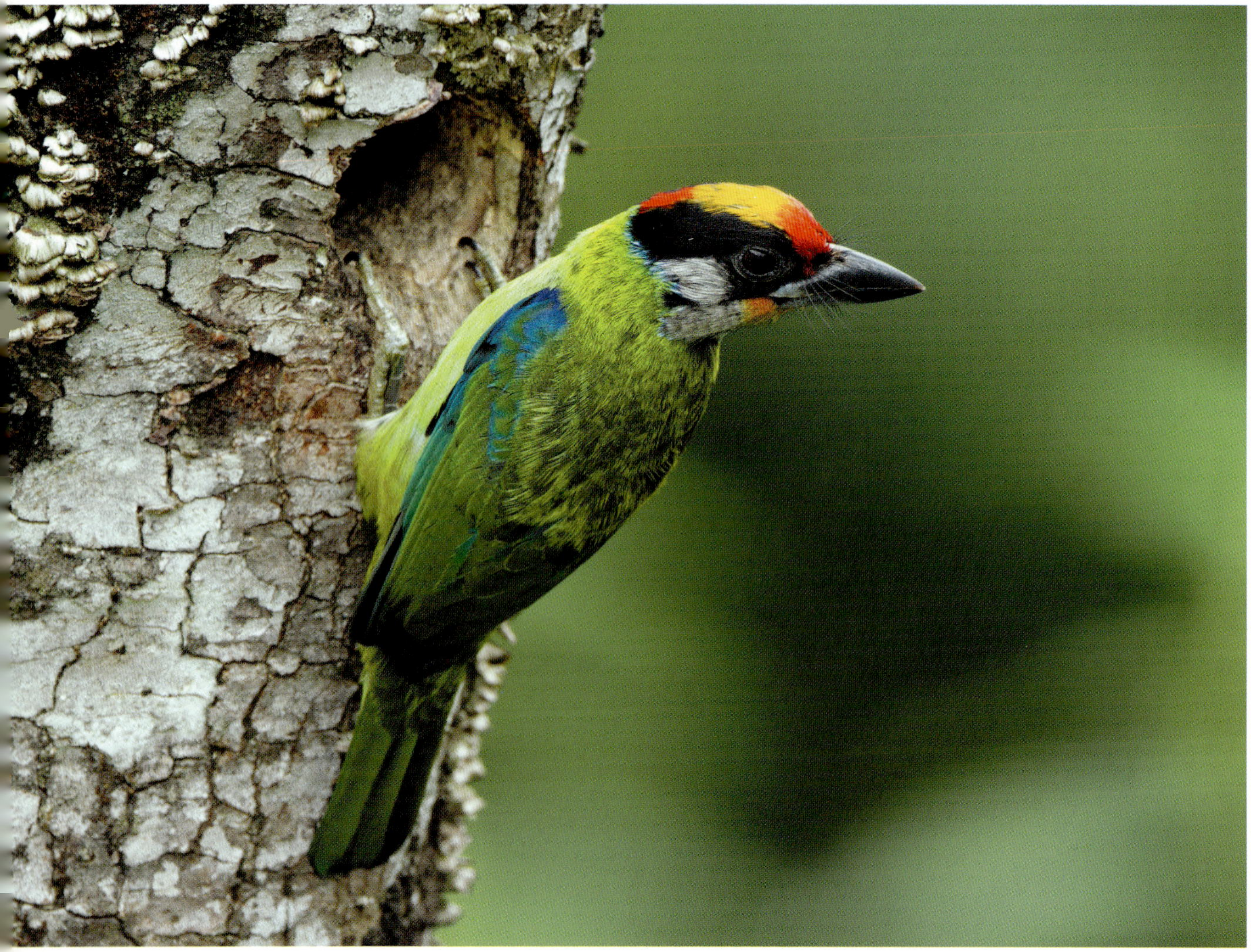

Golden-throated barbets are distributed in Nepal, southern China, and Southeast Asia. In China, they are seen in southeastern Tibet, the western, southern, and southeastern areas of Yunnan province, and southwestern Guangxi Autonomous Region. *M. F. Ramsayi*, a sub-species, is found in southwestern Yunnan province. Mainly living in evergreen broad-leaved forests at 500 to 2,500 meters above sea level, they mostly move around individually and prefer to perch on arbor trees with dense branches and leaves. Compared with other kinds of barbets, golden-throated barbets live closer to mountains. Males declare their territory with loud screams.

They chiefly eat nuts, seeds, and flowers, as well as insects and larvae. In the period between April and August, they would build up nests in evergreen broad-leaved forests, particularly in gulleys in forests and along streams. They peck at withered tree trunks or tree stakes to make holes for their nests in which there is no cushion at all. Two to five white eggs (usually three to four eggs) are laid in each nest. The male and the female would hatch eggs and feed the juveniles in turn. The parents would bring food back every ten minutes.

As a species with gorgeous feathers and loud chirps in the sub-tropical forests, barbets mainly eat berries and insects.

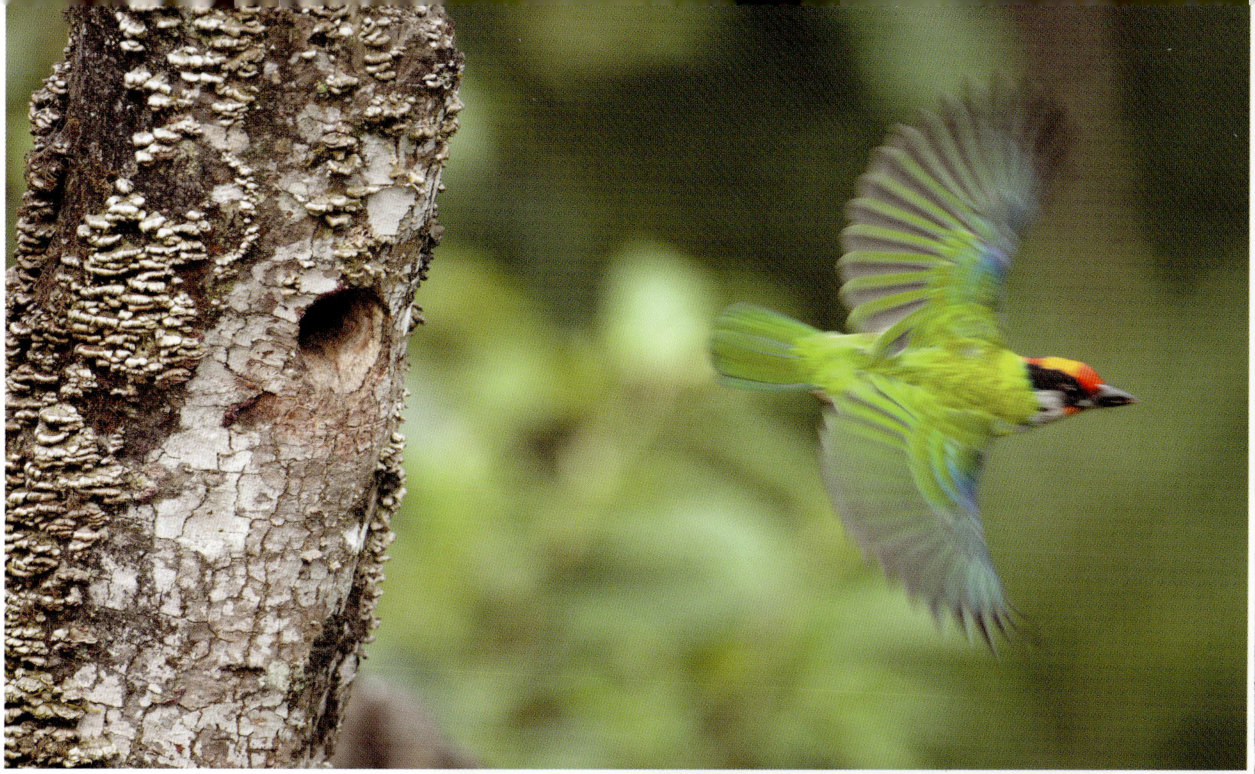

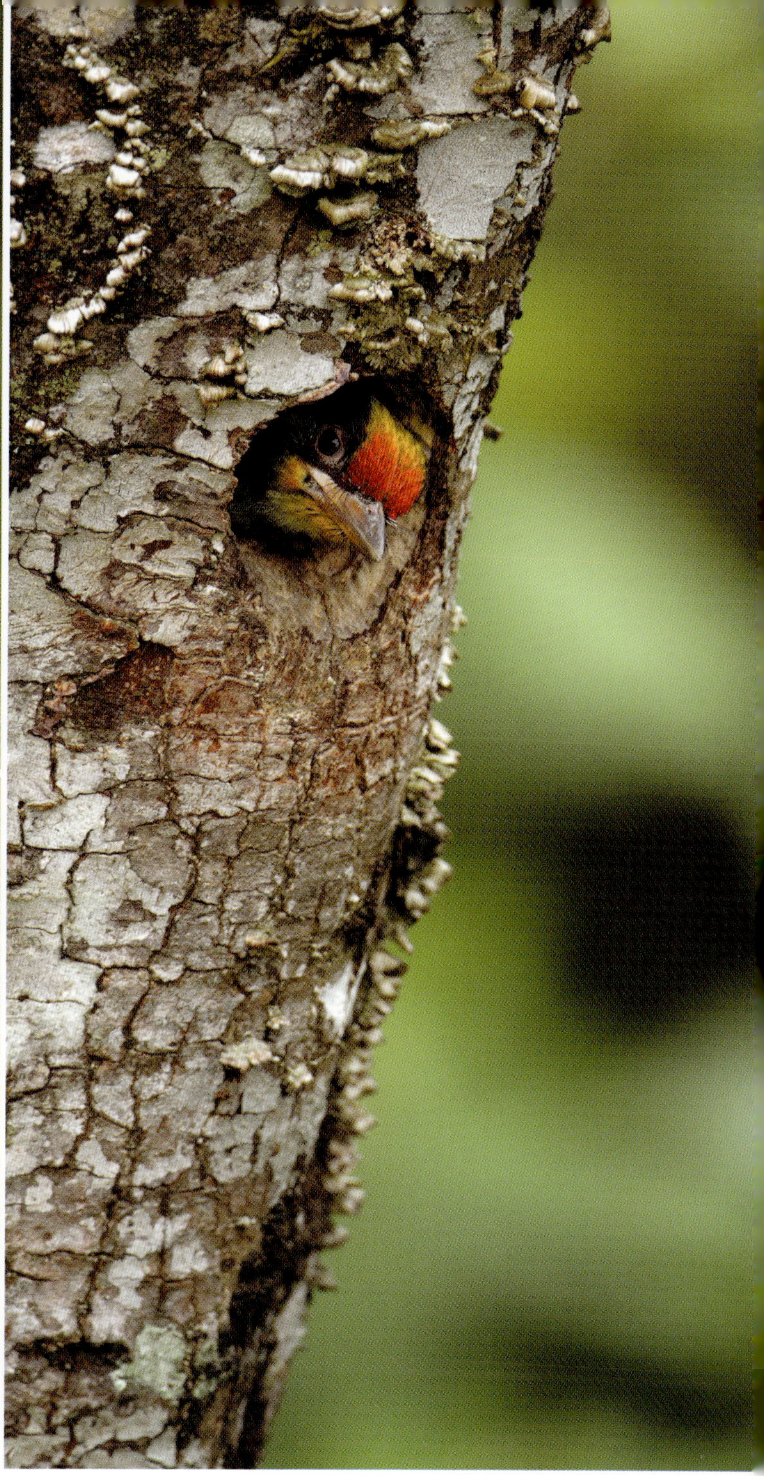

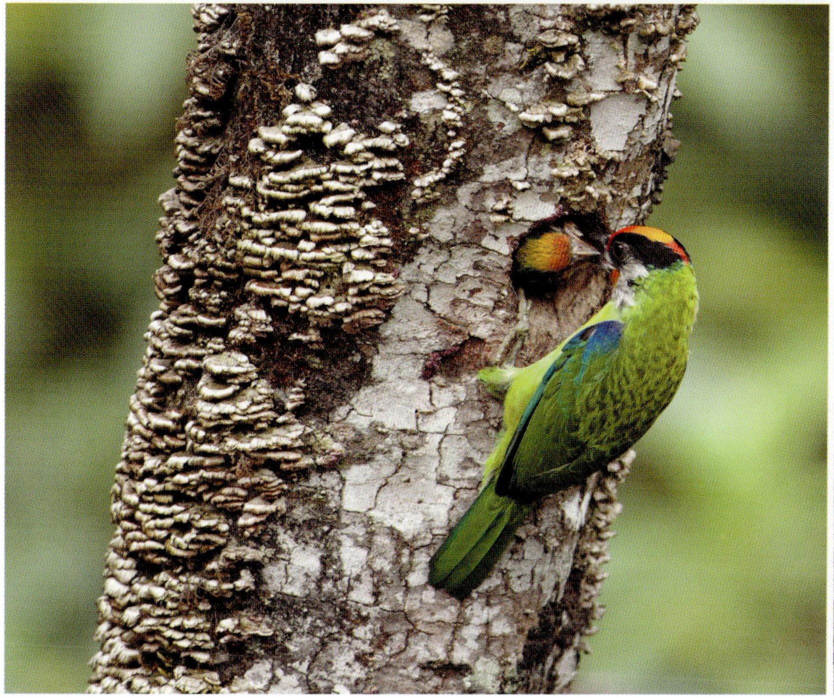

Golden-throated barbets usually build up nests by pecking holes in a withered tree. Throughout the period of breeding their infants, parents travel dozens of times daily between the place of their food source and the tree hole, bringing back food and taking away the droppings of their babies.

Blue-Tailed Bee-Eater

Merops philippinus
IUCN Red List: Least Concern

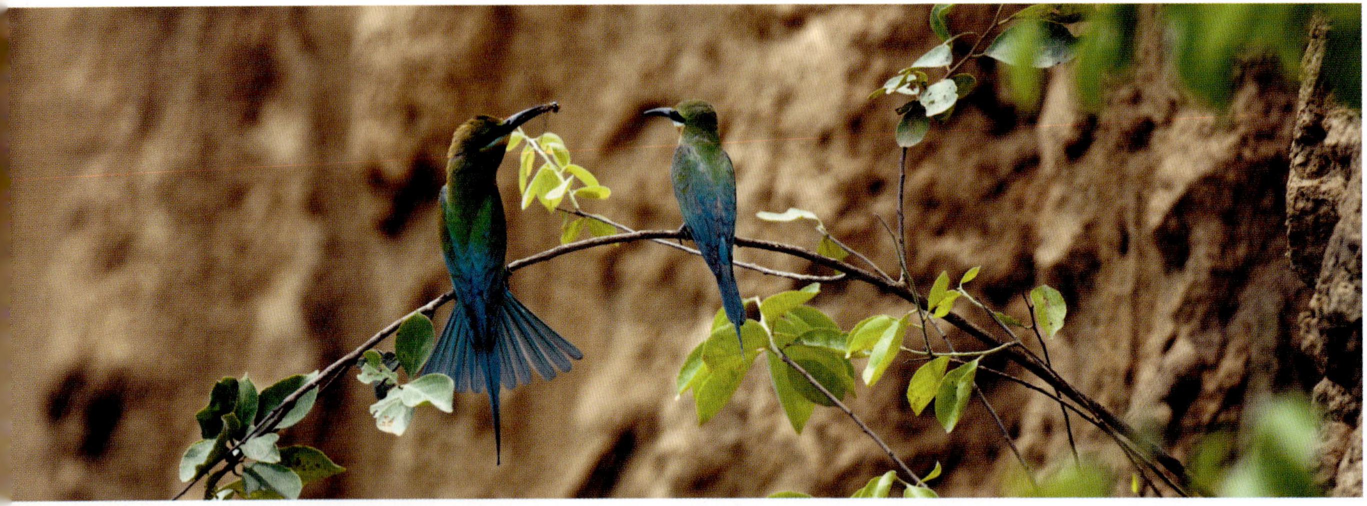

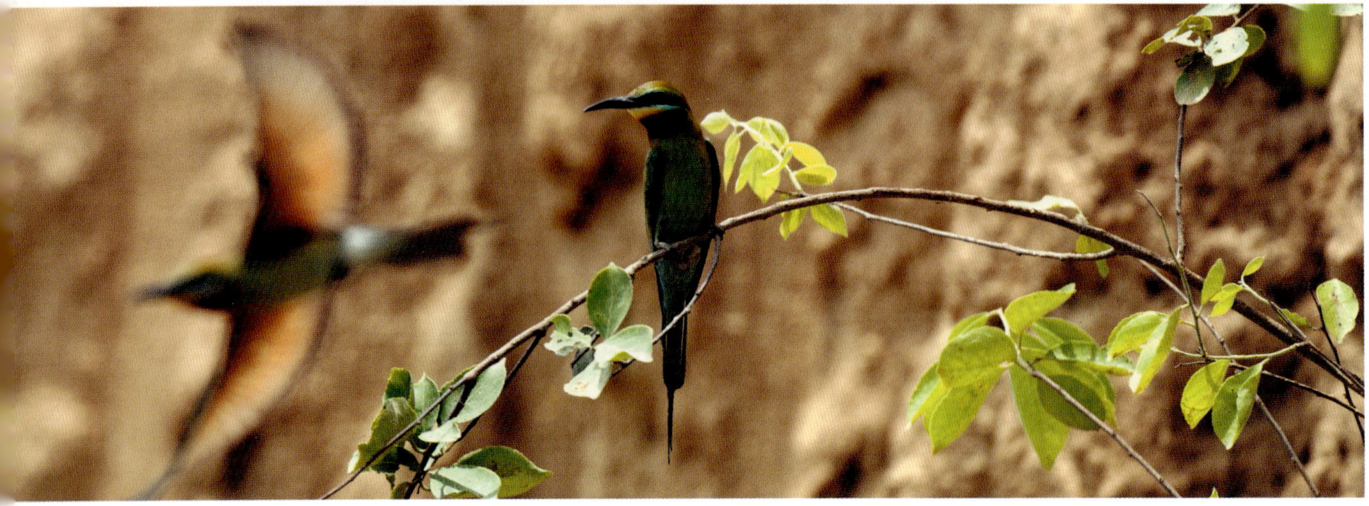

Blue-tailed bee-eaters are chiefly distributed in Southeast Asia. In China, they are only seen in some parts of Yunnan province, Hainan province, Hong Kong, and some coastal areas in Guangdong province and Fujian province.

At the end of April and in early May, they would seek their mates at the place of propagation. At this time, people can often see the male bring food to the female. They look for appropriate earthen and sandy walls for building up nests. Through collective efforts, they dig holes of about one meter deep in the wall, using their beaks and claws as tools. Around the end of July, juveniles step out of the nest to learn to fly and catch prey. Blue-tailed bee-eaters would move around near their habitats. The juveniles would be able to fly on their own in the period between August and October before winter comes around.

With earthen holes as nests, they would be inevitably attached with parasites. Therefore, they would all take sunbaths on the sand under the scorching heat to get rid of the parasites on their bodies. Sometimes, they would shake their wings to let sand enter into the feathers to slough off the parasites.

Above left
The vertical earthen cliff is the most ideal place for blue-tailed bee-eaters to build up their nests.

Below left
The tree branches beside the earthen cliff serve as a stop over before they enter their nest.

Indian Giant Flying Squirrel

Petaurista philippensis

IUCN Red List: Least Concern

With a big size in the tribe of Pteromyini, an Indian giant flying squirrel can be 60 centimeters long. So far, not much research has been conducted on them and there is still controversy over their classification. Generally, they are regarded as being mainly distributed in Yunnan, Sichuan, and Hainan provinces. Most of them live in tropical rain forests, seasonal rain forests, and south subtropical monsoon evergreen broad-leaved forests. They are featured by thick hair, a dark brown back, bright brown neck, and patagium, hair with white and grayish-white colors on the point over the head and back, just like a layer of frost. Their abdomen appears light orange brown and dark brown.

Building up nests on tall tree canopies, they generally move around in the evening mostly in pairs. Sometimes, they jump and glide over the tree canopies in groups, taking tender leaves, nuts, and berries as their food. A female Indian giant flying squirrel gives birth to two to three infants annually in the period from June to July.

Right

An Indian giant flying squirrel is on a tree branch, taking it as a transit platform before seeking for a starting point to fly to a higher tree tip.

Below

This Indian giant flying squirrel spreads its patagium between the front and rear limbs to help it glide quickly amidst the trees. It can use its wrists to adjust the patagium to change direction and speed, while the fluffy tail helps it to fly steadily and serves as an air brake when landing on another tree.

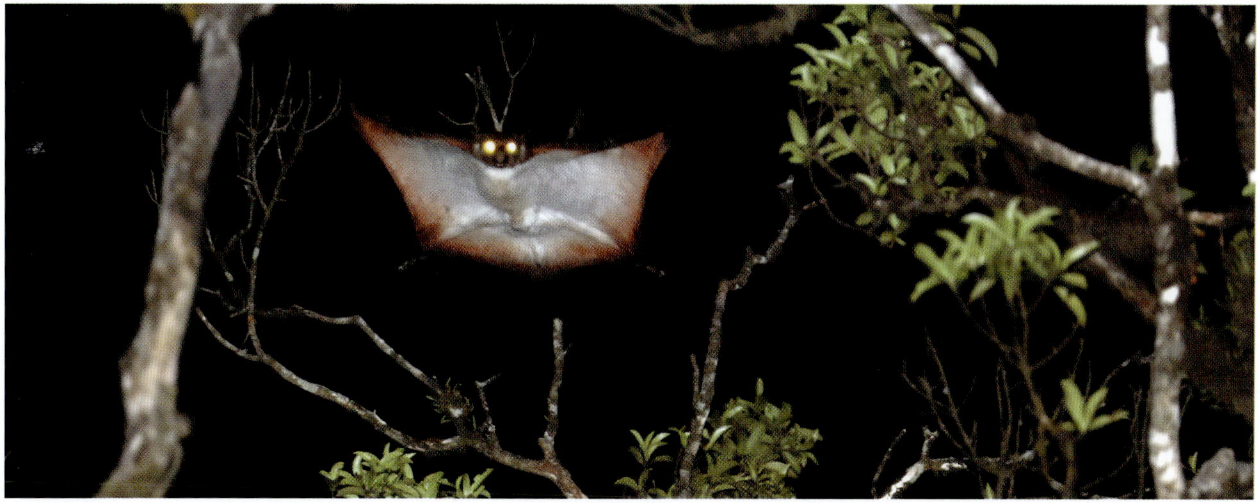

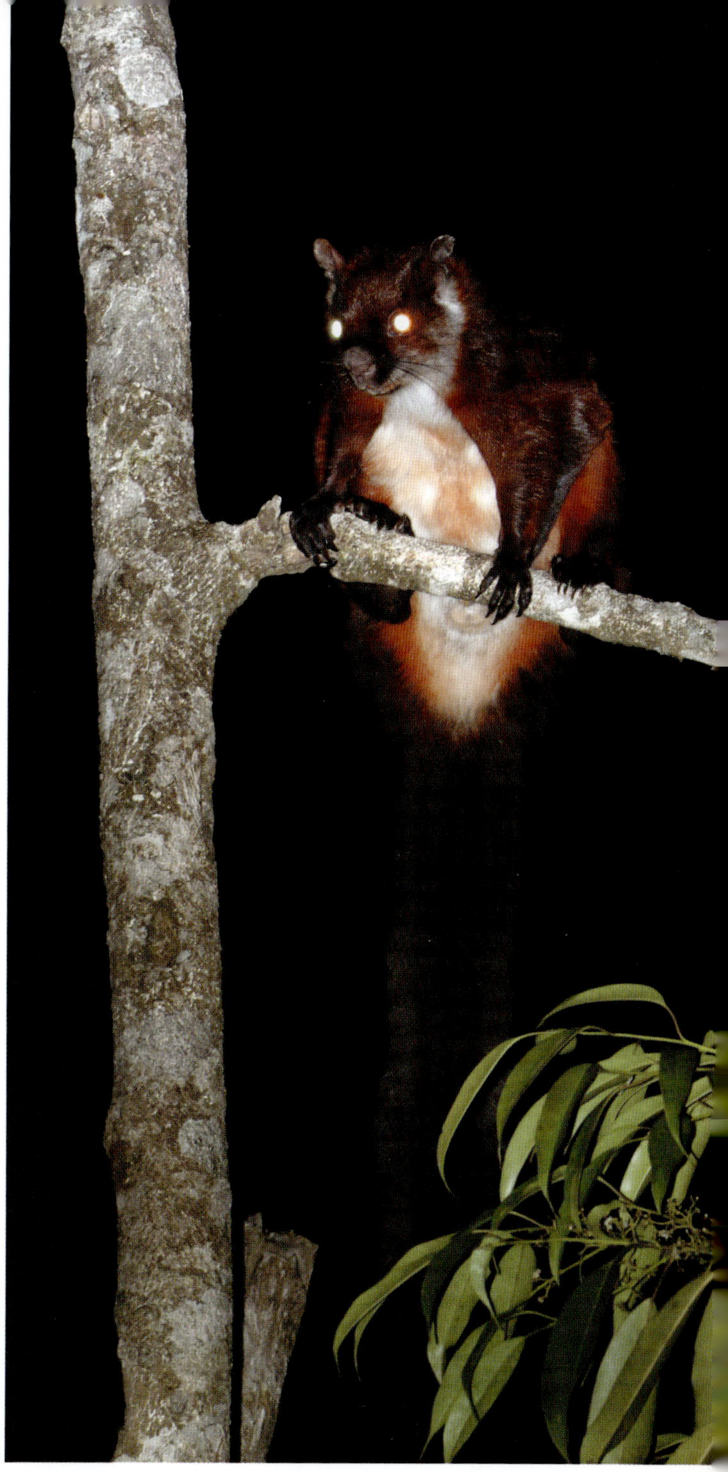

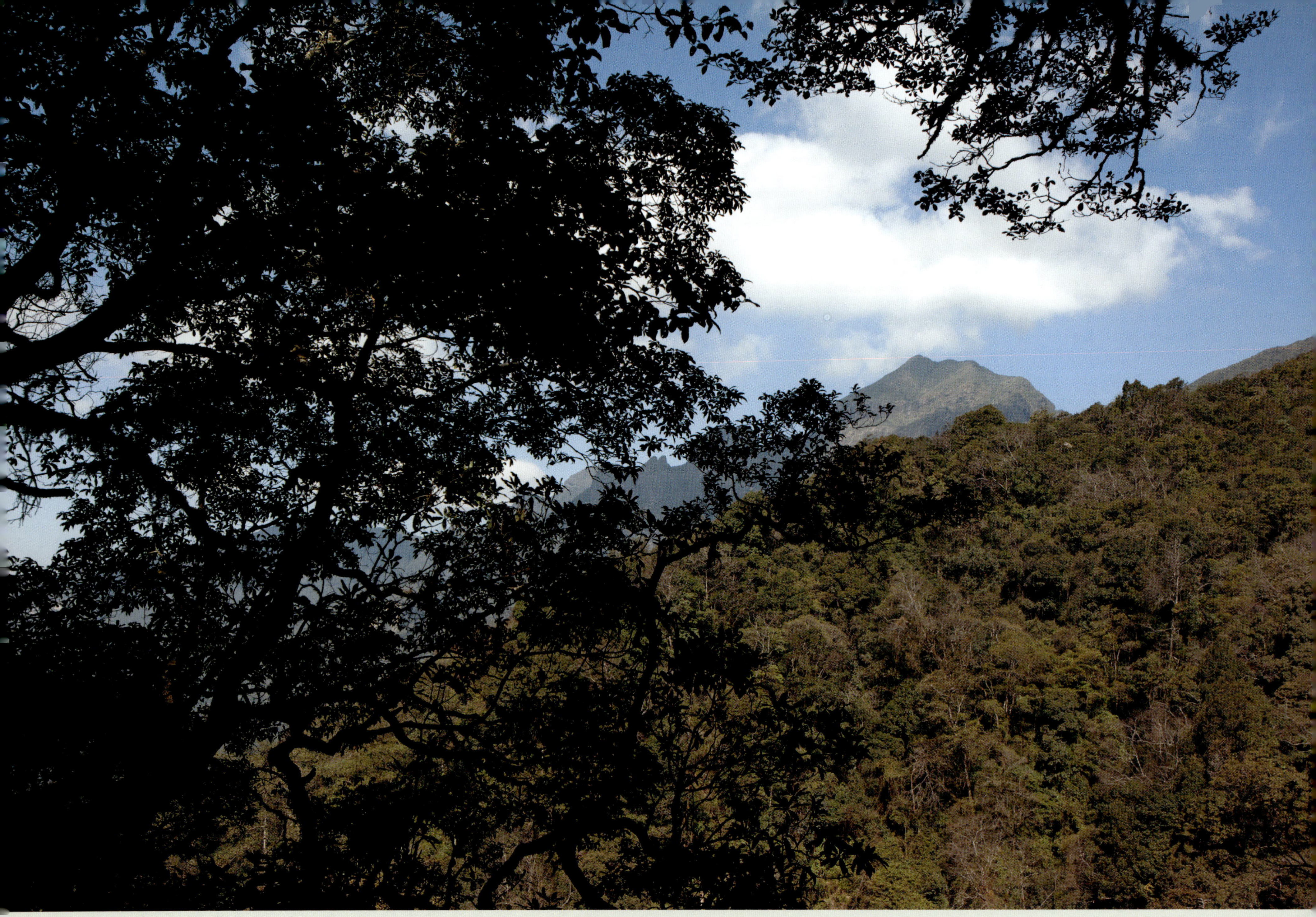

Chapter Nine

Wuliang Mountains—Inside the World of the Western Black Crested Gibbons

Situated where Jingdong Yi Nationality Autonomous County of Pu'er joins Nanjian Yi Nationality Autonomous County of Dali, the Wuliang Mountains National Nature Reserve in Yunnan province is the merger of Jingdong Nature Reserve and Nanjian Nature Reserve. As a nature reserve for protecting wild animals, it is about 83km long from north to south and about 5 to 7 km wide from east to the west, with a total area of 30,938 hectares.

As one of the famous mountains in Yunnan province, it is reputed as "Small Huangshan Mountain," marked by magnificent and steep terrains, dense and lush forests, and the absence of human beings in many places there. The Wuliang Mountains Nature Reserve lies at the joint of the Tibetan Plateau, Hengduan Mountains, and Yunnan Plateau as three big geographic areas of nature. With high and steep mountainous terrains, its highest sea level reaches 2,206 meters while its lowest sea level is over 1,000 meters. So far, the Wuliang Mountains is still a mysterious big mountain unknown to people. Thanks to its unique three-dimensional climate, there are extremely rich resources of animals and plants. Its ecosystem of mesic evergreen broad-leaved forests gives birth to many wild animals, such as black crested gibbons, Mrs. Hume's pheasant, as well as many precious and rare plants, such as Chinese yews and China bretschneidera. Black crested gibbons are first-grade animals under national protection as they are on the verge of extinction. So far, they are seen only in Dahei Mountains in Hainan province and the Wuliang Mountains in Jingdong.

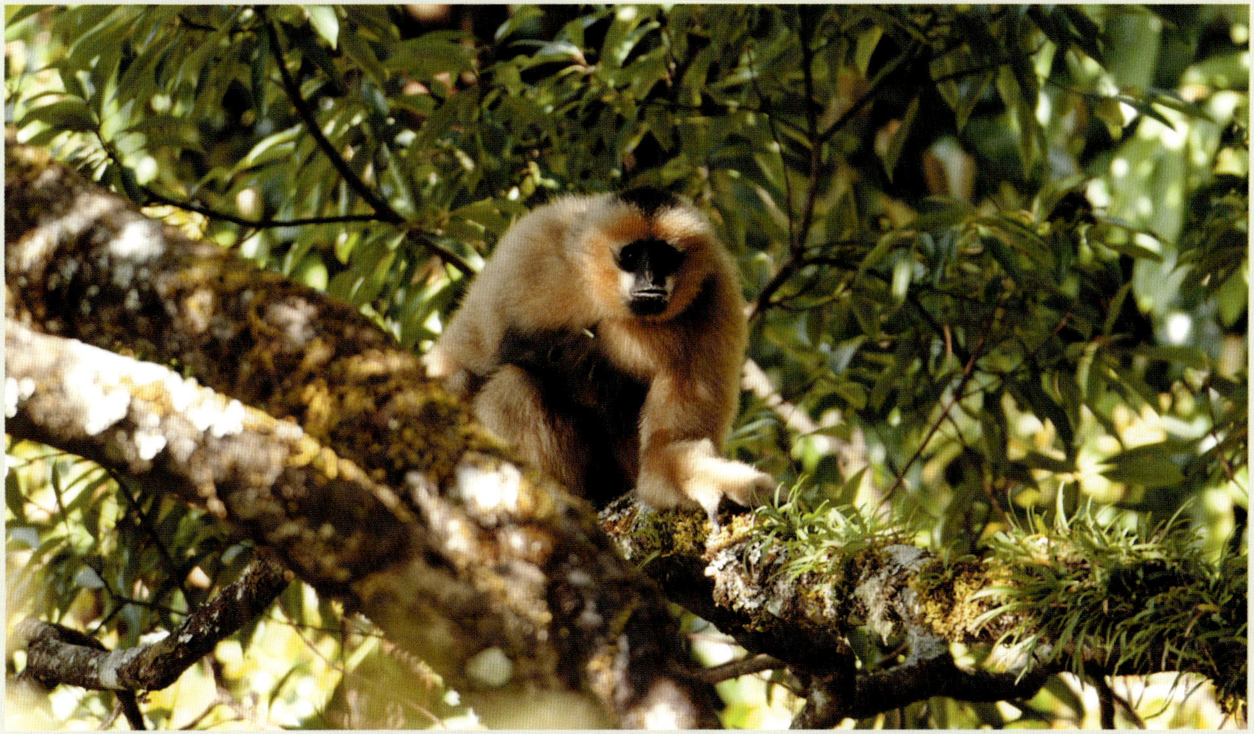

On facing page
The magnificent, steep, and unique Wuliang Mountains.

So far, the Wuliang Mountains is only one of the two habitats for western black crested gibbons, which are facing stern crisis of survival.

Western Black Crested Gibbon

Nomascus concolor

IUCN Red List: Critically Endangered

There are a total of about 1,100 to 1,400 western black crested gibbons in the world. In addition to about 100 in Vietnam and Laos, the rest of them live in Yunnan province with a number of about 1,000 to 1,300. Western black crested gibbons are the most extensively distributed gibbons with the greatest number among all of the different kinds of gibbons in China. These medium-sized gibbons chiefly live in tropical rains forests and south subtropical montane humid evergreen broad-leaved forests. Their habitats range from 1,000 meters to 2,500 meters above sea level. They live at places at the highest sea level of all the gibbons already known. They move around and look for food amidst canopies of tall arbor trees 15 meters above the ground or the medium layer, seldom going to perch on small trees of less than five meters above the ground. Western black crested gibbons differ from other kinds of gibbons in their bigger-sized groups. Monogamy and polygamy co-exist. The range of their activities covers more than 100 hectares, larger than that of other kinds of gibbons.

The Wuliang Mountains is the only area distributed with the sub-species of western black crested gibbons, *N.c.jingdongensis*. They mostly live in mesic evergreen broad-leaved forests at 2,000 to 2,600 meters above sea level. In of the last twelve years, the influence of human activities, particularly the destruction and loss of habitats, have reduced the range of their life and their number and led to the fragmentation of the species groups.

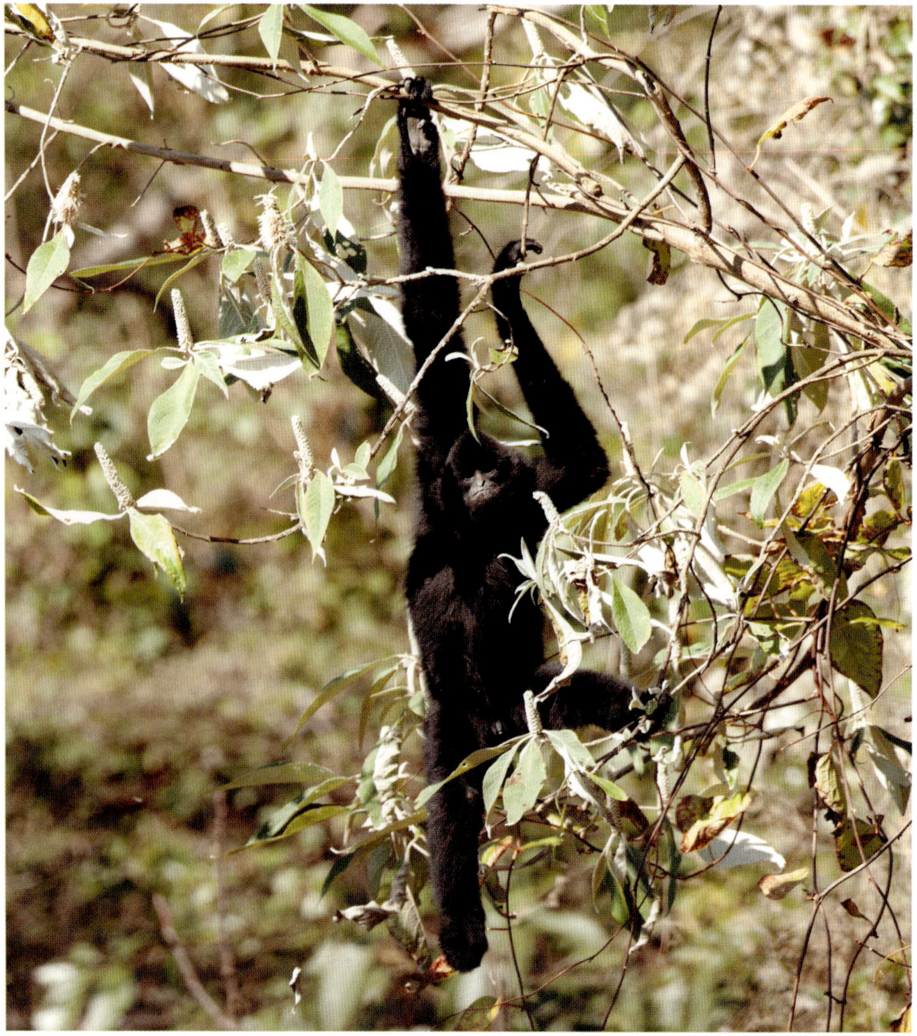

Among all the gibbons, western black crested gibbons have the greatest number in a relatively stable state of survival.

On facing page
The females' bodies can be grey-yellow, brown-yellow, or orange-yellow, and their heads have a diamond-shaped or multi-angle black-brown crest spots, while their chest and abdomen are light grey-yellow and often black-brown.

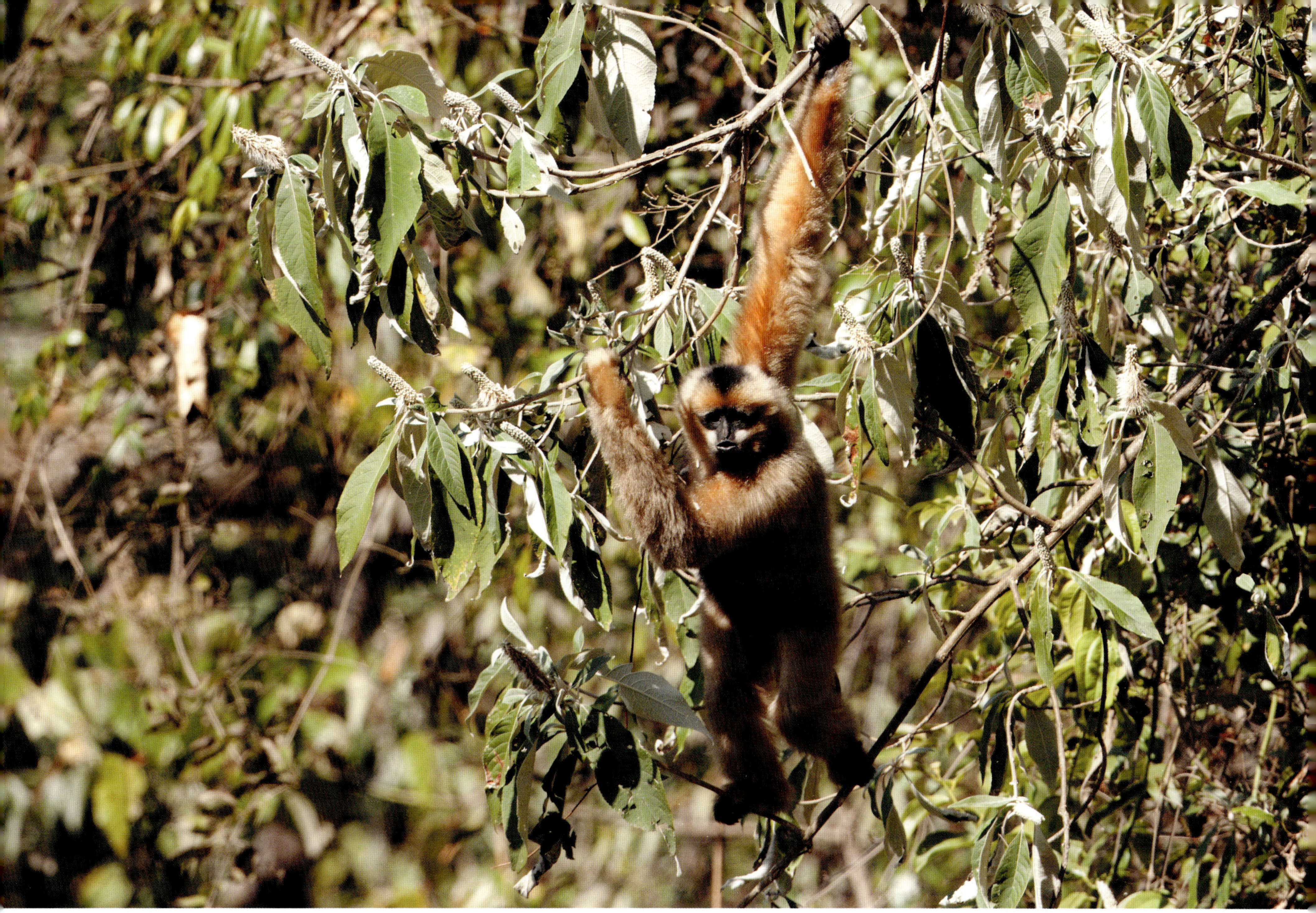

Oriental Pied Hornbill

Anthracoceros albirostris
IUCN Red List: Least Concern

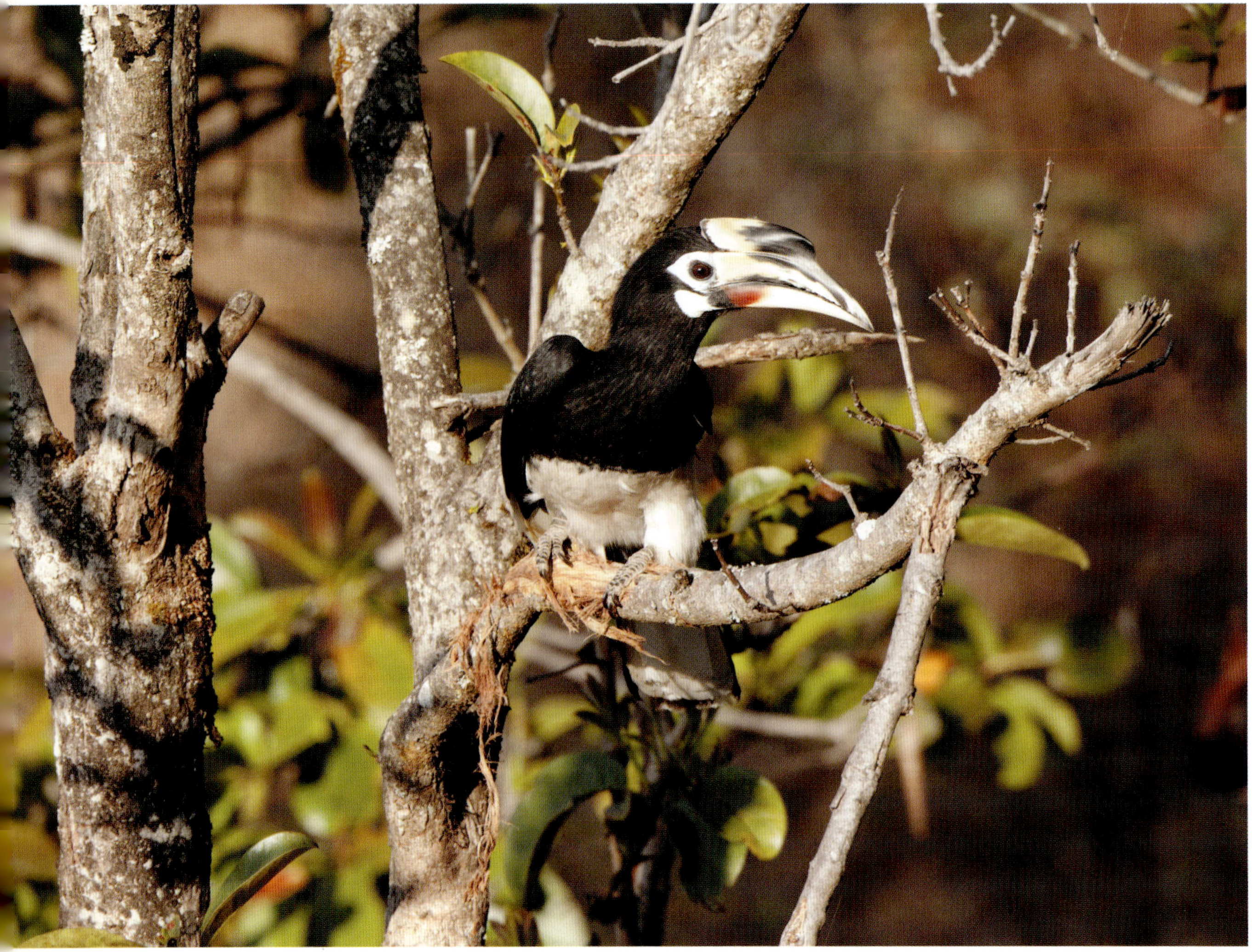

As typical birds in tropical forests, hornbills with big beaks are marked by interesting habits of propagation. They choose to lay eggs in big natural tree holes. After the laying eggs, the female would crouch in the hole to hatch them, while the male seals off the hole opening with mud, only leaving a small hole for delivering food to the female and infants until the latter grows all their feathers. The male looks for food far and wide each day, flying between the forest and his family. At night, the male would perch outside of the tree, standing guard against invasion from the enemy. The male and the female will not be united until the infants become fully grown. By then, they would take juveniles to practice flying and looking for food. This unique way of bringing up babies is conducive to preventing the younger generation from being harmed by snakes and other natural predators.

There are five kinds of hornbills in China. Among them, the oriental pied hornbills with a length of 75 centimeters are the most extensively distributed. They are seen in southwestern Yunnan

Hornbills are representative species in the tropical forests of Yunnan province. Due to the quick disappearance of tropical forests, hornbills are rarely seen now.

On facing page
Oriental pied hornbills, after having disappeared for nearly 30 years in the Wuliang Mountains, have appeared in the pinewoods.

province, southern Xishuangbanna, and a few areas in western Guangxi. They mainly live in tropical rain forests in low mountains at less than 1,500 meters above sea level or at the foot of mountains. Most of them rest and move around in trees and go to look for food on the ground. They eat the fruit of such plants as banyans and seeds, as well as snails, worms, insects, rats, and snakes. When eating, they would first throw food up towards the sky, catch it with their beaks, and then swallow it up.

Since the 1960s, lots of tropical rain forests have been cut down, hence having seriously damaged the habitats of these birds and greatly reduced the range of their activities.

My Preordained Relationship with Oriental Pied Hornbills

My preordained relationship with the oriental pied hornbills can be traced back to 2008 when some villagers in Jingdong county found two strange big birds in the mountain. Zhang Xingwei, the head of Jingdong Nature Reserve Administration at that time, took a picture of them and passed it to me. However, I was not sure about what kind of hornbills they were. From January 30 to February 1, 2009, I went to Jingdong with some others to conduct a three-day follow-up picture taking of and investigation into those two hornbills. It was finally proven that they were indeed oriental pied hornbills.

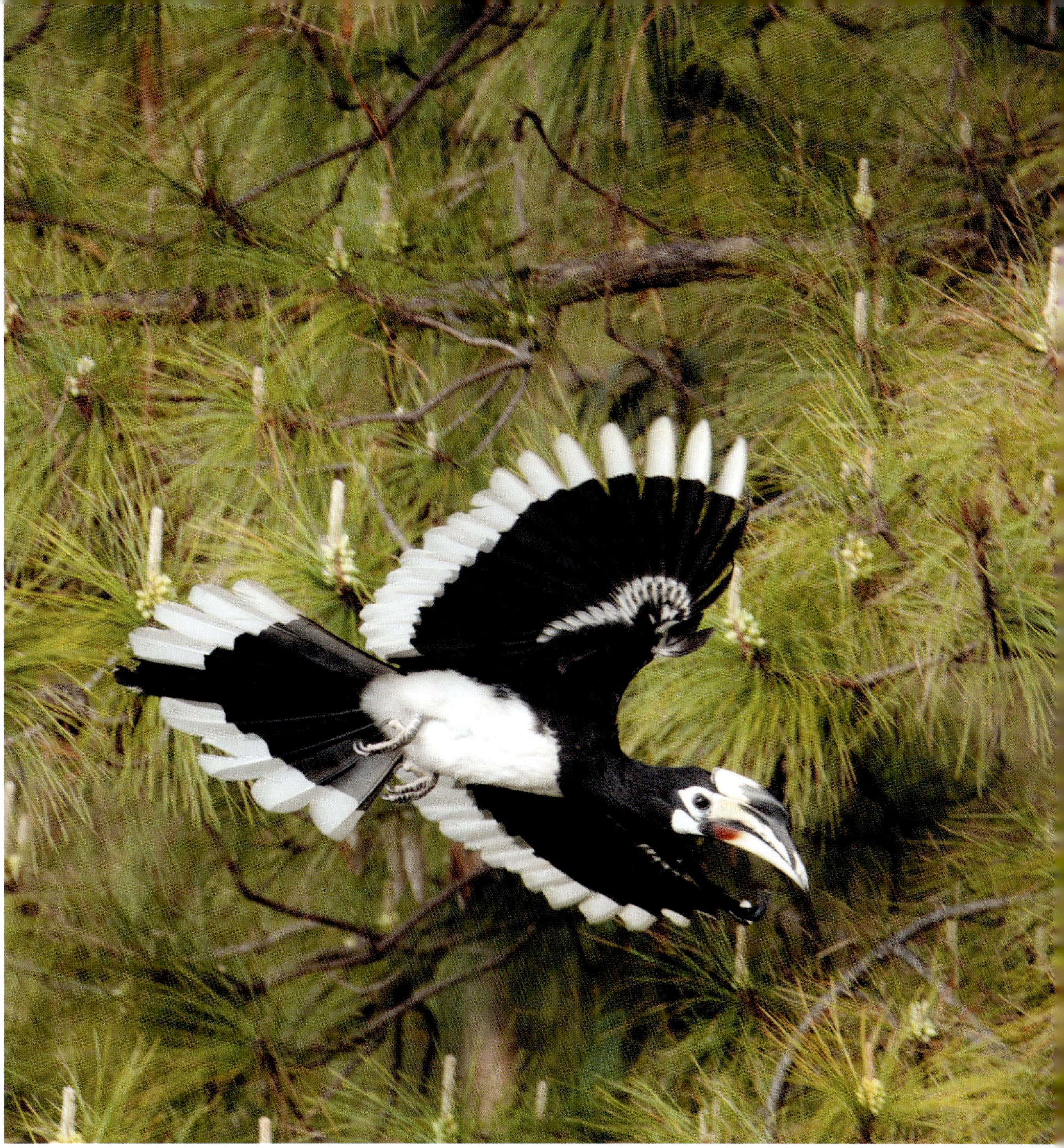

Lady Amherst's Pheasant

Chrysolophus amherstiae

IUCN Red List: Least Concern

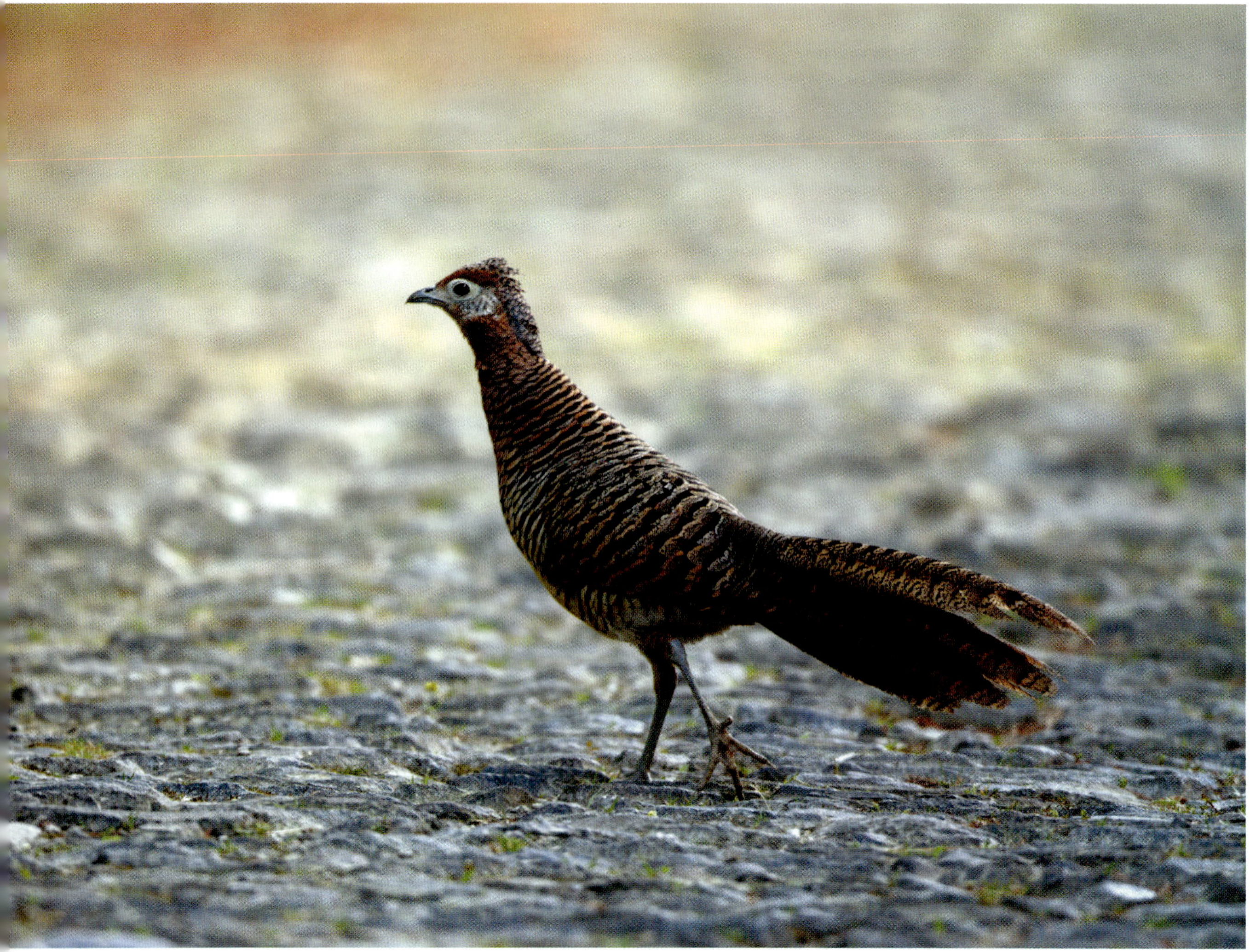

As one of the most beautiful pheasants in China, Lady Amherst's pheasants are chiefly distributed in southeastern Tibet, southwestern Sichuan province, western Guizhou province, western Guangxi, and most parts of Yunnan province. They live in mountain evergreen broad-leaved forests, coniferous and broad-leaved mixed forests, as well as coniferous forests at about 1,000 to 4,000 meters above sea level. They also live in bushes at forest edges as well as amidst grassy slopes and short bamboo groves. In the winter, they look for food near farmland. At night, they perch on tree canopies for shelter. In the daytime, they would come down to move around on the ground. They usually form into small groups of 4 to 5, or over ten. In the winter when there is a lack of food, they form bigger groups with as many as 20 to 30. Their robust feet enable them to run very fast in the forests. However, they seldom fly since their flying capacity is not very good. When encountering danger, they mostly run fast or hide to escape from the enemy. They will not fly onto trees or slide down along the slope unless it is very urgent and dangerous.

They mainly eat plants as well as insects. They chiefly look for food on the ground, sometimes fly onto trees to eat fruit. They mostly look for food in

Compared with males, females are less eye-catching. Female Lady Amherst's pheasants are very similar to female golden pheasants, but the former's head has a darker color and the veins of their abdomen are not so obvious.

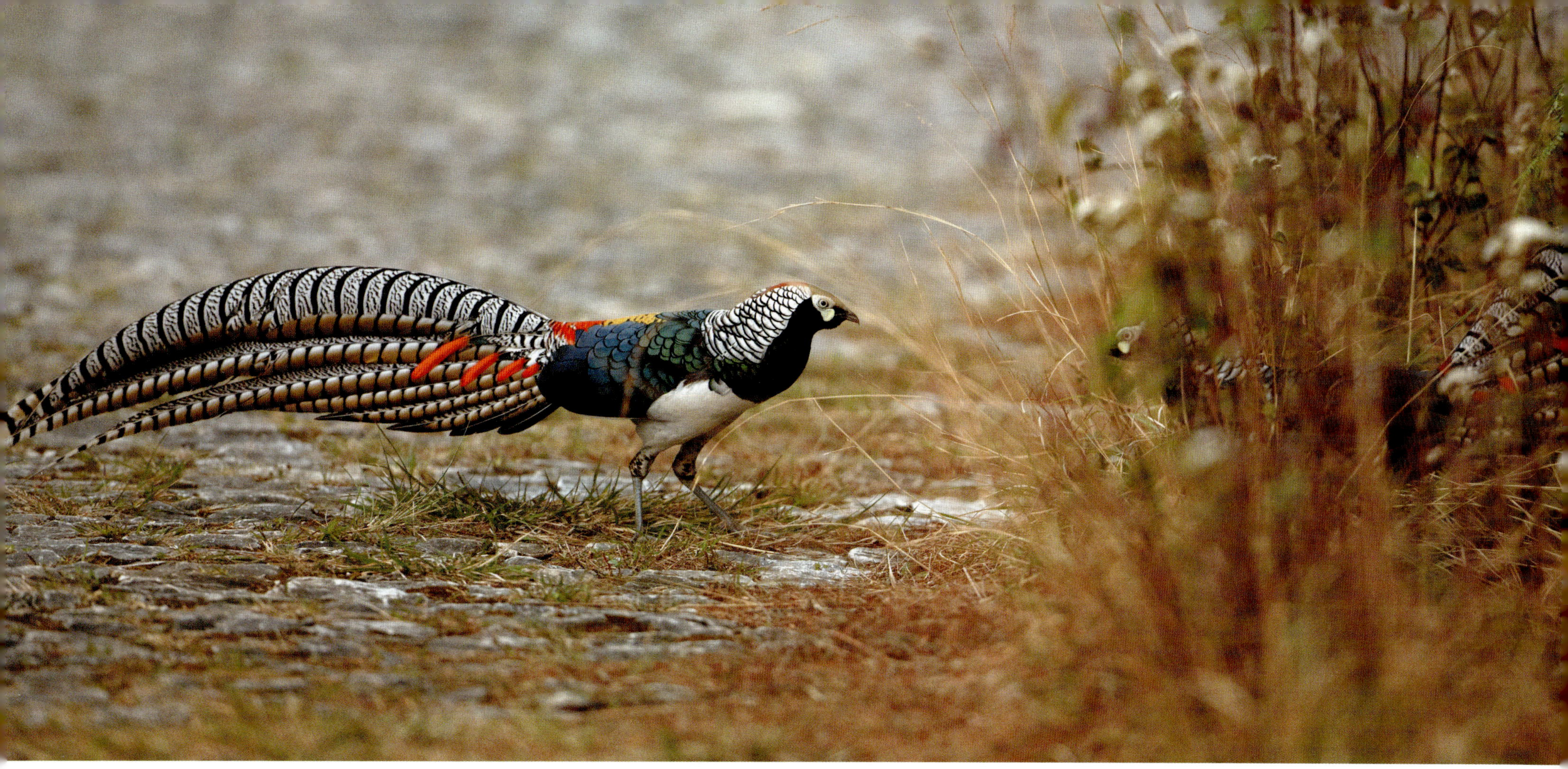

Lady Amherst's pheasants are probably the most extensively distributed and the most commonly seen pheasants with the most gorgeous feathers in southwestern China.

the morning and afternoon, with higher frequency particularly in the early morning or near dusk. They would rest beneath trees.

Their propagation takes place in the period from April to June. In March, the male would begin to occupy places as their territory and drive away other males. They would scream to declare their ownership. Male Lady Amherst's pheasants conduct themselves very interestingly when seeking for mates. The pastel green wattle under their eyes become inflated while the white ruff over their nape spread like a fan. They would keep showing off around the females and frequently extend the cape facing one side of the female into the low part forward as much as possible, with their wings drooping and the whole back leaning against the female to show their gorgeous back feathers. Meanwhile, they would spread their tail feathers like a fan toward the female, moving around the female in an arc or semi-arc manner. Such performance of seeking for a mate lasts for as short as 7 minutes and as long as 45 minutes. The female builds up the nest in bushes or under the fallen log, a nest which cannot be easily found.

Lady Amherst's pheasants were quite noble birds in ancient China. Those with their image embroidered on official robes were grade-two officials. However, there is a dense human population in areas distributed with them and reclamation for farmland is continuously nibbling at their habitats. In order to get their beautiful feathers, excessive hunting also poses a serious threat to their survival.

Jingdong Toothed Toad

Oreolalax jingdongensis

IUCN Red List: Vulnerable

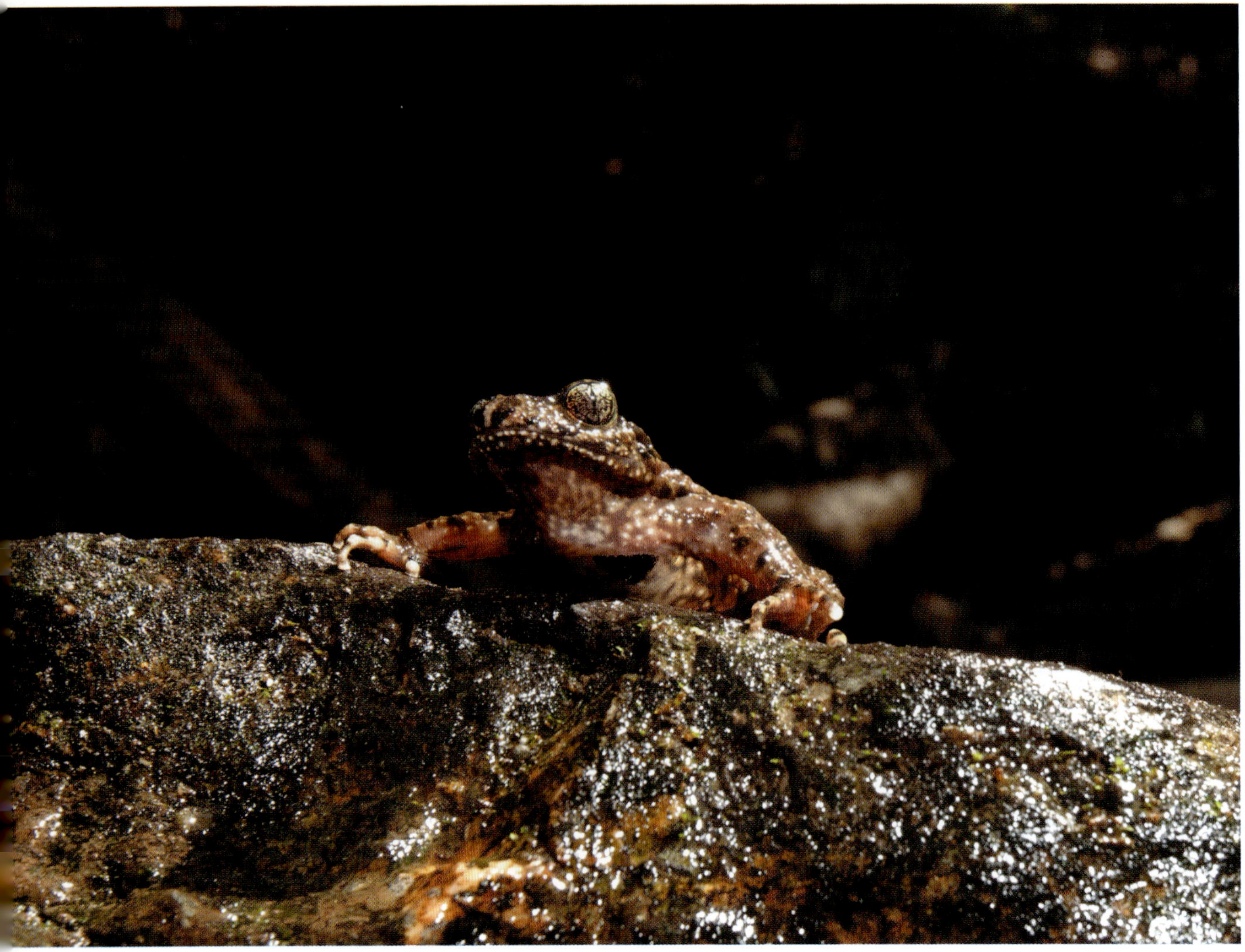

In the Wuliang Mountains, the ecosystem of south subtropical mesic evergreen broad-leaved forests has provided desirable habitats for amphibious animals and reptiles. Such unique amphibious animals as the Ailao moustache toad (*Vibrissaphoras ailaonica*) and the Jingdong toothed toads live in areas with slow flowing mountain streams, and pebble filled streams in evergreen broad-leaved forests at 2,400 meters above sea level.

Toothed toads are unique to China. Jingdong toothed toads are only distributed in Jingdong, Shuangbai, and Xinping in Yunnan province. The area of their distribution is narrow since it only covers an area of less than 2,000 square kilometers. Due to the serious fragmentation of distribution, the range and quality of their habitats have also been continuously declining.

The male Jingdong toothed toad is about 55 mm long and the back is earthen black with many black spots. The head and back are coarse, full of warts.

Chapter Ten
Other Areas

Mandarin Duck (Beijing)

Aix galericulata

IUCN Red List: Least Concern

The Mandarin duck is a kind of small duck, with the males being very gorgeous. They live in coniferous and broad-leaved mixed forests in nearby streams, marshes, reed fields, and lakes. They are fond of group activities. A group usually consists of over 20. Sometimes, they mingle with other wild ducks. Every day before the morning, mist fully disperses; they fly out of their habitats in the woods and gather beside ponds. They float and take food over the water covered with tree shade or reeds, and then fly to the woods to look for food. In about one to two hours, they would successively come back to rest on tree branches or rocks near flood land or ponds. While playing in water, they stretch their necks and drift with the water flow. Sometimes, they would also beat the water with their wings, throwing themselves in and out of the surface and stirring up a spray of glistening water. At dusk, they fly back to the woods or earthen pits, or caves near the water to sleep. During sleep, they put their head under their wings with one foot standing. They also doze off sometimes while floating on the water.

Mandarin ducks are species occurring with very high frequency in traditional Chinese culture. Nowadays, Beijing has become an important place for their propagation. They can be seen in ancient royal gardens or on the waters of new urban areas.

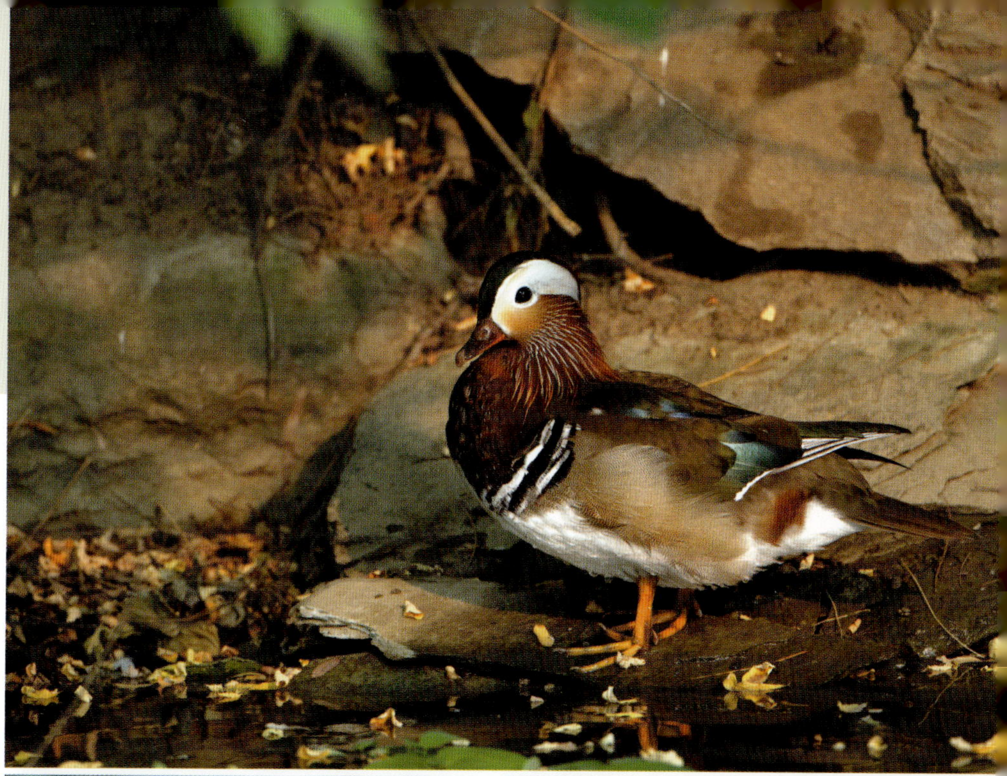

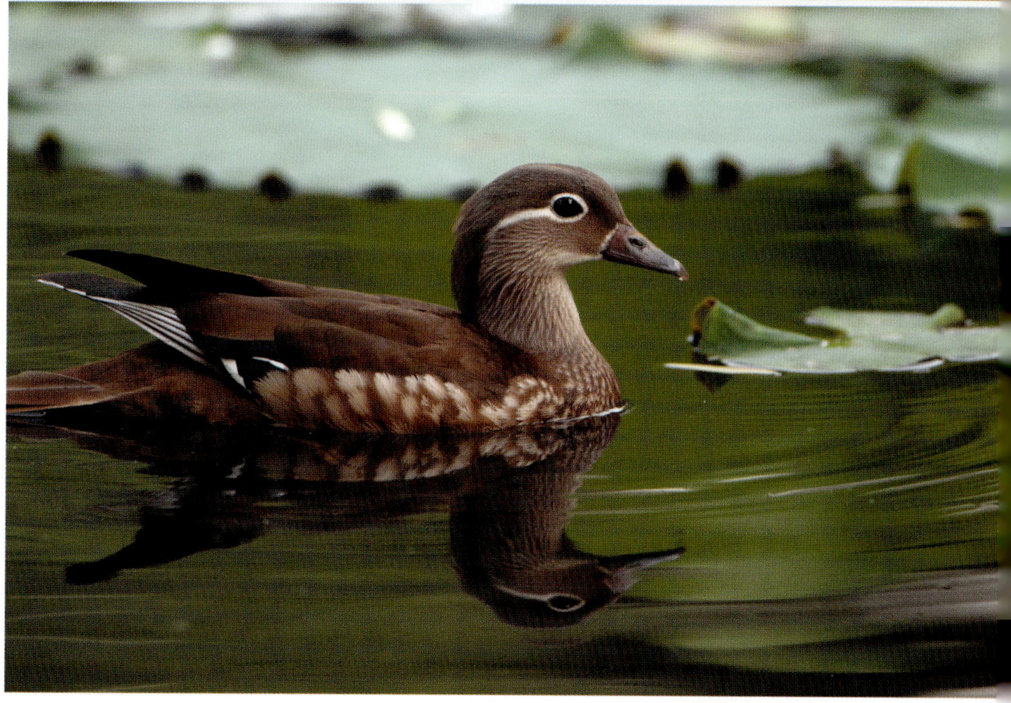

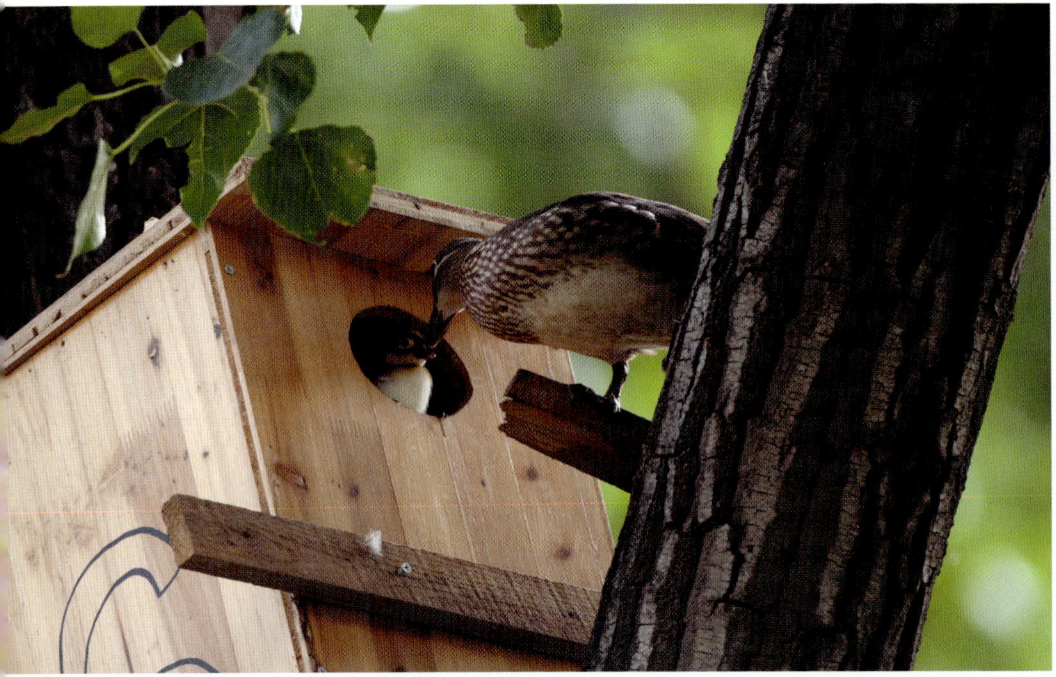

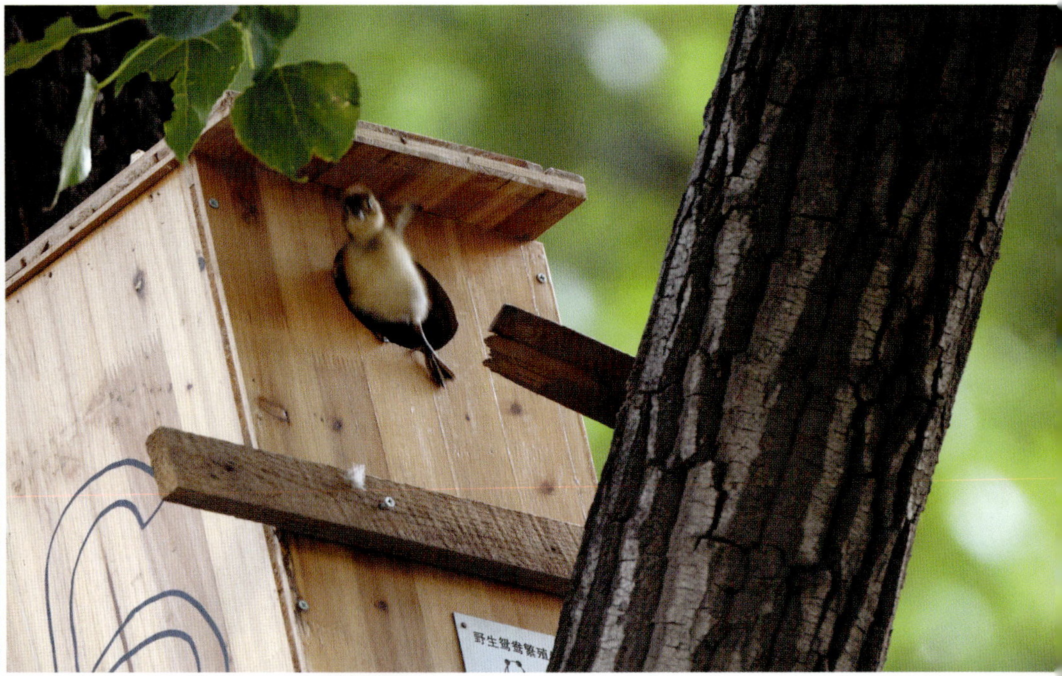
野生鸳鸯繁殖

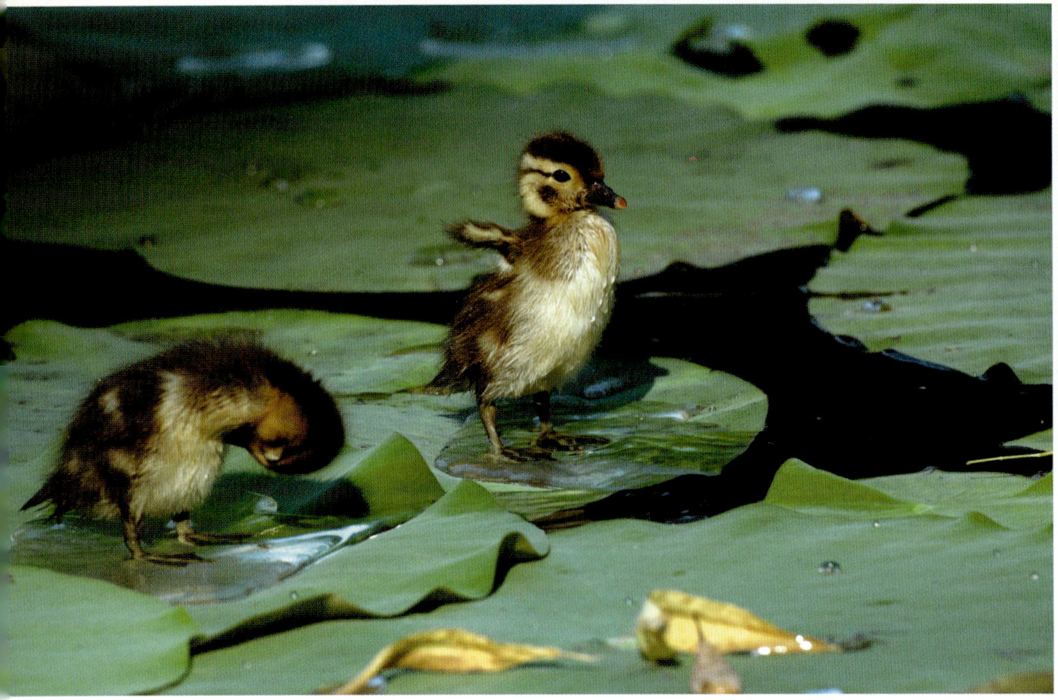

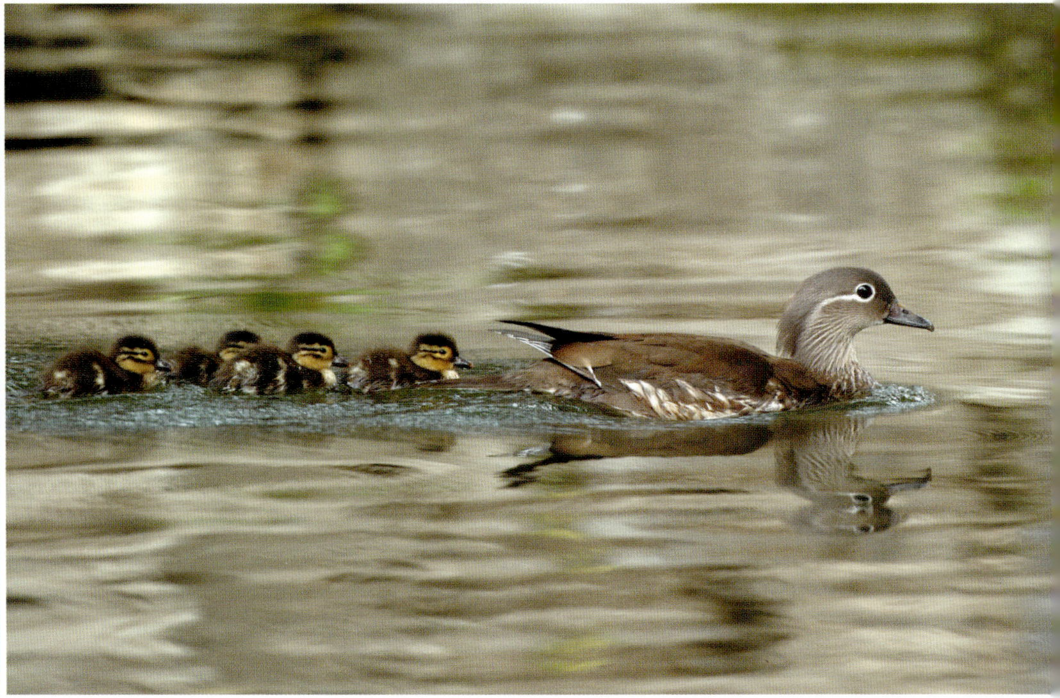

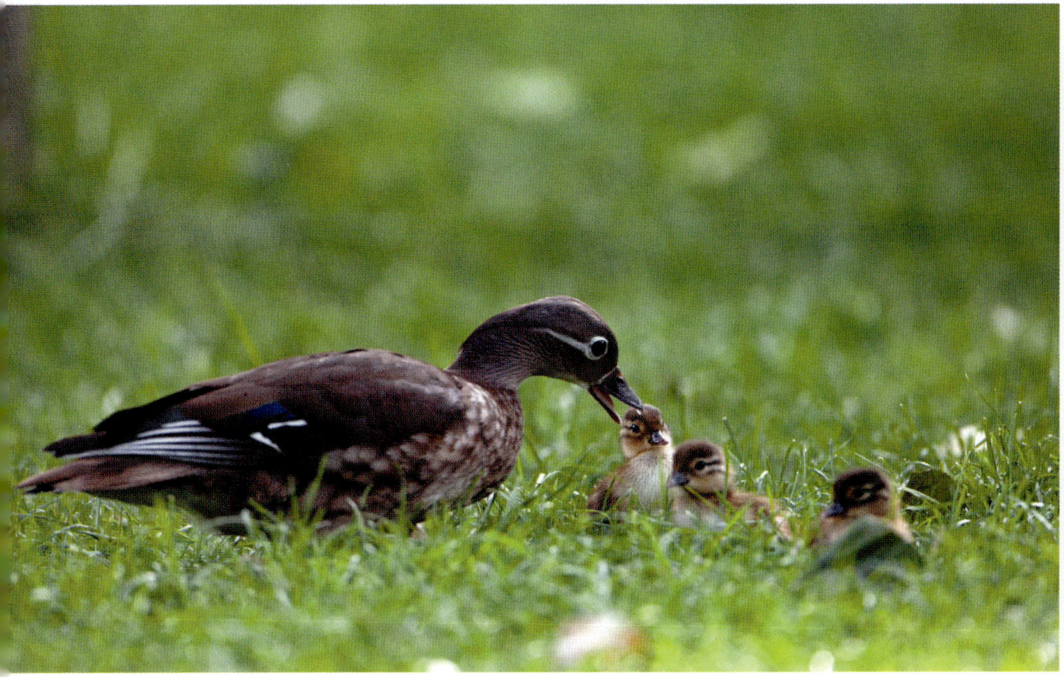

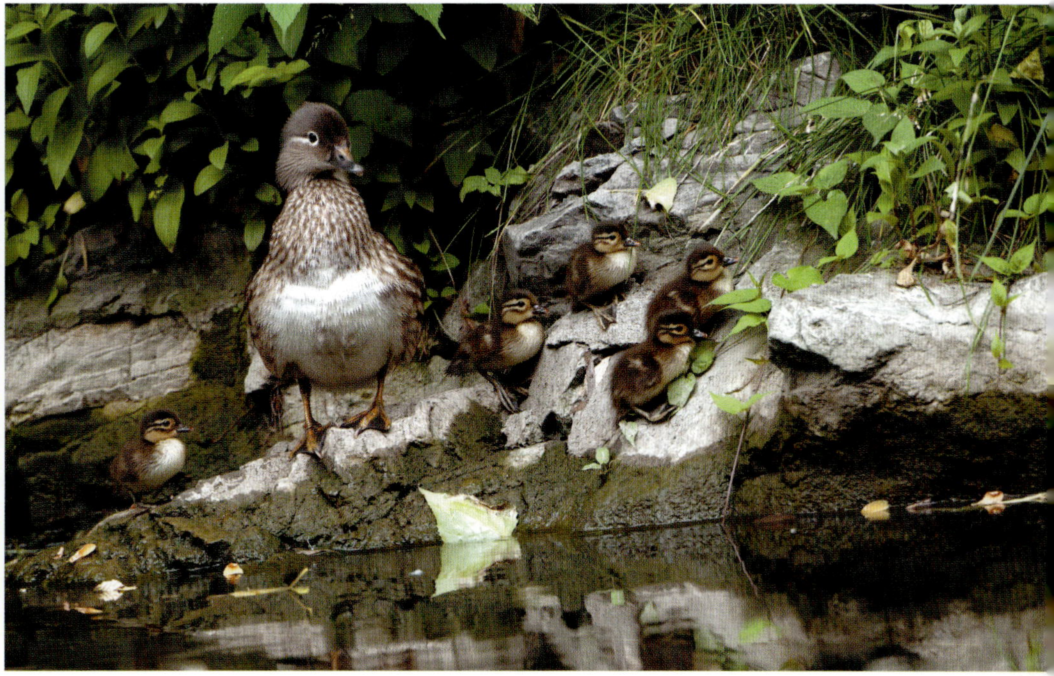

1 2 3 4
5 6

After mating, males moult by the water at other places while the females lay their eggs and take care of the infants in natural holes in big old trees. If there are not enough tree holes, man-made nests are OK. The nest is laid with scraps of wood and soft adult feathers. The female begins to lay eggs at the end of May. After 28 to 29 days of hatching, when all the infants are born, the female prepares to take them to leave the nest. The mother kisses her babies for encouragement. Then, it would chirp and about an hour later, it flies out of the tree hole. An infant chirps as it slowly moves half of its body out of the tree hole, flutters its wings, and jumps down to the grass. The mother pecks its head and takes it to the riverside. The mother jumps into the water first as the two infants stand on the lotus leaf. One withdraws its head while the other shakes its wings, getting ready to jump into the water. After a short while, several infants are able to swim decently while following their mother.

Mandarin ducks eat different kinds of things and the variety of their food changes according to different seasons and habitats. In the season of propagation, they would eat chiefly animal-based foods. In the winter, their food includes almost all kinds of nuts from such plants as oaks.

They mostly spend winter at places with lots of food and convenience for getting them. In February, they begin to seek out their mates. Having found mates, they would move around in pairs in paddy fields or oak woods and occasionally in ponds. In April, when the accumulated snow in northern China is not completely thawed, they fly impatiently over plains and high mountains to get to northern China and northeastern China to build up nests for propagation. Ducklings grow up gradually. Males and females begin the plumage exchange prepare for a long trudge to the place for spending the winter. In the period from the end of September to early October, they leave the place of propagation and fly to southern China. During the migration, they fall into groups of about ten and sometimes as many as over 50. In the period from the end of March to early April, they migrate to the place of propagation in northern China.

Guizhou Snub-Nosed Monkey

(Fanjing Mountains, Guizhou Province)

Rhinopithecus brelichi

IUCN Red List: Endangered

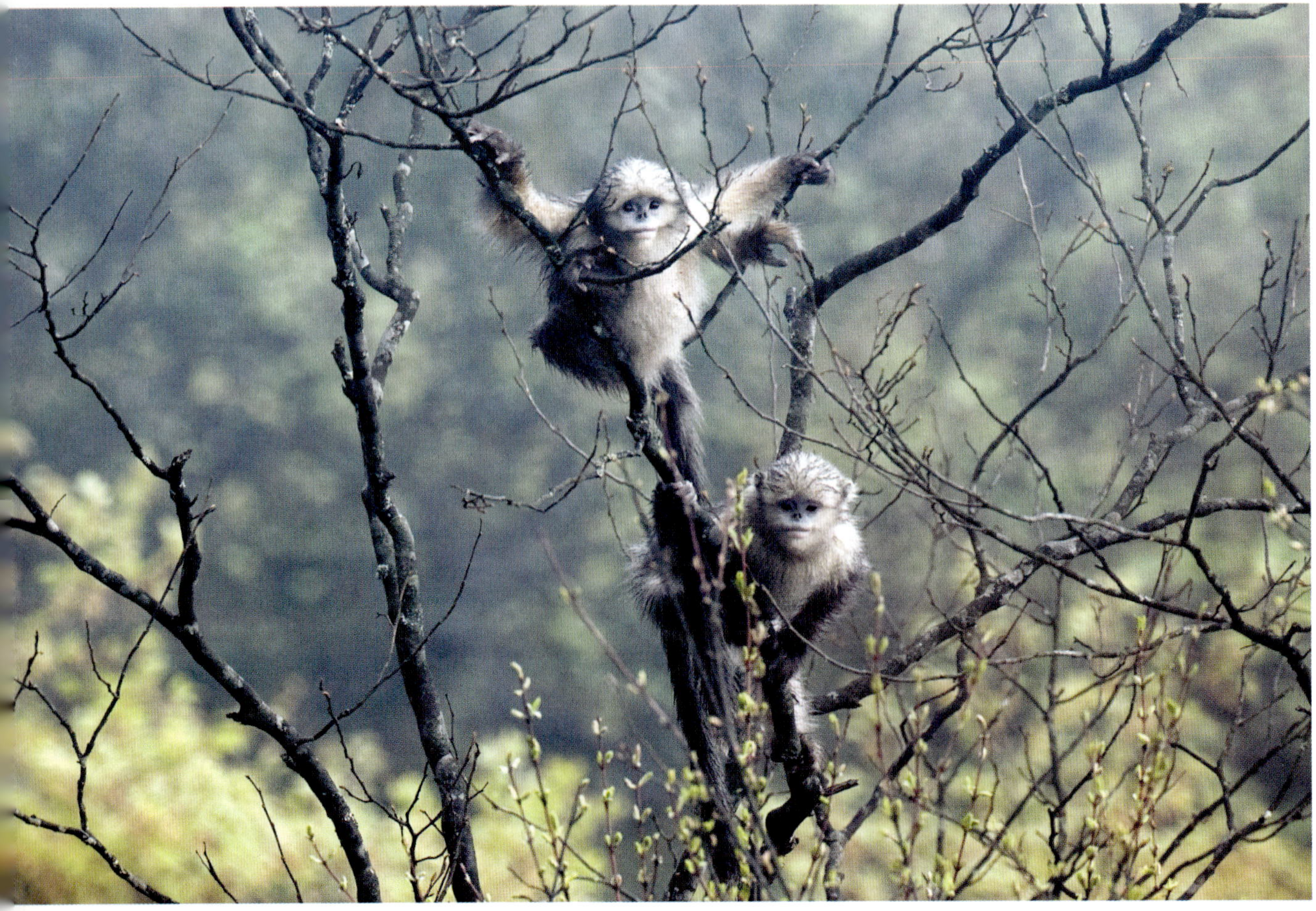

Among the four kinds of snub-nosed monkeys in China, the number of Guizhou snub-nosed monkeys is the smallest (less than 800) and they are distributed in the narrowest area. As primates right on the verge of extinction, they are only seen in the Fanjing Mountains Nature Reserve in northeastern Guizhou province.

The males are big while females are obviously small. They move around in large groups with as many as over 400. The group is composed of small families; each family has an adult male, 2 to 3 females, and 1 to 3 infants. As the head of the family, the male is in charge of their safety and takes the lead in jumping from one tree to another, and inspects the tree to make sure there is no danger before situating his family there.

In the river-valleys at 500 to 800 meters above sea level in the Fanjing Mountains, there are deciduous broad-leaved forests, i.e. lampstand trees, mountain ashes, and hollies, as well as dove trees, a kind of precious and rare plant. Guizhou snub-nosed monkeys like to eat them very much, particularly the tender buds of dove trees.

These two small monkeys are looking at the spot where the photographer is hiding as they climb up to the tree top.

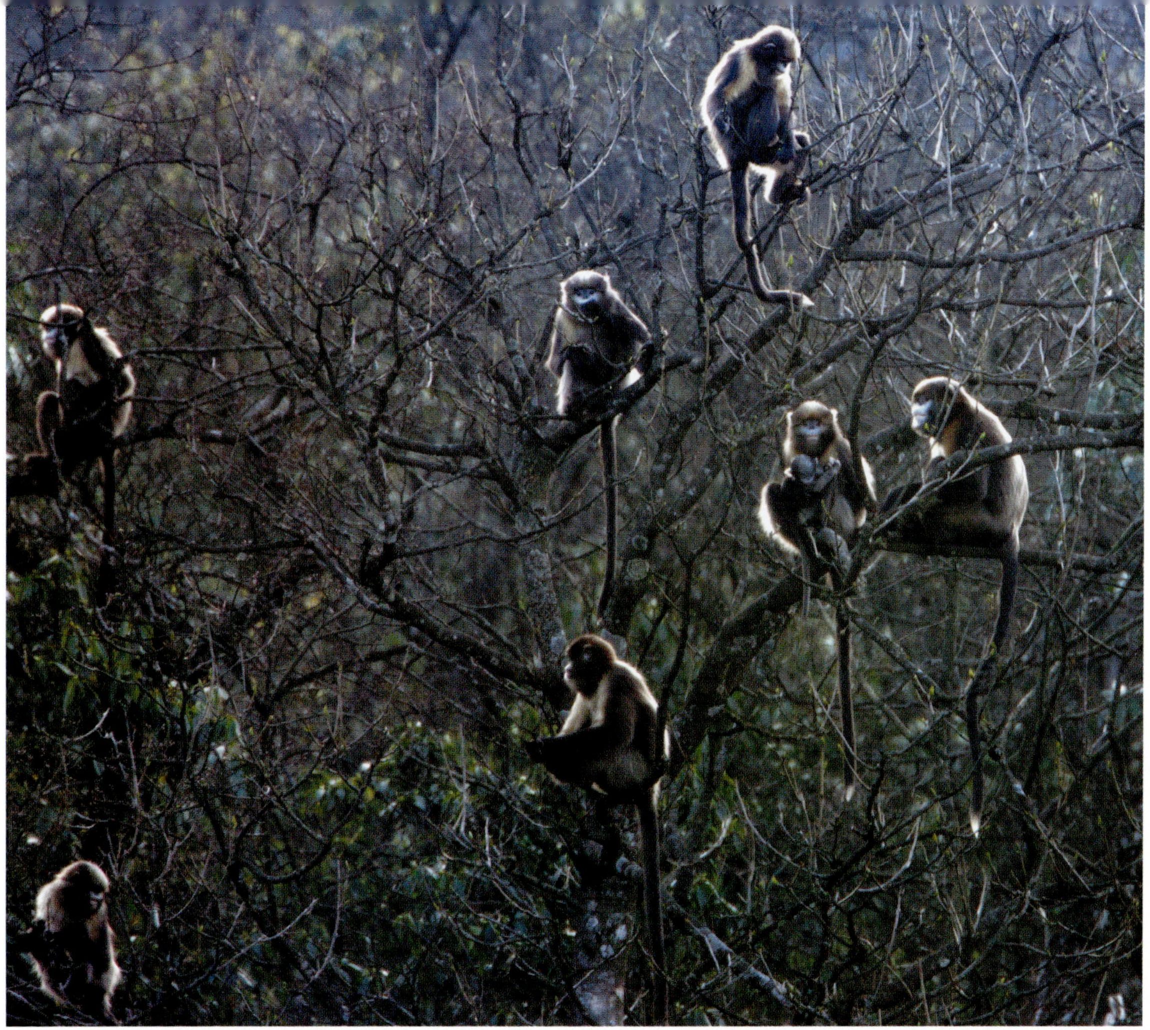

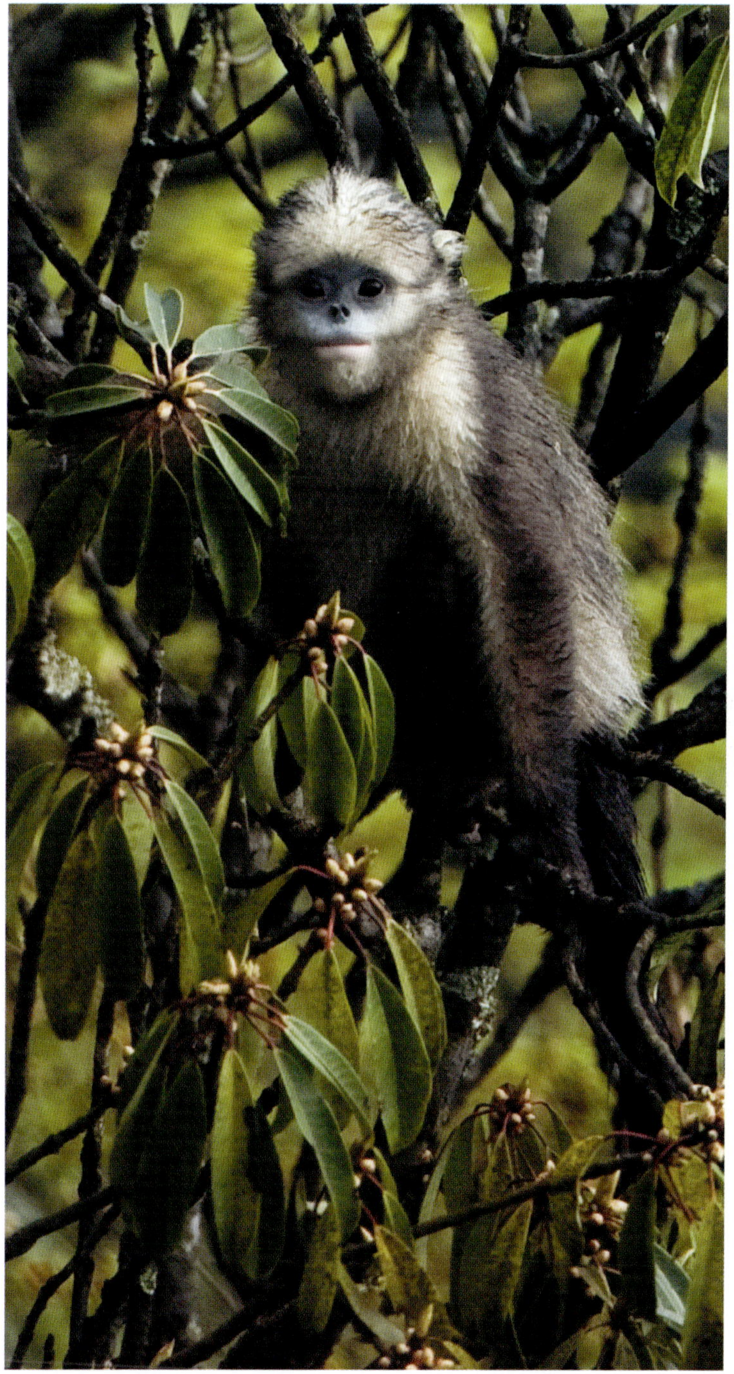

Before the establishment of the Fanjing Mountains Nature Reserve, the cut-down of forests and mining did serious damage to the habitats of the Guizhou snub-nosed monkeys. Worse still, local people have the tradition of hunting. According to incomplete statistics, the most serious damage caused by hunting took place in the period between 1962 and 1977, in which 317 Guizhou snub-nosed monkeys were killed. At present, despite alleviation of damage to their habitats and hunting, tourism has exerted new pressure on this species.

Above
Like other kinds of snub-nosed monkeys, Guizhou snub-nosed monkeys move around in large groups consisting of many families.

Right
The Guizhou snub-nosed monkey has a brown back, yellow abdomen, and black limbs. When compared to the Yunnan snub-nosed monkeys and the golden snub-nosed monkeys, the white tipped tail of the Guizhou snub-nosed monkeys is the longest. They have a large golden patch and a light-blue face, similar to that of the golden snub-nosed monkeys. The color of the female Guizhou snub-nosed monkeys is lighter than that of the male ones.

White-Tailed Eagle (Napahai Lake, Yunnan Province)

Haliaeetus albicilla

IUCN Red List: Least Concern

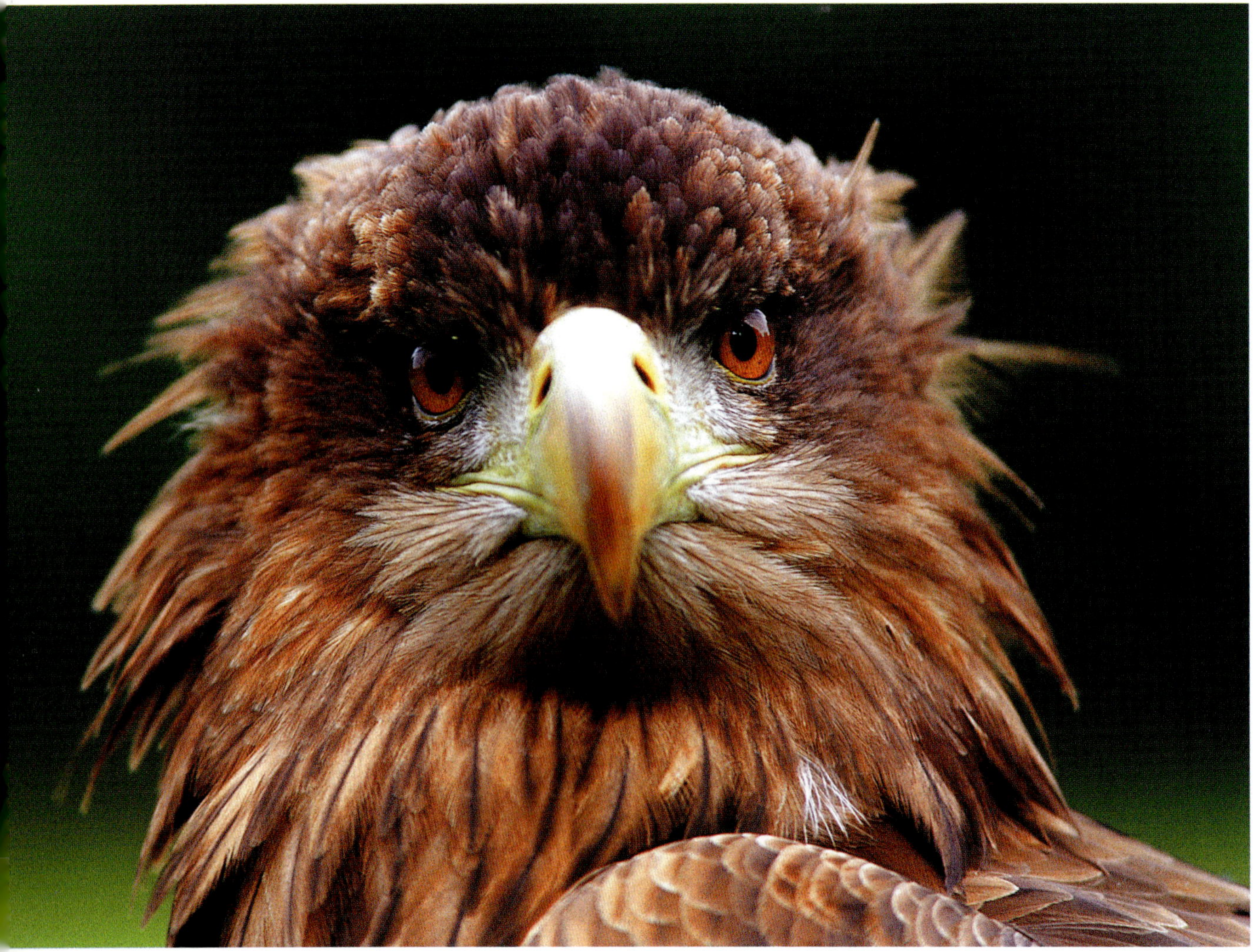

As large fish-eating birds of prey, white-tailed eagles often live near rivers and lakes. While flying just over water, they catch fish with their claws when they spot them. They hunt birds and mammals when they have the opportunity. They snatch prey from the mouth of otters and other kinds of fish-eating waterfowls and birds of prey. In the season when there is a lack of food, they would even eat rotten food.

In the period from April to June, they often build up nests by the lake, on riverbanks, or in nearby tall trees. Provided there is no interference, a nest can be used for many years, e.g. 30 years is the longest on record. The nest is over 2 meters in diameter.

In many areas in China, such majestic large birds of prey can be seen when winter comes around, but there are records about their propagation only in northeastern China and Inner Mongolia. Their number is increasing in the world. However, in China, due to the reduction of the area of wetland and economic development by human beings, white-tailed eagles spending the winter find it more and more difficult to find a suitable environment for their habitats and food. Since they are at the top of the food chain, the poisoning of the fish in some areas also does harm to them.

They fall into the category of sea eagles. The adult white-tailed eagle has yellow beak and purely white tail.

On facing page
The white tailed-eagle is nearly one meter long and its wings, when spread, can be 2.5 meters wide.

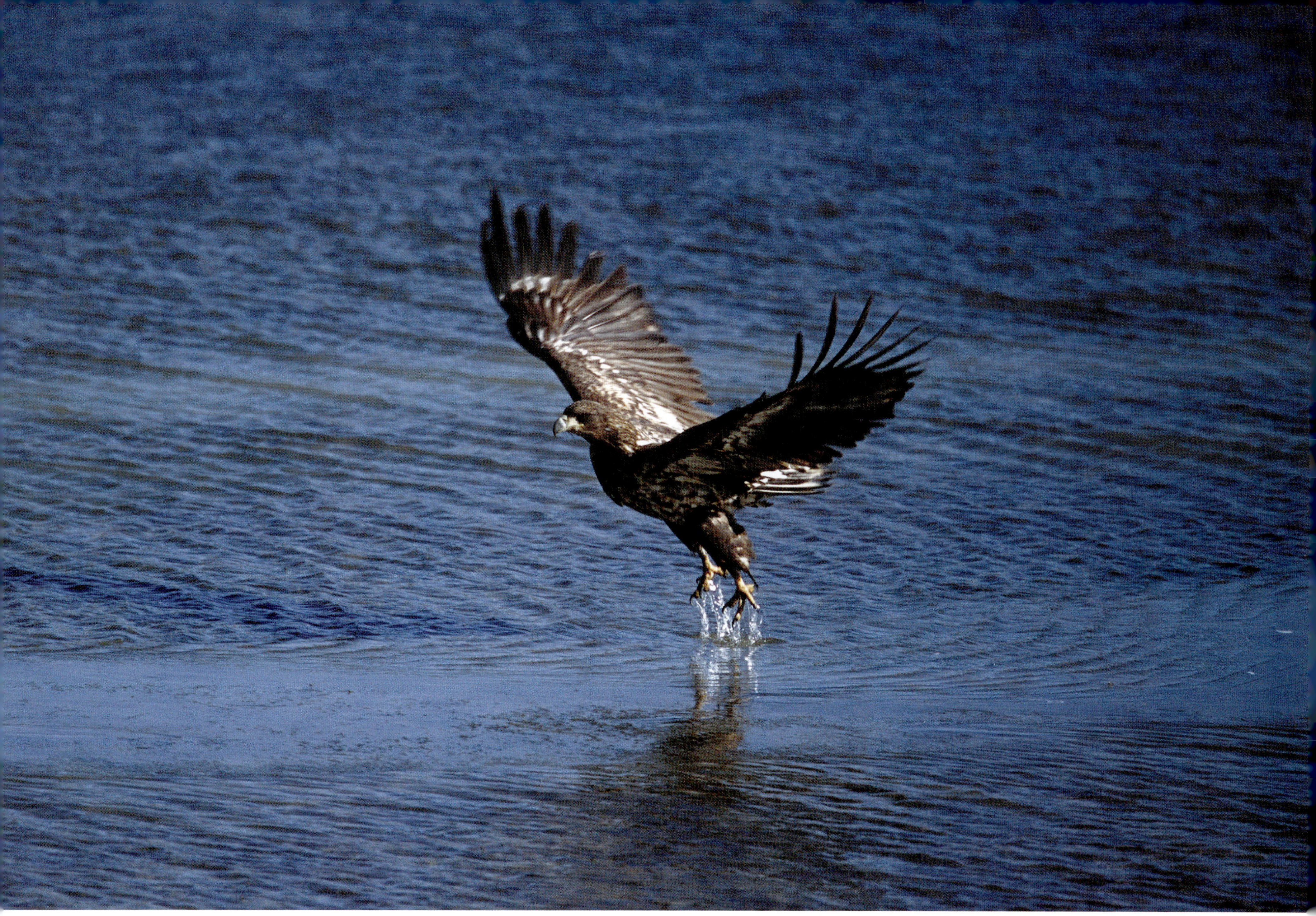

White Wagtail (Napahai Lake, Yunnan Province)

Motacilla alba

IUCN Red List: Least Concern

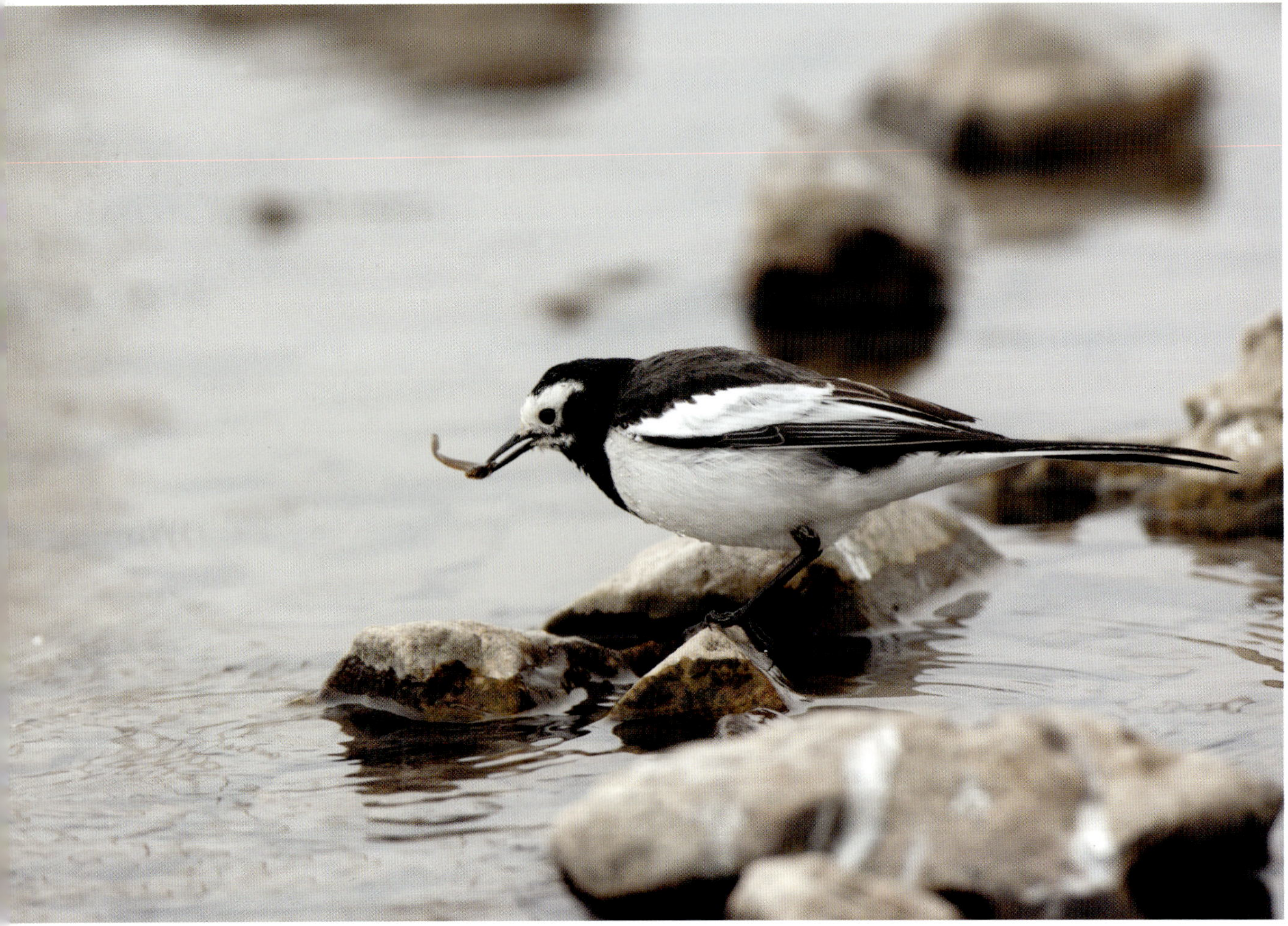

As a kind of small songbird, it is about 18 cm long and its wings, when spread, can be 31 cm wide. It weighs 23 grams. The feathers are black and white.

White wagtails are one of the most extensively distributed birds in the world and in China. They are named "wagtail" since they walk quickly while swaying their tail. These kinds of birds were mentioned in the *Classic of Poetry* (*Shi Jing*) written over 2,000 years ago in China.

Staying in pairs or groups, they often live near villages, rivers, small streams, and ponds. They eat insects, either looking for food on the ground or in the sky. They also eat spiders and other kinds of invertebrates, and occasionally eat plant seeds and berries. While flying, they advance like waves, often screaming, making it very easy to identify them.

In the period from April to July, they build up nests in caves, cliff-cracks, earthen mounds, and stone-cracks by the farmland near small streams and rivers, as well as on riverbanks, in bushes, and grass. They also build up nests on the roof ridges of homes and wall-cracks, and even in the holes of withered trees and artificially made nests.

There are over ten sub-species in the world, with four of them in China. Some migratory white wagtails of different sub-species in southeastern China move to propagate in northeastern China and further north of China in the period from March to April, while some others are non-migratory white wagtails. There are also white wagtails having migrated from southern China to propagate in northwestern China.

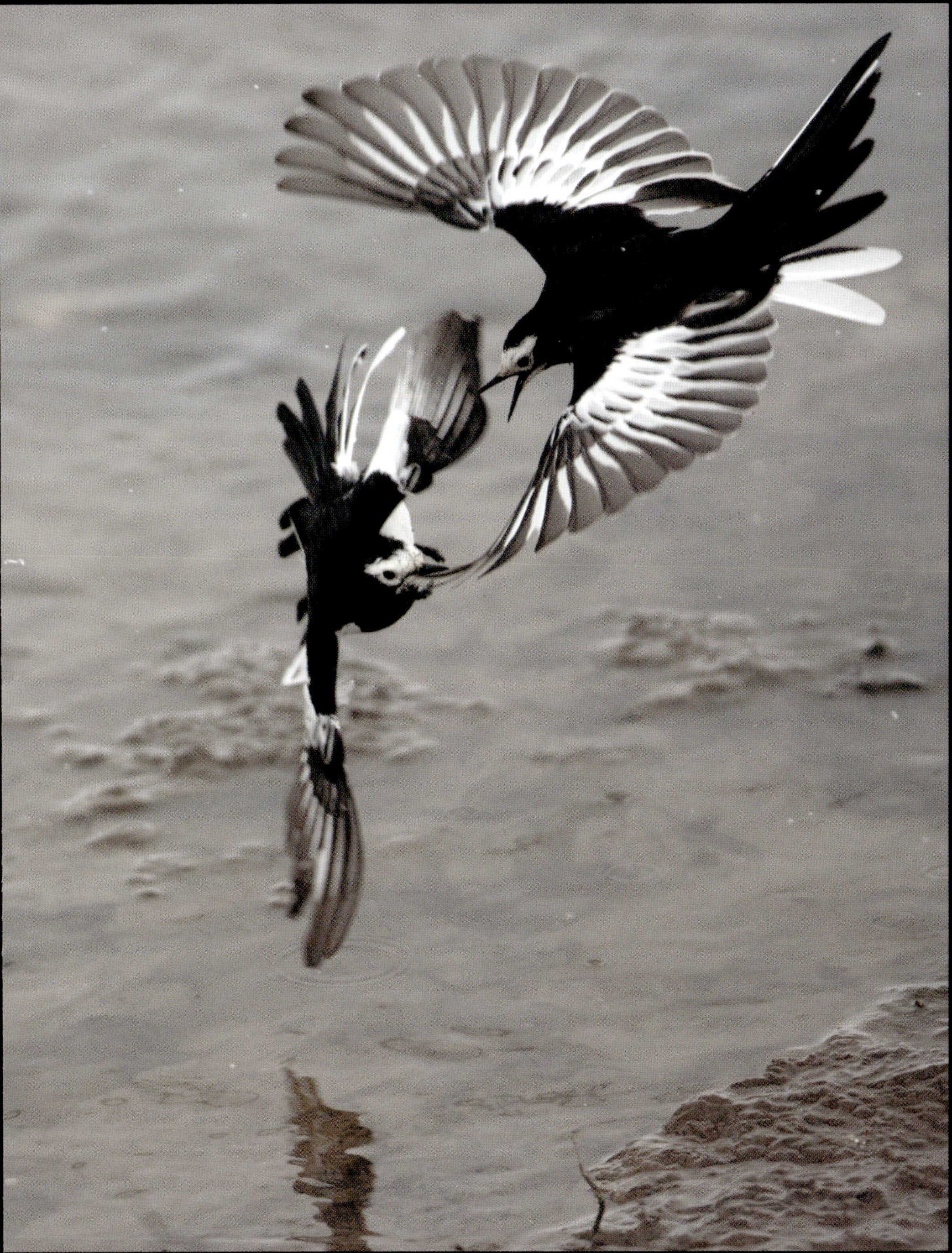

Left
Two white wagtails are competing for a small fish. However, they look like a pair of dancers on the water.

Below
With the ground covered by heavy snow, white wagtails can only look for food in this small pond of water. Though it is accustomed to eating insects, it has to catch fish. Its fine long legs gently touch the water, like the hero in a Chinese kung fu novel displaying his flying skills.

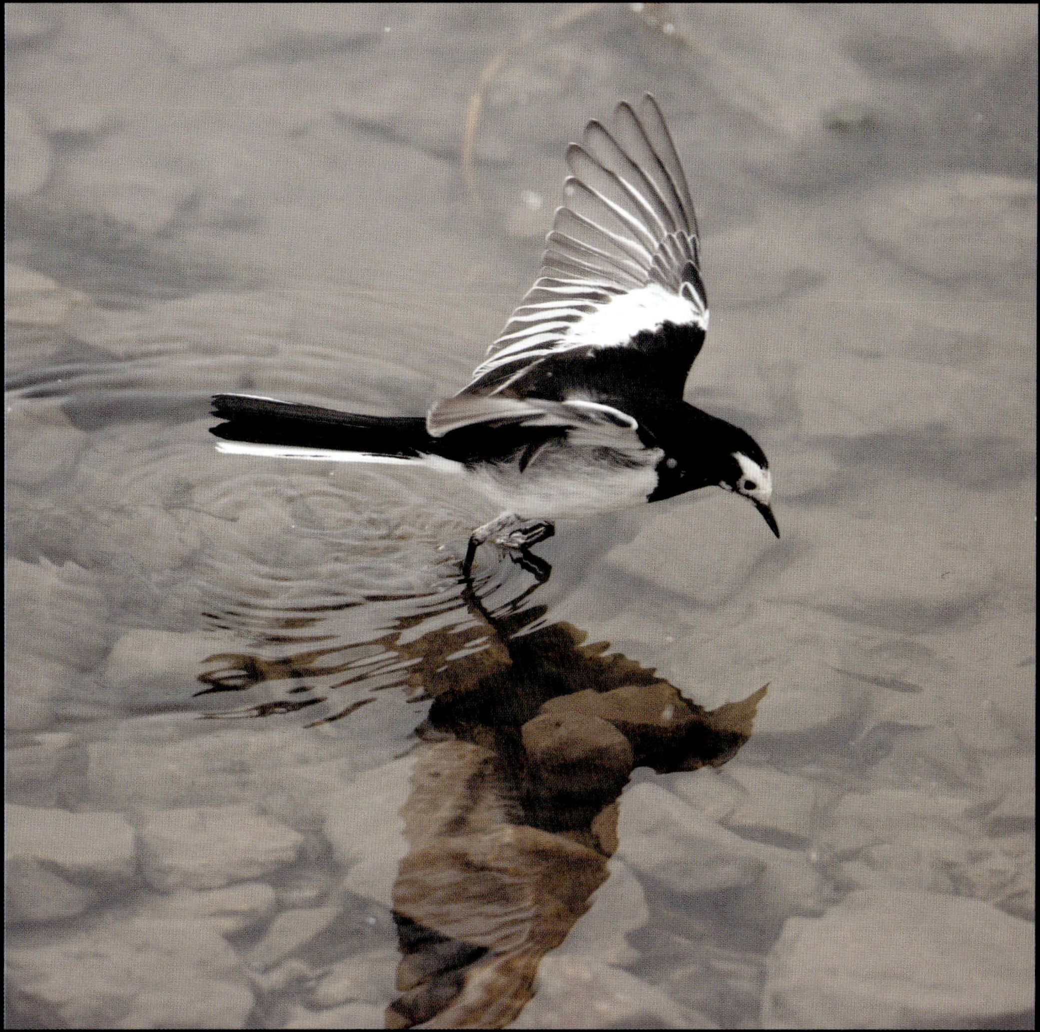

Purple Swamphen (Eryuan, Yunnan Province)

Porphyrio porphyria

IUCN Red List: Least Concern

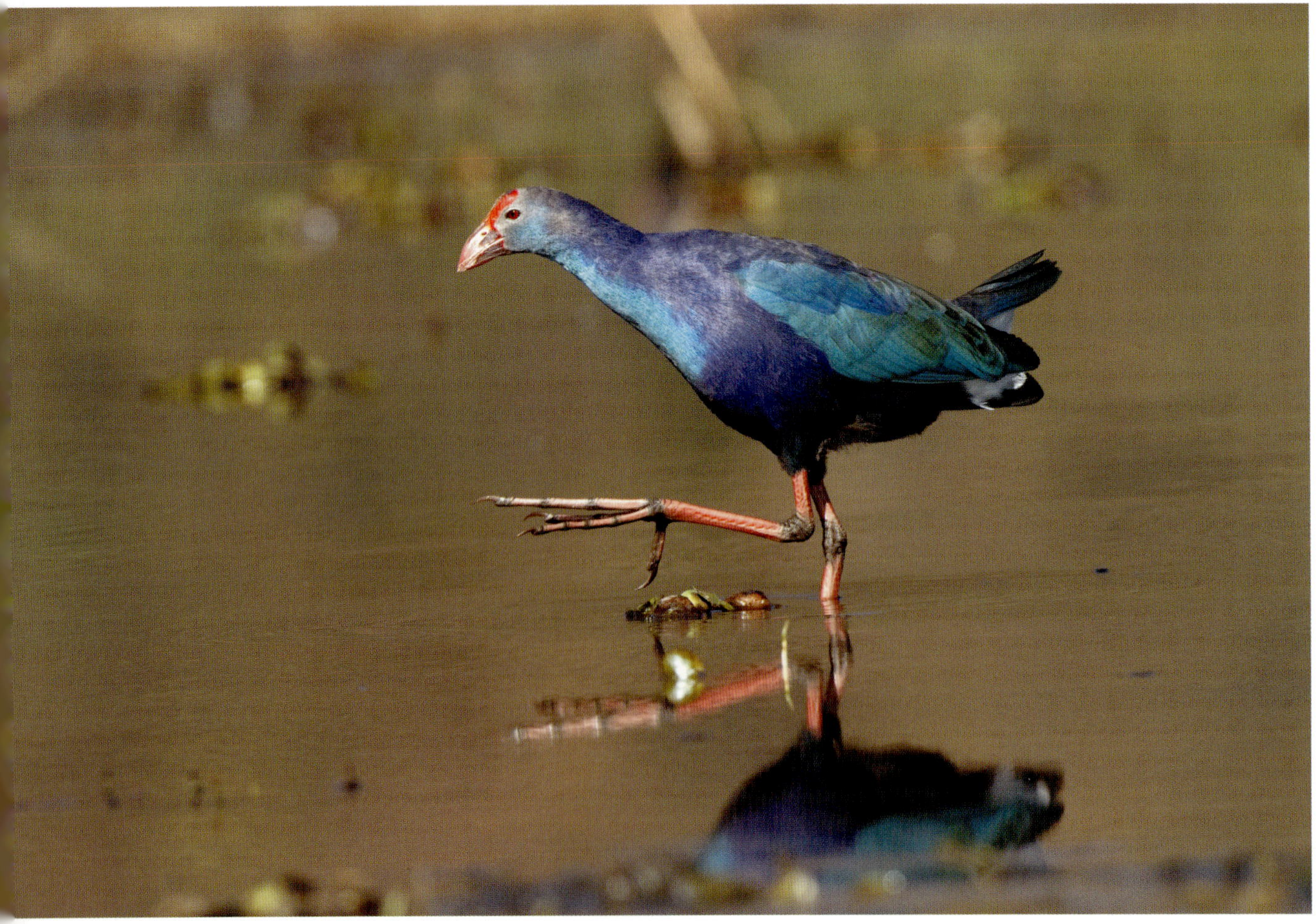

Among birds of the Rallidae family, purple swamphens are probably the most gorgeous. Except for the white feathers under its tail, the body is blue and purple. Its crown, like its beak, is a bright red color. With long red legs, they are good at strolling and running on the ground. They can also climb onto reed stems, or stroll and rest on the plants and leaves floating over the water.

As species of tropical and sub-tropical zones extensively distributed in the world, purple swamphens are seen in Guangxi, Fujian, Guangdong, Sichuan, and Yunnan provinces. Situated in the northwest of Yunnan province, Eryuan is an important place for migratory birds in western China to spend the winter and rest.

They live in reed swamp, lakes, streams, and ditches full of aquatic plants, as well as islands and swamp thickets along the coast, and sometimes in paddy fields. Purple swamphens chiefly eat tender leaves, buds, and seeds of aquatic plants, as well as land and aquatic insects, larva, and mollusks.

Docile and timid, they often move around in pairs or family groups. They are mostly seen at dawn and dusk. In the daytime, they hide themselves in reeds. When moving around, they utter noisy sounds, frequently clucking and humming. When on the alert, they frequently sway their tails up and down, showing their white undertails.

In the season of propagation, they build up nests amidst reeds and water grass. Their disc-shaped nests are built with reed-stems or other kinds of water grass. These nests cannot be easily found. Cooperative breeding is practiced among them, i.e. a nest is jointly used by a few pairs for propagation, or a pair of purple swamphens, together with those they gave birth to last year, would hatch eggs and take care of newborn infants through concerted efforts.

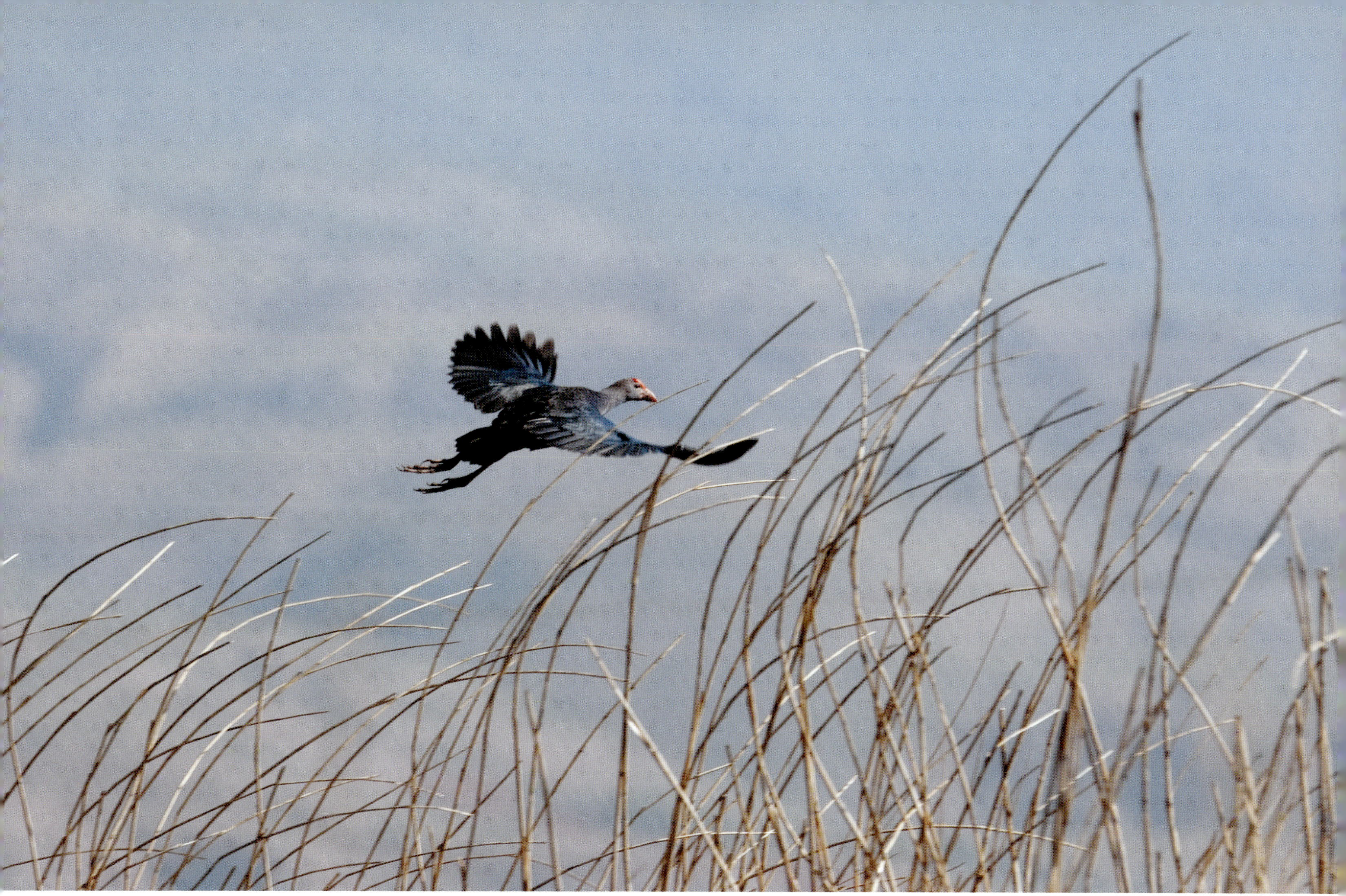

They seldom fly or swim, and when they have to, they would land after flying for a short distance. While they are flying, their wings flutter slowly with their long legs drooping, looking quite clumsy.

Asian Elephant (Xishuangbanna, Yunnan Province)

Elephas maximus

IUCN Red List: Endangered

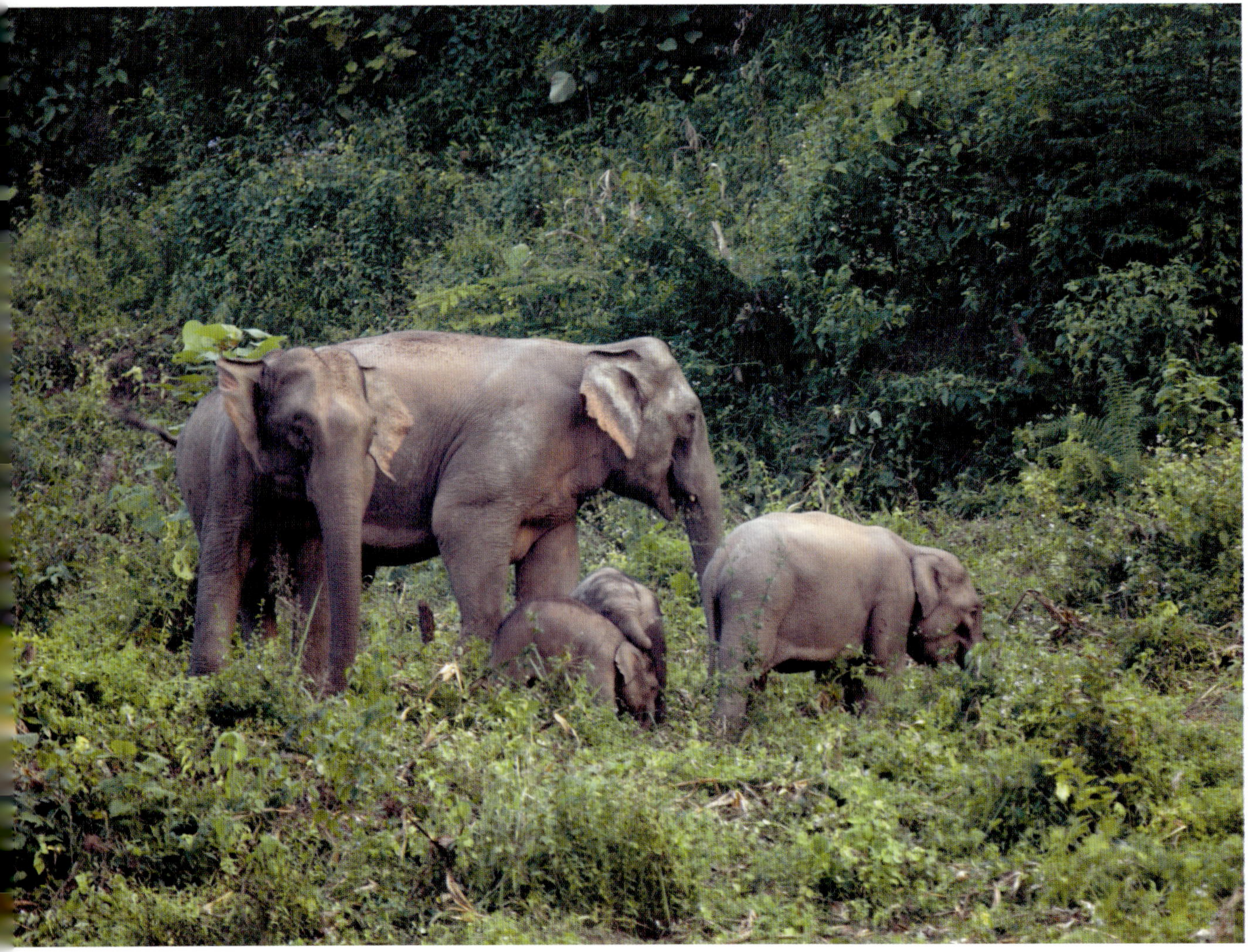

As the biggest terrestrial animals in China and even the entire Asia, they are about 2.9 meters high and weigh as much as 6 tons. There have long been records of Asian elephants in China. According to ancient Chinese mythology, the monarch of early times, Shun, used to fight against elephants many times until the latter were finally subdued and tamed. At present, such huge animals can only be seen in Xishuangbanna and Simao in Yunnan province.

Asian elephants are smaller than their relatives in Africa. The easiest way to tell Asian elephants from African elephants is from the ears and temperament of the former, which are smaller and milder than that of the latter, respectively. Only tigers and leopards in the wilderness, as well as human beings are their natural enemies.

Generally, Asian elephants live in groups in evergreen or semi-evergreen lowland hills and forests, often with bamboo groves. Each group consists of several or dozens of them led by an adult female elephant in their activities. Without fixed habitats, they move around extensively. The males live by themselves, or move around in a small group of 2 to 3. Families led by a few females often gather at places where they can lick salt and take mud baths.

A female elephant is taking several small elephants to cross the slope. Small elephants flutter their fan-like big ears, sway their tails, stroll, and play all the way.

Above right
Living in tropical forests, Asian elephants often go to ponds and streams to look for some earth, which is rich in minerals, to replenish the microelements they need. While moving in the pond, they would utter different kinds of low rumbling sounds to keep their small community close.

Below right
A mud bath is the best way for Asian elephants to deal with annoying insects.

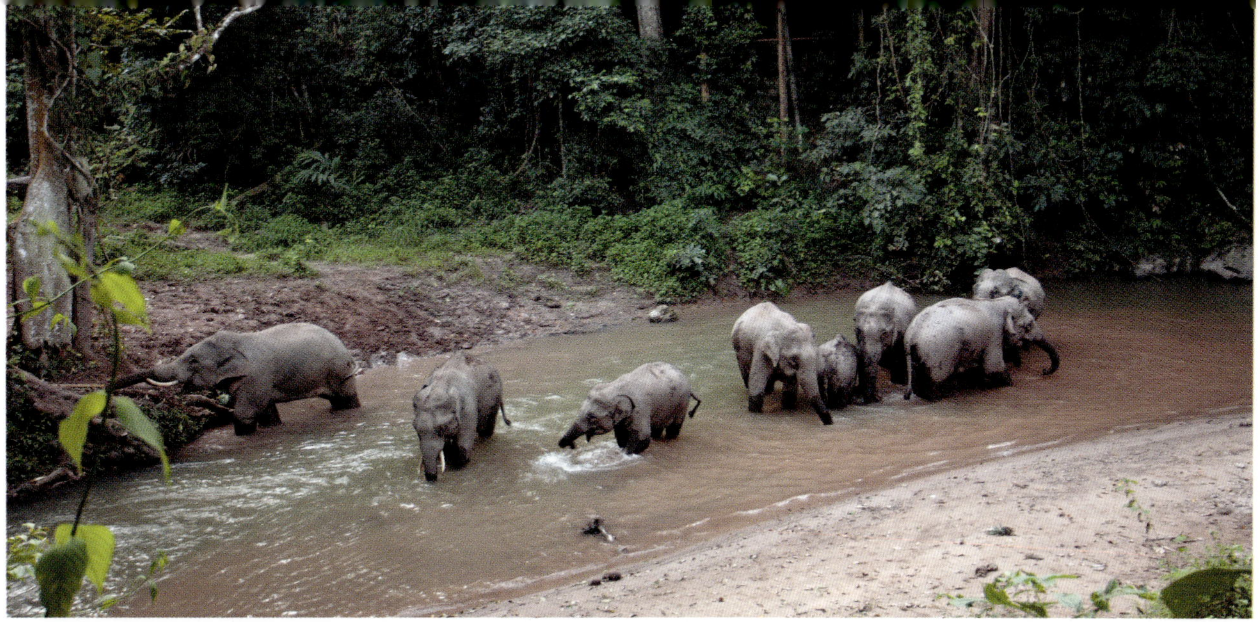

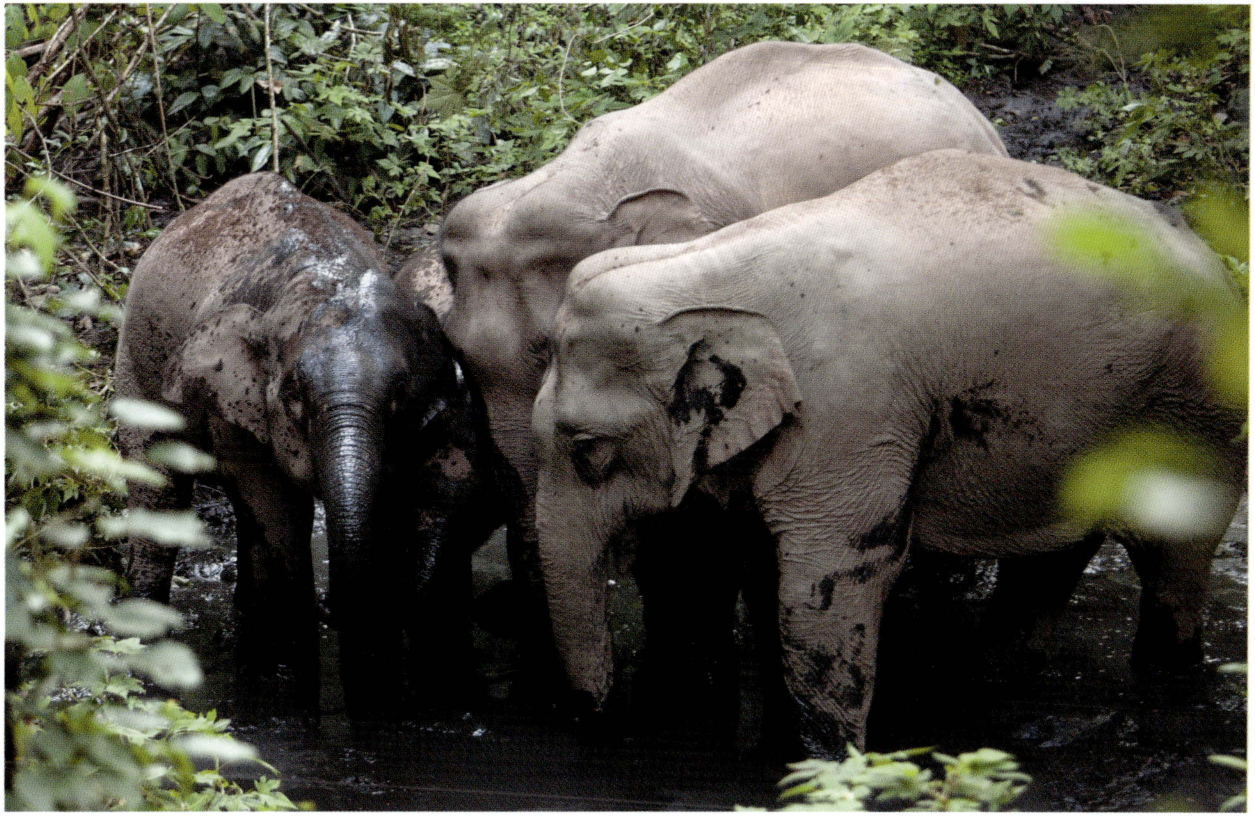

Unlike African elephants, only male Asian elephants have tusks with which they attack others and defend themselves, as well as remove obstacles in the forests and dig earth with rich minerals at places with salt for licking. As herbivorous animals, they are particularly fond of eating plants from the grass and palm family since those can provide them with a substantial amount of carbohydrates.

Since the overwhelming majority of their habitats have been developed and transformed into farmland or rubber tree plantations, elephants still in existence have to leave the forests to eat the crops of nearby farmlands on a large scale. Therefore, local farmers use guns, traps, and toxicants to deal with them.

Greed for their tusks in Asia has almost driven these elephants into a corner. Nowadays, there are only 40,000 wild elephants in Asia and the number in China is less than 250. Illegal hunting for their tusks has seriously imbalanced the proportion between the male Asian elephants and female ones. In some areas, the proportion between the males and females is 1:100, which is a very abnormal phenomenon. Because of such imbalance, only 1/3 of the female elephants can give birth to offsprings.

Moreover, their only existing habitats have been seriously carved up by roads and villages, resulting in the lack of gene exchange among the Asian elephants. Consequently, another change has taken place in the gene pool, i.e. there are more male elephants without tusks.

White-Headed Langur (Guangxi Autonomous Region)

Trachypithecus poliocephalus

IUCN Red List: Critically Endangered

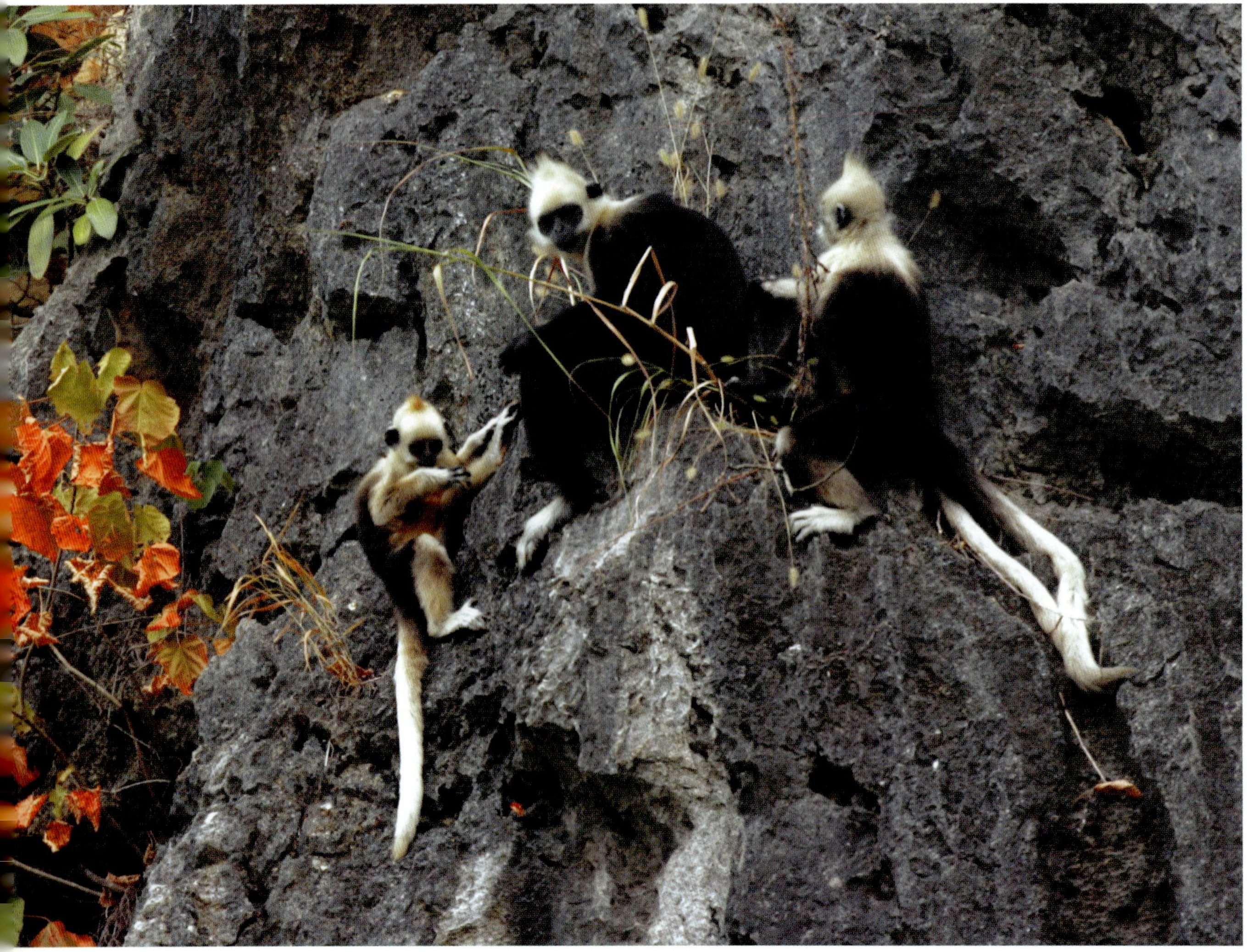

Looking very much like François' langurs, white-headed langurs are unique to China. They are mainly distributed in a narrow and small triangle area of 200 square kilometers encircled by Zuojiang River (literally Left River), Mingjiang River (literally Clear River), and Shiwan Mountains (literally Hundred Thousand Mountains) in Guangxi, areas chiefly marked by Karst topography.

Often living in small groups, they have a fixed range of activities and routes. They live in cliff caves and rock-cracks. Depending on the season, they eat tender leaves, buds, flowers, and fruit, as well as dodders, which is a kind of parasitic plant.

They mate in the autumn and give birth to infants in the spring. The color of newborn babies is quite similar to that of François' langurs, i.e. golden color all over. They can only move their head freely when sucking milk in the arms of their mother or during sleep. The lower part of the vertex and tail of a 7-day-old baby turns milky yellow, their head can move around flexibly, and their spirited eyes begin to look around. They usually grasp their mother tightly, unwilling to be hugged by other females. A 20-day-old baby begins to have some crest-hair, in addition to being able to crawl or leap on the ground without its mother's help.

A family of white headed langurs is crouching on the cliff. The female is gingerly combing her husband's hair while the infant is playing on the tree branches.

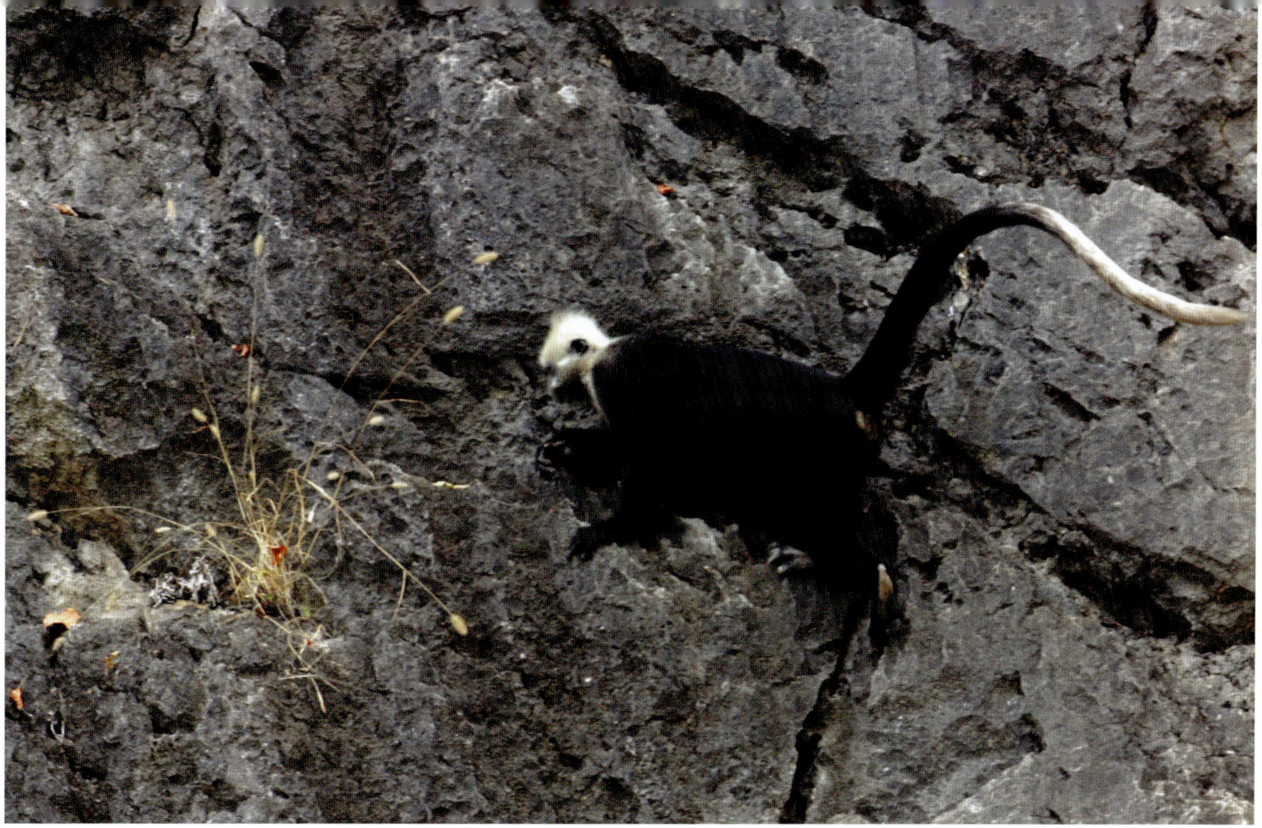

Above
White-headed langurs are good at climbing. They can not only swing on trees, but also climb cliffs, since their long tail helps them to keep balance.

Right
The rocky mountains of the Karst areas are representative habitats of the white-headed langurs.

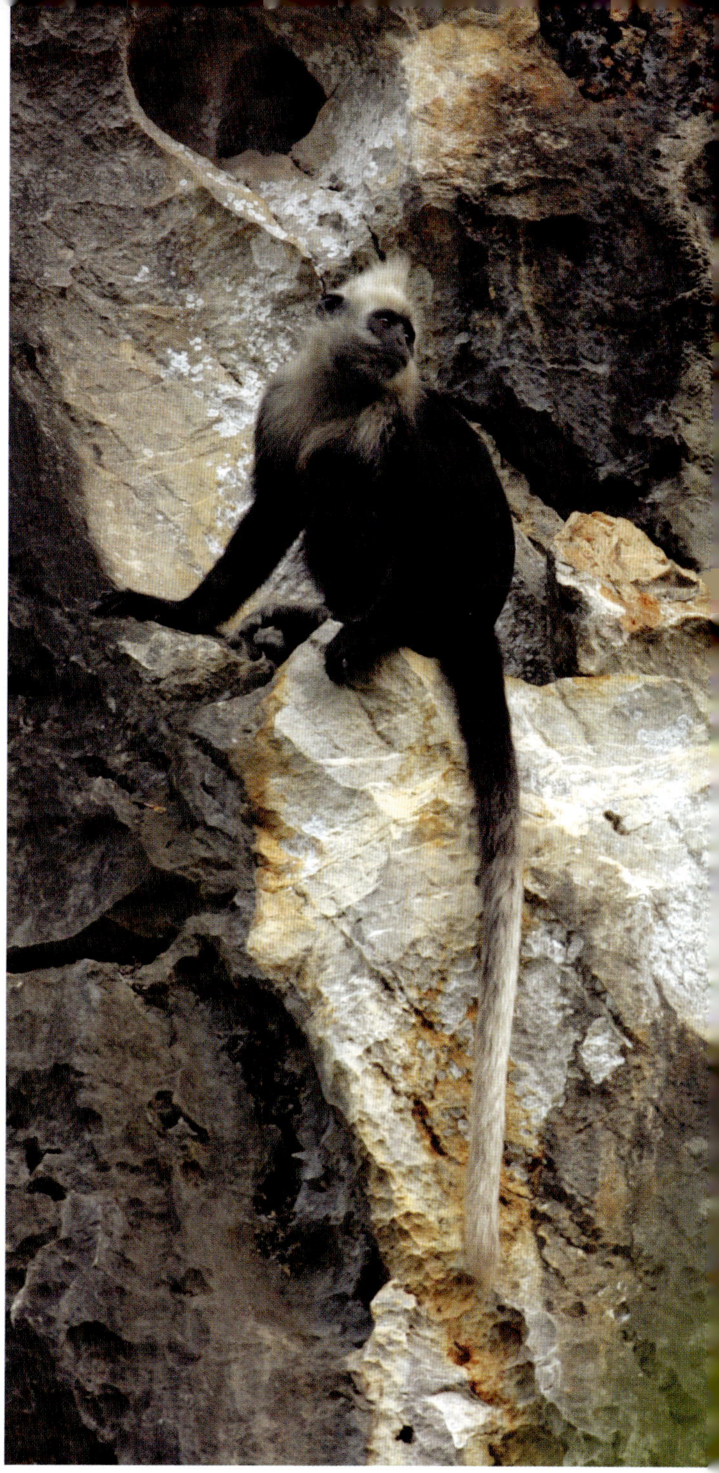

A two-month-old baby is quite different from that of François' langurs, as it has some fairly long black hair on the back and many parts of the body appear white, such as the vertex, face, abdomen, four limbs, and the lower part of the tail, gradually resembling the fur color of an adult. At the age of six months, they are able to live independently and look for food on their own. However, they still sleep in their mother's arms.

Over the past 30 years, human population in areas distributed with white-headed langurs has been increasing rapidly. Soil erosion caused by cut-down of forests and reclamation for farmland has sharply reduced the number of their habitats. In the 1960s, the total area of their habitats was 500 square kilometers. At the end of the 1980s, there were only 200 square kilometers left. Meanwhile, white-headed langurs were separated into 16 isolated groups in different places. In 1996, there were only two habitats left.

So far, there are only over 800 in the world. More than 400 are distributed in Bapen in the Chongzuo Nature Reserve of White-Headed Langurs, Guangxi. This is the area with the greatest number of white-headed langurs and the biggest density of the species.

Hainan Gibbon (Hainan Province)

Nomascus concolor

IUCN Red List: Critically Endangered

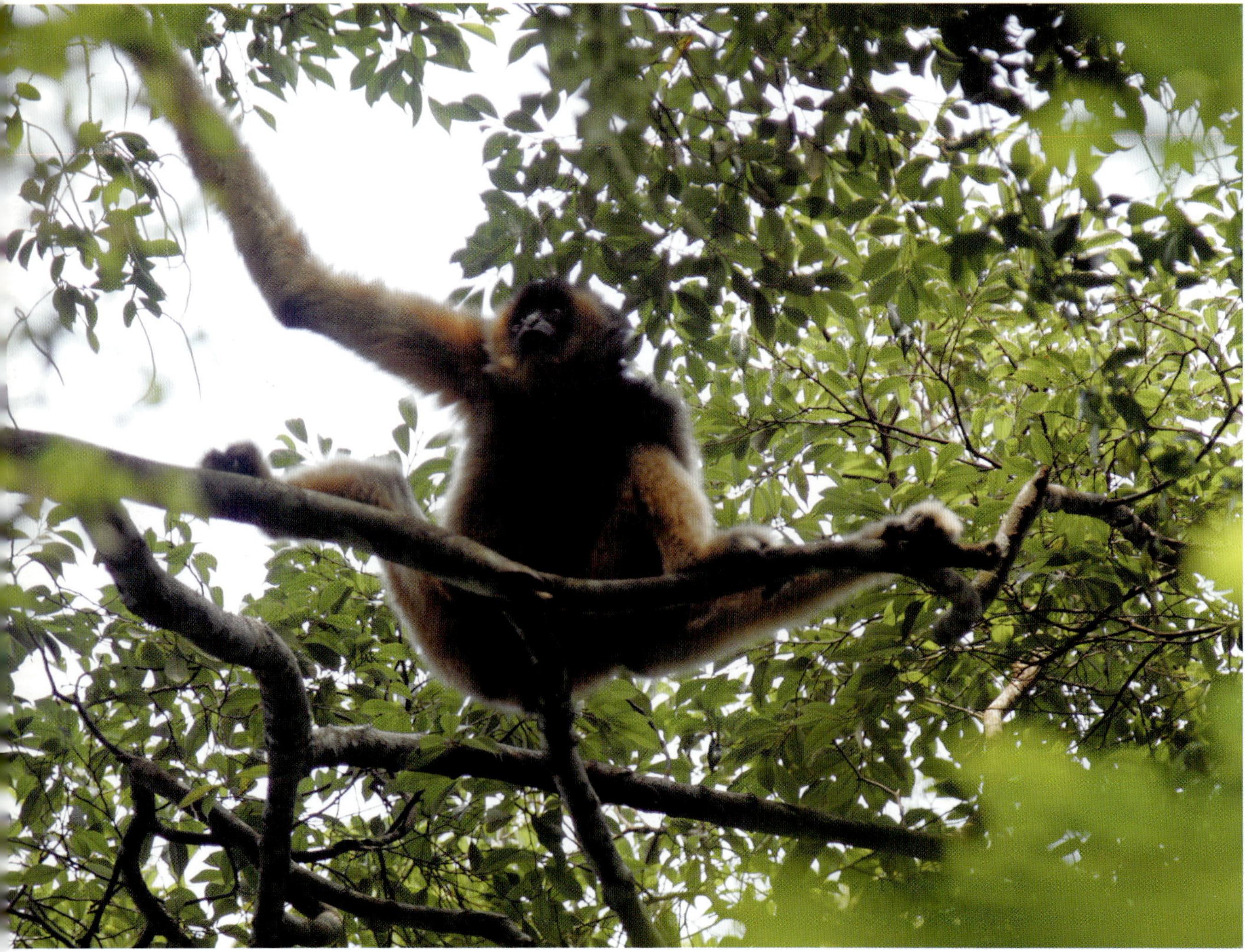

As primates right on the verge of extinction now, Hainan gibbons mainly live in mountain seasonal rain forests and gully rain forests of tropical areas on Hainan Island. They are partial to lowland tropical rain forests at less than 600 meters above sea level. They eat various tropical wild fruits, tender leaves, and flower buds, and occasionally some insects and bird's eggs. Hainan gibbons seldom drink water on the ground. They mainly drink the dew from blades of leaves and scoop water out of tree holes.

They move around in relatively fixed places without seasonal migration. As arboreal gibbons, they can climb trees freely and they always move around and look for food on canopies of tall arbor trees or across the medium layer. They do not have fixed places for sleep, nor are they able to build up dens. They curl up on trees and sometimes sleep on their back on tree trunks

Generally, they move around in a family group of 3 to 5 or 7 to 8. The system of "one husband and two wives" is practiced among them; an adult male and two adult females form the family. Monogamy takes place only when there is an imbalance between the male and the female due to interference against the small group. The range of a group of Hainan gibbons' activities is nearly 400

Whether or not this species unique to China can survive is completely dependent on human action.

hectares, far larger than the ranges of other kinds of gibbons.

Like other kinds of gibbons, they start to call for the first time at dawn. The males call loudly first, followed by the chorus of males and females that lasts for 15 minutes. Then, led by the male, they begin to look for food in their territory. At eight or nine o'clock a.m., after the meal and rest, they begin to call for the second time. Then, they inspect their territory while looking for food. If the weather is fine along with ample food and they are in a good mood, they call once again at noon. In the afternoon, they still roam around while eating, but do not call anymore.

They are dependent on the living environment very much. They can only survive in primitive seasonal rain forests, but cannot survive in man-made forests with single species of trees or secondary forests having been cut down. In the 1960s, Hainan gibbons could be found everywhere on Hainan Island, with the number over 1,000. However, the tropical rain forests almost disappear on Hainan Island. At present, over 20 Hainan gibbons in Bawangling Nature Reserve are the last hope of this species.

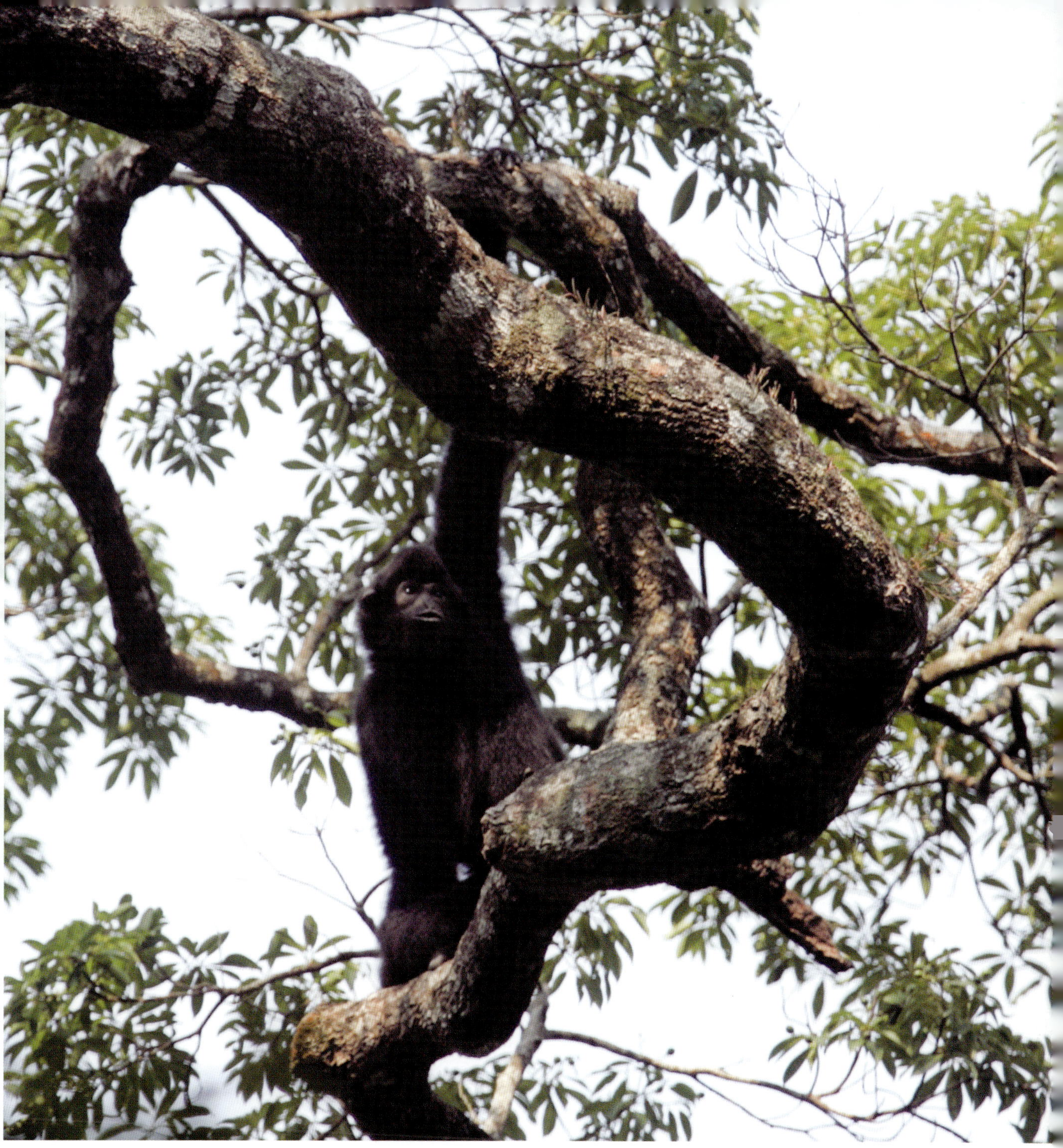

Along with the reduction of the area of tropical rain forests on Hainan Island, the number of Hainan gibbons has dropped sharply. Now, there are only over 20 left.

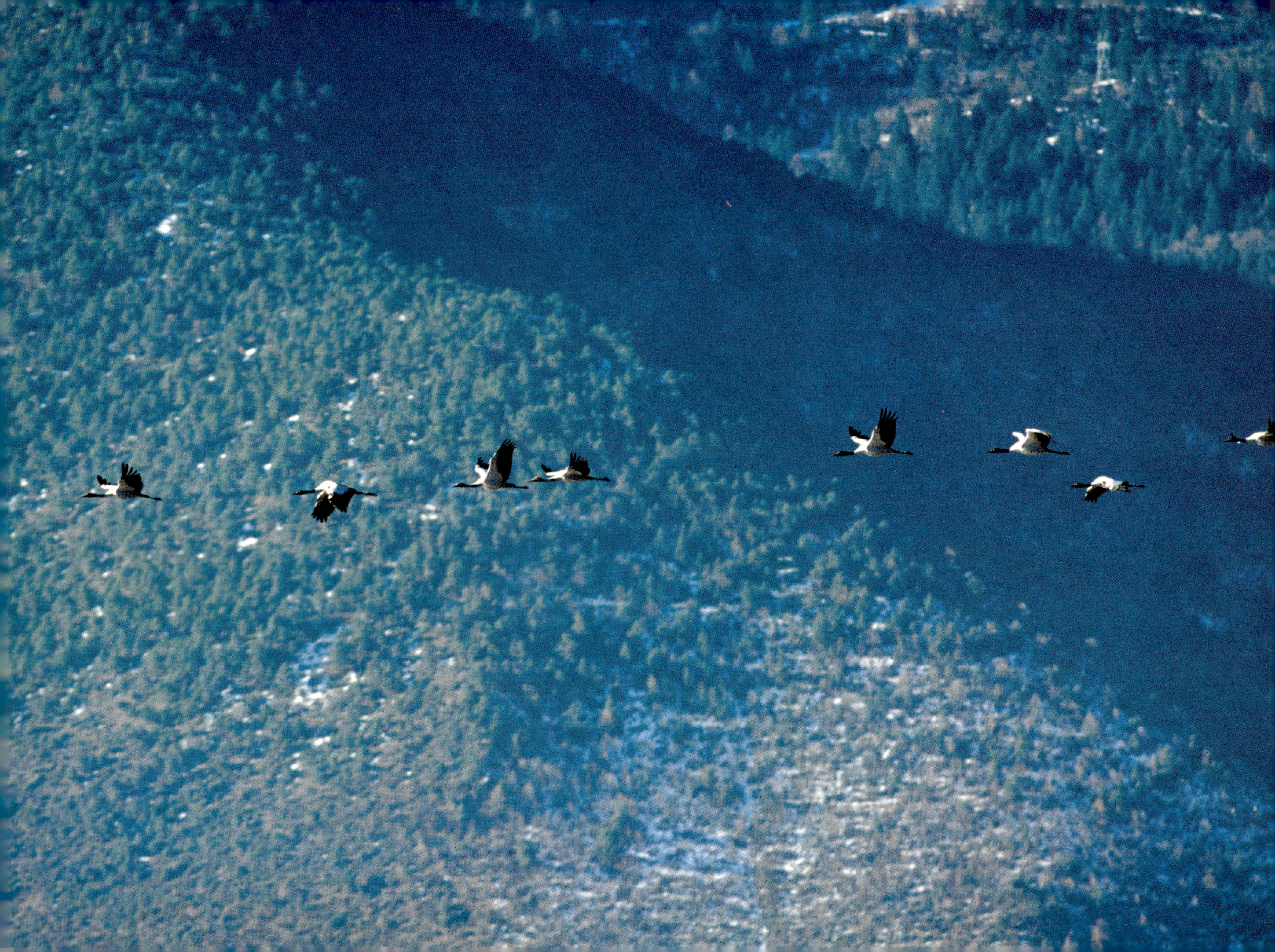

Part Four
Bird Migration

Huge territory and diversified environments for habitats in China have blessed China with a very rich bio-diversity. As far as the variety of birds is concerned, there are over 1,300 kinds of birds recorded in China, including many kinds of migratory birds. As compared with mammals, birds with wings can migrate to larger areas thousands of kilometers away. In the spring and autumn, they would gather in large groups and migrate between the place for spending the winter and the place for propagation along relatively fixed routes.

Roughly speaking, bird migration in China has three major areas of migration and three different routes. The first is the western area of migration and western route, including the summer migratory birds of dry steppe, semi-deserts, alpine meadows, and steppes in western Inner Mongolia, Ningxia, Tibet, Gansu, and Qinghai provinces. They winter in western Sichuan Basin, Yunnan-Guizhou Plateau, and even Indian Peninsula, flying from Amne Machen Mountains to the Qionglai Mountains, and southwards to Hengduan Mountains. Black-necked cranes are typical migratory birds following this route. Parts of the big and medium migratory birds in Tibet, apart from migrating along the Tanggula Mountains and the Himalayan Mountains southeastwards, probably go wintering by flying over the Himalayan Mountains in India and Nepal.

The second is the central area of migration and central route, including migratory birds propagating in central and eastern Inner Mongolia and the west of northern China. They would winter in Sichuan Basin, central China, and even further south via the Taihang Mountains, Lüliang Mountains, Qinling Mountains, and Daba Mountains. There is a small variety and number of migratory birds in this area of migration and route.

The third is the eastern area of migration and eastern route, including migratory birds propagating in northeastern China and the east of northern China. They winter by flying along the eastern coast of China southwards to central China or southern China, and even to various countries in Southeast Asia, or they may winter along the coast in Japan, Malaysia, the Philippines, and Australia. There is a great variety and number of migratory birds in this area of migration and route.

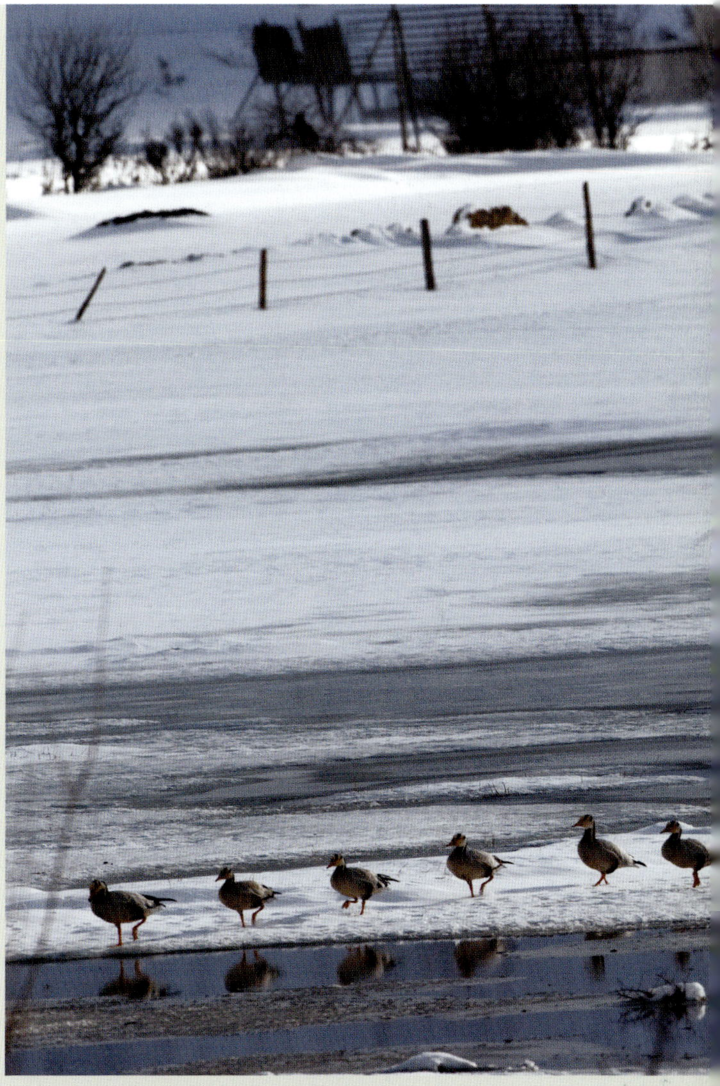

On facing page
A group of black-necked cranes forms a horizontal line as they fly over vast forests.

Six bar-headed geese are strolling across the snowy ground in a horizontal line.

Chapter Eleven
A Great Journey

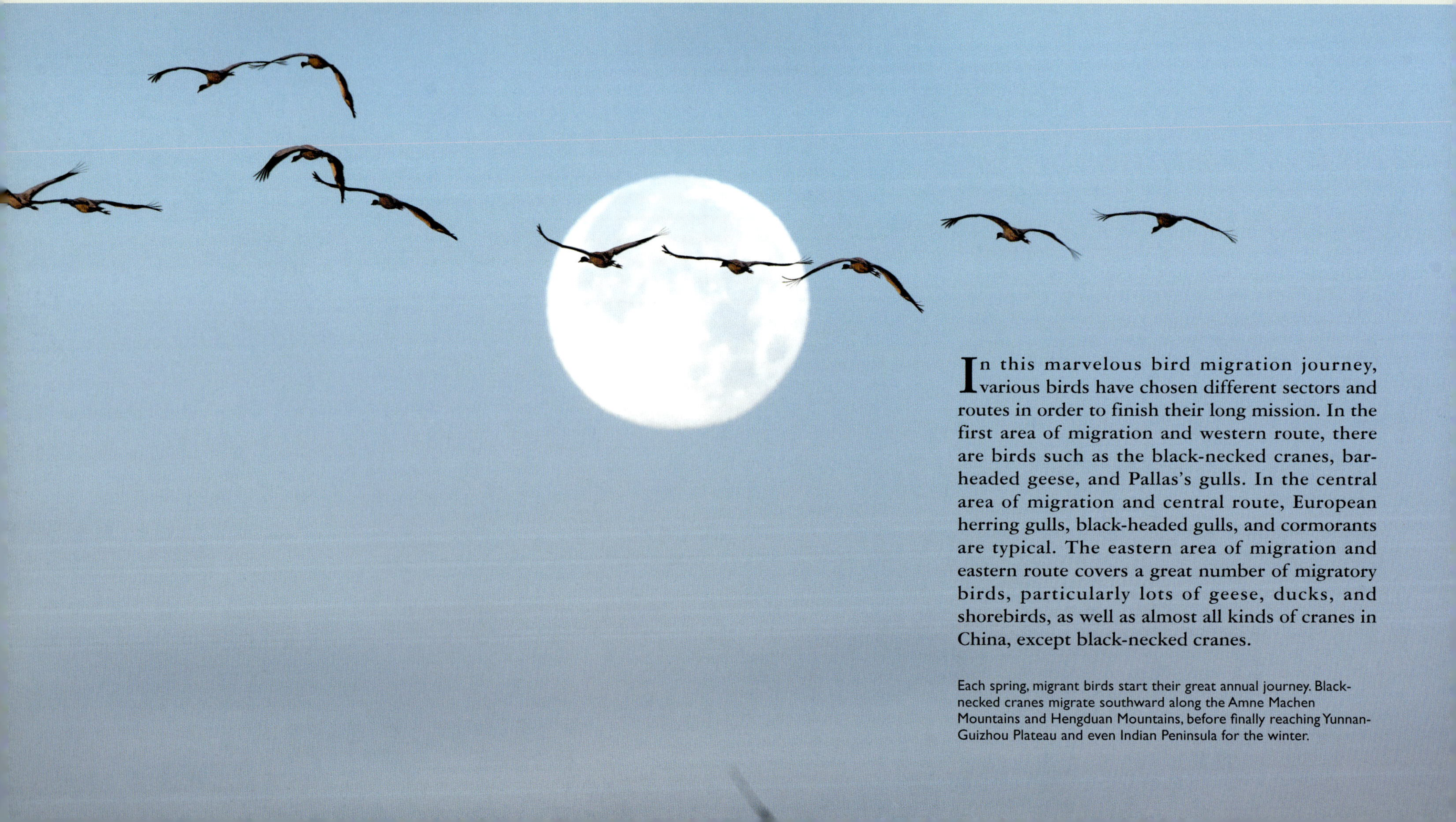

In this marvelous bird migration journey, various birds have chosen different sectors and routes in order to finish their long mission. In the first area of migration and western route, there are birds such as the black-necked cranes, bar-headed geese, and Pallas's gulls. In the central area of migration and central route, European herring gulls, black-headed gulls, and cormorants are typical. The eastern area of migration and eastern route covers a great number of migratory birds, particularly lots of geese, ducks, and shorebirds, as well as almost all kinds of cranes in China, except black-necked cranes.

Each spring, migrant birds start their great annual journey. Black-necked cranes migrate southward along the Amne Machen Mountains and Hengduan Mountains, before finally reaching Yunnan-Guizhou Plateau and even Indian Peninsula for the winter.

Black-Necked Crane

Grus nigricollis

IUCN Red List: Vulnerable

There are 15 kinds of cranes in the world and eight of them are in China. Cranes are migratory birds. In the spring, summer, and autumn, after spending a long period of propagation in marshes at high latitude almost without human beings, most of these cranes in China would fly in groups to spend the winter in central China, as well as the middle and lower reaches of the Yangtze River, on shallow wetland, lakes, and islands. Only black-necked cranes and another kind of Sarus cranes migrate from southwest China to northwest China.

Black-necked cranes are the only cranes living on plateaus. In 1876, Przhevalsk, a Russian explorer, got their samples from Qinghai Lake. This species of crane was identified the latest. It was not until the 1980s that people began to make a study of these plateau-based cranes.

Each March, black-necked cranes in different groups and batches leave places for spending the winter in Yunnan-Guizhou Plateau of southwest China and the western Wumeng Mountains, and fly to places of propagation in Qinghai province, northern Tibet, and A'li of Tibet in northwest China. Some of them would go to Ladakh in India. Black-necked cranes would make stopovers to rest on the high mountains of the Tibetan Plateau and its neighboring areas, as well as western Sichuan

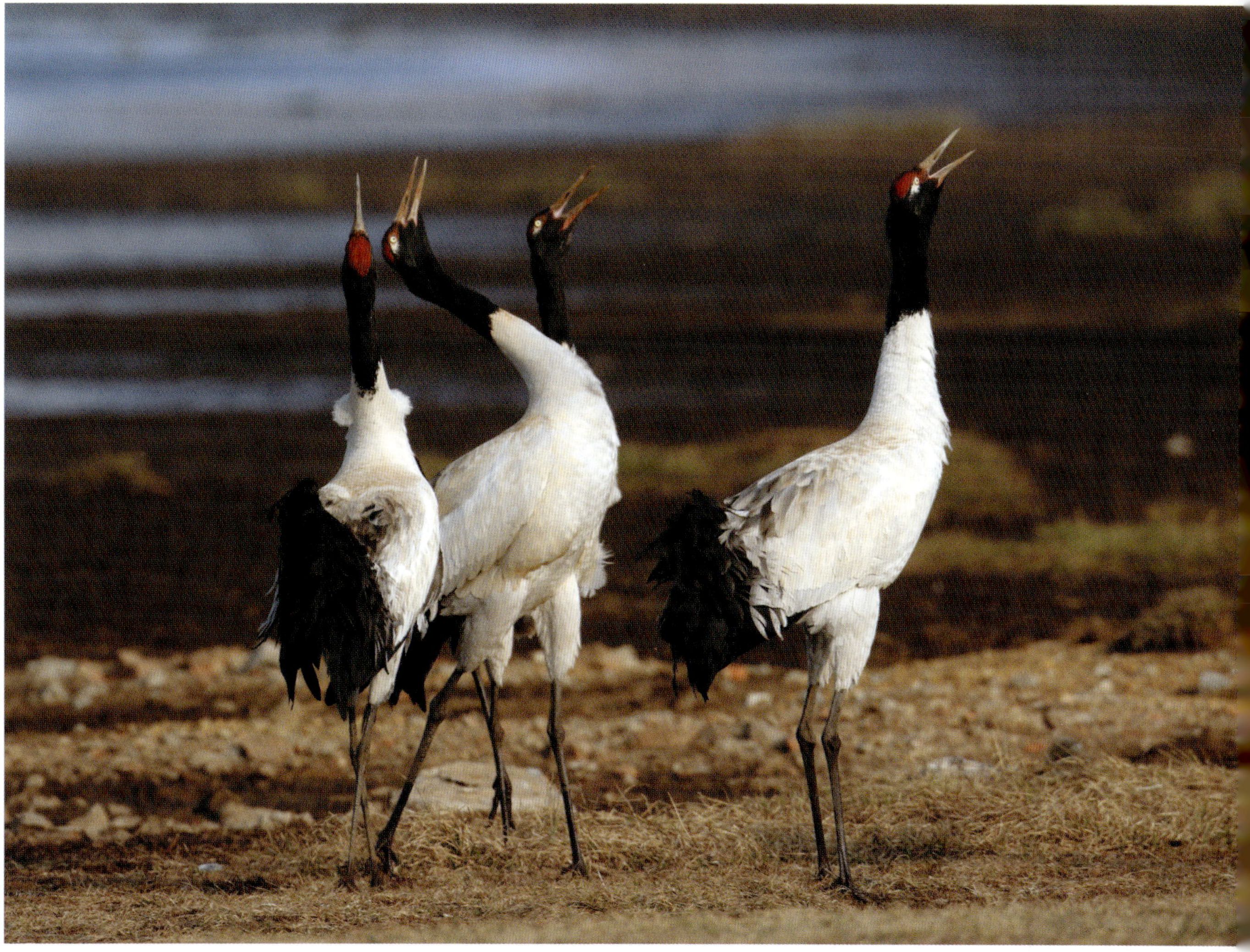

As the weather gets warmer, sexually mature black-necked cranes extend their necks and utter trumpeting calls to seek out their mates.

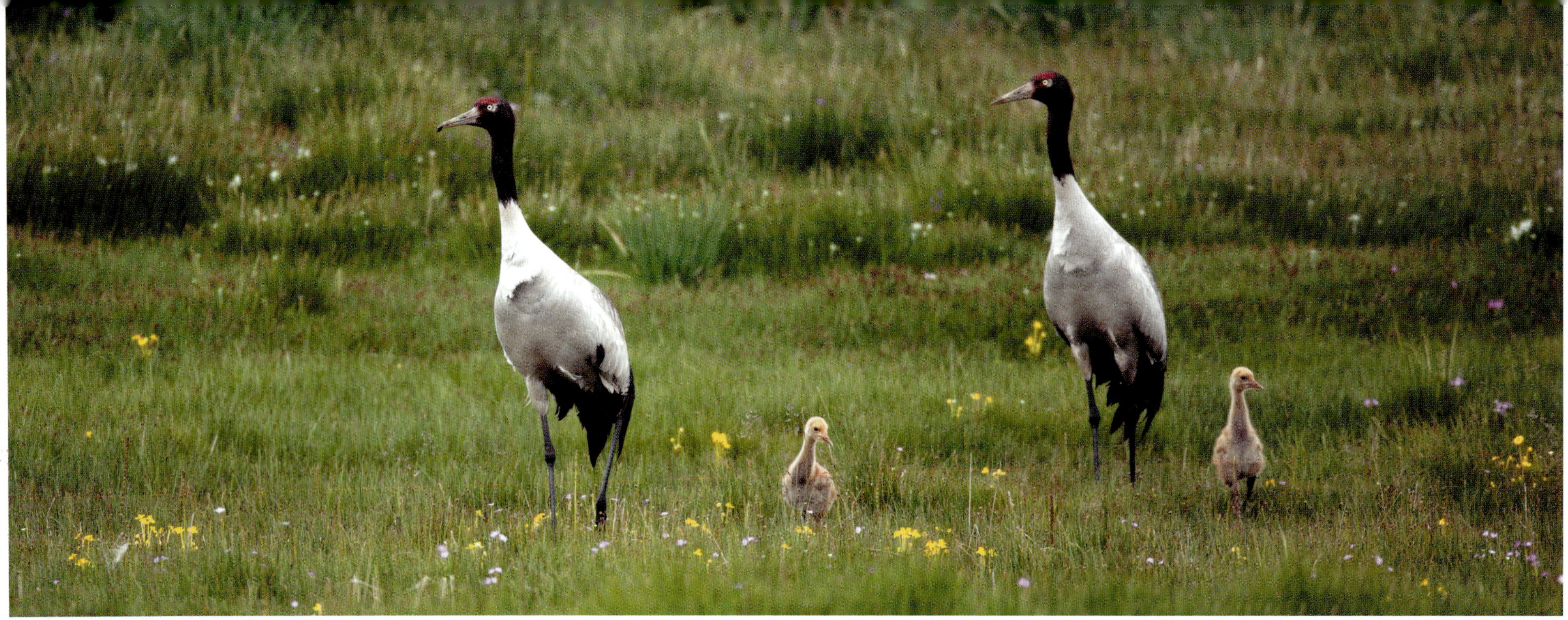

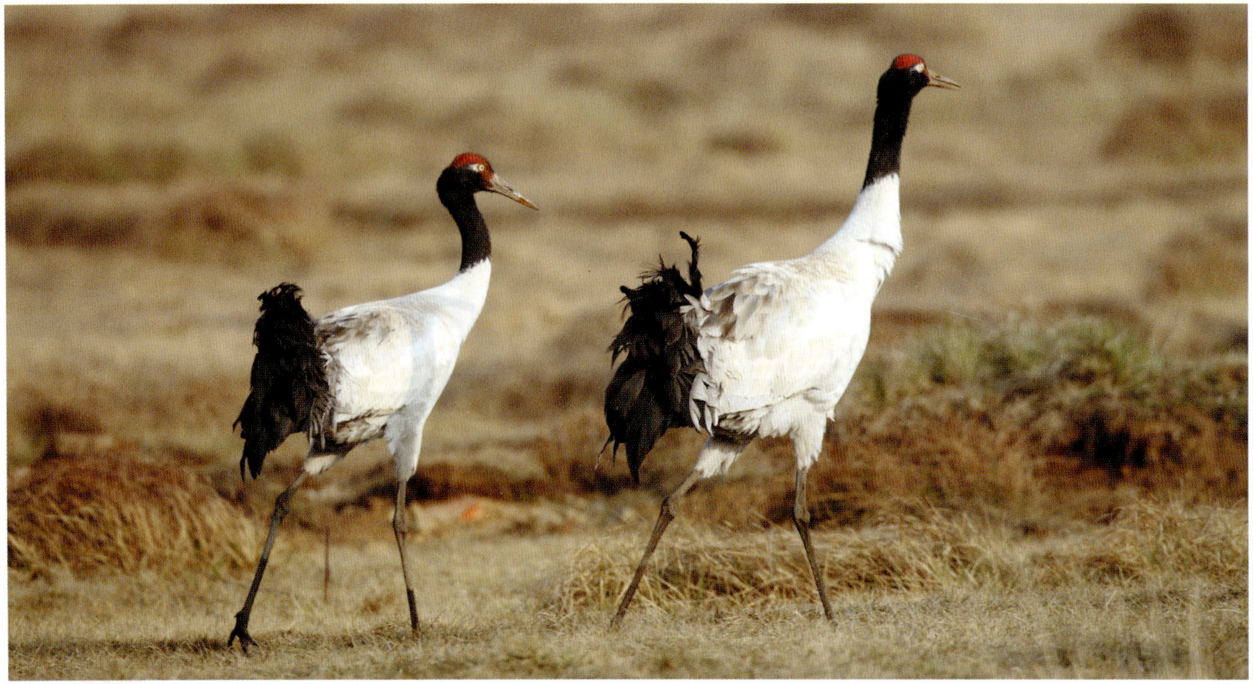

Above
On the Five Flowers Meadow wetland beside Qinghai Lake, juvenile black-necked cranes, following their parents, learn how to survive.

Left
This is a pair of successfully mated black-necked cranes in the last period of wintering.

province, starting from the Songpan grasslands to the Caohai wetland in Guizhou province. Migration of black-necked cranes in the spring also takes place in different batches. Adults in the period of propagation and their families would leave for places for the winter earlier, while sub-adults leave quite late. It would take them 15 days in a distance of about 800 kilometers to reach their places of propagation.

In such places of propagation as Qinghai Lake, at the end of March, people would see black-necked cranes in groups. Black-necked cranes having newly

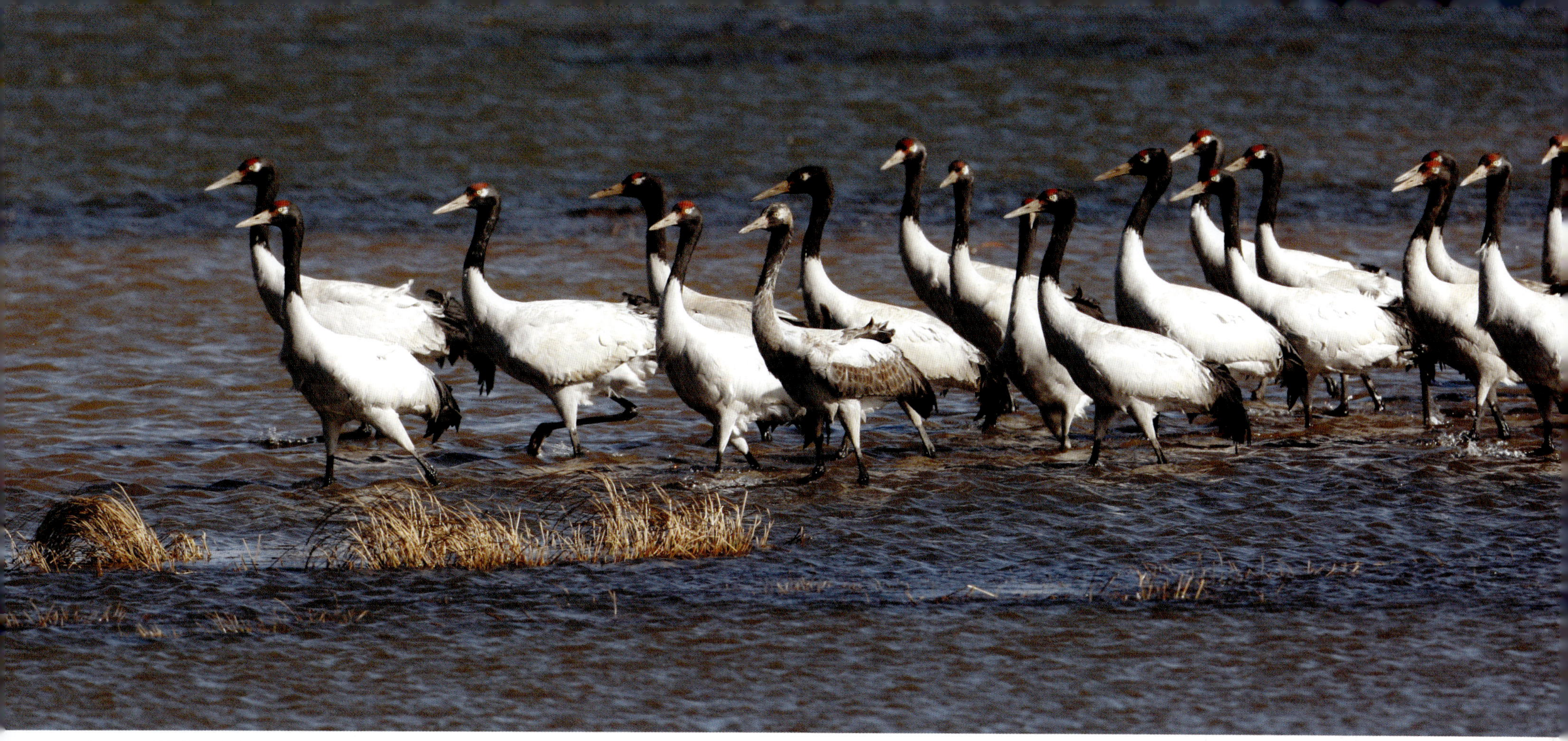

A group of black-necked cranes wade in a river. The one with smeared feathers is an immature crane. The black feathers on their necks are their most distinctive features.

arrived at places of propagation still live in groups. In order to establish proper areas for propagation, those couples ready for propagation fight each other very fiercely. Sub-adults arriving late would be squeezed out of the areas for propagation by the couples that settled there earlier, and would have to look for food in small groups to spend the summer.

One to two eggs are laid in each nest. Summer on the Tibetan Plateau is marked by inconsistent weather, i.e. a cloudless fine day with sunshine would change into a day of wild wind, rain, and snow in a short time. Black-necked cranes hatching eggs sit tight in the nest, sticking to their post, as if nothing has happened. The male and female hatch eggs in turn. There would be a change of duty 5 to 6 times a day and sometimes only 2 to 3 times a day. Hatching lasts for one month or so. By the time the juveniles are born, the parents would be exhausted. Due to the harsh climate, the survival rate of juveniles is very low. As shown by research, only 60% of newborn black-necked cranes survive three days after birth. There would be fighting among juveniles in the same nest and the weaker would often be injured or die. Sometimes, the females give birth late. When the severe winter comes around, juveniles, not fully-fledged, are very weak in their flying ability. When large groups of black-necked cranes begin to migrate southward, these late born juveniles have to stay at the places of their birth since they cannot follow the team to fly over high mountains. Soon, they would be frozen to death or hunted by their natural predators.

Caohai wetland in Guizhou province and

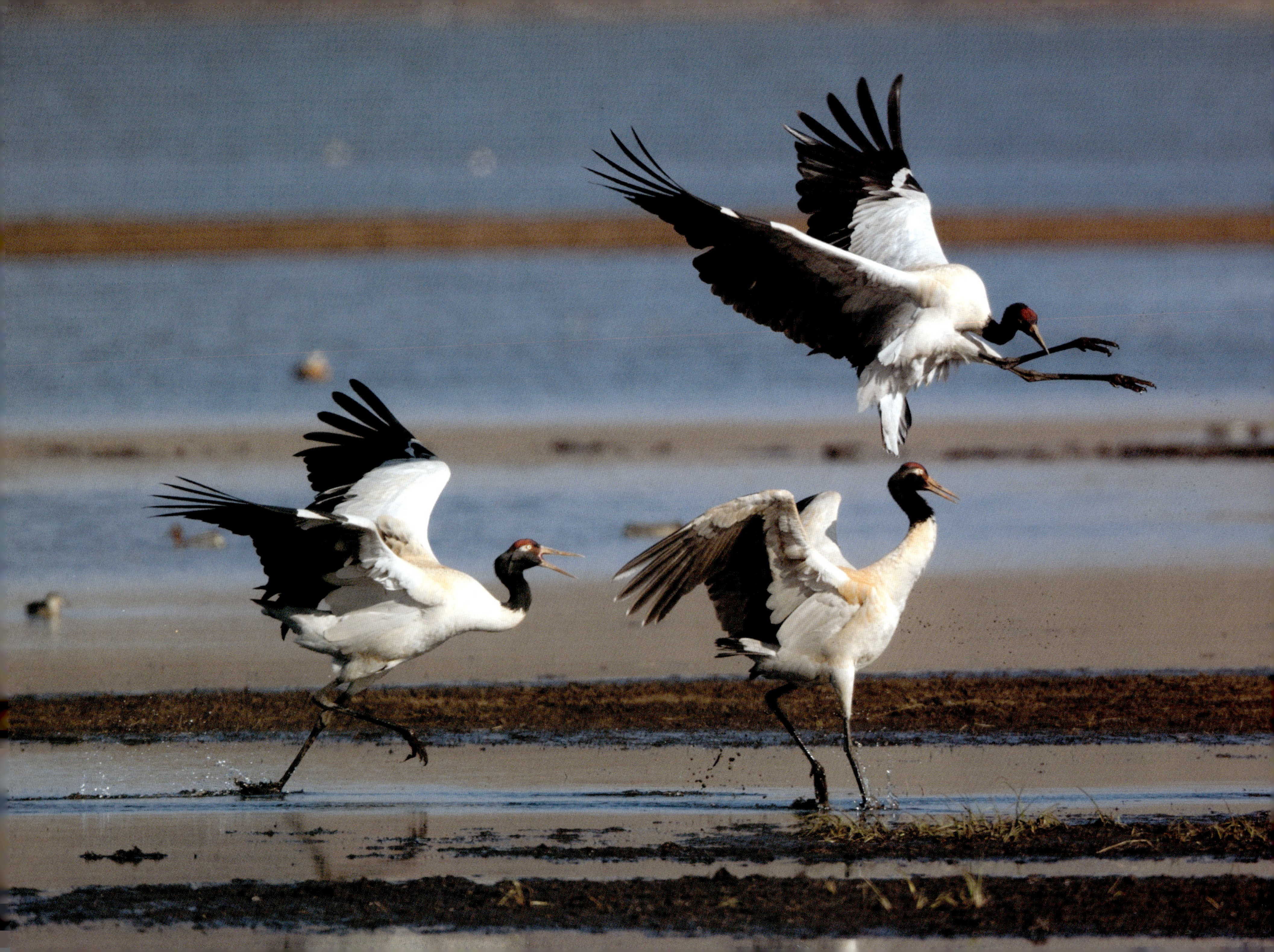

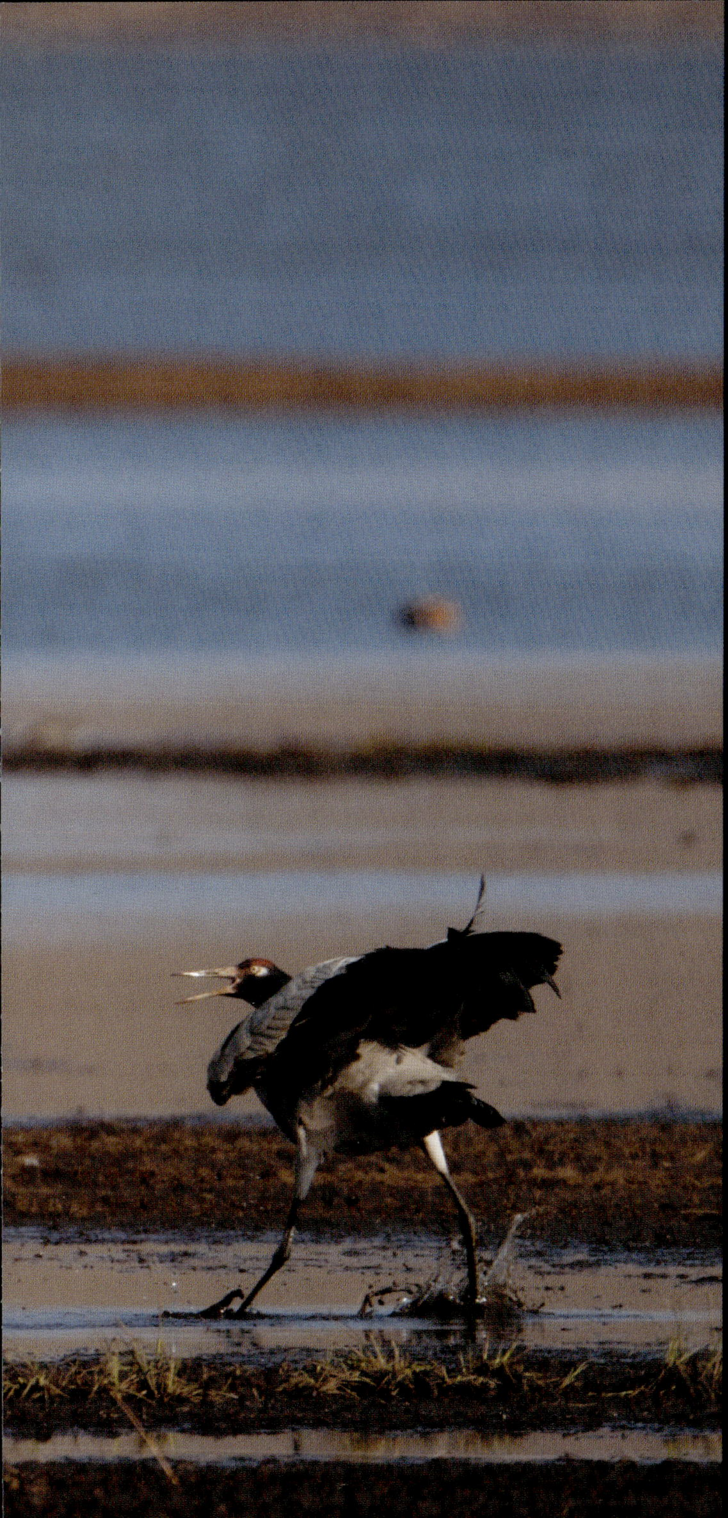

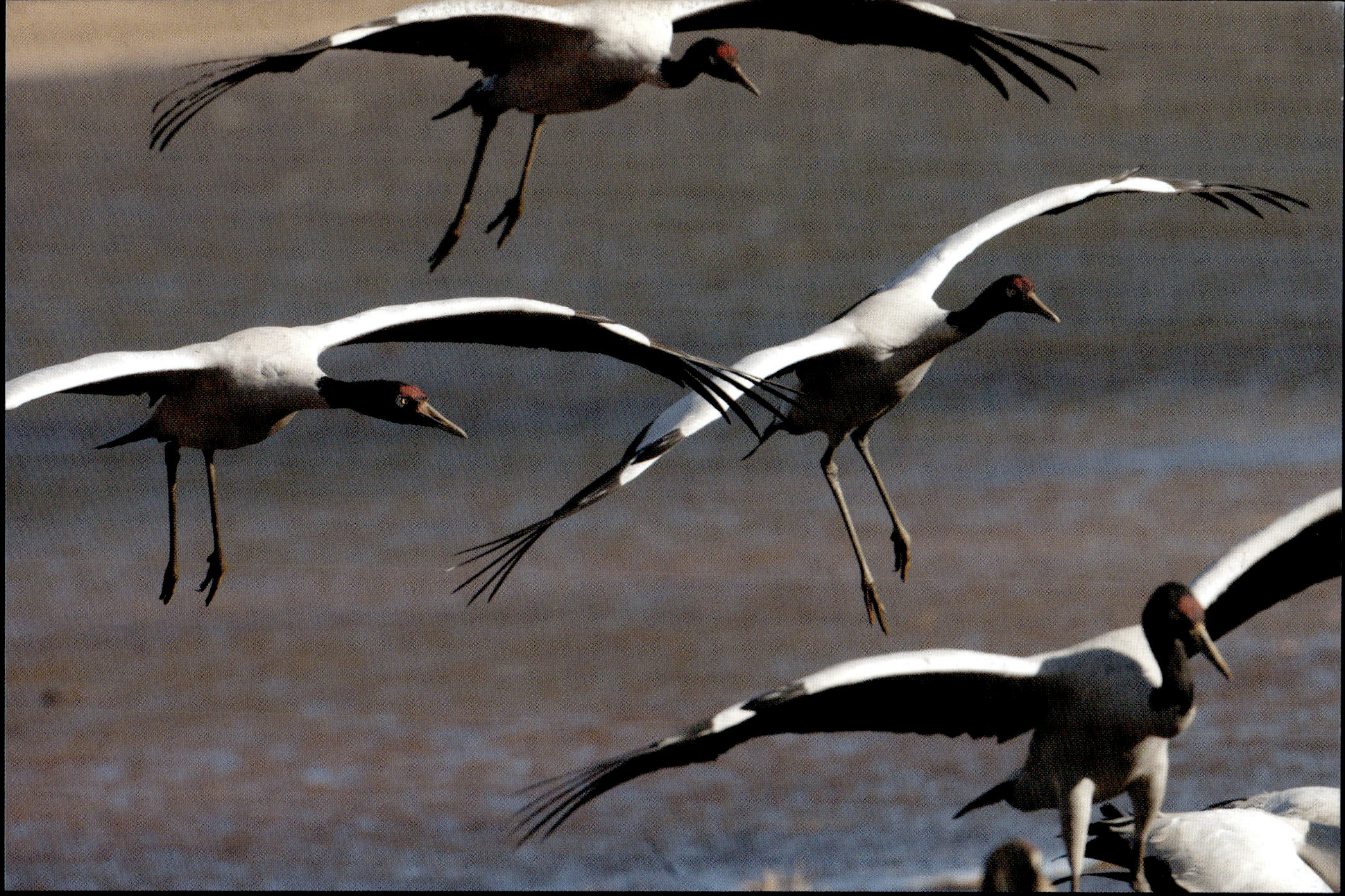

Above
Several black-necked cranes spread their wings and land gracefully.

Left
Fighting is inevitable when black-necked cranes are looking for their mates.

Dashanbao wetland of Zhaotong in Yunnan province are noted places for black-necked cranes to spend the winter. Black-necked cranes use over 60% of the daytime to look for food. They mainly eat bulbs from the sedge family, those potatoes left in the farmlands after harvest as well as some animal-based foods, such as small fish or spiral shells and even peck at small rodents. In central and southern Tibet, black-necked cranes spending the winter chiefly by eating cereal leftovers on farmland, since cereal can provide them with high-energy carbohydrates that can be easily absorbed.

At present, due to fish breeding, irrigation, dam building, expansion for farmland, development, and utilization of high mountains and lakes, the habitats of black-necked cranes are subject to constant damage and reduction in areas, in addition to the lack of food in the winter. Consequently, the number of black-necked cranes has been declining continuously. For instance, there is only a small number of them in Qinghai Lake where they were first discovered.

Bar-Headed Goose

Anser indicus
IUCN Red List: Least Concern

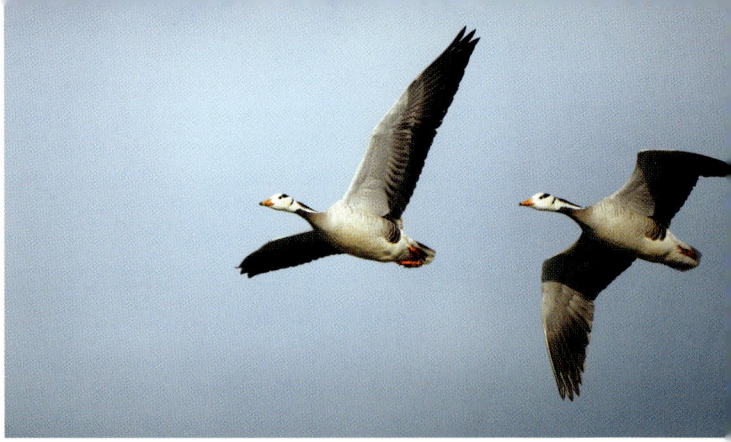

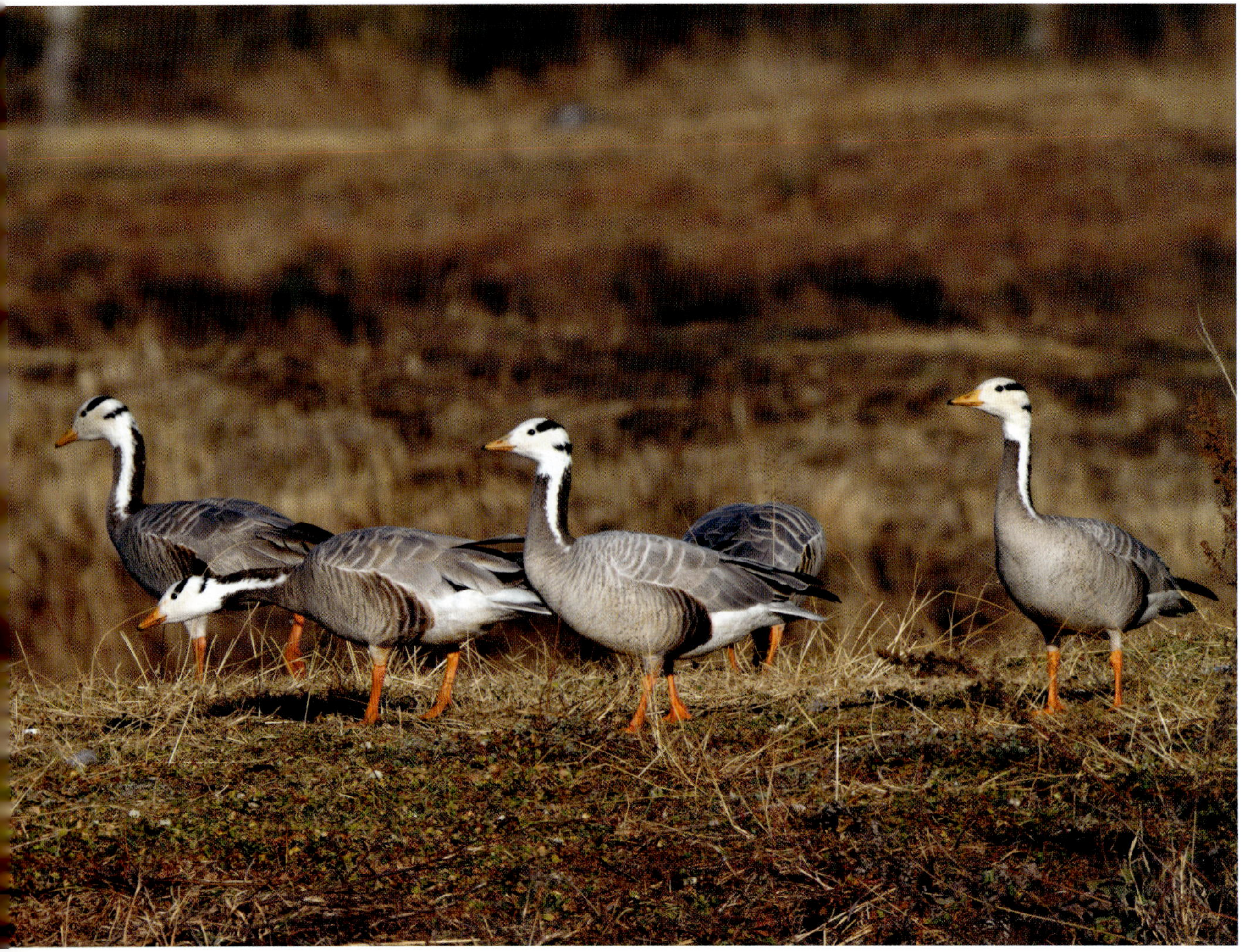

In the period from April to May, the Bird Island in Qinghai Lake would see lots of various waterfowls coming for propagation. The majority of them during the peak time would be 6,000 to 7,000 bar-headed geese, which are one of the biggest waterfowl populations in the summer in Qinghai Lake.

They eat green grass from the grass and sedge family, as well as the seeds of the leguminosae family, and occasionally, some mollusks. When looking for food in groups on the grassland, they would discharge excrements while eating just like lawn mowers, which play a considerable role in the adjusting ecology.

In the first half of April, they mate in the water and build up nests on the Bird Island. Marked by a great density of bird's nests on the island, there is a nest at every square meter or less.

Above
Two bar-headed geese flying in the air.

Left
Propagating on the Tibetan Plateau, they would come to the Yunnan-Guizhou Plateau to winter, and even fly over Himalayan Mountains to spend winter in southern Asia.

With a very simple structure, the nest is only a round small pit on the sandy ground dug by the female, a nest laid with feathers on the abdomen of the female, a few small pebbles, and collected withered plant stems. Two to eight eggs are laid in each nest. The female hatches eggs on her own while the male guards the area with the nest as the center. 29 days later, juveniles are born and move around with their parents. They will become adults 70 days later.

In July, adult bar-headed geese begin the postnuptial molt. As they would lose the flying ability for the time being, they are concentrated in lake bays with lush water grass. In September, with new feathers grown all over, they begin to migrate to the lakesides of the Indian Peninsula and southern China for the winter.

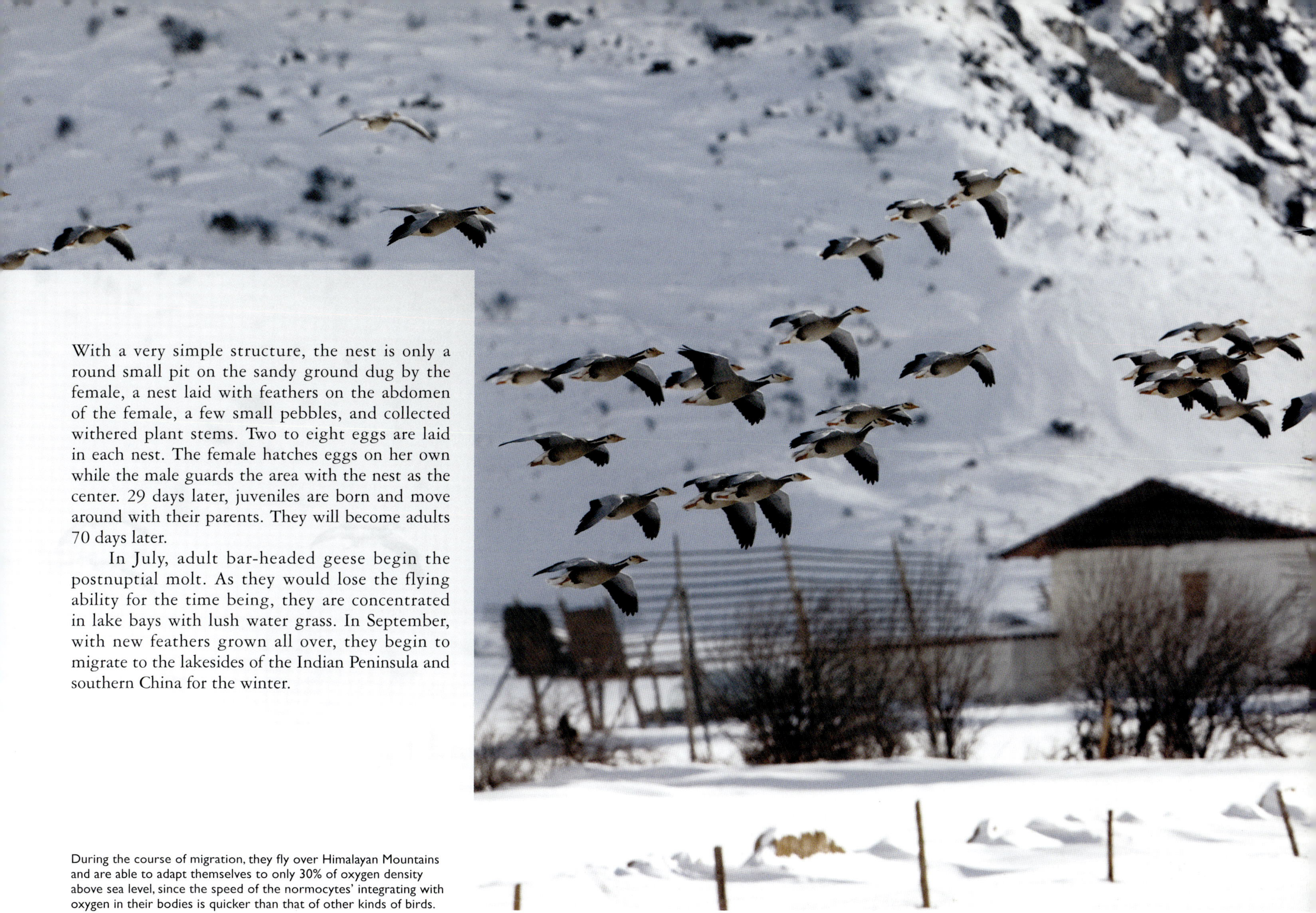

During the course of migration, they fly over Himalayan Mountains and are able to adapt themselves to only 30% of oxygen density above sea level, since the speed of the normocytes' integrating with oxygen in their bodies is quicker than that of other kinds of birds.

Ruddy Shelduck

Tadorna ferruginea

IUCN Red List: Least Concern

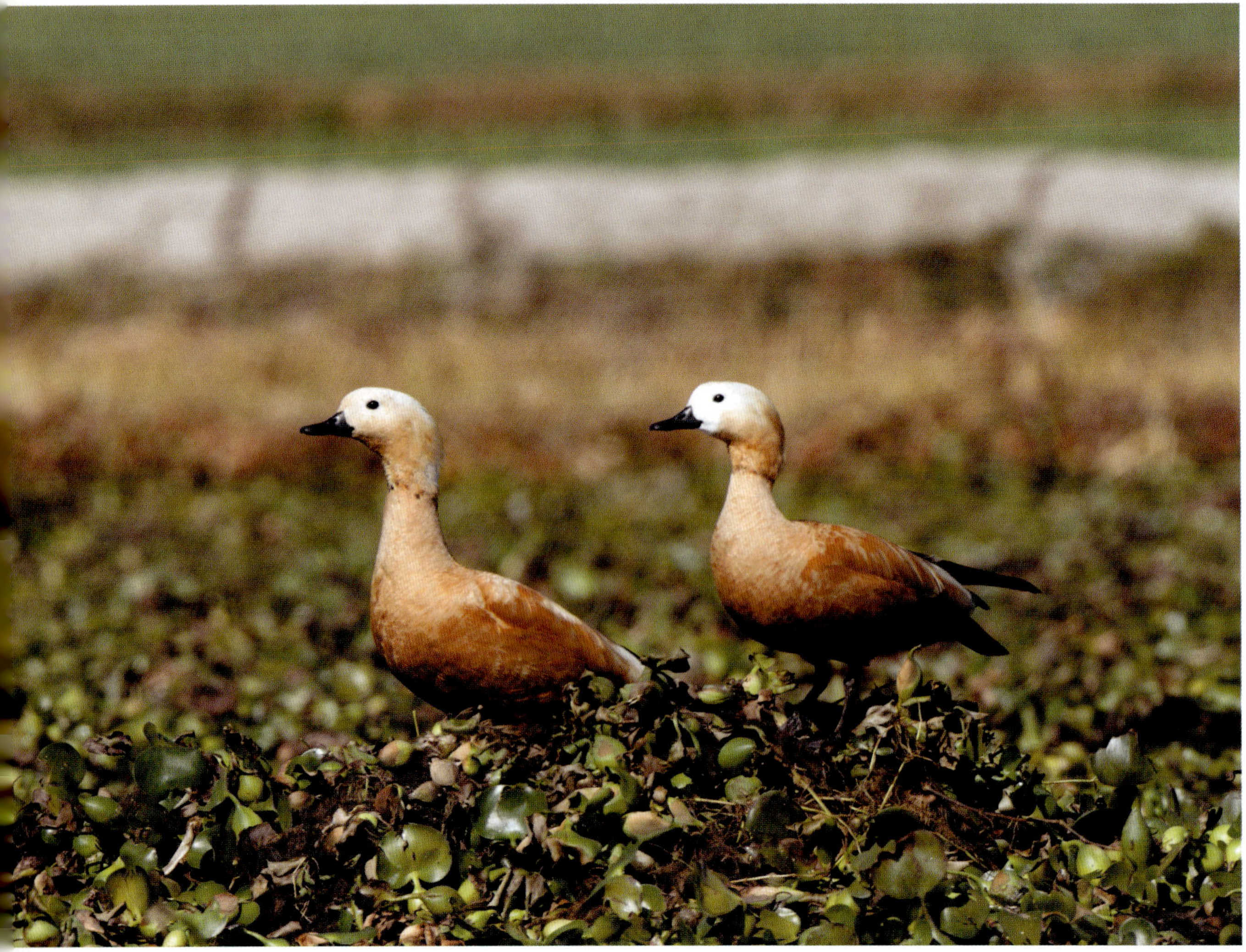

Generally, they live on the wetland by rivers and lakes, as well as nearby grasslands, marshes, sand beaches, and plain woodlands. They are particularly fond of lakes on plains. Most of them rely on inland fresh water and sometimes they are seen on sand beaches by the sea, saline lakes, and on expansive grasslands far away from water.

As migratory birds, they come from places to spend the winter during early to mid-March when the ice and snow at the places of propagation begin to thaw. In the period from the end of October to early November, they fly in groups from the places of propagation to places for spending the winter. Mostly, they migrate in the form of family groups or bigger flocks composed of different family groups. They scream while flying in a straight or horizontal array, constantly resting and looking for food on the way. Very often, they fall into bigger groups consisting of dozens or even nearly a hundred at the stop over.

They eat the leaves and buds of aquatic plants, as well as insects and beetles. They mostly look for food at dawn and dusk, and sometimes during the day. In the autumn and winter in particular, on farmlands beside rivers, small groups of several or over twenty ruddy shelducks are seen looking for cereal seeds scattered on the ground as well as looking for food over shallow water by the river and on the water surface.

They often move around in pairs.

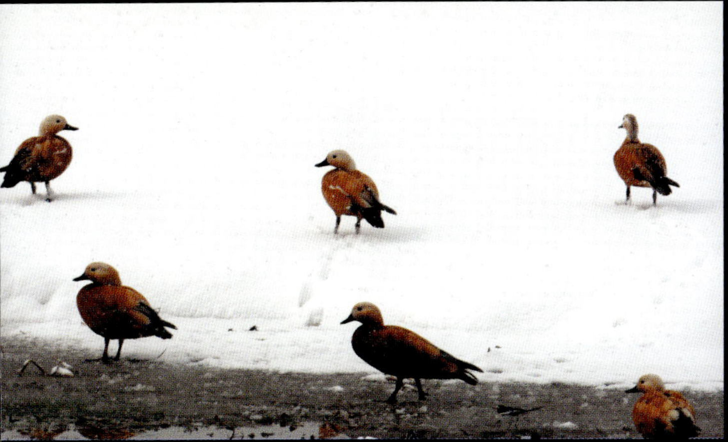

Above
A small group of ruddy shelducks looks for food in the shallow water.

Right
The range of their migration is larger than that of the bar-headed geese.

Becoming sexually mature at the age of two, they usually propagate once each year. The place of their propagation is generally on expansive plains, natural holes on grassland, holes abandoned by other animals, earthen holes, stone caves in mountains, and on islands over lakes. Sometimes, they choose holes in Euphrates poplars. Their nests are made up of a little withered grass and lots of feathers. The female lays one egg each day, with a total of 8 to 10 in the end. With eggs laid, the female would begin to hatch them on her own. The male stands on sentry nearby and utters alarm with loud screams when encountering danger. Sometimes, the male would fly against the intruder and pose attack as threat. After the hatching of 27 to 30 days, newborn juveniles swim with their parents in ponds and small streams. When encountering danger, they would hide at once in the grass by the riverside. Fifty days later, full-fledged juveniles with the ability to fly would gradually go off by themselves.

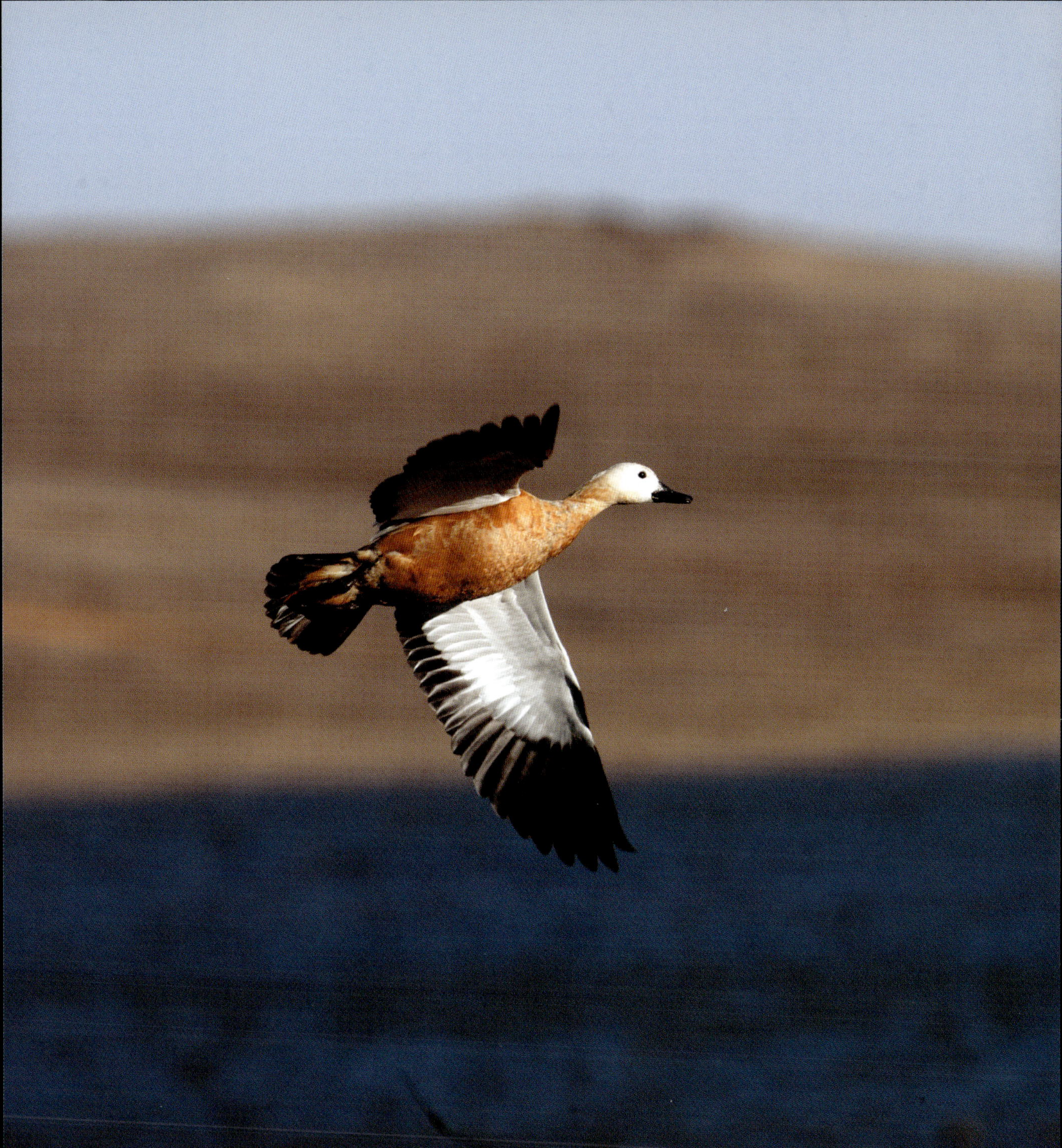

Common Redshank

Tringa totanus

IUCN Red List: Least Concern

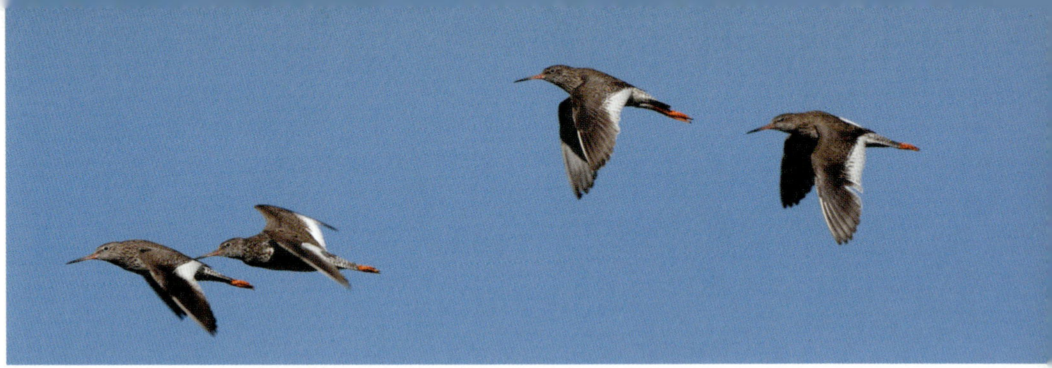

Four common redshanks fly across the sky.

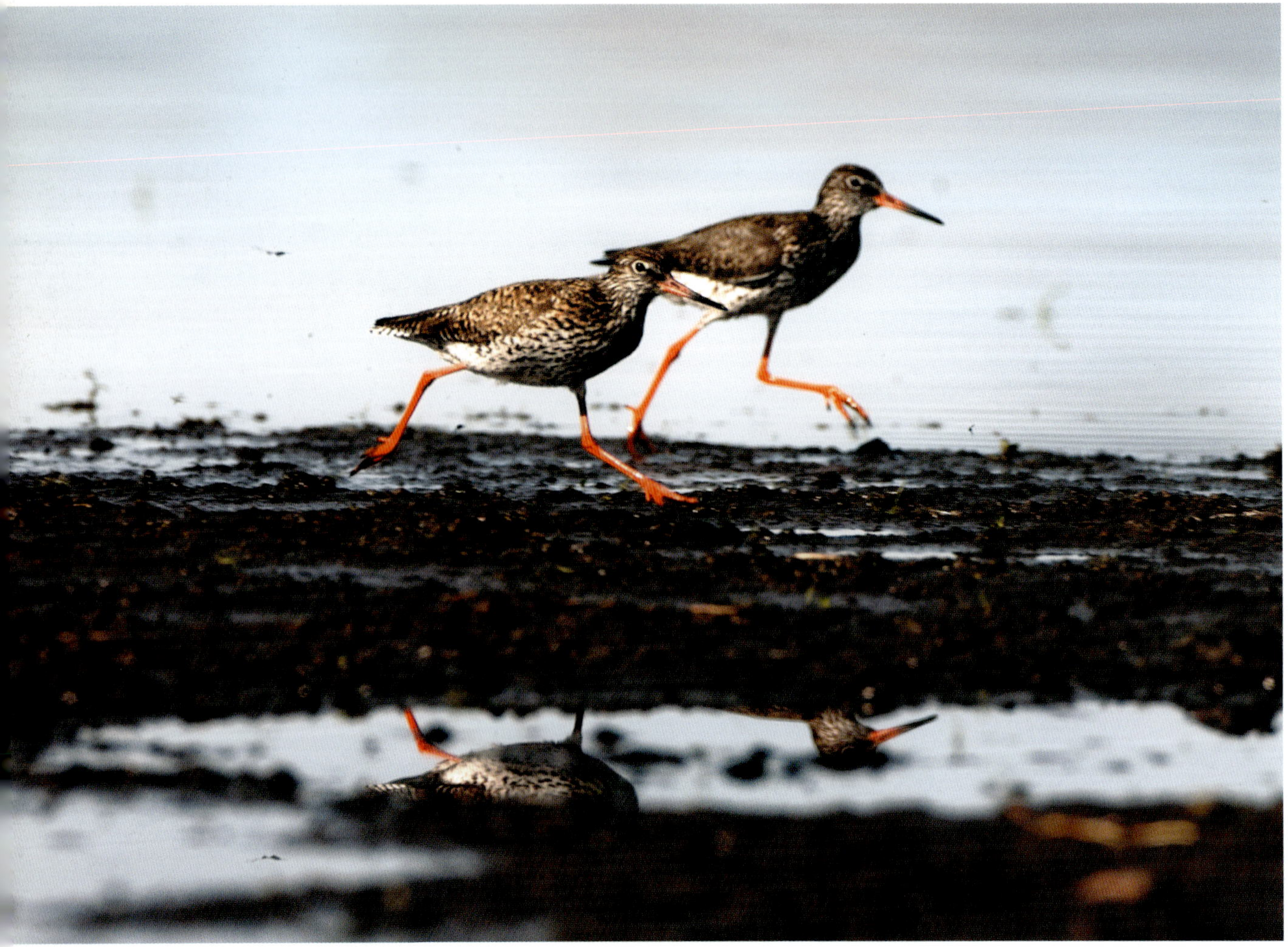

Two common redshanks neatly step forward with their orange-red long legs, running constantly.

In the temperate zones of Eurasia, common redshanks are breeders that are distributed extensively. However, they only propagate in northwestern China, the Tibetan Plateau, and eastern Inner Mongolia. Common redshanks migrate via southern China and eastern China while those wintering stay in the Yangtze River reaches, different provinces in southern China, Hainan Island, and Taiwan.

Also living on such wetlands as the seaside, river mouths, lakes, mud flats, and marshes, they eat small fish, insects, crustacean, earthworms, and tadpoles.

At places of propagation, they would begin to move around in pairs in middle and late April to choose the area for their nests. After mating, the female would lay four eggs in the nest, with the hatching jointly done by the female and the male. For most of the time, when the female is hatching in the nest, the male stands on guard and look for food ten meters away from the nest, and then enter the nest to hatch eggs when the female leaves to look for food.

Only half of the juveniles can survive since many of their natural predators cast covetous eyes on the eggs and juveniles of common redshanks, such as snakes, Amur falcons and foxes. Juveniles move around the nest under the care and protection of their parents until the season of migration comes around.

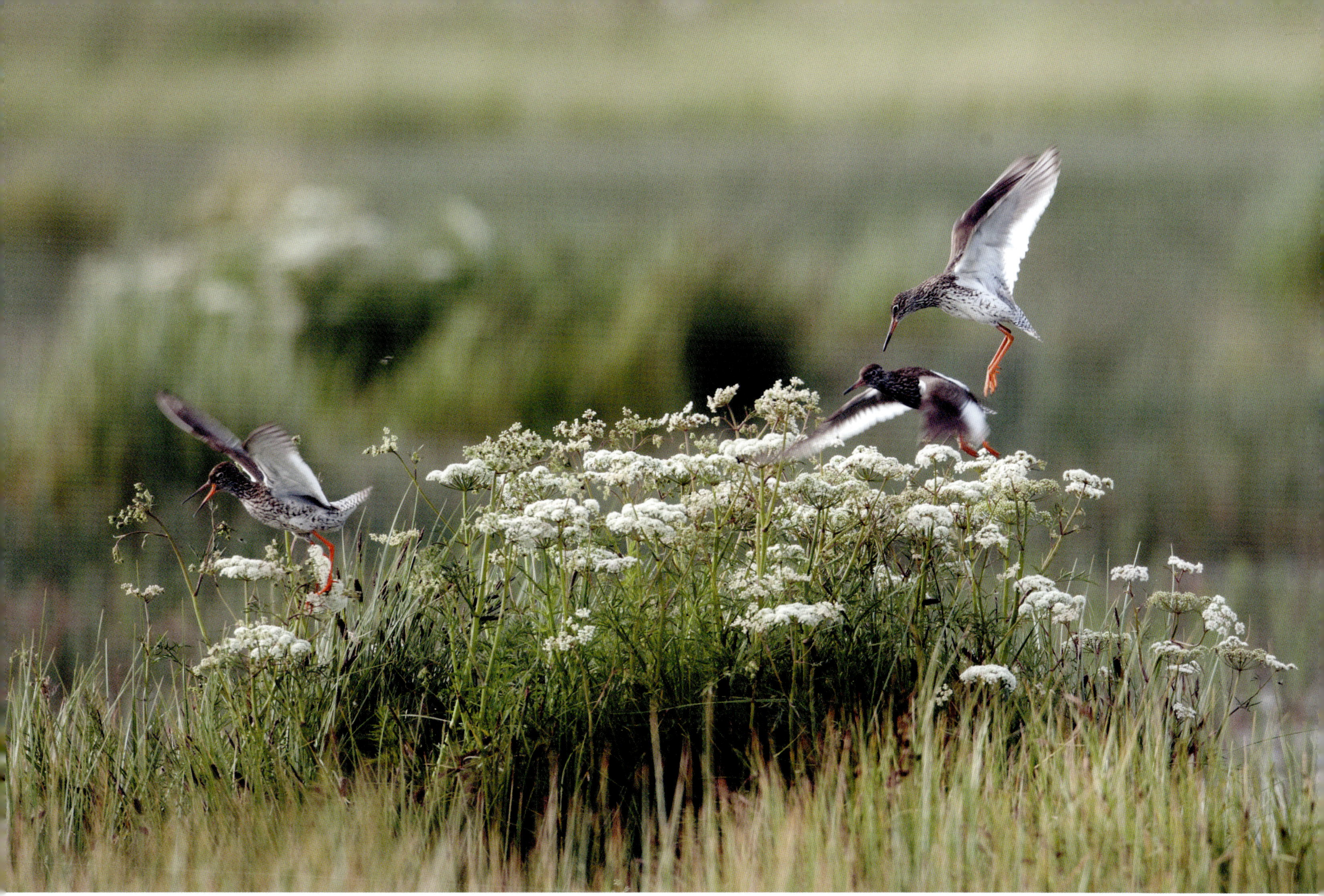

Three common redshanks vying with one another, try to land on a patch of white flowers in blossom.

Appendix I National Nature Reserves in China

Since the 1950s, there has been construction for the establishment of nature reserves across China. In recent years, the number of nature reserves has been rapidly on the rise. So far, over 300 national nature reserves have been established, with different targets under protection, as well as different aims and types. A brief introduction is given to one nature reserve in each province, each municipality under direct jurisdiction of the central government, and each autonomous region as follows.

Anhui Province
Number: 7
National Nature Reserve of Chinese Alligators

Situated in Xuancheng district, the Nationa Nature Reserve of Chinese Alligators covers a total area of 43,333 hectares as a transit area between Ghiangnania and Jinling Sag. This area is marked by a warm climate and ample rainfall. There is a complex system of ditches, ponds, and dams. In ponds and the hills' low lands and reservoirs, there are Chinese alligators known as "living fossils." They are ancient reptiles unique to China.

Beijing
Number: 2
Songshan National Nature Reserve

Situated at the southern foot of the Haituo Mountains in Yanqing county, it covers a total area of 4,660 hectares. The chief target under protection is the ecosystem of temperate forests mainly represented by the natural Chinese red pine forest. In this area, there are over 600 kinds of seed plants and more than 70 kinds of higher animals. Wild animals under national protection as important species include gorals and golden eagles.

Chongqing
Number: 4
Daba Mountains National Nature Reserve

Situated in Chengkou county, Daba Mountains National Nature Reserve covers a total area of 136,017 hectares, chiefly protecting the forest ecosystem of the central subtropical zones. There are a wide variety of wild animals and plants under protection dating back to ancient times. They are typical, representative, fragile, and unique. 656 kinds of wild animals have been discovered, such as leopards, clouded leopards, golden eagles, Asian golden cats, Asian black bears, macaques, and Chinese giant salamanders.

Fujian Province
Number: 12
Wuyi Mountains National Nature Reserve

Situated at the joint of Jianyang county, the city of Wuyi, and Guangze county, the Wuyi Mountains National Nature Reserve covers a total area of 56,527 hectares, chiefly protecting the mountain forests ecosystem of the central subtropical zone, as well as precious and rare species. Primitive forests and secondary primitive forests in this area look neat, in addition to the largest subtropical evergreen broad-leaved forests. There are over 400 kinds of higher animals, such as clouded leopards. There are more than 5,000 kinds of nomenclatorial insects, such as golden kaiserihind. It is also one of the areas most famous for insect type specimens in the world.

Gansu Province
Number: 16
An'nanba National Nature Reserve of Bactrian Camels

Situated in the Aksai Kazakh Autonomous County, the An'nanba National Nature Reserve of Bactrian Camels covers a total area of 396,000 hectares. There are roughly five kinds of vegetation, i.e. broad-leaved forests, steppes, deserts, bushes, and meadows. The area has 121 kinds of vertebrates, including 7 kinds of reptiles, 72 kinds of birds, and 42 kinds of mammals. Important animals under protection include Bactrian camels, kiangs, golden eagles, snow leopards, eastern imperial eagles, white-tailed eagles, and lammergeiers.

Guangdong Province
Number: 11
Nanling National Nature Reserve

Situated in Ruyuan, Lianxian, and Yangshan counties, the Nanling National Nature Reserve covers a total area of 58,924 hectares, chiefly protecting sub-tropical forests, as well as precious and rare animals and plants. Such vegetation as subtropical evergreen broad-leaved forests, mountain elfin forests, and coniferous forests are well preserved in this area. There are 70 kinds of mammals, 125 kinds of birds, and 41 kinds of reptiles.

Guangxi Autonomous Region
Number: 16
Nonggang National Nature Reserve

Situated at a place bordering Longshen and Ningming counties, the Nonggang National Nature Reserve covers a total area of 10,080 hectares, chiefly protecting the Karst seasonal rain forest ecosystem, other precious and rare species, and the Karst topography. Tropical seasonal rain forests in the Karst area rarely seen in the world are best preserved here. There are 123 kinds of higher animals, such as white-headed langurs, François' langurs, and clouded leopards.

Guizhou Province

Number: 8

Fanjing Mountains National Nature Reserve

Situated at a place bordering Jiangkou, Yinjiang, and Songtao counties, the Fanjing Mountains National Nature Reserve covers a total area of 41,900 hectares. There is a rich diversity of precious and rare plants, such as dove trees. With 382 kinds of vertebrates, this is the only area distributed with Guizhou snub-nosed monkeys, a precious and rare species.

Hainan Province

Number: 9

Bawangling National Nature Reserve

Situated at a place bordering Changjiang and Baisha counties, the Bawangling National Nature Reserve covers an area of 29,980 hectares. This area is marked by a humid tropical climate and tropical rain forests, chiefly protecting a very small number of endemic Hainan gibbons.

Hebei Province

Number: 12

Hengshui Lake National Nature Reserve

Situated in the city of Hengshui, the Hengshui Lake National Nature Reserve covers a total area of 18,787 hectares. This is a nature reserve chiefly protecting the ecosystem of inland wetlands, as well as precious and rare birds. It is a dense area that converges with the different routes through which a variety of migratory birds travel between south and north. This is an important habitat for birds to spend the winter, and a stop over for migratory birds to rest and propagate. According to statistics through investigation, there are 370 kinds of higher plants, 17 kinds of mammals, 286 kinds of birds, 17 kinds of amphibious animals, 26 kinds of fish, and 194 kinds of insects.

Heilongjiang Province

Number: 24

Xingkai Lake National Nature Reserve

Situated in the city of Mishan, the Xingkai Lake National Nature Reserve covers a total area of 222,488 hectares, chiefly protecting the wetland ecosystem as well as precious and rare birds. With marshes distributed extensively in the area, it is the stop over for birds migrating between south and north and the habitat for non-migratory birds. With rich bird resources, there are over 180 kinds of birds, such as red-crowned cranes, oriental storks, swans, white-naped cranes, and white-tailed eagles.

Henan Province

Number: 11

Dongzhai National Nature Reserve of Birds

Situated in Luoshan county, the Dongzhai National Nature Reserve of Birds covers a total area of 46,800 hectares, chiefly protecting precious and rare birds, as well as their habitats. The vegetation of this area is mainly marked by evergreen and deciduous broad-leaved mixed forests. There are 779 kinds of wild animals and 233 kinds of birds, such as oriental storks, Reeves's pheasants, and mandarin ducks. The number of birds in this area amounts to over 200,000.

Hubei Province

Number: 11

Shishou National Nature Reserve of Père David's Deer

Situated in the city of Shishou, the Shishou National Nature Reserve of Père David's Deer covers a total area of 1,567 hectares, chiefly protecting Père David's deer and their habitats. The area is marked by fertile soil, good water quality, and lush forage, with expansive reed swamps. There are over 100 vertebrates, such as great bustards and white storks. This nature reserve is also established to bring Père David's deer back to nature.

Hunan Province

Number: 18

Zhangjiajie National Nature Reserve of Chinese Giant Salamander

Situated in Wulingyuan district in the city of Zhangjiajie, the Zhangjiajie National Nature Reserve of Chinese Giant Salamander covers a total area of 14,285 hectares. This area is marked by four distinctive seasons, since there is no scorching heat in the summer, nor is there severe cold in the winter. Suitable climate and a well-developed water system have provided a desirable environment for the inhabitation and propagation of the Chinese giant salamanders as major targets under protection. Apart from the Chinese giant salamanders, there is also a rich resource of other kinds of wild animals, such as clouded leopards, large Indian civets, Temminck's Tragopan, and otters.

Inner Mongolia Autonomous Region

Number: 24

Ordos Relict Gull National Nature Reserve

Situated in the center of the city of Ordos, the Ordos Relict Gull National Reserve covers a total area of 14,770 hectares. This is a national nature reserve chiefly protecting relict gulls and its habitats. With sparse vegetation, it has the biggest and the most stable population of relict gulls in the world. Thanks to its environment suitable for the existence of birds, there are as many as 82 kinds of birds, making itself an important stop over for migratory birds.

Jiangsu Province

Number: 3

Yancheng National Nature Reserve of Coastal Beaches and Precious Birds

Situated in the coastal areas of Yancheng, this national nature reserve covers an area of 453,000 hectares. Beaches in this area extend 444 kilometers along the coast, with the ecosystem of the core area being basically in a primitive state. There are 315 kinds of birds. It is the biggest place for red-crowned cranes to spend winter and an important place of propagation for the Saunders's gulls, a species on the verge of extinction in the world.

Jiangxi Province

Number: 9

Boyang Lake National Nature Reserve of Migratory Birds

Situated in Yongxiu county, the Boyang Lake National Nature Reserve of Migratory Birds covers a total area of 22,400 hectares, chiefly protecting precious and rare migratory birds and the wetland ecosystem. The whole area has a rich variety of wild animals. There are 258 kinds of birds. As the biggest place for Siberian cranes to spend the winter, about 95% of them in the world spend the winter here. It is also the biggest place for swan geese to spend the winter.

Jilin Province

Number: 14

Huichun National Nature Reserve of Siberian Tigers

Situated in the southeast in the city of Huichun, the Huichun National Nature Reserve of Siberian Tigers covers a total area of 108,700 hectares. This is an area bordering China, Russia, and North Korea with a unique geographic location. There are 316 kinds of vertebrates, such as Siberian tigers, leopards, Siberian musk deer, sika deer, and red-crowned cranes. It is also an area with the biggest number and the greatest density of Siberian tigers of China.

Liaoning Province

Number: 13

Laotie Mountains—Shedao Island (Snake Island) National Nature Reserve

Situated in Lüshunkou district in the city of Dalian, this national nature reserve covers a total area of 14,595 hectares, chiefly protecting the Shedao island pit vipers (*Gloydius shedaoensis*), the special ecosystem of the Snake Island and migratory birds. The Snake Island covers an area of 73 hectares at its highest sea level being 216.9 meters. There are many natural rock cracks, caves, and bushes. The whole island is occupied by nearly 20,000 Shedao island pit vipers, poisonous snakes of the mono-type. The Laotie Mountains is one of the passages for the migration of birds from the continent of northeastern Asia. In the spring and autumn, over one million migratory birds of over 200 kinds stop here to rest.

Ningxia Autonomous Region

Number: 6

Helan Mountains National Nature Reserve

Situated in the northwest of the Yinchuan Plain, the Helan Mountains National Nature Reserve covers an area of 206,266 hectares. The area is mainly marked by the arid sandy area forest ecosystem. It has many precious and rare animals and plants. There are 135 kinds of wild terrestrial vertebrates, such as the forest musk deer and blue eared pheasants.

Qinghai Province

Number: 5

Hoh Xil National Nature Reserve

Situated in Zhiduo and Qumalai counties, the Hoh Xil National Reserve covers an area of 4,500,000 hectares. There are many lakes. The vegetation is chiefly marked by highland steppes and meadows. There are 16 kinds of mammals and about 30 kinds of birds in this area. Among them, 18 kinds of precious and rare wild animals endemic to the Tibetan Plateau are provided with the inhabitation and propagation by this area. There are many kiangs, wild yaks, Tibetan gazelles, and Tibetan antelopes, amounting to 30,000 to 40,000 in total.

Shandong Province

Number: 7

Yellow River Delta National Nature Reserve

Situated in the city of Dongying, the Yellow River Delta National Nature Reserve covers a total area of 15,300 hectares, chiefly protecting the original wetland ecosystem and birds. This area has a rich resource of living creatures of the wetlands. There are 116 kinds of higher plants, over 800 kinds of marine life, and 187 kinds of birds, such as red-crowned cranes and hooded cranes. It is an important stop over as well as an important wintering site for migratory birds from the northeastern Asia inland and the Pacific Rim.

Shanghai

Number: 2

Chongming Dongtan National Nature Reserve of Birds

Situated in the extreme east in Chongming Island, Chongming Dongtan National Nature Reserve covers a total area of 24,155 hectares, chiefly protecting the wetland ecosystem, as well as precious and rare birds. This is an important stop over on the way of bird migration and important place for waterfowls to spend winter in Asia-Pacific Region. There are 265 kinds of birds, such as oriental storks, white storks, Siberian cranes, common cranes, and white-naped cranes, as well as 73 kinds of fish, such as Chinese sturgeons and Chinese paddle fish. In 2002, it was designated as a piece of important wetland in the world.

Shaanxi Province
Number: 14
Hanzhong National Nature Reserve of Crested Ibises
Situated in Yangxian county, the Hanzhong National Nature Reserve of Crested Ibises covers a total area of 37,549 hectares. There are 314 kinds of wild vertebrates, including 18 kinds of fish, 28 kinds of reptiles, 205 kinds of birds, and 63 kinds of mammals. Apart from crested ibises under major protection, there are other kinds of important animals under protection, such as black storks, oriental storks, clouded leopards, forest musk deer, snub-nosed monkeys, and golden eagles.

Shanxi Province
Number: 5
Luya Mountains National Nature Reserve
Situated in Ningwu county, the Luya Mountains National Reserve covers an area of 21,453 hectares, chiefly protecting brown eared pheasants and the forest ecosystem. With a complex flora in this area, there have been over 700 kinds of higher plants and 232 kinds of vertebrates discovered. Among them, brown eared pheasants, with their number reaching nearly 3,000, accounts for a large part of all the animals.

Sichuan Province
Number: 24
Tangjiahe National Nature Reserve
Situated in Qingchuan county, the Tangjiahe National Nature Reserve covers an area of 40,000 hectares. The area is characterized by rich forest resources, well-preserved natural sceneries, and fairly obvious altitudinal vegetation zone. Lush and dense bamboo groves in places at 2,200 to 3,200 meters above sea level are suitable for the inhabitation and propagation of giant pandas. There are also other kinds of wild animals, such as snub-nosed monkeys, takins, clouded leopards, and Chinese monals.

Tianjin
Number: 3
Baxian Mountains National Nature Reserve
Situated in Jixian county, the Baxian Mountains National Nature Reserve covers an area of 1,049 hectares. The chief target under protection is the ecosystem of secondary forests. There is a rich variety of living creatures and a complete populative structure marked by considerable rarity and uniqueness. According to investigation, there are 362 kinds of higher plants and 172 kinds of vertebrates.

Tibet Autonomous Region
Number: 9
Mangkang National Nature Reserve of Yunnan Snub-Nosed Monkeys
Situated in Mangkang county, the Mangkang National Nature Reserve of Yunnan Snub-Nosed Monkeys covers a total area of 185,300 hectares, chiefly protecting such wild animals as the Yunnan snub-nosed monkeys and the forest ecosystem. The vegetation of this area is mainly marked by mountain coniferous forests, evergreen broad-leaved forests, deciduous broad-leaved forests, and bushes. There are 158 kinds of terrestrial vertebrates, such as the Yunnan snub-nosed monkeys, sun bears, snow leopards, white-lipped deer, macaques, Tibetan macaques, pangolins, dholes, and red pandas. It is one of the most important places distributed with Yunnan snub-nosed monkeys in China.

Xinjiang Autonomous Region
Number: 9
Altun Mountains National Nature Reserve
Situated in Ruoqiang county, it covers an area of 4,500,000 hectares. There are alpine steppes of large areas without human presence. The plateau ecosystem is in a primitive state, hence making it a paradise for the propagation of many plateau wild animals. There are 63 kinds of higher animals, including wild yaks, kiangs, Tibetan antelopes, Tibetan gazelles, snow leopards, black-necked cranes, and Tibetan snowcocks, which are marked by larger population quantity and greater density. Therefore, it is reputed as a natural zoo and as "the world of ungulates."

Yunnan Province
Number: 17
Gaoligong Mountains National Nature Reserve
Situated at a place bordering Tenchong, Baoshan, and Lushui counties, the Gaoligong Mountains National Nature Reserve covers a total area of 405,200 hectares. Plants in this area are mixed with those from the south and north of China, new and old. There are six vegetation zones starting from the river-valley of the Nujiang River to the peak of the Gaoligong Mountains. There are 440 kinds of higher animals, including over 30 kinds of important animals under national protection, such as takins, white-browed gibbons, and red slender lorises.

Zhejiang Province
Number: 10
Wuyanling Mountains National Nature Reserve
Situated in Taishun county, the Wuyanling Mountains National Nature Reserve covers a total area of 18,862 hectares, chiefly protecting Cabot's tragopan endemic to China, a species on the verge of extinction, as well as their habitats. Typical evergreen broad-leaved forests in the central sub-tropical zone are well preserved. There are 28 kinds of wild plants under protection, such as the Douglas fir. In addition, there are 42 kinds of animals under protection, such as leopards and macaques.

Note: The national nature reserves above do not include those in Hong Kong, Macao, and Taiwan.

Appendix II Index

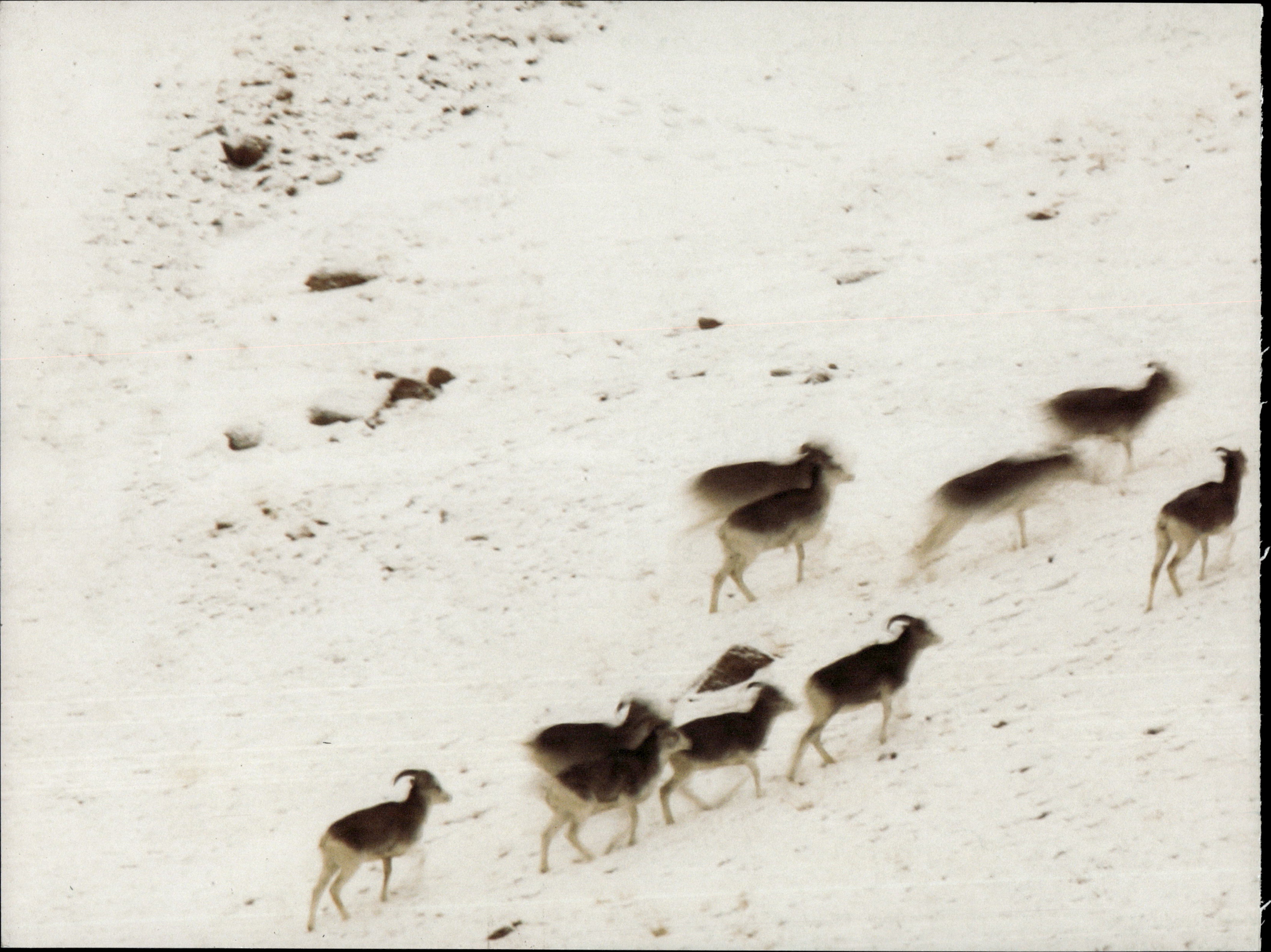